THE ROUTLEDGE COMPANION TO NONPROFIT MANAGEMENT

Over the past three decades or so, the nonprofit, voluntary, or third sector has undergone a major transformation from a small cottage industry to a major economic force in virtually every part of the developed world as well as elsewhere around the globe. Nonprofit organizations are now major providers of public services working in close cooperation with governments at all levels and increasingly find themselves in competition with commercial firms across various social marketplaces. This transformation has come with ever-increasing demands for enhancing the organizational capacities and professionalizing the management of nonprofit institutions. *The Routledge Companion to Nonprofit Management* is the first internationally focused effort to capture the full breadth of current nonprofit management research and knowledge that has arisen in response to these developments.

With newly commissioned contributions from an international set of scholars at the forefront of nonprofit management research, this volume provides a thorough overview of the most current management thinking in this field. It contextualizes nonprofit management globally, provides an extensive introduction to key management functions, core revenue sources and the emerging social enterprise space, and raises a number of emerging topics and issues that will shape nonprofit management in future decades. As graduate programs continue to evolve to serve the training needs in the field, *The Routledge Companion to Nonprofit Management* is an essential reference and resource for graduate students, researchers, and practitioners interested in a deeper understanding of the operation of the nonprofit sector.

Helmut K. Anheier is a Professor at the Hertie School of Governance, Berlin, Germany, and the Luskin School of Public Affairs at UCLA. His most recent books include *Nonprofit Organizations: Theory, Management, and Policy, Performance Measurement in Philanthropic Foundations: The Ambiguity of Success and Failure, Social Innovation – Comparative Perspectives,* and *Governance Indicators: Approaches, Progress, Promise.* Currently, he co-edits the *International Encyclopedia of Civil Society.*

Stefan Toepler is Professor of Nonprofit Studies and Director of the Master of Public Administration Program in the Schar School of Policy and Government, George Mason University, Arlington, VA. He has written broadly on nonprofit management and policy, philanthropy and global civil society. Among other books, he co-edited *Legitimacy of Philanthropic Foundations: United States and European Perspectives* and also co-edits the *International Encyclopedia of Civil Society.*

ROUTLEDGE COMPANIONS IN BUSINESS, MANAGEMENT AND ACCOUNTING

Routledge Companions in Business, Management and Accounting are prestige reference works providing an overview of a whole subject area or sub-discipline. These books survey the state of the discipline including emerging and cutting-edge areas. Providing a comprehensive, up to date, definitive work of reference, Routledge Companions can be cited as an authoritative source on the subject.

A key aspect of these Routledge Companions is their international scope and relevance. Edited by an array of highly regarded scholars, these volumes also benefit from teams of contributors which reflect an international range of perspectives.

Individually, Routledge Companions in Business, Management and Accounting provide an impactful one-stop-shop resource for each theme covered. Collectively, they represent a comprehensive learning and research resource for researchers, postgraduate students and practitioners.

Published titles in this series include:

The Routledge Companion to Critical Marketing
Edited by Mark Tadajewski, Matthew Higgins, Janice Denegri Knott and Rohit Varman

The Routledge Companion to the History of Retailing
Edited by Jon Stobart and Vicki Howard

The Routledge Companion to Innovation Management
Edited by Jin Chen, Alexander Brem, Eric Viardot and Poh Kam Wong

The Routledge Companion to the Makers of Global Business
Edited by Teresa da Silva Lopes, Christina Lubinski and Heidi J.S. Tworek

The Routledge Companion to Accounting in Emerging Economies
Edited by Pauline Weetman and Ioannis Tsalavoutas

The Routledge Companion to Career Studies
Edited by Hugh Gunz, Mila Lazarova andWolfgang Mayrhofer

The Routledge Companion to Nonprofit Management
Edited by Helmut K. Anheier and Stefan Toepler

The Routledge Companion to Inclusive Leadership
Edited by Joan Marques

For more information about this series, please visit: www.routledge.com/Routledge-Companions-in-Business-Management-and-Accounting/book-series/RCBMA

THE ROUTLEDGE COMPANION TO NONPROFIT MANAGEMENT

Edited by Helmut K. Anheier and Stefan Toepler

Routledge
Taylor & Francis Group

LONDON AND NEW YORK

First published 2020
by Routledge
4 Park Square, Milton Park, Abingdon, Oxon OX14 4RN
605 Third Avenue, New York, NY 10017

First issued in paperback 2023

Routledge is an imprint of the Taylor & Francis Group, an informa business

Publisher's Note
The publisher has gone to great lengths to ensure the quality of this reprint but
points out that some imperfections in the original copies may be apparent.

British Library Cataloguing-in-Publication Data
A catalogue record for this book is available from the British Library

Library of Congress Cataloging-in-Publication Data
Names: Anheier, Helmut K., 1954– editor. | Toepler, Stefan, editor.
Title: The Routledge companion to nonprofit management /
edited by Helmut K. Anheier and Stefan Toepler.
Description: First Edition. | New York : Routledge, 2020. |
Series: Routledge companions in business, management and accounting |
Includes bibliographical references and index. |
Identifiers: LCCN 2019046836 (print) | LCCN 2019046837 (ebook) |
ISBN 9781138744462 (hardback) | ISBN 9781315181011 (ebook)
Subjects: LCSH: Nonprofit organizations—Management.
Classification: LCC HD62.6 .R688 2020 (print) | LCC HD62.6 (ebook) |
DDC 658/.048—dc23
LC record available at https://lccn.loc.gov/2019046836
LC ebook record available at https://lccn.loc.gov/2019046837

Typeset in Bembo
by Apex CoVantage, LLC

Cover Art by Emilia Birlo.

ISBN 13: 978-1-03-265251-1 (pbk)
ISBN 13: 978-1-138-74446-2 (hbk)
ISBN 13: 978-1-315-18101-1 (ebk)

DOI: 10.4324/9781315181011

CONTENTS

CONTRIBUTORS

Alan J. Abramson, Professor of Government and Politics, Schar School of Policy and Government, George Mason University, Arlington, VA, USA

Theresa Anasti, Assistant Professor, Department of Sociology, Anthropology, Social Work, and Criminal Justice, Oakland University, Rochester, MI, USA

Helmut K. Anheier, Professor, Hertie School of Governance, Berlin, Germany, and Luskin School of Public Affairs at UCLA, CA, USA

Bob Beatty, Adjunct Faculty, University of San Diego, School of Leadership and Education Sciences, Department of Leadership Studies, San Diego, CA, USA

Lehn M. Benjamin, Associate Professor, The Lilly Family School of Philanthropy, Indiana University-Purdue University-Indianapolis, Indianapolis, IN, USA

Kara C. Billings, Graduate Research Assistant, Schar School of Policy and Government, George Mason University, Arlington, VA, USA

Omar Bortolazzi, Assistant Professor of International Studies, School of Arts & Sciences, American University in Dubai, Dubai, United Arab Emirates

Taco Brandsen, Professor, Institute for Management Research, Radboud University, Nijmegen, The Netherlands

Beth Breeze, Director, Centre for Philanthropy, University of Kent, Canterbury, UK

William A. Brown, Professor, Bush School of Government & Public Service, Texas A&M University, College Station, Texas, USA

David A. Campbell, Associate Professor, Department of Public Administration, College of Community and Public Affairs, Binghamton University, Binghamton, New York, USA

Wendy Chen, PhD Candidate, Schar School of Policy and Government, George Mason University, Arlington, VA, USA

Ki Joo Choi, Associate Professor and Chair, Department of Religion, Seton Hall University, South Orange, NJ, USA

Mary K. Feeney, Professor and Lincoln Professor of Ethics in Public Affairs, School of Public Administration, Arizona State University, Phoenix, AZ, USA

Nathan J. Grasse, Associate Professor, School of Public Policy and Administration, Carleton University Ottawa, ON, Canada

Roberto Gutiérrez, Associate Professor, School of Management, Universidad de los Andes, Bogotá, Colombia

Mark A. Hager, Associate Professor, School of Community Resources & Development, Arizona State University, Phoenix, AZ, USA

Jun Han, Adjunct Professor, McCourt School of Public Policy, Georgetown University, Washington, DC, USA

Femida Handy, Professor and Director, PhD Program in Social Welfare, School of Social Policy and Practice, University of Pennsylvania, Philadelphia, PA, USA

Alice Hengevoss, Research Assistant, Center for Philanthropy Studies, University of Basel, Basel, Switzerland

Jane Hudson, Lecturer in Marketing, Plymouth Business School, University of Plymouth, Plymouth, UK

Hokyu Hwang, Associate Professor, UNSW Business School, UNSW Sydney, Sydney, Australia

Natalya Ivanova, Senior Research Fellow, Center for Studies of Civil Society and the Nonprofit Sector, National Research University Higher School of Economics, Moscow, Russia

Urs Jäger, Associate Professor, INCAE Business School and Academic Director, VIVA Idea, Costa Rica

Lev Jakobson, Professor and Vice President of the National Research University Higher School of Economics, Research Supervisor of Center for Studies of Civil Society and the Nonprofit Sector at the National Research University Higher School of Economics, Moscow, Russia

Tobias Jung, Professor of Management and Director, Centre for the Study of Philanthropy & Public Good, School of Management, University of St. Andrews, St. Andrews, Scotland, UK

Janelle A. Kerlin, Associate Professor, Department of Public Management and Policy, Georgia State University, Atlanta, GA, USA

Gorgi Krlev, Postdoctoral Researcher, Centre for Social Investment (CSI), University of Heidelberg, Heidelberg, Germany

Marcus Lam, Assistant Professor, University of San Diego, School of Leadership and Education Sciences, Department of Leadership Studies, San Diego, CA, USA

Kelly LeRoux, Professor, Department of Public Administration, College of Urban Planning and Public Affairs, University of Illinois at Chicago, Chicago, IL, USA

Ian MacQuillin, Director, Rogare: The Fundraising Think Tank, London, UK

Jacob Mwathi Mati, Senior Lecturer, School of Humanities, Sol Plaatje University, Kimberly, South Africa and Associate Research Fellow, Society, Work and Politics (SWOP) Institute, The University of Witwatersrand, Johannesburg, South Africa

John McNutt, Professor, The Joseph R. Biden, Jr. School of Public Policy and Administration, University of Delaware, Newark, DE 19716, USA

Lucas C.P.M. Meijs, Professor of Strategic Philanthropy and Volunteering, Business-Society Management Department, Rotterdam School of Management, Erasmus University, Rotterdam, The Netherlands

Irina Mersianova, Director of the Center for Studies of Civil Society and the Nonprofit Sector and Head of the Chair of NPO Economics and Management, National Research University Higher School of Economics, Moscow, Russia

Michael Meyer, Professor, Department of Management, Institute of Nonprofit-Management, WU Vienna University of Economics and Business, Vienna, Austria

Georg Mildenberger, Head of Research, Centre for Social Investment (CSI), University of Heidelberg, Heidelberg, Germany

Roseanne Mirabella, Professor, Department of Political Science and Public Affairs, Seton Hall University, South Orange, NJ, USA

Clara Moder, University Assistant, Department of Political Science, University of Vienna, Vienna, Austria

Jennifer E. Mosley, Associate Professor, School of Social Service Administration, University of Chicago, Chicago, IL, USA

Daniel Gordon Neely, Associate Professor, Sheldon B. Lubar School of Business, University of Wisconsin-Milwaukee, Milwaukee, WI, USA

Michaela Neumayr, Assistant Professor, Institute for Nonprofit Management, WU Vienna University of Economics and Business, Vienna, Austria

Tamaki Onishi, Associate Professor, Department of Political Science, University of North Carolina at Greensboro, Greensboro, NC, USA

Astrid Pennerstorfer, Assistant Professor, Institute for Social Policy, WU Vienna University of Economics and Business, Vienna, Austria

Susan D. Phillips, Professor and Supervisor, Master of Philanthropy and Nonprofit Leadership, School of Public Policy and Administration, Carleton University, Ottawa, ON, Canada

Kathy T. Renfro, Doctoral Student, School of Community Resources & Development, Arizona State University, Phoenix, AZ, USA

Lonneke Roza, Assistant Professor, Business-Society Management Department, Rotterdam School of Management, Erasmus University, Rotterdam, The Netherlands

Allison R. Russell, Postdoctoral Fellow, School of Social Policy and Practice, University of Pennsylvania, Philadelphia, PA, USA

Adrian Sargeant, Director, Institute for Sustainable Philanthropy, Plymouth, UK

Ruth Simsa, Associate Professor, Department of Socioeconomics and Head of the Institute for Nonprofit Organizations, WU Vienna University of Economics and Business, Vienna, Austria

Trui Steen, Professor, KU Leuven Public Governance Institute, KU Leuven, Leuven, Belgium

David Suárez, Associate Professor, Evans School of Public Policy and Governance, University of Washington, Seattle, WA, USA

Felipe Symmes, PhD Candidate, University of St. Gallen, Switzerland, and Senior Researcher VIVA Idea, Costa Rica

Stefan Toepler, Professor of Nonprofit Studies and MPA Director, Schar School of Policy and Government, George Mason University, Arlington, VA, USA

Mary Tschirhart, Director and Professor, The Trachtenberg School of Public Policy and Public Administration, The George Washington University, Washington, DC, USA

Peter Vandor, Senior Researcher and Co-Founder, Social Entrepreneurship Center, WU Vienna University of Economics and Business, Vienna, Austria

Bram Verschuere, Associate Professor, Department of Public Governance and Management, Ghent University, Ghent, Belgium

Georg von Schnurbein, Professor of Philanthropy Studies, Center for Philanthropy Studies, University of Basel, Basel, Switzerland

Marlene Walk, Assistant Professor, Paul H. O'Neill School of Public and Environmental Affairs, Indiana University-Purdue University, Indianapolis, IN, USA

Tadeo Weiner-Davis, Doctoral Student, School of Social Service Administration, University of Chicago, Chicago, IL, USA

Naoto Yamauchi, Professor, Osaka School of International Public Policy, Osaka University, Osaka, Japan

1

NONPROFIT MANAGEMENT

Introduction and overview

Stefan Toepler

PROFESSOR OF NONPROFIT STUDIES AND MPA DIRECTOR, SCHAR SCHOOL OF POLICY
AND GOVERNMENT, GEORGE MASON UNIVERSITY, ARLINGTON, VA

Helmut K. Anheier

PROFESSOR, HERTIE SCHOOL, BERLIN, GERMANY, AND LUSKIN SCHOOL
OF PUBLIC AFFAIRS, UCLA, CA, USA

Introduction

Nonprofit organizations (NPOs), also known as civil society and non-governmental organizations (CSOs; NGOs) and a myriad of other designations depending on context, are private, voluntary organizations that are self-governed and legally required to apply surplus ("profit") to the pursuit of their mission rather than distributing it to members, officers, or directors (Anheier, 2014). Over the past three decades or so, these organizations have experienced significant growth in terms of their socio-economic importance. As increasingly indispensable providers of key social, healthcare, educational and cultural services, they account for significant shares of overall employment and economic value generation in many parts of the world (Salamon et al., 1999). Simultaneously, the stature of nonprofits and NGOs has also grown in the context of civic participation, social engagement, giving voice to minority interests, and the promulgation of values. The resurgence of civil society concepts and the evolution of neo-Tocquevillean thought, triggered by Robert Putnam's social capital argument (2000), placed additional spotlights on nonprofits and led to a worldwide increase in the visibility of the sector, but also brought a new set of challenges and expectations (Anheier, 2014). In a way, this has been both a boon and a bane for nonprofits. While favorable political rhetoric and expressions of support for the sector have increased, so have public scrutiny and critical media coverage of misconduct and management scandals (Eng et al., 2016; Smith, 2017).

The greater policy relevance has come with a diverse set of expectations of what nonprofits could and should do (Anheier et al., 2019): New public management and governance approaches have focused attention on nonprofit service provision, which is expected to be more efficient than government agencies and more trustworthy than for-profit alternatives (Salamon and Toepler, 2015). Nonprofits are also seen as a key mechanism for achieving social cohesion, serving as a locus of social capital creation and contributing to community resilience. Finally, social innovation is emerging as a new area of emphasis (Anheier et al., 2018), as governments aim at identifying, vetting, and scaling up new solutions to build more flexible responses to entrenched public problems.

Nonprofits accordingly find themselves cast into a variety of different roles, which are not always easily reconciled. But how to combine service provision, social innovation, and cohesion? Neo-Tocquevillean visions of civic activities may at some point run counter to the increasingly complex and competitive management reality of nonprofit service providers and social enterprises. Perceptions of a misfit between new political visions and organizational realities bring with it the potential for eventual public disillusionment and the risk of political backlash. This in turn makes it harder for nonprofit managers to find their way around the new and at times conflicting demands and expectations that they are facing.

To address the challenges inherent in these developments, there has been a surge of interest in, and need for, management knowledge, skills, and training that are specific to the characteristics of nonprofit organizations. Student demand at both undergraduate and master's levels has globally led to a mushrooming of the field of nonprofit studies (Mirabella and McDonald, 2012; Mirabella et al., 2015), which in turn fostered an increase in the number of PhD students entering the field (Jackson et al., 2014; Shier and Handy, 2014) and led NASPAA, the Network of Schools of Public Policy, Affairs, and Administration, to recognize nonprofit studies as a core element of public affairs education in 2019.

The proliferation of nonprofit management graduate programs over the past decade, particularly within the public administration discipline (Mirabella et al., 2015), has been fed by various ideas and concepts emanating either from the business world or public administration itself. The new public management and more recent collaborative governance strands in the public sector have brought concerns about outcomes versus outputs, efficiency versus effectiveness, as well as accountability and performance measurement to nonprofit management (Salamon and Toepler, 2015). From the business side, an increased consumer-orientation, marketing management concepts, social entrepreneurship (Defourney et al., 2014; Kerlin, 2017; Young et al., 2016), and hybridization (Skelcher and Smith, 2015) entered the field. Between these various concepts and pressures, nonprofit management teeters on a narrow edge: On one hand, nonprofits run the danger of losing their community-rootedness and turning into mere implementers of government policies (e.g., Banks et al., 2015), or of becoming too business-like, on the other (Maier et al., 2016). Social enterprises and newly emerging hybrid forms, moreover, are perceived by some as a potential threat to traditional nonprofits (Toepler, 2018).

Structural differences between nonprofits, business, and government

A key challenge for nonprofit management and nonprofit management educators, therefore, is to maintain a sense of the distinctiveness of nonprofits. They differ structurally from both the business corporations and government agencies, with which they frequently engage in complementary or competitive relationships. These differences occur along a number of key dimensions, including objective functions, outputs, resources, distribution criteria, goals, accountabilities, participants, and work motivation, among others (see Toepler and Anheier, 2004; and Anheier, 2014, for more detailed discussion).

More specifically, as shown in Table 1.1, government is concerned with optimizing overall social welfare by redistributing resources and providing for basic needs that are not otherwise met. Outputs are pure and impure public or collective goods that are not privately provided due to the free-rider problem or where market provision would lead to socially inefficient solutions. Equity and social justice are the primary distribution criteria for publicly provided goods and services. Private firms pursue the key objective of profit-maximization for owners through the production of private goods. Production is regulated by the interplay of supply and demand and the distribution is based on exchange relationships. Nonprofits typically aim at maximizing often value-based member or client group benefits (e.g., the homeless, students, opera lovers, faith adherents). Products have either club or collective good character and distribution is based on solidarity between members or with the client groups. Nonprofits also produce private goods, but do so to cross-subsidize their collective good provision (James, 1983; Weisbrod, 1998). Accordingly, organizations across the three sectors principally differ in the way they generate financial resources as well. Public agencies are predominantly financed in a coercive manner through the government's power to tax. Business firms employ commercial means of financing by way of charging market prices. Nonprofits, by contrast, ideal-typically rely on donative resources, dues, and public subsidies.

At the organizational-structural level, the bottom-line measure of profit allows business firms to set clear and specific goals that are also easily monitored and measured. High goal specificity translates into clearly delineated tasks and a formalized structure. Decision-making is top-down and the controlling authority is vested in the owners or shareholders to whom the firm is also primarily accountable. Government agencies, by contrast, lack a clear bottom-line measure. Goals and mandates are both complex and ambiguous due to changing and at times conflicting political imperatives as well as interventions of outside interest groups. External accountability and the locus of control are split with public agencies being ultimately accountable to the voters, while direct control is vested in elected officials which serve as the electorate's proxies. Similar to public agencies, nonprofits also lack clear-cut bottom lines. Missions tend to be broad and vague and members and stakeholders may join and support the organization for a diverse set of reasons leading to complex and diffuse sets of goals.

Regarding organizational participants, participation in the state is typically automatic (citizenship) and, given eligibility requirements, the same is also true for public sector agencies for entitlements. In some types of public agencies, such as schools, prisons, or the military, participation is or can also be coercive. Participation in business firms is voluntary, although necessitated by economic needs. Participation in nonprofits is typically purely voluntary. Choices concerning work participation can also be understood as a managerial sorting process (Weisbrod, 1988; Steinberg, 1993) that depends on organizational objective functions and individual preferences,

Table 1.1 Selected differences between nonprofits, government agencies and business firms

	Government Agency	*Nonprofit Organization*	*Business Firms*
Objective Function	Social welfare maximization	Member or client group benefit maximization	Profit-maximization
Outputs	Public/collective goods	Club/collective goods	Private goods
Resources	Coercive (taxation)	Donative	Commercial
Distribution criteria	Equity	Solidarity	Exchange
Goals	Complex, ambiguous	Complex, diffuse	Specific, clear
Accountability	Voters	Members	Owners/shareholders
Participants	Automatic/coercive	Voluntary	Quasi-voluntary (economic needs)
Motivation	Purposive	Solidary/Purposive	Material

Source: Based on Toepler and Anheier, 2004; and Anheier, 2014.

motivations, and perceived incentives. There are basically three types of incentives and corresponding organizational logics: material, solidary, and purposive incentives (Clark and Wilson, 1961; Etzioni, 1975). Material incentives, such as tangible, monetary rewards, dominate in business firms; whereas government agencies attract participants that respond more to purposive incentives, that is goal-related, intangible rewards. Many nonprofits, by contrast, are associated with intangible solidary incentives resulting from the act of association itself, but purposive incentives frequently also motivate participants (e.g., religious and political groups, human rights campaigns).

Distinctive functions

Whether collaborating with government or competing with private firms in mixed industries, based on these differences, nonprofits typically perform a set of special roles and functions that makes them further distinctive from the other sectors. Ralph Kramer (1981, 1987) distilled these distinctive functions into four key roles:

Service Provider Role: Since government programs are typically large scale and uniform, NPOs perform various important functions in the delivery of collective goods and services. They can be primary service providers, where neither government nor the business sector are either willing or able to act. They can provide services that complement the service delivery of other sectors, but differ qualitatively from it. Or they can supplement essentially similar services, where the provision of government or the market is insufficient in scope or not easily affordable.

Vanguard Role: NPOs innovate by experimenting with and pioneering new approaches, processes, or programs in service delivery. In their fields, they serve as change agents. If innovations prove successful after being developed and tested by NPOs, other service providers, particularly government agencies with broader reach, may adopt and scale them up.

Value Guardian Role: Governmental agencies are frequently constrained – either on constitutional grounds or by majority will – to foster and help express diverse values that various parts of the electorate may hold. Businesses similarly do not pursue the expression of values, since this is rarely profitable. NPOs are thus the primary mechanism to promote and guard particularistic values and allow societal groups to express and promulgate religious, ideological, political, cultural, social and other views and preferences. The resulting expressive diversity in society in turn contributes to pluralism and democratization.

Advocacy Role: In the political process which determines the design and contours of policies, the needs of underrepresented or discriminated groups are not always considered. NPOs thus fill in to give voice to the minority and particularistic interests and values they represent. In turn, they serve as critics and watchdogs of government with the aim of affecting change or improvements in social and other policies.

But despite this common core of features and functions, the nonprofit sector is nevertheless marked by its notable diversity, including the diversity of organizational types: Not all nonprofits are alike and not every nonprofit performs each of Kramer's four roles. But the great significance of Kramer's role conception is that it focuses attention beyond the economic aspects of service delivery to the value base that underlies all nonprofit activity. Indeed, despite their great diversity in purpose and form, among the many ways nonprofits are distinct from both business firms and public agencies (Table 1.1), three dimensions are particularly salient:

First, most nonprofits are based on values and have a distinct normative foundation. These values can be religious, political, humanitarian, moral, and even highly esoteric. The realization of these values is the *raison d'être* of nonprofits. These values can be deeply embedded in the organization, and their role is complex: From a management perspective, they can be enabling or restraining, protecting or stifling, leading or misleading, as well as invigorating or distracting.

Second, to a greater extent than business firms and public agencies, nonprofits have, and are subject to, the presence and influence of multiple stakeholders. These include trustees, staff, volunteers, users, clients, members, public and private funders, regulatory agencies, among many others. These stakeholders can have very different expectations of nonprofit operations and performance that reflect their respective normative foundations. As a result, many nonprofits become inherently political organizations.

Finally, managing nonprofits means managing multiple revenue sources – from market or quasi-market income to membership fees and sales, from various forms of transfers from, and contracts with, government to different kinds of monetary and in-kind donations by private funders, etc. At the same time, price mechanisms, the best indicators of performance, are absent, which means that nonprofits manage multiple revenue streams under performance uncertainty.

With the resulting managerial and governance complexities, nonprofits are fundamentally motivated by solidarity based on some kind of normative value base rather than purposive or material motivations (Etzioni, 1975). The key task of the nonprofit manager is to maintain their organizations' own distinguishing characteristics in order to protect the value-based core of nonprofits from getting crowded out by often predominant political considerations and economic necessities.

Structure of the volume

The purpose of this *Companion* is to present the state of the art and lay out current thinking across a broad range of nonprofit management issues. As the field is gaining academic currency, it is intended to help create a solid base for, and contribute to, strengthening graduate education in nonprofit management.

We do so with a global outlook. Therefore, the first part contextualizes nonprofit management in major world regions. Allison Graham's classic question of whether "public and private management are alike in all unimportant respects" has its correspondence in the relatively separate evolution of the Western "nonprofit management" and the development-oriented "NGO management" discourses (Lewis, 2015). Many aspects of managing nonprofits, however, are generic due to common legal systems and traditions and the projection of Western management approaches abroad through requirements of official public donors and preferences of private funders (Hammack and Heydemann, 2009; Spires, 2011). However, nonprofits are not closed systems, but highly dependent on their environments and context still matters. Chapters in Part I outline the current state of nonprofit and civil society development and core issues and challenges within the regions with bearing on managing nonprofits, NGOs, and CSOs. This serves to sensitize the reader to subtle and not-so-subtle differences in which nonprofit management paradigms and concepts that largely originated in the Anglo-Saxon space apply and adapt to different social-economic, political, regulatory, cultural, and historical contexts.

The following three parts focus on the managerial tasks and functions that lie at the heart of nonprofit management. Part II addresses Henry Mintzberg's (1983) strategic apex. It discusses board governance and composition, leadership, strategy development, and – given the centrality of trust for nonprofits – values and ethical considerations. Parts III and IV then look at the managerial tasks at the techno-structure and support staff around the operating core, to stay in Mintzberg's parlance. They function to sustain and enhance the operating core, which is comprised of the people, like case workers, doctors, teachers, curators, and so on, who actually produce the services. Part III discusses evaluation and performance measurement in the core, the marshalling of people for service delivery through staff and volunteer management and client involvement through co-production. For some types of nonprofits, members are a crucial part of the picture. Financial management and internal controlling are essential parts of the techno-structure and the use of information and communications technology has rapidly developed into an indispensable support tool.

Another function of the techno and support structure is to cushion the operating core from environmental interference and turbulence. Part IV thus examines the more externally oriented management tasks. Chapters here discuss collaborations and networks, as many nonprofits are increasingly drawn into New (or Collaborative or Networked) Governance approaches. Essential here is also the intersection with political and policy processes through nonprofit advocacy and lobbying, while engaging political participation more broadly. These address two of Kramer's core functions – advocacy and value guardianship – that nonprofits focused on service delivery too often fall woefully short on. Marketing and relationship fundraising chapters close the part out and provide a transition Part V, which is devoted to the major funding sources. Chapters in this part cover individual as well as institutional philanthropy – the latter by foundations and corporations – and the various forms of government support.

Earned income strategies are one element of the broader social enterprise space, which is considered in Part V. Social enterprise continues to be a big tent term that encompasses a significant variety of organizational models and approaches between the ideal-typical donative nonprofit, on the one hand, and strictly profit-maximizing business enterprise, on the other. It intends to create value towards a social purpose by utilizing business methods and approaches. The value these enterprises can pursue includes the pursuit of social innovation. To support these pursuits, new forms of social finance are emerging, that is financing and investment schemes that seek to achieve social outcomes and financial returns at the same time, such as impact investing and social impact bonds, or provide alternatives to traditional fundraising, such as crowdfunding. Within this overall space, new legal hybrid forms have emerged that could potentially evolve into new competitive threats for nonprofits and the exploration of hybridity and hybridization is rapidly emerging as a key issue.

Although still a relatively young specialty, nonprofit management emerges as a vibrant, ever-evolving field that continues to track the evolution of these organizations which remain central to future of public problem solving.

References

Anheier, H.K. (2014). *Nonprofit Organizations: Theory, Management, Policy* (2nd Revised edition). Abingdon, Oxon: Taylor & Francis.

Anheier, H., Krlev, G., & Mildenberger, G. (2018). *Social Innovation [Open Access]: Comparative Perspectives*. New York: Routledge.

Anheier, H., Lang, M., & Toepler, S. (2019). Civil Society in Times of Change: Shrinking, Changing and Expanding Spaces and the Need for new Regulatory Approaches. *Economics: The Open-Access, Open-Assessment E-Journal*, 13(2019–8), 1–27.

Banks, N., Hulme, D., & Edwards, M. (2015). NGOs, States, and Donors Revisited: Still Too Close for Comfort? *World Development*, 66, 707–718.

Clark, P. and Wilson, J. (1961). Incentive Systems: A Theory of Organizations. *Administrative Science Quarterly*, 6,129–166.

Defourny, J., Hulgård, L., & Pestoff, V. (Eds.). (2014). *Social Enterprise and the Third Sector: Changing European Landscapes in a Comparative Perspective*. Abingdon, Oxon: Routledge.

Eng, S., Smith, D.H., Al-Ekry, A.H., Brilliant, E.L., Farruggia, G., Faulkner, L., & Subianto, B. (2016). Crime, Misconduct, and Dysfunctions in and by Associations. In *The Palgrave Handbook of Volunteering, Civic Participation, and Nonprofit Associations* (pp. 1331–1359). London: Palgrave Macmillan.

Etzioni, Amitai (1975). *A Comparative Analysis of Complex Organizations*. New York: Free Press.

Graham, A. (2012). Public and Private Management: Are They Fundamentally Alike in All Unimportant Respects? In *Classics of Public Administration*, ed. Jay Shafritz and Albert Hyde (pp. 395–411). Boston: Wadsworth.

Hammack, D. C., & Heydemann, S. (Eds.). (2009). *Globalization, Philanthropy, and Civil Society: Projecting Institutional Logics Abroad*. Bloomington: Indiana University Press.

Jackson, S.K., Guerrero, S., & Appe, S. (2014). The State of Nonprofit and Philanthropic Studies Doctoral Education. *Nonprofit and Voluntary Sector Quarterly*, 43(5), 795–811.

James, E. (1983). Why Nonprofits Grow: A Model. *Journal of Policy Analysis and Management*, 2(3), 350–366.

Kerlin, J.A. (Ed.). (2017). *Shaping Social Enterprise: Understanding Institutional Context and Influence*. Bingley: Emerald Publishing.

Kramer, Ralph (1981). *Voluntary Agencies in the Welfare State*. Berkeley: University of California Press.

Kramer, Ralph (1987). Voluntary Agencies and the Personal Social Services. In Powell, Walter (Ed.), *The Nonprofit Sector: A Research Handbook* (pp. 240–257). New Haven, CT: Yale University Press.

Lewis, D. (2015). Contesting Parallel Worlds: Time to Abandon the Distinction between the 'International' and 'Domestic' contexts of Third Sector Scholarship? *VOLUNTAS: International Journal of Voluntary and Nonprofit Organizations*, 26(5), 2084–2103.

Maier, F., Meyer, M., & Steinbereithner, M. (2016). Nonprofit Organizations Becoming Business-Like: A Systematic Review. *Nonprofit and Voluntary Sector Quarterly*, 45(1), 64–86.

Mintzberg, Henry (1983). *Structures in Fives: Designing Effective Organizations*. Englewood Cliffs, NJ: Prentice Hall.

Mirabella, R., Hvenmark, J., & Larsson, O.S. (2015). Civil Society Education: International Perspectives. *Journal of Nonprofit Education and Leadership*, 5(4), 213–218.

Mirabella, R., & McDonald, M. (2012). University-based Education Programs in Nonprofit Management and Philanthropic Studies: Current State of the Field and Future Directions. In Burke, R.J., & Cooper, C.L. (Eds.), *Human Resource Management in the Nonprofit Sector: Passion, Purpose and Professionalism* (pp. 243–255). Northampton, MA: Edward Elgar.

Putnam, Robert (2000). *Bowling Alone: The Collapse and Revival of American Community*. New York: Simon & Schuster.

Salamon, L.M., Anheier, H.K., List, R., Toepler, S., Sokolowski, S.W., & Associates (1999). *Global Civil Society: Dimensions of the Nonprofit Sector*. Baltimore, MD: Johns Hopkins Center for Civil Society Studies.

Salamon, L.M., & Toepler, S. (2015). Government–Nonprofit Cooperation: Anomaly or Necessity? *VOLUNTAS: International Journal of Voluntary and Nonprofit Organizations*, 26(6), 2155–2177. https://doi.org/10.1007/s11266-015-9651-6

Shier, M.L., & Handy, F. (2014). Research Trends in Nonprofit Graduate Studies: A Growing Interdisciplinary Field. *Nonprofit and Voluntary Sector Quarterly*, 43(5), 812–831.

Skelcher, C., & Smith, S.R. (2015). Theorizing Hybridity: Institutional Logics, Complex Organizations, and Actor Identities: The Case of Nonprofits. *Public Administration*, 93(2), 433–448.

Smith, D.H. (2017). Misconduct and Deviance in and by Nonprofit Organizations. *Global Encyclopedia of Public Administration, Public Policy, and Governance*. New York: Springer.

Spires, A.J. (2011). Organizational Homophily in International Grantmaking: US-based Foundations and their Grantees in China. *Journal of Civil Society*, 7(3), 305–331.

Steinberg, R. (1993). Public Policy and the Performance of Nonprofit Organizations: A General Framework. *Nonprofit and Voluntary Sector Quarterly*, 22(1), 13–31.

Toepler, S. (2018). Do Benefit Corporations Represent a Policy Threat to Nonprofits? *Nonprofit Policy Forum* 9(4). https://doi.org/10.1515/npf-2018-0021

Toepler, S. & Anheier, H. (2004). Organizational Theory and Nonprofit Management: An Overview. In Zimmer, A. and Priller, E. (Eds.), *Future of Civil Society: Making Central European Nonprofit-Organizations Work* (pp. 253–270). Wiesbaden: VS Verlag für Sozialwissenschaften.

Weisbrod, B. (1988). *The Nonprofit Economy*. Cambridge: Harvard University Press.

Weisbrod, B. (1998). Modeling the Nonprofit Organization as a Multiproduct Firm: A Framework for Choice. In Weisbrod, B. (Ed.), *To Profit or Not to Profit: The Commercial Transformation of the Nonprofit Sector* (pp. 47–64). Cambridge: Cambridge University Press.

Young, D.R., Searing, E.A., & Brewer, C.V. (Eds.). (2016). *The Social Enterprise Zoo: A Guide for Perplexed Scholars, Entrepreneurs, Philanthropists, Leaders, Investors, and Policymakers*. Cheltenham: Edward Elgar Publishing.

PART I

Management context

2

A CHANGING MANAGEMENT CONTEXT

The US, UK, Canada and Australia

Susan D. Phillips

PROFESSOR AND SUPERVISOR, MASTER OF PHILANTHROPY AND NONPROFIT LEADERSHIP,
SCHOOL OF PUBLIC POLICY AND ADMINISTRATION, CARLETON UNIVERSITY,
OTTAWA, ON, CANADA

Introduction

The nonprofit sectors in the 'Anglo-Saxon' countries – for this chapter, focusing on the US, UK, Canada and Australia – have the advantage of operating in contexts featuring strong traditions of philanthropy, legal protections of freedom of speech and association, regulatory frameworks that are conducive to forming and operating civil society organizations, and governments that are, at least rhetorically, supportive of their work. Set in liberal welfare states in which governments have privatized or contract for a wide range of public services, nonprofits deliver services that are essential to the wellbeing of citizens. In addition, they serve as expressions of faith and 'community,' however defined, and as advocates for these identities and interests.

These contexts are undergoing significant change which have quite dramatic implications for the strategic direction, financing and management of nonprofits. These changes reflect and, in part, are driven by concerns with demonstrating impact and ensuring transparency that have come to dominate the expectations of donors and funders, state regulators and the public at large. This chapter assesses recent and unfolding developments in three key aspects of these contexts: the legal and regulatory regimes; philanthropy and social finance; and contracting and delivery of social services.

Composition of the nonprofit sector

In all of the Anglo-Saxon countries, the nonprofit sectors are large and diverse, important contributors to the economy and integral to the fabric of the social safety nets. In an effort to demonstrate the economic significance of the sector, and thus increase awareness by politicians and the public, sector leaders often compare its contribution to gross domestic product (GDP) to that of other industries. In Australia and Canada, for instance, the sector is described as larger than the construction or extractive industries and about the size of the retail sector, constituting about 9 percent of the workforce (Emmett and Emmett, 2015; Deloitte, 2017). In a comparison of the relative size of the nonprofit sectors in 41 countries, including their staff and volunteers as a total percentage of paid employment, Canada ranked no. 3, UK no. 5, US no. 9 and Australia no. 11 (Salamon, Sokolowski and Haddock, 2017). In terms of absolute number of nonprofits, the US is by far the largest (1.4 million), with about 170,000 to 180,000 in each of the other countries (Hall et al., 2005; Australian Government, 2010; McKeever, 2015; Australian Government et al., 2016; Blumberg, 2017; Keen and Audickas, 2017).

How we normally assess what constitutes the 'nonprofit' sector and its activities, however, is only a partial reflection of organized civil society because it relies on the data available. From a legal and data analytical perspective, organized civil society has two parts: 'charities' – nonprofits with charitable purposes or designated as equivalent by legislation (known as 501c(3)s in the US); and other nonprofits that include, among others, professional and industry associations, self-help groups and clubs, and organizations with policy advocacy as a primary purpose. All are tax exempt, but only charities may also issue tax receipts for donations, and they have more extensive requirements for registration and annual reporting to government. While the number of other types of nonprofits is as large as the 'charitable' sector, relatively little is known about them due to the lack of mandatory reporting. Thus, in analyzing the sector, this chapter – like most studies – focuses on registered charities and 501c(3)s, although they will be referred to as 'nonprofits.'

Two factors stand out about the sector. First, it is bifurcated between a small number of very large nonprofits and a plethora of small ones: more than half have one or no staff and limited budgets. Second, because the distribution of nonprofits is shaped to a significant degree by public policy, its composition and revenues vary by policy field, making it dangerous to generalize about the sector as a whole (Grønbjerg and Smith, 2014). There are also some important differences by subsectors across the four countries. As shown in Figure 2.1, nonprofits in social services and health constitute much larger proportions of the sector, by numbers and by revenues, in the US than in the other countries. Australia is an outlier in education (including primary through higher education) as a percentage of total income. Contrary to popular perception that religion is more dominant in the US, religious organizations form a larger percentage of the sector in Australia and Canada, although they represent a small portion of total income because

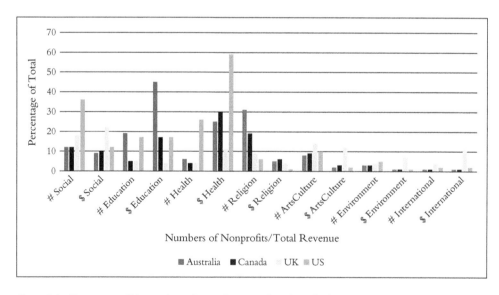

Figure 2.1 Percentage of the total number and revenue by selected subsectors

Sources: Hall et al., 2005; Imagine Canada and Rideau Hall Foundation, 2018; McKeever, 2015; Australian Government *et al.*, 2016; Keen and Audickas, 2017.

faith organizations rely heavily on donations and volunteers. The environment and international development represent very small parts of the sector, with spending on both higher in the UK than elsewhere. A much finer grained analysis is needed to explain these differences, but they provide a general caution about the need to account for diversity within the sector.

Regulation and government relations

Given the importance of maintaining public trust and confidence in nonprofits, and the availability of tax incentives for donations, all of the Anglo-Saxon countries have established extensive regulatory regimes, involving both state and self-regulation. These regulatory frameworks determine the kinds of causes considered 'charitable' and eligible for tax incentives, require them to register and report to the national regulator on an annual basis, and set the parameters for undertaking business, political and other activities. As common law jurisdictions, the legal foundations are rooted in the interpretation of 'charity' stemming from the Statute of Elizabeth in 1601, the four heads of charity articulated by the British Pemsel case in the late 1800s and subsequent case law. The eligible purposes of charity under common law are: advancement of education, advancement of religion, relief of poverty and other purposes beneficial to community (as the law regards as charitable). In all but Canada, the common law approach to charity has been codified and expanded in statute: in the tax code in the US and in dedicated charity legislation in the UK and Australia. In each of the UK jurisdictions (England and Wales; Scotland; and Northern Ireland) and Australia the national regulator is housed in an independent commission, whereas in the US and Canada it is located in the tax agency. These institutional differences are reflected in their independence and philosophies of regulation. For charity regulators located in a tax agency, their mandate includes protecting the integrity of the tax system, which may limit their autonomy and tilt their decisions about the boundaries of charity in favour of the 'fisc' (McGregor-Lowndes and Wyatt, 2017a). While the discourse of the independent commissions has focused on maintaining public trust and confidence and providing guidance to charities through a 'responsive,' education-first approach to regulation, the tax agencies are more likely to frame their roles as compliance, accountability and oversight (McGregor-Lowndes and Wyatt, 2017a; Owens, 2017).

The boundaries of 'nonprofit' and 'charity'

The regulation of charities in all four countries has undergone more significant change in the last 25 years than in the previous century (McGregor-Lowndes and Wyatt, 2017b), and arguably the pace and extent of change is accelerating as the sector becomes more complex. A fundamental but increasingly tricky question is: What are the boundaries of 'charity' or 'nonprofit'? This has implications for the kinds of organizations that are provided tax incentives and state regulated. The demonstration of 'public benefit' has become central to the evolution of the legal framework. In the UK jurisdictions and Australia, a public benefit test (which under common law is presumed by having charitable purposes) was enshrined in charity legislation, and has become 'the lens through which difficult modern issues affecting the charitable sector are evaluated and resolved' (Chan, 2015). The tensions over what entails a public benefit quickly became apparent in the cases of fee-charging, elite independent schools and religious organizations that do not respect minority rights as protected by human rights law (Parachin, 2015b; Etherington, 2017). One implication has been to place a greater responsibility on boards of directors to ensure they are achieving, assessing and communicating a public benefit (Morgan, 2012; Morgan and Fletcher, 2013).

In increasingly secular societies, the role of religion as charity receiving tax benefits is facing greater scrutiny. Although religion is regarded as politically sacrosanct in the US, UK and Canada, critical questions about religion as a private versus public benefit are very much alive in Australia (Michael, 2018a). There, religious organizations are recognized as charitable and are exempt from reporting on their finances and governance as other charities must do, but they do not automatically qualify to issue tax receipts for donations; rather they must demonstrate a public benefit (such as also providing some social service). On the basis of promoting transparency, there have been recent calls to remove the automatic qualification as charitable, and potentially tax any commercial activities undertaken by faith-based charities (Williams, 2017; Michael, 2018a). The political consequences of such a move suggest it is unlikely, but the overall secularization across the countries has long-term implications for patterns of giving and ongoing debates about public benefit.

The growing hybridity of this sector caused by organizations that combine social missions with commercial business models has brought a different set of pressures. Charities are allowed to carry on some business activities, albeit with differing treatment and restrictions: business activities are taxed in the US, UK and Australia, depending on the type of activity, but only those related to the charitable purposes or run by volunteers are allowed in Canada. Many charities set up subsidiaries to carry out their commercial activities, adding to the hybridization of this sector. The popularity of 'social enterprise' has also led to the creation of new legal corporate forms in the UK (community interest companies – CICs) and in many US states (low-profit limited liability companies – L3Cs) as well as in two Canadian provinces (see Abramson and Billings, Chapter 35 this volume). These hybrid forms must have a community interest while operating through commercial activities, and their main advantage is the ability to attract capital by issuing shares, albeit with limits on the extent to which profits can be distributed to shareholders. In the UK, a light touch regulator has been created to oversee the operation of CICs (Nicholls, 2010), and support for them and other forms of social enterprise has been reinforced with a tax benefit for social investment (a deduction for investing and deferral of capital gains on it). As a result, the creation of CICs in the UK has greatly outpaced the use of L3Cs in the US (over 13,000 compared to 1,530) (Regulator of Community Interest Companies, 2017; InterSector Partners, 2018). While there is considerable hype about these hybrid forms, the potential for mission drift or tension between the social and business logics is significant (Cornforth, 2014; Ebrahim, Battilana and Mair, 2014), and the failure rate is high, with 40 percent of the CICs approved since they were first introduced in 2005 no longer operating a decade later (Regulator of Community Interest Companies, 2017).

Particularly in the US, another fundamental boundary question has arisen: when is a nonprofit actually nonprofit? This issue is clouded by the needs of cash-strapped state and local governments to raise revenues and of the federal government to finance corporate tax cuts. Still, the principle of the character of being nonprofit is at its core, and the issue plays out in several ways. First, the tax exemptions of very large nonprofits, which are seen as indistinct from their for-profit competitors, are being rolled back. A number of US municipalities have begun to collect 'voluntary' payments-in-lieu (PILOTS) of property taxes (Grønbjerg and McGiverin-Bohan, 2016), and nonprofit hospitals have had their status revoked (Meiksins, 2015). Second, 'excessive' reserves and endowments of large nonprofits are seen by some as an abuse, and the 2018 Republican tax bill imposed an excise tax on the investment earnings of the endowments of large private universities (Wong and Fattal, 2017). A third trend, being felt in all of the jurisdictions, is greater scrutiny – and efforts to cap – the salaries of nonprofit executives. Although often wrapped in arguments about preventing abuse, there is an underlying perception that nonprofits are small, uncomplicated organizations and that it is unethical for their staff to accept high salaries for doing social good (Canada House of Commons, 2009). As a result of public and political pressure, sector leaders in the UK and Australia have initiated greater reporting on executive salaries (although these are already transparent in the annual reports), a proposed salary cap was narrowly avoided in Canada, but succeeded in the US where in 2018 a 21 percent excise tax was imposed on nonprofits that pay more than $1 million in compensation to any of their five highest-paid employees (Delaney, 2018). The serious consequence of this focus on executive salaries is not to reduce the pay of a few, but to divert attention from the real issue of compensation in this sector – low pay, job insecurity and lack of benefits for far too many nonprofit employees.

The limits on advocacy

Perhaps the most contentious aspect of the government–nonprofit relationship pertains to rules on advocacy, broadly defined as 'the attempt to influence public policy, either directly or indirectly' (Pekkanen and Smith, 2014: 3; see also Mosley et al., Chapter 23 this volume). The shared common law doctrine is that charities cannot have political purposes, but they may engage in non-partisan political activities as long as these are incidental and ancillary to their charitable work. Over the years, court decisions and legislative change have created open water among the four jurisdictions as to how advocacy is treated, although this space has recently converged on a more permissive approach. Australia has been at the liberal end as a result of the landmark decision in the 2010 Aid Watch court case which determined that advocacy is a charitable purpose when it aims to achieve another charitable purpose (Parachin, 2015a). This principle was then affirmed in guidance under Australia's 2013 charity legislation providing open-ended opportunities to engage in public policy debate, including criticizing or promoting the policies of political parties, albeit not to blatantly endorse or oppose candidates or parties. Despite such principles, in recent years Commonwealth and state governments have attempted to impose tighter limits. In 2018 the sector (with extensive public support) managed to roll back restrictions in a pending electoral funding reform bill that sought to ban foreign donations and prevent charities from speaking publicly about policy issues during elections (Michael, 2018b). In addition, the government of the most populous state, New South Wales, has announced it will cease funding for disability advocacy groups in 2020 when its budget for disability services is transitioned to a national program (Michael, 2018c).

The UK's approach has also been generally facilitating of advocacy, with recent efforts to make aspects of the system less so. In particular, changes to the Lobbying Act in 2017 set spending limits on third parties in England and Wales, including nonprofits and corporations, for a year prior to an election and requires them to register in order to spend (Electoral Commission UK, 2017).

Canada had long been positioned on the restrictive end with regulations that permitted between 10 percent (for large) and 20 percent (for small) of a charity's resources to be used for certain kinds of advocacy. This changed dramatically in 2019, however, making Canada very liberal in its treatment of advocacy, with the exception of election laws that continue to severely restrict advertising and participation during campaigns. Although the old '10 percent rule' still left more scope for advocacy than charities actually used, confusion over specifics and extensive auditing of political activities under the previous Conservative government had created an advocacy 'chill' by encouraging self-censorship. When elected in 2015, the Trudeau government promised to 'modernize' and clarify the rules on political activities, and appointed an independent panel to review them, which recommended a model akin to Australia's. The government initially delayed on implementing the panel's recommendations, and in 2018 a provincial court ruled that limiting non-partisan political activities by charities infringes their right to freedom of expression (*Canada Without Poverty v AG Canada*, 2018 ONSC 4147), a decision that the government appealed. In a surprise move in early 2019, it dropped the appeal and changed the rules to allow unlimited engagement in (non-partisan) 'public policy dialogue and development,' as long as such activities further charitable purposes.

The Trump administration has taken a different direction than any of its counterparts by seeking to repeal the 60-year-old 'Johnson Amendment' that prevents 501c(3)s, including religious organizations, from participating in political campaigns. The rationale was that the limitation is an impediment to free speech 'especially for [some] church leaders who believe they should be able to speak to their congregations and communities to endorse or oppose candidates in the context of their faith and the tenets of their religion' (Wyland, 2017). The move was strongly resisted by leaders of both secular nonprofits and religious organizations who feared the potential politicization by parties and wealthy donors, and ultimately was not included as part of the 2018 tax bill, but may yet return.

At their core, these debates are about principles and philosophies of whether nonprofits are integral or a threat to democracy, and they are a signal of whether governments seek a controlling or enabling role for this sector.

Credibility and capacity of the regulator

Serious compromises to the credibility and capacity of the regulators have contributed to uncertainty, generated demands for greater sector self-regulation and, in the US, prompted expanded, haphazard sets of rules by subnational governments. Across all of the countries, the regulator's legitimacy has been diminished in recent years by political interference in their work, highly contentious appointments to their leadership and major cuts to their funding. Indeed, the fall of the Charity Commission of England and Wales, which had long been held up as a 'model' regulator, is instructive. It has suffered perceptions of political bias in the appointment of commissioners and had its budget cut in half since 2008, forcing it to narrow its scope to a control function and diminishing its once important role in providing education and guidance for the good governance of charities. Its effectiveness was so compromised that parliamentary oversight bodies declared it a failing regulator in need of radical reform (Morris, 2016). At the same time, several scandals related to fundraising have given rise to a new fundraising regulator.

The Australian Charities and Not-for-Profits Commission is a relative newbie, established in 2012; it survived an attempt by the government to dismantle it a year later, but quickly became a respected, responsive regulator. The appointment in 2017 of an outspoken critic of charities as its second commissioner signals that it may take a more assertive stance toward charities, pushing for greater transparency and assuming a command-and-control approach. Like the US, Australia has a complicated, inconsistent and outdated set of rules related to fundraising, and the sector has led a campaign over the past decade to '#fixfundraising,' which is as yet not fixed. In spite of its commitment to modernize Canada's regulatory regime the Liberal government seems to have found such reform more complicated than anticipated, and the political gains less apparent, so the process is stalled awaiting implementation of recommendations of a parliamentary committee. The situation in the US is the most extreme where the vacuum created by the loss of credibility, funding and personnel in the Tax Exempt Office of Internal Revenue Service (IRS) has prompted states to expand their jurisdictional reach with multiple new sets of rules and oversight, in addition to the extensive state rules that already governed fundraising (Barber and Farwell, 2016). The combination of the measures noted above, coupled with what are likely to be de facto limitations on charitable giving, has produced what the National Council of Nonprofits calls 'the most dangerous policy environment' in decades (Delaney and Thompson, 2018).

Self-regulation

The rise of self-regulation has a causal relationship with state regulation, argue Breen and colleagues (2016), whether self-regulation is intended to ward off greater statutory regulation, fill gaps or is a parallel response to a changing environment. Professional and peak associations manage a wide range of standards and codes for nonprofits, which have become so extensive that Breen et al. describe this as an 'industry' onto itself. Most of these operate as voluntary codes to which adherence is promised in exchange for a 'hallmark' of quality assurance. Alternatively, they accredit by particular subsectors, often as a requirement to become a member of the umbrella organization. A more rigorous, sector-wide accreditation system was launched by Canada's national peak association in 2012 that involves self-assessment and peer review according to 73 standards, and monitoring of compliance through investigation of complaints and selected audits (ImagineCanada, 2017). Although the accredited nonprofits number only about 250, a mix of large and medium-sized organizations, the system has shifted the discourse of self-regulation from one of compliance to one of continuous self-improvement.

Internationally, a new urgency for more effective self- (and state) regulation has been sparked by the scandal over sexual exploitation by senior aid workers of Oxfam and several other international aid NGOs. Although Oxfam was regarded as having one of the best systems of safeguards among international NGOs, the misconduct has opened a serious discussion about toxic cultures and moral leadership of nonprofits. The UK Parliamentary committee that investigated the incidents found that sexual abuse is 'endemic' in the international aid community and pointed to a 'collective failure of leadership' (House of Commons, 2018). While such failures were first exposed in the aid sector, they are not confined to it, nor to the UK. The founding director of the Silicon Valley Community Foundation (US), the world's largest community foundation, was forced to resign in 2018 for permitting the existence of a culture of bullying and harassment in the interests of growth (SVCF, 2018). In the six months following the Oxfam scandal, reporting of incidents of abuse and inappropriate behaviour by UK charities, including those in disability, religion, education and youth, increased threefold (to over 2,100) over the previous two years (CCEW, 2018). Consequently, the Charity Commission has doubled down on ensuring better safeguards, enabling whistleblowing and dealing with reports of wrongdoing (CCEW, 2018). Key nonprofit leaders have also committed to change: as the head of the UK network of aid agencies noted, '"business as usual" is not going to cut it ... We need to see increased resourcing in safeguarding, particularly for smaller NGOs, more collaboration across organisations, donors and governments, better transparency, unwavering leadership and measures to ensure whistle-blowers and survivors are at the heart of any solutions' (quoted in Sharman, 2018). Across the nonprofit sector, we can anticipate greater pressure on boards of directors to improve their governance systems and exercise and oversee good leadership practices, and can expect demands for more stringent state and self-regulation.

The changing context of philanthropy and social finance

Philanthropy, both individual and institutionalized, is well established and robust in all of the Anglo-Saxon countries, serving as an important source of financing, volunteers and supporting culture for nonprofits. But, it is also changing in important ways that will affect the management of nonprofits.

Giving and volunteering

As Table 2.1 shows, philanthropy averages about 12 percent of the total revenue of the nonprofit sector in these countries; almost 75 percent of philanthropy is provided by individuals, about 15 percent by foundations and 8 percent by corporations (Hall et al., 2005; McKeever, 2015; Australian Government et al., 2016; Keen and Audickas, 2017). Giving and volunteering are widespread across the populations, with between 60 to 83 percent of people reporting they give to charity and 25 to 45 percent of people saying they volunteer. Although tax incentives are not the primarily reason for charitable giving, donors are nevertheless responsive to them and these incentives are comparatively generous in the Anglo-Saxon countries (Charities Aid Foundation, 2016). Indeed, the systems of incentives have expanded over the past two decades with no discussion of reducing them except in the US. The Obama administration repeatedly proposed but did not enact a cap on the deduction for charitable giving and, while the Trump administration has not directly lowered it, the 2018 changes that allow more taxfilers to take standard deductions rather than itemize them is predicted to suppress charitable giving by \$13 billion to \$20 billion annually (Delaney and Thompson, 2018).

Philanthropy supports a wide range of causes in all four countries, although very large non-profits are the beneficiaries to a much greater extent than small ones. In the US, for example, the top 400 nonprofits attract one-quarter of donations (Joslyn and Olsen-Phillips, 2017). In contrast, small, community-based organizations are struggling to raise new revenues and maintain enough revenue to stay afloat for the next fiscal year (Charles Stanley, 2018; Morris et al., 2018). In terms of the types of causes supported, the patterns are similar with religion, followed by health/medical and education, garnering the largest shares of philanthropy, although volunteering for these causes appears to be diminishing. Increasingly, people of all ages are seeking particular experiences and personal rewards in their volunteering, rather seeing volunteering as a means of pursuing a cause (Rochester, 2018).

Although the aggregate levels of philanthropy have been relatively stable, even rising slightly in the US (Giving USA, 2017), its composition and donor expectations are changing. Both giving and volunteering have become increasingly concentrated and reliant on older people (CAF, 2019). Overall, fewer people are giving and the rate of household donations (on average 3 percent of their income in the US, about 0.4 percent in the UK) has been stagnant, or declining slightly, for over a decade (Imagine Canada and Rideau Hall Foundation, 2018). As a result, philanthropy has become more reliant on High Net Worth (HNW) individuals and families making large gifts, yet HNW donors are not giving as much as they have the capacity to give (Baker, Barraket and Elmes, 2017). HNW donors, particularly those who earned their wealth at a relatively young age as entrepreneurs are tech-savvy, impatient and risk taking,

Table 2.1 Aggregate and distribution of philanthropy

	Australia	*Canada*	*UK*	*US*
Total Amount of Philanthropy \$US billion	\$23.6	\$15.9	\$26.8	\$390.1
Philanthropy as a % of Total Nonprofit Revenues	7.3	10.8	17	13.3
% of Population reporting Giving	81	82	61	83
% of Population reporting Volunteering	44	44	42–51	25
% to Religion	28	26–40	20	32

Sources: Imagine Canada and Rideau Hall Foundation, 2018; McKeever, 2015; Australian Government et al., 2016; Keen and Audickas, 2017.

desirous of maintaining control over their philanthropy, and have high expectations of achieving results, for which they want metrics. In short, 'they aren't satisfied to slap Band-Aids on social problems but want to rebuild entire systems' (Joslyn and Olsen-Phillips, 2017). HNW individuals often engage quite extensively with a nonprofit before contributing, or operate their own foundations and donor advised funds (DAFs), and look to social investing for which they anticipate a financial as well as a social return. Given that DAFs are much more flexible than foundations and enable gifts to be anonymous (for donors who do not wish to be 'cultivated' by many other organizations when their gifts are public), they have boomed in popularity in recent years, becoming the fastest growing destination for charitable giving in the US and Canada (Rooney, 2017). At the same time, the federated United Way campaigns are in trouble in the US and to a lesser extent in Canada, and giving to social services has flatlined (Blum, 2017; Paarlberg and Hwang, 2017).

Alongside the implications of growing income inequality, changing demographics are reshaping philanthropy in significant ways. The Baby Boom generation (born between 1946 and 1964), particularly women, has long been counted on as the stalwarts of philanthropy. They still account for over 40 percent of giving (Cowley et al., 2011; Pharoah, 2011) and their passing over the next few decades will result in a transfer of trillions of dollars of their wealth to their children and some portion to charity, producing predictions of a 'new golden age' of philanthropy. The Boomer cohort has been surpassed in size, generosity and civic engagement, however, by the Millennials (born between 1980 and 2000). The Millennials are already giving at higher rates, if not yet in greater amounts, than the Boomers (84 percent compared to 72 percent) and much higher than their Gen X parents (at 59 percent) (Rovner, 2013). As digital natives, they are predisposed to contributing through online platforms, enjoy 'micro' volunteering, mainly using their smart phones, and quite carefully investigate a nonprofit before engaging with it. They thus have high expectations that these organizations will be transparent adept with data and online technologies, and sophisticated in their storytelling about results (Gorczyca and Hartman, 2017). Retaining Millennials takes some work because they are not loyal to a brand or institution, with the result that the once-safe 'mega' brands – the well-known mid-sized and large social service and health agencies – are having to work much harder to remain relevant for younger donors, and the complacent are falling behind. As staff and leaders in the nonprofit sector, Millennials are also shaking things up as they look to greater diversity, anticipate inter-organizational collaboration rather than competition, and value both life balance and decent compensation (Joslyn, 2018). Because it has proven difficult to advance to higher positions within many nonprofits, the Millennials are very likely to work in startups or found their own organizations, with the result that their potential in many parts of the sector is untapped.

Finally, in spite of how diverse these societies have become, philanthropy still lacks a good understanding of how to engage or fundraise among cultural minority groups (Weisinger, Borges-Méndez and Milofsky, 2016), and nonprofits have substantial work to do in promoting greater diversity through meaningful participation among their boards, volunteers and staff.

Social finance

Although not a new invention, social finance has expanded and diversified over the past decade, led by the Anglo-Saxon countries, resulting in new instruments, institutions and exchanges (see Han et al., Chapter 33 this volume; Salamon, 2014; Nicholls, Paton and Emerson, 2015). The primary goals are to generate new sources of private capital for nonprofits, offer new tools and new markets for investors who seek to achieve social and environmental goals combined with the possibility of financial returns, and elevate performance incentives by linking these returns with results-based metrics. The UK took an early lead when in 2012 the government, working with a number of banks, established Big Society Capital, an independent institution intended to catalyze the social investment market and fund projects in the social sector. By 2017 Big Society Capital reported that, with its co-investors, about 590 million GBP (about $820 million US) had been drawn upon by charities and social enterprises. Its US counterpart, the Social Innovation Fund, was established by the Obama administration with a goal of linking evidence to funding, although the ability of nonprofit grantees to undertake rigorous evaluation was more challenging than anticipated (Zandniapour and Deterding, 2017), and the Fund was eliminated by the Trump administration. Until recently a laggard in this area, the Canadian government in 2018 committed $755 million (about $560 millions US) over ten years to a new social finance fund and an additional $50 million ($37 million US) over two years towards making the sector 'investment ready.'

Since being pioneered with a plan to reduce recidivism in a UK prison in 2010, all of the governments have become enthusiastic supporters of pay-for-performance contracts, often called social impact bonds (SIBs). From a policy perspective, SIBs aim to drive innovation and systems change in service delivery, particularly social services, and save money in the long run by supporting prevention rather than remedies at a later date. They operate by having a nonprofit contract to meet certain performance targets, funded by private investors, and these investors are repaid their investment as well as a return on their risk by government if the social outcomes are achieved. Although more than 60 SIBs have been issued by state and national governments in the four countries across a wide range of social services and health prevention (Del Giudice and Migliavacca, 2018; Khovrenkov and Kobayaski, 2018; Tomkinson, 2018), the evidence base of their effectiveness – in prompting innovation, improving outcomes and financial benefits – is still limited and 'maturing' (Department of Social Services Partnership, 2016).

With these public sector initiatives, as well as engagement by foundations in impact investing, the supply of new private capital for public purposes has substantially expanded, but significant barriers still exist on the demand side – in the ability of the nonprofits to fully exploit the potential. These barriers include lack of financial literacy, data analysis and knowledge about the marketplace, inadequate technology and other infrastructure, the challenges of producing robust metrics, and a misfit between the investment tools being offered and those needed by nonprofits (Rosener, 2013; Daggers and Nicholls, 2016; Phillips and Johnson, 2019). Moreover, the capital needs, risks, intermediaries and suppliers are quite different in different subsectors, making social impact investing increasingly variable across subsectors. The emerging implications of social finance are a growing gap between the organizations that can effectively operate in this space and those that lack the capacity or interest in doing so. In addition, the pressure to measure and demonstrate impact, often with standardized metrics, will continue to grow and will require new skills and capacities across the sector.

Contracting and service delivery

The Anglo-Saxon countries are regarded as exemplars of a liberal welfare state, as defined in Esping-Andersen's (1990) typology and its adaption for the nonprofit sector by Salamon and Anheier (1998). In the typical liberal welfare state, public spending on social welfare is relatively low, governments have a preference for market solutions in service delivery and, partly as a substitute for governments, the nonprofit sector is relatively large. When liberal welfare states enthusiastically embraced New Public Management (NPM) beginning in the 1980s, the existing contracting-out of services to the nonprofit and private sectors expanded. Under NPM, service delivery became highly fragmented, with different government departments managing different sets of contracts in an uncoordinated manner, each with their distinctive regulations and accountability requirements. This led to increased competition among nonprofits and with for-profits, extensive administrative burdens of compliance, and significant barriers to access for service users (Phillips and Smith, 2011). Continued austerity pressures have further cut program budgets and offloaded services.

It is important to note, however, that the implementation of NPM across these liberal welfare states and across service fields in each varied considerably. Moreover, as federations (and with devolution in the UK), the funding and delivery of services, especially human services, differs within each of these countries. Rather than concentrating on these differences, this section identifies several recent trends, within a context of extensive marketization of human services, that are generating new kinds of challenges for nonprofits.

The first is an emphasis on putting the user first through systems-based approaches and greater integration of services (Halligan, 2015; Smith and Phillips, 2016). This is manifest in greater coordination of programming and back office operations, co-location of services and collaboration among service providers. The popularity of the 'collective impact' model (Kania and Kramer, 2011), which specifies a series of steps for achieving sustained collaboration and shared measurement systems, has extended partnership into cross-sector arrangements. A different approach to user-centered services comes under the label of 'personalization' through voucher systems and personal accounts (envelopes of funding that the users manage to pay for an individualized basket of services). Although vouchers have long been used to purchase education and childcare services in the US and personal budgets for seniors and persons with disability have been implemented in the UK, perhaps the most dramatic experiment in personalization is occurring in Australia which in 2013 rolled its state level services for persons with disabilities into a national system of personal accounts (Carey et al., 2018). The results of these personal account systems have been mixed, often due to the fact that the nonprofit 'market' of suppliers is fragile and the need to invest in new technology, employee training, advertising to users and open retail outlets is not feasible for many nonprofits (Cunningham and Nickson, 2010; National Audit Office, 2016).

A second trend that is closely aligned with a system-based approach is an emphasis on design thinking and co-production. Design thinking has been described as 'crafting new solutions with people, not just for them' (Carstensen and Bason, 2012; McGann, Blomkamp and Lewis, 2018); who is involved and how they are engaged lends legitimacy to the process, and supposedly generates better results. More broadly, co-production refers to the active involvement of citizens, stakeholders and their organizations, not just as service users and not only as service contractors, but as co-creators in the design and joint delivery of public services, working closely with professionals (Fledderus, Brandsen and Honingh, 2015; Bovaird et al., 2016; Brandsen et al., Chapter 20 this volume). Although the concept of co-production has focused on how governments engage with stakeholders, nonprofits are also under pressure to more fully engage their users, members and stakeholders, and to be more diverse and inclusive in their governance, employment and operations.

Third, while innovation may be the by-product of these approaches, innovation has become valued as an end in itself. Foundations and other funders seek to support social innovation – projects that promise something new – rather than financing longstanding, well-run programs. Although there is little question that innovation is needed to find better ways of addressing a myriad of societal and environmental issues, the innovation proponents often do not recognize the inherent difficulties. Capital lacks the necessary patience to see results and take them to scale. Funders are not prepared to support the operational infrastructure required to enable nonprofits to innovate and are not equipped for the high risk of failure. There is also a perception that social enterprises or startups may be more adept at innovation than established nonprofits, which may make it more difficult for the latter to raise venture capital. In short, the expectations on nonprofits to be innovative may be over inflated.

Fourth, impact has become the mantra of strategic philanthropy, and performance targets remain a central requirement of the bulk of government funding and are at the core of SIBs (Mosley and Smith, 2018). Indeed, impact has become commodified through impact investing where metrics that compare impacts across different types of projects are the basis for trading these investments on a variety of new social exchanges. Yet, nonprofits and their funders often do not adequately support outcome measurement, either financially or in the time frames needed to assess impacts. In particular, methodical measurement of impact may not sit well with innovation that is moving fast and has many moving parts (Phillips and Carlan, 2018). The data environment itself presents an additional challenge. As Benjamin, Voida and Bopp (2018) report, the environment in which most nonprofits work is partial and fragmented, duplication common and, coupled with inadequate data analytical skills, inhibits the use of data in managing and monitoring outcomes. The availability of big, open data is quickly reshaping the data landscape, however, at least for the nonproifts with the skills and technology to navigate it (see McNutt, Chapter 17 this volume).

Although the specific implications of these trends in service delivery vary by policy field, several effects are widely reported across the Anglo-Saxon countries. Under continued financial constraints and service integration, larger, multiservice nonprofits have fared better than smaller, specialized ones, often landing major funding and subcontracting to community-specific nonprofits. As a result, power dynamics within many subsectors are being reconfigured, and whether these tiered arrangements serve minority communities well is an open question. While competition for contracts and other funding remains strong, so too are the pressures from governments and foundations for collaboration, so that nonprofits often find themselves having to partner with the same organizations that are their competitors (Mosley and Smith, 2018). Anecdotal evidence suggests that mergers are becoming more common due to financial pressures or interventions by foundations.

Contract management continues to have negative effects. It is all too common that government contracts are signed late and do not cover the full costs of these services and other funders have been reluctant to support 'overhead' that pays for technology, management systems and core staff, perpetuating a 'starvation cycle' (Lecy and Searing, 2015). Philanthropic gifts are widely used to subsidize government contracts – the magnitude of which is impossible to calculate – and even very large nonprofits have engaged in risky behaviour leading to bankruptcy (Human Services Council, 2016). This is compounded by declining individual donations for social services, other than foodbanks (Blum, 2017), in part because many have taken their brand for granted among a generation that is not brand loyal and failed to invest in new approaches to fundraising.

As a consequence of this interplay between public and private funding, the nonprofit sector and its ability to deliver services is becoming more differentiated by place, with abundant organizations in some and relative 'charity deserts' in other places (Breeze and Mohan, 2016). Over time, economically disadvantaged communities may be served by fewer nonprofits, and government austerity may disproportionately hollow out networks in poorer places, thereby reinforcing disadvantage (Lam and McDougle, 2015; Jones et al., 2016). In this environment of change, often with conflicting pressures, the demands on boards of directors to be strategic, ensure that effective planning, control, evaluation and fundraising systems exist, and take diversity and inclusion seriously is indeed daunting.

Conclusion: Tectonic shifts

The unfolding developments in regulation, philanthropy and service delivery in the Anglo-Saxon countries discussed in this chapter are signs of major shifts, akin to a tectonic scale, in the relationship of nonprofits to governments and societies at large.

Growing income inequality is generating new questions about the public responsibilities of private wealth. It is connected to the interest in public benefit tests to qualify as charitable, and underpins such issues as: Does the distribution of philanthropy serve societies well? What is the value of perpetuity for funds held in DAFs and private foundations? Are nonprofits sufficiently inclusive? At the same time, shifting demographics are producing different expectations and ways of giving, volunteering and activism. Not only are the Millennials, the largest, most diverse cohort in history, more tech-savvy and less brand loyal, but they have different expectations than their Gen X parents and Boomer grandparents about inclusion, collaboration, decent work and effective leadership. Big data combines with the Millennials' hardwired assumptions about transparency to create new norms of voluntary reporting by nonprofits. The increased hybridization of the nonprofit sector has blurred the lines between non- and for-profit, which is raising some fundamental questions as to when a nonprofit is actually nonprofit. In addition, the new markets for social investments have monetized impacts, creating a new industry of metrics and reinforcing the expectations of individual donors and institutional funders for performance measurement of their gifts and grants. A focus on working collaboratively for greater impact is causing many to ask whether there are simply too many nonprofits doing similar things. Finally, differing assumptions about the role that nonprofits play in democracy are playing out in divergent ways: through attempts to restrict nonprofit advocacy and, in the US, to politicize the sector by facilitating greater participation in partisan politics.

In spite of its economic and social importance and the magnitude of these long-term shifts, the nonprofit sector seems to have faded from governments' agenda. Even in the UK where both Labour and Conservative-led governments over the past 20 years had articulated strategies for the sector, these have been lost. Canada is awaiting delivery of the Liberal government's commitment to modernize the policy framework, and Australia's sector rightly has a skeptical stance toward the policies of the national government. Whether intentional or inadvertent, the main policies emanating from the Trump administration have been mainly harmful to the sector. In sum, it seems that both nonprofits and governments have substantial work ahead in order to be quake-ready.

References

Australian Government. (2010) *Contributions of the not-for-profit sector, Productivity Commission Research report.* Canberra: Productivity Commission.

Australian Government, Australian Charities and Not-for-Profits Commission (ACNC), Centre for Social Impact and Social Policy Research Centre. (2016) *Australian charities report 2016.* Melbourne: ACNC.

Baker, C., Barraket, J. and Elmes, A. (2017) *Philanthropy and philanthropists: Giving Australia.* Canberra and Brisbane: Commonwealth of Australia and Australian Centre for Philanthropy and Nonprofit Stuides, Queensland University of Technology.

Barber, P. and Farwell, M. (2016) The relationships between state and nonstate interventions in charitable solicitation law in the United States. In O.B. Breen, A. Dunn and M. Sidel (eds.). *Regulatory waves: Comparative perspectives on state regulation and self-regulation policies in the nonprofit sector.* Cambridge: Cambridge University Press, 199–220.

Benjamin, L.M., Voida, A. and Bopp, C. (2018) Policy fields, data systems, and the performance of nonprofit human service organizations, *Human Service Organizations: Management, Leadership & Governance,* 42(2): 185–204.

Blum, D.E. (2017) Social-service groups fight to reverse a slide in donations, *Chronicle of Philanthropy,* 1 November.

Blumberg, M. (2017) *Blumbergs' snapshot of the Canadian charity sector 2015.* www.globalphilanthropy.ca/blog/blumbergs_canadian_charity_sector_snapshot_2015 (Accessed 20 August 2018).

Bovaird, T., Stoker, G., Jones, T., Loeffler, E. and Pinilla Roncancio, M. (2016) Activating collective co-production of public services: Influencing citizens to participate in complex governance mechanisms in the UK, *International Review of Administrative Sciences*, 82(1): 47–68.

Breen, O.B., Dunn, A. and Sidel, M. (eds.). (2016). *Regulatory waves: Comparative perspectives on state regulation and self-regulation policies in the nonprofit sector.* Cambridge: Cambridge University Press.

Breeze, B. and Mohan, J. (2016) *The logic of charity: Great Expectations in hard times.* Basingstoke, UK: Palgrave Macmillan.

Canada House of Commons. (2009) Debate on Bill C-470. Hansard. https://openparliament.ca/bills/40-3/C-470/%0A%0A (Accessed 15 May 2018).

Carey, G., Dickinson, H., Malbon, E. and Reeders, D. (2018) The vexed question of market stewardship in the public sector: Examining equity and the social contract through the Australian National Disability Insurance Scheme, *Social Policy and Administration*, 52(1): 387–407.

Carstensen, H. V and Bason, C. (2012) Powering collaborative policy innovation: Can innovation labs help?, *The Innovation Journal*, 17(1): 2–26.

Chan, K. (2015) The UK's raging public benefit debate and its relevance in Canada. Unpublished paper.

Charities Aid Foundation. (2019) *World giving index: Ten years of giving trends.* London: Charities Aid Foundation.

Charities Aid Foundation. (2016) *Donation states: An international comparison of the tax treatment of dontations.* London: Charities Aid Foundation.

CCEW – Charity Commission for England and Wales. (2018) *Final report of the Charity Commission Safeguarding Task Force.* London: Charity Commission. https://www.gov.uk/government/publications/final-report-of-charity-commission-safeguarding-taskforce/final-report-of-charity-commission-safeguarding-taskforce (Accessed 22 October 2018).

Charles Stanley & Co. (2018) *Charity income spotlight.* London: Charles Stanley.

Cornforth, C. (2014) Understanding and combating mission drift in social enterprises, *Social Enterprise Journal*, 10(1): 3–20.

Cowley, E., McKenzie, T., Pharoah, C. and Smith, S. (2011) *The new state of donation: Three decades of household giving to charity 1978–2008.* London: Centre for Charitable Giving and Philanthropy, Cass Business School, City University London.

Cunningham, I. and Nickson, D. (2010) *Personalisation and its implications for work and employment in the voluntary sector.* Glasgow: Scottish Centre for Employment Research/University of Strathclyde Business School. https://strathprints.strath.ac.uk/30955/ (Accessed 15 June 2018).

Daggers, J. and Nicholls, A. (2016) *The landscape of social impact investment research: Trends and opportunities.* Oxford: Saïd Business School, University of Oxford.

Delaney, T. (2018) New threat in Congress to politicize nonprofits and foundations: An Interview with Tim Delaney, *Nonprofit Quarterly.* https://nonprofitquarterly.org/2018/03/09/new-threat-in-congress-to-politicize-nonprofits-foundations-interview-tim-delaney/ (Accessed 10 June 2018).

Delaney, T. and Thompson, D.L. (2018) Opinion: Nonprofits must move swiftly to fight for sound public policies, *Chronicle of Philanthropy*, 3 January.

Del Giudice, A. and Migliavacca, M. (2018) Social impact bonds and institutional investors: An empirical analysis of a complicated relationship, *Nonprofit and Voluntary Sector Quarterly*, Online First 3 September.

Deloitte. (2017) *Economic contribution of the Australian charity sector.* Canberra: Deloitte Access Economics Touche Tohmatsu.

Department of Social Services Partnership. (2016) *Social impact investing research.* Canberra: Department of Social Services Partnership for the Prime Minister's Community Business Partnership.

Ebrahim, A., Battilana, J. and Mair, J. (2014) The governance of social enterprises: Mission drift and accountability challenges in hybrid organizations, *Research in Organizational Behavio,*. 34(November): 81–100.

Electoral Commission UK (2017) *Overview of regulated non-party campaigning.* London: Electoral Commission.

Emmett, B. and Emmett, G. (2015) *Charities in Canada as an economic sector.* Toronto, ON: Imagine Canada.

Esping-Andersen, G. (1990) *The three worlds of welfare capitalism.* Princeton, NJ: Princeton University Press.

Etherington, S.S. (2017) Reflections on Modernizing and Reforming Regulation. In M. McGregor-Lowndes and B. Wyatt (eds.). *Regulating charities: The inside story.* London: Routledge, 59–77.

Fledderus, J., Brandsen, T. and Honingh, M.E. (2015) User co-production of public service delivery: An uncertainty approach, *Public Policy and Administration*, 30(2): 145–164.

Giving USA. (2017) *Giving USA 2017: The annual report on philanthropy for the Year 2016.* Chicago, IL and Indianapolis, IN: Giving USA Foundation and Lilly Family School of Philanthropy.

Gorczyca, M. and Hartman, R.L. (2017) The new face of philanthropy: The role of intrinsic motivation in millennials' attitudes and intent to donate to charitable organizations, *Journal of Nonprofit & Public Sector Marketing,* 29(4): 415–453.

Grønbjerg, K.A. and Smith, S.R. (2014) *The changing dynamics of government–nonprofit relations: Advancing the field – a review essay.* Paper presented to the International Society for Third Sector Research, Münster, Germany. https://www.researchgate.net/publication/301291814_The_Changing_Dynamics_of_Gov ernment-Nonprofit_Relations_Advancing_the_Field_-_A_Review_Essay (Accessed 5 May 2018).

Grønbjerg, K.A. and McGiverin-Bohan, K. (2016) Local government interest in and justifications for collecting payments-in-lieu of (property) taxes from charities, *Nonprofit Policy Forum,* 7(1): 7.

Hall, M.H., Barr, C.W., Easwaramoorthy, M., Sokolowski, S.W. and Salamon, L.M. (2005) *The Canadian nonprofit and voluntary sector in comparative perspective.* Baltimore, MD: Johns Hopkins Center for Civil Society Studies.

Halligan, J. (2015) Coordination of welfare through a large integrated organization: The Australian Department of Human Services, *Public Management Review,* 17(7): 1002–1020.

House of Commons International Development Committee, UK Parliament. (2018) *Sexual exploitation and abuse in the aid sector,* 31 July. London: UK Parliament. https://publications.parliament.uk/pa/ cm201719/cmselect/cmintdev/840/840.pdf (Accessed 20 October 2018).

Human Services Council. (2016) *New York nonprofits in the aftermath of FEGS : A call to action.* New York City, NH: Human Services Council. www.nysba.org/LessonsFromtheFEGSCollapse/ (Accessed 18 May 2018).

Imagine Canada. (2017) *Imagine Canada Standards Program.* www.imaginecanada.ca/our-programs/stand ards-program (Accessed 15 July 2018).

Imagine Canada and Rideau Hall Foundation (2018) *30 Years of giving in Canada.* Toronto: Rideau Hall Foundation.

InterSector Partners (2018) *Latest L3C tally.* https://www.intersectorl3c.com/l3c (Accessed 15 October 2018).

Jones, G., Meegan, R., Kennett, P. and Croft, J. (2016) The uneven impact of austerity on the voluntary and community sector: A tale of two cities, *Urban Studies,* 53(10): 2064–2080.

Joslyn, H. (2018) How Millennials lead, *Chronicle of Philanthropy,* 9 January.

Joslyn, H. and Olsen-Phillips, P. (2017) Philanthropy 400 special report: Top charities appeal to impatient, policy-minded donors, *Chronicle of Philanthropy,* 1 November.

Kania, J. and Kramer, M. (2011) Collective impact, *Stanford Social Innovation Review,* (Winter): 36–41.

Keen, R. and Audickas, L. (2017) *Charities and the voluntary sector: Statistics. Briefing Paper SN05428.* London: UK Parliament. http://researchbriefings.parliament.uk/ResearchBriefing/Summary/SN05428#fullre port (Accessed 12 July 2018).

Khovrenkov, I. and Kobayaski, C. (2018) *Assessing social impact bonds in Canada.* Regina, SK: Johnson-Shoyama Graduate School of Public Policy. https://www.schoolofpublicpolicy.sk.ca/documents/research/ policy-briefs/JSGS-policybriefs-Social-Impact-Bonds_FINAL.pdf (Accessed 5 October 2018).

Lam, M. and McDougle, L. (2015) Community variation in the financial health of nonprofit human service organizations: An examination of organizational and contextual effects, *Nonprofit and Voluntary Sector Quarterly,* 45(3): 500–525.

Lecy, J.D. and Searing, E.A.M. (2015) Anatomy of the nonprofit starvation cycle: An analysis of falling overhead ratios in the nonprofit sector, *Nonprofit and Voluntary Sector Quarterly,* 44(3): 39–563.

McGann, M., Blomkamp, E. and Lewis, J.M. (2018) The rise of public sector innovation labs: Experiments in design thinking for policy, *Policy Sciences,* 51(3): 249–267.

McGregor-Lowndes, M. and Wyatt, B. (2017a) Conclusion. In M. McGregor-Lowndes and B. Wyatt (eds.). *Regulating charities: The inside story.* London: Routledge, 261–292.

McGregor-Lowndes, M. and Wyatt, B. (2017b) Introduction. In M. McGregor-Lowndes and B. Wyatt (eds.). *Regulating charities: The inside story.* London: Routledge, 1–14.

McKeever, B. (2015) *The nonprofit sector in brief.* Washington, DC: Urban Institute.

Meiksins, R. (2015) Judge terms modern nonprofit hospitals a 'legal fiction', *Nonprofit Quarterly,* 7 July. https://nonprofitquarterly.org/2015/07/07/judge-terms-modern-nonprofit-hospitals-a-legal-fiction/ (Accessed 3 October 2018).

Michael, L. (2018a) Calls to abolish basic religious charity category from ACNC legislation, *ProBono Australia,* 1 March. https://probonoaustralia.com.au/news/2018/03/calls-abolish-basic-religious-charity-category-acnc-legislation/ (Accessed 5 October 2018).

Michael, L. (2018b) Foreign Donations Bill changes labelled a win for charities, *ProBono Australia*, 21 September. https://probonoaustralia.com.au/news/2018/09/foreign-donations-bill-changes-labelled-win-charities/ (Accessed 5 October 2018).

Michael, L. (2018c). Disability advocacy in NSW under threat, *ProBono Australia*, 3 October. https://probono australia.com.au/news/2018/10/disability-advocacy-nsw-threat/ (Accessed 22 October 2018).

Morgan, G.G. (2012) Public benefit and charitable status: Assessing a 20 year process of reforming the primary legal framework for voluntary activity in the UK, *Voluntary Sector Review*, 3(1): 67–91.

Morgan, G.G. and Fletcher, N.J. (2013) Mandatory public benefit reporting as a basis for charity accountability: Findings from England and Wales, *Voluntas*, 24(3): 805–830.

Morris, D. (2016) The Charity Commission for England and Wales: A fine example or another fine mess?, *Chicago-Kent Law Review*, 91(3): 965–990.

Morris, G., Roberts, D., MacIntosh, J. and Bordone, A. (2018) *The financial health of the United States nonprofit sector*. New York, NY: Oliver Wyman.

Mosley, J. and Smith, S.R. (2018) Human service agencies and the question of impact: Lessons for theory, policy, and practice, *Human Service Organizations Management, Leadership and Governance*, 40(2): 187–188.

National Audit Office, UK. (2016) *Personalised commissioning in adult social care: Report by the Comptroller and Auditor General*. London: House of Commons. https://www.nao.org.uk/wp-content/uploads/2016/03/Personalised-commissioning-in-adult-social-care-update.pdf%0Ahttps://www.nao.org.uk/wp-content/uploads/2016/03/Personalised-commissioning-in-adult-social-care-summary-update.pdf (Accessed 20 July 2018).

Nicholls, A. (2010) Institutionalizing social entrepreneurship in regulatory space: Reporting and disclosure by community interest companies, *Accounting, Organizations and Society*, 35(4): 394–415.

Nicholls, A., Paton, R. and Emerson, J. (eds.). (2015) *Social finance*. Oxford: Oxford University Press.

Owens, M. (2017) Challenged regulators. In M. McGregor-Lowndes and B. Wyatt (eds.). *Regulating charities: The inside story*. London: Routledge, 81–96.

Paarlberg, L. and Hwang, H. (2017) The heterogeneity of competitive forces: The impact of competition for resources on United Way fundraising, *Nonprofit and Voluntary Sector Quarterly*, 45(5): 897–921.

Parachin, A. (2015a) Charitable foundations and advocacy; Reimagining the doctrine of political purposes. Montreal: Montreal Research Laboratory on Canadian Philanthropy.

Parachin, A. (2015b) Charity, politics and neutrality, *Charity Law and Practice Review*, 18: 23–56.

Pekkanen, R.J. and Smith, S.R. (2014) Nonprofits and advocacy. In R.J. Pekkanen, S.R. Smith and Y. Tsujinaka (eds.). *Nonprofits and advocacy*. Baltimore, MD: Johns Hopkins University Press, 1–17.

Pharoah, C. (2011) Private giving and philanthropy – Their place in the Big Society, *People, Place and Policy Online*, 52: 65–75.

Phillips, S.D. and Carlan, V. (2018) On impact: Emerging challenges of evaluation for Canada's nonprofit sector. In K. Seel (ed.). *Management of nonprofit and charitable organizations in Canada*, 3rd ed. Toronto: LexisNexus.

Phillips, S.D. and Johnson, B. (2019) Inching to impact: The demand side of social impact investing, *Journal of Business Ethics*, Online First, June: 1–15.

Phillips, S.D. and Smith, S.R. (2011) Introduction. In S.D. Phillips and S.R. Smith (eds.). *Governance and regulation in the third sector: International perspective*. London: Routledge, 1–36.

Regulator of Community Interest Companies. (2017) *Annual report 2016–2017*. London, Department for Business, Energy & Industrial Strategy.

Rochester, C. (2018) *Trends in volunteering*. Building Change Trust. www.volunteernow.co.uk/fs/doc/publications/trends-in-volunteering-final.pdf (Accessed 2 August 2018).

Rooney, P. (2017) Have donor-advised funds and other philanthropic innovations changed the flow of giving in the United States?, *Nonprofit Quarterly*, 7 November. https://nonprofitquarterly.org/2017/11/07/have-donor-advised-funds-and-other-philanthropic-innovations-changed-the-flow-of-giving-in-the-united-states/ (Accessed 3 August 2018).

Rosener, A. (2013) Leveraging the power of foundations: An analysis of program-related investing, *Foundation Review*, 5(3): 70–71.

Rovner, M. (2013) *The next generation of giving – American giving*. Charleston, SC: Blackbaud. https://www.michiganfoundations.org/sites/default/files/resources/Next-Generation-of-Giving-Blackbaud-Study.pdf (Accessed 15 September 2018).

Salamon, L.M. (ed.). (2014) *New frontiers of philanthropy*. Oxford: Oxford University Press.

Salamon, L.M. and Anheier, H.K. (1998) Social origins of civil society: Explaining the nonprofit sector cross-nationally, *Voluntas*, 9(3): 213–248.

Salamon, L.M., Sokolowski, S.W. and Haddock, M.A. (2017). *Explaining civil society development: A social origins approach*. Baltimore, MD: Johns Hopkins University Press.

Sharman, A. (2018). Charities accept 'painful' findings of MPs' aid inquiry and promise improvements, *Civil Society*, 31 July. https://www.civilsociety.co.uk/news/charities-accept-painful-findings-of-mps-aid-in quiry-and-promise-improvements.html (Accessed 20 October 2018).

SVCF – Silicon Valley Community Foundation. (2018) Update from Silicon Valley Community Foundation board of directors, 27 June. https://www.siliconvalleycf.org/blog/announcements/update-silicon-val ley-community-foundation-board-directors (Accessed 20 October 2018).

Smith, S.R. and Phillips, S.D. (2016) The changing and challenging environment of nonprofit human services: Implications for governance and program implementation, *Nonprofit Policy Forum*, 7(1): 63–76.

Tomkinson, E. (2018) *Social impact bond (SIB) UK v. world map*. https://emmatomkinson.com/category/ world-map/ (Accessed 20 October 2018).

Weisinger, J.Y., Borges-Méndez, R. and Milofsky, C. (2016) Diversity in the nonprofit and voluntary sector, *Nonprofit and Voluntary Sector Quarterly*, 45(Supplemental): 3S–27S.

Williams, W. (2017) Advancement of religion as charitable purpose in question, *Pro Bono Australia*, 15 December. https://probonoaustralia.com.au/news/2017/12/advancement-religion-charitable-purpose-question/ (Accessed 21 September 2018).

Wong, A. and Fattal, I. (2017) The tax-bill provision that would cost Harvard millions, *The Atlantic*, 30 November. https://www.theatlantic.com/education/archive/2017/11/the-tax-bill-provision-that- would-cost-harvard-millions/547175/ (Accessed 22 September 2018).

Wyland, M. (2017) Tax reform measure passes Senate without repeal of Johnson Amendment attached, *Non-profit Quarterly*, 4 December. https://nonprofitquarterly.org/2017/12/04/tax-reform-measure-passes- senate-without-repeal-johnson-amendment-attached/ (Accessed 23 September 2018).

Zandniapour, L. and Deterding, N.M. (2017) Lessons from the Social Innovation Fund, *American Journal of Evaluation*, 39(1): 27–41.

3

NONPROFIT MANAGEMENT CONTEXT

Continental Europe and Scandinavia

Georg von Schnurbein

PROFESSOR OF PHILANTHROPY STUDIES, CENTER FOR PHILANTHROPY STUDIES,
UNIVERSITY OF BASEL, BASEL, SWITZERLAND

Alice Hengevoss

RESEARCH ASSISTANT, CENTER FOR PHILANTHROPY STUDIES, UNIVERSITY
OF BASEL, BASEL, SWITZERLAND

Socio-economic framework

As one of the wealthiest regions in the world, the economic environment in Europe has been favorable for nonprofits in recent decades. Especially, after the fall of the iron curtain, the non-profit sector has grown in all Western European countries as a consequence of economic growth and European integration. However, the situation changed to some extent after the economic and financial crisis in 2007/2008. There is a general trend to reduce government deficits and public debt in Europe (Davies, 2014). In most European countries public funding is the most important source of revenue for nonprofits, so the nonprofit sector had to deal with rationing and cutbacks. The crisis meant that in many European countries public spending on social welfare was insufficient and social services could not be adequately provided. Increases in donations and philanthropy could not substitute the lack of public funding in many countries. While in countries such as France the economic crisis caused severe social problems, in others such as Germany or Sweden the impact was much weaker.

Accordingly, research suggests a broad variety of national welfare systems across Europe which significantly define the role of the third sector in the individual countries (Salamon and Sokolowski, 2016). According to the works by Esping-Andersen (1990) and Salamon and Anheier (1998), the corporatist model dominates in countries such as Austria, France, Germany, or the Netherlands. These states have to a large extent subsidized the provision of public services to private nonprofit organizations, while the government acts as main funding source and regulator. The Scandinavian countries are usually described as the social-democratic model characterized by high levels of welfare spending. However, empiric evidence for the common distinction of the social origins theory (Salamon and Anheier, 1998) remains vague and it seems that many mixed-forms exist (Einolf, 2015). For instance, the Belgian welfare model is a combination of the principle of subsidiarity and a centralized public administration that allows for a close cooperation between nonprofits and the state. In Switzerland, one can find aspects of the corporatist model as well as of the liberal model (Helmig et al., 2010). The Southern countries of Italy, Spain, and Portugal have a third sector that is mainly focused on the areas of social services and health care (Salamon et al., 2012). While Italy has high state welfare spending, the third sector in the other Southern countries relies more heavily on private fees and charges for its income. Additionally, in the Southern countries the church still has a high influence on the third sector compared to other European countries.

In general, the legal framework for nonprofits is well developed in all European countries and offers a lot of opportunities for civic engagement. However, despite action towards a more uniform framework across Europe, significant differences between countries remain. The attempts for a European foundation statute as well as for other legal alignments on the European level have not been successful so far (Jakob, 2014). Tax ruling still differs significantly between countries. Moreover, transparency disclosure on nonprofits is still much less developed in Europe than in Anglo-Saxon countries. In most Western European countries, public registers on nonprofits are weak or non-existent. Although the statistical knowledge on nonprofits has been improved by several research studies and public programs, data records are far from comprehensive.

Important improvements have been made in regards to a court ruling by the European Court of Justice facilitating the tax exemption of cross-national donations within the European Union (Hüttemann and Helios, 2009). Additionally, most European countries have taken actions to increase private engagement for public purposes. For instance, most countries have passed laws to further incentivize the establishment of charitable foundations and the donation of money. Finally, the international fight on terrorism in recent years has led to a higher pressure on countries to increase transparency and accountability in the nonprofit sector (Then, 2006). As a consequence, many European countries (e.g., Germany and Switzerland) have introduced obligatory registration of nonprofits and board members, and organizations have to deal with stricter rules regarding their asset management.

Besides increased legal regulation, there is a strong trend towards self-regulation amongst European third sector organizations. The oldest self-regulation initiatives for nonprofits in Europe date back to the 1950s when first certificates for fundraising organizations where established. Today, there are certificates for fundraising organizations or governance codes for different types of nonprofit organizations. The idea of all these self-regulation initiatives is to reduce uncertainty for representatives of nonprofits and to increase transparency in the sector since legal obligation for disclosure is limited in most countries (Bies, 2010). However, the heterogeneity of the nonprofit sector and the missing external pressure for alignment (for instance by a stock market) lead to many different and competing solutions. For Germany and Switzerland, von Schnurbein and Stöckli (2013) found over 15 different governance codes for nonprofits directed to single organizations, federal structured systems, or to members of an association. For grant-making foundations, Sprecher, Egger, and von Schnurbein (2016) list governance codes or codes of conduct in 22 European countries.

Composition of the nonprofit sector

Table 3.1 gives an overview of the most important statistical information on the nonprofit sector in the different countries. The nonprofits' field of activities and the relationship with governmental agencies have grown through different political and economic contexts and thus vary significantly between countries. However, more recently, there seems to be a trend across Europe of increased cooperation between the public and third sector (Salamon and Toepler, 2015). In the following we group countries in four regions that are similar in their welfare state system, and describe the development and the composition of the nonprofit sector in each country.

Table 3.1 Statistical information on nonprofit sectors

Country	Total number of nonprofits	Most important field of activity[1] (ICNPO)	FTE[2] (share of total workforce)	Amount of volunteering[3]	Share GDP	Year of most recent data
France	400,000	41.6% Culture and Recreation 20.7% Social Services 15.7% Education and Research	1,435,330 (8.1%)	1,115,000	2.9%	2002
Belgium	17,794	41.4 % Culture and Recreation 12.4 % Education and Research 12.1% Social Services	368,300 (10%)		4.6%	2008
Netherlands		41.8% Health 27.8% Education and Research 19.2% Social Services	652,800 (11.9%)	390,000	15.3%	1995
Germany	589,000	38.8% Social Services 30.6% Health 11.7% Education and Research	1,440,000 (4.9%)	1,000,000	3.9%	2011
Austria	120,246	36.5% Social Services 19.6% Advocacy 14.26% Education and Research	210,000 (5.4%)	201,493	1.1%	2005
Switzerland	99,133	35.3% Social Services 32.4% Health 10.4% Education and Research	180,000 (4.5%)	80,000	6.0%	2005
Italy	208,718	26% Social Services 18% Health 15% Education and Research	580,000 (3.8%)	430,130	3.1%	2001
Spain	153,414	32% Social Services 25% Education and Research 14.5% Advocacy	475,179	253,599	4%	2005

Portugal		52% Social Services 16% Advocacy 11% Education	185,000 (4.3%)		2%	2006
Sweden	200,000	27% Culture and Recreation 21% Education and Research 18% Social Services	100,000	2,600,000	3.6 %	1992
Denmark	156,000	48% Culture and Recreation, and Education and Research 19% Social Services	140,620	110,041	6.6%	2006
Norway		61% Advocacy, and Culture and Recreation 35% Social Services	80,105	115,149	3.7%	1997
Finland	130,000	65% Education and Research, Health, and Social Services	181,500 (8.3%)		3.8%	2006

Source: Information compiled by the authors, references in the chapter.

Notes

ICNPO International Classification of Non-profit Organizations.
FTE Full-time equivalent.
GDP Gross domestic product.

1 Share of paid workforce.
2 FTE of paid workforce.
3 Additional FTE of volunteer workforce.

France, Belgium, and the Netherlands

The countries France, Belgium, and the Netherlands have a sizable and constantly growing third sector that plays an important role in the provision of social welfare. In France, the third sector experienced constant growth, with over 400,000 in the year 2002 (Archambault et al., 1999). Of these, associations constitute the major segment of nonprofit organizations, followed by a much smaller share of foundations, labor unions, political parties, and churches. Some 80.4% of all French nonprofit organizations are engaged in the field of public services, such as health care, social services, and education. The remaining 19.6% of nonprofits were engaged in civic and advocacy work, professional associations, and international activities (Archambault et al., 1999). The government accounts for more than half the funding of these nonprofit organizations; 57.8% of the organizations' revenue stems from public institutions, 34.7% from fees, and 7.5% of private giving by individuals or corporations (Archambault et al., 1999).

In Belgium, the third sector was established as a major provider of social welfare and public goods after the World War II (Mertens et al., 1999). In 2008, 17,794 *associations without profit purpose* (AWPPs) were registered in the *Non-profit Institution Satellite Account*[1] (National Account Institute, 2010). Similarly to the French context, Belgian nonprofits are highly concentrated in the fields of public services. In 2004, 71% of its activities went to the provision of health care, education and research, and social services. Advocacy activities accounted for 15% of nonprofit activity (National Account Institute, 2010). The nonprofit sector's funding structure underlines the principle of subsidiarity. In 1995, 76.5% of the nonprofit revenue stemmed from public sources, while private sales and membership dues only accounted for 18.7% of the income. Private donations only covered 4.8% of nonprofit revenue. Further, over two-thirds of government funding went to the fields of health care and education (Mertens et al., 1999). The high share of nonprofit employment in Belgium's total workforce is explained by the fact that hospitals and private schools, highly professionalized institutions, account for a large part of the third sector (National Account Institute, 2010).

The Netherlands has in relative terms the largest third sector of the countries analyzed in the *Johns Hopkins Comparative Nonprofit Sector Project* (CNP). Dutch nonprofits are often referred to as "private initiatives" or "societal midfield". The third sector has grown through a long tradition of private initiatives and – in contrast to the Belgian context – in the absence of a centralized state (Burger et al., 1999). As in France and Belgium, the Dutch third sector is an important pillar in the provision of public services, while the government is mostly restricted to funding. Some 41% of the nonprofits engage in the field of health care, 28% of private initiatives engage in education, and 19% in social services. The public sector thereby accounts for 60% of the nonprofit organization's funding, 37% services and membership fees, and 3% of private donations. The deliberate labor division between private initiatives and the public sector becomes apparent as the health care sector consists of 70% nonprofit employment (Burger et al., 1999). Further, the Netherlands stands out for the liberties extended by the state to nonprofits: They are free from minimum capital requirement, can register in a single day, allow foreigners or minors to serve as founders, and are generally free from reporting requirements except when they provide public services paid for by the government (Center for Global Prosperity, 2015).

Germany, Austria, and Switzerland

In Germany, Austria, and Switzerland the third sector is generally characterized by a cooperative relationship with governmental agencies. The government particularly promotes public services provided by nonprofit organizations through significant funding. As a result, the third sector is highly concentrated in the fields of health care and social services.

In Germany, nonprofit organizations, particularly associations, have an important role in the country's policy-making processes. After World War II, associations also started to play a more important role in the fields of sports, leisure, and education. The sector has experienced continued growth over the past two decades and had grown to include 580,000 associations in 2011. This development was pushed by reforms in 2002 and 2007 that raised the tax exemption for initial endowments (Zimmer, Priller, and Anheier, 2013). In 1995, over 80% of German nonprofit employees were engaged in core welfare areas: 40% operated in the field of social services, 31% in health care, and 12% in education (Priller et al., 1999). In the same year, government funding accounted for 64% of nonprofit revenue, private fees and charges accounted for 32.3% of the income, and private donations for 3.4% (Zimmer et al., 2013). The German third sector has important economic relevance for the country. In 1995, German nonprofits had operating expenditures in the amount of 94 billion USD corresponding to 3.9% of the country's GDP. The sector was a major employer with 1.44 million full-time equivalent (FTE) in paid workers and an additional 1 million FTE in volunteers (Zimmer et al., 2013). In 2007, nonprofits' expenditures were calculated to be 104.44 billion USD (Zimmer et al., 2013).

Similarly to the German context, Austrian nonprofit organizations not only play an important role in public services, but also have an important stake in political decision processes and policy making. In 2010, the Austrian third sector comprised 116,556 associations, 3,595 foundations, and 95 cooperatives (Pennerstorfer, Schneider, and Badelt, 2013). The composition and economic force of the Austrian third sector can best be represented through its revenue structure. In 2010, the third sector had a revenue of 4.4 billion USD (5.9 billion Euros[2]) corresponding to 1.1% of the Austrian GDP. Thereof, 29% went to social services and 21.5% to advocacy activities (the latter comprises a significant percentage compared to advocacy activity in other Western European countries). Public funding accounts for 52.5% of the nonprofits' revenue, 36% comes from own provided services and fees, and 11.5% stem from private donations. Between the years 2000 and 2010, the third sector experienced a growth of 39% in its employment rate. In 2010, nonprofit organizations employed 210,000 workers, which corresponded to 5.4% of the country's total workforce. For the same year, 36% of the employees were engaged in the field of public services and 20% pursued advocacy work (Pennerstorfer et al., 2013). In regards to its regulation and incentive structure for philanthropic activities, Austria lags behind other Western European countries in key areas (Center for Global Prosperity, 2015). Nevertheless, more recently there have been developments to liberalize Austria's third sector.

Switzerland's nonprofit sector, particularly the number of foundations, has experienced significant growth in the past 25 years. In 2000, the sector comprised 8,123 foundations, which had grown to 13,172 foundations in 2016 (Eckhardt, Jakob, and von Schnurbein, 2017). For the year 2010, the sector is further estimated to have comprised 76,438 associations (Helmig et al., 2010). The Swiss nonprofit sector is highly concentrated in the field of public services; 82% percent of the paid nonprofit workforce is engaged in the fields of social services, health care, education and research, and work integration. Labor associations, sports, culture, and religion account for a total of 14% in the nonprofit paid engagement. Accordingly, the government particularly supports nonprofits in the fields of social services and health care, accounting for approximately 45% of their revenue and underlining the principle of subsidiarity in the provision of public services (von Schnurbein, 2013). However, looking at the revenue composition of the entire nonprofit sector, governmental funding accounts for a relatively small share, compared to other Western European countries. Public funding only covers 35% of the organizations' total revenue. The major share of 57% of nonprofit revenue for the entire sector stems from private donations, which are particularly important in the fields of religion and international activities. The revenue share from fees is 8% (Helmig et al., 2010). In 2005, Swiss nonprofit organizations benefited from a total revenue of 33.1 billion USD (25.3 billion CHF[3]).

Italy, Spain, and Portugal

In Italy, despite the dominance of the public welfare system, the private civil society sector has experienced significant quantitative growth since the 1990s. In recent years, the various organizational types that compose the third sector have not grown at the same rate; whereas voluntary organizations and traditional associations have registered a slight growth, productive (social cooperatives and associations) and grant-making organizations (particularly banking foundations) have increased more markedly. In 2001, the country's nonprofit sector comprised 202,059 associations, 4,651 cooperatives, and 2,008 foundations (Barbetta et al., 2004). As for most of the Western European third sector, a major share of the Italian nonprofit workforce (paid and unpaid) is engaged in social services. In 1999, 62% of nonprofits were engaged in that field, while the fields of culture and recreation, labor unions, and advocacy occupied 34% of the nonprofit workforce. Governmental funding, in comparison to other Western European counterparts, accounts for a relatively small share of the third sector's revenue. For the year 1999, 37% of the revenue was reported to stem from public agencies, underlining the country's dual service system. For the same year, 61% of the sector's income came from fees and charges of offered services. Philanthropic donations only accounted for 3% of the total income. More recent information suggests that public resources for the provision of core welfare are further shrinking (Barbetta et al., 2004). There is a trend of re-publicization, on the one hand, and the entry of new, for-profit providers, in the field of public services, on the other hand. In 1999, nonprofit organizations contributed 36 billion USD to the country's economy corresponding to 3.1% of the GDP (Barbetta et al., 2004).

In Spain the third sector comprises 26,000 cooperatives and 127,414 nonprofit organizations accounting for 5% of the country's registered organizations (Defourny and Pestoff, 2008). Cooperatives, associations, and foundations have a strong presence in activities related to public services. For the year 1995, 32% of nonprofits were engaged in social services, 25% were active in the field of education, 12.2% in health, and 11.8% in culture. Further, there is an unusually large share of nonprofits active in the field of advocacy and development (14.5%). In 1995, almost half of the nonprofit sector's income (49%) stemmed from fees and charges for services offered by the organizations. A significant share of income, much larger compared to other Western European nonprofit funding structures, came from private philanthropic donations (18.8%). The dual welfare regime of Spain is underlined by the government's comparatively small contribution to the nonprofit sector; only 32.1% of the income stemmed from public sources (Olabuénaga et al., 1999). Private philanthropic contributions are promoted by tax incentives (Center for Global Prosperity, 2015).

The Portuguese third sector covers a wide range of organizations, including charitable organizations closely related to the Catholic Church, mutual benefit associations, private institutions of social solidarity and cooperatives, mainly from the social solidarity branch (Salamon et al., 2012). As in the two other Southern countries, Portuguese nonprofits are highly concentrated in the fields of public services, but benefit very little from governmental funding. In 2006, 52% of the nonprofits were engaged in social services, 16% in membership organizations, 11% in education, and 7% in health care. Government funding for these activities accounted for 41% of the sector's revenue. Fees accounted for 31% of the revenue and private donations for 10%. In spite of the general underfunding of social welfare by public agencies, the Portuguese philanthropic environment is relatively liberal by global standards promoting the growth of private nonprofit initiatives (Salamon et al., 2012). The Portuguese nonprofit sector has a significant economic presence. In 2006, the sector contributed 2.7 billion Euros (2.05 billion USD[4]) of Gross Value Added (GVA) to the national economy which corresponded to 2% of the national economy.

Sweden, Denmark, Norway, and Finland

In the Nordic countries there is traditionally a clear division of responsibilities between the three societal components: the state is to deliver welfare, business organizations ensure production and the creation of jobs, and civil society is to articulate interests and shaping the societal agenda. This division is also reflected in the countries' nonprofit activities and funding structure. In the last decades, however, the public sector and the third sector have become closer regarding forms of practice. The public sector has started to involve voluntary organizations in the carrying out of political decisions, particularly in the social service area.

In 1992, the third sector in Sweden counted 200,000 nonprofit organizations (Lundström and Wijkström, 1995). Historically seen, civil society movements have played an important role in the preservation of the Swedish culture and advocacy of civil society's interests. This role is still apparent in the third sector's composition. Sweden's nonprofit organizations are highly concentrated in the fields of culture and recreation (27% of all paid nonprofit employees), and in education and research (21% of all paid nonprofit employees). Contrary to most other Western European countries, the social service sector accounts for a relatively small share of non-profit employment occupying only 18% of the sector's workforce. Accordingly, public spending on the third sector is relatively low compared to other European countries. In 1992, govern-ment funding accounted for 29% of the nonprofit revenue. The major source of income was the organizations' fees and charges accounting for 62% of the revenue. Private philanthropy accounted for only 9% of the nonprofits' income (Lundström and Wijkström, 1995). Due to its significant private activities, the Swedish nonprofit sector is an important economic driving force. In 1992, the sector's operating expenditures amounted to 10.3 billion USD. Nonprofits occupied 100,000 paid workers and benefited from another 2.6 million volunteers. In spite of the clear labor division between the public and the third sector, more recently governmental agencies and nonprofits have followed a more cooperative approach in the provision of social ser-vices. The government further incentivizes the creation of new nonprofit organizations through a relatively liberal regulatory framework (Center for Global Prosperity, 2015).

The Danish nonprofit sector experienced significant quantitative growth in the 1980s when the welfare state developed to such a degree that it assumed responsibility for almost everything. Third sector organizations emerged to counterbalance the public power and represent civil society's interests. In a Danish context, the definition of voluntary sector includes three differ-ent forms of organizations: the association, the self-governing institution, and the public utility fund (Defourny and Pestoff, 2008). Estimates suggest that in 2006 the Danish voluntary sector comprised more than 83,000 local associations, 62,000 funds, nearly 8,000 independent insti-tutions in the area of education and the care of disabled people, and 3,000 nationwide associ-ations (Defourny and Pestoff, 2008). The Danish third sector's composition is best represented through the share of nonprofit employees per field. In the year 2004, nonprofits were predom-inantly active in the fields of culture and recreation, and in education and research accounting for 48% of the nonprofits employment. Given the dominant role of the state in providing social welfare, it is not surprising that only 19% of the third sector employment is engaged in the field of social services. Government funding is a little more generous than in Sweden, accounting for 40% of the nonprofits' revenue. Yet, the major share of income stems from fees and charges covering 53% of the organizations' revenue. Private philanthropy accounts for 7% of the income (Defourny and Pestoff, 2008).

In Norway, the third sector is that of "voluntary organizations", which are primarily associated with membership, participation, volunteering, and democratic structures. Many civil associations in Norway were formed during the 19th century as a consequence of social movements to mobilize the population towards the promotion of democratic governance, self-help, and community welfare (Sivesind et al., 2004). As is the case in much of Scandinavia, the Norwegian third sector is highly concentrated in the field of expressive activities. In 1997, 61% of the organizations were engaged in advocacy and professions, and culture and recreation. For the same year, a relatively small 35% share of the organizations was engaged in the field of social services. Fees, charges, and membership dues were the main source of nonprofit revenue accounting for 58% of the income. Governmental funding contributed to 35% of the income and private donations accounted for 7% of total revenue. Accounting for volunteer work the revenue structure shifts significantly: 33% of the revenue stems from fees, 20% from government funds, and 47% from private philanthropy (Sivesind et al., 2004). The Norwegian third sector is a growing economic force. In 1997, the sector's expenditures amounted to 5.5 billion USD corresponding to 3.7% of the country's GDP (Sivesind et al., 2004).

In Finland, like in the other Scandinavian countries, a strong tradition of popular social movements has significantly influenced the country's third sector. The sector is rather small in terms of paid employment, mostly concentrated in the fields of expressive activities, and plays an important role in the process of policy making. Taking into account cooperatives, mutual societies, foundations, and associations, we obtain total figures of some 130,000 organizations for the year 2006. The country's 5.4 million citizens were represented by 70,000 associations leading to one of the highest rates of associations per capita in Europe. More recently, voluntary organizations in Finland have established closer contact and cooperation with public authorities for the provision of social services (Defourny and Pestoff, 2008). For the year 2006, a shift towards a higher share of nonprofit organizations active in social services and health care was reported. The sector is most importantly funded by fees and charges for the organizations' service, which in 2006 accounted for 57.9% of their income (Defourny and Pestoff, 2008). Public funding accounted for 36.2% of the income and was mostly invested into health care and social services. Private philanthropy covered 5.9% of the sector's income.

Resources for the nonprofit-sector

Financial resources

Nonprofit organizations rely on three main sources for financial means: public funding, private donations, and own revenues (Salamon and Sokolowski, 2016). Cross-regional studies, such as the *Comparative Nonprofit Sector Project* (CNP), reveal significant differences in the organizations' funding structure between countries. Whereas in North-western European countries third sector organizations primarily rely on their own revenue and private donations, nonprofits in the Southern countries are to a large extent funded through public contributions.

Table 3.2 gives an overview of the total amount of revenues of nonprofits and the share of public funding, private donations, and own revenues. It becomes clear that nonprofits in all countries receive funds from all three different categories. Overall, either government funding or own revenues add the highest shares to the revenues of nonprofits, whereas private donations are of minor importance. However, this impression does not count for the single organization which can have very different proportions of the three revenue sources. Additionally, the

Table 3.2 Revenue sources of nonprofits

Country	Total revenue (billion USD)	Government funding	Private donations	Fees, own revenues, etc.	Year of most recent data
France	58	57.8%	7.5%	34.7%	1999
Belgium	25	76.5%	4.8%	18.7%	1995
Netherlands	60	60%	3%	37%	1999
Germany	69	64%	3.4%	32.3%	1995
Austria	3.4	52.5%	11.5%	36%	2005
Switzerland	33.1	35%	8%	57%	2005
Italy	36	37%	3%	61%	1999
Spain	22.6	32.1%	18.8%	49%	1999
Portugal	2.7	41%	10%	31%	2006
Sweden	10.3	29%	9%	62%	1992
Denmark	16.6	40%	7%	53%	2004
Norway	5.5	35%	7%	58%	1997
Finland	4.7	36.2%	5.9%	57.9%	2008
Total	338.8				

Source: Information compiled by the authors.

Note
May not always add up to 100% due to rounding.

aggregation reduces the information on changes or substitutions within the three major revenue categories (Chikoto-Schultz and Neely, 2016). Thus, from a management perspective, a more detailed analysis is necessary in order to enable strategic planning of the financial development of nonprofits (von Schnurbein and Fritz, 2017).

Labor and volunteering

In Europe, the third sector relies extensively on both volunteer and paid employment. For the year 2014, the European third sector was reported to have engaged an estimated 28.3 million FTE workers (paid and volunteer) in the 28 EU countries and Norway (GHK, 2010). Remarkably, 55% were volunteers. This large share of voluntary workforce significantly contributes to the reach and power of the European third sector. However, individual country-level data reveals that the third sector's workforce composition strongly varies within Europe (see e.g., CNP). The variations are explained by different variables. For example, in countries where third sector organizations are importantly engaged in social services or more professionalized activities, the overall level of paid workers tends to be higher. Also, the country's volunteering traditions and attitude towards voluntary work, and regulation framework for volunteer work, significantly influence the composition of its third sector workforce (Angermann and Sittermann, 2010). In 2008, the European Parliament published a report on the "Role of volunteering" for member states to recognize the value of volunteering in promoting social and economic cohesion. Different countries have since established national volunteer promotion programs and strategies to promote volunteering in the third sector (Angermann and Sittermann, 2010).

Despite these efforts, the European third sector faces some important challenges. Particularly, the phenomenon of episodic volunteering hinders the professionalization of the third sector;

it is getting more difficult for organizations to find people who are willing to volunteer for the long term or who are ready to assume responsibility in organizations (e.g., becoming a board member) (Angermann and Sittermann, 2010).

Sector infrastructure

Europe's third sector also includes a variety of infrastructure organizations (IOs) that support traditional nonprofit organizations and seek to improve their effectiveness. They particularly provide research and management assistance to help strengthen the sector. These organizations facilitate the exchange of nonprofits on a national and international level.

In spite of the large number of such IOs there is a general call for a more "enabling" environment, particularly on an international level (Pfitzer and Stamp, 2010). Presently, service organizations face a number challenges impacting their effectiveness in fostering the philanthropic sector. There are major differences in the quality and number of infrastructure organizations across European countries hindering a consistent network and thus exchange of best practices. Subsequently, technical assistance resources, while plentiful in some places, are lacking in others. Further, there often is reluctance by nonprofits themselves to join infrastructure networks. Many European foundations, for example, are not yet convinced that collaboration creates sufficient additional value to merit the effort it requires (Pfitzer and Stamp, 2010). Finally, research and university-based education on philanthropy lags behind in many European countries. A study by Keidan, Jung, and Pharoah (2014) reveals that in most Northern and Eastern European countries, philanthropy education is only discernible within related subjects or altogether absent.

Trends in nonprofit management styles, organizational structure, and capacities

Social entrepreneurship has gained much attention through both research and practice in Europe. Some argue that the concept leads to more professionalism and a broader financing of the nonprofit sector, others criticize the increased managerialism and the pressure on nonprofits to increase own revenues (Eikenberry and Kluver, 2004). In general, social enterprises are located between the market and the nonprofit sector and can be part of both (Battilana and Lee, 2014). The organizations take the legal form of cooperatives or associations but follow the principle of limited distribution of profits. The concept has become particularly popular in France where in the context of persistent unemployment of low-qualified people, the most recognized field of activity of social enterprises is that of work integration. Comparable developments are reported from other countries such as Belgium, Italy, Germany, and Finland (Defourny and Pestoff, 2008). However, in general there is no real governmental support, either at the regional or the national level. As the enterprises do not benefit from any public support, they have no specific restrictions on how to use their surplus.

With the rise of social enterprises, the more or less clear separation of business and nonprofit has become blurred. This has consequences for the management styles and organizational structures of the traditional nonprofits. In terms of management style, nonprofits are less oriented towards the state as cooperative partner, but follow more the management trends in business, e.g., human resource management, marketing, or strategic development. Additionally, the organizational structures of social enterprises are less hierarchical and more flexible. For the future development of the national nonprofit sectors it will be of great interest to observe the relationships between nonprofits and social enterprises (Khan, Lacity, and Carmel, 2018). Both parties would benefit from increased collaboration; while traditional nonprofits have existing structure, high recognition, and a strong network, social enterprises offer innovative ideas, and access to the younger generations. Cooperation or even mergers may be promising options for nonprofit management and even better service provision in the future.

Another trend of economization concerns new forms of financing nonprofits. Especially since the financial crisis and its consequences on the financial markets, institutional funders such as grant-making foundations are looking for new ways to invest their assets. Concepts such as micro-finance, impact investing, and venture philanthropy have gained increased attention. However, the development is still in the pioneer phase.

The concept of social investment, also often referred to as venture philanthropy, has become increasingly popular in different European countries. A popular form of social investment is the *social investment bond* (SIB) (Jackson, 2013). The European Commission recognized the need for more private funding for social enterprises and promised in 2013 to facilitate the exchange amongst member states about their experience with SIBs. In the same year, the European Investment Fund (EIF) launched the *Social Impact Accelerator* (SIA), a pan-European public–private partnership for social impact investing. The SIA is designed to provide initial equity financing of 60 million Euros to investment funds that target social enterprises across Europe. The aim is to encourage the long-term sustainability of the social investment sector (Davies, 2014).

As a consequence of increased regulation, difficulties in funding, and decreasing membership, the role of nonprofits is questioned. Especially in the areas of social services, leisure and sports, and health services, mergers among nonprofits have increased (von Schnurbein, 2013). Trade unions, sports associations, and charities have merged as a consequence of decreasing membership or increasing costs. Especially in charities, the pressure for reducing administrative costs leads to a need for more economies of scale (Lecy and Searing, 2015). So far, mergers of nonprofits have not gained a lot of attention by researchers, but several questions result (Fischer, Vadapalli, and Coulton, 2017). For instance, what role do values and culture of the involved organizations play for the success of the merger? What are legal options, requirements, and limitations for mergers in different countries? Additionally, the managerial consequences of a merger have to be taken into account. Costs might decrease and the organization may gain the ability to plan larger projects. However, the linkage to the member or donor basis might become more distinct, investments in infrastructure might be necessary, and a new reputation has to be built up.

An alternative solution to cooperation or merger is the dissolution of an organization. In recent years, the number of nonprofits dissolving has increased. The reasons for these developments are manifold. First, organizations have difficulties in finding active members or board representatives. Second, reduced public funding, low returns on investments, or decreasing donations impede the organizations' operative capacity. Third, many of the nonprofits established in the past two decades are now getting to the end of the founder generation. As this first generation of intrinsically motivated people leaves, the organization comes to a crossroad of either professionalizing or reduction. Finally, societal changes make some of the organizations' purposes obsolete. In some cases, the purpose is out of fashion (e.g., for specific sports), for others, the state has taken over the activity (e.g., in the field of social integration), or new technologies create alternative and more attractive solutions (e.g., Facebook groups or other platforms).

As with all parts of society, nonprofits in Europe have had to change with the fast development of digitalization. New opportunities in fundraising, changes in communication, and new fields of activities (digital rights) are only the beginning of a new way of how nonprofits will serve the society. In an early study, Finn, Maher, and Forster (2006) showed that nonprofits were slowly adapting to the use of information and communications technology (ICT). Their findings proved that larger nonprofits are more likely and more eager to use ICT. Raman (2016) highlights the positive influence on organizational effectiveness through social media, mobility, analytics, and cloud computing (SMAC). For nonprofits, the challenge with new technologies touches both mission and organization. In regards to their mission, nonprofits face new opportunities in advocacy (Johnson and Prakash, 2007; Guo and Saxton, 2012) or medical treatments (Bram et al., 2015). Based on case studies, (Schneider, 2003) emphasizes that nonprofits should focus less on access to technology or technical assistance, but more on how to make use of the technology available. At the same time, nonprofits have to manage the use of new technologies in their organization (Kang and Norton, 2004) including the question of technological and administrative leadership (Jaskyte, 2011).

Consequences for managing nonprofits

Managing a nonprofit in Europe today means adapting to the challenges mentioned before. After two decades of professionalization, nonprofit leaders have to deal with the inherent consequences: There are many well-educated and experienced collaborators; donors turn into investors with clear strategies for how they want to create impact; and in fields of development aid, health, or education state agencies are challenged by supranational nonprofit organizations. Today, there are still significant differences between managing a business enterprise and managing a nonprofit organization. These differences, however, are not so marked in their tools, methods, or reporting obligations (Maier, Meyer, and Steinbereithner, 2016). In these areas, mainly due to government regulation and isomorphic pressure, nonprofits have actually become similar to business organizations of their respective size. The differences rather lie in the primary purposes of nonprofits and business organizations: Businesses are designed to make money and increase profits, whereas nonprofits are primarily about a social cause and about how to spend money (and other resources) on that respective cause. Nonprofit leaders have to be excellent in explaining the "reason why" of their organization. Otherwise, they may face allegations of mission drift or conformity in case of too much business alignment. In other cases, potential major donors or investors will identify a lack of compassion, if the organization does not present visionary aims.

Thus, while operating with hybrid structures, with profit and nonprofit revenue sources, and with entrepreneurial and philanthropic engagements, nonprofit organizations deal with a more competitive and more critical environment (Hielscher et al., 2017). This calls for more transparency and better communication. Important elements of nonprofit communication are authentic stories, emotions, and diversity in the communicated content. The more fragmented society becomes, the more organizational communication needs to be adapted to different societal contexts in order to transmit stories and content to a broad part of the society.

In terms of organizational structures, technological development and increasing parallel projects lead to a lean and decentralized organization. Especially in recent years, new organizational models of agility and self-organization are discussed as organizations become more project-oriented. These models follow the idea that responsibilities and tasks are not assigned top-down (as the top management is not able to keep up with recent developments in all areas), but the team members take over tasks in their business area and find the relevant and necessary partners in the organization on their own.

Additionally, new professions have emerged or will emerge in the years to come. One is the increasing need of volunteer coordinators. While this position has been created in many UK- or US-based nonprofits, it is still rare in organizations in Continental Europe. However, today's volunteers demand more flexibility and better support. Thus, nonprofits need to develop a more professional guidance of volunteers, if they want to attract more of them (Studer and von Schnurbein, 2013). Another profession developing in the nonprofit sector is the impact measurement officer. Until now, impact measurement has usually been carried out by external evaluators and was restricted to single organizations. But the more it becomes a common demand, the more it will be embedded in the organization itself. So far, few organizations have created impact measurement units in order to create a homogeneous and constant impact measurement for the whole organization.

Conclusion

The nonprofit sector in Europe has a very long tradition and is well established in terms of political participation, legal regulation, public and private funding, and professionalization. However, the past decade has shown that the future outlook is less about growth than about reorganization and new organizational structures. We may expect closer collaboration between governmental organization and private nonprofits, as well as increased cooperation between traditional nonprofits and innovative social enterprises. In order to evaluate the outcome of such developments, research will rely on adequate qualitative and quantitative information. National accounts and other initiatives to increase transparency and accountability in the sector have improved the quality of country-level data on Europe's third sector. Nevertheless, much of the empirical data on nonprofits in most European countries remains sparse or is outdated. Research may therefore benefit from more recent data in order to provide a more comprehensive picture of the European third sector of the future.

Notes

1   The NPI Satellite Account was established by the University of Liège to account for the economic activity of all "associations without profit purpose" in Belgium. It resulted from the recommendation in the United Nations' publication, the *Handbook on Non-profit Institutions in the System of National Accounts* in 2003.
2   The calculation is based on an exchange rate of 1.342 Euro/USD for the end of the year 2010.
3   The calculation is based on an exchange rate of 0.7452 CHF/USD for the end of the year 2005.
4   The calculation is based on an exchange rate of 1.3186 Euro/USD for the end of the year 2006.

References

Angermann, A. & Sittermann, B., 2010. Volunteering in the Member States of the European Union – Evaluation and summary of current studies. *Working Paper no. 5*. Frankfurt: Observatory for Sociopolitical Developments in Europe.

Archambault, É., Gariazzo, M., Anheier, H.K. & Salamon, L.M., 1999. France: From Jacobin tradition to decentralization. In: *Global Civil Society – Dimensions of the Nonprofit Sector*. Baltimore, MD: Johns Hopkins Center for Civil Society Studies, pp. 81–97.

Barbetta, G.P. et al., 2004. Italy. In: *Global Civil Society – Dimensions of the Nonprofit Sector Volume 2*. Bloomfield, CT: Kumarian Press, pp. 245–261.

Battilana, J. & Lee, M., 2014. Advancing research on hybrid organizing – Insights from the study of social enterprises. *Academy of Management Annals,* 8(1), pp. 397–441.

Bies, A.L., 2010. Evolution of nonprofit self-regulation in Europe. *Nonprofit and Voluntary Sector Quarterly,* 39, pp. 1057–1086.

Bram, J.T., Warwick-Clark, B., Obeysekare, E. & Mehta, K., 2015. Utilization and monetization of healthcare data in developing countries. *Big Data,* 3(2), pp. 59–66.

Burger, A. et al., 1999. The Netherlands: Key features of the Dutch nonprofit sector. In: *Global Civil Society – Dimensions of the Nonprofit Sector*. Baltimore, MD: Johns Hopkins Center for Civil Society Studies, pp. 145–162.

Center for Global Prosperity, 2015. *The Index of Philanthropic Freedom 2015*. Washington, DC: Hudson Institute.

Chikoto-Schultz, G.L. & Neely, D.G., 2016. Exploring the nexus of nonprofit financial stability and financial growth. *VOLUNTAS: International Journal of Voluntary and Nonprofit Organizations,* 27(6), pp. 2561–2575.

Davies, D., 2014. *Social impact bonds – Private finance that generates social returns.* European Parliament Research Service.

Defourny, J. & Pestoff, V., 2008. Images and concepts of the third sector in Europe. In: *EMES Working Papers, no 08/02.* Liège: EMES European Research Network.

Eckhardt, B., Jakob, D. & von Schnurbein, G., 2017. Der Schweizer Stiftungsreport 2017. In: *CEPS Forschung und Praxis.* Basel: CEPS.

Eikenberry, A.M. & Kluver, J.D., 2004. The marketization of the nonprofit sector: Civil society at risk?. *Public Administration Review,* 64(2), pp. 132–140.

Einolf, C.J., 2015. The social origins of the nonprofit sector and charitable giving. In: *The Palgrave Handbook of Global Philanthropy.* Basingstoke: Palgrave Macmillan.

Esping-Andersen, G., 1990. *The Three Worlds of Welfare Capitalism.* Princeton, NJ: Princeton University Press.

Finn, S., Maher, J.K. & Forster, J., 2006. Indicators of information and communication technology adoption in the nonprofit sector: Changes between 2000 and 2004. *Nonprofit Management & Leadership,* 16(3), pp. 277–295.

Fischer, R.L., Vadapalli, D. & Coulton, C., 2017. Merging ahead, increase speed: A pilot of funder-driven nonprofit restructuring. *Journal of Public and Nonprofit Affairs,* 3(1), pp. 40–54.

GHK, 2010. *Volunteering in the European Union.* Brussels: GHK.

Guo, C. & Saxton, G., 2012. Tweeting social change: How social media are changing nonprofit advocacy. *Nonprofit and Voluntary Sector Quarterly,* 41, pp. 1051–1071.

Helmig, B. et al., 2010. Statistik des Dritten Sektors in der Schweiz. In: D.D.S. d. Schweiz, ed. *Der Dritte Sektor der Schweiz.* Bern: s.n., pp. 173–206.

Hielscher, S., Winkin, J., Crack, A. & Pies, I., 2017. Saving the moral capital of NGOs: Identifying one-sided and many-sided social dilemmas in NGO accountability. *VOLUNTAS: International Journal of Voluntary and Nonprofit Organizations,* 28(4), pp. 1562–1594.

Hüttemann, R. & Helios, M., 2009. Zum grenzüberschreitenden Spendenabzug in Europa nach EuGH-Urteil vom 27.1.2009. *Persche, DB 2009,* pp. 701–707.

Jackson, E.T., 2013. Evaluating social impact bonds: Questions, challenges, innovations, and possibilities in measuring outcomes in impact investing. *Community Development,* 44(5), p. 608.

Jakob, D., 2014. Stand und Zukunft der "Europäischen Stiftung" – Wie gelingt ein europäisches Stiftungs- und Gemeinnützigkeitsrecht?. In: M. Institut, ed. *Das Europäische Stiftungsstatut, Europa Bottom-Up Nr. 8.* Berlin: Maecenata Institut, pp. 29–41.

Jaskyte, K., 2011. Predictors of administrative and technological innovations in nonprofit organizations. *Public Administration Review,* 71(1), pp. 77–86.

Johnson, E. & Prakash, A., 2007. NGO research program: A collective action perspective. *Policy Sciences,* 40(3), pp. 221–240.

Kang, S. & Norton, H.E., 2004. Nonprofit organizations' use of the World Wide Web: Are they sufficiently fulfilling organizational goals? *Public Relations Review,* 30(3), pp. 279–284.

Keidan, C., Jung, T. & Pharoah, C., 2014. *Philanthropy education in the UK and Continental Europe: Current provision, perceptions and opportunities,* London: Centre for Charitable Giving and Philanthropy, Cass Business School City University London.

Khan, S., Lacity, M. & Carmel, E., 2018. Entrepreneurial impact sourcing: A conceptual framework of social and commercial institutional logics. *Information Systems Journal,* 28(3), pp. 538–562.

Lecy, J.D. & Searing, E.A.M., 2015. Anatomy of the nonprofit starvation cycle: An analysis of falling overhead ratios in the nonprofit sector. *Nonprofit and Voluntary Sector Quarterly,* 44(3), pp. 539–563.

Lundström, T. & Wijkström, F., 1995. Working paper defining the nonprofit sector: Sweden. Johns Hopkins University Institute for Policy Studies. Baltimore, MD: Johns Hopkins University.

Maier, F., Meyer, M. & Steinbereithner, M., 2016. Nonprofit organizations becoming business-like: A systematic review. *Nonprofit and Voluntary Sector Quarterly,* 45(1), pp. 64–86.

Mertens, S. et al., 1999. Belgium. In: *Global Civil Society – Dimensions of the Nonprofit Sector.* Baltimore, MD: Johns Hopkins Center for Civil Society Studies, pp. 43–61.

National Account Institute, 2010. *Le compte satellite des institutions sans but lucratif,* Belgium: Institut des comptes nationaux.

Olabuénaga, J.I.R., Lara, A.J., Anheier, H.K. & Salamon, L.K., 1999. Spain. In: *Global Civil Society – Dimensions of the Nonprofit Sector.* Baltimore, MD: Johns Hopkins Center for Civil Society Studies, pp. 163–178.

Pennerstorfer, A., Schneider, U. & Badelt, C., 2013. Der Nonprofit-Sektor in Österreich. In: *Handbuch der Nonprofit-Organisationen*. Stuttgart: Schäffer Poeschel, pp. 55–75.

Pfitzer, M. & Stamp, M., 2010. *Multiplying Impact through Philanthropic Collaboration*. European Foundation Centre.

Priller, E. et al., 1999. Germany: Unification and change. In: *Global Civil Society – Dimensions of the Nonprofit Sector*. Baltimore, MD: Johns Hopkins Center for Civil Society Studies, pp. 99–118.

Raman, A., 2016. How do social media, mobility, analytics and cloud computing impact nonprofit organizations? A pluralistic study of information and communication technologies in Indian context. *Information Technology for Development*, 22(3), pp. 400–421.

Salamon, L.M. & Anheier, H.K., 1998. Social origins of civil society: Explaining the nonprofit sector cross-nationally. *Voluntas: International Journal of Voluntary and Nonprofit Organizations*, 9(3), pp. 213–248.

Salamon, L.M. & Sokolowski, W., 2016. The size and scope of the European third sector. *Working Paper No. 13/2016*.

Salamon, L.M., Sokolowski, W.S., Haddock, M. & Stone Tice, H., 2012. *Portugal's Nonprofit Sector in Comparative Context*. Baltimore, MD: John Hopkins Center for Civil Society Studies.

Salamon, L.M. & Toepler, S., 2015. Government–nonprofit cooperation: Anomaly or necessity? *Voluntas*, 26(6), pp. 2155–2177.

Schneider, J.A., 2003. Small, minority-based nonprofits in the information age. *Nonprofit Management & Leadership*, 16(3), pp. 383–399.

Sivesind, K.H. et al., 2004. Norway. In: *Global Civil Society – Dimensions of the Nonprofit Sector Volume 2*. Bloomfield, CT: Kumarian Press, pp. 261–275.

Sprecher, T., Egger, P. & von Schnurbein, G., 2016. Swiss foundation code. In: *Foundation Governance*. Basel: Helbing Lichtenhahn.

Studer, S. & von Schnurbein, G., 2013. Organizational factors affecting volunteers: A literature review on volunteer coordination. *VOLUNTAS: International Journal of Voluntary and Nonprofit Organizations*, 24(2), pp. 403–440.

Then, V., 2006. Non-profit corporate governance in Europa – Regulierung oder Selbstregulierung. In: *Non Profit Law Yearbook 2006*. Köln: Carl Heymanns Verlag, pp. 123–137.

von Schnurbein, G., 2013. Der Nonprofit-Sektor in der Schweiz. In: *Handbuch der Nonprofit-Organisationen*. Stuttgart: Schäffer Poeschel, pp. 37–54.

von Schnurbein, G. & Fritz, T., 2017. Benefits and drivers of nonprofit revenue concentration. *Nonprofit and Voluntary Sector Quarterly*, 46(5), pp. 922–943.

von Schnurbein, G. & Stöckli, S., 2013. The codification of nonprofit governance – A comparative analysis of Swiss and German nonprofit governance codes. In: *Conceptualizing and Researching Governance in Public and Non-profit Organizations*. Bingley: Emerald Group Publishing, pp. 179–202.

Zimmer, A., Priller, E. & Anheier, H.K., 2013. Der Nonprofit-Sektor in Deutschland. In: *Handbuch der Nonprofit-Organisationen*. Stuttgart: Schäffer Poeschel, pp. 15–36.

4

NONPROFIT MANAGEMENT CONTEXT

Central and Eastern Europe

Peter Vandor

SENIOR RESEARCHER, CO-FOUNDER, SOCIAL ENTREPRENEURSHIP CENTER, WU VIENNA
UNIVERSITY OF ECONOMICS AND BUSINESS, VIENNA, AUSTRIA

Clara Moder

UNIVERSITY ASSISTANT, DEPARTMENT OF POLITICAL SCIENCE, UNIVERSITY
OF VIENNA, VIENNA, AUSTRIA

Michaela Neumayr

ASSISTANT PROFESSOR, INSTITUTE FOR NONPROFIT MANAGEMENT, WU VIENNA
UNIVERSITY OF ECONOMICS AND BUSINESS, VIENNA, AUSTRIA

Introduction

Three decades have passed since the region of Central and Eastern Europe emerged as a new area of interest among nonprofit researchers (Bernhard 1993; Howard 2003; Toepler and Salamon 2003). After the collapse of the communist regimes across the region in 1989/1990, scholars noticed the development of new nonprofit actors and were curious to understand the role these actors would play in their societies.

Since that time, the countries of Central and Eastern Europe (CEE) have experienced intensive periods of transformation, conflict and renewal. They have gone through changes in political systems, ethnic tensions and conflicts, economic turmoil and growth as well as the development of new relationships with their European neighbors. Many of these changes have affected the nonprofit sector directly or indirectly.

This chapter provides an introduction to this dynamic region and its management context for nonprofit organizations. First, we outline the recent history of the nonprofit sector and the development of its legal framework since the early 1990s. Next, we describe its composition, economic contribution and funding sources. Finally, we give an overview of the diverse institutional landscapes in which nonprofit organizations operate as well as the main trends in the region.

Historical context

Despite the vast diversity of the countries of Central and Eastern Europe and their historical development, some historical patterns are shared across countries. First, a large part of the region was under foreign rule for centuries, as parts or vassal states of Byzantine, Ottoman, Habsburg and other empires. The presence of religious and dynastic empires challenged the process of nation building and civic development. There was a strong link between social and ethnic segregation, which gave nationalism an anti-elitist component (Szabó 2004). Second, they share a communist past, although it has to be noted that communism took very different shapes in the respective countries. Whereas the Baltic countries were part of the USSR, facing a higher degree of control and repression (Maciukaite-Zviniene 2008; Uhlin 2006), the Visegrád countries (the Czech Republic, Hungary, Poland and Slovakia) had comparatively more freedom, which led to a stronger dissident movement and the development of civic initiatives already under communist rule (Ekiert and Kubik 2014; Piotrowski 2009). Finally, all countries have undergone a transition process since the early 1990s. They all experienced painful economic reforms introduced to establish market economies, which led to a steep rise in unemployment and inflation, and a decrease in disposable income and standard of living (Podkaminer 2013). These reforms were often the subject of civic protest in the 1990s (Ekiert and Kubik 2010).

With respect to their recent historical development, the Western Balkans (Albania, Bosnia and Herzegovina, Kosovo, Serbia, Montenegro, Republic of North Macedonia) have additional commonalities, as they are the successor states of the Socialist Republic of Yugoslavia (except for Albania), and were involved in the Yugoslav wars in the 1990s (Spahić-Šiljak 2017; Spasojević 2017). In many countries of the Western Balkans, the process of nation building is still ongoing, which is illustrated by the comparatively recent declarations of independence by both Montenegro in 2006 and Kosovo in 2008 (Musliu 2017; Vujović 2017). Figure 4.1 provides a schematic overview of recent historical events (and development) that can be considered crucial for the development of civil society and the nonprofit sector in the region. The remainder of this section is dedicated to two major developments, namely the process of European Union (EU) accession and the introduction of new legal frameworks for nonprofit organizations and civic engagement.

European integration and the nonprofit sector in CEE

Concerning the more recent historical developments in the region, probably the most important has been the process of European integration. While some CEE countries are still in the pre-accession phase or have announced their intentions to commence negotiations, many have become members of the European Union in the 2004 and 2007 accession rounds. The process of EU accession had and continues to have far-reaching consequences for nonprofit

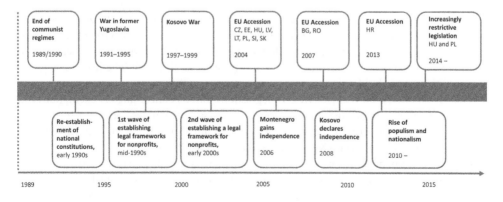

Figure 4.1 Timeline of historical developments

organizations. It influences, amongst others, the amounts and types of funding that are available to them as well as the national legal frameworks in which they operate (Börzel 2010; Brusis 2010). It is notable that EU accession itself is often described as a rather symbolic event, whereas the pre-accession phase is understood to be more impactful for civil society (Ekiert et al. 2017a; Fink-Hafner and Novak 2017; Navrátil and Pecjal 2017). During the pre-accession process, country legislators are required to align their institutions and certain laws with EU directives. Among these, many are concerned with the promotion of political participation of nonprofit organizations. Furthermore, the EU provides dedicated funding opportunities to nonprofit organizations during the pre-accession phase (e.g., PHARE) which also contributes to the development of the nonprofit sector.

However, the process of EU accession has led to different outcomes in the various CEE countries. While eight countries became EU members as early as in 2004 – Czech Republic (CZ), Estonia (EE), Hungary (HU), Latvia (LV), Lithuania (LT), Poland (PL), Slovakia (SK), Slovenia (SI) – and Bulgaria (BG) and Romania (RO) joined in 2007, other countries are still in the pre-accession or accession negotiations. Also, in recent years, some of the early EU members have experienced what has been described as "democratic backsliding" (Greskovits 2015; Krastev 2016), and have seen the establishment of governments with authoritarian tendencies.

Parallel to the process of EU accession, or in some cases preceding it, the presence of foreign donor institutions increased. In the early 1990s, many donors set up programs to support civil society in post-communist countries in Central and Eastern Europe (Aksartova 2009). Foreign donor funding, regardless of whether public or private, had a big impact on civil societies in CEE. This impact has been described as ambiguous by both researchers and practitioners: On the one hand, it provided an important source of otherwise unavailable funding; on the other, the supported organizations were often not rooted in local communities but rather emerged with the main purpose of obtaining funding (see also Political instrumentalization of civil society as an "imported concept" below).

Development of legal frameworks for the nonprofit sector in CEE

Another important factor for civil society activity, besides funding, is a stable legal framework. After 1989, the legal framework for voluntary action and participation of nonprofit organizations developed very quickly in CEE. By the mid-1990s, most countries had established laws providing a regulatory framework for setting up nonprofit organizations. The two dominant legal forms in the region are membership-based associations and foundations, the latter usually demanding an initial financial endowment. These basic types are often broadly defined, therefore encompassing a wide range of organizational purposes and forms. In some countries, additional legal forms for nonprofit organizations are available, such as "open foundations", representing hybrids between associations or foundations. Some jurisdictions distinguish between social service nonprofits and advocacy nonprofits (Rutzen et al. 2009). The legal frameworks for establishing and dissolving nonprofit organizations in CEE can be characterized as well developed and often even outstand Western legislations. Efforts concerning tax exemptions and deductions for nonprofit organizations are however often still in their developmental stage. Nevertheless, there is some form of tax relief on income for nonprofit organizations in all countries in CEE, except Slovakia (Hadzi-Miceva 2008; Rutzen et al. 2009).

Regarding tax deductions of private donations, there is a high degree of variation in the region. The most notable regulation is the "percentage philanthropy rule," which allows private individuals to donate 1–2 percent of their personal income tax to eligible nonprofit organizations. It was first introduced in Hungary in 1996, and Lithuania, Poland, Slovakia and Romania followed consecutively (Strečanský and Török 2016). Some countries (e.g., Estonia) considered a similar mechanism, but concluded that it would harm, rather than foster, the development of their nonprofit sector (Hadzi-Miceva 2008; Rutzen et al. 2009).

In recent years, the governments of Hungary and Poland have introduced restrictive legislation concerning nonprofit organizations as well as public protests and assembly. A law passed in December 2016 by the Polish Parliament for instance, prioritizes "circular" protests over spontaneous protests. These circular protests are regular public meetings, always organized by the same people and take place at the same venue each time. Protests that are taking place only once must keep a distance of at least 100 meters to circular protests (Anheier 2017). In Hungary, law requires nonprofit organizations to declare the amount and the provider of foreign funding (Anheier 2017). In 2018, the Hungarian government announced the introduction of a 25 percent penalty tax for civil society organizations working with refugees. The latter was declared as part of the government's official campaign directed against the American-Hungarian philanthropist Georg Soros, who has been an active supporter of civil society and academic life in Central and Eastern Europe since the late 1970s. These actions are exemplary for what can be described as a government-led "intimidation campaign" against civil society organizations since the return of the populist Fidesz party to power in 2010 (Kuti 2017). These are only two examples of how the rise of populism and nationalism in some countries of the region affect civil societies' legal framework and activities.

Characteristics and composition of the nonprofit sector

While several features of civil society in Central and Eastern Europe reflect very recent events, some of its main characteristics are still influenced by the regions' communist past. These include nonprofits' most prevalent fields of activities, the economic relevance of formal civil society and the nonprofit sectors' funding structures. In the following sections, we discuss these characteristics along with an updated and extended version of a framework developed by Meyer et al. (2019), forming four country groups on the basis of shared patterns in the institutional environments and historical events in CEE: the Baltic group; the Visegrád group and Slovenia; the group of Bulgaria, Croatia and Romania; and finally, the group of countries in the Western Balkans.

Composition of the nonprofit sector

In the majority of countries of CEE, the most prevalent field of nonprofits' activities today is culture and recreation. This particularly applies to the Visegrád countries, Bulgaria, Croatia and Romania. Accordingly, in Hungary, Poland and Croatia more than 40 percent, 47 percent and 50 percent respectively of all nonprofits are active in culture, arts, sports, or leisure activities (Bežovan et al. 2017; Kuti 2017; Pazderski 2017). While the relative importance of the field of culture and recreation has diminished over the last three decades due to the vast number of nonprofit organizations that have been founded since 1989 in all fields of activity, the composition of the sector still differs from the rest of Europe, at least in Western Continental and Mediterranean countries (Salamon and Sokolowski 2016; Salamon et al. 2004). This difference is often explained by the countries' communist legacy, as culture and recreation were among the few social activities tolerated or even encouraged under communist rule (Toepler and Salamon 2003). It is worth noting that some of these nonprofits might have "operated under a false flag" as some nonprofits that officially engaged in culture and recreation were actually working on civil rights and advocacy issues, which was otherwise prohibited by communist authorities (Navrátil and Pecjal 2017). In light of the dominant role of culture and recreation, the field of social services is relatively less significant as a field of activity in CEE. While commonly ranked first in Western Europe, it is typically only the second most common form of activity in the Visegrád group and Bulgaria, Croatia and Romania. The comparatively lower importance might also result from a lack of nonprofits' resources to provide these capital-intensive services and from the reluctance of governments to share core welfare responsibilities with nonprofit organizations (Toepler and Salamon 2003).

In the group of countries in the Western Balkans, nonprofits' predominant activities are civil rights and advocacy issues such as human rights, combating corruption, democratic consolidation, and the support of marginalized groups and women's rights (Meyer et al. 2017). The presence of advocacy and civil rights organizations is particularly strong in Kosovo, Montenegro, Republic of North Macedonia and Serbia. Among other things, this is due to the fact that large parts of the sector have emerged only recently, in about the last decade, in which Western donor institutions have often provided funding for such issues (Navrátil and Pecjal 2017; Toepler and Salamon 2003).

In the Baltic group, nonprofits' main activities are quite diverse. In Estonia, several organizations in the field of sports, culture and recreation were brought back to life after five decades of Soviet occupation, making up approximately 20 percent of the country's nonprofits today. Employment initiatives and professional associations play a large role too, and half of all nonprofits are housing associations (European Commission 2010a; Lepp 2015). In Lithuania, the main activities of nonprofits comprise social services and health care (55 percent), sports and culture (18 percent) and childcare and youth affairs (8 percent) (European Commission 2010b). In comparison, Latvian nonprofits tend to be more active in economic, social and community development, advocacy and education, followed by culture, recreation and social services (Caune et al. 2016).

Economic (contribution) and civic relevance of the nonprofit sector

Data on the economic relevance of the nonprofit sectors in CEE underline that nonprofits in the four country groups indeed operate in different environments. Most indicators suggest that countries of the Visegrád group and Slovenia as well as the Baltic countries are ahead, the group of Bulgaria, Croatia and Romania is mid table, and the group of countries in the Western Balkans trails behind (see Table 4.1). This pattern for instance applies to the share of the countries' employees that work in nonprofit organizations, which on average is 1.8 percent in the Visegrád group and Slovenia, 1.1 percent in Bulgaria, Croatia and Romania, and 0.8 percent in the Western Balkans. Likewise, it relates to the sector's value added to GDP: It is approximately 1.6 percent in the Visegrád group and Slovenia, 1.3 percent in the Baltic countries but lower than 1 percent in the remaining groups (Meyer et al. 2017; Salamon et al. 2004).

A similar distribution can be observed concerning the density of nonprofit organizations. While there are about 12 nonprofits per 1,000 capita in the Baltics, the respective figure is 9 for the Visegrád group and Slovenia, 8 for the group of Bulgaria, Croatia and Romania, and 5 for the countries in the Western Balkans. More meaningful, however, are the numbers of active nonprofits per 1,000 capita, which are much lower in all country groups than the number of registered organizations.

These data do not only demonstrate variance across CEE, but also show that the nonprofit sectors in CEE score lower in almost every aspect than their Western European counterparts: CEE countries have fewer nonprofits per capita as well as lower levels of employment in nonprofits and formal volunteering. Civic participation is also lower in terms of voter turnout, which averages 54.9 percent in the region, as compared to 72.7 percent in Western Europe (IDEA 2018). Such empirical findings have led some scholars to claim civil society in CEE to be "weak"

Table 4.1 Comparison of key characteristics of the nonprofit sector and civil society in CEE

	Population in millions	GDP per capita in PPS (Index EU28=100)	Nonprofit sector value added as % of GDP	Share of total employment in NPOs	Number of nonprofits	Number of active nonprofits	Nonprofits per 1,000 capita	Active nonprofits per 1,000 citizens	Volunteer engagement (in %)	Voter turnout (in %)
Czech Republic	10.55	88	1.77	2.1	127300	n.a.	12.1	n.a	26.8	60.8
Hungary	9.83	67	1.55	3.7	81000	64000	8.2	6.5	12.2	61.8
Poland	38.0	68	1.40	0.9	117000	80000	3.1	2.1	8.5	50.9
Slovakia	5.4	77	0.98	1.5	53000	13400	9.8	2.5	13.5	59.8
Slovenia	2.1	83	2.06	1.0	28600	n.a.	13.9	n.a	32.1	51.7
Group 1	**65.8**	**77**	**1.55**	**1.8**	**406900**	**157400**	**9.4**	**3.7**	**18.6**	**57.0**
Croatia	4.2	60	n.a.	1.6	68000	57900	16.2	13.8	n.a.	52.6
Bulgaria	7.1	49	n.a.	0.6	41500	9500	5.9	1.3	11.9	53.9
Romania	19.8	58	0.60	1.2	62600	26000	3.2	1.3	13.2	37.8
Group 2	**31.0**	**56**	**0.60**	**1.1**	**172100**	**93400**	**8.4**	**5.5**	**12.6**	**48.1**
Albania	2.9	30	0.28	0.7	2400	2400	0.8	0.8	19.7	46.8
Bosnia & Herzegov.	3.5	29	0.60	0.4	23000	6600	6.5	1.9	8.3	54.5
Kosovo	1.8	n.a.	n.a.	2.6	8000	8000	4.5	4.5	10.4	41.3
Macedonia	2.1	37	0.96	0.4	13600	4200	6.6	2.0	n.a.	66.8
Montenegro	0.6	45	0.58	0.4	3950	1100	6.3	1.8	7.5	73.4
Serbia	7.1	37	1.34	0.3	50300	37700	7.1	5.3	11.2	56.1
Group 3	**17.9**	**36**	**0.75**	**0.8**	**101250**	**60000**	**5.3**	**2.7**	**11.4**	**56.5**
Estonia	1.3	75		4.5	30331		23.0		22.7	64.2
Latvia	2.0	65	1.30		7000		3.6		22.4	58.8
Lithuania	2.9	75			30000		10.4		16.0	50.6
Group 4	**6.2**	**72**	**1.30**	**4.5**	**67331**	**0**	**12.3**	**0.0**	**20.4**	**57.9**
TOTAL	**121.0**	**60**	**1.05**	**2.1**	**747581**	**310800**	**8.9**	**3.0**	**15.7**	**54.9**
Western Europe										**72.7**

Sources: Population: Eurostat per 01.01.2016; GDP per Capita: Eurostat for 2016; Nonprofit Sector value added, Share of total employment in NPOs, Number of Non-profits per 1,000 capita, Number of active NPOs per 1,000 capita: Vandor et al. 2017; Share of Volunteers: European Values Study Group 2011 (EVS 2008 data); Voter turnout: IDEA, 2018; additional sources for Estonia: Lepp, 2015; Lithuania: Jatautaite and Vaidelyte 2015.

(Howard 2003). Nevertheless, the potential for mobilization is considerably high in many CEE countries, as for instance mass protests have shown in recent years in Poland or Romania. Nonprofit organizations and civic initiatives thus often exert more influence on decision- and policy-making than mere numbers would suggest (Ekiert et al. 2017b; Piotrowski 2015).

Funding structure of the nonprofit sector

The funding structure of the nonprofit sector in CEE also differs distinctively from that of many Western European countries and the USA: Government funding is less important while membership fees and foreign philanthropic donations play a much larger role (Salamon and Sokolowski 2016). Similarly, domestic philanthropy, both corporate and individual, is less developed.

The nonprofit sectors in the Visegrád group and Slovenia rely heavily on fees, which corresponds with the high share of organizations in culture and recreation that are typically funded by their members. While in the mid-1990s, more than 50 percent of the sectors' revenue stemmed from this source of income (Salamon et al. 2004), its relevance has decreased slightly until today (e.g., Czech Republic: 22 percent; Navrátil and Pecjal 2017; Salamon and Sokolowski 2016). Likewise, income from philanthropic sources had greater significance in the 1990s and early 2000s than it currently has, largely because of the extensive degree of public and private democracy assistance at that time. While international funding in the 1990s mainly stemmed from embassies, governments and philanthropic foundations, predominantly from Western Europe and North America (e.g., USA, Canada, the Netherlands, Open Society Fund, German Marshall Fund), many of these actors ceased their support once the EU started to provide funding. Conversely, domestic public funding somewhat increased during the same time in many countries. Domestic donations originate mainly from corporate giving or, as in Hungary, Poland, Romania and Slovakia, from private income tax donations (Strečanský and Török 2016). The funding sources of nonprofits in Bulgaria, Croatia and Romania are very similar to those in the Visegrád countries and Slovenia. In both country groups, EU funding, contributions from international foundations and government funding provide the majority of nonprofits' income.

In the Western Balkans, the role of foreign donors is even larger than in the two country groups discussed above. In course of the rebuilding efforts after the Yugoslav wars as well as the beginning of the process of EU accession, numerous foreign donors have become active in the region. EU funds are thereby mainly provided through programs focusing on civil society (Instrument for Pre-Accession Assistance – IPA) and are among the most important funding sources. The share of the sectors' income from foreign donations is therefore very high, reaching about 75 percent in both Kosovo and Montenegro, and 66 percent in the Republic of North Macedonia (Musliu 2017; Vujović 2017). Since funding from national or local governments is rare or difficult to obtain – though its share has been increasing lately – the nonprofit sector in the Western Balkans is highly dependent on foreign funding for now (Musliu 2017).

In the three Baltic States, the nonprofit sectors rely on different income sources. In Estonia, membership fees are the most frequent source, followed by income from local governments and state-run foundations (Lagerspetz et al. 2002). In Latvia, donations and gifts make up the largest part of nonprofits' revenues (37 percent), followed by government funding and membership fees (15 percent each) (Vilka et al. 2004). In Lithuania, however, funding provided by the government is the sector's main source of income (30 percent), closely followed by donations (28 percent) (European Commission 2010b).

Overall, the nonprofit sectors in CEE have made remarkable progress over the last three decades in terms of numbers and today comprise of more than 750,000 registered nonprofit organizations. While comparison data are hard to obtain, this almost certainly represents a substantial increase, as reflected in data on individual countries. In Croatia, for example, the number of associations has more than quadrupled between 1990 (12,000 organizations) and the end of 2015 (53,000 organizations) (Bežovan et al. 2017). Similar increases are documented in many other countries, including Bulgaria, Hungary and Romania (e.g., Kuti 2017; Lambru 2017; Smilova 2017). Even if we consider methodological challenges and acknowledge that not all registered organizations are still active, this amounts to substantial growth. The rising importance of the nonprofit sector has also been visible in its increased importance as an employer. In the four countries (Czech Republic, Hungary, Romania and Slovakia) for which comparative data are available, the share of the countries' employees working for nonprofit organizations has risen from an average of 1.1 percent of the workforce in 1995 to 2.1 percent in 2015 (Salamon et al. 2004; Vandor et al. 2017). Employment growth rates of the nonprofit sector in Poland for example, have also drastically surpassed other parts of the economy (Salamon and Sokolowski 2016).

The institutional environment of the nonprofit sector

Nonprofit organizations do not operate in a vacuum. As the description of the historical context and the legal framework above has shown, they are influenced by a multitude of economic, political, social and human forces and are embedded in the institutional context of their countries. One way of understanding the state and role of the nonprofit sector is through an analysis of the institutional environment and its key actors, including domestic public authorities, international donors, private philanthropists and the media (see also Meyer et al. 2019).

Institutional environment in the Baltic countries

The Baltic countries share a past as member states of the Soviet Union and joined the European Union as early as 2004. In spite of their different civil society traditions, they share some characteristics with respect to the influence that is exerted on nonprofits through the institutional environment.

Domestic public authorities: Around the transition years of 1989/1990, civil movements in Central and Eastern Europe mainly emerged in opposition to the state authority. In the following years, however, one of the main lessons that the nonprofit sector in these countries had to learn, was how to cooperate with the state (Rikmann and Keedus 2013). Such cooperation was not only undertaken to preserve legitimacy and access resources, but also to ensure the influence of nonprofits on policy making in the legal and administrative reforms after independence (Hadzi-Miceva 2008; Rikmann and Keedus 2013). One can argue that this learning process was successful in the Baltic States. Today, all three countries employ reliable legal frameworks for operating nonprofit organizations and have well-established advocacy and communication structures between the nonprofit sector and official bodies (Rikmann and Keedus 2013; USAID 2015, 2017). Central and regional governments routinely engage in contracting social services to nonprofits, even though their overall funding volume for nonprofit organizations does not reach the level of Western Europe or the Visegrád countries (Caune et al. 2016; Ilgius 2016; USAID 2017).

European Union and foreign funders: Arguably, the EU accession process deserves some credit for the comparatively fast development of stable legal frameworks and nonprofit–state relationships (Börzel 2010). Currently, the EU is still one of the major funders for research and development (R&D) (Jatautaite and Vaidelyte 2015; Lepp 2015; Miezaine 2015), but its contribution to the nonprofit sector has declined in recent years.

Public and private foreign funders were particularly important in helping to facilitate the fast initial growth of nonprofit organizations right after the declarations of independence in the 1990s (Maciukaite-Zviniene 2008). Their involvement decreased notably once Estonia, Latvia and Lithuania became members of the EU. Nevertheless, a number of public foreign funders are still active in the region, including, amongst others, the European Economic Area (EEA) and Norwegian grants program, which has announced to continue its commitment at least until 2021.

Private philanthropy and the media: Private philanthropy is not very developed in the region, probably owing to the fact that private foundations had been illegal during Soviet rule (Ilgius 2016). Nevertheless, stimulated by public interventions such as the Lithuanian percentage tax designation, private and institutional contributions have increased over the years in all three countries (Ilgius 2016). Another notable factor is the media. Unlike in most other countries in the region, the relationship between media and nonprofit organizations is generally regarded as positive and constructive. Activists are perceived as opinion leaders and trusted sources, and there is positive coverage on nonprofit-related topics (USAID 2017).

Institutional environment in the Visegrád countries and Slovenia

Overall, the institutional environment in the Visegrád countries and Slovenia is comparable to the Baltic countries. Like Estonia, Latvia and Lithuania, the Visegrád countries and Slovenia underwent a relatively swift economic and political transition after the collapse of communism. The Czech Republic, Hungary, Poland, Slovakia and Slovenia joined the European Union in the same 2004 accession round as the Baltic countries. In spite of these similarities, the institutional frameworks of these groups show differences.

Domestic public authorities: The role of public authorities in these five countries has been mixed and somewhat volatile. In the 1990s and early 2000s, most national governments operated along a predominantly nonprofit-friendly agenda. However, relationships with civil society deteriorated over time, most notably in Hungary, where the government has openly accused various nonprofit organizations of being part of an illegitimate liberal opposition (Bozóki 2015).

Today, central governments are perceived as the most powerful actors in this country group and their influence on civil society is regarded as higher than in other countries in the region. Central governments are perceived as more powerful in shaping civil society than foreign funders and the EU (Meyer et al. 2019). Even though federal state funding for nonprofits has considerably decreased in recent years, it is still an important source of funding and more frequent than in other country groups (Fink-Hafner and Novak 2017; Kuti 2017; Szabó 2015).

European Union and foreign funders: Like in Estonia, Latvia and Lithuania, the process of EU accession is widely considered a success story. This process of EU accession and the associated legislative and monetary support has often been credited for having a very positive influence on the process of transformation, the promotion of democratic consolidation, as well for providing funding and legitimacy to nonprofit organizations (Grabbe 2006).

Although the EU remains a significant funder, its overall influence has been declining since the five countries were granted EU membership. This has direct consequences for nonprofit organizations, as the European Union had previously been a more active advocate for the rights of the nonprofit sector (Kuti 2017). Additionally, decision-making processes about the allocation of EU funds are now often firmly in the hands of local public authorities. The influence of international aid agencies and foreign donors has similarly declined over the past two decades and many international funders have reduced their support (Navrátil and Pecjal 2017; Strečanský 2017).

Private philanthropy and the media: The public image of private philanthropy is rather positive among nonprofit practitioners and experts (Meyer et al. 2017). As highlighted above, three of the five countries have established income tax designation schemes (Hungary, Poland and Slovakia), which have contributed to the development of private philanthropic giving (Strečanský and Török 2016). The role of the media is however more ambivalent in this region than in the Baltics. In the Czech Republic, Slovakia and Slovenia, media are mostly supportive of nonprofit organizations (Fink-Hafner and Novak 2017; Navrátil and Pecjal 2017). In Hungary and Poland, the media is increasingly controlled by the right-wing governments, leading to more critical or even hostile coverage of the nonprofit sector (Bajomi-Lázár 2015; Ekiert et al. 2017a).

Institutional environment in the Western Balkans

The institutional environment in Albania, Bosnia and Herzegovina, Kosovo, Montenegro, Republic of North Macedonia and Serbia differs from the first two groups. In contrast to the state-dominated institutional environments in the previous two groups (the Baltics, Visegrád countries and Slovenia), the influence of domestic public institutions is much less pronounced. At the same time, foreign institutions play a pivotal role as partners of the nonprofit sector.

Domestic public authorities: Central governments are frequently characterized as powerful but corrupt and paternalistic actors who try to exert control over civil society (Meyer et al. 2019). As a consequence, nonprofits which are critical of public authorities are frequently threatened and limited in their ability to perform advocacy functions (Freedom House 2017). Nonprofits in this country group therefore operate under less sustainable conditions than nonprofits in the Baltics and the Visegrád group (USAID 2017).

European Union and foreign funders: The European Union is the most important and influential actor for the development of the nonprofit sector. Apart from being an active funder, the EU enables dialogue between public authorities and the nonprofit sector. The European Commission has emphasized that it sees EU accession being a realistic long-term perspective for all countries in the region and has presented a roadmap for an EU accession of Montenegro and Serbia by 2025 (European Commission 2018). Foreign donors, such as USAID or EEA and the Norwegian grants program, are also very active in the Western Balkans.

Private philanthropy and the media: Individual domestic donors and corporations are rather insignificant in the region. According to estimates, corporate and individual donations across the six countries constitute only between 36 and 44 million USD per year (Catalyst Balkans 2017). With respect to the media and the public perception of the nonprofit sector, the institutional environment can be assessed as challenging. Foa and Ekiert (2017: 428) remark that the public's evaluation of the nonprofit sector in other parts of Central and Eastern Europe is "notably ahead of the Balkans." Comparative studies such as conducted by Reporters Without Borders and Freedom House generally do not consider the Western Balkans to have a free press and report problematic ownership structures, journalistic self-censorship, attacks by the government and a lack of funding for alternative media (see e.g., Freedom House 2017).

Institutional environment in Croatia, Bulgaria and Romania

A mix of strong domestic public authorities and substantial, but decreasing, influence of the European Union and foreign donors shape the institutional environment in Bulgaria, Croatia and Romania.

Domestic public authorities: Over the past decades, public authorities in all three countries have undertaken reforms that benefited the nonprofit sector. These include the introduction of legal frameworks for nonprofit entities, regulations for collaboration between nonprofits and the state as well as some degree of social service marketization. Public authorities have also started to directly finance nonprofit activities. At the same time, corruption and paternalism represent serious challenges to the nonprofit sector. In Croatia, a survey conducted between 2008 and 2010 found that almost 80 percent of all nonprofit organizations had experienced unlawful restrictions by the local or central government (Bežovan et al. 2017). In Bulgaria, relatives of local officials (or even the officials themselves) are reported to sometimes register their own nonprofits in order to siphon off public resources (Smilova 2017).

European Union and foreign funders: The three countries are the 'youngest' members of the European Union, which Romania and Bulgaria joined in 2007 and Croatia in 2013. Overall, EU accession is considered to have successfully facilitated the development of a largely stable legal and political framework for nonprofits (Grabbe 2006; Lambru 2017; Parau 2009; Smilova 2017). Together with foreign donor institutions, the European Union is also still an important partner in terms of funding. The same can be said about other foreign donors, although the activities of many aid agencies are expected to be curbed in the near future.

Private philanthropy and the media: Private philanthropy has become a small but relevant source of funding in all three countries. All three provide some form of tax benefits or deductions for charitable giving of individuals and companies. The role of the media is mixed. While the relationship between the media and nonprofits is often fruitful at the local level, all three countries have witnessed attacks against nonprofit organizations and their funders through media sources close to the government. As in many other CEE countries, negative campaigns often use narratives which de-legitimize nonprofits, civil protesters or philanthropic foundations, claiming them to be "foreign agents" (Bežovan et al. 2017; Lambru 2017; Smilova 2017; USAID 2017).

Trends and implications for managing nonprofit organizations

As the preceding sections have shown, the nonprofit sector in Central and Eastern Europe has been shaped by many developments in recent decades and changed at a faster pace than in most other regions of the world. Meyer et al. (2017) identified a number of areas in which civil society experts in the region expect changes in the next ten to fifteen years. Some of these trends are shared with other parts of the world, such as the growing popularity of social entrepreneurship and earned-income orientation, the development of new forms of fundraising, or increasing professionalization and formalization of civil society, while others are more idiosyncratic for the region. In the following, we will focus on the latter.

Political instrumentalization of civil society as an "imported concept"

One remarkable difference to most parts of Western Europe and North America is the relationship of the public with the concepts of civil society and nonprofits. In many countries, the very idea of civil society and nonprofit organizations is seen as something "imported". In the 1980s and 1990s, much of the language and many conceptions of civil society were modeled after practices of "the West", filling a (perceived) gap of civic identity and know-how that had been created by the suppression of large parts of civil society during Socialist and Soviet rule (Fink-Hafner and Novak 2017; Spahić-Šiljak 2017). In addition to ideas and concepts, Western European and North American institutions also contributed tangible resources to support the development of civil society, such as funding and staff, and were actively engaged in agenda setting. As highlighted, a good degree of nonprofit sectors' funding was (and partially still is) provided by the European Union and foreign aid agencies. Many individuals and organizations in the nonprofit sector who were concerned with the rebuilding efforts after the Yugoslav wars were foreigners (Aksartova 2009; Fagan 2011; Sterland 2006). As Bežovan et al. (2017: 113) argue for the case of Croatia, this high level of involvement has sometimes led to the perception of civil society being illegitimate: "Civil society was seen as speaking a 'foreign' language and as lacking roots in local communities and in the consciousness of Croatian citizens. Due to the absence of such a basis in Croatian society, the public was unwilling to acknowledge those agencies as stakeholders in contemporary development projects and required nonprofits to justify both their existence and activities."

This notion of foreignness provides a problematic frame for civil society, as it leads to a powerful narrative of de-legitimization of nonprofit organizations and their supporters. Together with the broader trope of political heteronomy that is widespread across the region, the idea of civil society as an "imported concept" has added to the success of anti-civic campaigns in recent years. Labeling nonprofits as "foreign spies" or the campaign against the US-Hungarian philanthropist Georg Soros are examples of this phenomenon.

Withdrawal of European Union and foreign donor funds

Foreign funders and the European Union have contributed greatly to the development of the nonprofit sector throughout the region. In addition to providing funding opportunities, the EU has had (or in the case of the Western Balkans, is expected to have) a positive impact on state legislation, international networking, and the public legitimacy of civil society and nonprofit organizations (Börzel 2010; Grabbe 2006).

In spite of these positive effects, a number of challenges arise in connection with foreign funding. One of these challenges is the high dependence on foreign funds, in particular in the Western Balkans. As Sterland (2006: 17) remarks for the case of Bosnia and Herzegovina as well as Kosovo, international aid was partially perceived to create a "large, non-specialized, short-term oriented, financially insecure sector." This notion has been echoed by authors who have highlighted that donor dependency can hamper the development of self-sustaining, professional organizations (Aksartova 2009; Bežovan et al. 2017; Ordanoski 2017). The dependency on foreign donors becomes an even bigger problem, once international donors withdraw, as has been largely the case in current EU member states in the 1990s and early 2000s and in recent years in the Western Balkans. Some of the funds can be compensated for with resources from the European Union. However, these funds also tend to come with strings attached and are often accompanied by problems such as bureaucracy, challenging co-funding and liquidity requirements, and limited access for small organizations (Kutter and Trappmann 2010; Sudbery 2010).

The challenges of donor dependency and the withdrawal of foreign funds are expected to continue in the coming ten to fifteen years (Meyer et al. 2017). These issues hold direct management implications for organizations in the region: Organizations that find themselves in such a challenging environment need to diversify income, e.g. through developing community-based forms of funding, building consortia with other nonprofits for accessing EU funds or through generating earned income. Other dominant trends in the region, such as the growing ecosystem and acceptance for social entrepreneurship, professionalization and expected positive developments in private philanthropy might provide opportunities for doing so (Meyer et al. 2017).

Increased government control over the nonprofit sector

Finally, another worrisome trend is the increasing tendency of governments to seek control over nonprofit organizations and their work, by influencing funds, regulations and public perception. This trend is particularly strong in the authoritarian and nativist governments of Hungary and Poland, as well as Montenegro, the Republic of North Macedonia and Serbia (Bajomi-Lázár 2015; Ekiert et al. 2017a; Greskovits 2015; Ordanoski 2017; Spasojević 2017). As a consequence, nonprofits that are critical of public authorities are limited in their ability to perform advocacy functions. Ironically, this development has also been fueled by international attempts to foster collaboration between the state and nonprofits, which has increased the dependency and vulnerability of nonprofits to interventions by public authorities (Meyer et al. 2019). In addition, the state's control over the allocation of EU funding is a powerful instrument for public authorities, allowing them to tie nonprofit organizations closer to their interests and limit activities that are not politically convenient. This creates challenges for many nonprofits, particularly in the field of advocacy and work with minorities. Some organizations attempt to cope with this situation by seeking independence from public authorities through accessing alternative sources of funding, but also by increasing collaboration with other nonprofit organizations within and across domestic borders.

Conclusion

Over the last three decades, the nonprofit sector in Central and Eastern Europe has undergone remarkable development and has grown profoundly in terms of size, scope and impact. In spite of many differences, the sector resembles Western countries today much more than just a few years ago. Nonprofit organizations are now more often the kind of formalized and well-organized service providers which are typical for the sector in Western Europe, and less frequently the informal, often oppositional movements and initiatives associated with the region at the time of the regime changes of 1989/1991.

In spite of this remarkable growth, recent years have also brought along challenges. Some, such as the withdrawal of foreign donors, the lack of domestic income sources and the perceived illegitimacy of the sector, have been very persistent over time (Toepler and Salamon 2003). Others, such as narratives of de-legitimization, decreasing trust and open hostility of autocratic governments are comparably new challenges for nonprofits and their members. Nevertheless, experts and practitioners in the region have a predominantly optimistic outlook: In a recent survey among over 350 civil society experts in the region, 75 percent expected a moderately or very positive development for civil society in the next ten to fifteen years (Vandor et al. 2017). Given the many hurdles that the nonprofit organizations in the region have managed to successfully overcome in the past decades, this optimism seems warranted.

References

Aksartova, S. (2009) Promoting civil society or diffusing NGOs? In D. Hammack and S. Heydemann (eds.), *Globalization, Philanthropy, and Civil Society: Projecting Institutional Logics Abroad*. Bloomington: Indiana University Press, 160–191.

Anheier, H.K. (2017) Civil society challenged: Towards an enabling policy environment, *Economics Discussion Papers*, no. 2017–45.

Bajomi-Lázár, P. (2015) Party colonization of the media: The case of Hungary. In P. Krasztev and J. Van Til (eds.), *The Hungarian Patient: Social Opposition to an Illiberal Democracy*. Budapest: Central European University Press, 59–80.

Bernhard, M. (1993) Civil society and democratic transition in East Central Europe, *Political Science Quarterly*, 108(2): 307–326.

Bežovan, G., Matančević, J. and Baturina, D. (2017) Country report: Croatia. In P. Vandor, N. Traxler, R. Millner and M. Meyer (eds.), *Civil Society in Central and Eastern Europe: Challenges and Opportunities*. Vienna: ERSTE Foundation, 111–125.

Börzel, T.A. (2010) Why you don't always get what you want: EU enlargement and civil society in Central and Eastern Europe, *Acta Politica*, 45(1–2): 1–10.

Bozóki, A. (2015) Broken democracy, predatory state, and nationalist populism. In P. Krasztev and J. Van Til (eds.), *The Hungarian Patient. Social Opposition to an Illiberal Democracy*. Budapest: Central European University Press, 3–36.

Brusis, M. (2010) European incentives and regional interest representation in Central and Eastern European countries, *Acta Politica*, 45(1/2): 70–89.

Catalyst Balkans. (2017) Current State of Philanthropy in the Western Balkans. www.catalystbalkans.org/en/home/resources [Accessed 28 September 2018].

Caune, E., Neilande, J., Krieviņa-Sutora, B. and Pīpiķe, R. (2016) *The Review of the NGO Sector in Latvia. 2015*. Civic Alliance Latvia.

Ekiert, G. and Kubik, J. (2010) *Rebellious Civil Society: Popular Protest and Democratic Consolidation in Poland, 1989–1993*. Ann Arbor: University of Michigan Press.

Ekiert, G. and Kubik, J. (2014) Myths and realities of civil society, *Journal of Democracy*, 25(1): 46–58.

Ekiert, G., Kubik, J. and Wenzel, M. (2017a) Country report: Poland. In P. Vandor, N. Traxler, R. Millner and M. Meyer (eds.), *Civil Society in Central and Eastern Europe: Challenges and Opportunities*. Vienna: ERSTE Foundation, 76–91.

Ekiert, G., Kubik, J. and Wenzel, M. (2017b) Civil society and three dimensions of inequality in post-1989 Poland, *Comparative Politics*, 49(3): 331–350.

European Commission. (2010a) Volunteering in the European Union: Country Report – Estonia. http://ec.europa.eu/citizenship/pdf/national_report_ee_en.pdf [Accessed 28 September 2018].

European Commission. (2010b) Volunteering in the European Union: Country Report – Lithuania. http://ec.europa.eu/citizenship/pdf/national_report_lt_en.pdf [Accessed 28 September 2018].

European Commission. (2018) Policy: Western Balkans. http://ec.europa.eu/research/iscp/index.cfm?pg=west_balk [Accessed 15 March 2018].

European Values Study Group. (2011) European Values Study 2008: Integrated dataset (EVS 2008). Cologne, Germany: GESIS Data Archive.

Eurostat. (2016a) Statistics explained: GDP per capita. Brussles: Eurostat.

Eurostat. (2016b) Statistics explained: Unemployment rates. Brussels: Eurostat.

Fagan, A. (2011) EU assistance for civil society in Kosovo: A step too far for democracy promotion?, *Democratization*, 18(3): 707–730.

Fink-Hafner, D. and Novak, M. (2017) Country report: Slovenia. In P. Vandor, N. Traxler, R. Millner and M. Meyer (eds.), *Civil Society in Central and Eastern Europe: Challenges and Opportunities*. Vienna: ERSTE Foundation, 126–142.

Foa, R. and Ekiert, G. (2017) The weakness of postcommunist civil society reassessed, *European Journal of Political Research*, (56): 419–439.

Freedom House. (2017) Freedom in the World 2017. https://freedomhouse.org/sites/default/files/FH_FIW_2017_Report_Final.pdf [Accessed 28 September 2018].

Grabbe, H. (2006) *The EU's Transformative Power. Europeanization through Conditionality in Central and Eastern Europe*. Basingstoke: Palgrave Macmillan.

Greskovits, B. (2015) The hollowing and backsliding of democracy in East Central Europe, *Global Policy*, 6: 28–37.

Hadzi-Miceva, K. (2008) Legal and institutional mechanisms for NGO–government cooperation in Croatia, Estonia, and Hungary, *International Journal of Not-for-Profit Law*, 10(4): 43–72.

Howard, M.M. (2003) *The Weakness of Civil Society in Post-Communist Europe*. Cambridge: Cambridge University Press.

IDEA. (2018) IDEA Voter Turnout Database. https://www.idea.int/data-tools/data/voter-turnout [Accessed 28 September 2018].

Ilgius, V. (2016) Country report: Lithuania. In B. Strečanský and M. Török (eds.), *Assessment of the Impact of the Percentage Tax Designations: Past, Present, Future*. Vienna: ERSTE Foundation, 86–89.

Jatautaite, B. and Vaidelyte, E. (2015) *EUFORI Study: Lithuania Country Report*. Brussels: European Commission, DG for Research and Innovation.

Krastev, I. (2016) Liberalism's failure to deliver, *Journal of Democracy*, 27(1): 35–38.

Kuti, É. (2017) Country report: Hungary. In P. Vandor, N. Traxler, R. Millner and M. Meyer (eds.), *Civil Society in Central and Eastern Europe: Challenges and Opportunities*. Vienna: ERSTE Foundation, 58–75.

Kutter, A. and Trappmann, V. (2010) Civil society in Central and Eastern Europe: The ambivalent legacy of accession, *Acta Politica*, 45(1/2): 41–69.

Lagerspetz, M., Rikmann, E. and Ruutsoo, R. (2002) The structure and resources of NGOs in Estonia, *Voluntas: International Journal of Voluntary and Nonprofit Organizations*, 13(1): 73–87.

Lambru, M. (2017) Country report: Romania. In P. Vandor, N. Traxler, R. Millner and M. Meyer (eds.), *Civil Society in Central and Eastern Europe: Challenges and Opportunities*. Vienna: ERSTE Foundation, 158–172.

Lepp, Ü. (2015) *EUFORI Study: Estonia Country Report*. Brussels: European Commission.

Maciukaite-Zviniene, S. (2008) Challenges for civil society: Participation in the Baltic States region building, *Viesoji Politika ir Administravimas*, (26): 113–121.

Meyer, M., Moder, C.M., Neumayr, M., Traxler, N. and Vandor, P. (2017) Patterns in civil society in Central and Eastern Europe: A synthesis of 16 Country Reports and an Expert Survey. In P. Vandor, N. Traxler, R. Millner and M. Meyer (eds.), *Civil Society in Central and Eastern Europe: Challenges and Opportunities*. Vienna: ERSTE Foundation, 12–42.

Meyer, M., Moder, C., Neumayr, M. and Vandor, P. (2019) Civil society and its institutional context in CEE. *Voluntas: International Journal of Voluntary and Nonprofit Organizations*, 1–17.

Miezaine, Z. (2015) *EUFORI Study: Latvia Country Report*. Brussels: European Commission, DG for Research and Innovation.

Musliu, V. (2017) Country report: Kosovo. In P. Vandor, N. Traxler, R. Millner and M. Meyer (eds.), *Civil Society in Central and Eastern Europe: Challenges and Opportunities*. Vienna: ERSTE Foundation, 204–215.

Navrátil, J. and Pecjal, J. (2017) Country report: Czech Republic. In P. Vandor, N. Traxler, R. Millner and M. Meyer (eds.), *Civil Society in Central and Eastern Europe: Challenges and Opportunities*. Vienna: ERSTE Foundation, 43–57.

Ordanoski, S. (2017) Country report: Macedonia. In P. Vandor, N. Traxler, R. Millner and M. Meyer (eds.), *Civil Society in Central and Eastern Europe: Challenges and Opportunities*. Vienna: ERSTE Foundation, 216–231.

Parau, C.E. (2009) Impaling Dracula: How EU accession empowered civil society in Romania, *West European Politics*, 32(1): 119–141.

Pazderski, F. (2017) Poland: Expecting negative trends. In EU–Russia Civil Society Forum (ed.), *2016 Report on the State of Civil Society in the EU and Russia*. Berlin: EU–Russia Civil Society Forum, 75–97.

Piotrowski, G. (2009) Civil society, un-civil society and the social movements, *Interface: A Journal for and about Social Movements*, 1(2): 166–189.

Piotrowski, G. (2015) What are Eastern European social movements and how to study them?, *Intersections. East European Journal of Society and Politics*, 1(3): 4–15.

Podkaminer, L. (2013) *Development Patterns of Central and East European Countries (in the course of transition and following EU accession)*. Vienna: Vienna Institute for International Economic Studies.

Rikmann, E. and Keedus, L. (2013) Civil sectors in transformation and beyond: Preliminaries for a comparison of six Central and Eastern European societies, *Voluntas*, 24: 149–166.

Rutzen, D., Moore, D. and Durham, M. (2009) The legal framework for not-for-profit organizations in Central and Eastern Europe, *International Journal of Not-for-Profit Law*, 11(2): 25–75.

Salamon, L.M. and Sokolowski, S.W. (2016) The size and scope of the European third sector. TSI Working Paper No. 13/2016. Brussels: Third Sector Impact.

Salamon, L.M., Sokolowski, S.W. and List, R. (2004) *Global Civil Society. Dimensions of the Nonprofit Sector* (Vol. 2). Bloomfield, CT: Kumarian.

Smilova, R. (2017) Country report: Bulgaria. In P. Vandor, N. Traxler, R. Millner and M. Meyer (eds.), *Civil Society in Central and Eastern Europe: Challenges and Opportunities*. Vienna: ERSTE Foundation, 143–152.

Spahić-Šiljak, Z. (2017) Country report: Bosnia and Herzegovina. In P. Vandor, N. Traxler, R. Millner and M. Meyer (eds.), *Civil Society in Central and Eastern Europe: Challenges and Opportunities*. Vienna: ERSTE Foundation, 188–203.

Spasojević, D. (2017) Country report: Serbia. In P. Vandor, N. Traxler, R. Millner and M. Meyer (eds.), *Civil Society in Central and Eastern Europe: Challenges and Opportunities*. Vienna: ERSTE Foundation, 266–281.

Sterland, B. (2006) Civil Society capacity building in post-conflict societies: The experience of Bosnia and Herzegovina and Kosovo, Praxis Paper no. 9. Oxford: INTRAC.

Strečanský, B. (2017) Country report: Slovakia. In P. Vandor, N. Traxler, R. Millner and M. Meyer (eds.), *Civil Society in Central and Eastern Europe: Challenges and Opportunities*. Vienna: ERSTE Foundation, 92–110.

Strečanský, B. and Török, M. (2016) *Assessment of the Impact of the Percentage Tax Designations: Past, Present, Future*. Vienna: ERSTE Foundation and Centrum Pre Filantropiu.

Sudbery, I. (2010) The European Union as political resource: NGOs as change agents?, *Acta Politica*, 45(1–2): 136–157.

Szabó, M. (2004) Civic engagement in East-Central Europe. In A. Zimmer and E. Priller (eds.), *Future of Civil Society*. Wiesbaden: Springer, 77–97.

Szabó, M. and Márkus, E. (2015) Civil society in Hungary. In C. Schreier (ed.), *25 Years After. Mapping Civil Society in the Visegrad Countries*. Berlin: Maecenata Institute, 9–59.

Toepler, S. and Salamon, L.M. (2003) NGO development in Central and Eastern Europe: An empirical overview, *East European Quarterly*, 37(3): 365–378.

Uhlin, A. (2006) *Post-Soviet Civil Society: Democratization in Russia and the Baltic States*. London: Routledge.

USAID. (2015) *The 2014 CSO Sustainability Index for Central and Eastern Europe and Eurasia* (17th edition). Washington, DC: U.S. Agency for International Development.

USAID. (2017) *The 2016 CSO Sustainability Index for Central and Eastern Europe and Eurasia* (20th edition). Washington, DC: U.S. Agency for International Development.

Vandor, P., Traxler, N., Millner, R. and Meyer, M. (2017) *Civil Society in Central and Eastern Europe: Challenges and Opportunities*. Vienna: ERSTE Foundation.

Vilka, I., Strupiss, A., Strode, I., Balodis, O. and Simane, M. (2004) The development of civil society in Latvia: An analysis. www.mfa.gov.lv/data/file/e/mso35b.pdf [Accessed 28 September 2018].

Vujović, Z. (2017) Country report: Montenegro. In P. Vandor, N. Traxler, R. Millner and M. Meyer (eds.), *Civil Society in Central and Eastern Europe: Challenges and Opportunities*. Vienna: ERSTE Foundation, 246–265.

5

NONPROFIT MANAGEMENT CONTEXT

Russia and the FSU

Lev Jakobson

PROFESSOR AND VICE PRESIDENT OF THE NATIONAL
RESEARCH UNIVERSITY HIGHER SCHOOL OF ECONOMICS, RESEARCH SUPERVISOR
OF THE CENTER FOR STUDIES OF CIVIL SOCIETY AND THE NONPROFIT SECTOR, NATIONAL
RESEARCH UNIVERSITY HIGHER SCHOOL OF ECONOMICS, MOSCOW, RUSSIA

Irina Mersianova

DIRECTOR OF THE CENTER FOR STUDIES OF CIVIL SOCIETY
AND THE NONPROFIT SECTOR, HEAD OF THE CHAIR OF NPO ECONOMICS AND MANAGEMENT,
NATIONAL RESEARCH UNIVERSITY HIGHER SCHOOL OF ECONOMICS, MOSCOW, RUSSIA

Natalya Ivanova

SENIOR RESEARCH FELLOW, CENTER FOR STUDIES OF CIVIL
SOCIETY AND THE NONPROFIT SECTOR, NATIONAL RESEARCH UNIVERSITY HIGHER
SCHOOL OF ECONOMICS, MOSCOW, RUSSIA

Introduction

The Russian third sector has been developing now for about three decades or so. Over the last five to seven years, growth has accelerated due to public policies aimed at supporting nonprofit entities as service providers in the social sphere, as well as the population's growing involvement in volunteering. While Russia's third sector had been stuck in a statist model with a generally limited scope, low level of volunteering, small financial support from the government, and a focus on advocacy, culture and leisure, it is now moving to another model with stronger volunteer participation, more government spending for NPOs and a higher profile of NPO as social service providers. This chapter will provide a description of the dynamically changing context of NPO governance which is important for understanding not only the Russian specifics but also for casting more light on developments relating to NPOs in other former Soviet Union (FSU) countries outside the Baltics, which are covered in Chapter 4.

Historical background and legal environment of third sector development in Russia

The Russian third sector in the post-Soviet period

The emergence of rudiments of social activities in Russia pursued by non-governmental entities not associated with the church dates back to the reign of Empress Catherine II (1762–1796). But the modern history of the Russian third sector had its starting point in the "perestroika" period when the economy dramatically stagnated and authorities faced a crisis of legitimacy, while the emerging discussions on the ways to reform the economic and political system of the Soviet society focused on reducing the government's intervention into the economic and social life. The late 1980s witnessed a fairly boisterous process of civil society self-organization at the grass-roots level. Environmental clubs, unheard of in Russia before, would number several dozen in the late 1980s, with teenager and family clubs, charity groups, etc. emerging by the hundreds. According to some estimates, bottom-up initiatives involved 7–8 percent of the urban population (Zhukova et al. 1988).

Dramatically falling living standards of the population in the 1990s led to the creation of many mutual aid entities and groups. Shrinking social, cultural and humanitarian spending spurred the establishment of civil society associations to save culture, arts, education and science. Preferential policies for specific types of civil society associations (for example, those of disabled persons) encouraged their creation. The USSR Law "On Civil Society Associations" adopted in 1990 and Resolution of the Presidium of the RSFSR [Russian Soviet Federative Socialist Republic] Supreme Soviet "On the Procedure for Registration of Statutes of Political Parties, Trade Unions and Other Civil Society Associations in the RSFSR" of January 15, 1991, invited the population to create formal nonprofit entities. Meanwhile, local Soviets of people's deputies took the initiatives without waiting for the relevant RSFSR legislation to be developed. In the summer of 1990, for example, the Leningrad Soviet adopted provisional registration procedures, which increased the number of civil society associations in the city from 58 (March 1990) to 1,500 in February 2001 (Sungurov & Nezdyurov 2008: 218).

The 1990s were characterized by an 'import-dependent development model' of Russia's third sector in Russia. International donors acted as key agents for supply of both resources and institutions. They not only provided funds but also ensured – through training programs for activists, study tours, etc. – a transfer of the Western (primarily US) third sector culture to Russia. The government's role was largely reduced to benevolent non-interference in the third sector, given a very limited budget for NPO support (Jakobson & Sanovich 2010). By 2000–2001, the Russian third sector had grown quite numerous. As of January 1, 2000, according to Rosstat, the State Statistics Agency, there were a total of 144,000 civil society and religious organizations registered in the country, more than 17,000 foundations, and NPOs totaling 275,000 (Sevortian 2000: 1), although not all of them were operational.

The 2000s were characterized by a process of import substitution of the third sector institutions and resources in Russia: While domestic sources took up the role of foreign ones in providing NPOs with funding, the influence of international donors subsided, self-organization of individuals (associated primarily with the middle class) and charitable activities of businesses stepped up, thus laying the ground for consolidation of the third sector (Jakobson & Sanovich 2010).

The legal environment of the third sector in Russia

The introduction of a new legal framework for nonprofits began in the early 1990s and has proceeded through a number of stages since (Abrosimova 2016). The right to association is guaranteed by the Russian Federation Constitution (Article 30). According to the Federal Law "On Nonprofit Organizations" of 1996, NPOs are established to achieve social, charitable, cultural, educational, research and governance objectives, as well as other purposes. Since 2014, the forms of incorporation of NPOs are listed in Article 50 of the Civil Code of Russia. Thus, nonprofit legal entities can be incorporated in the form of consumer cooperatives; civil society organizations and movements; associations (unions); state institutions; and religious organizations, among others.

The principal rules of NPO management are provided by the Civil Code. The management structure of an NPO will normally include two supervisory bodies: a supreme (governing) and executive (implementing) body. The supreme body in membership-based entities is a meeting or conference (congress) of participants to be attended by their elected representatives (delegates, proxies). For non-membership-based entities the functions of a supreme body are assumed by a special body determined in the incorporation documents; this can be a council of founders or specific persons appointed by it (supervisory and/or guardianship board). With some exceptions, no restriction as to the nominees to such a body is envisaged by law. Standing collective management bodies of this kind (guardianship and supervisory councils, arts councils, partners' councils, etc.) can be also established at membership-based nonprofit entities. The structure and competence of executive bodies of the majority of nonprofit entities are prescribed by law only in general terms. The regulatory center of gravity is shifted towards incorporation documents of a specific organization. NPOs normally have a collective (presidium, board or council) and/ or an individual executive to be appointed by, and accountable to, the entity's supreme body or the founder.

According to an All-Russia NPO survey,[1] 72 percent of respondent NPOs had a collective management body, of which 55 percent were managed by the collective body only, whereas 17 percent of NPOs had both a collective body plus a guardianship board. Among foundations obliged to have a guardianship board by law, only 43 percent of those sampled had it in practice. On average, collective management bodies are composed of eight members, and guardianship boards, six members. Members of the collective bodies would have a meeting seven times a year, members of guardianship boards, four times.

Sector parameters: size, revenues, contribution

NPO number, forms and focus areas

According to the Ministry of Justice (2018), a total of 220,154 nonprofit entities were registered in Russia, as of January 1, 2018. NPOs formally also include public and municipal institutions as well as state corporations. To distinguish those that pursue nonprofit purposes of social importance, a new category, socially oriented NPOs (SONPOs), was introduced by law in 2010. The range of purposes covered under this status is broad and roughly compatible with the charitable status in the US (Benevolenski and Toepler 2017), excluding state corporations. To qualify for this status, it is enough for an NPO to note in its statute at least one of the qualifying activities. According to Rosstat's official estimates, nearly 143,000 SONPOs were in operation in 2017. All-Russia NPO survey data show the principal activity areas of nonprofits and SONPOs (Table 5.1) heavily focusing on the areas of culture and recreation, social services and advocacy and other social activities.

Table 5.1 Activity areas of Russian nonprofits and SONPOs in %

NPO activity areas	All NPOs	SONPOs
Culture and recreation (culture and arts, sports, recreation and social clubs, other in the area of culture and recreation)	22	20
Education and research (basic and secondary education, higher education, supplementary education, other types of education, research)	7	7
Health (rehabilitation, protection of mental health and effects of crises, other health services, other in the area of health care)	5	7
Social services (social services, extraordinary and emergency aid, income support and assurance, other social services)	14	20
Environment (environment, animal protection, other in the environmental area)	5	4
Development and housing (economic, social and community development, territorial social self-governance, housing, employment and vocational re-training, other in the area of development and housing)	6	5
Advocacy and other social activities (advocacy and other civil society entities, law and legal services, political organizations, other in the area of advocacy and social activities)	12	14
Charity and promotion of volunteering (grant-giving foundations, other organizations for charity and promotion of volunteering, other in the area of charitable activities)	2	3
Religion	7	6
Business and industry associations, unions (business associations, industry associations, trade unions, other business and industry associations and unions)	8	3
Other	11	11
No answer	1	1

Source: All-Russia NPO survey.

Note
CEO answers to the question: "What is the main activity area of your NPO?" (% of those polled for the sample as a whole n = 852, and % of those who believe their NPO to be socially focused).

Sector employment and resources

The nonprofit sector is a major part of the national economy as a whole and of the social infra-structure in particular. Thus, Rosstat estimated that SONPOs had an average total employment of 630,000 in 2017 (On the Development . . . 2018: 31). According to our All-Russia NPO poll, 73 percent of NPOs had employees, but with only less than one in five having more than 11 employees.

SONPOs had total revenues of RUB 686 billion in 2015, 831 billion in 2016 and 848 bil-lion in 2017 (On the Development . . . 2018). Table 5.2 shows findings of the All-Russia NPO poll, giving a sense of the respective relevance of various revenue sources. The largest average revenue amounts came from the following sources: paid services provision and the sale of goods; subsidies/grants from the federal authorities; and cash contributed by international NPOs. The smallest average amounts came from local governments' and regional authorities' subsidies/grants; and contributions by businesses.

Despite a fairly large and growing amount of revenues in the SONPO sector, a vast major-ity of CEOs believe that the available sources of funds (62 percent) and funding amounts (63 percent) are inadequate to continue operations. These data were confirmed by the same poll

Table 5.2 Frequencies of various revenue sources of NPOs and SONPOs

Sources of funds	All NPOs	SONPOs
Membership fees	33	30
Contributions by founders or owners	21	21
Proceeds from sales of services (goods)	27	21
Personal funds of members, employees, founders (other than fees)	21	23
Subsidies, grants by federal authorities (including "presidential" grants and subsidies issued by the Ministry of Economic Development)	14	17
Subsidies, grants by regional authorities (from budgets of constituent territories)	19	25
Subsidies, grants by local governments (from local municipal budgets)	21	26
Funding from public extrabudgetary funds (pension fund, medical insurance fund, social insurance fund)	3	4
Private donations in cash	39	45
Cash contributed by domestic businesses	27	28
Cash contributed by international businesses	2	2
Cash/grants contributed by other Russian NPOs including foundations	8	10
Contributions by local community funds	6	6
Cash/grants contributed by other international NPOs including foundations	3	4
None	5	4
Other	3	4
No answer	4	3

Source: All-Russia NPO survey.

Note
Distribution of answers to the question: "What were the sources of funds of NPO over the last year?" for the NPO sample as a whole as well as among those who believe their NPO to be socially focused.

of CEOs asked to evaluate their economic situation. Only 26 percent of those polled did not experience problems due to a lack of funds. Four percent of NPOs currently have adequate funds for all their needs including the creation of financial reserves. Twenty-two percent generally have funds to implement all their plans. Approximately one-fourth (27 percent) have funds for an adequate performance but many new ideas remain unimplemented due to a shortage of resources. Sixteen percent of CEOs admitted that their NPO had enough funds to retain workers of relevant skill but not enough to upgrade a full-fledged technical inventory and cover other necessary costs. Three percent of NPOs had to hire lower skills workers due to a shortage of funds. Every fifth entity had financial problems due to a shortage of funds. Nine percent of CEOs said that to avoid closure, they spent too much effort on the search for funds to the detriment of the main mission. To 11 percent of NPOs operating largely due to good will of their personnel, a lack of funds means an eventual closure.

Volunteering

The past few years have witnessed a noticeable growth of volunteering. According to an All-Russia population poll conducted in 2018,[2] 35 percent of adults participated in unremunerated public activities over the past year (other than helping their family members or close relatives).

However, despite President Putin's declaration of 2018 as the Year of Volunteering, the term volunteering is yet to be fully embraced by the population at large. While significant numbers of respondents indicated participation in various volunteer activities, only 11–16 percent of them self-identified as "volunteers." In part, this may be due to the fact that "community work" became somewhat discredited during the Soviet period.

According to findings of the All-Russia NPO poll, 66 percent of NPOs used volunteer labor. The use of volunteers is particularly prevalent among NPOs providing social services; those with a longer than 10-year record of social services; those focused on people in hardship; those with an experience of raising charitable contributions and recruiting volunteers; those which provided services to 100 or more individuals. Most NPOs involve relatively small numbers of volunteers, with only one-fifth reporting more than 20 volunteers.

Public policies regarding NPOs

Perception of public policies regarding NPOs

Developing public support streams for NPOs is one form of institutionalizing the relationships between the government and civil society in this country (Mersianova & Jakobson 2011). Currently, a whole range of financial and non-financial support for NPOs has been developed. This includes subsidies to NPOs on a targeted and tender basis, tax benefits and access to government assets as well as informational, advisory and educational support.

The forms of cooperation between authorities and NPOs emerged initially on the municipal level, then were taken up at the regional level, and only the early 2000s witnessed a change of attitude in favor of supporting NPOs at the federal level (Sungurov & Nezdyurov 2008; Mersianova 2004). Since then, the amounts of public support have been constantly increasing (Gromova & Mersianova 2016). According to the All-Russia NPO poll, 50 percent of nonprofit CEOs believe that the government stance on NPOs is appropriate, whereas a little over a quarter believe that the government's position is wrong-headed. While most of Russian NPOs are supportive of the policies towards the sector, one-third of nonprofit leaders, particularly of smaller and under-resourced NPOs, still perceive a considerable gap between declared and actual public policies in respect of civil initiatives, community-based and nonprofit entities. For another 30 percent, existing policies lack consistency.

Financial support for SONPOs

According to the Russian Ministry of Economic Development, the amount of federal budget financial support for SONPOs grew from RUB 5.2 billion in 2012 to RUB 12.9 billion in 2017 (Report on Performance . . . 2018: 1). The Presidential Grant Foundation established in early 2017 became a sole operator of federal grant support to nonprofit entities, which has been in existence since 2006. In the grant competitions of 2017–2018, 6,786 projects received support totaling RUB 14.5 billion (On the Development . . . 2018: 35). A number of federal ministries provide additional subsidies.

SONPOs are furthermore supported by regional and local governments from the executive authorities of the constituent territories and local governments. Following the federal impetus, government support programs are implemented in 74 regions (cf. Toepler et al. 2019). In 2017, regional support reached RUB 27 billion, but it is highly concentrated. The Moscow budget alone accounted for RUB 5.4 billion and St. Petersburg and an additional seven regions for another RUB 12.5 billion.

In-kind support

Governments are authorized to provide in-kind support in form of privileged leases of non-residential spaces to grant SONPOs free or low-cost offices or space to provide programs. According to Rosstat, while almost 8,000 SONPOs in Russia own their property, nearly 32,000 enjoy a free lease of space owned by public, municipal or private organizations, with 26,000 more using non-residential space on a rental basis. Experts believe that a vast majority of SONPOs neither own nor have in use any property. Some entities are constantly seeking space to hold specific events while others operate out of public and municipal agencies.

Tax benefits

The modern NPO taxation system has been taking shape in Russia over the last 20 years in a spontaneous process affected by political and economic considerations. For this reason, the taxation problems currently faced by Russian NPOs have not been, until recently, a product of deliberate policies (Grishchenko 2013). NPOs taxes include 1) corporate profit tax; 2) value-added tax; 3) insurance contributions; 4) unified tax (simplified taxation system); 5) corporate property tax; 6) transport tax; and 7) land tax. However, tax benefits provision depends on what NPOs actually do. Therefore, the determination of an organization's taxation regime depends on a variety of factors (Grischenko 2016: 63–64), including the type of organization, its field of operation, sources and types of funding, whether it has membership and others.

NPO management: trends and problems

Public trust in NPOs

The All-Russia representative population poll showed that two-thirds of all those polled (66 percent) expressed trust in specific types of NPOs. Gardening and datcha owner associations, veteran associations, and charitable initiatives tend to be more credible. Nationalist and patriotic movements, youth patriotic associations, ethnic communities and diasporas inspire the least degree of trust. Political parties inspire the highest mistrust among the respondents (29 percent). Various religious organizations and movements, associations of property owners also have a relatively low level of credibility (12 percent). Officially registered NPOs inspired trust considerably more often than informal associations and civil society initiatives

It is worth noting though that despite the growing trust of Russians in nonprofits (Study: . . . 2017), NPOs are yet short of fully implementing their potential as a channel to mobilize charitable giving, including cash donations, which is the most widespread form (Mersianova & Korneeva 2017). People prefer to provide aid to those in need directly rather than channeling it through NPOs.

The problem of trust has acquired a new dimension lately as charitable organizations in Russia faced large-scale fraudulent practices of collecting donations on behalf of non-existing charitable foundations. Since charitable brand names (unlike commercial ones) are not protected by Russian law, there were frequent cases of illegal collection (mis)using the names of the well-known charities. Thus, up to 19 sham entities are reported to work on the Internet under the name "Gift of Life," which is a credible charitable foundation (Mursalieva 2017). The practices of collecting cash under the pretext of charitable aid in the streets, through the Internet and social media are also on the rise. The nonprofit sector responded to a lack of regulation of charitable donation procedures by self-organization of charities staging a campaign "Together Against Fraudsters." Ultimately over 290 charitable foundations signed the Declaration of Fairness stating that uncontrolled collection of cash undermined trust in charitable activities as a whole. Thus the Russian nonprofit sector, with its self-organization initiatives, is developing a clear understanding of the major role of trust as a guarantee of public support for NPOs.

Information transparency practices

Transparency is often identified as one of the conditions of building trust in NPOs. In the Russian sociopolitical context, the term "transparency" does not have the same connotations as in the US and Western Europe. For this reason, NPO researchers and practitioners in Russia tend to mix the notions of transparency and openness and use them interchangeably in describing the disclosure practices at NPOs. For example, the Transparency International – R report (2013) equates information transparency and openness understood as the organization's desire to publish the information about it on the Internet to advise the public of its activities, retain volunteers and donors, as well as establish communication with stakeholders (A Study of Information Transparency: . . . 2013: 5).

Several Russian studies, however, attempt to draw a distinction between openness and transparency but without a consistent basis. Overall, there is a trend to distinguish two aspects: Corporate efforts to publish information on the performance and opportunities available to the public to have the required information. However, there is no consistency in identifying these aspects. Thus, according to Nezhina et al. (2016: 17),

> a review of literature on NPO openness and transparency can be divided into two key theoretic areas. The first identifies the purpose of transparency as provision of information on how efficiently NPOs operate while the second regards openness and transparency instrumentally as an opportunity for donors, volunteers and service users to quickly find and assess the information on the entity and its activities.

According to some experts, openness means the availability of NPO reports while transparency means that they are accessible. Other experts believe that quality public reports fall within the notion of "transparency" to which they also add other corporate practices: availability of a corporate website, independent public assessment of corporate performance, voluntary financial and/or legal audit and internal assessment of performance, etc. The above practices describe external transparency of a nonprofit entity, to be accompanied by internal or managerial transparency, which is ensured by the existence of business procedures of the management and the guardianship board, accounting for staff opinions in the decision-making process, involving target groups into NPO work, etc. (Muravieva 2010).

To address this issue, an expert group launched the "Standards of NPO Information Openness" calling for NPOs to disclose information on their operations and the sources and amounts of their revenues/expenditures. The disclosure of information includes three levels of openness – basic (structure and contacts), extended (performance and funding report) and full which assumes the disclosure of all information of the basic and extended levels as well as the description of managerial processes (NGO Disclosure Standards . . . 2018).

Empirical studies of the NPO disclosure practices in Russia are few. However, according to the All-Russia NPO poll, 88 percent of NPOs use various elements of information transparency (e.g., websites, social media, participation in public events, ensuring availability of various reports), which represents a 12-percentage point increase from 2014. Although debates around this issue continue, Russian NPOs are already becoming more transparent.

Official reporting

The progress of NPO reporting in Russia has to a large extent been determined by the evolving context of relationships between the nonprofit sector and the government throughout the last decade, ranging from conflict to close cooperation (Jakobson & Sanovich 2010). On the conflicting side, researchers noted that the amendments to the nonprofit sector legislation in 2006 and the introduction of Federal Law No. 18 dated January 10, 2006, "On Amending Specific Regulations of the Russian Federation," which complicated the process of registration and reporting for NPOs, led to high transaction costs (especially for smaller NPOs), reduction or transformation of their operations (for example, registration as commercial businesses) or the closure of some bona fide organizations due to high operating costs (Economic Implications . . . 2007). Formally designed to improve NPO transparency, the Federal Law of 2006 was a serious burden on the reporting and audit requirements for NPOs, tightening the government control in the sector (Benevolenski & Toepler 2017).

On the cooperative side, it is worth mentioning reform of the NPO legislation, in particular the removal of cumbersome administrative barriers in critical areas of cooperation between the nonprofit sector and the government such as NPO registration, inspections and reporting. Thus, Federal Law No. 170-FZ "On Amending the Federal Law On Nonprofit Organizations" dated July 17, 2009, envisioned a simplified reporting procedure for organizations with annual revenues under RUB 3 million without foreign funds or any form of foreign participation in their budget. The simplified reporting meant that such entities had to provide information to confirm their status as a going concern, their management structure and their address once a year. This affects more than 80 percent of Russian nonprofits.

As noted by Jakobson et al. (2012), the resulting development vector suggests a movement towards harmonizing different aspects of accounting. This is largely helped by the increasingly active, albeit uneven, dissemination of information on Western technologies for accountability of the nonprofit sector among Russian NPOs. This indicates that the introduction of reporting practices in the nonprofit sector in Russia is driven to a certain extent by a desire to comply with the generally accepted Western standards (Jakobson et al. 2012: 18).

NPO management in the FSU

Similarly to Russia, NPOs started to emerge all over the former Soviet Union after the perestroika period, once the Soviet republics gained independence. However, the newly emerging civil society of the 1990s was to an extent shaped by its Soviet predecessors (Buxton 2017). Leaders of the new non-governmental entities were shaped as individuals at Komsomol, the Communist Party, trade unions and other social mass organizations. While the dissident movement was not as important in Central Asia as it was in Eastern Europe and Russia in the mid-1980s, it still seeded the emergence of new NPOs fostering a sense of the national identities and environmental activism, as well as the increasing role of women in society (Buxton 2017: 24–25). Environmental concerns for example became the breeding ground for the inception of NPOs in Armenia: The environmental movement emerging in Yerevan in 1989 resulted in the closure of harmful industrial facilities. These movements found their point of convergence in the national idea and a strife for independence and reunion with Artsakh (Nagorno-Karabakh Autonomous Region). These organizations as well as spontaneous initiatives aiding the victims of the earthquake which struck in Leninakan on December 7, 1988, eventually made up the mosaic of the civil society sector in Armenia by gradually laying down its legal and financial groundwork (Asoyan 2018: 405).

The NPO sector development in the FSU followed a path similar to that of the import substitution model in Russia, with international donors acting as the key agents for supply of the third sector resources and institutions. While international agencies issued grants to NPOs, they focused also on training NPO staff in operational, managerial and fundraising skills. At the time, the national law in the FSU countries generally encouraged and invited international funding through a favorable regulation and removal of administrative barriers to make foreign aid available to local organizations. Currently, despite legal restrictions of NPO access to foreign funding in a number of FSU countries,[3] it continues to play a significant role. Western foundations operating in Armenia, for example, play an important role in civil society development and implementing humanitarian, economic and intercultural cooperation programs (Tatsis 2017).

In the 1990s, large nationwide organizations also received, apart from international funds, direct funding from their governments (Legal Framework . . . 2017: 4). In the early 2000s, the arrangements for tender-based public financing of NPOs were introduced in a number of countries, once they understood the importance of involving NPOs in addressing social issues. For example, Kazakhstan, Kyrgyzstan and Tajikistan adopted laws on government-commissioned social services. In Uzbekistan, a special body – the Public Foundation for the Support of NPOs and other civil society institutions – was established to distribute grants and commission social services. These NPO funding mechanisms are based on a competitive selection of social service providers from among NPOs. Government funding is becoming increasingly important for NPOs financial sustainability. However, both in the past and today, government funding is limited in all countries and cannot alone make NPOs financially sustainable. At the same time, traditional sources of revenues which are essential for NPOs elsewhere, such as business income and donations by local donors, are not yet significant for a majority of NPOs in the FSU countries.

In terms of NPO legal regulation, the FSU countries have much in common with Russia since their law was based on the Soviet law, at least in Central Asia. Thus, the term "managing body" defines NPO management bodies, with collective and sole bodies existing everywhere. There are differences though regarding the powers (or obligations) of management bodies. For example, in Tajikistan the management body of a civil society association is obliged to communicate its decisions to the Justice Ministry – not just a protocol but the actual decision-making procedure. Some details of NPO governance are linked to the area of their activities and the law applicable to the particular activity area/type – such as participation in government procurement, international cooperation and foreign funding, etc.

The progress of the modern NPO sector is country-dependent. For example, studies conducted in Belarus suggest that, according to rough estimates, the number of non-governmental organizations is around 3,000. This number seems extremely low for a country such as Belarus. Compared to other countries of the Eastern Partnership, Belarus has the lowest number of NPOs both in absolute terms and as per 100 thousand of the population (Yegorov et al. 2017: 5). Meanwhile, Turkmenistan has only 118 registered civil society associations for a population of more than 5 million. An opposite situation is observed in Armenia with its 4,000 NGOs and a population almost three times smaller than that of Belarus. Moreover, it takes just two people as the founders to register a civil society organization in Armenia. An NPO can be registered in any apartment or house. With no mandatory requirement to the statutory capital of a civil society oganization to be established, it is enough to pay a state duty. This liberal practice gives rise to abuse as NGOs may be registered in an empty apartment to have access to government grants and subsidies (Tatsis 2017: 114).

Conclusion

The third sector in Russia and elsewhere in the FSU has been in existence for only a little more than a quarter of a century. However, it has become a major component of the national economy and social infrastructure. This is promoted by targeted public policies implemented throughout the executive hierarchy – from the federal down to the regional level – including a wide range of financial (subsidies, tax benefits) and non-financial (physical, information, advisory, educational) policies to support the nonprofit sector. It is only natural that two-thirds of CEOs polled by the Center for Civil Society and the Nonprofit Sector Studies believe the government support to be an important factor of the development of civil society in Russia.

The Russian population has grown more involved in volunteering lately. So it is especially important to have an adequate statistical accounting of how many nonprofit entities are actually in operation and how many volunteers constitute the sector's key resource. Thus, the shortcomings of statistical accounting for these key parameters are a major problem to be addressed by the public authorities and the expert community.

Empirical data suggest that the third sector in Russia has developed somewhat unevenly with considerable variations at the regional level regarding the number and the level of professionalism, cooperation with the authorities and public recognition. However, it is also evident that the NPO sector in Russia is undergoing the processes of self-organization to gain the public's trust, promote transparency and accountability although these processes penetrate various segments of the NPO sector to a different extent due to its considerable heterogeneity. But these processes are among the most crucial areas of nonprofit sector development currently.

At the same time and with few exceptions, such as the work of the Center for Civil Society and Nonprofit Sector Studies at the NRU "Higher School of Economic," nonprofit research in Russia and the region still lags behind in describing emergent practices and trends which determine the sector's development vectors, as well as in analyzing the specifics of adaptation of international approaches to building trust in the third sector and improving its transparency, accountability and the effectiveness of these approaches in the post-Soviet context.

Acknowledgment

The research leading to these results has received funding from the Basic Research Program at the National Research University Higher School of Economics.

Notes

1   Throughout the chapter, we will reference findings of an All-Russia NPO poll conducted by the Center for Studies of Civil Society and the Nonprofit Sector under the National Research University (NRU) Higher School of Economics in 2017 in 33 constituent territories of Russia on a quota-based sample of 852 NPOs with representative quotas across NPO incorporation forms and years of registration. In accordance with the assigned quotas, heads of organizations in municipal districts, urban settlements and other municipal areas across the 33 territories were polled. The regions were selected on the basis of typology of constituent territories of Russia in three groups of parameters: the urban development index; the nonprofit sector development indicator (on quantitative terms); and the regional economic development expressed as per capita gross regional product (GRP) to countrywide average. Respondents were selected on the basis of registers of nonprofit entities and civil society associations in the given

constituent territories. The selection was mechanic. Not more than two-thirds of all respondents per region were polled at its administrative center (except Moscow and St. Petersburg).

2   The Center for Studies of Civil Society and the Nonprofit Sector at the NRU Higher School of Economics also conducted an All-Russia population poll, which will be occasionally referenced in the remainder of the chapter. From October 29 to November 14, 2018, a total of 2012 respondents were polled. The sample is representative of the adult population of Russia (older than 18) by sex, age, education attainment and type of settlement where the respondents have their residence. The poll involved the inhabitants of all federal districts of Russia, 80 regions, urban and rural population. Polling method: CATI-based telephone interviewing.

3   For example, it is quite difficult for NPOs in Uzbekistan and Turkmenistan to have access to foreign grants. Kazakhstan and Tajikistan introduced a requirement to advise the authorities on provision of foreign aid and to report on how it is used. Belarus has a criminal liability for violation of the procedure for access to and use of foreign aid effective since 2011.

References

A Study of Information Transparency of the NGO State Support System/Report prepared by the Center for Anticorruption Research and Initiatives Transparency International-Russia (2013) (in Russian)

Abrosimova E.A. (2016). Nonprofit organizations in economics: Legal regulation issues. *Russian Law Journal*. No. 1 (229), pp. 9–13 (in Russian).

Asoyan L. (2018). Social sector in Armenia: Stages of development and modern state. In: *XXI Urals Sociological Readings. The Social Dimension and Time of the Region: Sustainable Development Issues:* Papers of the International Academic and Practical Conference. Yekaterinburg, March 15–16. Edited by Yu. R. Vishnevskiy. Yekayerinburg: Humanitarian University, pp. 404–407 (in Russian).

Benevolenski V.B., & Toepler S. (2017). Modernising social service delivery in Russia: Evolving government support for non-profit organizations. *Development in Practice*. 27(1), pp. 64–76. DOI: 10.1080/09614524.2017.1259392

Buxton Ch. (2017). *Civil Society in Central Asia: Overcoming post-Soviet crises*. V.R.S. Company (in Russian).

Economic implications of the new nonprofit legislation. (2007). In: A.V. Zolotov & A.A. Auzan (eds.), *The National Project Institute "Public Agreement"*. Moscow: ZAO "Book and Business".

Grishchenko A.V. (2013). Theoretical aspects of NGO taxation. *Nonprofit Organizations in Russia*. No. 2, pp. 13–19 (in Russian).

Grishchenko A.V. (2016) Trends in the development of taxation policy with regard to the nonprofit sector. *Nonprofit Organizations in Russia*. No. 1 (90), pp. 59–67 (in Russian).

Gromova M.N., & Mersianova I.V. (2016). Government support of NGOs and evaluating its effectiveness. *Civil Society in Russia and Abroad*. No. 1, pp. 39–44 (in Russian).

Jakobson L.I., & Sanovich S.V. (2010). The changing models of the Russian third sector: Import substitution phase. *Journal of Civil Society*. 6(3), pp. 279–300.

Jakobson L.I., Mersianova I.V., & Efremov S. (2012). Challenges and new trends for nonprofit accountability in Russia. NRU Higher School of Economics. Public Administration Series. No. 03.

Legal Framework for NGO Financial Sustainability in the Countries of Central Asia. (2017). International Center for Nonprofit Law.Mersianova I.V. (2004). *Citizen Voluntary Associations in Territorial Self-governance: Institutionalization Issues*. Moscow: Academia (in Russian).Mersianova I.V., & Jakobson L.I. (2011). Collaboration between the state and civil society institutions in alleviating social problems. *Public Administration Issues*. No. 2, pp. 5–24 (in Russian).

Mersianova I.V., & Korneeva I.E. (2017). The impact of trust on Russians' participation in charities. *Monitoring of Public Opinion: Economic and Social Changes*. No. 2, pp. 145–159 (in Russian).

Ministry of Justice. (2018). *Main Operational Outcomes of the Ministry of Justice of the Russian Federation in 2017*. Report. Available at: https://minjust.ru/osnovnye-itogi-deyatelnosti-ministerstva-yusticii

Muravieva V. (2010). Transparency and accountability of Russian NGOs as a resource for improving their effectiveness. In: *Increasing Trust in Nongovernmental Organizations: Russia's Context*. St. Petersburg: Agency for Social Information, Center for NGO Development, pp. 12–13 (in Russian).

Mursalieva G. (2017). Fraudsters steal half of charitable donations. Available at: https://www.novayagazeta.ru/articles/2017/05/17/72478-moshenniki-otbirayut-polovinu (in Russian).

Nezhina T.G., Gombozhapova B.S., & Pavlovskaya S.V. (2016). Methods of evaluating the transparency and openness of socially oriented NGOs in Russia. *Moscow University Bulletin*. Series 21. Governance (the state and society). No. 4, pp. 13–42 (in Russian).

NGO Disclosure Standards. Methodological Recommendations. (2018). Available at: https://www.infocul ture.ru/wp-content/uploads/2018/03/Standart-informacionnoi-otkrytosti-NKO.-Metodicheskie-re komendacii-po-primeneniju.pdf (in Russian).

On the Development of Volunteerism and Socially Oriented Non-commercial Organizations. (2018). Report of the State Council of the Russian Federation (in Russian).

Report on Performance and Development of Socially Oriented NGOs in 2017. Ministry of Economic Development. (2018) Available at: http://nko.economy.gov.ru/PortalNews/Read/4439 (Accessed 18 April 2019) (in Russian).

Sevortian A.R. (2000). NGO territory: The borders are open. *Information and Analytical Bulletin of the Agency for Social Information.* No. 16 (46). (in Russian).

Sungurov A. Yu., & Nezdyurov A.L. (2008). Interaction of authorities and civil society institutions: Potential models and their implementation in the social and political life of contemporary Russia. In: *Factors of Civil Society Development and the Mechanisms of its Interaction with the State.* Edited by L.I. Jakobson. Moscow: Vershina, pp. 209–236 (in Russian).

Study: Russians' level of trust in the performance of NGOs and civic associations has grown to 66%. (2017). Agency for Social Information. 7 April. Available at: https://www.asi.org.ru/news/2017/04/07/issle dovanie-doverie-k-nko (in Russian).

Tatsis K.I. (2017). Western humanitarian funds in Armenia as "soft power" instruments. *National Strategy Problems.* No. 5 (44), pp. 112–130 (in Russian).

Toepler S., Pape U., & Benevolenski V. (2019). Subnational variations in government-nonprofit relations: A comparative analysis of regional differences within Russia. *Journal of Comparative Policy Analysis: Research and Practice,* 1–19. DOI: 10.1080/13876988.2019.1584446

Yegorov A., Shutov A., & Katsuk N. (eds.). (2017). *Civil Society in Belarus: The Actual State and Conditions of Development.* Analytical Overview. Minsk: Centre for European Transformation (in Russian).

Zhukova I., Kononov V., Kotov Yu. et al. (1988). Citizens' independent initiatives. An Informal View. *The Communist.* No. 9, pp. 95–106 (in Russian).

6

NONPROFIT MANAGEMENT IN ASIA

Tamaki Onishi

ASSOCIATE PROFESSOR, DEPARTMENT OF POLITICAL SCIENCE, UNIVERSITY OF NORTH
CAROLINA AT GREENSBORO, GREENSBORO, NC, USA

Naoto Yamauchi

PROFESSOR, OSAKA SCHOOL OF INTERNATIONAL PUBLIC POLICY,
OSAKA UNIVERSITY, OSAKA, JAPAN

Introduction

Asia is not only the most populous continent, with over 50 percent of the world's population, it also is becoming an influential economic power as the "world's growth center," producing more than half the world's GDP. Like other societal institutions, the state of nonprofit management in Asia is affected by these changes, specifically by the following factors. The first factor is rapid economic growth in the Asian region. As income per capita increases, it enhances the financial capacity of both individuals and businesses; we expect a significant growth in philanthropy, too. The second factor is the growing presence of high net-worth individuals (HNWIs). Today, HNWIs are prominent in China and Singapore, but the HNWI class is sprouting in Malaysia, Thailand, and Indonesia, also. The third factor is wealth inequality. The recent economic growth in Asia has contributed to widening income and asset disparities and aggravating poverty. Beyond these economic trends, Asian countries have distinct religious and cultural traditions, which are deeply tied to the way of managing nonprofits and philanthropy.

Given these, we first examine the socio-cultural, political, and economic backgrounds of Asia. We then offer an overview of the nonprofit sector, philanthropy, and social enterprises of each nation, and discuss issues surrounding nonprofit management in Asia, including accountability, internal governance, and board management. The chapter concludes with a discussion about challenges, prospects, and future research.

Socio-cultural, political, and economic backgrounds

Religious traditions

Religions have underpinned a strong tradition of philanthropy, and with it, the nonprofit sector. As the world's largest, most populous continent, Asia encompasses a considerable diversity of cultural and religious traditions, with each country containing distinct religious and cultural characteristics. Table 6.1 summarizes the results of a recent Pew Research Center study

73

Table 6.1 Religious affiliation of selected Asian countries (%) (2010)

Country	Buddhists★	Christians★	Folk religions	Hindus	Jews	Muslims	Other religions	Unaffiliated
China	18.2	5.1	21.9	<1	<1	1.8	<1	**52.2**
Indonesia	<1	9.9	<1	1.7	<1	**87.2**	<1	<1
Japan	**36.2**	1.6	<1	<1	<1	<1	4.7	**57.0**
Korea	22.9	29.4	<1	<1	<1	<1	<1	**46.4**
Malaysia	17.7	9.4	2.3	6.0	<1	**63.7**	<1	<1
Philippines	<1	**92.6**	1.5	<1	<1	5.5	<1	<1
Singapore	**33.9**	18.2	2.3	5.2	<1	14.3	9.7	16.4
Taiwan	21.3	5.5	**44.2**	<1	<1	<1	16.2	12.7
Thailand	**93.2**	<1	<1	<1	<1	5.5	<1	<1
Vietnam	16.4	8.2	**45.3**	<1	<1	<1	<1	29.6

Source: The authors compiled the table based on the Pew–Templeton: Global Religious Futures Project data (Pew Research Center).

Notes

The largest group in each country is highlighted in bold. ★The Pew–Templeton Global Religious Futures Project does not show breakdown of different Christian denominations and other Eastern religions. East Asian Buddhism is characterized by a number of different schools, and Buddhists often simultaneously practice other religions, such as Confucianism, Shintoism, or Taoism, which are often merged into folk religions. The data also do not contain information on religious upbringing, but just on current religious affiliation.

regarding religious affiliations in the countries examined in this chapter. The prevailing religions in East Asia are eastern religions and thoughts, such as Buddhism, Confucianism, and Taoism. Islam and Christianity have also influenced Asian nations; while they are not the religion of the majority, they are often minority religions in the countries (Domingo, 2010).

Buddhism is particularly influential in Thailand (93.2 percent). Other Buddhism-influenced countries include Japan (36.2 percent), Singapore (33.9 percent), South Korea (22.9 percent), Taiwan (21.3 percent), and China (18.2 percent), although other belief systems, such as Confucian thought, also have deeply shaped their traditional values. Yet, a religious profile of certain countries has been transforming. Singapore, Malaysia, China, and Taiwan are religiously more heterogeneous than might be expected. Table 6.1 indicates that the group identified as "unaffiliated" is the largest in China (52.2 percent), Japan (57.0 percent) and South Korea (46.4 percent). Despite about 50 percent of its population being religiously unaffiliated, South Korea has a significant presence of Protestant and Catholic communities, which surpass the Buddhist community (Pew Research Center, no date). Protestant and Catholic churches and individuals are the most active in supporting both religious and secular causes in South Korea (Kang, Auh, and Hur, 2015). The private nonprofit activities of Japan's ancient period were Buddhism-oriented (Yamaoka, 1998). Even today, the 2013 statistics of the Ministry of Education, Culture, Sports, Science, and Technology found that the dominant religions in Japan are Shinto, and Buddhism (78.7 percent and 66.1 percent of the total population, respectively) (Okuyama and Yamauchi, 2015). Yet, Japan has the largest group of the unaffiliated. Giving to temples and shrines are not necessarily a monetary expression of gratitude, but rather ritualized or almost obligatory (Okuyama and Yamauchi, 2015). Furthermore, folk beliefs, which are a combination of Buddhism, Taoism, and Confucianism, are the most popular informal religion in Taiwan: the 2009 Taiwan Social Change Survey revealed that 42.8 percent of those self-identified as religious have folk beliefs, followed by Buddhism (19.7 percent), Taoism (13.5 percent), Protestant (4 percent), and Roman Catholic (1.5 percent) (Lo and Wu, 2015).

Islam is the leading religion in Indonesia (87.2 percent) and Malaysia (63.7 percent). Islamic philanthropy in Asia takes the form of *zakat* (almsgiving, obligatory monetary payments), *sadaqa* (voluntary charitable acts which may be monetary or in-kind), and *waqaf* (religious endowment), as in other Islamic communities (Fauzia, 2013). Islamic philanthropy in Indonesia has been highly institutionalized through government policies (Domingo, 2010). Major examples include Badan Amil Zakat, Infak dan Sedekah (BAZIS), quasi-state agencies that President Suharto helped establish for the nationwide *zakat* collection in 1968 (Alfitri, 2005). Presidential decision further created the National Zakat Collector Body (BAZNAS) in 2001 as the highest body in the organizational structure of the semi-government *zakat* collectors in Indonesia (Alfitri, 2005). The highly institutionalized *zakat* collection system in Indonesia has contributed to rising religious donations and the emergence of nonprofit organizations (NPOs) engaged in the professional management of *zakat* to benefit public welfare (Mahmood and Santos, 2011). The state's prominent role in supporting Islamic philanthropy under regulation, however, has also become controversial (Wiepking and Handy, 2015). Conversely, *zakat* in Malaysia is collected through a private professional organization supervised by the Islamic Council, while a government agency distributes the funds to beneficiaries (Domingo, 2010).

The Philippines became the most Christian nation in Asia through its history as a colony first of Spain and then the United States (Lyons and Hasan, 2002), and the Catholic religion has permeated Filipino culture. Catholics in the Philippines give voluntary cash contributions during church services. They also make donations in cash or in-kind whenever there is a solicitation for typhoon victims, the poor, the repair of the church, or other special projects (Domingo, 2010). The Roman Catholic Church has also contributed significantly to the development of Philippine's nonprofit sector, introducing and developing the organizational form (Cariño and PNSP Project Staff, 2001).

Political factors

In many Asian countries, the government traditionally has been a powerful actor providing social welfare to the public. The government's dominant role and policies historically have suppressed the growth of philanthropy and the nonprofit sector. For instance, the 1949 founding of the People's Republic of China halted philanthropy in the new socialist country, because the state was supposed to provide all social welfare for its citizens. This drastic shift also dissolved extant philanthropic organizations or assimilated them into the government because these organizations had been founded by missionaries, business owners, and social elites, who were unaffiliated with the new Socialist party. Consequently, non-state philanthropy did not revive in China until the 1990s, when the government started to allow NPOs to be more involved in disaster relief and other social services (Xinsong et al., 2015). Taiwan's martial law, imposed by the Kuomintang from 1949–1987, severely restricted civil rights, freedom of association, and free speech, thereby hindering the growth of NPOs (Wang, 2007). In Japan, due to state dominance established during the Meiji Restoration of 1868 (Yamamoto, 1998), coupled with the absence of a strong religious tradition, the nonprofit sector has been proportionately smaller (Salamon and Anheier, 1997).

More recent government policies and laws have promoted the growth of NPOs and philanthropy in Asia. One such example is the "New Order" (1967–1998) of Indonesia's Suharto government, which emphasized the importance of collaboration with NPOs in the areas of education, health, and environment for the purpose of program-cost sharing (Antlöv, Ibrahim, and van Tuijl, 2006). In Taiwan, the 1987 abolishment of martial law contributed to the development of nonprofit activities (Lo and Wu, 2015).

The growth of the nonprofit sector was triggered by not only public perception of government inefficiency but also by a growing middle class during socioeconomic crises and regime change. In the 1980s, when Taiwan's first political opposition party was established, the democratic political environment raised awareness that the government was incapable of solving growing social problems (Lo and Wu, 2015). In Japan, the 1995 Kobe earthquake alerted the Japanese people to the greater effectiveness of nonprofit and voluntary groups, compared to government agencies, and provided the impetus for the growth of voluntarism and the nonprofit sector (Yamamoto, 1998; Yamauchi et al., 1999). South Korea's 1997–1998 economic crisis accelerated the public's challenge to the government monopoly of social services (Kim and Hwang, 2002). In the recent histories of the Philippines and Thailand, a widely ramified network of NPOs helped the middle classes overthrow unpopular regimes (Lyons and Hasan, 2002). When the People Power Revolution in 1986 ended 20 years of dictatorship under Ferdinand Marcos in the Philippines, its progressive legal and political environment, combined with a massive influx of foreign grants in the aftermath of the revolution, prompted the rapid growth of the Philippine's nonprofit sector (Cariño and PNSP Project Staff, 2001). The grassroots groups' call for constitutional recognition of civil society's contribution led to the 1987 Constitution of the Philippines that explicitly acknowledged civil society's vital role and affirmed its right to participate in decision-making (Anand, 2014).

Economic factors

National economies, often associated with state policies, have exerted multifaceted influences on Asian philanthropy and NPOs. Recent economic shocks, such as the 1997 Asian Financial Crisis, the 2005 Asian Tsunami, and the 2008 Global Financial Crisis, provided NPOs with both challenges and opportunities in such areas as employment, poverty alleviation, health, and education (The Asia Foundation, 1998; Wiepking and Handy, 2015). A shift from planned to market economies in China and Vietnam has enabled grassroots activities and transformed party-controlled mass movements into an independent nonprofit sector (Antlöv et al., 2006). In Thailand, dramatic economic growth from 1977 to 1997 created a supportive environment for nonprofit activities, prompting rapid growth in the nonprofit sector during the 1980s–1990s (Asian Development Bank, 2011). Vietnam implemented a policy of reform ("Doi Moi") in 1986 and joined the World Trade Organization in 2008. Accordingly, steady economic development and exposure to international business practices have helped advance corporate giving and increased the number of domestic and international NPOs (Nguyen and Doan, 2015). In Singapore, total charitable giving nearly doubled between 2001 (US\$ 308 million) and 2009 (US\$ 556 million), due to the strong economy (Mahmood and Santos, 2011). Chinese philanthropy has witnessed a dramatic advancement recently; the number of private foundations rapidly increased from 436 in 2007 to 846 in 2009 (Mahmood and Santos, 2011).

Nonprofit sectors and social enterprises

Emerging nonprofit sectors

Although nonprofit sectors in Asian countries are not as mature as those in the UK and the US, scale and systems in Asia's nonprofit sectors have expanded more rapidly than have those in the UK and the US. Available data explicate this. The Hudson Institute released the Index

Table 6.2 Index of Philanthropic Freedom in Asian countries

Overall Rank	Rank in Asia	Country	Overall Score	CSO	Taxes	Cross Border	GDP per capita	Ln(GDP)
2	1	United States	4.7	4.7	5.0	4.5	52,392	10.9
9	2	Japan	4.4	4.7	4.5	4.0	38,528	10.6
19	3	Philippines	4.1	4.3	4.0	4.0	2,765	7.9
36	4	Thailand	3.5	3.2	3.8	3.5	6,270	8.7
35	5	Kyrgyz Republic	3.5	3.8	3.0	3.6	1,303	7.2
40	6	Malaysia	3.2	2.5	3.2	4.0	10,514	9.3
46	7	India	3.2	3.5	4.0	2.1	1,548	7.3
43	8	Kazakhstan	3.2	3.2	2.9	3.5	13,650	9.5
44	9	Pakistan	3.2	3.3	3.5	2.8	1,238	7.1
52	10	China	2.7	2.1	2.4	3.5	6,626	8.8
55	11	Vietnam	2.6	2.3	3.4	2.0	1,868	7.5
56	12	Indonesia	2.5	3.0	2.5	2.0	3,475	8.2
58	13	Myanmar	2.4	2.8	2.0	2.5	1,183	7.1
62	14	Nepal	1.9	2.1	1.9	1.7	654	6.5

Data: Hudson Institute (2015).

of Philanthropic Freedom (IPF) for 64 countries, including 13 Asian countries, in 2015. The IPF consists of three main indicators: (1) ease of registering and operating civil society organizations (CSOs); (2) tax policies for deductions, credits, and exemptions; and (3) ease of sending and receiving cash and in-kind goods across borders. Asian countries, with the exception of Japan and the Philippines, scored below average on all three indicators. As Table 6.2 shows, out of 64 surveyed countries, the US was ranked 2nd, Japan was ranked 9th, followed by the Philippines (19th), Thailand (36th), Malaysia (40th), China (52th), Vietnam (55th), and Indonesia (56th).

Figure 6.1 presents a considerably strong and positive correlation (coefficient of correlation higher than 0.5) between the IPF and per capita GDP (measured by the natural log). This indicates that the conditions surrounding NPOs and philanthropy are likely to improve as per capita income increases due to economic development in the Asian region. However, this varies from country to country. For instance, the Philippines' IPF was relatively high despite its low per capita GDP, while the IPF of Malaysia and China was relatively low (Figure 6.1).

A state's restrictions on NPO activities makes the registration process particularly difficult in most Asian countries. As the Hudson Institute (2015) has pointed out, while these registration fees are not high by North American or European standards, they can be a deterrent for applicants, given the higher poverty rate in the Asian region. As such, more generous tax incentives are likely to lead to future growth of the nonprofit sector in Asia. Legal and policy frameworks for cross-border philanthropy are similarly underdeveloped. Consequently, most Asian countries offer few, if any, incentives for international donors to give to NPOs.

Japan's legal and tax systems for NPOs have been modernized by the 1999 NPO law and 2008 PIC reform (Okada, Ishida, Nakajima and Kotagiri, 2017). There are over 300,000 NPOs, out of which approximately 180,000 are religious corporations, 40,000 are medical corporations, 20,000 or fewer are social welfare corporations, 10,000 or fewer are school corporations, and 10,000 or fewer are public interest corporations. The number of general incorporated

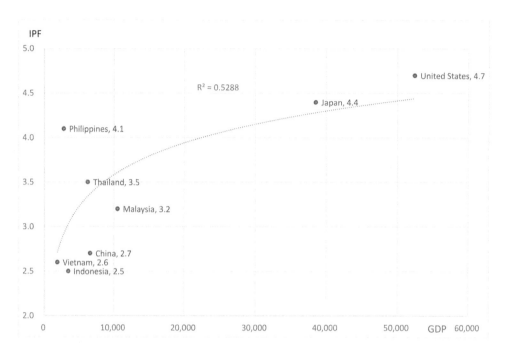

Figure 6.1 Relationship between IPF and per capita GDP

Data: IPF from Hudson Institute (2015) and per capita GDP from UN Statistical Office.

associations and foundations has increased significantly. The number of newly established general corporations after the PIC reform has already reached 40,000, whereas approximately 10,000 general corporations have been converted from public interest corporations built upon the old legal regime. The value generated by organizations broadly defined as NPOs (e.g., school corporations, social welfare corporations, and medical corporations) is estimated to be at least 4 percent of Japan's GDP.

South Korea's nonprofit sector consists of formally organized institutions supplementing government-provided services and informally organized social movement and highly political organizations intending to create social change through advocacy (Kang et al., 2015). The dramatic rise of these social movement organizations during the late 1980s and early 1990s was promoted by the rapid democratization beginning in the mid-1980s. The Korean non-profit sector has grown steadily by various measures, such as giving levels and the number of nonprofit corporations (excluding school corporations and medical corporations), especially since the IMF crisis when NPOs became new actors in South Korean society (Kim and Hwang, 2002).

In China, where the government is a dominant power and enjoys a high level of trust from the public, NPOs are still unfamiliar concepts. Public trust of NPOs remains low, and the Chinese government strictly regulates NPOs' activities. However, grassroots organizations have emerged since the 2008 Great Sichuan Earthquake.

Taiwan offers two types of Civil Code nonprofit corporations: incorporated associations and foundations. The government's statistical data show over 40,000 social organizations, approximately 30,000 of which were registered with local governments. Social organizations have contributed approximately 4 percent of Taiwan's GDP.

The Philippines has the most advanced nonprofit sector in Southeast Asia; nonprofits are viewed as partners leading national development efforts. As such, legal and tax systems are well developed, granting favorable treatment to nonprofits, since democratization in 1986. The Philippine Council for NGO Certification evaluates financial reports and accountability of NPOs and grants them the status of receiving tax-deductible giving.

In Thailand, the 1970's democratization movements, along with Cambodian refugee problems, poverty issues, and government inability to solve social problems, have contributed to the nonprofit sector's development. Buddhism has influenced Thailand's nonprofit sector and philanthropy. Both NPOs and people's organizations have played an instrumental role in Thailand's local communities.

The Indonesian nonprofit sector consists of foundations, NPOs, and grassroots organizations with no particular legal statuses. Most NPOs were founded in the 1980s and after; they are often small and suffer from a lack of funding.

Malaysia's nonprofit sector has been attracting attention in recent years due to its contribution to national development. NPOs must register within a specific category (e.g., culture, youth, women, charity, and mutual benefits). The Malaysian government competes with, and at the same time depends on, NPOs as a community-based vehicle expanding the provision of social services.

Singapore's nonprofit sector has been small, yet recently, it has been growing rapidly. There are over 2,000 registered NPOs, the majority of which are religious organizations. The nonprofit sector in Singapore consists of a small number of large NPOs and a large number of small NPOs; many rely on government grants.

In Vietnam, it is widely recognized that the nonprofit sector has been tackling certain social problems under the current political regime. Since the introduction of the Doi Moi policy, privately funded innovative programs have been underway, especially in the rural areas. Professional associations exist in the fields of sports, culture, business, and charity.

Giving and volunteering

Philanthropy, both monetary giving and volunteering, is vital for effective nonprofit management. While "chequebook charity" has been a common practice by the wealthy in many Asian countries, available data give evidence of recent dramatic growth in Asian philanthropy, thanks to growing economies.

The Johns Hopkins Comparative Nonprofit Sector Project (JHCNP) found, on average, the percentage of philanthropic support (the sum of donations and the monetary value of volunteering) within the total revenue of NPOs is 53.1 percent in Pakistan, 43.2 percent in the Philippines, 39.9 percent in India, 14.9 percent in South Korea, and 10.7 percent in Japan. Charities Aid Foundation's 2017 study revealed a rather high World Giving Index in some Asian countries in recent years. In terms of the percentage of people donating money compared to the total population, Myanmar ranked first, Indonesia second, and Thailand ranked fifth among 139 countries. In terms of the number of people donating money, seven among the top ten countries were from Asia – India ranked first, followed by Indonesia (second), China (fourth), Pakistan (fifth), Thailand (seventh), Japan (eighth), and Myanmar (tenth). In terms of volunteer time, Indonesia ranked first, Myanmar third, and Tajikistan ranked fifth. For number of volunteers, India ranked first, followed by Indonesia (third), China (fourth), the Philippines (seventh), Japan (eighth), and Myanmar (ninth).

Corporate giving is an essential part of philanthropy and foundations also have a long history in many Asian countries. Asian philanthropy is becoming more strategic, addressing social issues in a more systematic manner (Anand, 2014). Some foundations are implementing professional management styles learned from US foundations and employing professional staff.

Japanese corporate and individual giving totals well over one trillion yen annually, which accounts for only 0.2 percent of the national GDP (Japan Fundraising Association, 2017). There are around 3,000 grant-making foundations in Japan (Japan Foundation Center, no date), and the number of community foundations and civic funds has grown in recent years. Grant sizes are small, relative to the size of foundations' assets, due to a long-term low-interest rate in Japan.

In South Korea, the total amount of giving has increased sharply since 2000, and crowd-funding has increasingly become popular. Unlike American foundations that develop a close partnership with NPOs, Korean foundations' partnerships with NPOs have been limited. They instead tend to give directly to individuals in the form of scholarships.

China's growing economy and recent large-scale disasters and events (e.g., the Sichuan Earthquake and the Beijing Olympics) have significantly advanced volunteering. The China Foundation Center has evaluated information disclosures of each foundation and calculated a transparency index.

In Taiwan, both the volunteer rate and giving have increased since the 2001 Volunteer Act enactment. Established under the civil code, foundations in Taiwan are relatively new phenomena. Many foundations are small (as measured by endowments and staff) and are located in Taipei.

The Philippines' philanthropic sector has been the most sophisticated in East Asia. The number of high net-worth individuals has increased due to economic growth. Two-thirds of their giving support human services (e.g., services for the poor), education, and healthcare. Most foundation giving comes from a small number of large foundations, while small community foundations actively support their local communities.

Thailand has highly advanced tax systems for giving; giving to registered NPOs is 100 percent deductible (200 percent deductible for educational organizations). Foundations, both grant-making and operating foundations, are incorporated to pursue public purposes. Many foundations are related to the royal family. Some international NGOs created foundations in Thailand to support local communities.

Indonesians are estimated to give more than 1 percent of their annual income (*zakat*). Volunteering is religiously motivated and based on mutual assistance (e.g., Gotong Royong). Although most Indonesian foundations are still in their infancy, the scale and management styles of some foundations are comparable to those in developed countries.

In Malaysia, Muslims give 2.5 percent of their income to charitable purposes and receive income deductions for their gifts; HNWIs' giving has increased. Corporations actively engage in corporate social responsibility (CSR) activities in order to reduce their tax liability and cultivate relationships with both government and consumers. Numerous family foundations were founded by successful corporate owners.

In Singapore, the increased number of HNWIs has boosted giving. Both giving and volunteering are typically daily activities and often informal in Singapore. While the number of foundations has increased since the 1970s, the amount of giving to foundations is rather small, despite high per capita income. While many existing foundations are family foundations, corporate and institutional giving and community foundations are becoming increasingly important.

Multiple Vietnamese corporations provide grants. While monetary giving is the most popular, in-kind donations may be easily managed to directly reach the recipients. It is estimated that over 1,000 foundations were created under the law allowing the establishment of social funds and charitable funds. A charitable fund, in particular, is typically established to help disaster victims, as well as patients with terminal illnesses and other difficult conditions.

Social enterprises

Overall, the Asian social enterprise landscape is marked by a strong influence of historical, sociopolitical, and cultural realities (Kerlin, 2009; Defourny and Kim, 2011; Sengupta and Sahay, 2017). Impetuses for the emergence of social enterprises include societal needs, public policies, and the development phase of each country, which in turn affects the nature of social enterprises' work. For instance, the 1997 financial crisis, followed by a rapidly increasing unemployment rate in South Korea and Taiwan, advanced the need to reform their welfare and employment policies and encourage the privatization of welfare services (Kerlin, 2010; Defourny and Kim, 2011). Social enterprises in these nations were created mostly to address unemployment and alleviate poverty (Chan, Kuan, and Wang, 2011). Japan is facing a rapidly aging population and the need for an inclusive labor market if it is to retain its economic clout. Consequently, some Japanese social enterprises – work integration social enterprises (WISEs) often called "workers' cooperatives" in Japan – provide not only long-term care for the elderly and disabled but also childcare for working mothers. Many workers' collectives in Japan were established by married women who also had encountered obstacles when obtaining full-time jobs (Laratta, Nakagawa, and Sakurai, 2011). In resource-rich Indonesia and the Philippines, social enterprises may focus on environmental stewardship and management of a more inclusive value chain (Sengupta and Sahay, 2017). In China, the reformation from a communist system to a market-based economy triggered the emergence of social enterprises (Lan et al., 2014). Chinese social enterprises, usually located in rural areas, have implemented social welfare and economic transformation, as well as engaged in policy reformation in the post-reformation phase (Sengupta and Sahay, 2017).

Existing studies have found a variety of organizational forms among Asian social enterprises. Defourny and Kim (2011) observed: (1) traditional NPOs, (2) work-integration social enterprises (WISEs), (3) nonprofit cooperative enterprises, (4) hybrid nonprofit/for-profit partnerships, and (5) community development enterprises in China, Hong Kong, Taiwan, Japan, and South Korea. Santos and Macatangay (2009) suggested that social enterprises in the Philippines, Malaysia, Thailand, Singapore, Bangladesh, and Indonesia are grouped into four major categories: (1) cooperative enterprises, (2) civic foundations of corporations, (3) religious-based organizations, and (4) associations started by leading social entrepreneurs.

The major contemporary issues constraining social enterprises in Asia include the absence of a separate legal framework and policies dedicated to social enterprises. Asia has lagged behind Western Europe, the UK, and the US in developing such legal frameworks for social enterprises (Kerlin, 2010). Hence, many social entrepreneurs in Asia have structured their organizations by using one of the available legal statuses. Studies about countries like China (Yu, 2011) and Japan (Laratta et al., 2011) stress that using a conventional status may suppress their unique activities. Social enterprises registered as commercial businesses are forced to compete with well-financed mainstream businesses, whereas social enterprises structured as traditional NPOs may face restrictive government oversight and limited funding opportunities. The government support and institutional capabilities assisting social enterprises are still in the nascent stages in Indonesia and Vietnam (Santos and Macatangay, 2009)

However, recent years have witnessed a considerable advancement in the legal and regulatory regimes for Asia's social enterprises. For instance, South Korea enacted the Social Enterprise Promotion Act (SEPA) in 2006 to facilitate the launch of social enterprises and to create a more favorable atmosphere for their successes (Jeong, 2017). The Philippine government has adopted policies and reforms to provide indirect support (e.g., decentralization, empowerment of local government units, and strengthening of government financial institutions and direct support) (Santos and Macatangay, 2009). Albeit limited, this support includes technical training, education, and funding.

Both individual and institutional funders in Asia are increasingly aware of the need for greater financial support for social enterprises. Mahmood and Santos (2011) found that 36 percent of survey respondents ranked social entrepreneurship as the most important trend affecting philanthropy in Asia, indicating a growing interest among philanthropists. The concepts of venture philanthropy and impact investing have also drawn great enthusiasm in Asia for the last decade. Leading network associations include the Asian Venture Philanthropy Network (AVPN), which was established in Singapore in 2011 to promote venture philanthropy and impact investing across Asia (Asian Venture Philanthropy Network, no date). Governments in countries such as Singapore, Thailand, South Korea, Malaysia, Taiwan, and Indonesia also launched new funds and support programs for social enterprises (Shapiro, 2018). Examples include Singapore's Ministry of Social and Family Development, which currently administers three funds for social enterprises – the ComCare Enterprise Fund, the Youth Social Entrepreneurship Programme for Start-Ups, and the Central Co-operative Fund (Chhina et al., 2014). Besides local impact investing and venture philanthropy investors, international impact investors, such as LGTV and Bamboo, have identified some Asian countries, such as Indonesia, as countries with significant market potential (Chhina et al., 2014).

Organizational management

Accountability and governance

Asia's nonprofit sectors did not have systematic self-regulation mechanisms before the late 1990s because the focus of NPOs in most countries was to fend off strict governmental regulation (Sidel, 2010). A growing presence of the nonprofit sector in Asia, however, prompted the public and other stakeholders to demand a higher standard of accountability from NPOs. As such, accountability and governance are among the most explored topics in extant studies about nonprofit management in Asia (and other regions). External/public accountability (Kim, 2003; Zhang, Guo, and Cai, 2011) takes a variety of forms, such as direct governmental regulatory enforcement and legal requirements for the sector and self-regulation systems adopted voluntarily by the nonprofit sector itself (Kim, 2003; Sidel, 2003, 2010; Zhang et al., 2011).

Government enforcement

The 2003 study commissioned by the Asia Pacific Philanthropy Consortium (Kim, 2003) noted that the varying levels of governmental regulatory enforcement and scrutiny of the nonprofit sector in Asia led to two different models of nonprofit governance: independent governance and heavily regulated models. In Indonesia, the Philippines, and Taiwan (independent governance models), the government rarely intervenes in setting standards for nonprofit accountability, affording almost free rein to each NPO in terms of organizational governance roles and structures. In contrast, the nonprofit sectors in China, Japan, Korea, and Thailand (heavily regulated models) have traditionally faced a high level of governmental control and scrutiny (Kim, 2003; Zhang et al., 2011), as described next.

Examining the heavily regulated models, Kim (2003) found that governing boards of Chinese NPOs exist, but their roles are highly restricted by the government, which selects 60 percent of the members, and they are required by law to hold regular meetings. Another restriction on NPO governance is strict donor rules imposed by the Regulation on the Administration of Foundations enacted in 2004, which allows only governmental or government-sponsored foundations to raise funds from the public (Zhang et al., 2011). However, the Chinese government has recently begun initiating policies to facilitate NPOs' work. The most significant case is the abolition of the dual administration system: NPOs for technology, social welfare, and community services are no longer required to affiliate with a professional supervisory agency before they register with the Ministry of Civil Affairs (Yang, Wilkinson, and Zhang, 2014). While this policy cedes greater autonomy to China's NPOs, it has brought many challenges for funding and self-governance (Yang et al. 2014).

In Japan, the government enforces NPO governance. For instance, NPOs must have more than three boards of directors in accordance with the NPO Law to obtain legal NPO status, which then contributes to a high level of internal governance (Yamauchi, Okuyama, and Matsushima, 2011). Disclosure rules vary for different types of NPOs. For instance, general NPOs, without tax-exempt status, are not required to submit their financial statements and activity reports to the government but are still required to keep these documents available for those interested. In contrast, Public Interest Corporations and Specified Nonprofit Corporations are required to submit those documents to the government as well as to keep them available for interested parties to view (Yoshioka and Onishi, 2018).

In the 1990s in South Korea – the decade often labeled the "age of civil society" – a deepened democracy enhanced the public expectation of greater accountability for NPOs than for the government (Jeong and Kearns, 2015). A series of high-profile scandals in the 2000s have also intensified public concerns about accountability in the growing nonprofit sector. Consequently, recent legislative initiatives have pushed for greater transparency and oversight of Korea's NPOs, including the Ministry of Public Administration and Security's comprehensive measures to root out nonprofit grantees' inappropriate use of government grants (Ministry of Public Administration and Security 2014, cited in Jeong and Kearns, 2015).

In Thailand, the government has historically focused on controlling rather than promoting NPOs through cumbersome laws and regulations (The Asia Foundation, 1998). External accountability and reporting requirements include submission of annual reports and other documents. Among Thailand's registered NPOs, those registered as foundations are required to submit copies of their annual reports including financial statements prepared by an authorized auditor, along with copies of the agendas of committee meetings, to provincial offices of the Ministry of the Interior. In addition, associations or foundations designated as Public Charitable Institutions by the Ministry of Finance must submit their reports to the Revenue Department (Anand, 2014).

Self-regulation

Because the nonprofit sectors in many Asian countries have faced legitimacy problems due to a series of scandals, leading to diminished public trust (Zhou and Pan, 2016), the focus on self-regulation has increased since the late 1990s. A variety of nonprofit self-regulation measures were implemented to defend against intensifying state pressures and regulations, improve the perceptions of key stakeholders, and strengthen the quality of governance (Sidel, 2003). Main examples include accreditation, certification and validation, evaluation, ratings, rankings and grading, codes of conduct, self-regulatory registers or charity commissions, and disciplinary measures (Sidel, 2003). Table 6.3 presents examples of the countries this chapter examines, based on Sidel's classifications.

Table 6.3 Accountability and self-regulation mechanisms of the nonprofit sector in selected Asian countries

Category	Description	Examples
Accreditation/certification	Adopted either by the umbrella group, or the government for tax or other purposes	• Indonesia (The Satunama Foundation Certification of Indonesian NGOs) • Japan (Japan Fundraising Association certification) • Korea (Korea Society of Philanthropy CFRE certification) • Philippines (Philippine Council for Nonprofit Certification)
Evaluative measures	Ratings, rankings, or grading (may overlap with accreditation measures)	• Indonesia (YAPPIKA Civil Society Index) • Philippines (rating systems by Partnership for Philippine Service Agencies and the Association of Foundations)
Codes of conduct	Standards governing conduct, program or financial information disclosure	• China (Prof. Shang/Chinese NPO Network Nine Standards for NPO Self-Regulation) • Indonesia (NGO Code of Ethics by Agency for Research, Education, Economic and Social Development) • Japan (JANIC Code of Conduct for NGOs; JACO Non-Profit Organizations Database System "NOPODAS"; Japan NGO Center database) • Korea (Guidestar Korea accreditation criteria; Korea Society of Philanthropy Code of Governance) • Philippines (Code of Conduct for Development NGOs "Code-NGO"; The Philippine Association of Foundations Code of Ethics/NGO Mega Databank Project; the Children and Youth Foundation of the Philippines standards and self-assessment) • Singapore (National Council of Social Service Code of Governance and Management for voluntary welfare organizations) • Taiwan (United Way Taiwan) • Vietnam (Code of Practice on Transparency and Accountability for Civil Society Organizations in Vietnam)
Disciplinary measures	Measures used by the nonprofit sector with respect to nonprofits	• Found in the Philippines, and under discussion elsewhere (Sidel, 2003)

Sources: Concerning examples include Anand (2014); Antlöv, Ibrahim, and van Tuijl (2006); Breen, Dunn, and Sidel (2016); Cagney (2018); Kim (2003); Lee and Haque (2008); Mahmood and Santos (2011); Shigetomi (2002); Sidel (2003, 2010).

Note
Categories along with descriptions are based on Sidel's typology (2003).

The degree of experiments and initiatives in nonprofit self-regulation across Asian countries varies significantly. The Philippines is known for its success in pioneering self-regulation in Asia, especially the Philippine Council for NGO Certification (PCNC), a partnership program established in 1998 between national NGO networks, the Department of Finance and the Bureau of Internal Revenue (Mahmood and Santos, 2011; Sidel, 2010). The PCNC reviews NGO credentials for receiving official "donee" status and tax incentives. Other government bodies (e.g., Department of Health, Department of Social Welfare and Development, Department of Environment and Natural Resources and the Department of Agriculture) have also developed their own NGO accreditation procedures (Mahmood and Santos, 2011). Sidel (2003) reported that China, Indonesia, and Thailand were among other Asian countries in which extensive discussions had taken place regarding nonprofit self-regulation and emerging efforts to develop new programs. Thailand's nonprofit sector lacks systematic explicit self-regulation systems but has been exploring formal self-regulation and accreditation systems (Sidel, 2003). Furthermore, the Ministry of Social Development and Human Security was reportedly forming working groups to develop standardization of development work, including NPO standards. A recent publication by BoardSource discussed cultural factors, such as unanimity in decision-making and in-group solidarity, as being so significant in Indonesia that traditional decision-making still outweighs nonprofit self-regulation (Cagney, 2018).

Korea and Japan established two major self-regulation programs based on US and UK models, especially a database that discloses financial and programs information and a certificate for professional fundraisers. GuideStar Korea, a development partner of GuideStar International, was founded by the Kids and Future Foundation in 2008. Japan Association of Charitable Organizations (JACO), too, has also followed the GuideStar system to launch the Non-Profit Organizations Database System (NOPODAS). GuideStar International and JACO are exploring the possibility of creating an English version of the database (GuideStar International, no date). For certification, Korea Society of Philanthropy and Japan Fundraising Association (JFRA) became participating organizations that endorse the Certified Fund Raising Executive (CFRE) certification. JFRA issues its own certification, Certified Fundraiser program as a CFRE's participating organization (CFRE International, no date). The 2018 publication by BoardSource notes the public's demand for government to create a Korean charity commission (Cagney, 2018).

Internal governance and board management

Nonprofits' self-regulation also signifies the effort to develop their internal governance (Sidel, 2010). In some countries, a discourse on nonprofit governance has emerged from regime changes and the ensuing democratization process (e.g., Indonesia; in Antlöv et al., 2006; Kim, 2003). As such, effective management and governance have been discussed along with nonprofit accountability and self-regulation (Kim, 2003; Sidel, 2003, 2010). The burgeoning literature illustrates recent improvements in Asian NPOs' internal governance and management issues. Key topics include board structure, functions, efficiency, transparency and information disclosure, and representational capacity (Jeong and Kearns, 2015; Jiangang, Xiaojun, Univesrity, and Yifei, 2014; Zhang et al., 2011). The nonprofit sector has begun focusing on internal governance in many Asian countries. This trend is reflected in the focus of institutional funders on supporting capacity building (e.g., The Asia Foundation, Kemitraan, and Tifa Foundation in democratic Indonesia; Peace and Equity Foundation in the Philippines) and training programs(e.g., Centre for Philanthropy and Civil Society in Thailand) (Anand, 2014).

While the quality of nonprofit governance varies among countries and findings are often mixed (e.g., China; Zhang et al., 2011), general patterns emerge from recent studies. First, considering that boards are among the top stakeholders, many NPOs in Asia (e.g., South Korea in Jeong and Kearns, 2015) are keenly aware of the importance of internal governance, and often set up a board of directors to improve their internal governance. Yamauchi et al. (2011) found that 95.3 percent of the surveyed NPOs in Japan followed the NPO Law to obtain legal nonprofit status by establishing a board of directors or formal steering committee. A 2009 study by Japan's Cabinet Office (cited by Yamauchi et al., 2011) also identified the same pattern among organizations without legal status. Yamauchi et al. (2011) further found that NPOs in Japan think highly of their well-established and well-functioning internal governance. Jiangang et al. (2014) surveyed Chinese NPOs and found 69.20 percent of participants had established a board of directors, and 66.66 percent evaluated their board positively, while 12.90 percent evaluated it as "poor." Zhang et al. (2011) further found that in China, the board's roles and responsibilities are wide-ranging from program development and oversight to resource acquisition. In some countries (e.g., Korea), NPOs have utilized Internet-based technology to facilitate more effective and active communication for improving internal governance and collective decision-making systems (Kim, 2003).

Second, studies have also revealed that NPOs' governing boards are often ineffective in Asian countries. A study by JACO (cited in Kim, 2003) found that the governing boards of Japanese NPOs were more of a mere formality, without properly fulfilling their fiduciary duties. Jiangang et al. (2014) found that 4.09 percent, and 55.97 percent of Chinese NPOs surveyed never held a meeting, or held meetings on an irregular basis, respectively. Other recent studies about Chinese NPOs (Huang, Deng, Wang, and Edwards, 2013; Jiangang et al., 2014) suggest that the majority of grassroots NPOs, especially those established prior to 2000, lack proper internal governance. Perhaps because the Chinese government's intervention is limited and foreign funders make administrative decisions for their fundees, the NPO boards' functions, such as decision-making, supervising, and supporting the organization, are generally not fully realized. NPOs in Indonesia have not implemented many of the principles of good internal governance despite their awareness of them (YAPPIKA, 2006). The boards of Korean NPOs, too, often function poorly (Kim, 2003). In Korea, charismatic founders tend to seize significant decision-making power. Due to a lack of systematic self-regulation mechanisms to ensure transparency in Korea's nonprofit sector, government regulation and supervision is the strongest factor in ensuring NPOs' financial transparency. Such long-term government controls have also hindered Korean NPOs from developing internal governance (Kim, 2003).

Prospects, challenges, and future research

Medium and long-term prospects

While the pace of Asia's economic growth may slow in the near future, we still expect Asian economies to continue to grow and maintain overall economic trends and the number of Asian HNWIs to increase, contributing to increased philanthropic giving and volunteering.

Just like the United States today, in Asian countries with growing aging populations, inter-generational wealth transfers are likely in coming years. This will provide the nonprofit sector with a viable fundraising opportunity. The demands of social services, such as healthcare, social welfare, nursing care, and education, will intensify due to an increase in the poverty rate and population inflow to metropolitan areas.

As discussed previously, the development of the nonprofit sector, at least in terms of IPF, will highly depend on economic development (e.g., per capita income). Political systems (e.g., China and Vietnam) and state–nonprofit relationships (e.g., the Philippines and Malaysia) should be considered as factors affecting the growth of the nonprofit sector in Asia. History, religions, and culture are other important factors contributing to the different growth patterns of Asia's nonprofit sectors.

Challenges to NPOs and social enterprises

When the government is unable to manage highly diverse demands of social services, the role of NPOs, social enterprises, and foundations become even more critical in Asia. To meet this need, NPOs must strengthen their organizational capacity for effective fundraising and professional staff training. Partnerships among NPOs, government, and business will become more important. The government should invest in modernizing legal and tax systems to facilitate the development of the nonprofit sector. Currently, many foundations in Asia are small family foundations, but they are likely to become more professionalized by acquiring advanced grant-making and management skills in the future.

The absence of a specific legal framework can create the sectoral blur between NPOs and for-profits in some Asian countries, unlike those based in the highly institutionalized social sector of developed countries. This condition, in turn, may facilitate activities of social enterprises and impact investing, thereby offering novel financing opportunities for social enterprises through market-based tools, such as equity investment and loans.

Challenges to nonprofit management

As the role of NPOs and social enterprises is becoming more prominent, public accountability and effective governance will continue to be a major focus of nonprofit management in Asian countries. However, formulating and implementing self-regulation experiments are often longer and slower processes (Sidel, 2010). A hasty expansion of self-regulatory initiatives can unintentionally create obstacles that would be more problematic in the long term. To avoid this, self-regulatory initiatives should be developed and implemented through collaborative and collective efforts between NPOs and different stakeholder groups, such as government and community leaders. As aforementioned, certain self-regulation methods have been brought from US and UK models (e.g., GuideStar International). Using a method proven in the United States can help make the development processes more efficient, but a nation's cultural and historical factors should always be considered.

Need for continued comparative research

Launched by Lester Salamon and Helmut Anheier in the late 1980s, the Johns Hopkins Comparative Nonprofit Sector Project (JHCNP) has covered approximately 40 countries, including a few Asian countries. CIVICUS Civil Society Index Project also covered over 40 countries, including several Asian countries. Those comparative studies have been instrumental in advancing nonprofit and philanthropy scholarship. However, there are not as many comparative studies today as during the 1990s and 2000s.

Founded in 1994, Asia Pacific Philanthropy Consortium (APPC) strengthened the philanthropy network in the Asia Pacific region under the leadership of Barnett Baron, former president and CEO of Give2Asia and previous executive vice president of the Asia Foundation, and Tadashi Yamamoto, founder and former president of the Japan Center for International Exchange. APPC was in the process of organizing APPIN (Asia Pacific Philanthropy Information Network) as a clearinghouse for philanthropic and NPO data in Asia. However, their research programs were eliminated several years ago. Currently, there are few major research projects studying Asian NPOs and philanthropy.

The nonprofit sector in Asia, especially those in developing countries, will benefit from interaction with developed countries, such as the United States, and vice versa. Hence, continued efforts should be made to gather data for comparative research in Asia, including Asian countries that have not been part of the JHCNP. We suggest that a portal site or a data center can be instrumental in active discourses and sharing information about the state and challenges that NPOs face in the different countries of Asia.

References

Alfitri, B. (2005) The law of zakat management and non-governmental zakat collectors in Indonesia, *International Journal of Not-for-Profit Law*, 8, pp. 55–64.

Anand, P.U. (2014) *Levers for change: Philanthropy in select South East Asian countries*. Lien Centre for Social Innovation.

Antlöv, H., Ibrahim, R. and van Tuijl, P. (2006) NGO governance and accountability in Indonesia: Challenges in a newly democratizing country. In L. Jordan and P. van Tuijl (eds.), *NGO accountability: Politics, principles and innovations*. London: Earthscan, pp. 147–163.

Asian Development Bank (2011) *Civil society briefs: Thailand*. Metro Manila, Philippines: Asian Development Bank. Available at: https://www.adb.org/publications/civil-society-briefs-thailand (Accessed: 19 May 2018).

Asian Venture Philanthropy Network (no date) *About AVPN*. Available at: https://avpn.asia/about-us/ (Accessed: 2 June 2018).

Breen, O.B., Dunn, A. and Sidel, M. (eds) (2016) *Regulatory waves: Comparative perspectives on state regulation and self-regulation policies in the nonprofit sector*. Cambridge: Cambridge University Press.

Cagney, P. (2018) *Global best practices for CSO, NGO, and other nonprofit boards: Lessons from around the world*. Hoboken, NJ: Wiley.

Cariño, L.V. and PNSP Project Staff (2001) *Defining the nonprofit sector: The Philippines*. Baltimore, MD: Johns Hopkins University Centre for Civil Society Studies.

CFRE International (no date) Korea Society of Philanthropy joins CFRE International as a Participating Organization. *CFRE International*. Available at: http://www.cfre.org/news/ksop_po_annnouncment/

Chan, K.-T., Kuan, Y.-Y. and Wang, S.-T. (2011) Similarities and divergences: Comparison of social enterprises in Hong Kong and Taiwan, *Social Enterprise Journal*, 7(1), pp. 33–49.

Charities Aid Foundation (ed.) (2017) CAF World Giving Index 2017, Charities Aid Foundation. Available at: https://www.cafonline.org/docs/default-source/about-us-publications/cafworldgivingindex 2017_2167a_web_210917.pdf?sfvrsn=ed1dac40_10

Chhina, S. et al. (2014) From charity to change: Social investment in selected Southeast Asian countries, Lien Centre for Social Innovation. Available at: https://lcsi.smu.edu.sg/publications/charity-change-socialinvestment-selected-southeastasian-countries

CIVICUS Civil Society Index Project. Available at: http://www.civicus.org/csi/

Defourny, J. and Kim, S.-Y. (2011) Emerging models of social enterprise in Eastern Asia: A cross-country analysis, *Social Enterprise Journal*, 7(1), pp. 86–111.

Domingo, M.O.Z. (2010) Philanthropy in South East Asia. In Anheier, H.K. and Toepler, S. (eds) *International encyclopedia of civil society*. New York, NY: Springer US, pp. 1220–1226.

Fauzia, A. (2013) *Faith and the state: A history of Islamic philanthropy in Indonesia*. Leiden: Brill.

GuideStar International (no date) Current Engagements – South Korea. Available at: http://www.guidestarinternational.org/southkorea.aspx

Huang, C.-C., Deng, G., Wang, Z. and Edwards, R.L. (2013) *China's nonprofit sector: Progress and challenges*. New York: Routledge.

Hudson Institute (2015) *Index of Philanthropic Freedom 2015*. Available at: https://s3.amazonaws.com/media.hudson.org/files/publications/2015.06.15IndexofPhilanthropicFreedom2015.pdf

Japan Fundraising Association. (2017) *Giving Japan 2017*, Japan Fundraising Association.

Jeong, B. (2017) South Korea: Government directed social enterprise development: Toward a New Asian Social Enterprise Country Model. In J.A. Kerlin (ed.) *Shaping social enterprise*. Bingley: Emerald Publishing Limited, pp. 49–77.

Jeong, B. and Kearns, K. (2015) Accountability in Korean NPOs: Perceptions and strategies of NPO Leaders. *VOLUNTAS*, 26(5), pp. 1975–2001.

Jiangang, Z., Xiaojun, H., Univesrity, S.Y. andYifei, L. (2014) Accountability of civic philanthropy organizations in China: Findings from a national survey. *Initiative on Philanthropy in China*. Presented at the China Philanthropy Summit, Indianapolis: Indiana University Research Center for Chinese Politics and Business and the Lilly Family School of Philanthropy.

Johns Hopkins Comparative Nonprofit Sector Project (JHCNP), Johns Hopkins Center for Civil Society Studies. Available at: http://ccss.jhu.edu/research-projects/comparative-nonprofit-sector-project/

Kang, C., Auh, E.Y. and Hur, Y. (2015) Giving in South Korea: A nation of givers for the population under public assistance. In *The Palgrave Handbook of Global Philanthropy*. Basingstoke: Palgrave Macmillan, pp. 426–454.

Kerlin, J.A. (2009) *Social enterprise: A global comparison*. UPNE.

Kerlin, J.A. (2010) A comparative analysis of the global emergence of social enterprise, *VOLUNTAS*, 21(2), pp. 162–179.

Kim, I. and Hwang, C. (2002) *Defining the nonprofit sector: South Korea*. Baltimore, MD: Johns Hopkins University Center for Civil Society.

Kim, J. (2003) Accountability, governance, and non-governmental organizations: A comparative study of twelve Asia-Pacific nations. In Asia-Pacific Philanthropy Consortium conference: Governance, organizational effectiveness, and the non-profit sector in Asia-Pacific. September.

Lan, H., Zhu, Y., Ness, D., Xing, K. and Schneider, K. (2014) The role and characteristics of social entrepreneurs in contemporary rural cooperative development in China: Case studies of rural social entrepreneurship, *Asia Pacific Business Review*, 20(3), pp. 379–400.

Laratta, R., Nakagawa, S. and Sakurai, M. (2011) Japanese social enterprises: Major contemporary issues and key challenges, *Social Enterprise Journal*, 7(1), pp. 50–68.

Lee, E.W. and Haque, M.S. (2008) Development of the nonprofit sector in Hong Kong and Singapore: A comparison of two statist-corporatist regimes, *Journal of Civil Society*, 4(2), pp. 97–112.

Lo, K.-T. and Wu, S.-Y. (2015) Giving in Taiwan: On the rise following economic growth and political democratization. In *The Palgrave Handbook of Global Philanthropy*. Basingstoke: Palgrave Macmillan, pp. 455–472.

Lyons, M. and Hasan, S. (2002) Researching Asia's third sector, *VOLUNTAS*, 13(2), pp. 107–112.

Mahmood, M. and Santos, F. (2011) UBS-INSEAD study on family philanthropy in Asia, Zurich/Singapore: UBS Philanthropy Services/INSEAD.

Nguyen, P.A. and Doan, D.R. (2015) Giving inVietnam: A nascent third sector with potential for growth. In *The Palgrave Handbook of Global Philanthropy*. Basingstoke: Palgrave Macmillan, pp. 473–487.

Okada, A., Ishida, Y., Nakajima, T. and Kotagiri, Y. (2017) The state of nonprofit sector research in Japan: A literature review. *Voluntaristics Review*, 2(3), pp. 1–68.

Okuyama, N. and Yamauchi, N. (2015) Giving in Japan: The role of philanthropy in strengthening civil society. In *The Palgrave Handbook of Global Philanthropy*. Basingstoke: Palgrave Macmillan, pp. 404–425.

Pew Research Center (no date) *Pew-Templeton: Global Religious Futures Project*. Available at: http://www.globalreligiousfutures.org

Salamon, L.M. and Anheier, H.K. (1997) *Defining the nonprofit sector: A cross-national analysis*. Manchester: Manchester University Press.

Santos, J. and Macatangay, L. (2009) Southeast Asia. In J.A. Kerlin (ed.) *Social enterprise: A global comparison*. UPNE, p. 64.

Sengupta, S. and Sahay, A. (2017) Social entrepreneurship research in Asia-Pacific: Perspectives and opportunities, *Social Enterprise Journal*, 13(1), pp. 17–37.

Shapiro, R.A. (2018) Impact investing in Asia: Just getting started. In *Pragmatic Philanthropy*. Springer, pp. 145–158.

Shigetomi, S. (2002) *The State and NGOs: Perspective from Asia*. Institute of Southeast Asian Studies.

Sidel, M. (2003) Trends in nonprofit self-regulation in the Asia Pacific region: Initial data on initiatives, experiments and models in seventeen countries, Asia Pacific Philanthropy Consortium.

Sidel, M. (2010) The promise and limits of collective action for nonprofit self-regulation: Evidence from Asia, *Nonprofit and Voluntary Sector Quarterly*, 39, pp. 1039–1056.

The Asia Foundation (1998) International conference on supporting the nonprofit sector in Asia. In *The Asia Foundation. Asia Pacific Philanthropy Consortium*. Bangkok, Thailand. Available at: http://unpan1.un.org/intradoc/groups/public/documents/apcity/unpan005476.pdf

The Japan Foundation Center. (no date) JFCWEB | Overview. *Definition of Grant-Making Foundations.* Available at: http://www.jfc.or.jp/eng/introduction/

Wang, F.T.Y. (2007) From charity to citizenship: NPOs in Taiwan, *Asia Pacific Journal of Social Work and Development*, 17(1), pp. 53–68.

Wiepking, P. and Handy, F. (2015) *The Palgrave Handbook of Global Philanthropy.* Basingstoke: Palgrave Macmillan.

Xinsong, W. et al. (2015) Giving in China: An emerging nonprofit sector embedded within a strong state. In *The Palgrave Handbook of Global Philanthropy.* Basingstoke: Palgrave Macmillan, pp. 354–368.

Yamamoto, T. (1998) *The nonprofit sector in Japan.* Manchester: Manchester University Press.

Yamaoka, Y. (1998) On the history of the nonprofit sector in Japan. In Yamamoto, T. (ed.) *The nonprofit sector in Japan.* Manchester: Manchester University Press, pp. 19–58.

Yamauchi, N. et al. (1999) Japan. In Salamon, L.M. et al. (eds) *Global civil society. Dimensions of the nonprofit sector.* Baltimore, MD: Johns Hopkins University, pp. 243–260.

Yamauchi, N., Okuyama, N, Matsushima M. (2011) *Japanese civil society at a crossroad: CIVICUS Civil Society Index Report for Japan*, Center for Nonprofit Research and Information, OSIPP, Osaka University.

Yang, Y., Wilkinson, M. and Zhang, X. (2014) Beyond the abolition of dual administration: The challenges to NGO governance in 21st century China, *VOLUNTAS*, 27(5), pp. 2292–2310.

YAPPIKA (2006) *CIVICUS Civil Society Index Report for the Republic of Indonesia.* Jakarta: CIVICUS.

Yoshioka, T. and Onishi, T. (2018) Country Report 2018: Japan. The global philanthropy indices. Indianapolis: Indiana University Lilly Family School of Philanthropy. Available at: https://scholarworks.iupui.edu/handle/1805/15994

Yu, X. (2011) Social enterprise in China: Driving forces, development patterns and legal framework, *Social Enterprise Journal*, 7(1), pp. 9–32.

Zhang, Z., Guo, C. and Cai, D. (2011) Governing Chinese nonprofit organizations: The promise and limits of the "third way", *International Review of Public Administration*, 16(1), pp. 11–30.

Zhou, H. and Pan, Q. (2016) Information, community, and action on Sina-Weibo: How Chinese philanthropic NGOs use social media, *VOLUNTAS*, 27(5), pp. 2433–2457.

7

NONPROFIT MANAGEMENT CONTEXT

The Middle East and North Africa

Omar Bortolazzi

ASSISTANT PROFESSOR OF INTERNATIONAL STUDIES, SCHOOL OF ARTS &
SCIENCES, AMERICAN UNIVERSITY IN DUBAI, DUBAI, UNITED ARAB EMIRATES

Introduction

The Middle East and North Africa (MENA) region continues to experience social and economic challenges related to poverty, illiteracy, and inaccessibility to basic social services. These problems have encouraged the growth of humanitarian efforts spearheaded by governments, private institutions, and individuals to provide aid and other support services to needy populations. The entry of international nonprofit organizations (NPOs), facilitated by the necessity to develop and sustain social capabilities, cultivates collaborative efforts to alleviate the socioeconomic problems faced in remote and neglected regions (Kinzey, 2013).

Although the data relative to the nonprofit sector around the world is substantial, the representation of Arab countries in the research is significantly lacking. Prior to the 2011 political and social uprisings in the region, the preponderance of authoritarian and single-party regimes in the second half of the 20th century kept civil societies under a tight scrutiny (Brown and Pierce, 2013) and massively restricted the work of researchers, academics, practitioners, and analysts. NPOs in the MENA region also compete against the historic institutionalization of charity, social, and welfare services through faith-based organizations. This practice is based on the religious traditional precepts of *zakat, sadaqa,* and *waqf*.[1] In a few countries, social services are provided through non-religious/secular nonprofit organizations and thus are subject to the same oversight requirements as other nonprofits. However, in most countries in the region, welfare services are generally delivered directly by the religious institutions and thus continue to be outside the taxation system and other regulatory oversight (Casey, 2016). Because most Islamic philanthropy lacks oversight and regulation and is sometimes distributed through informal channels, it is consequently very difficult to analyze scientifically (Bortolazzi, 2013). Extreme diversity within the MENA countries is also an important consideration. The Middle East is not a monolithic entity: there are a wide variety of laws and practices throughout the region, and there is an enormous difference between a country such as Tunisia and the Kingdom of Saudi Arabia.

While the 2011 uprisings across the Middle East and North Africa posed immediate challenges for charities, many nonprofit analysts started to envisage new opportunities for philanthropy and

NPOs in the region. Nonprofits once repressed by the governments found themselves advising political transitions. As a transition occurs – or just the prospect – Western nonprofit organizations appear. Working alone or with local partners, they reconsolidate autochthonous NPOs that were outlawed by the previous governments or simply create *ex novo* realities. Unfortunately, some nonprofit entities were left dealing with their affiliation to preceeding regimes. Decades of corrupt administrations result in government officials sitting on the boards of various organizations. Some were legitimate organizations providing meaningful grants, but with others, the legitimacy was more questionable.

The development of the philanthropic/nonprofit sector in the contemporary MENA region is also tied to the provision of corporate social responsibility (CSR) activities. The creation of the Global Compact Unit by the United Nations and its subsequent operations in the Middle East led to the signing of many public and private institutions to participate in the humanitarian and charity work for the community. The transformation from individual or corporate philanthropy to CSR was cultivated by increased efforts towards addressing social issues such as disability, food, clothing for the poor, and housing and education for the underprivileged. Nonetheless, many shifts and changes that occurred in the nonprofit sector in the Middle East and North Africa are not comparable to ones that took place in the West. While philanthropic practices are deeply rooted in the Arab/Islamic tradition, practices labeled as CSR are still very much in their infancy in the Middle East. Where it exists, CSR's evolution in the region is similar to that in Europe and the United States. Companies are exploring ways to formalize giving to help solve pressing social challenges and to build CSR into their business blueprint.

A substantial number of individuals involved in charity and humanitarian activities in the MENA region are motivated by religion (The Conversation, 2017). Even though the Arab world is not monolithic, the concept of *ummah* – referring to the supra-national Muslim community with a common history and bound together by ties of religion – has led to large donations towards charity activities. While Western professionalism has infiltrated the management of the Muslim NPOs, the conventional motivation for their activities is still retained. The philanthropic elements cultivated by the Islam faith – mainly *zakat, sadaqa, waqf* – compel individuals to contribute a certain amount of their wealth towards helping individuals in need.

The MENA region receives an annual average of more than 500 billion US dollars in the form of donations from individuals and corporations to advance philanthropic activities (Islamic Development Bank, 2019). Donations are mainly channeled in projects that seek to eradicate poverty, provide education facilities in the less developed areas, offer better health, create an inclusive society through an understanding of individual rights, and build an environment for the disadvantaged social groups (Fishman, Schwarz, and Mayor, 2015). The increase in particular social and health issues such as untreatable diseases, poverty, hunger, floods, political oppression, and poor economic levels in the MENA region has led to the growth of NPOs that implement programs targeted towards these issues. The increase in international nonprofit institutions has spurred governments to create avenues for growth of national and regional relief and humanitarian programs.

Humanitarian organizations in the MENA region rely on contributions from volunteers and donors to meet their objectives. Domestic and foreign NPOs working in the region collaborate with governments and religious institutions to solicit more resources through regulations that require individuals and companies to contribute a percentage of wealth towards helping the disadvantaged in the society. Countries with stable political administrations and strict religious beliefs report more contributions. Within the region, North Africa accounts for the highest number of NPOs. The majority of these institutions focus on improving education services, alleviating poverty, and reforming health services.

Historical development of nonprofits in the Middle East and North Africa

Civil society and modern forms of voluntary association were first introduced to the Arab world during the colonial era. At the time, the field was dominated by community-based self groups, guilds (*asnaf*), merchants, religiously oriented charitable trusts, and charitable and educational institutions; and funded by Islamic endowments (Bortolazzi, 2015; Vallianatos, 2013). Colonialism enabled the creation of a number of institutions such as clubs, trade unions, professional associations, etc. After regaining independence from their European colonizers, civil society was co-opted by the new nationalist and reformist regimes. It became either a tool of the state or was simply prevented from effectively functioning (Bortolazzi, 2015). After the 1970s, due to the nationalist impulse, civil society organizations (CSOs) multiplied – but always under the surveillance of the regimes. Many CSOs lived under draconian laws imposed by governments, which severely impacted their operational activities (Bortolazzi, 2015; Hawthorne, 2004). CSOs throughout the Arab world saw further development in the 1990s, when the NGOs actively worked to push governments to amend laws and regulations concerning them. This resulted in a positive outcome for civic development (Abdelaziz, 2017). However, as an outgrowth of the 2011 uprisings, many Arab governments imposed restrictions on the operations of NGOs. They imposed increasingly restrictive laws on local NGOs, specifically those working on human rights and democracy-related issues.[2] These government impositions on NGOs have enabled the emergence of GONGOs (government-organized NGOs). Since these organizations are funded, staffed, and in general supported by government, they do not tend to propose societal change, but rather control and manage it.

The failure of governments to meet the economic and social demands of their citizens was a major driver behind the emergence of NGOs providing necessary services. Ibrahim and Sherrif (2008) explored the extent of these activities in countries in the MENA region such as Egypt, Lebanon, Jordan, Saudi Arabia, Kuwait, Qatar, United Arab Emirates (UAE), and Palestine. Oil deposits and other resources have created unprecedented wealth in some of these countries. While the resources have fueled positive economic growth, the political environment in some states has led to increased levels of poverty, unemployment, poor health services, wars, environment pollution, among other critical social economic challenges.

Families, individuals, and private companies have amassed wealth from the oil trade, and have sought methods to utilize their resources to improve the livelihood of their fellow local citizens as well as impoverished societies across the region. The increase in philanthropic activities in the MENA region has been spurred by the availability of these resources in the hands of private individuals and institutions and the willingness of such entities to participate in the public welfare. According to Ibrahim and Sherrif (2008), the main humanitarian activities in the region have included voluntary contributions to the various causes and programs initiated to serve the public good. In contemporary society, the religious ethos continues to influence the trends in charitable activities. There is a notable shift towards strategic philanthropy where contributors are concentrating on establishing the cause of social challenges and finding methods to resolve them.

On the other hand, philanthropic activities in the MENA region have seen the transformation of many individual contributions into institutional programs. Humanitarian activities provided through institutions are considered more effective and impactful compared to individual efforts. Individuals seeking to leave a legacy have institutionalized their activities to attract more donors and contributors while reaching wider populations (Ibrahim and Sherrif, 2008). However, the influence of religious, clan, tribal, family ties in both individual and organizational philanthropy is still remarkable throughout the Middle East and North Africa. Clan, tribal, and religious affiliations tend to provide security and fill the void left by unstable, weak governments. At the same time, these relations hijack the formation of civil society and social capital.

Shaw notes that the increased levels of poverty in marginalized areas and the lack of education, water, and healthcare facilities in such areas, created an imbalance in social and economic development (Shaw, 2011). Nonprofits that focused initial efforts in North Africa sought to fight poverty, illiteracy levels, and provide better healthcare services to the poor and disenfranchised. Such perennial social, political, and economic challenges have turned the Middle East and North Africa into a region with the highest presence of international nonprofit organizations in the world. The MENA region is served by institutions that operate collaboratively due to the similarity of social and economic challenges facing the population (Hoque and Parker, 2014).

However, the spread of NPOs in the MENA region depends on the needs and objectives of the humanitarian institutions. The America–Mideast Educational and Training Services, Inc. (AMIDEAST) is one of the top NPOs in the Middle East that creates and strengthens cordial relations between America and the Middle East and North Africa through educational training and skill exchange programs. The Anna Lindh Foundation is another organization that promotes integration, peaceful relations, and coexistence between cultures through respectful dialogue and diversity (Tanielian, 2017). The Middle East Youth Initiative offers economic empowerment and inclusion of young people in the region by building partnerships and strategic alliances among policymakers, investors, youth leaders, governments, civil society, academics, and the private sector. The Said Foundation works towards assuring a better future for children by investing in their education, development, and understanding of different cultures. Save the Children offers programs to uplift and sustain living conditions for children in difficult social and economic situations. The program has expanded in North Africa to promote the possibilities of parents and guardians to achieve better lives for their children.

Northern Africa is served by similar organizations that have comparable objectives and goals. Action for Africa is a nonprofit organization that advocates for the development of productive and healthier young lives by supporting early child development, education especially for girls and orphans who have a higher risk of illnesses, social violence, and neglect. The Fistula Foundation focuses on restoring health for African women suffering from obstetric fistula (Anderson, 2015). It is a response to the increased number of women who deliver without medical help due to unavailability of facilities or resources. World Conservation Network (WCN) has programs in Northern Africa that include the identification and preservation of endangered species of wild animals and their habitats such as lions, elephants, cheetahs, and rhinos. The NPO promotes coexistence between local population and wildlife through awareness and advocacy programs. The Search for Common Ground (SFCG) is another Northern Africa and Middle East nonprofit organization that seeks to improve women's participation in the social, economic, and political processes. The institution focuses on rights of women through inclusive dialogues with leaders in various sectors (Halpem, 2015).

It can be concluded, therefore, that the historical development of nonprofits in the Middle East and North Africa has been widely determined by the recurrent social and economic issues facilitated by poor governance and improper use of available resources (Driver, 2010). In addition, a number of broad trends can be identified. Among the most important: (1) an increase in activism among successful and affluent business leaders who bring innovation and resources; (2) a significant number of foundations and NGOs churning out from the vision of reformist ruling families, especially in the Gulf countries (e.g.: the Mohammed Bin Rashid Al Maktoum Foundation and the Mohammed Bin Rashid Al Maktoum Global Initiatives in Dubai), enhancing the collaboration between the public and private sector (Emirates Foundation in the UAE); (3) religion as an enduring motivator of giving and a revival of endowed *awaqf* institutions.

Philanthropic traditions

Islam has inspired charitable giving for over fourteen centuries. The calculation, payment, and distribution of *zakat* and *sadaqa*, along with other traditional forms of solidarity, have been the backbone of Islamic societies, characterizing charity as both religious ideal and social practice. At the root of Islamic charity is a desire (and obligation, in the case of *zakat*) to honor and connect with God in everyday actions to strengthen the bond with their Creator (Singer, 2008). This bond is realized through acts of solidarity towards others in the community. Consequently, a special value is placed on public good, "characterized by understandings of social justice and equal relations between people and helping to forge bonds across and within the community" (Celal, 2009). Religious and cultural values and practices are overlapping and synergic concepts in Islam. These articulated webs of practices help to understand another concept which is at the core of Islam: *al-'adalah ijtima'iah* (social justice). While there is no single definition of social justice within the literature on charity and Islam, throughout the region the concept is understood to represent a fundamental aspect of Islamic charity and philanthropy:

> Islam, a religion of peace through the submission to the will and laws of God, advocates the establishment of social justice in order to achieve peace. The Qur"an does not specify the basic feature of social justice, but outlines the purpose and objectives of human life and human beings, interrelationships and relationship to God . . . it includes interconnected divine obligations guiding the individual, social, and public lives of Muslims, mutual obligation of commercial and social contracts, treaty-based obligations as citizens of states, and tacit obligations living in a civil society. These obligations are the basis of human relationships in Islam.[3]

Several other resources refer to *al-'adalah ijtima'iah* as the fair and equitable distribution of resources as essential to ensuring human dignity and in general to a culturally legitimated normative orientation towards what is considered a fair distribution of wealth in society.[4]

In the contemporary MENA region, this concept of "social solidarity" is still at the basis of the newly emerging institutions that are addressing a number of issues related to effective philanthropy: how to structure and channel effective philanthropic support, "what types of organizations or programs to support and how to operate effectively within the complex legal landscape."[5]

Denhardt, Denhardt, and Aristigueta assert that top-performing NPOs across the world are better organized with strict regulations, traditions, and principles that lead to effectiveness in operations and excellence in services.[6] The traditional philanthropic activities in the MENA region have included the works of civil society organizations that respond to societal issues such as famine, floods, refugee crisis, and water shortages.[7] The CSO activities have been very prominent in Palestine due to the lack of a functioning political administration. The organizations have provided basic social services such as food, shelter, education, and sanitation. In other Arab countries with better sustainable economic development, the affluence in these societies has stimulated positive contribution from the public towards humanitarian activities.

Ibrahim and Shneif (2017) explore the transformations in the Arab world concerning the impact of politics, employment, wealth creation, education, relationships, and other social impacts on the advancement of philanthropic activities. Arab countries have a culture of sharing that is based on the legacies of families and social institutions. Parents have traditions of guiding their children through values of sharing financial resources and principles to enable improvement of social welfare and economic changes (Budrys, 2013). Therefore, the philanthropic activities in the Middle East and North Africa have been positively impacted by the strong values that are attached to sharing and promoting public welfare.

Traditional Islamic principles, and the increase in the number of institutions and individuals involved in philanthropic activities, have helped the region to collaborate effectively in redistributing wealth, while creating at the same time an attractive environment for international charitable organizations and new models of institutionalized philanthropy.

The resemblance of the Middle East and Northern Africa in terms of social environment, and religious systems helps the NPOs to interrelate in the provision of the selected services (Kumar, 2006). The collaboration among the humanitarian institutions and the governments to improve the quality of healthcare, education, literacy, sanitation, and provision of water resources fits into the objectives and tradition of most NPOs and their donors, along with tradition and religious duties. Empowering the population reduces the overreliance on external help in the future through the creation of a self-sustainable society (Svara, 2014). Most NPOs recognize poverty, illiteracy, religious discrimination, and racial differences as the huge challenges facing developing and underdeveloped countries (Hoque and Parker, 2014). Establishing accurate and proper social values and rules is significant in the functioning of social, political, and economic systems. It is necessary to create an empowering legal environment for strategic philanthropy and to enhance the professionalization of the sector. Philanthropists and donors require legal structures that provide straightforward and non-intrusive relationships with regulatory authorities (Ibrahim and Sherrif, 2008).

Regulatory and tax environment: key features

The success of nonprofit organizations is guaranteed by the availability of a friendly and legal regulatory system that enables such organizations to operate and adhere to the internal, national, and international regulations. While countries in the Middle East and North Africa region have received many nonprofit institutions, their increased presence is not facilitated by the laxity of laws, regulations, or the protocols needed to allow and manage the operations of these relief entities (Svara, 2014).

The regulation of NPOs varies from region to region due to the diversity in political, policy, regulatory, and income laws. The universal goal of the majority of nonprofit organizations has led to the unification of taxation and regulation mechanisms that seek to create a global environment where the organizations can work without excessive control and monitoring (Anheier, 2014). The high number of conflicts between the nonprofits and governments in the Middle East and North Africa stem from the differences in regulation and taxation (Osula and Ng, 2014). Some governments have mandated all organizations in their territory pay and file tax returns to support government activities. With regard to their nonprofit legal systems, MENA countries can be divided into three main categories: (1) countries that highly restrict civil society and a general lack of codified regulations for the nonprofit sector; (2) countries with a law governing the NPOs, but one that public authorities use as a tool for restricting civil society organizations; (3) countries with relatively liberal laws (or a laissez-faire approach to NGO regulation) that enable a space for NPOs, but with some problems in implementing the law that hinder civil society (Abdel Samad, 2007).

However, the vital element of these regulatory processes is the exemption from income tax and other forms of taxes by the government and government-affiliated entities. While some countries and regions have indirectly dictated the utilization of the funds collected by the organizations, some nonprofits select the projects to invest in economic, social, education, infrastructure, religious, and research settings.

Nevertheless, the exemption from the tax system requires the NPO to submit an application and subsequent review and approval from the government. In the United States, for example, the Internal Revenue Service (IRS) is responsible for receiving tax exemption applications from NPOs, then vetting such organizations to determine their operations, sources of revenue, expenditure, and other financial processes before issuing them with tax exemption certificates.[8] The governments have a regulatory role of examining and reviewing the operations of these institutions to ensure that they abide by the mission, objectives, and strategies.[9] There are various cases where business frauds have registered NPOs with a mission of executing illegal business in foreign countries as well as evasion of taxes.

Notably, nonprofit organizations working in the MENA region have faced the same procedures in complying with the regulations and tax systems. In the MENA region, the tax authorities or services work with the NPO organizations to provide exemptions on the payment and filing of tax returns. The lifting of tax levies for the international relief organizations in these regions has been attributed to a high number of humanitarian activities in the Middle East and North Africa. More organizations are preferring countries that have fewer restrictions on financial control and other regulations that may limit the implementation of social and economic projects.[10]

However, organizations that do not follow through on their mandate in bettering the lives of the population may be forced out of these regions through the imposition of taxes that render the operation futile.[11] The exemption from taxes is a method by governments to enable the nonprofit organizations to expand their activities in the humanitarian, development, and relief efforts. Additionally, the sources of finances for the institutions have also been considered in exempting them from income levies due to the understanding that majority of donors and volunteers are subjected to normal incomes taxes such as Pay As You Earn or income withholding taxes.

On the other hand, the regulation of nonprofit organizations in Northern Africa and the Middle East is carried out by specific government authorities that oversee the operation of these institutions. The authorities ensure that the NPOs meet their objectives in the charters agreed to by the governments. The organizations are not allowed to interfere with the national political, social, and economic landscape (Maier, Meyer, and Steinbereithner, 2016). The mandate of most NPOs includes providing relief, responding to calamities, and supporting social processes such as education and healthcare. The governments have strict rules that bar organizations from interfering with the political and economic sectors.

Nonprofit organizations that participate in the political processes, such as campaigns and elections, have often found themselves unregistered and blocked from operating in these regions. This also applies to such institutions that go beyond the scope of work agreed to in the charters. The power struggles between governments in developing countries and NPOs are a result of increased activities by NPOs, that influence the population to view the NPOs as more important in the provision of necessary services, leading to conflicts and eventual registration of such institutions.

For instance, the civil wars in the Middle East determine which countries the NPOs should engage with to seek financial or material support (Kovacs and Spens, 2012). While the governments have laws and rules that guide the operations of NPOs, such regulations only apply to general processes. The control and management of internal activities are left to the organizations to manage. The NPOs operating in the Middle East and North Africa have shown high self-regulation levels leading to their success in meeting their goals and objectives.

The NPOs in the MENA region fit in the third sector of a typical economy which includes institutions providing support in social, health medical, human rights, sports, and other activities. The self-governing nature of these institutions continues to raise regulation and administration debates. The separation of the NPOs from government laws and regulations has created conflicts with some countries in the Middle East, such as Saudi Arabia banning most of the internal and global private organizations. At the same time, some Western countries have viewed the MENA governments as unstable political administration systems, and thus are unable to successfully regulate the works of NPOs in the regions.

The post-2011 uprisings saw a renewed local and international interest in the creation of new organizations, nonprofit corporations, and non-governmental organizations alike. In some cases like Tunisia, the political and governance reforms have created an environment where philanthropic activities can thrive through laws and regulations that guide the registration and implementation of relief activities. In others, like Egypt, new regimes targeted NGOs as sources of national discord and instability. Meanwhile, NGO development underwent severe regression in Yemen after the uprisings, and intensified the sectarian divisions between the organizations (Erakat and Saghiyeh, 2016). Overall, the execution of the laws, practices, and regulations greatly differs among countries. For instance, Egypt has over 20,000 registered NPOs working on various social projects while UAE and Saudi Arabia have relatively few organizations due to their political administration and economic stability.

At any rate, the proliferation and – in some cases – endurance of NGOs, in countries with more liberal NGO laws and even in those with more repressive laws, suggest significant potential for the not-for-profit sector in the MENA region. In this regard, the Middle East may not be different from other areas of the world that have undergone major political transitions, and the domestic nonprofit sector could effectively contribute to lasting changes in the region (Elbayar, 2005).

The social, economic, and political environments in the Middle East and North Africa have influenced the management and structuring of the nonprofit institutions that have a presence in the region (Gould, 2015). The religious backgrounds in some MENA region countries have adversely affected the works and management of humanitarian organizations. At the same time, some Gulf Cooperation Council (GCC) countries could rely on extensive oil resources that have led to an increase in donations through the responsible government ministries and religious institutions.

The regulation policy frameworks have increased the micromanagement of many nonprofit organizations and NGOs in the MENA region. Countries with unstable political systems have influenced the operations of these institutions through direct interference with their strategies and management (Epstein and Yuthas, 2014). Fundraising policies relating to the procedures and rules on raising resources for the various humanitarian projects have also impacted the capabilities of the NPOs. Most organizations are used to an environment where they solicit funds from various sources such as religious institutions, communities, and schools without dictation from the governments (Flynn and Hodgkinson, 2013). The NPOs consider the restriction on collection of funds as the major challenge to their functioning in the Middle East and North African countries. The difficult relations among countries in these regions also negatively impacts the number of donor and volunteers.

Comparison with standard Western nonprofit management model

According to Irwin (2013), the standard Western nonprofit management model includes a board that is responsible for the strategic functioning of the institution in the various regions selected as candidates for the humanitarian aid. The boards are usually composed of founders and major financiers. The structure of the board determines the success of the operations through the development of various committees that are charged with separate responsibilities that develop the mission, vision, and core values of the NPO. The effectiveness of this management model is identified in the composition of the critical committees that handle finance, program, planning, fundraising, and personnel activities. The implementation of this standard management model in the MENA region is affected by the local regulations and rules that govern both home-based and foreign NPOs (Slim, 2015).

While the NPOs are not business entities, their management and operations should meet some of the requirements of profit organizations because they work with finances, personnel, infrastructure, and other resources and thus are required to be responsible in terms of professionalism and financial control. The personnel and other human resources should include experts in employee relations, project management, accounting, management, coordination, risk management, and auditing to ensure that the operations of the institutions meet the required standards and can be comparable to business entities.

The administration of the NPOs in the MENA region is different from the standard Western nonprofit management model. While the not-for-profit sector in Western countries is largely institutionalized, the NPOs in the Middle East and North Africa are still widely guided by religiously driven altruistic principles. Another difference between the Western and MENA nonprofit management model is the perception of CSR activities. Nonprofit organizations in the Western nations view corporate social responsibility as a strategy to reinforce core social and economic issues such as environment, health, and education while the organizations in MENA consider CSR as a channel to provide support to charity towards managing social problems. However, the institutionalization of philanthropy is a new but expanding concept in the Middle East and North Africa. Those countries with expanded wealth through oil and other resources have allied with NPOs to help them provide contributions and monitor their utilization.

Conclusion

The management of nonprofit organizations in Northern Africa and the Middle East has been subject to various internal and external issues that have impacted the execution of projects and programs. The nature of the political environment, religious systems, and the cultural background has affected the entry and the operations of these NPOs. The political unrests in some countries in the Middle East and North Africa have also resulted in limited relief and humanitarian programs implemented in these regions. However, the study has identified some key aspects that have guided the success in improving the operations of NGOs in some countries.

Relief, improvement, social reform, and response principles are some of the features that are considered in management and operations of the nonprofit organizations in the selected regions. The regulatory framework by some of the home and host governments has also affected – and continues to affect – the organization and management of nonprofit institutions operating in the North Africa and Middle East region. Some governments have facilitated a cordial environment for the institutions through a framework of policies and regulations that prevent maltreatment, while affording them access to the government infrastructure and resources required in reaching the most remote areas. In other cases, the political instability of some countries has rendered inapplicable an efficient management of civil society organizations, NGOs, NOPs, etc.

The exemption from taxes and levies both at the institutional and employee level encourages initiation of more programs that result in economic and social benefits for the population. This chapter has highlighted how the various economic and political policies impact the management and functioning of the NPOs. The financial, regulation, economic, and fundraising procedures determine the levels of investment. Governments that are extremely strict on the work of external stakeholders create challenges for these institutions to achieve their goals.

The diversity of policies within the MENA region is considered one of the the major problems for humanitarian and relief organizations. The mismanagement and misappropriation of natural resources due to poor political administration and instability create an economy with few wealthy individuals and many middle and low-income earners. The analysis of the standard Western nonprofit management model compared the changes that the NPOs have made to ensure full assimilation in the targeted regions through an understanding of the local political, social, and economic systems. The success of managing nonprofit organizations in the Northern Africa and the Middle East countries is based on the relationship that the entities create with the governments, as well as the adherence to the conventional management models and regulation that have helped the institutions succeed in other parts of the world.

The Middle East and North Africa persist to be a turbulent region. Several places continue to experience political instability, turmoil, or civil war. Several trends affecting civil society organizations and NGOs remain in existence in the region in 2018. While several governments still maintain closed civic space, others increasingly acknowledged the nonprofit sector's influence through formal dialogues and documents, such as in Morocco (USAID, 2013). At the same time, the ongoing civil war in Syria continues to affect the neighboring countries of Iraq, Jordan, and Lebanon, influencing the implementation of several aspects related to NPOs' sustainability, including service provision, organizational capacity, financial viability, and public image (USAID, 2013).

Notes

1 *Zakat* is the third pillar of Islam, the giving of wealth required of all believers. Often translated as "alms" or "charitable giving." Muslims must give 2.5 percent of their annual savings to help the poor, the needy, and the oppressed (and other categories). This act of devotion acknowledges that all wealth comes from God and purifies the soul from material greed. In addition, Islam encourages voluntary acts of charity, be they monetary or physical. *Sadaqa* refers to an act of "benevolence," connoting voluntary charitable giving and beneficence of all types. It differs from *zakat* which is obligatory. *Waqf* (pl. *awaqf*) is one of the oldest examples of an endowment. If we refer to the the root of the word, literally to stop, confine, isolate, or preserve in perpetuity certain revenue or property for religious or philanthropic purposes.

2 E.g.: Law 70 /2017 gives Egypt's NGOs one year to comply or face being dissolved in court. Among its restrictions are a ban on field research and surveys without government permission, forcing NGOs to adapt their activities to government priorities and plans or face up to five years in prison. The law also gives the authorities wide powers to dissolve NGOs, dismiss their board of administration, and subject their staff to criminal prosecution based on vaguely worded terms including "harming national unity and disturbing public order" ("Egypt: NGO law threatens to annihilate human rights groups", Amnesty International, May 30, 2017).

3 Hasan, Samiul. (2007). "Islamic Concept of Social Justice: Its Possible Contribution to Ensuring Harmony and Peaceful Coexistence in a Globalized World", *Macquarie Law Journal*, vol. 7, 168–183.

4 Schultz Hafid (2009); Ismael and Ismael (2008: 23–44).

5 Ismael and Ismael (2008: 23–44).

6 Denhardt, Denhardt, and Aristigueta (2012).

7 Ibrahim and Sherrif (2008: 72).

8 Meier (2015).

9 Singh (2014: 79).

10 Arvidson and Lyon (2014: 881).

11 Berman (2014).

Bibliography

Abdelaziz, Mohamed. "The Hard Reality of Civil Society in the Arab World". The Washington Institute for Near East Policy. December 11, 2017.

Abdel Samad, Ziad. "Civil Society in the Arab Region: Its Necessary Role and the Obstacles to Fulfillment", *International Journal of Not-for-Profit Law*, 9, no. 2, April 2007/3.

Anderson, Ronald. *World Suffering and Quality of Life*. New York: Springer, 2015.

Anheier, Helmut. *Nonprofit Organizations: Theory, Management, Policy*. New York: Routledge, 2014.

Aoki, Masahiko, Kuran, Timur, Roland, Gerard. *Institutions and Comparative Economic Development*. Basingstoke: Palgrave Macmillan, 2012.

Arvidson, Malin, Lyon, Fergus. "Social Impact Measurement and Non-profit Organizations: Compliance, Resistance, and Promotion", *International Journal of Voluntary and Nonprofit Organizations*, 25, no. 4 (2014): 869–886.

Berman, Margo. *Productivity in Public and Nonprofit Organizations*. New York: Routledge, 2014.

Bonner, Michael., Ener, Mine, Singer, Amy. *Poverty and Charity in Middle Eastern Contexts*. New York: SUNY Press, 2012.

Bortolazzi, Omar (ed.). *Youth Networks, Civil Society and Social Entrepreneurship. Case Studies in Post-Revolutionary Arab World*. Bologna: Bononia University Press, 2015.

Bortolazzi, Omar. "Zakat: The Islamic Tradition of Formalized Compulsory Giving", *Africa e Mediterraneo*, July 2013.

Brown, R.A., Pierce, J. (eds.). *Charities in the Non-Western World: The Development and Regulation of Indigenous and Islamic Charities*. New York: Routledge, 2013.

Budrys, Grace. *How Nonprofits Work: Case Studies in Nonprofit Organizations*. Lanham, MD: Rowman & Littlefield, 2013.

Casey, John. "Comparing Nonprofit Sectors Around the World: What Do We Know and How Do We Know It?". *Journal of Nonprofit Education and Leadership*, 6, no. 3 (2016): 187–223.

Celal, Rana. "Charity in Islamic Societies", *Alliance Magazine*, September 2009.

Ceptureanu, Sebastian, Ceptureanu, Eduard, Bogdan, Liviu, Radulescu, Violeta. "Sustainability Perceptions in Romanian Non-Profit Organizations: An Exploratory Study Using Success Factor Analysis", *Sustainability*, 10, no. 2 (2018).

Denhardt, Robert, Denhardt, Jane, Aristigueta, Maria. *Managing Human Behavior in Public and Nonprofit Organizations*. Thousand Oaks, CA: Sage, 2012.

Driver, Carolyn. *Guidelines for Writing Successful Grant Proposals for Nonprofit Organizations*. Bloomington, IN: AuthorHouse, 2010.

Elbayar, Kareem. "NGO Laws in Selected Arab States", *International Journal for Not-for-Profit Law*, 7, no. 4, September 2005/3.

Epstein, Marc, Yuthas, Kristi. *Measuring and Improving Social Impacts: A Guide for Nonprofits, Companies, and Impact Investors*. Oakland, CA: Berrett-Koehler Publishers, 2014.

Erakat, Noura, Saghiyeh, Nizar (eds.). *NGOs in the Arab World Post-Arab Uprisings: Domestic and International Politics of Funding and Regulation*. ASI-FAMA Incorporated, 2016.

Eweje, Gabriel. *Corporate Social Responsibility and Sustainability: Emerging Trends in Developing Economies*. Auckland: Emerald Group Publishing, 2014.

Fishman, James, Schwarz, Stephen, Mayor, Lloyd. *Nonprofit Organizations: Cases and Materials*. New York: Foundation Press, 2015.

Flynn, Patrice, Hodgkinson, Virginia. *Measuring the Impact of the Nonprofit Sector*. Washington, DC: Springer Science & Business Media, 2013.

Gould, Julie. "Non-profit Organizations: Scientists on a Mission", *Nature,* 527, no. 7577 (2015): 265–266.

Halpem, Mafred. *Politics of Social Change: In the Middle East and North Africa*. Princeton, NJ: Princeton University Press, 2015.

Hawthorne, Amy. *Middle Eastern Democracy. Is Civil Society the Answer?*. Washington, DC: Carnegie Endowment for International Peace. Carnegie Papers Middle East Series, no. 44, 2004.

Hoque, Zahirul, Parker, Lee. *Performance Management in Nonprofit Organizations: Global Perspectives*. New York: Routledge, 2014.

Ibrahim, Barbara, Sherrif, Dina. *From Charity to Social Change: Trends in Arab Philanthropy*. New York: American University in Cairo Press, 2008.

Ibrahim, Barbara, Shnief, Heba. *Family Legacies: Wealth and Philanthropy in the Arab World*. New York: American University in Cairo Press, 2017.

Irwin, Julia. *Making the World Safe: The American Red Cross and a Nation's Humanitarian Awakening*. New York: OUP USA, 2013.

Islamic Development Bank. Annual Report 2018. Jeddah: Islamic Development Bank, 2019.

Ismael, Jaqueline S., Ismael, Shereen T. "Social Policy in the Arab World: The Search for Social Justice", *Arab Studies Quarterly*, 30, no. 2 (2008): 23–44.

Kinzey, Ruth. *Promoting Nonprofit Organizations: A Reputation Management Approach*. New York: Routledge, 2013.

Kovacs, Gyongyi, Spens, Karen. *Relief Supply Chain Management for Disasters: Humanitarian Aid and Emergency Logistics*. Hershey, PA: Information Science Reference, 2012.

Kumar, Anuradha. *Human Rights Development of Under Privileged*. New Delhi: Sarup & Sons, 2006.

Maier, Florentine, Meyer, Michael, Steinbereithner, Martin. "Nonprofit Organizations Becoming Business-Like: A Systematic Review", *Nonprofit and Voluntary Sector Quarterly*, 45, no. 1 (2016).

Meier, Patrick. *Digital Humanitarians: How Big Data Is Changing the Face of Humanitarian Response*. Boca Raton, FL: CRC Press, 2015.

Osula, Bwamwell, Ng, Eddie. "Toward a Collaborative, Transformative Model of Non-Profit Leadership: Some Conceptual Building Blocks", *Leadership in Non-Profit Organizations*, 4, no. 2 (2014).

Potluka, Oto, Spacek, Martin, Schnurbein, Georg. "Impact of the EU Structural Funds on Financial Capacities of Non-profit Organizations", *International Journal of Voluntary and Nonprofit Organizations*, 28, no. 5 (2017).

Schultz Hafid, Molly. "Emerging Trends in Social Justice Philanthropy in Egypt", John D. Gerhart Center for Philanthropy and Civic Engagement, the American University in Cairo, 2009.

Shaw, John. *The World's Largest Humanitarian Agency: The Transformation of the UN World Food Programme and of Food Aid*. Basingstoke: Palgrave Macmillan, 2011.

Sheehan, Robert. *Mission Impact: Breakthrough Strategies for Non-profits*. New York: John Wiley, 2010.

Singer, Amy. *Charity in Islamic Societies*. Cambridge: Cambridge University Press, 2008.

Singh, Ardhendu. "Conducting Case Study Research in Non-Profit Organizations", *Qualitative Market Research: An International Journal*, 17, no. 1 (2014).

Slim, Yugo. *Humanitarian Ethics: A Guide to the Morality of Aid in War and Disaster*. New York: Oxford University Press, 2015.

Svara, James. *The Ethics Primer for Public Administrators in Government and Nonprofit Organizations*. Burlington, MA: Jones & Bartlett Publishers, 2014.

Tanielian, Melaine. *The Charity of War: Famine, Humanitarian Aid, and World War I in the Middle East*. Palo Alto, CA: Stanford University Press, 2017.

The Conversation. "How Religion Motivates People to Give and Serve", August 19, 2017. Available at https://theconversation.com/how-religion-motivates-people-to-give-and-serve-81662

Turton, Tine, Torres, Nicholas. *Social Innovation and Impact in Nonprofit Leadership*. New York: Springer, 2014.

USAID. The 2013 CSO Sustainability Index for the Middle East and North Africa. United States Agency for International Development; Bureau for Democracy, Conflict, and Humanitarian Assistance: Center of Excellence on Democracy, Human Rights, and Governance; Bureau for the Middle East: Office of Middle East Programs. US Agency for International Development. Third Edition, 2013.

Vallianatos, Stefanos. Arab Civil Society at the Crossroad of Democratisation: The Arab Spring Impact, CIES (Centre for International and European Studies), Neighbourhood Policy Paper, no. 10, February 2013.

Walker, Peter, Maxwell, Daniel. *Shaping the Humanitarian World*. New York: Routledge, 2014.

Wang, Jiane-Ye. *What Drives China's Growing Role in Africa?* Washington, DC: International Monetary Fund, 2007.

Wang, XiaoHu. *Performance Analysis for Public and Nonprofit Organizations*. Sudbury, MA: Jones & Bartlett Learning, 2010.

Weikart, Lynne, Chen, Greg. *Budgeting and Financial Management for Nonprofit Organizations*. Thousand Oaks, CA: Sage, 2012.

Wolf, Thomas. *Managing a Nonprofit Organization: Updated Twenty-First-Century Edition*. New York: Simon and Schuster, 2012.

8

NONPROFIT MANAGEMENT CONTEXT

Africa

Jacob Mwathi Mati

SENIOR LECTURER, SCHOOL OF HUMANITIES, SOL PLAATJE UNIVERSITY, KIMBERLY,
SOUTH AFRICA, AND ASSOCIATE RESEARCH FELLOW, SOCIETY, WORK AND POLITICS (SWOP)
INSTITUTE, THE UNIVERSITY OF WITWATERSRAND, JOHANNESBURG, SOUTH AFRICA

Introduction

This chapter examines the nonprofit sector management context in Africa. Aware that an analysis of a phenomenon straddling 54 odd countries and dearth of reliable data across them portends great limitations and risks of overlooking each country's unique features, the chapter attempts to be as illustrative as possible while alerting readers to convergences and differences. The chapter begins with a brief conceptual overview of what is meant by nonprofit organizations (NPOs) in Africa. This is followed by a discussion of the historical development of nonprofits in Africa and how this shapes the context of their management. Then follows a discussion of how the nature of socio-political and economic operating environment shapes nonprofits regulation and management. A discussion on nonprofit resourcing and its implications on the management context is next. Finally, based on a review of the environmental context, the chapter reflects on challenges and opportunities and future implications for NPOs management context.

Nonprofit management context in Africa

The nonprofit management context in Africa reflects the hybrid milieu of their production. In essence, African NPOs are products of a triple fusion of Euro-Americanism, Orientalism and local adaptations. This reflects in the diversity of organizations occupying the nonprofit space in many African countries. Non-governmental organizations, faith-based organizations, trade unions, women's organizations, student and youth organizations, nonprofit schools, educational associations (parents–teachers, alumni), nonprofit healthcare service organizations, nonprofit media groups, social movements, social service charities, professional and business organizations, grassroots community organizations (such as village associations, neighbourhood committees), burial societies, self-help groups, indigenous peoples associations, economic interest organizations (e.g., cooperatives, credit unions, mutual saving associations), ethnic, traditional or indigenous associations or organizations, environmental organizations, culture, arts and social and recreational organizations and networks of organizations all carry the nonprofit tag. These have differing management needs and practices.

According to Toepler and Anheier (2004), existing theorizations of the context of nonprofits management broadly relies on four approaches. These are the *systems theory, contingency theory, resource dependency theory* and *neo-institutionalism.* Systems-theory inspired approaches see NPOs as complex conglomerates of multiple agents – employees, volunteers, board members, funders and beneficiaries or client communities – with varied value motivations and bottom lines, pursuing diffuse and often changing goals and interests (Toepler and Anheier 2004; Anheier 2000; Claeyé 2012). This characteristic diversity of agents, their motivations and bottom lines, demands a variety of management approaches and styles.

For contingency theories NPOs are open systems constantly adapting to succeed/survive, where organizations survive based on "the appropriateness of their structure in relation to their environments" (Toepler and Anheier 2004: 263). An organization's management approach, therefore, is geared at ensuring "goodness of fit between key characteristics of task environments and organizational structure (Lawrence/Lorsch, 1967)" (Toepler and Anheier 2004: 263).

The resource dependency theory treats resource control as the key determinant of NPO management. Simply put, resource dependency theorists argue that because organizations depend on resources that they do not control, they are vulnerable to managerial direction from actors who control the critical resources that NPOs need. Financial donors, for example, influence NPO management. Organization's continued survival therefore is contingent upon "operational efficiency" and conformity to donors when mobilizing and utilizing resources (Toepler and Anheier 2004: 263). Existing research discounts that NPOs simply comply with external demands. Instead, nonprofits employ a variety of "strategies to manage dependencies and regain managerial freedom and autonomy" in effect influencing and changing their environment (Toepler and Anheier 2004: 263; Claeyé 2012).

For neo-institutionalists, organizational actions are formed, shaped and constrained by institutions – the prevailing, usually taken-for-granted social rules, norms and values (Powell and DiMaggio 1991). Institutions delineate the range of available options perceived legitimate/allowable and critically important for organization's long-term survival (Toepler and Anheier 2004). Neo-institutionalists further argue that NPOs sharing the same environment are subject to the same institutional expectations and constraints. Over time, the application of similar management practices results in institutional "isomorphism" (Kostova et al. 2008; Toepler and Anheier 2004). While largely true, universal isomorphism does not always ensue due to differential treatment of various types of organization in many Africa states. This suggests that in Africa only similar NPO types are likely to be isomorphic.

Powell and DiMaggio (1991) suggest three mechanisms of institutional isomorphic change: coercive, mimetic and normative. Coercive isomorphism is a reaction to direct or indirect pressure to abide by institutional expectations. In coercive isomorphism, pressures are typically exerted by institutions upon which the pressured organization depends, such as state regulatory authorities (Toepler and Anheier 2004). Mimetic isomorphism "occurs in situations of technological or environmental uncertainty which makes organizations to mimic" other organizations that are perceived successful (Toepler and Anheier 2004: 265). Lastly, normative isomorphism "derives from professional norms and standards that guide the work of professionals in organizations and thus shape organizational behavior" (Toepler and Anheier 2004: 265). Industry-wide self-regulation regimes typify this.

In his study of NPO management in Africa, Claeyé (2012) invokes Homi Bhabha's (1994) hybridity to argue that the African NPO is a hybrid fusion of cultures and relationships. Contextually, African NPOs are products of geopolitical power dynamics in their origin, the cultures within which they exist and are produced, and their location. As a result, the African NPO management context is also a hybrid "outcome of an on-going process of appropriation, translation, interpretation and re-interpretation" of multiple managerialist discourses (Claeyé 2012: 163). Specifically, the nonprofit management context in Africa is shaped by, among others, history, social, economic, political and cultural milieus within which it has emerged and operates. Before delving into the discussion of these factors, it is important to clarify what we mean by nonprofit organization in Africa.

Nonprofits in Africa: A conceptual recapitulation

Substantial amount of descriptive intellectual effort has gone towards conceptualizing what constitutes the nonprofit sector in Africa. Besides a host of individual scholarly efforts, prominent cross-country initiatives include the CIVICUS Civil Society Index (CSI),[1] the Johns Hopkins Comparative Nonprofit Sector Project,[2] and the USAID CSO Sustainability Index.[3] An evaluation of conceptions, methodologies and results of these comparative studies suggests that they collectively suffer from over-concentration of their analytical gaze on formal non-governmental organizations (NGOs) as the sum total of NPOs (Obadare 2014). This bias emanates, in part, from the Euro-American inspired NGOs (a phenomenon that arrived on the continent in the early 1990s) ostensive "prostitution of the term civil society to suit own ambiguous agendas" (Obadare 2004: 155).

The effect of this bias is two-fold. First, it leaves out the rich tapestry of informal and often unregistered traditional forms of associations (e.g., village associations, homeboy associations, craft unions and title societies) that arguably outnumber the formal organizations in the continent (Mbaye 2011; FDC 2008). Second, it introduces an elitist bias in the thinking of what constitutes NPOs in Africa given that most formal African NGOs tend to be elitist, exclusionary, and often started by educated urban citizens vainly claiming to represent interests of communities (Mbaye 2011; CNOSCG 2011; FDC 2008).

Relatedly, existing studies of NPO management in Africa are, by extension, burdened by the obsession with the formal registered organization. The Johns Hopkins CNP as well as the USAID CSO Sustainability Index are arguably more outright in their organizational bias. The Johns Hopkins CNP approach for example uses five key criteria for distinguishing the "bewildering array" of nonprofit entities from state and market-oriented organizations: NPOs are *organized, private, self-governing, nonprofit distributing, and voluntary* (Salamon et al. 1999: 3; Salamon and Anheier 1997).

CNP's conceptualization has been criticized on at least two fronts. First, it ignores the rich cultural milieu and specificity (Heinrich 2005) especially of informal organizations across Africa. The review-based nature of this chapter does not help remedy this shortcoming in the literature. However, it suffices to note that the management of informal types of NPOs is itself informed by informal norms and institutions. There is also substantial mimicry of the formal management structures across these informal organizations. Specifically, the informal organization's leadership structure may include a chairperson, a secretary and a treasurer. In some instances, the same person performs all the three roles. Being self-resourced organizations, accountability is directly to members.

The second criticism is the interchangeable usage of "nonprofit" and "civil society." This is charged as conceptually unsound because the two are dissimilar phenomena, rooted in different perspectives: nonprofits in economic and social policy debates, and civil society being embedded in democratic political and social theory (Heinrich 2005: 219). Even then, contestation, fluidity and controversy on terminology and the constitutive elements of the "nonprofit sector" and "civil society" in Africa is widespread. Obadare (2004, 2014) broadly categorizes existing works in this regard as either rejectionists (Gellner 1994; Mamdani 1995; Bereketeab 2009; Chabal and

Daloz 1999), "conditional accepters" (Blaney and Pasha 1993; Ekeh 1992; Mustapha 1998) or "positive affirmationists" (Chan 2002; Comaroff and Comaroff 1999).

The persistent debate over existence and the utility of "nonprofit" and "civil society" concepts in Africa emanates, in part, from disciplinary differences between economics and sociology on the primary defining characteristics of the constitutive organizations in this sphere (Mati 2012; Corry 2010). Economists for example, focus on the non-redistribution constraints while "sociologists look at value-based motivations, persuasions, normative appeals, communicative rationality and idealism of participants as key generative and operative drivers of civil society" (Mati 2012: 42). Additionally, there is a perverse normative bias towards civility and free will of the associating human agents in the empirical–analytical projects such as CIVICUS CSI and the Johns Hopkins CNP (Obadare 2004; Heinrich 2005). This normative orientation determines conceptions of what the sector ought to look like. The implication is that many nonprofits outside this normative fit are excluded in existing analysis. An example is ethnic-based associations whose membership is by ascription and contributions are demanded/required and therefore not necessarily "voluntary" (Aina 2013). Another consequence, as we will see later in this chapter, is that governments and donors, often blinded by normative views of 'good/preferred' characteristics of NPOs devoid of "warts" (Van Rooy 1998), have co-created (albeit mostly separately) the associated institutional isomorphism of nonprofits.

History and nonprofit management context in Africa

Despite disagreements on constitutive elements, various forms of associations falling under nonprofits have been a significant feature of the socioeconomic and political landscape of many African societies since pre-colonial times (ForDIA 2011; CGG 2006; Darkwa et al. 2006); CDS 2005; FDC 2008; Makumbe 1998). Colonialism violently transformed existing African social structures, discouraged and banned traditional associations as barbaric and uncivilized, only selectively utilizing those that facilitated the advance of colonial objectives (ForDIA 2011; Mbaye 2011; Maina 1998). Free association of Africans was further impeded through introduction of regulatory systems such as identity cards, licensing and formal policing. These, alongside colonialism's political economy of taxation and migrant labour system, exposed Africans to geophysical and cultural dislocation-associated hardships.

Africans reacted to these developments in two ways. First, the dislocated labourers in the emergent centres of economic exploitation – mines, large-scale plantations and towns – formed unions as a means for dealing with the alienation associated with the colonial system. Second, there emerged, initially, informal ethnic-based organizations that served both cultural and resource mobilization purposes which operated 'below the radar' of the colonial state. The management of these types of organizations had no legal encumbrances and therefore remained largely informal.

Activities of the new formal organizations were under a constant gaze of the colonial state which did not hesitate to ban those suspected of disturbing colonial order. Various coercive legislations were also used in governing African associational life and in effect, setting the stage for practices of governmental control and regulation of nonprofit organizations. Some of the strict colonial era NPO regulatory laws are still the superstructures of regimes of governmentality of associational life in many countries (DENIVA 2006; Darkwa et al. 2006; FONGTO 2006). Though highly regulated by the state, these organizations (especially labour) played an important role in the anti-colonial struggles (Scott 1967; Millen 1963; Akue and Coulibaly 2004; FONGTO 2006).

Other nonprofits emerging during the colonial period were those exclusively of white colonial settlers especially in the settler colonies – South Africa, Zimbabwe, Kenya and Algeria.

These included cooperatives of export crop growers and professional associations (Nzomo 2003). Additionally, Christian missionary-run hospitals, schools and other charitable institutions emerged. Besides ameliorating sharper, dehumanizing facets of colonial rule, these had a pacifying effect on indigenous Africans (Page and Sonnenburg 2003; Nzomo 2003; Fowler and Mati 2019). In some cases, faith organizations later became important civic umbrellas, sheltering and giving sanctuary even to groups that the state may otherwise have considered illegitimate, unauthorized and illegal (Nzomo 2003). Examples of such include the Christian Council of Kenya whose first African bishop, consecrated at the height of Mau Mau insurgency, lobbied for dialogue (Mati 2015). To date, some churches continue to be refuge centres for nascent democratic forces (often regarded by government as "dissident" groups) confronting the state (Nzomo 2003: 186; for examples across Africa, see Ranger 2008). Religion also played a role in subversive political mobilizations by groups like Dini ya Msambwa and Legio Maria in Kenya (Mati 2015) or the Muslim Brotherhood in Egypt and Sudan (Munson 2001; Zahid and Medley 2006).

The interwar period witnessed increased activism as Africans started demanding for themselves the same rights the European colonizers enjoyed (Mati 2012). This resulted from increased African consciousness of their alienation by the bifurcated colonial state that governed its white *citizenry* "by the rule of law and associated regime of rights" while its African *subjects* were governed by a "regime of extra-economic coercion and administratively driven justice" (Mamdani 1996: 19). Many indigenous associations emerging during this time agitated against the economic and political domination by the colonial system. By the middle of the 20th century, this agitation converged into an anti-colonial movement incorporating various African associational formations.

In the last three decades there has been tremendous growth of NPOs as part of the contemporary global "associational revolution" (Salamon 1994; Smith et al. 2016) across Africa. The specific rate of growth remains unknown and varies across countries. In countries like Kenya the number of registered NPOs grew from 113,259 to 347,387 (i.e. 307 per cent) between 1997 and 2005 (Kanyinga et al. 2007). In South Africa, the first five post-apartheid years saw over 7,000 new NPOs established (Swilling and Russell 2002). CIVICUS CSI reports for Egypt (CDS 2005), Ghana (Darkwa et al. 2006), Guinea (CNOSCG 2011), Nigeria (Action Aid Nigeria et al. 2007), Morocco (Akesbi 2011), Togo (FONGTO 2006), Uganda (DENIVA 2006), Zambia (ZCSD 2010), Mozambique (FDC 2008), Rwanda (CCOAIB 2011), Senegal (Mbaye 2011), Sierra Leone (CGG 2006), and Tanzania (ForDIA 2011) show comparable trends.

The significant growth of NPOs has been attributed partly to a crisis of legitimacy of the post-independence one-party African state. Specifically, the immediate post-independence colonial state applied coercive or co-optive strategies in systematically stifling alternative mass mobilization bases such as trades unions by integrating them into the single-party structures or military dictatorships of the time. Such usurpation resulted in single-party states that excluded large sections of citizens especially the intelligentsia, students and a wide array of urban educated professional middle classes. Some of these resorted to formation of radical underground resistance movements (Pinkney 1972; Mati 2012; Gyimah-Boadi et al. 2000).

Given significant personal risks to activists, to ensure their survival, the organizational structures of these underground movements mirrored those outlined in contingency theory which later saw them crystallize as pro-democracy movements that anchored on African shores in the late 1980s to early 1990s. Teaming up with religious organizations and professional associations (especially Bar) these movements morphed into aided forms of civil society organizations that underwrote the democratic transitions in many African countries (Nzomo 2003; Action Aid Nigeria et al. 2007; Darkwa et al. 2006; DENIVA 2006; CNOSCG 2011).

Contemporary NPO growth is also a product of global geopolitical and economic developments from the late 1980s after the fall of the Berlin Wall. Without the ideological encumbrances that had characterized development assistance during the Cold War, Western democracies started pegging aid to democratization, human rights and good governance goals (Mati 2014). On the economic front, the 1980s were characterized by decay of African states' capacity to deliver welfare services. This was driven by internal bureaucratic inefficiencies, dwindling support from external aid, and the neoliberal push towards markets as the primary sphere for meeting social and material needs of citizens. In the absence of reliable government safety nets, a plethora of NGOs emerged providing assistance to the poor (Action Aid Nigeria et al. 2007: 23). These were favoured by the same neoliberal forces in the global aid system which pushed NGOs as the magic sponges for absorbing the toxic effects of economic neoliberalism (Mati 2014, 2017; Ullman 1998 cited in Casey 2016). Many NGOs emerged aided by either external donors or development agencies, or as subsidiaries of international NPOs, often resulting in greater complexities of African nonprofit organizations, their relationships and management contexts. Additionally, a category of NPOs (mainly social movements) opposed to the effects of neoliberal economic policies also emerged (Mati 2014; Action Aid Nigeria et al. 2007).

With increasing prominence of new forms of nonprofits, demands for professionalization of their management and governance practices ensued. The initial impetus came from both governments and donors pushing NPOs to establish the first-generation institutional infrastructures (especially Codes of Conduct for NPOs) for enhancing accountability as well as maximization of impacts through establishing of networks (James and Malunga 2006; Mati 2009). Consequently, management ideas from the for-profit management scene found their way into discourses and practices on NPO management (Anheier 2000). These developments were possible largely because these new organizations, unlike their predecessors, had few linkages (if any) to African social bases and heavily relied on external sources of funding.

The increasing role of NGOs in the aid system in Africa defined the management context due to different expectations and their relationship with their funders, which include international NPOs development organizations, the state, citizens/beneficiaries and, increasingly today, the private sector (Lewis 2003; Gyimah-Boadi, et al. 2000). For example, internal nonprofit stakeholders (members, staff, volunteers, board members) have complex motivational structures and values – an interplay of altruistic and egotistical goals (Anheier 2000). In addition, NPOs have to address "interests and needs of clients who may not be in a position to reveal their preferences (e.g., people with disabilities, children and older people) nor able to pay prices that cover the cost of service delivery" (Anheier 2000: 6). All these aspects exert different types of demands to force organizations to borrow and improvise on their management styles (Lewis 2003).

Modern-day NPOs are "more complex than business firms of comparable size" (Anheier 2000: 7). They are often "several organisations or organisational components in one" (Handy 1988 cited in Anheier 2000: 7). For example, NPOs are:

> Markedly more secular and nonpartisan in their affiliations, more universalist in their service delivery and policy-making aspirations, and more professionalized and commercialized in their operations than earlier iterations rooted in religious charity, political movements, or grassroots collective and voluntary action.
>
> *(Casey 2016: 188)*

This complexity goes hand in hand with a need for concomitant evolution of their management practices. We turn next to analysing the socio-political and economic environmental complexity shaping the management of NPOs in Africa.

Socio-political and economic environment

The salience of the socio-political and economic environment in shaping the NPO management context is captured by, among others, Lewis (2001: 3) who argues that NPO management challenges emanate from the "types of roles and strategies being undertaken by different kinds of NGOs in the struggle against poverty." For example, "efforts to catalyse social, economic and political change processes at the level of group or individual action" are more contentious and result in tensions with the state (Lewis 2001: 3; see also Oyugi 2004 for similar arguments). Arguing along the same lines Obadare (2014: 1) observes that "both the discourse and the advocacy of civil society has often been at cross purposes." This is illustrated in a "co-operation and rebuff" relationship between the state and nonprofits (Ndegwa 1996: 10; Bratton 1989) where states embrace certain organizations as "partners in development" but hostile to those involved in political advocacy.

Certain nonprofits therefore operate in difficult environments often riddled with "multiple externalities that make straightforward transactions [or activities] more precarious and ... perhaps even inequitable" (Anheier 2000: 7). In Egypt, for example, even before the February 2011 revolution that overthrew Hosni Mubarak's regime, the relationship between government and NPOs was an ambiguous one. Yet, government narrative suggested that it worked with nonprofits to address social challenges in Egyptian society (CDS 2005). In fact, the government was the single-most contributor of NPOs' financial resources (34 per cent). However, government excluded NPOs dealing with democracy and human rights issues in their funding (CDS 2005).

The other extreme of this ambiguity is illustrated in Nigeria, Morocco, Uganda, Mozambique, Tanzania, Senegal and Guinea where governments' support for NPOs remains insignificant compared to other sources of funding (cf. Action Aid Nigeria et al. 2007; Akesbi 2011; CNOSCG 2011; DENIVA 2006: FDC 2007; ForDIA 2011; Mbaye 2011). The few that receive government support in Nigeria, for instance, are perceived by other organizations as co-opted by the government (Action Aid et al. 2007).

Legal environment and coercive isomorphism

The relationship between NPOs and the state is defined not just by cooperation or support or lack thereof. Across Africa, state-induced coercive isomorphism in NPO management is pervasive. Many countries have Acts of Parliament or Executive Decrees that govern registration and operations of NPOs (USAID 2016; see also various CIVICUS CSI reports and Freedom House reports[4] for examples). In addition, the legal-regulatory environment dictates the allowable practices in, for more example, the hiring of international staff (e.g., whether entitled to equal pay or not), registration frameworks, tax regimes and allowable (legitimate) management practices.

In Kenya, for instance, formal NPOs must meet stringent registration, operational and management requirements, including the recruitment of any foreign staff, their duties and staff remuneration as laid down in the recent Public Benefit Organizations (PBO) Act (2013) and earlier in the NGO Co-ordination Act (1990). Interestingly, there has been widespread support of the PBO Act especially by some local NGO workers as it is deemed that it will have an equalizing effect especially as it requires equal treatment (e.g., on salaries) of expatriates and local staff. However, the Act remains in limbo six years after its enactment. This is due to the ruling regime's hostility towards governance and human rights NGOs. The regime continues to rely on the 1990 NGO Co-ordination Act to harass these NPOs (The Observatory of Human Rights Defenders 2018).

In Guinea, though the state is alive to the idea of an independent civil society, occasional illegal government interventions occur. The Ministry of Interior and Political Affairs has to vet and approve any organization before registration; those considered anti-establishment are denied registration (CNOSCG 2011). As such, many NPOs are forced to kowtow to state-dictated managerial and operational requirements.

Coercive isomorphism has become particularly pronounced in the post 9–11 War on Terror era with increasing securitization of aid, demands for bureaucratization of NPO management and the tightening of regulatory frameworks. For authoritarian regimes in Africa, these global developments are the perfect scapegoats for establishing more restrictions especially against externally funded advocacy NPOs. In Ethiopia, for instance, NGOs involved in human rights advocacy are restricted from receiving external funding; and those receiving foreign funding are registered as foreign NPOs and therefore cannot partake in human rights work (USAID 2016).

State regulation also impacts on tax benefit status for NPOs as well as tax credit incentives for local donations (both individual and corporate) and, by extension, affects fundraising opportunities and the nature of allowable/legitimate activities and projects. In Togo, for example, every association has to be accredited by the Ministry of Home Affairs and Security before it can register with the Ministry of Territorial Management and Development which further evaluates the specifications of the NGO and accords it tax benefits (FONGTO 2006). In most African countries, tax credit incentives for local giving are non-existent (Mati 2017).

The above-mentioned factors impact mainly on those NPOs that depend on extra-membership support to fund their operations and not the small mainly informal NPOs that rely on membership dues, or those operating as social enterprises that survive on service fees. The NPOs affected by these factors constantly adjust their management practices, organizational structure and capacities to meet state and, as we will soon see, donor demands. While donor conditions may be based on a desire for accountability, especially given numerous reports of dark-side practices of NPOs (Smith et al. 2016), African states desirous to dominate have crafted disenabling regimes of governmentalities. Various CIVICUS CSI reports suggest that most NPOs are 'coerced' into particular managerialism dictated by states and donors due to their financial and other resource dependency. Government regulations, as do donor requirements, therefore shape, among other practices, organization's management culture, accountability and modes of popular participation (Beddoe and Maidment 2009; Anheier 2000).

Resourcing and managing resources

While sources of funding support for NPOs are theoretically diverse (ranging from government, business sector, foreign agencies, individuals, membership fees and fees from services), most organizations in Africa rely predominantly on external donors. NGOs are particularly dependent on external donor funds. Exceptions to this are the informal traditional associations, professional associations, trade unions and faith-based groups financed largely from membership fees, or service-fee charging organizations especially in healthcare and education sector. This has created conditions for external resource dependency, and by extension created conditions for donors to influence management of NPOs across Africa (ForDIA 2011; CGG 2006; CCOAIB 2011; FDC 2008; Akesbi 2011; FONGTO 2006; DENIVA 2006; ZCSD 2010).

As African NPOs face greater funding uncertainty, they have become more beholden to external donors for their survival and, by extension, donor-imposed managerial conditions (Fowler 1997; Van Rooy 1998; Pfeffer and Salancik 1978; Anheier 2000; Malatesta and Smith

2014) due to traditional power asymmetries between the giver and receiver in these arrangements. To survive, NGOs conform to management practices and accountabilities demanded by their donors (ZCSD 2010; Frenkel 2008 cited in Claeyé 2012; FCD 2006).

Such imposition by donors and internalization of the managerialist discourse of the international aid system can also result in managerial mimicry (Claeyé 2012; Maier 2011; Roberts et al. 2005; Wallace et al. 2006). This mimicry results because NPOs feel coerced to donor reporting requirements, while organizations do not fully buy into the ethics and cultures of what they are subscribing to or doing. This mimicry, Claeyé (2012: 162 citing Bhabha 1984: 126) argues, "is constructed around ambivalence . . . in order to be effective, mimicry must continually produce its slippage, its excess, its difference . . . As such, it constructs a subject that is almost the same, but not quite." Managerial mimicry, therefore, is a dynamic process of translation and appropriation, of interpretation and reconfiguration of managerialist discourse mediated through cultural lens. Its outcomes are "hybrid ways of managing that seek to reconcile Western instrumental rationality with an African way of being" (Claeyé 2012: 162). In effect, African NPO management involves construction of an object that is a new hybrid that can no longer be traced back to its "authentic 'roots'" (Frenkel 2008 cited in Claeyé 2012: 163). Mimetic isomorphism is the name Powell and DiMaggio (1991) gives to this managerial mimicry.

Self-regulation and industry standards

Self-regulation initiatives have also shaped the nature and context of NPO management especially of professional associations and, more recently, NGOs in Africa. Here, self-regulation initiatives are prototype normative isomorphism when driven by normative ideals of the types of preferred or legitimate behaviours that associations themselves create. Self-regulation works better for professional associations because the predominant practice model has been for individual accreditation as opposed to organizational accreditation or licensing. However, there are emergent organizational self-regulation initiatives especially among NGOs. These have often been mimetic decoys for forestalling external regulation (especially government-imposed) (Heinrich et al. 2008). In this case, NGOs voluntarily subscribe to self-regulation ideals and mechanisms such as codes of conduct promising to freely adhere to set governance and management practices, but the actually existing management practices are mimetic (Claeyé 2012). Several CIVICUS CSI country reports point to such mimicry despite the existence of first-generation self-accountability mechanisms whose performances have been disappointing, often with "little real impact on organizational practices because of their voluntary nature" (Heinrich et al. 2008: 335; FONGTO 2006; CDS 2005; DENIVA 2006).

While a majority of NGOs' self-regulation mechanisms are driven by donor and state legal conditions, a number of self-regulation initiatives have also been driven by normative accountability imperatives. This is best illustrated in countries lacking self-regulation but that feel the need for it. For some though, this desire is based on the fear that the accountability noose will tighten soon because both donors and governments are calling for the tightening of the rudimentary and weak accountability practices in the sector (see for example CIVICUS CSI reports for Nigeria, Rwanda, Ghana and Tanzania).

Although self-regulation is criticized as ineffective in arresting aberrations in NGO management and operations (see for example CDS 2005: 32) it has nonetheless been popular and instrumental in shaping management context by stipulating minimum standards of allowable managerial practices for NPOs. In Guinea, for example, CIVICUS CSI data shows that 62.5 per cent of NGOs adhere to self-regulation mechanisms, which "include a manual of administrative and accounting procedures and an internal code of conduct. These are additional to any requirements entailed in the official organizational registration by the state" (CNOSCG 2011: 23).

In addition to codes of conduct, in some countries NPOs have developed second-generation self-regulation and industry best practices in areas such as results measurement and accreditation. For example, Zimbabwe advocacy NGOs developed the *Advocacy Index* as a managerial monitoring, evaluation and reporting tool. The Moroccan CIVICUS CSI reported a combination of normative and coercive isomorphism where NPOs have adapted to undertaking internal auditing as this gives them the advantage in clarifying relations between public authorities and organizations and, at the same time, improving the accountability of decision-making (Akesbi 2011). Akesbi (2011: 74) notes that the adoption of internal auditing standards was necessary since "CSOs manage important budgets, often in conditions of insufficient transparency, relying only on people's will to ensure ethical practice is not enough." Internal auditing standards therefore meet two goals: legal regulations requirements and self-governmentality.

In some countries, NPOs, probably pushing towards higher normative isomorphism, have moved to set standards and accreditation mechanisms. Kenya with Viwango[5] and Uganda with NGO Quality Assurance Mechanism (QuAM)[6] are some leading examples that require specific management and governance parameters that NGOs must meet to be accredited. The push for these initiatives has been 'dark side' practices blemishing the sector. As such, like their predecessors, these second-generation self-regulation tools are reactionary. However, as we will see below, they are also products of nonprofit mimetic appropriation of mechanisms borrowed from private sector self-regulatory frameworks.

Nonprofits and market-inspired management practices

Many market-based ideas prevalent in the private sector have been imported into the nonprofit sector. Some of the practices have been introduced as part of funding arrangements from the private sector, while others have been imposed by other funding forces. Other corporate managerial practices have found their way into nonprofits through what Anheier (2000) calls copy-cutting to deal with the uncertainty created by financial resource precarity. In this context,

> Organisations in distress look for outside models they perceive as successful and promising (DiMaggio and Powell, 1983) ... "successful" models are more likely assumed to be found in the more self-confident world of business than among governments that have grown insecure about their role in society. Nonprofit organisations, therefore, look more to for-profit corporations and commercial enterprises for management tools and models in the hope of finding solutions to real or perceived financial challenges.
>
> *(Anheier 2000: 4)*

The impact of this corporate orientation to NPOs management, Anheier (2000: 4) argues, is that "management of nonprofit organizations frequently means financial management" because the source of uncertainty for NPOs is primarily seen as financial. This means, first and foremost, prioritizing management practices that "improve financial accountability and reporting ... and adaptation of fundraising and other practices to diversify revenue" (Anheier 2000: 5). These practices have resulted into fundamental contradictions whose central import for Africa is the tendency to forget value motivations that are as important as financial resources in driving NPOs (Anheier 2000).

Challenges and opportunities ahead

In the last decade, Africa's economic situation has greatly improved, leading to development of indigenous foundations resourcing NPOs that hitherto depended on external sources of funding (Mati 2017; Atibil 2013; Wilkinson-Maposa et al. 2005; AGN 2013). Community foundations for instance, have emerged across several countries (*Community Foundations Atlas* 2018).[7] However, the number of politically oriented foundations with dubious public integrity records have also increased. Such foundations have been conduits for neopatrimonialism, laundering ill-gotten wealth and stealing from the civic public and distributing some of the loot to the primordial public (Mati 2017). As these foundations do not necessarily care about integrity or sound management, some of the gains made towards NPOs managerial integrity might be eroded. A related threat is the increase in politically motivated repression targeted at politically purposed NPOs. In Kenya, for example, accounts of several foundations of leading opposition figures were frozen in the lead up to the 2017 election over what the state indicated were questionable transactions (Mosoku 2017; Thiong'o 2017).

Revenue generated from external donors continues to diminish in the context of the War on Terror and especially after the 2008 financial crisis in the West. As Western donors lose clout while new funding sources emerge, these developments will affect the present management context. The jury is still out on the nature of the impacts of funding from these emergent sources.

On a positive note, higher rates of economic growth have meant a growing middle class and High Net Worth Individuals (HNWI) in the philanthropic landscape (AGN 2013; BoE Private Clients 2011). This, combined with increasing diaspora remittances (Copeland-Carson 2007; Adelman 2009), means that a diversified source of funding is emerging. In addition, innovations in NPOs through social investments offer opportunities for some currently donor-dependent NPOs to reduce levels of dependency and even transition towards self-sustainability (Fowler 2002). For example, the Kenya Red Cross Society investments in building and running hotels have transformed the financial status of the society (KTN News 2013). Such organizations join church-run education institutions, hospitals and healthcare centres across Africa that traditionally raise revenue through services.

Another development is an increase in formal volunteering in the continent which calls for greater attention to management of volunteers as a resource. The recent wave of volunteer management charters and policies established across several countries attests to some emergent changes in the volunteer management context (Graham et al. 2013: 21). Even then, there are gaps in how market-oriented models such as voluntourism and employee volunteering are managed and its implications to the larger sector.

The question then is, what have been the impacts of these developments on the NPO management context in Africa? With increasing numbers of HNWI, it is hoped that African governments will ultimately reform the tax and legal environment with a view to encourage private and corporate giving. A number of countries have already enacted laws for guiding corporate social responsibility (Mati 2017). However, even with the new opportunities, the obsession with the promotion of Euro-American management styles in formal organizations has meant that the African NPO management mimics that of the West. This is reinforced by African foundations and HNWI borrowing scripts from the West in their grant-giving conditions. As such African NPOs will continue to account to their benefactors, be they local or foreign in origin. Resource dependency will therefore continue to determine the direction of African NPOs accountability.

Conclusion

There are multiple theoretical perspectives with varying saliences in explaining the nonprofit management context in Africa. This chapter has shown that the NPO management context in Africa is shaped first by the history and context of its production. Second, as elsewhere in the world, African NPOs operate in complex environments where core constituencies have different expectations and complex motivational structures that require a dynamic management context.

The nature of the regulatory environment (government and self-regulation) and the nature of the source of nonprofits' resources are other factors shaping the nonprofit management context in Africa. These, coupled with values (normative dimension) and strategic dimensions (e.g., resources for continued survival of the organizations and meeting competing demands of multiple stakeholders) define opportunities and constraints confronting NPOs as part of the larger political economy (Anheier 2000: 9) and therefore shape the management context for African NPOs. Finally, management is confronted with demands for "everyday functioning of organizations, such as administration and accounting, personnel and service-delivery" (Anheier 2000: 9). The interaction of these factors and demands indicates complex management imperatives that take into account the complexities of the operating environment, demands upon organizations, and the diversity of value orientations within and outside the organization (Anheier 2000). The result is a hybrid African NPO management practice.

Notes

1 CIVICUS CSI has been implemented in Egypt, Ghana, Guinea, Liberia, Morocco, Mozambique, Nigeria, Rwanda, Sierra Leone, South Africa, Tanzania, Togo, Uganda and Zambia. Various versions of CSI have been implemented more than once in some of these countries.
2 The Johns Hopkins Comparative Nonprofit Sector Study has been implemented in Egypt, Ghana, Kenya, Morocco, South Africa, Tanzania and Uganda.
3 By 2018, USAID CSO Sustainability Index had been implemented in at least 34 African countries including Burkina Faso, Burundi, Côte d'Ivoire, Democratic Republic of Congo, Egypt, Ethiopia, Gabon, Gambia, Ghana, Guinea, Kenya, Liberia, Madagascar, Mali, Malawi, Morocco, Mozambique, Namibia, Niger, Nigeria, Rwanda, Senegal, Sierra Leone, South Africa, Sudan, Tanzania, Togo, Uganda, Zambia and Zimbabwe. The USAID CSO Sustainability Index has been implemented for at least three rounds in some of these countries.
4 https://freedomhouse.org/report/freedom-world/freedom-world-2018
5 www.viwango.org
6 http://ngoforum.or.ug/quam
7 http://communityfoundationatlas.org/explore/#directory=1 | continent=Africa (Accessed February 10, 2018).

References

ActionAid Nigeria, DevNet, CIVICUS & UNDP. (2007) *Civil Society in Nigeria: Contribution to Positive Social Change*. CIVICUS Civil Society Index Report. https://www.issuelab.org/resources/19687/19687.pdf [Accessed 1 February 2018].
Adelman, C. (2009) Global Philanthropy and Remittances: Reinventing Foreign Aid, *Brown Journal of World Affairs*, 15 (2): 23–33.
African Grantmakers Network (AGN). (2013) *Sizing the Field: Frameworks for a New Narrative of African Philanthropy*. Johannesburg: African Grantmakers Network & Southern Africa Trust.
Aina, T. (2013) The State, Politics and Philanthropy in Africa: Framing the Context. In Aina, T. and Moyo, B. (eds.). *Giving to Help, Helping to Give: The Context and Politics of African Philanthropy*. Dakar: Amalion Press, 1–36.

Akesbi, A. (2011) *CIVICUS Civil Society Index Analytical Country Report for Morocco.* https://www.civicus. org/downloads/CSI/Morocco.pdf [Accessed 12 December 2019].

Akue, N.A.G. & Coulibaly, B. (2004) *Rapport de Conférence sur la Société Civile au Togo: Définition du Concept et État Des Lieux.* Lomé: Université de Lomé.

Anheier, H.K. (2000) *Managing Nonprofit Organisations: Towards a New Approach.* Civil Society Working Paper 1, LSE. http://eprints.lse.ac.uk/29022/1/cswp1.pdf [Accessed 1 February 2018].

Atibil, C.L. (2013) *Does It Matter Where the Money Comes From? African Civil Society and the Question of Dependency on Foreign Donors: Implications for Citizen Participation and Sustainability.* Paper presented at the ISTR/Africa Network Conference, Nairobi, Kenya, July 11–13, 2013.

Beddoe, L & Maidment, J. (2009) *Mapping Knowledge for Social Work Practice.* Melbourne: Cencage Learning.

Bereketeab, R. (2009) Conceptualizing Civil Society in Africa: The Case of Eritrea. *Journal of Civil Society,* 5 (1): 35–59.

Bhabha, H. (1984) Of Mimicry and Man: The Ambivalence of Colonial Discourse. *Discipleship: A Special Issue on Psychoanalysis,* 28: 125–133.

Bhabha, H.K. (1994) *The Location of Culture.* London: Routledge.

Blaney, D.L. & Pasha, M.K. (1993) Civil Society and Democracy in the Third World: Ambiguities and Historical Possibilities. *Studies in Comparative International Development,* 28 (1): 3–24.

BoE Private Clients. (2011) *The Giving Report 2010: A Survey on the Philanthropy Practices of High Net Worth Individuals in South Africa: Summary Results,* https://www.nedbankprivatewealth.co.za/nedbank_ wealth/action/media/downloadFile?media_fileid=369 [Accessed 1 February 2018].

Bratton, M. (1989) The Politics of Government-NGO in Africa. *World Development,* 17 (4): 569–587.

Campaign for Good Governance (CGG). (2006) *A Critical Time for Civil Society in Sierra Leone: A CIV-ICUS Civil Society Index Report for the Republic of Sierra Leone.* www.civicus.org/media/CSI_SierraLe one_Country_Report.pdf [Accessed 30 August 2017].

Casey, J. (2016) Comparing Nonprofit Sectors Around the World: What Do We Know and How Do We Know It? *Journal of Nonprofit Education and Leadership,* 6 (3): 187–223.

Center for Development Services (CDS). (2005) *An Overview of Civil Society in Egypt: Civil Society Index Report for the Arab Republic of Egypt.* Johannesburg: CIVICUS.

Chabal, P. & Daloz, J. (1999) *Africa Works: Disorder as Political Instrument.* London: International African Institute.

Chan, S. (2002) *Composing Africa: Civil Society and Its Discontents.* Vol. 86 of Tampere Peace Research Institute, Occasional papers. Tampere: Tampere Peace Research Institute.

Claeyé, F. (2012) Contextualising Non-profit Management in Sub-Sahara Africa: Understanding Cross-cultural Interaction at the Global/Local Interface. *African Journal of Economic and Management Studies,* 3 (2): 159–183.

Comaroff, J.L. & Comaroff, J. (eds.). (1999) *Civil Society and the Political Imagination in Africa: Critical Perspectives.* Chicago: University of Chicago Press.

Community Foundations. (2018) *Community Foundations Atlas* http://communityfoundationatlas.org/ explore/#directory=1|continent=Africa [Accessed 10 February 2018].

Conseil de Concertation des Organisations d'Appui aux Initiatives de Base (CCOAIB) (2011) *The State of Civil Society in Rwanda in National Development: Civil Society Index Rwanda Report.* https://www.civicus. org/downloads/CSI/Rwanda.pdf [Accessed 12 December 2019].

Conseil National des Organisations de la Société Civile Guinéenne (CNOSCG). (2011) *Guinean Civil Society: Between Activity and Impact.* CIVICUS Civil Society Index for Guinea. www.civicus.org/images/ stories/csi/csi_phase2/guinea%20acr.pdf [Accessed 30 August 2017].

Copeland-Carson, J. (2007) *Kenyan Diaspora Philanthropy: Key Practices, Trends and Issues.* Prepared for the Philanthropic Initiative, Inc. and the Global Equity Initiative, Harvard University.

Corry, O. (2010) Defining and Theorizing the Third Sector. In Taylor, R. (ed.). *Third Sector Research.* New York: Springer, 11–20.

Darkwa, A., Amponsah, N., & Gyampoh, E. (2006) *Civil Society in a Changing Ghana: An Assessment of the Current State of Civil Society in Ghana.* Accra: CIVICUS and GAPVOD.

Development Network of Indigenous Voluntary Associations (DENIVA) (2006) *Civil Society in Uganda: At the Crossroads?* www.civicus.org/media/CSI_Uganda_Country_Report.pdf [Accessed 12 December 2019].

Ekeh, P. (1992) Constitution of Civil Society in African History and Publics. In Caron, B., Gboyega, E., & Osaghae, E. (eds.). *Democratic Transition in Africa.* Ibadan: CREDU, 187–212.

FONGTO. (2006) *A Diagnostic Study of Togolese Civil Society*. www.civicus.org/media/CSI_Togo_Coun try_Report.pdf [Accessed 30 August 2017].

ForDIA. (2011) *Civil Society Index (CSI) Project Tanzania Country Report 2011. CIVICUS CSI Analytical Country Report for Tanzania*. www.civicus.org/downloads/CSI/Tanzania.pdf [Accessed 30 August 2017].

Foundation for Community Development (FDC). (2008) *Mozambican Civil Society Within: Evaluation, Challenges, Opportunities and Action*. www.civicus.org/media/CSI_Mozambique_Country_Report.pdf [Accessed 30 August 2017].

Fowler, A. (1997) *Striking a Balance: A Guide to Enhancing the Effectiveness of Non-Governmental Organisations in International Development*. London: Earthscan.

Fowler, A. (2002) NGOs as a Moment in History: Beyond Aid to Social Entrepreneurship or Civic Innovation?, *Third World Quarterly*, 21 (4): 637–654.

Fowler, A. and Mati, J.M. (2019) African Gifting: Pluralising the Concept of Philanthropy. *Voluntas*, 30(4): 724–737. DOI 10.1007/s11266-018-00079-z.

Gellner, E. (1994) *Conditions of Liberty: Civil Society and Its Rivals*. London: Allen Lane.

Graham, L., Patel, L., Ulriksen, M., Moodley, J., & Mavungu, E.M. (2013) *Volunteering in Africa: An Overview of Volunteer Effort in Africa and Its Potential to Contribute to Development*. https://www.uj.ac.za/faculties/humanities/csda/Documents/Research%20Report%20_%20Volunteering%20in%20Africa. pdf [Accessed 4 September 2017].

Gyimah-Boadi, E., Oquaye, M., & Drah, K. (2000) *Civil Society Organisations and Ghanaian Democratization*. CDD Ghana Research Paper No. 6. Accra: CDD-Ghana.

Heinrich, V.F. (2005) Studying Civil Society Across the World: Exploring the Thorny Issues of Conceptualization and Measurement. *Journal of Civil Society*, 1 (3): 211–228.

Heinrich, V.F., Mati, J.M., & Brown, L.D. (2008) The Varying Contexts for Civil Society Accountability: Insights from a Global Analysis of Country Level Assessments. In Heinrich, V.F. & Fioramonti, L. (eds.). *CIVICUS Global Survey on the State of Civil Society. Volume 2: Comparative Perspectives*. West Hartford, CT: Kumarian, 325–340.

James, R. & Malunga, C. (2006) Organisational Challenges Facing Civil Society Networks in Malawi. *Knowledge Management for Development Journal*, 2 (2): 48–63.

Kanyinga, K., Mitullah, W.V., & Njagi, S. (2007). *The Nonprofit Sector in Kenya: Size, Scope, and Financing*. Nairobi: IDS, University of Nairobi.

Kostova, T., Roth, K., & Dacin, M.T. (2008) Institutional Theory in the Study of Multinational Corporations: A Critique and New Directions. *Academy of Management Review*, 33 (4): 994–1006.

KTN News. (2013) *Kenya Red Cross Opens International Hotel*, 9 January. https://www.youtube.com/watch?v=eq_gmGdSmjY [Accessed 18 January 2018].

Lewis, D. (2001) *The Management of Non-Governmental Development Organizations*. London: Routledge.

Lewis, D. (2003) Theorizing the Organization and Management of Non-governmental Development Organizations: Towards a Composite Approach. *Public Management Review*, 5 (3): 325–344.

Maier, F. (2011) Philanthropy and Nonprofit Leaders. Rise of the Business Model in Philanthropy. In Agard, K.A. (ed.). *Leadership in Nonprofit Organizations*. Thousand Oaks, CA: Sage, 484–490.

Maina, W. (1998) Kenya: The State, Donors and the Politics of Democratization. In Van Rooy, A. (ed.). *Civil Society and the Aid Industry*. London: Earthscan, 134–167.

Makumbe, J. (1998) *Democracy and Development in Zimbabwe: Constraints of Decentralisation*. Harare: SAPES Books.

Malatesta, D. & Smith. C.R. (2014) Lessons from Resource Dependence Theory for Contemporary Public and Nonprofit Management. *Public Administration Review*, 74 (1): 4–25.

Mamdani, M. (1995) A Critique of the State and Civil Society Paradigm in Africanist Studies. In Mamdani, M. & Wamba-dia-Wamba, E. (eds.). *African Studies in Social Movements and Democracy*. Dakar: CODESRIA, 602–616.

Mamdani, M. (1996) *Citizens and Subjects: Contemporary Africa and the Legacy of Late Colonialism*. Princeton, NJ: Princeton University Press.

Mati, J.M. (2009) A Cartography of a Global Civil Society Alliance: The Case of the Global Call to Action against Poverty (GCAP). *Journal of Civil Society*, 5 (1): 83–105.

Mati, J.M. (2012) *The Power and Limits of Social Movements in Promoting Political and Constitutional Change: The Case of the Ufungamano Initiative in Kenya (1999–2005)*. PhD Diss. Johannesburg: University of the Witwatersrand.

Mati, J.M. (2014) Neoliberalism and the Forms of Civil Society in Kenya and South Africa. In E. Obadare (ed.). *Handbook of Civil Society in Africa*. New York: Springer, 215–232.

Mati, J.M. (2015) Constraining Political Transformation: The Two Faces of Activist Religious Organizations in the Search for a New Constitution in Kenya. *Journal of Civil Society*, 11 (4): 348–365.

Mati, J.M. (2017) *Philanthropy in Contemporary Africa*. Leiden: Brill.

Mbaye, M. (2011) *Engaging Together for Real Change: CIVICUS Civil Society Index Analytical Country Report for Senegal*. www.civicus.org/downloads/CSI/Senegal.pdf [Accessed 10 December 2017].

Millen, B.C. (1963) *The Political Role of Labour in Developing Countries*. Washington, DC: The Brookings Institution.

Mosoku, G. (2017) Kalonzo Musyoka Foundation Accounts Frozen over Unaccounted Funds, *Standard Digital*, 3 May 2017, https://www.standardmedia.co.ke/business/article/2001238393/kalonzo-musyoka-foundation-in-trouble-over-unaccounted-funds [Accessed 1 February 2018].

Munson, Z. (2001) Islamic Mobilization: Social Movement Theory and the Egyptian Muslim Brotherhood. *Sociological Quarterly*, 42 (4): 487–510.

Mustapha, A.R. (1998) When Will Independence End? Democratization and Civil Society in Rural Africa. In Rudebeck, L., Törnquist O., & Rojas, V. (eds.). *Democratization in the Third World: Concrete Cases in Comparative and Theoretical Perspectives*. Basingstoke: Macmillan, 222–233.

Ndegwa, S. (1996) *The Two Faces of Civil Society: NGOs and Politics in Africa*. West Hartford, CT: Kumarian.

Nzomo, M. (2003) Civil Society in the Kenyan Political Transition: 1992–2002. In Oyugi, W.O., Wanyande, P., & Odhiambo-Mbai, C. (eds.). *The Politics of Transition in Kenya: From KANU to NARC*. Nairobi: Heinrich Böll Foundation, 180–211.

Obadare, E. (2004) Civil Society in West Africa between Discourse and Reality. In Glasius, M., Lewis, D., & Seckinelgin, H. (eds.). *Exploring Civil Society: Political and Cultural Contexts*. London: Routledge, 154–162.

Obadare, E. (2014) Introduction: Turning the Table on Gellner: Alternative Discourses of Civil Society in Africa. In Obadare, E. (ed.). *The Handbook of Civil Society in Africa. Nonprofit and Civil Society Studies*. New York: Springer, 1–3.

Oyugi, W.O. (2004) The Role of NGOs in Fostering Development and Good Governance at the Local Level in Africa with a Focus on Kenya. *Africa Development*, 39 (4): 19–55.

Page, M. & Sonnenburg, P. (2003) *Colonialism: An International, Social, Cultural, and Political Encyclopaedia, Volume 1*. Santa Barbara, CA: ABC-CLIO.

Pfeffer, J. & Salancik, G.R. (1978) *The External Control of Organizations: A Resource Dependence Perspective*. New York: Harper & Row.

Pinkney, R. (1972) *Ghana Under Military Rule, 1966–1969*. London: Methuen.

Powell, W.W. & DiMaggio, P.J. (eds) (1991) *The New Institutionalism in Organizational Analysis*. Chicago: University of Chicago Press.

Ranger, T.O. (2008) *Evangelical Christianity and Democracy in Africa*. Oxford: Oxford University Press.

Roberts, S.M., Jones, J.P. III, & Fröling, O. (2005) NGOs and the Globalization of Managerialism: A Research Framework. *World Development*, 33 (11): 1845–1864.

Salamon, L.M. (1994) The Rise of the Nonprofit Sector. *Foreign Affairs*, 73 (4): 109–122.

Salamon, L.M. & Anheier, H. (eds.). (1997) *Defining the Nonprofit Sector*. Manchester: Manchester University Press.

Salamon, L.M., Anheier, H K., List, R., Toepler, S., & Sokolowski, S.W. & Associates. (1999) *Global Civil Society. Dimensions of the Nonprofit Sector*. Baltimore, MD: The Johns Hopkins Center for Civil Society Studies.

Scott, R. (1967) Are Trade Unions Still Necessary in Africa?, *Transition*, 33: 27–31.

Smith, D.H., Eng, S., & Albertson, K. (2016) The Darker Side of Philanthropy: How Self-Interest and Incompetence Can Overcome a Love of Mankind and Serving the Public Interest. In Jung, T., Phillips, S., & Harrow, J. (eds.). *The Routledge Companion to Philanthropy*. London: Routledge, 273–286.

Swilling, M. & Russell, B. (2002) *The Size and Scope of the Nonprofit Sector in South Africa*. Johannesburg: Wits University and University of Natal.

The Observatory of Human Rights Defenders. (2018) Kenya: After Years of Broken Promises, Will the PBO Act Become More Than Paper Tiger? www.omct.org/files/2018/07/24955/kenya_briefing_note_july_2018.pdf [Accessed 4 November 2018].

Thiong'o, J. (2017) Governor Evans Kidero Foundation Permit Revoked. *Standard Digital*, 23 February, https://www.standardmedia.co.ke/article/2001230393/governor-evans-kidero-foundation-permit-revoked [Accessed 10 January 2018].

Toepler, S. & Anheier H.K. (2004) Organizational Theory and Nonprofit Management: An Overview. In Zimmer, A. & Priller, E. (eds.). *Future of Civil Society*. Wiesbaden: VS Verlag für Sozialwissenschaften, 253–270.

Ullman, C. (1998) *The welfare state's other crisis: Explaining the new partnership between nonprofit organizations and the state in France*. Bloomington: Indiana University Press.

USAID. (2016) *The 2014 CSO Sustainability Index for Sub-Saharan Africa*. https://www.usaid.gov/sites/default/files/documents/1866/2016_Africa_CSOSI_-_508.pdf [Accessed 10 January 2018].

Van Rooy, A. (1998) Civil Society as Idea: An Analytical Hatstand? In Van Rooy, A. (ed.). *Civil Society and the Aid Industry*, London: Earthscan, 6–30.

Wallace, T., Bornstein, L., & Chapman, J. (2006) *The Aid Chain: Coercion and Commitment in Development NGOs*. Rugby, Warwickshire: Intermediate Technology Publications.

Wilkinson-Maposa, S., Fowler, A., Oliver-Evans, C., & Mulenga, C.F. (2005) *The Poor Philanthropist*. http://us-cdn.creamermedia.co.za/assets/articles/attachments/02846_poor_philanthropist_screen.pdf [Accessed 12 December 2019].

Zahid, M. & Medley, M. (2006) Muslim Brotherhood in Egypt & Sudan. *Review of African Political Economy*, 33 (110): 693–708.

Zambian Council for Social Development (ZCSD). (2010) *The Status of Civil Society in Zambia: Challenges and Future Prospects*. http://civicus.org/downloads/CSI/Zambia.pdf [Accessed 12 January 2018].

9

THE LATIN AMERICAN CONTEXT

The challenge of managing advocacy and impact inclusion

Urs Jäger

ASSOCIATE PROFESSOR, INCAE BUSINESS SCHOOL AND ACADEMIC
DIRECTOR VIVA IDEA, COSTA RICA

Felipe Symmes

PHD CANDIDATE, UNIVERSITY OF ST. GALLEN, SWITZERLAND, AND SENIOR
RESEARCHER VIVA IDEA, COSTA RICA

Roberto Gutiérrez

ASSOCIATE PROFESSOR, SCHOOL OF MANAGEMENT, UNIVERSIDAD
DE LOS ANDES, BOGOTÁ, COLOMBIA

This chapter uses the lens of "path dependency" (Ghezzi and Mingione, 2007), which assumes that future nonprofit organizations' (NPOs) management challenges partially depend on past developments. It outlines the evolution of NPOs' "role and function" (Tönnies, 2002/1887) over time and their respective management challenges in Latin America. Despite the wide and highly complex social structures in 33 Latin American countries, we generally deduce patterns of management challenges from the complex socio-economic and political history of Latin American countries, and specifically explore the importance of "inclusion" in NPO management.

Inclusion can be understood as a right (Gómez-Quintero, 2013), or it can be considered the result of initiatives that positively impact excluded populations (Vidal, 2005; Akaah, 1992; Fujimoto et al., 2014). Both perspectives on inclusion define different NPOs' roles and functions. In what we call *advocacy inclusion*, NPOs adopt a political role to claim the right of excluded groups to obtain access to resources of states and/or powerful elites; in what we call *impact inclusion*, NPOs assume an economic or social role and function to directly increase the life quality of excluded groups. In this chapter, we argue that Latin American NPOs have historical roots in managing advocacy inclusion, and have recently begun to strengthen their role and function in impact inclusion, which manifests in the rising discussion on social economy, social enterprise, social entrepreneurship, and cross-sectorial partnership (Gutiérrez et al., 2016; Austin et al., 2004; Ogliastri et al., 2016).

Our proposal is in line with development institutions, as we consider "inclusion" to be an essential challenge of functioning societies (World Bank, 2013). Our focus on "inclusion," therefore, differs from recent civil society literature that discusses inclusion mainly in relation to employment inclusion within companies (Nishii, 2013) of people with disabilities (Fujimoto et al., 2014), inclusion in the area of social enterprises (Vidal, 2005; Austin et al., 2006), inclusion of small and medium size enterprises into established markets (ECLAC, 2011), or inclusion as an ethical issue (Akaah, 1992).

The reason why the literature does not discuss "inclusion" as an essential challenge of functioning societies has contextual roots. Mainstream research on civil society generally refers to countries in the developed world where the emergence of the state and market institutions grew over centuries, and led to functioning democratic institutions that include marginalized groups. In these developed countries, the current discussion on the development of civil societies is characterized by blurring sectorial borders where NPOs include business-oriented practices or even market-oriented business models into their management (Evers, 2005). As a consequence, over the last 15 years, the literature on NPOs increasingly explored management challenges in hybrid organizations (Jäger and Schröer, 2013).

We argue that the emergence of organized civil society and therefore nonprofit organizations in European countries differs to Latin American history, where societies suffer from weak or non-functioning democratic institutions and informal markets, and accordingly large parts of the population are excluded from societal benefits (Ciravegna et al., 2013). This difference implies a theoretical shift from "blurring sectorial borders and hybrid organizations" – as discussed in regards to developed countries – to what we call "advocacy and impact inclusion" (Figure 9.1).

This theoretical shift has historical roots. Many Latin American countries were constructed formally as independent states during the first half of the 19th century. In most parts of the region, privileged families with Spanish roots (the "criollos") led this process of independence where European institutional structures "overlaid" (Rustow, 1980) Latin American cultures.

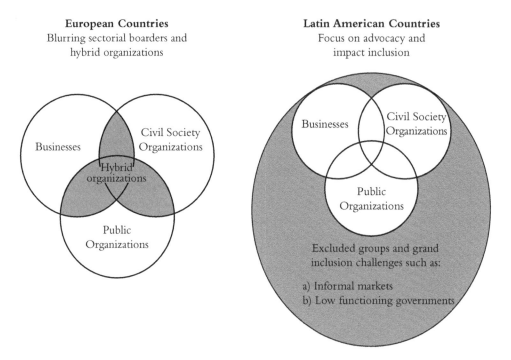

Figure 9.1   Focus on hybrid organizations and focus on inclusion

Market and democratic institutions that permit the emergence of the voice of minorities in public decisions did not arise due to this process. Furthermore, whereas Europe had a relatively long period of time to establish its democratic institutions, Latin America has had to develop its institutions in a "historical snapshot."

After independence, privileged groups that benefited from the overlaid institutions reproduced the colonial order without public spaces or democratic cultures, and conditioned an almost nonexistent organized civil society sector (Olvera, 1998). The cause of this goes back to the constitutional laws of Latin American countries, which were not constructed in relation to social needs, but rather copied directly from already established European constitutions and laid over their socio-economic structures and cultures (Touraine, 1988). Political and economic institutions were created following the schemes of European nation-states. The foreign and decontextualized solutions overlying Latin American structures and cultures led to systems with weak institutional support and with large portions of actors excluded from the process of development. In current times, a high number of groups are still excluded from institutional mechanisms. This has led to a society that is – in the present day – one of the most unequal in the world (Jäger and Sathe, 2014; Nicholls-Nixon et al., 2011).

As we will show below, Latin American NPOs emerged to politically and structurally counteract the process of the elites accumulating wealth and power. At first, networks of charities related to the Catholic Church, mainly of Jesuit influence, supported the advocacy inclusion of excluded groups. Then, in the first half of the 20th century, although the Catholic Church remained in an important role, NPOs were more related with the political struggles of the time and the demands from the excluded groups for more participation in the economic system. In the last two decades many NPOs transformed their role and function from advocacy to impact inclusion, as it became important to include those in poverty in centralized welfare systems, and informal market participants or first-nation tribes into formal market structures.

In this chapter, we show that Latin American countries are characterized by the historically rooted exclusion of groups, mainly due to limited functioning institutions. Two questions guided our analysis: *How have NPOs been contributing to reduce the inequality by advocacy and impact inclusion? And, what can we learn from the Latin American context about their future management challenges?*

We present an analysis of the history, governance, legal structures and tax benefits, collaborative endeavors, management issues, and current trends that illustrate how NPOs transformed from advocacy to impact inclusion. This transformation and the historical roots in advocacy inclusion explain the current NPO management challenges that we outline in the final section as programmatic questions.

NPOs' historical roots and the rise of advocacy inclusion

Already in the beginning of the 16th century, NPOs initiated inclusive activities based on charity and mainly occurred through European missionaries associated with the Catholic Church. Decisions about working areas and sectors for NPOs depended on the historical moments in each country (Agurto and Piña, 1988). Under the auspices of the Catholic Church, ideas and practices regarding charity and benevolence were spread during the 17th and 18th centuries in the American Spanish colonies (Landim and Thompson, 1997). Charity, usually in religious guise, provided relief to the poor, the needy, and the excluded. It also served as the key instrument for the evangelization of native tribes, imposing inclusion on groups with strong cultural ties that generally did not want to be included in formal structures of the Spanish colonies. Until the mid-19th century, the Church ran most of the educational, health, and social services organizations. As the independence movements of the first decades of that century took place, the provision of social services passed (at least in part) from the Church to governments.

Politicization of NPOs

With the advent of the 20th century, and still based on the notion of charity, the prevalent intention of NPO work was to empower the poor through education and economic support (Gómez, 1992). Although mutual benefits, self-help, and self-managed NPOs proliferated throughout the region (Landim and Thompson, 1997), Latin American societies' political processes mainly led to the rise of NPOs focusing on advocacy inclusion.

The Mexican Revolution (1910–1920) was the first inflection point in the politicization of NPOs. They claimed inclusion as a political right and turned away from focusing on services that supported the poor and excluded groups in obtaining access to secure housing, jobs, and other services. Different social movements started to claim social and civil rights for excluded actors. Most of them proposed local and national political structures that allowed more political participation of excluded actors and that opposed the dominant oligarchic–capitalistic structures. Workers organized themselves in unions and gained bargaining power, rural actors claimed more prominence and benefits in the national processes of development, and the "zapatistas" began demanding political autonomy and rights for endogenous processes of development.

During the 1960s in many Latin American countries, and likely inspired by the Mexican Revolution, different NPOs contributed to a common political discourse that offered an alternative to the elite-driven model. On the one hand, rural inhabitants started to organize and pushed for changes that could give them priority in public policies (Gómez, 1985). This process reduced the importance of "haciendas" (manors) as the rural economic power. On the other hand, in cities, construction workers, industrial workers, employees in service industries, and the unemployed started to realize that their political struggles were quite similar to the ones in rural areas; therefore, they also started to take on political advocacy roles and functions, which strengthened the coordination between rural and urban NPOs (Valdés, 1986).

The cooperative movement was also important at the time. For example, in Chile mainly European immigrants created cooperatives and financial and mutual relief funds during the rural–urban migration and industrialization of the 1950s (Gatica, 2017). After the 1960s and in parallel with the rise of NPOs, cooperatives experienced a boom as governments and the Catholic Church set up development promotion programs to include informal – mostly agricultural – producers in a formal structure and to strengthen their market power.

In many Latin American countries, governmental authorities and economic elites tried to hinder the emergence of these NPOs that were advocating for political inclusion from urban and rural areas. However, wherever NPOs were able to garner support from the state or from important actors like the Catholic Church, they participated in structural reforms, especially in rural areas (Gómez, 1985). A major part of their struggle was against social and economic dependency from the developed world (Cardoso, 1976); another part aimed for social consciousness and liberation, as the education movement led by Paulo Freire illustrates (Freire, 1970). Some of these struggles promoted local development with grassroots leadership (Gómez-Quintero, 2013). Grassroots organizations (e.g., neighborhood boards) became legitimized local power bases and, on occasions (for example, in the case of Chile), acted in the role and function of a local government (Valdés, 1986). Different political parties and even military regimes (such as that of Alvarado in Peru) promoted reforms that intended to diversify economic production and give more political participation to excluded groups and grassroots organizations.

Emergence of advocacy NPOs under rising populism and authoritarian regimes

From the 1960s onward, the rise of populism and authoritarian regimes[1] in Latin America further strengthened NPOs oriented toward advocacy inclusion (Touraine, 1988). Populism had pushed civil society to organize in a vertical, corporatist way, while authoritarian prohibitions forced the emergence of semi-legal anti-governmental organizations and guerrilla movements. In both cases, the capability of citizens to intervene in public causes were restricted (Landim and Thompson, 1997). In the 1970s, during the military dictatorships in Argentina, Bolivia, Chile, and Uruguay, cooperatives were repressed as well, and were eliminated by dictatorships or became controlled by popular movements.

NPOs then began to organize social protests, obtaining support from foreign organizations to defend human rights and civic participation and to construct opposition movements (Gómez, 1992). These organizations also aimed to solve problems of poverty that increased with cuts in social spending and neoliberal economic approaches. Most of the advocacy NPOs, especially those defending human rights, were strongly supported by the Catholic Church (Morello, 2012).

Due to their fight against authoritarian military regimes, Latin American NPOs became internationally popular (Cohen and Arato, 2000; Sorj, 2007). In countries like Mexico and Colombia, NPOs transitioned from social invisibility to an increasing presence in social and political realms (Gómez-Quintero, 2013). Notwithstanding the heterogeneous nature of NPOs, the common objective of fighting for democracy united many.

NPOs in search of an impact-oriented role and function

During the 1990s, as most of the authoritarian regimes ended, the political context of Latin America showed a great diversity in political tendencies and contexts for NPOs: from cases of political federalism (e.g., Argentina, Mexico) to unitary countries that constituted regional government entities above municipal powers (e.g., Bolivia, Colombia, Ecuador, Paraguay). From the 1980s onward, direct elections of state and municipal governors were introduced in 18 countries in the region as part of a (limited but existent) decentralization process that empowered local governments, organizations, and communities (Ferreiro and Symmes, 2013). In the case of Chile and Uruguay, most of these organizations reframed their focus on the reconstruction of democratic regimes. This was a critical moment because many NPOs had created strong competences in advocacy, but few capabilities in less ideological areas of impact inclusion (Gómez, 1992).

By the time the World Summit for Social Development was held in Copenhagen in 1995, arguments to support states by allowing NPOs to take on responsibilities for covering basic needs (impact inclusion) became internationally common. Many Latin American NPOs toned down their "revolutionary" character to accommodate an approach akin to the private sector (e.g., fundraising, crowdfunding, crowdsourcing) as they addressed social issues. The boom of foundations and their hierarchies came with a decline in grassroots organizations focused on advocacy and their popular support. During these changes on a global level, Latin American NPOs that aimed for impact inclusion received support from all sides of the political spectrum. They came to be considered as an alternative to ideological dogmatism, as they vindicated continuous reforms based on their practical knowledge of problems (Gaviria, 2017). For the political-right parties, NPOs' focus on impact inclusion partially replaced the social protections provided by states. As public spending decreased, outsourcing to NPOs increased. However, NPOs participated in the implementation of social programs, not in their planning and design phases, and therefore many NPOs depended – and still depend – on public decisions and resources. This dependency has diminished the critical stances of NPOs (Gómez-Quintero, 2013).

The legitimization of NPOs focused on impact inclusion did not bring the disappearance of NPOs focused on advocacy inclusion. NPOs continued to play an important role and function in advocacy inclusion. However, most of these initiatives did not wield political power, as it was often the case in previous decades, but spread public awareness about particular local, regional, and even global topics (Cohen and Arato, 2000). Furthermore, the political left defended NPOs that aimed for advocacy inclusion because they were still a vehicle to channel claims of justice after the demise of many socialist models (Sorj, 2007). An alternative development and local development paradigm supported these views (Tandon, 2004).

The case of cooperatives in the 1990s was particularly notable, as different views arose regarding their role. In the 1980s, in the midst of a global crisis, cooperatives lost credibility and had to reformulate their objectives within societies. Many critics claimed that cooperatives had failed and had little possibility of developing in free market economies (Radrigán et al., 1998). These critics also highlighted the abusive use of these organizations to make labor relations more flexible. Cooperative supporters, however, presented cooperatives as an alternative model of business development that balanced capital with work and had significant growth possibilities (Mogrovejo et al., 2012).

Despite these different perceptions, cooperatives have had strong economic and social impact in the region: for example, 13,000 cooperatives affiliated with the International Co-operative Alliance for the Americas (ACI Americas) represent more than 32 million citizens and workers (Mogrovejo et al., 2012). As a reaction to its lost legitimacy, the Organization of the Cooperatives of America (OCA) has promoted legal frameworks in the region. In 2008, ACI Americas achieved an egalitarian legal framework, as proposed by ILO Recommendation 193 (Mogrovejo et al., 2012). Furthermore, ACI Americas has contributed through building capacities to participate in the elaboration of public policies for cooperatives within the region's different countries (Mogrovejo et al., 2012).

Low-functioning governments fostered NPOs focused on impact inclusion

The relative inefficiency and ineffectiveness of Latin American governments raises inclusion challenges, as they face issues of access to social services for citizens. As we further argue, this reinforces the challenge of NPOs to take an impact inclusion role. During the last three decades, NPOs have been working in impact inclusion fields such as the following:

- Gender: mainly foundations against violence against women.
- Education: mainly foundations with programs in excluded communities.
- Culture and spare time: associations, cooperatives, and foundations.
- Health: mainly foundations and associations.
- Work and production: mainly cooperatives, associations, unions, and informal organizations.
- Economic inclusion: associations, cooperatives, foundations, and social enterprises.
- Environment: mainly foundations and research institutes.

Low-functioning welfare systems

The reason for the importance of impact inclusion NPOs lies in the structures of Latin American welfare systems. Most Latin American countries constructed welfare systems under a

Principal-Agent problem between different government levels. Public efficiency depended on the capacity of the central government (principal) to generate rules, incentives, and supervision for sub-national governments (agents) to achieve the objectives sought by national policies (IDB, 2010). These hierarchical relations between central and local governments had a centralized direction that did not adapt to local needs and desires, and lacked clarity regarding the responsibilities of each government level. The phenomenon of overlapping responsibilities can be seen in both federal and unitary states. Mexico is an example of the former, while Bolivia and Peru illustrate the latter (IDB, 2010).

In the absence of clear responsibilities, one might promote accountability through contracts between different levels of governments, as is the case in many European countries. However, most countries in the region lack the abilities to budget, regulate spending, create accountability and supervision systems, and evaluate the results required by contracts (IDB, 2010). The legal and institutional frameworks of Latin American countries do not help either, since inefficiency prevents sanctions for non-compliance with contracts. Under the condition of badly functioning governments, welfare provision became a combination of (1) a social security structure granting benefits to those linked to productive activities, and (2) an assistance structure in which delivery was split between governmental organizations and NPOs. The latter were granted exemptions, tax incentives, and funding for their operations (Landim and Thompson, 1997).

Tax systems are another strong limitation when constructing functioning welfare systems. Most countries have tax systems without functional clarity, their own resources, and a clear design of intergovernmental relations (Ciravegna et al., 2013). No tax transfer system in the region leans toward equality between territories and entities with different contexts, challenges, and capabilities (IDB, 2010). Furthermore, municipal governments generally have control over property taxes, but national governments have the power to define their base and rate. This generates a great difference in the resources of sub-national governments, increased by the low tax collection that results from their institutional weakness (World Bank, 2008).

Legal frameworks for NPOs and their tax benefits

In light of Latin American countries' significant challenges, governments established different legal forms of NPOs to support their effectiveness and efficiency. Although differences exist between countries, most of them occur in the following forms: functional community organizations, nonprofit corporations, foundations, first-nation associations, professional associations, labor unions, cooperatives, mutual organizations, and federations (Table 9.1).

Table 9.1 Legal forms of nonprofits

Legal forms	Definition
Functional Community Organizations	Nonprofit organizations that aim to represent and promote the values and specific interests of the community within the territory of the community or group of communities.
Nonprofit Corporations	Organizations formed by a number of individuals that pursue a common objective, giving origin to and determining their purpose and mission. They differ from foundations since the nature of their constitution is the association of people.

(Continued)

Table 9.1 (Continued)

Legal forms	Definition
Nonprofit Foundations	An organization in which agents administer a patrimony according to the will of its founder(s), who determine(s) the organization's goals, which must be directed to public-interest objectives.
First-Nation Organizations	Voluntary and functional groupings of certain groups of members of a first-nation group, based on a common interest or goal.
Trade Associations	Organizations that aim to promote, develop, and protect the activities they have in common, like professions, trade, industry production, or services.
Labor Unions	Legal persons governed by the labor code of each country. Their main objectives are to represent employees exercising rights arising from individual and collective labor contracts, ensuring compliance with labor laws and social security, and reporting non-compliance.
Cooperatives	Organizations based on the principle of reciprocity and the purpose of mutual aid for which the aim is to improve the lives of their members, and whose members have equal rights and obligations.
Unions and Federations	There can be two kinds of unions and federations. On the one hand, it can be an organization formed by the association of three or more cooperatives, in which each party has its own legal personality and full capacity to act. On the other hand, it can be the union of three or more unions, union confederations of five or more federations, or 20 or more unions. The union of 20 or more unions may give rise to either a federation or confederation.
Trade Unions	Organizations that aim to promote the development and protection of the activities they have in common, like professions, trade, or industry production or services.
Mutuals	Nonprofit organizations for which the objective is for their members to achieve service benefits on a reciprocal basis, based on the voluntary cooperation of people who unite on the basis of mutual help.

Source: Based on Gatica (2017).

One of the earliest legal forms to emerge were mutual organizations, and they did so to provide aid and collective action in areas where states were close to absent. Functional community organizations, nonprofit corporations, and foundations emerged during the proliferation and diversification of NPOs in the 1950s and 1960s when peasants, artisans, young people, and others started to organize. Other legal forms are more recent and express the long-standing exclusion of first-nation groups. First-nation associations were only accepted in the 1990s in most countries, despite the fact that most of these communities have existed for centuries.

Some NPOs have been exonerated from paying income taxes in most countries and, subsequently, there are restrictions on such designations. For example, in Chile, the fiscal approach considers the activity that generates the income rather than the legal form of the organization (Etchart et al., 2002).

Grand challenge of including informal market actors

Coming from a history of a strong orientation toward advocacy inclusion as well as the lack of well-functioning public institutions, NPOs needed to learn the capabilities of impact inclusion to tackle those challenges in Latin America. One of them is the inclusion of a high percentage of informal market actors which encompass small businesses, self-employed workers, and unregistered informal micro-enterprises (Godfrey, 2015). Informal employment is due to a lack of familiarity with the law and the inability to cover the cost of formalities. Informal workers do not fall under labor protection laws (Godfrey, 2015).

Informality in the region is prevalent for several reasons. First, in the 1990s, neo-liberal and autocratic governments reduced public employment within a few years. Second, Latin America has a strong urban population: 79 percent of the whole population. This is a relatively high number compared to Africa (39 percent) and Arab countries (56 percent) (UNFPA, 2008). Big cities accumulate millions of inhabitants and produce social and economic tensions, such as the creation of precarious urban slums with high numbers of scarcely educated, unskilled, and informal workers (Clichevsky, 2000). Third, traditional first-nation cultural roots and lifestyles remain outside formal markets.

Informality of non-agricultural employees varies among the countries in the region (from 30.7 percent in Costa Rica to 73.6 percent in Guatemala), and between sectors and population groups (IMF, 2017). Around 130 million Latin Americans have informal non-agricultural jobs (the number would be much higher when including agricultural jobs) including at least 27 million young people. Their labor conditions limit productivity and economic development in the region, and exclude workers from social and labor protections (IMF, 2017). Most of the Latin American countries have a percentage of informality close to or higher than 50 percent (e.g., Mexico, the Dominican Republic, Colombia, Paraguay, Peru, El Salvador, Honduras, and Guatemala).

Although some NPOs have begun to specialize in impact inclusion with informal market actors, different complex drivers of informality challenged the success of their work. Specific industries, such as agriculture and construction, have high degrees of informality because of their seasonal character. For example, data for Colombia show that among five million agricultural producers, 91 percent do not have access to credit, 83 percent do not have machinery, 62 percent do not use irrigation systems, 83 percent do not have technical assistance, 54 percent do not have property titles, and 42 percent do not have primary education (Estadística, 2014). In Brazil, the Landless Workers' Movement has been able to provide land to 500,000 families, but 100,000 wait in camps and four million still do not have access to land. Unfortunately, land-ownership concentration has increased since the military regime of the 1960s: the Gini index of land concentration was 0.854 in 2006.

NPOs focusing on the extractive industry face the challenge of a rising number of informal market actors that are not included in the strategic decisions and subsequent benefits of mining. The long tradition of NPOs focused on advocacy inclusion, due to abuse from multinational corporations or the state, precludes collaboration between formal and informal actors.

Extractive industries contribute importantly to the economies of Chile, Peru, Colombia, Bolivia, Venezuela, Ecuador, Mexico, and Guatemala. Only Costa Rica has forbidden mining activities in the country due to its long-standing focus on environmental protective policies. In most of these countries, mine ownership is retained by central governments or sold to multinational companies through licenses. This posits a problem, particularly for first-nation communities, which have not yet been formally included in the development of the industry (CEPAL, 1994).

NPOs working with extractive industries demand more participation in political and economic decisions about exploitation and more independence of labor unions (Ballón et al., 2017). In countries like Peru, Chile, Guatemala, and Bolivia, some communities demand a fair distribution of profits and have had a number of conflicts with mining companies. For example, in 2015, Chile had 102 cases of conflicts despite an international commitment to first consult communities (Toledo and Liberona, 2017). In Colombia and Guatemala, participative processes in decisions between local communities and companies have tried to reduce negative environmental and social impacts on communities (Velásquez et al., 2017). NPOs focused on impact inclusion can help to shift from conflicts to collaboration between multinational corporations or the state, which usually lead mining operations, and rural and first-nation communities that often live where operations are established.

Rising impact inclusion based on market solutions

The need for impact-inclusion NPOs has increased due to the significant challenges of informal markets and low-functioning governments. Therefore, practitioner and researcher discourses began to support NPO solutions that included markets in their organizational models (Austin et al., 2006; Gutiérrez et al., 2016; Ogliastri et al., 2016). This has led to cross-sectorial partnerships, but not to access to more resources as is the case in developed countries. However, it has increased the focus on impact in the management of NPOs for tackling inclusion challenges.

The social economy movement

In past decades, the social economy movement has promoted a social economy – different from private and public organizations – with different forms of organizations that primarily focus on increasing the family income of poor and excluded households (Razeto, 1986). Since families are at the center of the social economy, it promotes the welfare of each of its members in difficult socio-economic conditions. Support networks, solidary baskets, solidarity stores, and other forms of grassroots organizations are ways in which families cope with critical circumstances (Jiménez, 2015).

In particular, left-party governments in regions of Venezuela, Ecuador, Argentina, Nicaragua, and Bolivia have collaborated with social economy organizations to create solidarity bonds and distribute wealth to excluded groups. Under these governments, social economy organizations played a role in approaching the socialism of the 21st century (Coraggio, 2015). For example, since 2006 in Ecuador, President Correa has promoted a project called the "Citizens' Revolution" ("La Revolución Ciudadana"), which tried to include historic demands from different social movements in the public agenda (Ortiz Lemos, 2014), and was established with the creation of the Instituto de Economía Solidaria (Coraggio, 2015). This generated a patronage relationship between the state and NPOs with social economy orientations regarding their social demands (Becker, 2012). For example, Venezuela and Argentina also experienced the expansion of NPOs of this type – sponsored by the Chávez and Kirchner governments (Coraggio, 2015; Ellner, 2011); in Argentina, the "Plan Nacional de Desarrollo Local y Economía Social" has made the social economy part and parcel of economic policy; and proponents of the social economy in Brazil exhort it as another model of production, commercialization, and consumption. They state that it deserves its own ministry, and requires high-level conditions to maximize its potential to create employment and productivity.

In Bolivia, the rise of President Morales was accompanied by a strong discourse regarding the importance of social economy organizations as an alternative to the capitalist economic system. Its constitution defends participation by social economy organizations and prioritizes support to community organizations and "peasant" associations. Furthermore, the constitutional processes in Venezuela, Bolivia, and Ecuador have incorporated social economy in their proposals to change the regime of accumulation.

Nonetheless, while these governments supported social economy organizations, at the same time they created centralistic public policies that controlled them and left little room for non-dependent social movements (Coraggio, 2015). Therefore, the search for innovative solutions to increase inclusion through market solutions via social economy initiatives have been done mainly through top-down processes. This approach has encountered obstacles as the resistance of government bureaucracies and insufficient social economy organizations could make the movement scale.

Social enterprises and social entrepreneurship

The origin of social enterprises and social entrepreneurship is related to the social economy movement in Latin America (Gatica, 2017). Their conceptualization has a close relation with popular economic initiatives, which emerged from socio-political unrest at the end of various dictatorships and the rise of democracy in the region. In particular, scholars described the marginalization and poverty among some urban communities in their work about popular economic organizations, and referred to the difficulties of understanding the different logic behind these organizations within the context of mainstream economics (Singer, 2009).

Recently, the private sector started to participate more frequently in discussions about welfare, public goods, and social impact. Chile, for instance, has an ongoing discussion about for-profit companies carrying out public purposes. In Colombia, entrepreneurs are integrating social and economic dimensions into their ventures in diverse contexts.

In light of this development, the region has a delay of legal frameworks in recognizing these new organizational forms dedicated to social/environmental and economic value creation. In Latin America, the transformation of corporations toward more socially responsible participation is occurring without any legal framework. In some developed countries, corporations with economic, social, and environmental purposes can adopt new legal forms (e.g., low-profit limited liability companies (L3C), benefit corporations, and community interest companies). For some of these organizations in Latin America, a normative definition pushed by *Sistema B* sets the standards for businesses to run their assessment and be certified as a Benefit (B) Corporation.

Inclusive enterprises have become more important as well. These enterprises take the best of business ventures to address pressing social needs (Bucher et al., 2015). Inclusive enterprises usually arise from expanding into a new market or offering a new product in low-income markets, where traditional ways of doing business often do not work (Godfrey, 2015; Jäger and Sathe, 2014). Despite the difficulty of doing so, examples can be found in every country from Mexico to Suriname and Argentina.[2]

Cross-sector partnerships

A complex process unfolded in recent decades as corporations in Latin American markets started to explore social/environmental value creation in relation to their business, and Latin American NPOs focusing on poverty alleviation started to perceive markets as a solution rather than a problem (Gatica, 2017). Within this process, impact inclusion NPOs developed certain market strategies (Austin et al., 2006).

This convergence has caused cross-sector partnerships to increase. These partnerships span along a collaboration continuum. In order to increase the number of beneficiaries, capture organizational learning, or multiply value creation, organizations from different sectors engage in multi-party alliances (i.e., one company with several NPOs, one NPO with several companies, or multiple companies with multiple NPOs). As in the case of a single partnership, developing potential alliances involves building trust and deploying considerable coordination, as cases from Colombia illustrate (Gutiérrez et al., 2004).

The complexity of these collaborations calls for a "collaborative process" (McKaughan, 2018). In this century, Fundación Avina has been sponsoring networks of NPOs to address significant social challenges: environmental conservation, recycling, and inclusion, among others. Additionally, emerging trends of the social economy, social enterprise and entrepreneurship (Austin et al., 2006), B Corps, collaborative processes, and cross-sectorial partnerships can be seen as a starting point in searching for cross-sectorial solutions for impact inclusion.

In search of an agenda for NPO management challenges

In light of the highly complex and conflicting Latin American history, it is likely that implementing NPO theories, concepts, and solutions from developed countries in the context of Latin America is not enough to tackle the significant challenges of excluded groups. To respond to contextual challenges, NPO managers need theories, concepts, and tools adapted to the historical challenges of Latin America.

Assuming that NPO management challenges are path-dependent (Ghezzi and Mingione, 2007) and systematizing our previous analysis, in our final reflection, we pose the question: *What can we learn from the Latin American context for the future management challenges of NPOs?* Answering this question, we highlight essential issues in the form of programmatic questions. We define a priority of management challenges based on Latin American history. Further research needs to revise the literature to define the current knowledge on those programmatic questions and specify a research agenda on NPOs in Latin America.

As we have shown before, NPOs have been contributing to reduce inequality during Latin American history as it relates to the following essential topics: the influence of first nations in the development of the NPOs' role and function within Latin American societies; the influence of charity NPOs and the Catholic Church before independence in the 19th century; the advocacy inclusion role and function of NPOs during authoritarian and populist governments; and the present inclusion challenges of low-functioning governments and informal markets that condition market-based approaches.

We have organized future management challenges according to the analytical lens used in this chapter: advocacy inclusion and impact inclusion. It serves as a guideline to explore different issues from a practitioner or researcher point of view (Table 9.2).

Management challenges based on advocacy inclusion

We defined advocacy inclusion as NPOs that adopt a political role to claim the right of excluded groups to obtain access to resources of states and/or powerful elites. In Latin America, this role and function of NPOs have deep historical roots and are still highly relevant for NPOs in different areas.

As discussed in our analysis, colonization strongly affected and still affects first nations. Although most of them are considered to be informal and poor, what actually happens is that most of them relate to first-nation institutions such as tribe leadership structures and even different worldviews, and these are mostly unknown to Latin American formal and modern societies. Therefore, inclusion needs to be considered in both directions, from formal market actors to first-nation actors and vice versa. To tackle this issue, we propose the question: *How do effective first-nation initiatives advocate for their exclusion/inclusion?*

Table 9.2 Examples of essential NPO management challenges

Historical events	Advocacy inclusion	Impact inclusion
First nations	How can first-nation initiatives effectively advocate for their inclusion/exclusion?	How can NPOs effectively bridge the gap between first-nation cultures and market cultures?
Charities and Catholic Church	How did missionaries intervene in indigenous communities, and what can NPOs learn from those practices and their results?	How can charities and philanthropic initiatives effectively increase their positive impact on inclusion?
Authoritarian and populist governments	How can NPOs maintain their independence in situations of high repression?	How can NPOs effectively provide their services to beneficiaries even in the face of conflicts with governments?
Low-functioning governments	How can NPOs effectively support democratic decision-making in low-functioning governments?	How can NPOs collaborate with governments to strengthen their organizational capabilities and improve the provision of social services?
Informal markets and market-based approaches	How can NPOs effectively advocate for healthy markets to serve low-income populations (e.g., labor laws, consumer protection)?	How can NPOs effectively reach low-income markets by themselves or through corporations that produce social/environmental and economic value?

Also related to first nations, the Christian Church has a long missionary history of successes and failures of "inclusion." Thus, we propose the question: *How did missionaries intervene in indigenous communities, and what can NPOs learn from those practices and their results?*

In the 1980s, Latin American NPOs became internationally recognized when they needed to work under high political repression, which is still the case in some Latin American countries such as Nicaragua and Venezuela. This is why a historically rooted question is still relevant for the future: *How can NPOs effectively maintain their independence in situations of high repression?*

Furthermore, even countries with more established democratic structures suffer from low-functioning institutions. Thus, we propose the question: *How can NPOs effectively support democratic decision-making in low-functioning governments?*

Finally, in cases where NPOs try to collaborate with corporations, they need to learn the language of business. Therefore, we ask: *How can NPOs effectively advocate for healthy markets to serve low-income populations (e.g., labor laws, consumer protection)?*

Management challenges based on impact inclusion

We defined impact inclusion as NPOs that assume an economic or social role and function to increase the quality of life of excluded groups. As shown in our historical analysis, this role and function of NPOs became more important in recent times and its challenges are pressing.

Issues related to first nations are secondary in the political and research arenas despite the significant cultural influences of first nations on Latin American cultures. Hence, we propose the question: *How can NPOs effectively bridge the gap between first-nation cultures and market cultures?*

Although Latin American donor markets are relatively weak, international non-governmental organizations and private foundations invest considerably in Latin America. In order to examine their contributions, we propose the question: *How can charities and philanthropic initiatives effectively increase their positive impact on inclusion?*

Populist governments had and still have a strong influence on NPOs in some Latin American countries. For many NPOs, not working within those countries is not an option, and therefore we ask: *How can NPOs effectively provide their services to beneficiaries even in the face of conflicts with governments?* Where government organizations are weak, but have the political will to provide social services, public–private partnerships seem to be an effective option. We then highlight the following question: *How can NPOs collaborate with governments to strengthen their organizational capabilities and improve the provision of social services?*

As explained before, using markets to increase the effectiveness of social services is becoming a common practice. Thus, we propose the question: *How can NPOs effectively reach low-income markets by themselves or through collaborations with the private sector and produce social/environmental and economic value?*

Conclusion

As we outlined in the previous historical analysis of Latin American civil societies, nonprofits' management challenges have their roots in the initial foundation of the Latin American states. The then ruling powers overlaid constitutions, copied from European countries, over the Latin American cultures. In light of this history, analyzing the challenges of Latin American nonprofit management from the perspective of western welfare states, such as the European countries, seems to make sense. But taking this lens would likely show similar challenges that European nonprofits face such as fundraising, professionalization of management processes and the need for impact assessments. No doubt, those challenges are pressing; but they are not essential. In our historical analysis we highlight inclusion as the essential nonprofit management challenge. In most developed countries of the west, the democratic governments take the function to provide inclusion. But where governments cannot take this function – such as in Latin American states – nonprofits need to respond to this government failure.

An effective organizational response to these inclusion challenges of Latin America has likely to meet three fundamental characteristics: scale (increasing the number of beneficiaries), permanence (efforts will need to span generations), and efficiency (scarce resources have to be stretched). Many well-intended efforts of philanthropic initiatives do not pass the scale test. Public administrations do have scale, but they are the historical cause of the inclusion challenge and therefore it is unlikely that just transforming public administrations can be the solution; and multilateral agencies change their priorities, making it likely that public sectors fail the permanence and efficiency tests (Austin et al., 2006); and the private sector has accomplished scale, permanence, and efficiency but without eliminating poverty or diminishing inequalities yet (Austin and Chu, 2006).

The failures of philanthropy, public administrations, international multilateral agencies and companies put Latin American nonprofit managers on the spot. They have the opportunity to significantly contribute to solve the Latin American inclusion challenge by focusing on solutions that are scalable, permanent in their provision, and efficient in their execution. But as the inclusion challenges are immense nonprofit managers can likely not solve those alone. This is why they increasingly search for public–private partnerships or cross-sectorial collaborations, a still weak but powerful trend. Responding to this trend, nonprofit managers already develop successful solutions based on innovations that emerge from the specific Latin American inclusion challenges and less from a knowledge transfer from European and other developed countries. As the Latin American inclusion challenges are – in comparison to other regions of the world – immense, its solutions can likely teach European and other countries how to effectively manage advocacy and impact inclusion.

Notes

1   The list is long: Augusto Pinochet in Chile, Hugo Bánzer in Bolivia, Aparicio Méndez in Uruguay, Alfredo Stroessner in Paraguay, Juan Velasco Alvarado in Peru, Humberto Branco in Brazil, Manuel Antonio Noriega in Panama, Gustavo Rojas Pinilla in Colombia, Carlos Castillo Armas in Guatemala, Fidel Castro in Cuba, and François Duvalier in Haiti.
2   A glimpse into the mixed record of inclusive businesses, and their offspring inclusive distribution, can be observed at https://observatorioscala.uniandes.edu.co/es/negocios-inclusivos.

References

AGURTO, I. & PIÑA, C. 1988. Las organizaciones no gubernamentales de promoción y desarrollo urbano en Chile. Una propuesta de investigación. *FLACSO*.

AKAAH, I.P. 1992. Social Inclusion as a Marketing Ethics Correlate. *Journal of Business Ethics,* 11, 599–608.

AUSTIN, J., & CHU, M. 2006. Business and Low-Income Sectors: Finding a New Weapon to Attack Poverty. *Revista. Harvard Review of Latin America.* Autumn, pp. 3–5.

AUSTIN, J., GUTIÉRREZ, R., OGLIASTRI, E. & REFICCO, E. (eds.) 2006. *Effective Management of Social Enterprises. Lessons from Business and Civil Society Organizations in Iberoamerica.* Cambridge, MA: Harvard University Press.

AUSTIN, J., REFICCO, E., BERGER, G., FISCHER, R., GUTIÉRREZ, R., KOLJATIC, M., LOZANO, G. & OGLIASTRI, E. 2004. *Social Partnering in Latin America: Lessons Drawn from Collaborations of Businesses and Civil Society Organizations.* Cambridge, MA: Harvard University Press.

BALLÓN, E., VIALE, C., MONGE, C., PATZY, F. & DE LA PUENTE, L. 2017. La agenda de la sociedad civil frente a las industrias extractivas en América Latina. National Resource Governance Institute.

BECKER, M. 2012. *Pachakutik: Indigenous Movements and Electoral Politics in Ecuador.* Lanham, MD: Rownman & Littlefield.

BUCHER, S., JÄGER, U. & PRADO, A. 2015. Sistema Ser: Scaling Private Health Care for the Base of the Pyramid. *Journal of Business Research,* Online first.

CARDOSO, F.H. 1976. América Latina: Proceso interno y mundial. *FLACSO.* Santiago.

CEPAL. 1994. Revista de la CEPAL. 52.

CIRAVEGNA, L., FITZGERALD, R. & KUNDU, S. 2013. *Operating in Emerging Markets: A Guide to Management and Strategy in the New International Economy.* Upper Saddle River, NJ: FT Press.

CLICHEVSKY, N. 2000. Informalidad y segregación urbana en América Latina. *In:* CEPAL (ed.) *Serie Medio Ambiente y Desarrollo.* CEPAL.

COHEN, J. & ARATO, A. 2000. *Sociedad civil y teoría política,* México, Fondo de Cultura Económica.

CORAGGIO, J.L. 2015. La presencia de la economía social y solidaria (ESS) y su institucionalización en América Latina.

ECLAC. 2011. Innovating, Gaining Market Share and Fostering Social Inclusion: Success Stories in SME Development. Economic Commission for Latin America and the Caribbean. Santiago: ECLAC.

ELLNER, S. 2011. Venezuela's Social-based Democratic Model: Innovation and Limitations. *Journal of Latin American Studies,* 43, 29.

ESTADÍSTICA (National Admistrative Department of Statistics – DANE). 2014. National Agricultural Census. Bogotá.

ETCHART, N., MILDER, B., JARA, M.C. & DAVIS, L. 2002. The Legal and Regulatory Framework for CSO Self-Financing in Chile. Nonprofit Enterprise and Self-sustainability Team (NESsT). Santiago.

EVERS, A. 2005. Mixed Welfare Systems and Hybrid Organizations: Changes in the Governance and Provision of Social Services. *International Journal of Public Administration,* 28, 736–748.

FERREIRO, A. & SYMMES, F. 2013. Descentralización empoderando a las regiones. *95 propuestas para un Chile mejor.* Chile.

FREIRE, P. 1970. *La pedagogía del oprimido.* New York.

FUJIMOTO, Y., RENTSCHLER, R., LE, H., EDWARDS, D. & HÄRTEL, C.E.J. 2014. Lessons Learned from Community Organizations: Inclusion of People with Disabilities and Others. *British Journal of Management,* 25, 518–537.

GATICA, S. 2017. *The Role of the State in the Emergent Phenomenon of the Social Enterprises in Chile.* PhD, University College London.

GAVIRIA, A. 2017. *Alguien tiene que llevar la contraria*. Bogotá: Ariel.

GHEZZI, S. & MINGIONE, E. 2007. Embeddedness, Path Dependency and Social Institutions. *Current Sociology*, 55, 11–23.

GODFREY, P.C. (ed.) 2015. *Management, Society, and the Informal Economy*. New York: Routledge.

GÓMEZ, S. 1985. El movimiento campesino en Chile. *FLACSO*.

GÓMEZ, S. 1992. Dilemas de las ONGs rurales en el contexto democrático. *FLACSO*.

GÓMEZ-QUINTERO, J.D. 2013. Organizaciones no gubernamentales y entidades sin ánimo de lucro en Colombia: Despolitización de la sociedad civil y tercerización del Estado.

GUTIÉRREZ, R., MÁRQUEZ, P. & REFICCO, E. 2016. Configuration and Development of Alliance Portfolios: A Comparison of Same-Sector and Cross-Sector Partnerships. *Journal of Business Ethics*, 135, 55–69.

GUTIÉRREZ, R., TRUJILLO, D.M. & LOBO, I.D. 2004. Multi-party Alliance Development in Colombian Cases. I. *In:* Austin et al., *Social Partnering in Latin America: Lessons Drawn from Collaborations Between Business and Civil Society Organizations*. Washington, DC: Harvard University.

IDB. 2010. La alternativa local: Descentralización y desarrollo económico. Santiago, Chile.

IMF. 2017. www.imf.org [Online]. International Monetary Fund. [Accessed 28 January 2018].

JÄGER, U. & SATHE, V. (eds.) 2014. *Strategy and Competitiveness in Latin American Markets: The Sustainability Frontier*. Cheltenham: Edward Elgar.

JÄGER, U. & SCHRÖER, A. 2013. Integrated Organizational Identity: A Definition of Hybrid Organizations and a Research Agenda. *Voluntas*, Published online: 3 July.

JIMÉNEZ, J. 2015. Avances y desafíos de la economía social y solidaria en Ecuador. Universidad Central del Ecuador.

LANDIM, L. & THOMPSON, A. 1997. Non-governmental Organisations and Philanthropy in Latin America: An Overview. *Voluntas*, 8, 14.

McKAUGHAN, S. 2018. *Come Together – A Guide to the Collaborative Change Process*, Unpublished draft, Fundación Avina.

MOGROVEJO, R., MORA, A. & VANHUYNEGEM, P. 2012. El cooperativismo en América Latina: Una diversidad de contribuciones al desarrollo sostenible. *In:* ILO (ed.).

MORELLO, G. 2012. Secularización y derechos humanos: Actores católicos entre la dictadura argentina (1976) y la administración Carter (1977–1979). *Latin American Research Review*, 47.

NICHOLLS-NIXON, C.L., CASTILLA, J.A.D., GARCIA, J.S. & PESQUERA, M.R. 2011. Latin America Management Research: Review, Synthesis, and Extension. *Journal of Management*, 37, 1178–1227.

NISHII, L.H. 2013. The Benefits of Climate for Inclusion for Gender-Diverse Groups. *Academy of Management Journal*, 56, 1754–1774.

OGLIASTRI, E., JÄGER, U. & PRADO, A. 2016. Strategy and Structure in High-Performing Nonprofits: Insights from Iberoamerican Cases. *Voluntas*, Online first.

OLVERA, A. 1998. Problemas conceptuales en el estudio de las organizaciones civiles: De la sociedad civil al tercer sector. *Instituto de Investigaciones Histórico-Sociales-Universidad Veracruzana*.

ORTIZ LEMOS, A. 2014. Sociedad Civil y Revolución Ciudadana en Ecuador. *Revista mexicana de sociología*, 76.

RADRIGÁN, M., DEL CAMPO, P. & RUBIO, H. 1998. El sector cooperativo chileno. Tradición, experiencia, y proyecciones. *C.Gral. de Coops. de Chile*. Santiago.

RAZETO, L. 1986. *Economía popular de solidaridad*, Área Pastoral Social de la Conferencia Episcopal de Chile.

RUSTOW, A. 1980. *A Historical Critique of Civilization*. Princeton, NJ: Princeton University Press.

SINGER, P. 2009. *Relaciones entre sociedad y Estado en la economía solidaria*, Quito, Ecuador, FLACSO.

SORJ, B. 2007. ¿Pueden las ONGs reemplazar al Estado?: Sociedad civil y Estado en América Latina. *Nueva Sociedad*, 210, 15.

TANDON, R. 2004. En la cresta de la ola o cayendo en picado: Las ONGs de desarrollo en el nuevo milenio. *D. Eade y E. Ligteringen, El debate sobre el desarrollo y el futuro de las ong*, 19.

TOLEDO, C. & LIBERONA, F. 2017. La agenda de la sociedad civil frente a las industrias extractivas en Chile. Fundación Terram.

TÖNNIES, F. 2002/1887. *Community and Society*. Mineola, NY: Dover.

TOURAINE, A. 1988. *Le parole et le sang*. Paris: Odile Jacob.

UNFPA. 2008. State of the World Population. New York: United Nations Fund for Population Activities.

VALDÉS, T. 1986. El movimiento poblacional: La recomposición de las solidaridades sociales. *FLACSO.*

VELÁSQUEZ, F., MARTÍNEZ, M. & PEÑA, J. 2017. La agenda de la sociedad civil frente a las industrias extractivas en Colombia. Natural Resource Governance Institute.

VIDAL, I. 2005. Social Enterprise and Social Inclusion: Social Enterprise in the Sphere of Work Integration. *International Journal of Public Adiministration,* 28, 807–825.

WORLD BANK. 2008. Decentralization and Local Democracy in the World: 2008 First Global Report. Barcelona, Spain.

WORLD BANK. 2013. Inclusion Matters. The Foundation for Shared Prosperity. *New Frontiers of Social Policy.* Washington, DC: World Bank.

PART II

Leading and planning

10

COMPOSITION OF NONPROFIT BOARDS

Summary of factors that account for who governs nonprofits

William A. Brown

PROFESSOR, BUSH SCHOOL OF GOVERNMENT & PUBLIC SERVICE, TEXAS
A&M UNIVERSITY, COLLEGE STATION, TEXAS, USA

Introduction

This chapter summarizes nonprofit governance theoretical approaches and contextual factors to understand the task and composition demands of nonprofit governing boards or governing bodies. The theoretical background suggests key roles for the governing board and who is likely to govern nonprofit organizations. Then the chapter considers internal and external contextual factors that might influence why particular stakeholder groups gain access to governance roles. "Governance is defined as the system by which organizations are directed, controlled, and held accountable" (Cornforth, 2003). There is variation in the systems, structures and priorities of governance (Lane, Astrachan, Keyt, & McMillan, 2006), but fundamentally governing boards are expected to provide some degree of oversight and support for the organization (Hillman & Dalziel, 2003). Huybrechts et al. (2016) recognize that governance priorities are informed through interpretation of internal and external forces that influence governance needs and by extension governance structures (Van Puyvelde, Cornforth, Dansac, Guo, & Hough, 2017). The chapter argues that one way to understand composition of the governance team, those who exert control in governance activities, is associated with governance priorities. Governance priorities, in turn, are informed by the operating context. This recognizes that governance team composition reflects an interplay of internal and external factors (Ostrower & Stone, 2010).

Understanding composition of the governing body, typically the board of directors although the board is by no means the only entity involved in governance (Cornforth, 2012), has a long history in governance research. The composition of the board is important because boards hold formal legal and moral responsibly to oversee and guide the organization. Concern for the composition of the governing board reflects an understanding that individual actors influence priorities and practices undertaken (Callen, Klein, & Tinkelman, 2003). These actors are imbedded in structures and processes that facilitate or constrain behaviors (Brown, 2014; Leslie, 2010). As has been noted (Renz & Andersson, 2013), there is a substantive and developing field of study to explore how individual-level factors relate to structures and performance. One area identifies competencies (Balduck, Van Rossem, & Buelens, 2010; Brown, 2007) of board members. This line of study seeks to identify the capabilities of individual board members in relation to various performance measures, which include individual engagement, group or board-level performance and performance of the organization. Related is the concept of board capital (Haynes & Hillman, 2010, p. 1145), which is defined as the "breadth and depth of directors' human and social capital." These studies find unequivocal support for the conclusion that board member composition characteristics explain different levels of role performance. The chapter summarizes theoretical and empirical research to consider factors that explain why particular individuals are responsible for governance.

Theoretical background

Board composition in the US has remained relatively unchanged for nearly 20 years and the most recent BoardSoure report indicates it is "unlikely to change" (BoardSource, 2017, p. 8) because few organizations report systematic practices or efforts to change racial and ethnic composition of the board. We know less about the composition of boards in other parts of the world, but there are increasing number of studies that provide some descriptive information of particular industries or regions (Brunt, 2016; Mori, Randøy, & Golesorkhi, 2013). This section summaries several theoretical approaches to understanding governance priorities and the implications inherent in those approaches to suggest composition expectations or needs (see Table 10.1).

Agency theory is a widely utilized theoretical perspective in corporate governance research and posits the need for the board to monitor and control management behavior (Eisenhardt, 1989; Fama & Jenson, 1983). Agency theory is concerned with the potential that managers who are not owners of the institution may waste resources, either through malevolent misappropriation or poor judgment (Jegers, 2009). This is because the personal interests of the managers may not align with the best interests of the organization. Consequently effective governance retains sufficient control to monitor managers and thereby minimize the potential for "excessive rents." This misappropriation of resources ultimately hurts the bottom-line. The owners of the firm are disadvantaged because managers may take more than their share of the profits (Dalton, Hitt, Certo, & Dalton, 2008). Agency theory has been the basis of understanding corporate governance for more than 75 years and the premise that boards must watch over management remains solid. One solution to this oversight concern is for the board to contain a sufficient number of "outside" or independent directors who can ensure accountability to owners (Dalton, Daily, Ellstrand, & Johnson, 1998).

The nonprofit context complicates the agency problem because of ambiguous ownership rights (Jegers, 2009). Consequently, it is reasonable to consider if nonprofit organizations even have an agency problem (Miller, 2002). Hansmann (1980) makes a case that the non-distribution constraint mitigates the opportunity to extract excessive proceeds and creates a bond of

Table 10.1 Summary of theoretical perspectives on governance board composition

Theory	Summary role function	Composition expectation
Agency	Control and accountability	Independent outside directors
Stewardship	Functional and strategy partnership with leadership	Power and competency
Resource dependence	Secure and manage resource demands	Resource engagement and contribution
Institutional	Legitimacy concerns	Reputational attributes
Stakeholder	Relationship management	Representation from key groups

trustworthiness with stakeholders. Brody (1996) contends that the nonprofit context is perhaps even more problematic in relation to control and oversight because there are no owners. Consequently, nonprofit managers (agents) may operate the organization without any clear accountability partner (i.e., principals). In the nonprofit context, both the conceptualization of "owners" and "outside/independent" directors is problematic. For community-based nonprofits it is often difficult to clearly specify to whom they are accountable. Even if managers are trusted allies that consistently operate in the best interest of the organization they have limitations, which implies that oversight might help (Eisenberg, 1984; Hendry, 2002). The general consideration is that principal/agent concerns exist in nonprofit organizations as well (Bernstein, Buse, & Bilimoria, 2016; Steinberg, 2010) and the incorporation of some aspect of "independent" or outside directors may mitigate some of these concerns, but the determination of what constitutes an independent director and optimal structural considerations are less clear (Van Puyvelde, Caers, Du Bois, & Jegers, 2012). Independent directors are defined as having "no material relationship" with the firm (Clarke, 2007; Gordon, 2007) and can also be referred to as "outside" directors. In practice the nature of a material relationship is contingent on interpretation, but tends to reflect that the director does not have business interests with the organization. The intent is to bring a perspective which is independent of managerial perspectives.

Stewardship theory is a possible corollary to agency theory to understand management behavior that is organizationally focused as opposed to self-interested (Davis, Schoorman, & Donaldson, 1997; Donaldson & Davis, 1991). Stewardship theory helps explain when "agents" act collectively toward higher order goals that may or may not be in their own self-interest. Stewardship theory is proposed as a complementary and important contribution to understanding the roles and responsibilities of boards (Van Puyvelde et al., 2012). It also provides an excellent perspective to consider the dynamics of a negotiated relationship in which the partners share or are perceived to share a more balanced resource dynamic, which is reflective of boards working with staff to help create strategic direction. This suggests that in order for boards to be an equal partner in guiding the organizations, board members must possess sufficient knowledge, skills and understanding to contribute substantively to the designing and monitoring strategic priorities (Hillman & Dalziel, 2003; Jäger & Rehli, 2012). To be a partner in governance requires a level of sophistication, capabilities and knowledge that can guide organizational priorities. This stream of research considers the balance of power between board members and managers (Krause, Withers, & Semadeni, 2016) and the competencies board members need to be effective (Balduck et al., 2010). Research suggests that enhanced capabilities of board members is associated with improved performance at the board and organizational level (Brown, 2005).

Resource dependency theory (Pfeffer & Salancik, 1978) is a frequently used perspective in nonprofit governance, and is based on the assumption that organizations are dependent on their environment for various crucial resources. Resource dependency theory suggests that the board is part of both the organization and the resource environment, and that it functions as a boundary-spanning unit that reduces external dependencies through links to necessary resources (Middleton, 1987; Pfeffer, 1973). Organizations may seek to reduce these dependencies in a number of different ways, for example by adapting or altering the environmental challenge or constraints; by growing or merging, or by engaging in political action to alter or influence the power of external constituents (Alexander, 2000). Alternatively, they may seek to manage these dependencies by inviting key stakeholders into the organization (Young, 2011). Directors can serve a critical link to mitigate resource power differentials. In a governance capacity, this is commonly fulfilled by inviting influential or high status individuals on to the boards (Rehli & Jäger, 2011). Organizations can also form advisory structures that seek to integrate external stakeholders into the organizational system (Saidel, 1998). One implication of resource dependency theory is that individuals that bring key resources will gain power (Hillman, Withers, & Collins, 2009; Pfeffer & Salancik, 2003). This includes access to financial resources, but other resource elements might include skills or capabilities that fill particular gaps in leadership (Hillman & Dalziel, 2003). Generally it was found that funding dependencies seem to override community participation in decision-making (Hardina, 1993). Rehli and Jäger's (2011) findings support a resource-based perspective and that recruitment and composition are driven by resource power. They find that when primary funding is from particular constituencies (e.g., high networth individuals or governments) these stakeholders tend to participate in nominations for the board and have representation on the governing board.

Institutional theory recognizes that legal, regulatory, and normative forces have an impact on governance priorities and structures enacted (Aguilera & Jackson, 2010). A key concern for nonprofit organizations is the establishment and maintenance of legitimacy. Institutional forces are exerted through compliance, mimetic and isomorphic mechanisms to influence how organizations are governed (Powell & DiMaggio, 1991). Compliance pressures refer to the ability of some organizations to impose rules on others, for example government laws and regulations (Bloodgood, Tremblay-Boire, & Prakash, 2014). The development and adoption of governance codes of practice across different sectors are examples of normative pressures. Similarly, one way that beneficiaries gain access to the board is through government and regulatory expectations that require boards to include community or consumer representatives on the board (LeRoux, 2009). Mimetic pressures occur through the desire to copy other organizations. If an organization is uncertain how to act, it may copy another organization that it thinks has found a successful or legitimate way of dealing with the situation. Institutional theory suggests board members will be chosen that bring greater legitimacy to the organization (Abzug & Galaskiewicz, 2001; Renz & Andersson, 2013).

Stakeholder theory extends the discussion to consider how governance mechanisms can account for and manage stakeholders more broadly (beyond resource-based stakeholders). From this perspective boards serve to manage relationships with principal stakeholder groups often through the incorporation of stakeholders onto the board (Leardini, Rossi, & Moggi, 2014; Wellens & Jegers, 2014). Wellens and Jeger (2014) identify internal and external stakeholders that hold expectations of the organization and consider how governance structures and patterns can be instrumental to address performance demands from different groups. One pattern reflects the need to engage and support participation by salient stakeholder groups in organizational governance. Participation by diverse constituencies on the board comes at a cost of negotiating conflicting interests (Speckbacher, 2008) and so organizations evaluate the salience of multiple stakeholder demands. Mitchell, Agle and Wood (1997) suggest three attributes (power, legitimacy and urgency) of stakeholders that suggest salience to managers. Speckbacher (2008) makes a distinction between primary and secondary stakeholders in regards to those who hold or maintain more rights to influence or participate in governance and those that tend not to have those rights (Young, 2011). A stakeholder-informed governance system has to find the right balance of different constituencies to support the mission and sustain the organization, while ensuring the organization can maintain sufficient strategic focus. Another concern is related to the extent to which the organization is held captive by particular stakeholder groups.

The field of comparative corporate governance considers the "relationship between parties with a stake in the firm and how their influence on strategic corporate decision-making is shaped in different countries" (Aguilera & Jackson, 2010, p. 491). This perspective provides insight into how and why variation of governance structures is operationalized. Aguilera and Jackson (2003) emphasize the nature of relationships between different actors and forces in different social contexts. They consider three influential stakeholder groups – capital, management and labor – and explore how these groups influence governance structures. Capital structures includes how organizations gain sufficient capital to operate which has implications for ownership-related rights and control. Prior literature recognizes the capital constraints and resource dependences are experienced by many nonprofit organizations (Huybrechts, Mertens, & Rijpens, 2014; Young, 2011). As discussed, ownership in the nonprofit context is complicated, but the influence of capital suggests the degree and extent of influence. What is less well understood is how managerial norms and labor engagement dispositions tend to influence and relate to governance systems. For instance, a study exploring the participation of producers in cooperatives revealed that as few as 25 percent of the organizations have voting seats on the board for producers (Bennett, 2017). Furthermore, the nature and character of beneficiary engagement and disposition is potentially unique to the nonprofit context and also under-explored (Wellens & Jegers, 2011). Generally it seems that funding dependencies override community participation in decision-making (Hardina, 1993), but, in the following, this chapter will explore different context factors that might explain why particular groups or individuals tend to serve in governance roles.

Factors that influence governing board composition characteristics

Ostrower and Stone (2010) propose a contingency-based perspective to understand nonprofit governance and call for more research on the relationship between context and board practices. Central to the contingency-based framework is a recognition that context informs governance needs or roles (Huybrechts et al., 2016) and how organizations may enact different composition characteristics (Callen, Klein, & Tinkelman, 2010). Governance systems and practices are sensitive to organizational needs and environmental influences (Pettigrew, Woodman, & Cameron, 2001; Van de Ven & Sun, 2011). Widespread governance standards and best practices exist, but organizations adapt tactics and practices appropriate to the organizational context, especially in an international setting because Anglo-American and Continental European governance systems tend to dominate normative approaches in literature. As summarized, conceptual and theoretical approaches propose different expectations of composition. Consequently contextual factors might strengthen estimations of variation in composition. Of particular significance for boards are the decision-rights and authorities granted executives, staff or insiders who attend more directly to the operations of the organization. Ostrower and Stone (2010) suggest that there are three general areas that influence governance functions and board composition. These factors are: (1) features of the external environment; (2) internal organizational characteristics; and (3) board attributes. Environmental factors are the most distal and include concepts such as complexity and stability in the operating environments of nonprofits. Organizational factors include historal patterns of engagement, how the organization is structured and strategic priorities. Board-level attributes reflect interpersonal and group dynamic features that inform decision processes. Such as who exerts influence and how those constituencies exert control. The next section summarizes macro- and micro-context factors (Bradshaw, 2009) that influence governance needs and by extension composition expectations.

External factors

There are a variety of ways to organize or interpret the external environment. In strategic management literature the external environment influences an organization's approach to programs and services through the interpretation of forces by managers and leaders (Mintzberg, 1979). For instance as managers perceive threats or opportunities they respond appropriately to seize opportunities and buffer threats (Alexander, 1998). This matters for governance because governance structures help leaders identify and respond to external forces. Different forces and different strategic priorities suggest different governance needs. A classic approach considers how to describe and interpret significant environmental forces (Mintzberg, 1979; Schmid, 2009). The most basic of these consider the degree to which the external environment is *simple vs. complex*; and stable vs. turbulent. Environmental features can be fairly simple and easy to understand or they can be highly complex and variable. A complex environment has many different components, participants or forces that enact on the organization. Another feature is the extent to which the various stakeholder groups are relatively similar to each other (homogeneous) and alternatively stakeholder groups could be very heterogeneous suggesting that there are different priorities. Complex environments require more effort to monitor and respond to different constituencies. While a simple environment tends to require less attention to nuance and distinction among constituencies. Research suggests that organizations in highly complex task environments may be less likely to engage in monitoring functions and more likely to engage in boundary spanning activities (Callen et al., 2010; Miller-Millesen, 2003).

Next is the extent to which the environment is *stable vs. turbulent*. This has to do with the extent of change within or among participants and the attributes of those participants. Consider the nature of a volunteer membership base that is very stable. This includes such factors as long tenure in participation and consistency over time in support from volunteers. Organizations can accurately predict and anticipate the number and type of volunteers from year to year. A turbulent volunteer base indicates that the number and type of individuals who volunteer might change from year to year (increasing or decreasing) or volunteers might change preferences thereby shifting demand or support for services. Turbulence suggests increased difficulty in planning and operating because it is difficult to control or understand environmental features over time (see Table 10.2). There are a various response options available to boards in regards to external forces. In general, organizations seek understanding of how different forces may or may not influence organizational operations. In addition, organizations are looking for ways to exploit benefits or mitigate effects of external factors. The extent to which board members can facilitate understanding, limit impact or support the organization's ability to capture benefits suggests how composition might be influenced. This relates to both planning and external relations roles for boards. Boards with deeper understanding are able to engage in planning that better reflects operating context. Similarly boards that maintain functional external relations facilitate relationships that allow the organization to better respond to external opportunities or threats.

For instance in complex environments executives stated that the strategy role was important as well as the public relations or outreach role to manage legitimacy with more actors (Brown & Guo, 2010). Iecovich (2005) found increased collaboration with other nonprofits was associated with an increased number of board committees. Ostrower and Stone (2006) found that complexity of interorganizational ties makes power more differentiated and tended to shift some authority to the executives who can better attend and respond to the complexities (Callen et al., 2010). Several studies have found that boards tend to be larger when organizations operate in more complex environments (Abzug, 1996; Brown & Guo, 2010). Table 10.2 summarizes the contextual factors considered and implications for governance and composition.

Internal factors

Research at the organizational level is complex capturing a variety of factors and influences. Internal factors relate to features of the organization such as structure, complexity, strategic approach and history of the organization. These factors influence management and governance priorities (Toubiana, Oliver, & Bradshaw, 2016) and consequently have implications for the

Table 10.2 Summary of context factors and implications for governance composition

Context aspect	Governance implications	Composition implications
External		
Simple	Clear stakeholder groups and power dynamics	Easier to identify potential stakeholder participants and processes
Complex	Multiple and potentially conflicting stakeholder groups	Lack of clarity about who and how to include and as a result potentially larger boards
Stable	Easier to determine long-term plans	Historical knowledge and depth of power
Turbulent	Changes in pressures and priorities	Smaller core group to respond quicker
Internal/Organizational		
High level complexity	Difficult to understand internal operations and stakeholders	Potential need for internal expertise
Structure		
Decentralized	Potential complex political dynamics	Representatives from constituencies
Centralized	Dominate power disposition	Smaller dominate coalition
Strategic approach		
Prospector	Need for entrepreneurial perspectives	Larger more open systems
Defender	Need for efficiency and stability	Smaller more internal
Historical/cultural patterns		
Clear power disposition	Influential internal stakeholders gain power	Dominate coalition
Complex or changing power	Mediation and negotiation	Potential for conflicting interests and fault-lines

composition demands. These influences extend to micro-interactions in groups and among board members (Joshi & Roh, 2009) and the power disposition of different stakeholders to have influence in the organization (Fleming & Spicer, 2014; Pfeffer, 1992). A distinction to consider is the difference between centralized decision-making structures that consolidate decisions to core individuals or groups and a more decentralized structure that disburses decision authority downward and across the organization. Different decision-making arrangements place different demands on management and the board.

There is tendency to use age and size as a proxy for the stage of development or structure issues. Larger, older organizations are typically conceptualized as having more formal structures with professionalized staff and hence accountability controls in place (Cornforth & Simpson, 2002). While smaller, younger organizations might exhibit less formal structures with fewer accountability policies (Rochester, 2003). There is evidence to suggest that developmental changes such as organizational growth can impact governance structures and practices. These patterns suggest priorities and demands for governance needs (Filatotchev, Toms, & Wright, 2006) and issues can arise during transitions in life stages. Governance demands and competencies are substantively different during an early stage of development when compared to a mature organization. Understanding the stage of development and patterns of organizational growth (or decline) implies how governance needs might shift (Stone, 1996). Cornforth and Simpson (2002), in a survey of charities in England and Wales, showed that various board characteristics such as size, composition, the number of sub-committees, formalization and various board problems varied with size. Rochester (2003), based on case study research in the UK, suggests that organizations with few or no staff face a number of distinctive challenges in developing and maintaining an effective board. Similarly Kumar and Nunan (2002) suggest these organizations have distinctive support needs. Ostrower (2007) in a survey of the boards of mid-size nonprofits in the US identifies a number of distinctive weaknesses and challenges they face. Larger more complex organizations looked for the board to provide guidance on internal policies (Brown & Guo, 2010; Ostrower & Stone, 2010) and had more advising requirements. Complexity of organizational structure makes it harder to incorporate outsiders and those with less knowledge of the organization and as a result tends to shift power to executives (Jegers, 2008; Ostrower & Stone, 2006). Research has also found that organizational complexity is negatively associated with the board's role in strategy (Hendry & Kiel, 2004). Larger organizations also had larger boards with more outside directors (Coles, Daniel, & Naveen, 2008; de Andres-Alonso, Azofra-Palenzuala, & Elena Romero-Merino, 2009).

Another potentially significant internal contingency is the strategic disposition or approach an organization might utilize. Strategic management is a blend of management practices that entail interpreting environmental conditions and designing systems to foster success (Miles & Snow, 1978). "The effectiveness of organizational adaptation hinges on the dominant coalition's perceptions of environmental conditions and the decisions it makes concerning how well the organization will cope with these conditions" (p. 21). These strategic choices and priorities have implications for governance functions (Gabrielsson & Huse, 2004). A classic distinction of strategic priorities is to consider if an organization is more entrepreneurial or more conservative in regards to new programs and services (Miles & Snow, 1978). Those organizations that prioritize developing and experimenting with new programs, referred to as a prospector-type strategy, need a board to support innovation and accept risk. Conversely organizations that seek consistency and efficiency in services, referred to as a defender, needs a board to prioritize performance systems and accountability measures that drive that aspect of the organization. Conflict occurs when organizations try to shift strategic priorities and the board is unable to adjust practices. Consequently the strategic approach utilized or promulgated has governance implications and there is relatively limited study to explain this linkage. Brown and Iverson (2004) found linkages between approach and structure. Such that prospector-type organizations tended to have more committees and more engagement of diverse constituencies on those committees, while defender-oriented organizations tended to have fewer committees and fewer numbers of constituencies incorporated into the governance system.

Historical patterns and norms of behavior are also going to influence governance priorities. Stone (1996) investigated shifts in institutional logics and how a social service organization moved from a grassroots, community-based organization to a more professionalized, state-funded human service provider. This shift in operational practices had direct implications on governance priorities and participation on the board. As might be expected, community-based participants were less prevalent on the board in subsequent years while those with more expertise and access to resources gained more influence on the board. Maier and Meyer (2011) explored what they called discourses in NGO organizations and found the different perspectives (Managerialism, Domestic, Professionalism, Grassroots, and Civic) had a direct impact on how the board functioned (structures and process) and to whom they felt accountable (funders, local communities, etc.). Their study as well as Stone's reflect a deep appreciation for the cultural forces that operate in organizations and how those forces inform priorities and practices. There are broad trends in that some nonprofits are more community-based, while others tend to be more professionalized, and others are more market-oriented. Appreciating these forces and factors is an important distinction to understanding variation in governance systems.

The disposition and inclination of significant internal stakeholders do influence governance structures and priorities. Internal power dynamics are salient to changes in governance systems (Gazley & Kissman, 2015) as powerful groups and individuals can exert influence to facilitate or thwart change initiatives. It is not necessarily clear how CEOs, for instance, can influence governance process changes (Heimovics, Herman, & Jurkiewicz, 1993; O'Regan & Oster, 2005; Westphal & Zajac, 1995). There is some research to suggest CEOs can have a detrimental effect on governance accountability mechanisms (Joseph, Ocasio, & McDonnell, 2014). This is because CEOs tend to push the board toward fundraising in place of monitoring (O'Regan & Oster, 2005). Managerial tenure and level of expertise are associated with more influence (Ostrower & Stone, 2006). CEOs with less power (shorter tenure) were more likely to talk about the oversight role when compared to executives with more tenure (Brown & Guo, 2010). CEOs tend to want boards that are like them (Westphal & Zajac, 1995). CEOs are not the only constituency that might exert influence. Prestige or wealth of board members suggests that they may exert influence, while more female board members seem to make the board less influential (Ostrower & Stone, 2006).

Conclusion

Table 10.2 summarizes the context factors discussed and the implications for governance priorities and composition. It is the interpay of external environmental forces and multiple and at times conflicting internal dyanmics that ultimatly make the determination about how governance is enacted in particular nonprofit organizations. The extent that any particular force or influence is going to override others is difficult to explain or interpret in the nonprofit context as the variability of organizational priorities, structures and developmental influences creates a heterogeneity that complicates simple questions and tendencies to draw conclusions that are widely applicable. It is further recognized that the chapter does not fully summarize or identify all contextual factors that may influence governance priorities and composition. These are some of the most prevalent with some empirical studies to suggest them as substantive, but there are clearly other factors that might be more relevant for different organizations, industries or locations. As a scholarly community concerned about the governance of nonprofit organizations, an appreciation and incorporation of relevant context factors is important. Consequently, the field can utilize the framework proposed by Ostrower and Stone (2010), which suggests three general areas that influence governance functions: (1) features of the external environment; (2) internal organizational characteristics; and (3) board attributes. This chapter builds on that framework to identify specific features and considers how those features inform governance priorities and performance.

References

Abzug, R. (1996). The Evolution of Trusteeship in the United States: A Roundup of Findings from Six Cities. *Nonprofit Management and Leadership, 7*(1), 101–111. doi: 10.1002/nml.4130070110

Abzug, R., & Galaskiewicz, J. (2001). Nonprofit Boards: Crucibles of Expertise or Symbols of Local Identities? *Nonprofit and Voluntary Sector Quarterly, 30*(1), 51–73.

Aguilera, R.V., & Jackson, G. (2003). The Cross-National Diversity of Corporate Governance: Dimensions and Determinants. *Academy of Management Review, 28*(3), 447–465. doi: 10.5465/amr.2003.10196772

Aguilera, R.V., & Jackson, G. (2010). Comparative and International Corporate Governance. *Academy of Management Annals, 4*(1), 485–556. doi: 10.1080/19416520.2010.495525

Alexander, J. (2000). Adaptive Strategies of Nonprofit Human Service Organizations in an Era of Devolution and New Public Management. *Nonprofit Management and Leadership, 10*(3), 287–303. doi: 10.1002/nml.10305

Alexander, V.D. (1998). Environmental constraints and organizational strategy: Complexity, conflict, and coping in the nonprofit sector. In W.W. Powell & E.S. Clemens (Eds.), *Private Action and the Public Good*. New Haven, CT: Yale University Press.

Balduck, A.-L., Van Rossem, A., & Buelens, M. (2010). Identifying Competencies of Volunteer Board Members of Community Sports Clubs. *Nonprofit and Voluntary Sector Quarterly, 39*(2), 213–235. doi: 10.1177/0899764009334306

Bennett, E.A. (2017). Who Governs Socially-Oriented Voluntary Sustainability Standards? Not the Producers of Certified Products. *World Development, 91*(Supplement C), 53–69. doi: https://doi.org/10.1016/j.worlddev.2016.10.010

Bernstein, R., Buse, K., & Bilimoria, D. (2016). Revisiting Agency and Stewardship Theories. *Nonprofit Management and Leadership, 26*(4), 489–498.

Bloodgood, E.A., Tremblay-Boire, J., & Prakash, A. (2014). National Styles of NGO Regulation. *Nonprofit and Voluntary Sector Quarterly, 43*(4), 716–736. doi: 10.1177/0899764013481111

BoardSource. (2017). Leading with intent: 2017 National Index of nonprofit board practices. Washington, DC: BoardSource.

Bradshaw, P. (2009). A Contingency Approach to Nonprofit Governance. *Nonprofit Management and Leadership, 20*(1), 61–81. doi: 10.1002/nml.241

Brody, E. (1996). Agents Without Principals: The Economic Convergence of the Nonprofit and For-Profit Organizational Forms. *New York Law School Law Review, 40*(3), 457–536.

Brown, W.A. (2005). Exploring the Association Between Board and Organizational Performance in Nonprofit Organizations. *Nonprofit Management & Leadership, 15*(3), 317–339.

Brown, W.A. (2007). Board Development Practices and Competent Board Members. *Nonprofit Management & Leadership, 17*(3), 301–317.

Brown, W.A. (2014). Antecedents to board member engagement and participation in deliberation and decision-making. In C. Cornforth & W.A. Brown (Eds.), *Nonprofit Governance: Innovative Perspectives and Approaches* (pp. 84–100). Abingdon: Routledge.

Brown, W.A., & Guo, C. (2010). Exploring the Key Roles for Nonprofit Boards. *Nonprofit and Voluntary Sector Quarterly, 39*(3), 536–546. doi: 10.1177/0899764009334588

Brown, W.A., & Iverson, J.O. (2004). Exploring Strategy and Board Structure in Nonprofit Organizations. *Nonprofit and Voluntary Sector Quarterly, 33*(3), 377–400.

Brunt, C. (2016). Existing governance structure in international NGOs. In J. Nyigmah Bawole, F. Hossain, A.K. Ghalib, C.J. Rees, & A. Mamman (Eds.), *Development Management: Theory and Practice* (pp. 190–202). Abingdon: Routledge.

Callen, J.L., Klein, A., & Tinkelman, D. (2003). Board Composition, Committees, and Organizational Efficiency: The Case of Nonprofits. *Nonprofit and Voluntary Sector Quarterly, 32*(4), 493–520.

Callen, J.L., Klein, A., & Tinkelman, D. (2010). The Contextual Impact of Nonprofit Board Composition and Structure on Organizational Performance: Agency and Resource Dependence Perspectives. *Voluntas: International Journal of Voluntary and Nonprofit Organizations, 21*(1), 101–125. doi: 10.1007/s11266-009-9102-3

Clarke, D.C. (2007). Three Concepts of the Independent Director. *Deleware Journal of Corporate Law, 32*, 73–111.

Coles, J.L., Daniel, N.D., & Naveen, L. (2008). Boards: Does One Size Fit All? *Journal of Financial Economics, 87*(2), 329–356. doi: https://doi.org/10.1016/j.jfineco.2006.08.008

Cornforth, C. (2003). Introduction: The changing context of governance – emerging issues and paradoxes. In C. Cornforth (Ed.), *The Governance of Public and Non-profit Organisations: What Do Boards Do?* London: Routledge.

Cornforth, C. (2012). Nonprofit Governance Research. *Nonprofit and Voluntary Sector Quarterly, 41*(6), 1116–1135. doi: doi:10.1177/0899764011427959

Cornforth, C., & Simpson, C. (2002). Change and Continuity in the Governance of Nonprofit Organizations in the United Kingdom: The Impact of Organizational Size. *Nonprofit Management and Leadership, 12*(4), 451–470. doi: 10.1002/nml.12408

Dalton, D.R., Daily, C.M., Ellstrand, A.E., & Johnson, J.L. (1998). Meta-Analytic Reviews of Board Composition, Leadership Structure, and Financial Performance. *Strategic Management Journal, 19*(3), 269–290.

Dalton, D.R., Hitt, M.A., Certo, S.T., & Dalton, C.M. (2008). The Fundamental Agency Problem and Its Mitigation. *Academy of Management Annals, 1*(1), 1–64.

Davis, J.H., Schoorman, F.D., & Donaldson, L. (1997). Toward a Stewardship Theory of Management. *Academy of Management Review, 22*(1), 20–47.

de Andres-Alonso, P., Azofra-Palenzuala, V., & Elena Romero-Merino, M. (2009). Determinants of Nonprofit Board Size and Composition. *Nonprofit and Voluntary Sector Quarterly, 38*(5), 784–809.

Donaldson, L., & Davis, J.H. (1991). Stewardship Theory or Agency Theory: CEO Governance and Shareholder Returns. *Australian Journal of Management, 16*(1), 49–64.

Eisenberg, M.A. (1984). New Modes of Discourse in Corporate Law Literature. *George Washington Law Review, 52*, 582, 590.

Eisenhardt, K.M. (1989). Agency Theory: An Assessment and Review. *Academy of Management Review, 14*(1), 57–74. doi: 10.5465/amr.1989.4279003

Fama, E.F., & Jenson, M.C. (1983). Separation of Ownership and Control. *Journal of Law & Economics, 26*(June), 301–326.

Filatotchev, I., Toms, S., & Wright, M. (2006). The Firm's Strategic Dynamics and Corporate Governance Life-cycle. *International Journal of Managerial Finance, 2*(4), 256–279. doi: doi:10.1108/17439 130610705481

Fleming, P., & Spicer, A. (2014). Power in Management and Organization Science. *Academy of Management Annals, 8*(1), 237–298. doi: 10.1080/19416520.2014.875671

Gabrielsson, J., & Huse, M. (2004). Context, Behavior, and Evolution: Challenges in Research on Boards and Governance. *International Studies of Management & Organization, 34*(2), 11–36. doi: 10.1080/00208825.2004.11043704

Gazley, B., & Kissman, K. (2015). *Transformational Governance: How Boards Achieve Extraordinary Change.* Hoboken, NJ: John Wiley.

Gordon, J.N. (2007). The Rise of Independent Directors in the United States, 1950–2005: Of Shareholder Value and Stock Market Prices. *Stanford Law Review, 59*(6), 1465–1568.

Hansmann, H. (1980). The Role of the Nonprofit Enterprise. *Yale Law Journal, 89*, 835–901.

Hardina, D. (1993). The Impact of Funding Sources and Board Representation on Consumer Control of Service Delivery in Organizations Serving Low-income Communities. *Nonprofit Management and Leadership, 4*(1), 69–84. doi: 10.1002/nml.4130040106

Haynes, K.T., & Hillman, A.J. (2010). The Effect of Board Capital and CEO Power on Strategic Change. *Strategic Management Journal, 31*(11), 1145–1163.

Heimovics, R.D., Herman, R.D., & Jurkiewicz, C.L. (1993). Executive Leadership and Resource Dependence in Nonprofit Organizations: A Frame Analysis. *Public Administration & Management, 53*(5), 419–427.

Hendry, J. (2002). The Principal's Other Problems: Honest Incompetence and the Specification of Objectives. *Academy of Management Review, 27*(1), 98–113.

Hendry, K., & Kiel, G.C. (2004). The Role of the Board in Firm Strategy: Integrating Agency and Organisational Control Perspectives. *Corporate Governance: An International Review, 12*(4), 500–520. doi: 10.1111/j.1467-8683.2004.00390.x

Hillman, A.J., & Dalziel, T. (2003). Boards of Directors and Firm Performance: Integrating Agency and Resource Dependence Perspectives. *Academy of Management Review, 28*(3), 383–396.

Hillman, A.J., Withers, M.C., & Collins, B.J. (2009). Resource Dependence Theory: A Review. *Journal of Management, 35*(6), 1404–1427. doi: 10.1177/0149206309343469

Huybrechts, B., Mertens, S., & Rijpens, J. (2014). Explaining stakeholder involvement in social enterprise governance through resources and legitimacy. In J. Defourny, L. Hulgård, & V. Pestoff (Eds.), *Social Enterprise and the Third Sector: Changing European Landscapes in a Comparative Perspective* (pp. 157–175). New York: Routledge.

Huybrechts, J., Voordeckers, W., D'Espallier, B., Lybaert, N., & Van Gils, A. (2016). The Board's Demography—Firm Performance Relationship Revisited: A Bayesian Approach. *Journal of Small Business Management, 54*(3), 992–1007. doi: 10.1111/jsbm.12223

Iecovich, E. (2005). Environmental and Organizational Features and Their Impact on Structural and Functional Characteristics of Boards in Nonprofit Organizations. *Administration in Social Work, 29*(3), 43–59. doi: 10.1300/J147v29n03_04

Jäger, U., & Rehli, F. (2012). Cooperative power relations between nonprofit board chairs and executive directors. *Nonprofit Management and Leadership, 23*(2), 219–236. doi: 10.1002/nml.21061

Jegers, M. (2008). *Managerial Economics of Nonprofit Organizations*. New York: Routledge.

Jegers, M. (2009). "Corporate" Governance in Nonprofit Organizations. *Nonprofit Management and Leadership, 20*(2), 143–164. doi: 10.1002/nml.246

Joseph, J., Ocasio, W., & McDonnell, M.-H. (2014). The Structural Elaboration of Board Independence: Executive Power, Institutional Logics, and the Adoption of CEO-Only Board Structures in U.S. Corporate Governance. *Academy of Management Journal, 57*(6), 1834–1858. doi: 10.5465/amj.2012.0253

Joshi, A., & Roh, H. (2009). The Role of Context in Work Team Diversity Research: A Meta-analytic Review. *Academy of Management Journal, 52*(3), 599–627.

Krause, R., Withers, M., & Semadeni, M. (2016). Compromise on the Board: Investigating the Antecedents and Consequences of Lead Independent Director Appointment. *Academy of Management Journal.* doi: 10.5465/amj.2015.0852

Kumar, S., & Nunan, K. (2002). *A Lighter Touch: An Evaluation of the Governance Project*. York: Joseph Rowntree Foundation/YPS.

Lane, S., Astrachan, J., Keyt, A., & McMillan, K. (2006). Guidelines for Family Business Boards of Directors. *Family Business Review, 19*(2), 147–167. doi: 10.1111/j.1741-6248.2006.00052.x

Leardini, C., Rossi, G., & Moggi, S. (2014). Composition of the Boards. In *Board Governance in Bank Foundations: The Italian Experience* (pp. 51–69). Berlin: Springer.

LeRoux, K. (2009). Paternalistic or Participatory Governance? Examining Opportunities for Client Participation in Nonprofit Social Service Organizations. *Public Administration Review, 69*(3), 504–517. doi: 10.1111/j.1540-6210.2009.01996.x

Leslie, M. (2010). The Wisdom of Crowds – Groupthink and Nonprofit Governance. *Florida Law Review, 62*(5), 1179–1226.

Maier, F., & Meyer, M. (2011). Managerialism and Beyond: Discourses of Civil Society Organization and Their Governance Implications. *Voluntas: International Journal of Voluntary and Nonprofit Organizations, 22*(4), 731. doi: 10.1007/s11266-011-9202-8

Middleton, M. (1987). Nonprofit Boards of Directors: Beyond the Governance Function. In W.W. Powell & R. Steinberg (Eds.), *The Nonprofit Sector: A Research Handbook*. New Haven, CT: Yale University Press.

Miles, R.E., & Snow, C.C. (1978). *Organizational Strategy, Structure and Process*. New York: McGraw-Hill.

Miller, J.L. (2002). The Board as a Monitor of Organizational Activity: The Applicability of Agency Theory to Nonprofit Boards. *Nonprofit Management and Leadership, 12*(4), 429–450. doi: 10.1002/nml.12407

Miller-Millesen, J.L. (2003). Understanding the Behavior of Nonprofit Boards of Directors: A Theory-Based Approach. *Nonprofit and Voluntary Sector Quarterly, 32*(4), 521–547. doi: 10.1177/0899764003257463

Mintzberg, H. (1979). *The Structuring of Organizations*. Englewood Cliffs, NJ: Prentice Hall.

Mitchell, R.K., Agle, B.R., & Wood, D.J. (1997). Toward a Theory of Stakeholder Identification and Salience: Defining the Principle of Who and What Really Counts. *Academy of Management Review, 22*(4), 853–886. doi: 10.5465/amr.1997.9711022105

Mori, N., Randøy, T., & Golesorkhi, S. (2013). Determinants of Board Structure in Microfinance Institutions: Evidence from East Africa. *Journal of Emerging Market Finance, 12*(3), 323–365. doi: doi:10.1177/0972652713512916

O'Regan, K., & Oster, S.M. (2005). Does the Structure and Composition of the Board Matter? The Case of Nonprofit Organizations. *Journal of Law, Economics, and Organization, 21*(1), 205–227. doi: 10.1093/jleo/ewi009

Ostrower, F. (2007). Nonprofit Governance in the United States: Findings on Performance and Accountability from the First National Representative Study. Washinton, DC: Urban Institute.

Ostrower, F., & Stone, M.M. (2006). Boards of Nonprofit Organizations: Research Trends, Findings and Prospects for Future Research. In W.W. Powell & R. Steinberg (Eds.), *The Nonprofit Sector: A Research Handbook* (2nd ed.). New Haven, CT: Yale University Press.

Ostrower, F., & Stone, M.M. (2010). Moving Governance Research Forward: A Contingency-Based Framework and Data Application. *Nonprofit and Voluntary Sector Quarterly, 39*(5), 901–924. doi: 10.1177/0899764009338962

Pettigrew, A. M., Woodman, R.W., & Cameron, K.S. (2001). Studying Organizational Change and Development: Challenges for Future Research. *Academy of Management Journal, 44*(4), 697–713. doi: 10.2307/3069411

Pfeffer, J. (1973). Size, Composition, and Function of Hospital Boards of Directors: A Study of Organization–Environment Linkage. *Administrative Science Quarterly, 18*(3), 349–364.

Pfeffer, J. (1992). Understanding Power in Organizations. *California Management Review, 34*(2), 29–50.

Pfeffer, J., & Salancik, G.R. (1978). *The External Control of Organizations: A Resource Dependence Perspective.* New York: Harper & Row.

Pfeffer, J., & Salancik, G.R. (2003). The external control of organizations. In M.J. Handel (Ed.), *The Sociology of Organizations: Classic, Contemporary, and Critical Readings* (pp. 223–242). Thousand Oaks, CA: Sage.

Powell, W.W., & DiMaggio, P.J. (1991). The iron cage revisited: Institutional isomorphism and collective rationality. In P.J. DiMaggio & W.W. Powell (Eds.), *The New Institutionalism in Organizational Analysis.* Chicago: University of Chicago Press.

Rehli, F., & Jäger, U. (2011). The Governance of International Nongovernmental Organizations: How Funding and Volunteer Involvement Affect Board Nomination Modes and Stakeholder Representation in International Nongovernmental Organizations. *Voluntas: International Journal of Voluntary and Nonprofit Organizations,* 1–26. doi: 10.1007/s11266-011-9197-1

Renz, D.O., & Andersson, F.O. (2013). Nonprofit governance. In C. Cornforth & W. Brown (Eds.), *Nonprofit Governance: Innovative Perspectives and Approaches.* Abingdon: Routledge.

Rochester, C. (2003). The Role of Boards in Small Voluntary Organisations. In C. Cornforth (Ed.), *The Governance of Public and Non-profit Organizations: What Do Boards Do?* London: Routledge.

Saidel, J.R. (1998). Expanding the Governance Construct: Functions and Contributions of Nonprofit Advisory Groups. *Nonprofit and Voluntary Sector Quarterly, 27*(4), 421–436. doi: 10.1177/0899764098274003

Schmid, H. (2009). Agency–environmental relations: Understanding external and natural environments. In R.J. Patti (Ed.), *The Handbook of Human Services Management* (pp. 411–434). Thousand Oaks, CA: Sage.

Speckbacher, G. (2008). Nonprofit versus Corporate Governance: An Economic Approach. *Nonprofit Management and Leadership, 18*(3), 295–320. doi: 10.1002/nml.187

Steinberg, R. (2010). Principal-agent theory and nonprofit accountability. In K.J. Hopt & T. Von Hippel (Eds.), *Comparative Corporate Governance of Non-profit Organizations* (pp. 74–125). New York: Cambridge University Press.

Stone, M.M. (1996). Competing Contexts: The Evolution of a Nonprofit Organization's Governance System in Multiple Environments. *Administration & Society, 28*(1), 61.

Toubiana, M., Oliver, C., & Bradshaw, P. (2016). Beyond Differentiation and Integration: The Challenges of Managing Internal Complexity in Federations. *Organization Studies.* doi: 10.1177/0170840616670431

Van de Ven, A.H., & Sun, K. (2011). Breakdowns in Implementing Models of Organization Change. *Academy of Management Perspectives, 25*(3), 58–74. doi: 10.5465/amp.2011.63886530

Van Puyvelde, S., Caers, R., Du Bois, C., & Jegers, M. (2012). The Governance of Nonprofit Organizations: Integrating Agency Theory With Stakeholder and Stewardship Theories. *Nonprofit and Voluntary Sector Quarterly, 41*(3), 431–451. doi: 10.1177/0899764011409757

Van Puyvelde, S., Cornforth, C., Dansac, C., Guo, C., & Hough, A. (2017). Governance, boards, and the internal structure of associations. In D.H. Smith (Ed.), *The Palgrave Handbook of Volunteering, Civic Participation, and Nonprofit Associations* (pp. 894–914). Basingstoke: Macmillan.

Wellens, L., & Jegers, M. (2011). Beneficiaries' Participation in Nonprofit Organizations: A Theory-based Approach. *Public Money & Management, 31*(3), 175–182. doi: 10.1080/09540962.2011.573227

Wellens, L., & Jegers, M. (2014). Effective Governance in Nonprofit Organizations: A Literature Based Multiple Stakeholder Approach. *European Management Journal, 32*(2), 223–243. doi: http://dx.doi.org/10.1016/j.emj.2013.01.007

Westphal, J.D., & Zajac, E.J. (1995). Who Shall Govern? CEO/Board Power, Demographic Similarity, and New Director Selection. *Administrative Science Quarterly, 40*(1), 60–83.

Young, D.R. (2011). The Prospective Role of Economic Stakeholders in the Governance of Nonprofit Organizations. *Voluntas: International Journal of Voluntary and Nonprofit Organizations, 22*(4), 566. doi: 10.1007/s11266-011-9217-1

11

LEADERSHIP

Ruth Simsa

ASSOCIATE PROFESSOR, DEPARTMENT OF SOCIOECONOMICS & HEAD OF
THE INSTITUTE FOR NONPROFIT ORGANIZATIONS, WU VIENNA UNIVERSITY
OF ECONOMICS AND BUSINESS, VIENNA, AUSTRIA

Introduction

Leadership is a highly relevant topic for practitioners and is of significant academic interest in many disciplines with multifaceted focuses. This chapter will provide an overview on the topic related to the specific field of nonprofit organizations (NPO).

The notion of leadership goes beyond management by putting a stronger focus not only on methods and techniques, but also on the person of the leader, on his or her charisma and ability to motivate and inspire others. The Oxford Dictionary (2018) defines the term as "the action of leading a group of people or an organization," "the state or position of being a leader," or "the leaders of an organization, country, etc." Often, the term is used with romanticizing pathos: "Managers are people who do things right and leaders are people who do the right thing" (Bennis & Nanus, 2005, p. 20). Nevertheless, the distinction between management and leadership is blurring. In the following, leadership is to be understood as a value-, goal- and result-oriented, activating and reciprocal social influence for the fulfilment of common tasks in and with a structuring work situation (Wunderer, 2009).

The chapter first presents traditional and alternative theoretical approaches to leadership. Based on that, the specific conditions for leadership in NPOs will be discussed and an overview on NPO-specific research on leadership will be given, focusing on crucial topics of leadership research and on what we know about requirements for good leadership in these organizations. The chapter concludes with a discussion of the benefits of leadership and hierarchy on the one hand and critical leadership approaches on the other hand. It argues that there is no one best way of leadership and that the heterogeneous group of NPOs requires different leadership styles and practices.

Theories and concepts of leadership

Traditional approaches

Within the mainstream management literature, the assumption persists that leadership is the result of designated leaders and their actions. Therefore, an organization is perceived as shaped by its leader's decisions, style and personality. Leadership is ascribed to a person with certain qualities, a formal position within a hierarchy and the exercise of authority. Leadership theory thus assumes "that social action needs clearly identifiable, hierarchically positioned leaders" (Sutherland et al., 2014, p. 759).

Several different types of leadership theories can be distinguished: universal and situational theories on the one hand, and trait and behavioural theories on the other. Trait theories focus on personal characteristics of leaders, behavioural theories on their behaviour and leadership styles. Universal theories assume generally applicable attributes of effective leadership, whereas situational or contingency theories emphasize the context in which leadership is executed and suggest that specific styles of leadership are preferable in different situations (Fiedler et al., 1975; Hersey et al., 1988). Contingency theories have been the basis for much research, support and criticism (Ayman et al., 1995), nevertheless it is argued that the context of leadership still is not sufficiently taken into account (Osborn et al., 2002).

Trait theories focus on the personal characteristics of leaders which predestine them to lead. While early trait-based theories posited innate leadership traits as responsible for success, current trait theories claim that they can be learned and trained (Avolio & Gardner, 2005; Kibbe, 2004, p. 50). The roots of universal trait theory are old (Stogdill, 1948), but in practice, the belief in innate characteristics of leaders as a basis for success that are transferable to different situations persists. The same is true for situational trait theories, which also see innate traits of leaders as essential prerequisite for effectiveness but highlight situational conditions (the same leader might be successful in some situations but not in others) such that the leader and the situation must match (Fiedler et al., 1975).

Regarding the question of which traits of leaders are important, the empirically well-tested Big Five Model stresses five personality variables (Toegel & Barsoux, 2012). The model was derived from comprehensive analyses of adjectives used to describe personality and from numerous factor analyses (Goldberg, 1990; McCrae & Costa, 1985). It stresses the following personal characteristics: (1) *Emotional stability*: Emotional stability refers above all to dealing with unpleasant events and negative emotions. Emotionally stable people (low neuroticism values) describe themselves as calm, balanced and relaxed. (2) *Extraversion*: Extroverted people are sociable, active, energetic, cheerful and optimistic. They feel comfortable among people and like a stimulating and eventful environment. (3) *Openness to experience*: People with a high degree of openness describe themselves as inquisitive, imaginative, keen to experiment and unconventional. (4) *Social compatibility*: The central characteristics of tolerant people are altruism, the need for harmony, helpfulness and trust. Their dealings with others are characterized by understanding, goodwill and empathy. (5) *Conscientiousness*: This refers to planning and self-discipline in the execution of tasks. Conscientious people describe themselves as diligent, disciplined, ambitious, reliable, punctual and orderly.

Behavioural theories emphasize the behaviour and leadership style of leaders. Universal behavioural approaches share the belief that effective leadership depends on behaviour, which is more or less always the same (Blake & Mouton, 1964; Lewin, 1939). Situational behavioural theory suggests that leaders must adapt their leadership style to the specific context (Drucker, 2006; Hersey & Blanchard, 1977).

On the basis of behavioural theories, the classic dichotomy of employee and task orientation was developed. Employee-oriented leadership pays attention to the well-being of employees and strives for a good relationship with them, treating them as equal and supporting them. Task-oriented leadership places particular value on the quantity and quality of work, rebukes poor work, makes sure that the workers make full use of their labour force and spurs them on to greater efforts through pressure. Based on this distinction, Blake and Mouton presented the well-known distinction of leadership styles in the managerial grid model (Blake & Mouton, 1964), ranging from impoverished management with low concern for both tasks and people to team management with high concern for both aspects. According to the constituency theory (Fiedler et al., 1975), task-oriented leaders will be more successful in high- and low-control situations, and relationship-oriented leaders will be more successful in moderate control situations.

The dichotomy of employee and task orientation was sidelined in the mid-1980s by a concept that differentiated between "transactional" and "transformational" leadership (Bass & Avolio, 1990). Transactional leadership would function in the sense of a barter (Burns, 1978) by giving remuneration according to the achievement of goals, while transformational leadership would raise their followers to higher levels of satisfaction of needs, so that they would stand up for an idea or a collective beyond their own interests.

Another classic concept in understanding leadership is the distinction between personal-interactive leadership and structural-systemic leadership (Senge, 1990). Personal-interactive leadership aims at an immediate and direct influence through communication, feedback, perception, motivation, development, etc., while structural-systemic leadership refers to the factual-instrumental, indirect influence through context, culture, strategy or organization design. In everyday life, both are closely intertwined: personal-interactive leadership implements structural-systemic contents and vice versa; structural contents are negotiated via personal-interactive leadership.

Alternative approaches

Modern approaches put a stronger focus on the interaction between leaders and followers (Stippler & Dörffer, 2011) and thus characterize leadership as a process.

In recent years, a number of different styles and concepts were discussed in literature, including democratic leadership, oligarchy, leadership by default (Markham et al., 2001) and spiritual leadership (Cregård, 2017). Alternative forms of leadership are described with different terms, such as "shared" (Pearce & Conger, 2002), "collective" (Contractor et al., 2012), "collaborative" (Chrislip, 2002), "emergent," "co-democratic" or "distributed" leadership (Binci et al., 2016; Bolden, 2011; Gronn, 2002; Spillane, 2012; Spillane et al., 2004). They all understand leadership "as a dynamic, interactive influence process among individuals in groups for which the objective is to lead one another to the achievement of group or organizational goals or both" (Pearce & Conger, 2002, p. 1). This includes fluid processes of taking leadership roles according to contextual conditions (Pearce & Sims Jr, 2002), and outcomes understood as co-constructed by leaders and followers, thus "recognizing leadership as inherently a collaborative act" (Ruben & Gigliotti, 2016, p. 469).

Most of these concepts are situated in critical leadership studies (CLS). While the common feature of mainstream approaches is the emphasis on a clear top-down hierarchy and a clear distinction between leaders and followers (Collinson, 2011, p. 182), CLS by contrast interprets leadership as a process, which is a relational, socially constructed phenomenon realized through the interaction of diverse actors (Bolden, 2011; Gronn, 2002). They stress the importance of the management of meaning and the definition of reality (Smircich & Morgan, 1982) which is reflected, for example, in distributed leadership approaches (Bolden, 2011; Drath et al., 2008; Spillane, 2012). Distributed leadership considers leadership as something not done by an individual to others, but as a group activity (Bennett et al., 2003). Within critical leadership studies, the leader has been theoretically de-centred (Wood, 2005), and various aspects discussed may be subsumed under the term "post-heroic" (J.K. Fletcher, 2004), as opposed to the heroic "great leader" approach of the transformational leadership literature.

The systemic approach (Malik, 2006) and the symbolic approach (Neuberger, 1995) also apply social-constructivist perspectives, understanding leaders as an integral part of the entire system being influenced by this system (Mahlmann, 2011). If one understands organizations as social systems, then leadership is an effect of an order produced by the organization and its dynamics (Wimmer, 2009). Thus, the effects of leadership are not seen as resulting only from individual persons, but mainly from the dynamics within the respective system: "When placed in the same system, people, however different, tend to produce similar results" (Senge, 1990, p. 42). Willke also commented that once the rules of an institutionalized game have been established, it is more correct to say that the game is playing the people (players) than that the people are playing the game (Willke, 1995).

Both the systemic approach and critical leadership theories consider the influence of the leader to be limited. Systems theory attributes this to the self-referential character of social systems, which fundamentally limits their manageability and only allows for irritations of the system's patterns, which have indeterminable effects (Luhmann, 2011; Seidl & Becker, 2006). CLS stresses not so much systemic dynamics but interactions and the dynamics of relationships among the involved individuals. Also, CLS are sometimes based on normative approaches, documenting how leadership without leaders can be obtained (Sutherland et al., 2014).

Specific conditions for leadership in NPOs

Situational leadership theories state that "Leadership and its effectiveness, in large part, is dependent upon the context. Change the context and leadership changes as does what is sought and whether specific leadership patterns are considered effective" (Osborn et al., 2002, pp. 797f.). If this is presumed to be empirically convincing, the question of what is the context for leadership in NPOs becomes relevant.

There is wide consensus that NPOs need specific forms of leadership. Among practitioners, leadership as such or at least in its traditional ways is often discussed with certain scepticism. Grassroots organizations distance themselves from established organizations, emphasize self-organization and are highly sceptical of traditional forms of leadership. Scholars critically discuss the opportunities and threats of implementing management tools and leadership styles of the profit world in NPOs (Zimmer & Nährlich, 1993, 1997).

It also is widely acknowledged that leaders face specific conditions in NPOs. Although the sector encompasses a wide range of different organizations and these organizations differ not in all aspects from profit organizations (Helmig et al., 2004), a commonality of many NPOs seems to be the particularly challenging nature of leadership in these organizations (Meyer, 2007). Challenges result on the one hand from diversity and specific contradictions within NPOs (Stone et al., 1999), and on the other hand from the strong focus on values in organizational discourses, self-descriptions and decisions (Jeavons, 1992).

Regarding organizational contradictions, leaders typically have to balance between the economic rationale and the social mission (Jäger & Beyes, 2010) – the commercial-social paradox (Sharma & Bansal, 2017) – between task- and relationship-oriented leadership (Judge et al., 2004) and between different functions in society (Neumayr et al., 2009; Toepler & Anheier, 2004). Further, they typically can be characterized as multiple stakeholder organizations (Herman & Renz, 1997). Stakeholder interests in NPOs are often contradictory and in direct conflict with each other, thus posing diverse dilemmas for the organization and their leaders (Hielscher et al., 2017). As there is no simple bottom line as the ultimate decision-making criterion, NPOs are more dependent on legitimacy and the establishment of a balance between different stakeholders. Thus, while all organizations face dilemmas and contradictory expectations, NPOs have fewer possibilities to handle these problems since they cannot refer to one dominant external relationship. Typical organizational strategies of dealing with these contradictions are the ambiguity of goals, problems of performance measurement and difficulties in dealing with formal structures, authority and power. The high relevance of values and ideologies has motivating effects and adds to their moral capital. Executives generally perceive this as facilitating, but ideological overlays of certain topics can also make work more difficult. Usually, there are higher expectations of participation, which makes decision processes more complex, though sometimes of higher quality (Eckardstein & Simsa, 2004; Kane, 2001; Meyer & Simsa, 2013).

Another specific feature of many NPOs is the leadership of volunteers who work unpaid and thus expect more freedom, participation or being rewarded by positive emotions (Rowold & Rohmann, 2009a). Thus, their leaders have to be particularly sensitive to individual goals (Toepler and Anheier, 2004). To some extent, the leadership and motivation of members in membership associations poses a similar challenge for nonprofit leaders (see Chapter 21 Association and Membership Management).

NPO-specific research on leadership

Crucial research topics

Research generally describes leadership as important success factor for NPOs (Froelich et al., 2011) and argues that charismatic leaders influence both the performance of the organization and the motivation of members (De Hoogh et al., 2005), yet, the complex conditions in NPOs make it difficult to present empirical evidence for these assumptions.

An example of the complexity is diverging influences of formal positions (like voluntary boards) and of operative positions (executive director). Although the influence of executive directors is widely stated, so far there is little empirical evidence for this influence (exceptions e.g. Allison, 2002; Ritchie & Eastwood, 2006; Santora et al., 2007). Some authors see the executive director as most important factor for the performance (Herman & Heimovics, 1994), other studies stress the important role of board chairs (Harrison et al., 2013).

There is more agreement on the challenges that organizational and/or contextual conditions pose for nonprofit leaders (Dobbs, 2004; Green & Griesinger, 1996). Not surprisingly, empirical evidence shows that NPO leaders are particularly stressed (Bell et al., 2006) and are comparatively highly prone to burnout (Maunz & Steyrer, 2001). Another topic is the sector's lack of leadership, i.e. the lack of "strong" leaders, as the post-war generation of nonprofit executives is set to retire. Important questions are thus the difficulties of recruiting good leaders (Tierney, 2006), succession planning (Froelich et al., 2011), dealing with crisis (Gilstrap et al., 2016) and specific demands of leading volunteers (Connors, 2011; Leonard et al., 2004; Oostlander et al., 2014). However, it also is stated that, in general, NPO management has been widely professionalized over the last decades (Meyer & Simsa, 2014). Partly, this is due to New Public Management approaches and practices, which put more emphasis on performance (Pollitt & Bouckaert, 2011), and partly it is a response to economic pressure (Pape et al., 2016).

From the 1990s onwards, there has been a perceptible shift of leaders' orientation from a mission-driven to a resource-driven focus, and also from a focus on external linkages to a more inward- and funding-oriented focus that came about in connection with increasing resource shortages and competition (Adams & Perlmutter, 1995) and with the pressure to become more business-like in various dimensions (Maier et al., 2016). NPOs and their managers have widely adopted business-sector management methods. Nevertheless, they also need high competencies regarding the design of organizational structures, the management of diversity, contradictions, flexibility and external relationships (Zimmer & Pahl, 2016). Recently, increasing pressure to balance organizational values with business performance (and consequent higher demands on managerial capabilities, specifically with regard to personal skills) and commitment has been noted (Bish & Becker, 2015). Growing resource pressures in many NPOs likewise contribute to greater constraints on their leaders (Never, 2011).

Regarding different leadership styles, the results of meta-analyses of their effect on different aspects of success such as job satisfaction, employee satisfaction with the manager, or achievement of goals (Judge et al., 2004) have shown that employee orientation and transformational leadership are more effective in NPOs than in for-profit organizations. Conversely, transactional management in for-profit organizations is more effective than in NPOs (Simsa & Steyrer, 2013). In NPOs, positive emotions and motivation are more closely associated with transformational leadership than with transactional leadership (Rowold & Rohmann, 2009b).

Requirements for good leadership in NPOs

What are the requirements for good leadership in NPOs? Due to the different theoretical approaches, different contexts and organizational conditions and, most of all, due to the constructivist nature of the topic, this question cannot be answered objectively. Nevertheless, while keeping these inherent limitations in mind, a number of propositions can be offered.

According to the classic empirical findings of Herman and Heimovics (1994), which have been supplemented by the work of other authors, essential factors for the success of NPO leaders are the following:

Accepting the leadership role and its psychological significance: Acceptance of the leadership role is a central prerequisite for success. However, this often poses difficulties in NPOs: Management positions are frequently filled with front-line workers who are primarily interested in the client- or content-related work. Being promoted into management requires them to redefine their self-identity, especially in terms of balancing client-centred values with the focus on donors and funders, top management and the board as well as dealing with power and decision-making (Austin et al., 2011; Simsa & Patak, 2016).

Active leadership of the board: The relationship between the board of directors and the management is crucial for the success of NPOs, where the latter has an important – often underestimated – role in supporting and directing board members. The keyword here is "leading upwards," i.e. steering, moderating and influencing committees. Empirical results show that successful executives often perceive this role much more actively, consciously and creatively than less successful ones (K.B. Fletcher, 1992).

Leadership beyond the boundaries of the organization: One of the most important resources of a NPO is public credibility. An active strategic orientation towards the environment of the organization and the maintenance of community networks are thus another important success factor (Herman & Heimovics, 1994). Other authors also have highlighted the critical role of the external environment and a leadership focus on external strategies (Adams & Perlmutter, 1995) and the active design of "stakeholder relations" to manage external connections and accountability demands (Benjamin, 2008; Cordery & Baskerville, 2011).

(Micro-)political thinking and acting: At the intersection of interests and conflicting demands on the organization and against the background of low assertiveness towards donors, volunteers, supporters, etc., leaders require skills needed to manage micro-political negotiation

and cooperation processes. This includes the ability to improvise, integrate different points of view, accept compromises and partial solutions and a certain flexibility with regard to strategies and goals, an attitude that Herman and Heimovics call "creative leadership" (1994). In this context, with regard to the manifold contradictions of NPOs' roles and stakeholder expectations, conflict management skills are also of special importance.

A recent investigation of required leadership skills for third sector leaders in all European countries based on secondary data and reports of experts (Simsa et al., 2017) emphasizes to a high degree basic management skills and specific management capabilities, most of all in fundraising and financial management, innovation and public relations. Further, the following general leadership skills were named as currently particularly important: being mission-driving leaders (visionary skills, future thinking, securing the agility of the organization), motivating and inspiring others, strategy development, leading change (being emotionally able to cope with change, developing visions, establishing participatory processes, taking care of people), decision-making skills, dealing with conflicts and contradictions and being able to represent the organization. An American study on perceptions of organizational effectiveness came to compatible results: NGO leaders emphasized the importance of sound principles and strategies, a grassroots approach, large organizational size and resources, being collaborative, singleness of focus, campaigning abilities, funding and fundraising prowess, global scope and quality people (Mitchell, 2015). In another study that focused on leadership in crisis situations, nonprofit leaders identified six important personal characteristics: being a team player, strategic, transparent with stakeholders, quick to respond, self-composed and prepared (Gilstrap et al., 2016). Taking all these results together, NPO leaders should function like the proverbial Swiss army knife, being capable of performing in all possible situations, combining personal capabilities with basic management skills, balancing tensions and diverging demands, lead and ensure participation, being fast and reflexive, and so on.

Hierarchy and designated leaders versus autonomy and leadership without leaders

An ongoing discussion in the literature is whether leadership in NPOs requires the exertion of authority or if new, self-organized forms of leadership without leaders may provide a better alternative. NPOs often show a pronounced resistance to formal structures, authority and power. The reasons for this lie in the ideologies and value orientations of many NPOs – the desire for counter-worlds, co-determination and grassroots orientation – but also in stakeholder expectations, according to which NPOs should be more sympathetic, more participative and more humane than other organizations.

Nevertheless, with regard to the significance of hierarchy and strong leaders, there is a notable division within the sector. With tendencies towards professionalization and the adoption of business-like structures in many NPOs, they also adopt managerialist leadership structures, which result in clearly defined and empowered leadership positions. At the same time, grassroots and movement organizations are experimenting with new forms of leadership, attempting to enable leadership without designated leadership positions. Both positions have their merits.

On the one hand, oft-cited expressions concerning the "tyranny of structurelessness" (Freeman, 1970) and "freedom is an endless meeting" (Polletta, 2002) point out the drawbacks of leaderlessness which include hidden internal dynamics, informal power and inefficiencies. Epstein states that "[a]bsolute internal equality is hard to sustain" and that an "[a]nti-leadership ideology cannot eliminate leaders" but bears the risk of the emergence of informal authorities

(Epstein, 2001, p. 8). As soon as organizations exceed a certain minimum size, however, a hierarchy in the sense of clearly regulated supra- and subordinate relationships and decision-making powers is said to be required in order to be able to achieve goals (Reihlen, 2004). Hierarchy leads to stability and clarity. In the factual dimension, it helps to make decisions and deal with ambiguity: Contradictions and uncertainties can be pushed upwards until the matter is decided. In the social dimension, the possibility of delegation relieves conflicts and power struggles. In the time dimension, it has advantages, because decisions can be made without the time-consuming need to obtain consent. Hierarchy replaces individual power bases (competence, strength, social skills, etc.) with the authority of the function, thus simplifying matters by eliminating the need for repeated legitimization (Kühl, 2011). Furthermore, it is easier to control the opportunistic behaviour of individual persons by means of hierarchical instructions. In this sense, the active acceptance of the leadership role in NPOs might go along with the acceptance of power and hierarchy. Based on that, it should then be a question of how these structures can be reflected and made transparent. Further, even the clearest management structures do not mean that leadership is a one-way street from top to bottom. In all organizations, employees also influence their superiors.

On the other hand, there is evidence for the effective implementation of "non-hierarchical, informal and distributed forms of leadership" (Western, 2014, p. 673), of elaborated forms of self-organization and of radically participative decision-making practices (Simsa & Totter, 2017). Social movement and grassroots organizations thus often wish to put into practice what critical leadership studies theorize, namely, a focus not on leaders but on relations and leadership dynamics, thus "recognizing leadership as inherently a collaborative act" (Ruben et al., 2016, p. 469). These organizations reflect principles of anarchist thinking and the goal of leadership without leaders, emphasizing internal direct and participatory democracy, self-organization and autonomy (Benski et al., 2013; Flesher Fominaya, 2015; Gibson, 2013; Polletta, 2002). This horizontal distribution of leadership is often characterized as feminine or as resulting from feminist perspectives. In fact, research suggests that women often prefer democratic decision-making processes, and that their leadership style appears to be more consensus-oriented and participative, although evidence for these gender differences is not homogeneous and no consensus exists regarding underlying reasons (Barakso, 2007).

Specifically, activists of new social movements' organizations often aim at autonomous leadership. Leadership is thus seen as important, but it shall not imply any forms of hierarchy, formal authority or fixed roles; it shall enable more or less equal participation of all members and shall be transparent, empowering and open to everyone. Yet, the implementation of these ideals implies certain difficulties in practice, like the emergence of informal hierarchies and inefficiencies. Research on organizations of the Spanish protest movement showed that mainly collective reflection and elaborated and common rules are implemented as means to deal with these difficulties (Simsa & Totter, forthcoming). Collective reflection means regular and purposeful circles of review, interpretation, and understanding of experiences and experiments as a basis for collective learning. Leadership must thus be always open to collective reflection, contestation, change and reinterpretation (Fairhurst & Grant, 2010). Further alternative approaches to leadership need to be backed and safeguarded by collectively agreed upon and monitored rules (Simsa & Totter, forthcoming). Thus, while literature on social movements often stresses the aspects of freedom, fluidity and spontaneity (Western, 2014), these must be seen in a dialectic balance with clear, common, yet contested rules (Blee, 2012).

Sutherland et al. (2014) similarly analyse how leadership is understood and performed in anarchist organizations, calling these practices "anti-leader[ship]." They describe organizational practices and processes, which ensure non-hierarchical and shared leadership such as distributed and rotating formal roles, distributing tacit knowledge or enhancing accountability through symmetrical power relations. Although they describe these processes as challenging and conflictual, they stress their functionality and argue "that just because an organization is leaderless, it does not necessarily mean that it is also leadershipless" (Sutherland et al., 2014, p. 759). Establishing and maintaining leadership without leaders is demanding in daily practice, requiring experimentation with organizational forms and the development of reasonable organizational forms, but it is an integral part of the identity of these organizations.

Despite all difficulties in practice, the way leadership is lived or strived at in these organizations challenges the assumption that social action needs identifiable, hierarchically positioned leaders (Reedy, 2014).

Conclusion

NPO-specific research highlights major challenges for leaders, mainly the necessity to deal sustainably with organizational tensions that arise from the hybrid character of NPOs, their diverse stakeholders and varied societal functions. Financial success – the ultimate criterion in the profit world – is thus only one factor to estimate leadership success. Concurrently, external conditions for NPOs and therefore their leaders have become more demanding. Generally, the leadership culture in the sector has been professionalized and leaders seem to cope well with the demands of the role, yet many do so at high personal costs. Research on the success factors of nonprofit leadership focuses on behavioural attitudes like the acceptance of the leadership role; the active leading of boards; boundary spanning; and the ability to deal with sensitive issues (Austin et al., 2011; K.B. Fletcher, 1992). Due to growing financial pressures, specific competencies regarding funding, innovation and trust building have also gained in importance.

Given the heterogeneity of the sector, there is no one best way of leadership in NPOs. While in grassroots organizations, transformational and people-oriented leadership styles or the radical forms of leadership without leaders are culturally appropriate. In larger, traditional and market-driven NPOs, transactional and task-oriented styles will be more successful. However, critical leadership theory as well as systems theory suggest that we still overestimate the influence of individual persons and that outcomes of leadership are rather co-processed. Business administration scholars and political scientists as much as practitioners tend to heroize leadership. Due to their strong relationship orientation, NPOs are also very receptive to this point of view. However, the above-mentioned contradictions cannot be resolved by one person – not even by the most talented leaders. The task of leadership in this context is rather to notice them and orchestrate efforts to balance them out – over and over again.

References

Adams, C., & Perlmutter, F. (1995). Leadership in Hard Times: Are nonprofits Well-served? *Nonprofit and Voluntary Sector Quarterly, 24*(3), 253–262.

Allison, M. (2002). Into the Fire: Boards and Executive Transitions. *Nonprofit Management and Leadership, 12*(4), 341–351. doi: 10.1002/nml.12402

Austin, M., Regan, K., Samples, M., Schwartz, S., & Carnochan, S. (2011). Building Managerial and Organizational Capacity in Nonprofit Human Service Organizations Through a Leadership Development Program. *Administration in Social Work, 35*(3), 258–281. doi: 10.1080/03643107.2011.575339

Avolio, B.J., & Gardner, W.L. (2005). Authentic Leadership Development: Getting to the Root of Positive Forms of Leadership. *Leadership Quarterly, 16*(3), 315–338.

Ayman, R., Chemers, M.M., & Fiedler, F. (1995). The Contingency Model of Leadership Effectiveness: Its Levels of Analysis. *Leadership Quarterly, 6*(2), 147–167. doi: https://doi.org/10.1016/1048-9843(95)90032-2

Barakso, M. (2007). Is There a "Woman's Way" of Governing? Assessing the Organizational Structures of Women's Membership Associations. *Politics & Gender, 3*(2), 201–227. doi: 10.1017/S1743923X07000037

Bass, B.M., & Avolio, Bruce J. (1990). The Implications of Transactional and Transformational Leadership for Individual, Team, and Organizational Development. *Research in Organizational Change and Development, 4*(1), 231–272.

Bell, J., Moyers, R., & Wolfred, T. (2006). *Daring to Lead 2006: A National Study of Nonprofit Executive Leadership.* San Francisco.

Benjamin, L.M. (2008). Account Space: How Accountability Requirements Shape Nonprofit Practice. *Nonprofit and Voluntary Sector Quarterly, 37*(2), 201–223.

Bennett, N., Wise, C., Woods, P., & Harvey, J. (2003). *Distributed Leadership: Full Report.* National College for School Leadership Nottingham, UK.

Bennis, W.G., & Nanus, B. (2005). *Leaders: Strategies for Taking Charge,* 2nd Edition. New York: HarperBusiness.

Benski, T., Langman, L., Perugorría, I., & Tejerina, B. (2013). From the Streets and Squares to Social Movement Studies: What Have we Learned? *Current Sociology, 61*(4), 541–561. doi: 10.1177/0011392113479753

Binci, D., Cerruti, C., & Braganza, A. (2016). Do Vertical and Shared Leadership Need Each Other in Change Management? *Leadership & Organization Development Journal, 37*(5), 558–578.

Bish, A., & Becker, K. (2015). Exploring Expectations of Nonprofit Management Capabilities. *Nonprofit and Voluntary Sector Quarterly, 45*(3), 437–457. doi: 10.1177/0899764015583313

Blake, R.R., & Mouton, J.S. (1964). *The Managerial Grid: The Key to Leadership Excellence.* Houston, TX: Gulf Publishing.

Blee, K.M. (2012). *Democracy in the Making: How Activist Groups Form.* Oxford: Oxford University Press.

Bolden, R. (2011). Distributed Leadership in Organizations: A Review of Theory and Research. *International Journal of Management Reviews, 13*(3), 251–269. doi: 10.1111/j.1468-2370.2011.00306.x

Burns, J.M. (1978). *Leadership.* New York: Harper Collins.

Chrislip, D.D. (2002). *The Collaborative Leadership Fieldbook* (Vol. 255). Hoboken, NJ: John Wiley.

Collinson, D. (2011). Critical Leadership Studies. In A. Bryman, D. Collinson, K. Grint, B. Jackson, & M. Uhl-Bien (Eds.), *The Sage Handbook of Leadership* (pp. 179–192). London: Sage.

Connors, T.D. (Ed.). (2011). *The Volunteer Management Handbook: Leadership Strategies for Success,* 2nd Edition. Hoboken, NJ: Wiley

Contractor, N.S., DeChurch, L.A., Carson, J., Carter, D.R., & Keegan, B. (2012). The Topology of Collective Leadership. *Leadership Quarterly, 23*(6), 994–1011.

Cordery, C.J., & Baskerville, R.F. (2011). Charity Transgressions, Trust and Accountability. *VOLUNTAS: International Journal of Voluntary and Nonprofit Organizations, 22*(2), 197–213. doi: 10.1007/s11266-010-9132-x

Cregård, A. (2017). Investigating the Risks of Spiritual Leadership. *Nonprofit Management & Leadership, 27*(4), 533–547. doi: 10.1002/nml.21262

De Hoogh, A.H.B., Den Hartog, D.N., Koopman, P.L., Thierry, H., Van den Berg, P.T., Van der Weide, J.G., & Wilderom, C.P.M. (2005). Leader Motives, Charismatic Leadership, and Subordinates' Work Attitude in the Profit and Voluntary Sector. *Leadership Quarterly, 16*(1), 17–38. doi: http://dx.doi.org/10.1016/j.leaqua.2004.10.001

Dobbs, S. (2004). Some Thoughts about Nonprofit Leadership. In R.E. Riggio & S. Smith Orr (Eds.), *Improving Leadership in Nonprofit Organizations* (pp. 10–18). San Francisco: Jossey-Bass.

Drath, W.H., McCauley, C.D., Palus, C.J., Van Velsor, E., O'Connor, P. M., & McGuire, J.B. (2008). Direction, Alignment, Commitment: Toward a More Integrative Ontology of Leadership. *Leadership Quarterly, 19*(6), 635–653.

Drucker, P. (2006). *The Effective Executive: The Definitive Guide to Getting the Right Things Done.* New York: HarperBusiness.

Eckardstein, D. v., & Simsa, R. (2004). Strategic Management: A Stakeholder Based Approach. In A. Zimmer & E. Priller (Eds.), *Future of Civil Society: Making Central European Nonprofit-Organizations Work.* Wiesbaden: VS Verlag für Sozialwissenschaften.

Epstein, B. (2001). Anarchism and the Anti-Globalization Movement. *Monthly Review, 53*(4), 1–14.

Fairhurst, G.T., & Grant D. (2010). The Social Construction of Leadership: A Sailing Guide. *Management Communication Quarterly,* 24, 171–210.

Fiedler, F., Chemers, M. & Mahar, L. (1975). *Improving Leadership Effectiveness: The Leader Match Concept.* New York: John Wiley.

Flesher Fominaya, C. (2015). Debunking Spontaneity: Spain's 15-M/Indignados as Autonomous Movement. *Social Movement Studies, 14*(2), 142–163. doi: 10.1080/14742837.2014.945075

Fletcher, J.K. (2004). The Paradox of Postheroic Leadership: An Essay on Gender, Power, and Transformational Change. *Leadership Quarterly, 15*(5), 647–661.

Fletcher, K.B. (1992). Effective Boards: How Executive Directors Define and Develop Them. *Nonprofit Management and Leadership, 2*(3), 283–293. doi: 10.1002/nml.4130020307

Freeman, J. (1970). The Tyranny of Structurelessness. Retrieved 24.01.2017, from www.jofreeman.com/joreen/tyranny.htm

Froelich, K., McKee, G., & Rathge, R. (2011). Succession Planning in Nonprofit Organizations. *Nonprofit Management and Leadership, 22*(1), 3–20. doi: 10.1002/nml.20037

Gibson, M.R. (2013). The Anarchism of the Occupy Movement. *Australian Journal of Political Science, 48*(3), 335–348. doi: 10.1080/10361146.2013.820687

Gilstrap, C.A., Gilstrap, C.M., Holderby, K.N., & Valera, K.M. (2016). Sensegiving, Leadership, and Nonprofit Crises: How Nonprofit Leaders Make and Give Sense to Organizational Crisis. *VOLUNTAS: International Journal of Voluntary and Nonprofit Organizations, 27*(6), 2787–2806. doi: 10.1007/s11266-015-9648-1

Goldberg, L.R. (1990). An Alternative Description of Personality: The Big-Five Factor Structure. *Journal of Personality and Social Psychology, 59*(6), 1216–1229.

Green, J.C., & Griesinger, D.W. (1996). Board Performance and Organizational Effectiveness in Nonprofit Social Services Organizations. *Nonprofit Management and Leadership, 6*(4), 381–402.

Gronn, P. (2002). Distributed Leadership as a Unit of Analysis. *Leadership Quarterly, 13*(4), 423–451. doi: 10.1016/S1048-9843(02)00120-0

Harrison, Y., Murray, V., & Cornforth, C. (2013). Perceptions of Board Chair Leadership Effectiveness in Nonprofit and Voluntary Sector Organizations. *VOLUNTAS: International Journal of Voluntary and Nonprofit Organizations, 24*(3), 688–712. doi: 10.1007/s11266-012-9274-0

Helmig, B., Jegers, M., & Lapsley, I. (2004). Challenges in Managing Nonprofit Organizations: A Research Overview. *VOLUNTAS: International Journal of Voluntary and Nonprofit Organizations, 15*(2), 101–116. doi: 10.1023/b:volu.0000033176.34018.75

Herman, R.D., & Heimovics, R. (1994). Executive and Management Leadership. In R.D. Herman (Ed.), *The Jossey-Bass Handbook of Nonprofit Leadership and Management*. San Francisco: Jossey-Bass.

Herman, R.D., & Renz, D.O. (1997). Multiple Constituencies and the Social Construction of Nonprofit Organization Effectiveness. *Nonprofit and Voluntary Sector Quarterly, 26*(2), 185–206.

Hersey, P., & Blanchard, K.H. (1977). *The Management of Organizational Behaviour*. Upper Saddle River, NJ: Prentice Hall.

Hersey, P., Blanchard, K.H., & Johnson, D.E. (1988). *Management of Organizational Behavior: Utilizing Human Resources*. Englewood Cliffs, NJ: Prentice Hall.

Hielscher, S., Winkin, J., Crack, A., & Pies, I. (2017). Saving the Moral Capital of NGOs: Identifying One-Sided and Many-Sided Social Dilemmas in NGO Accountability. *VOLUNTAS: International Journal of Voluntary and Nonprofit Organizations, 28*(4), 1562–1594. doi: 10.1007/s11266-016-9807-z

Jäger, U., & Beyes, T. (2010). Strategizing in NPOs: A Case Study on the Practice of Organizational Change Between Social Mission and Economic Rationale. *VOLUNTAS: International Journal of Voluntary and Nonprofit Organizations, 21*(1), 82–100. doi: 10.1007/s11266-009-9108-x

Jeavons, T.H. (1992). When the Management Is the Message: Relating Values to Management Practice in Nonprofit Organizations. *Nonprofit Management & Leadership, 2*(4), 403–417.

Judge, T.A., Piccolo, R.F., & Ilies, R. (2004). The Forgotten Ones? The Validity of Consideration and Initiating Structure in Leadership Research. *Journal of Applied Psychology, 89*(1), 36–51.

Kane, J. (2001). *The Politics of Moral Capital*. Cambridge: Cambridge University Press.

Kibbe, B. (2004). *Funding Effectiveness: Lessons in Building Nonprofit Capacity*. San Francisco: Jossey-Bass.

Kühl, S. (2011). *Organisationen. Eine sehr kurze Einführung* (1. Aufl. ed.). Wiesbaden: VS Verl. für Sozialwiss.

Leonard, R., Onyx, J., & Hayward-Brown, H. (2004). Volunteer and Coordinator Perspectives on Managing Women Volunteers. *Nonprofit Management & Leadership, 15*(2), 205–219.

Lewin, K. (1939). Patterns of Aggressive Behavior in Experimentally Created Social Climates. *Journal of Social Psychology, 10*, 271–301.

Luhmann, N. (2011). *Organisation und Entscheidung* (3. Aufl. ed.). Wiesbaden: VS Verl für Sozialwiss.

Mahlmann, R. (2011). *Führungsstile gezielt einsetzen. Mitarbeiterorientiert, situativ und authentisch führen*. Weinheim: Beltz.

Maier, F., Meyer, M., & Steinbereithner, M. (2016). Nonprofit Organizations Becoming Business-Like: A Systematic Review. *Nonprofit and Voluntary Sector Quarterly, 45*(1), 64–86. doi: 10.1177/0899764014561796

Malik, F. (2006). *Führen, Leisten, Leben. Wirksames Management für eine neue Zeit.* Frankfurt am Main: Campus.

Markham, W.T., Walters, J., & Bonjean, C.M. (2001). Leadership in Voluntary Associations: The Case of the "International Association of Women". *VOLUNTAS: International Journal of Voluntary and Nonprofit Organizations, 12*(2), 103–130. doi: 10.1023/a:1011234618485

Maunz, S., & Steyrer, J. (2001). Das Burnout-Syndrom in der Krankenpflege: Ursachen – Folgen – Prävention. *Middle European Journal of Medicine 113*(7–8), 296–300.

McCrae, R.R., & Costa, P.T. (1985). *The NEO Personality Inventory.* Odessa.

Meyer, M. (2007). Stichwort: Nonprofit-Organisationen. In R. Köhler, H.-U. Küpper, & A. Pfingsten (Eds.), *Handwörterbuch der Betriebswirtschaftslehre* (pp. 1249–1258). Stuttgart: Schäffer-Poeschel.

Meyer, M., & Simsa, R. (2013). Besonderheiten des Managements von NPOs. In R. Simsa, M. Meyer, & C. Badelt (Eds.), *Handbuch der Nonprofit-Organisation. Strukturen und Management* (5., überarb. Aufl. ed., pp. 145–159). Stuttgart: Schäffer-Poeschel.

Meyer, M., & Simsa, R. (2014). Developments in the Third Sector – The Last Decade and a Cautious View into the Future. In M. Freise & T. Hallmann (Eds.), *Modernizing Democracy? Associations and Associating in the 21st Century* (pp. 203–215). New York: Springer.

Mitchell, G.E. (2015). The Attributes of Effective NGOs and the Leadership Values Associated with a Reputation for Organizational Effectiveness. *Nonprofit Management and Leadership, 26*(1), 39–57. doi: 10.1002/nml.21143

Neuberger, O. (1995). *Führen und geführt werden.* Oldenbourg: Lucius & Lucius.

Neumayr, M., Meyer, M., Pospíšil, M., Schneider, U., & Malý, I. (2009). The Role of Civil Society Organizations in Different Nonprofit Regimes: Evidence from Austria and the Czech Republic. *Comparative Social Research, 26*, 167–196.

Never, B. (2011). Understanding Constraints on Nonprofit Leadership Tactics in Times of Recession. *Nonprofit & Voluntary Sector Quarterly, 40*(6), 990–1004.

Oostlander, J., Güntert, S.T., & Wehner, T. (2014). Linking Autonomy-Supportive Leadership to Volunteer Satisfaction: A Self-Determination Theory Perspective. *VOLUNTAS: International Journal of Voluntary and Nonprofit Organizations, 25*(6), 1368–1387. doi: 10.1007/s11266-013-9395-0

Osborn, R.N., Hunt, J.G., & Jauch, L.R. (2002). Toward a Contextual Theory of Leadership. *Leadership Quarterly, 13*(6), 797–837. doi: https://doi.org/10.1016/S1048-9843(02)00154-6

Pape, U., Chaves-Ávila, R., Pahl, J.B., Petrella, F., Pieliński, B., & Savall-Morera, T. (2016). Working under Pressure: Economic Recession and Third Sector Development in Europe. *International Journal of Sociology and Social Policy, 36*(7/8), 547–566. doi: doi:10.1108/IJSSP-01-2016-0010

Pearce, C.L., & Conger, J.A. (2002). *Shared Leadership: Reframing the Hows and Whys of Leadership.* London: Sage.

Pearce, C.L., & Sims Jr, H.P. (2002). Vertical versus Shared Leadership as Predictors of the Effectiveness of Change Management Teams: An Examination of Aversive, Directive, Transactional, Transformational, and Empowering Leader Behaviors. *Group Dynamics: Theory, Research, and Practice, 6*(2), 172.

Polletta, F. (2002). *Freedom Is an Endless Meeting: Democracy in American Social Movements.* Chicago: University of Chicago Press.

Pollitt, C., & Bouckaert, G. (2011). *Public Management Reform. A Comparative Analysis: New Public Management, Governance, and the Neo-Weberian State*, 3rd Edition. Oxford: Oxford University Press.

Reedy, P. (2014). Impossible Organisations: Anarchism and Organisational Praxis. *Ephemera: Theory & Politics in Organization, 14*(4), 639–658.

Reihlen, M. (2004). Hierarchie. In G. Schreyögg & A. v. Werder (Eds.), *Handwörterbuch Unternehmensführung und Organisation* (Vol. 4, pp. 407–413). Stuttgart: Schäffer-Poeschel.

Ritchie, W.J., & Eastwood, K. (2006). Executive Functional Experience and its Relationship to the Financial Performance of Nonprofit Organizations. *Nonprofit Management and Leadership, 17*(1), 67–82. doi: 10.1002/nml.131

Rowold, J., & Rohmann, A. (2009a). Relationships between Leadership Styles and Followers' Emotional Experience and Effectiveness in the Voluntary Sector. *Nonprofit and Voluntary Sector Quarterly, 38*(2), 270–286.

Rowold, J., & Rohmann, A. (2009b). Transformational and Transactional Leadership Styles, Followers' Positive and Negative Emotions, and Performance in German Nonprofit Orchestras. *Nonprofit Management and Leadership, 20*(1), 41–59. doi: 10.1002/nml.240

Ruben, B.D., & Gigliotti, R.A. (2016). Leadership as Social Influence. *Journal of Leadership & Organizational Studies, 23*(4), 467–479. doi: doi:10.1177/1548051816641876

Santora, J.C., Caro, M.E., & Sarros, J.C. (2007). Succession in Nonprofit Organizations: An Insider/ Outsider Perspective. *S.A.M. Advanced Management Journal, 72*(4), 26–31.

Seidl, D., & Becker, K.H. (2006). Organizations as Distinction Generating and Processing Systems: Niklas Luhmann's Contribution to Organization Studies. *Organization, 13*(1), 9–35.

Senge, P. M. (1990). *The Fifth Discipline: The Art and Practice of the Learning Organization.* New York: Doubleday/Currency.

Sharma, G., & Bansal, P. (2017). Partners for Good: How Business and NGOs Engage the Commercial– Social Paradox. *Organization Studies, 38*(3–4), 341–364. doi: doi:10.1177/0170840616683739

Simsa, R., Hoff, M., Rameder, P., & Moder, C. (2017). The Third Sector in Europe: Challenges, Opportunities and Required Leadership Skills. Vienna: Vienna University of Economics and Business.

Simsa, R., & Patak, M. (2016). *Leadership in Nonprofit-Organisationen. Die Kunst der Führung ohne Profitdenken.* Wien: Linde Verlag.

Simsa, R., & Steyrer, J. (2013). Führung in NPOs. In R. Simsa, M. Meyer & C. Badelt (Eds.), *Handbuch der Nonprofit-Organisation. Strukturen und Management* (5., überarb. Aufl. ed., pp. 359–381). Stuttgart: Schäffer-Poeschel.

Simsa, R., & Totter, M. (2017). Social Movement Organizations in Spain – Being Partial as the Prefigurative Enactment of Social Change *Qualitative Research in Organizations and Management, 12*(4).

Simsa, R., & Totter, M. (2020). The Struggle for Good Leadership in social Movement Organizations: Collective Reflection and Rules as Basis for Autonomy. *ephemera: theory & politics in organization,* forthcoming.

Smircich, L., & Morgan, G. (1982). Leadership: The Management of Meaning. *Journal of Applied Behavioral Science, 18*(3), 257–273.

Spillane, J.P. (2012). *Distributed Leadership* (Vol. 4). Hoboken, NJ: John Wiley.

Spillane, J.P., Halverson, R., & Diamond, J.B. (2004). Towards a Theory of Leadership Practice: A Distributed Perspective. *Journal of Curriculum Studies, 36*(1), 3–34.

Stippler, M., & Dörffer, T. (2011). *Leadership – Approaches, Developments, Trends.* Gütersloh: Bertelsmann-Stiftung.

Stogdill, R.M. (1948). Personal Factors Associated with Leadership: A Survey of the Literature. *Journal of Psychology, 25,* 35–71.

Stone, M.M., Bigelow, B., & Crittenden, W. (1999). Research on Strategic Management in Nonprofit Organizations: Synthesis, Analysis, and Future Directions. *Administration & Society, 31*(3), 378–423.

Sutherland, N., Land, C., & Böhm, S. (2014). Anti-leaders(hip) in Social Movement Organizations: The Case of Autonomous Grassroots Groups. *Organization, 21*(6), 759–781. doi: 10.1177/1350508413480254

Tierney, T.J. (2006). The Leadership Deficit. *Stanford Social Innovation Review, 4*(2), S.26–35.

Toegel, G., & Barsoux, J.-L. (2012). How to Become a Better Leader. *MIT Sloan Management Review, 53*(3), 51–60.

Toepler, S., & Anheier, H.K. (2004). Organizational Theory and Nonprofit Management: An Overview. In A. Zimmer & E. Priller (Eds.), *Future of Civil Society: Making Central European Nonprofit-Organizations Work* (pp. 253–270). Wiesbaden: VS Verlag für Sozialwissenschaften.

Western, S. (2014). Autonomist Leadership in Leaderless Movements: Anarchists Leading the Way. *Ephemera. Theory and Politics in Organization, 14*(4), 673–698.

Willke, H. (1995). *Systemtheorie III. Steuerungstheorie.* Stuttgart: Fischer, UTB.

Wimmer, R. (2009). Führung und Organisation – zwei Seiten ein und derselben Medaille. *Revue für postheroisches Management, 4.*

Wood, M. (2005). The Fallacy of Misplaced Leadership. *Journal of Management Studies, 42*(6), 1101–1121.

Wunderer, R. (2009). *Führung und Zusammenarbeit.* München: Luchterhand.

Zimmer, A., & Nährlich, S. (1993). Nonprofit-Management und -Marketing mehr als Betriebsführung und Marktorientierung. *Zeitschrift für öffentliche und gemeinwirtschaftliche Unternehmen*(3), 345–354.

Zimmer, A., & Nährlich, S. (1997). Krise des Wohlfahrtsstaates und New Public Management. *Zeitschrift für Sozialreform*(9), 661–684.

Zimmer, A., & Pahl, B. (2016). Learning from Europe: *TSI Comparative Report No. 1.* Brussels.

12

BEYOND CODES

Values, virtues, and nonprofit ethics

Ki Joo Choi

ASSOCIATE PROFESSOR & CHAIR, DEPARTMENT OF RELIGION,
SETON HALL UNIVERSITY, SOUTH ORANGE, NJ, USA

Roseanne Mirabella

PROFESSOR, DEPARTMENT OF POLITICAL SCIENCE AND PUBLIC AFFAIRS,
SETON HALL UNIVERSITY, SOUTH ORANGE, NJ, USA

Introduction

Nonprofit sector values have historically been defined as and associated with fulfilling a social purpose (DiMaggio & Anheier, 1990; James, 2003; Moore, 2000; Weisbrod, 1998). As boundaries between the sectors have become increasingly blurred, nonprofit organizations struggle to define themselves as the values of "mission, markets, and politics collide" (Frumkin & Andre-Clark, 2000, 141). "One of the most profound trends in the social sector over the past thirty-five years has been its steady rationalization and marketization" (Ebrahim, Battilana, & Mair, 2014, 82) including its embrace of market and evidence-based strategies such as social enterprise, effective altruism, and philanthrocapitalism (Eikenberry & Mirabella, 2018, 43). The nonprofit sector has indeed entered uncharted waters as organizations struggle to balance the turn to the market with the sector's historic commitment to social purpose.

In this context, we ask: what are the distinctive contributions of nonprofit organizations to democratic life and civic society? How should their role and function be imagined? To ask such questions is to inquire about the centrality of values, about the values that ought to drive the work of nonprofits. This chapter pivots on the premise that the steady turn to rationalization and marketization in the nonprofit sector is not necessarily inevitable but are reflective of and aided by certain kinds of values that nonprofits either purposefully adopt or (more likely) simply assume. Human actions hardly take place within a moral vacuum, but always within a valuational context, or against a horizon of value (Taylor, 1991). In other words, these values are consequential (or are action guiding) insofar as they shape or inform our sense of self (either personal or corporate) and, ultimately, our choices.

What are the values underwriting the rationalization and marketization of nonprofits? As a point of departure, we turn to an assessment of nonprofit ethics, focusing on the sector's growing reliance on codes of conduct as the statement of values its presents to the community. Our aim is to indicate what reliance on such codes suggests about the kind of values that nonprofits embrace and whether nonprofits are well served by those values (or, put differently, whether they are serving well their various constituencies in light of those values). While there is no uniform code of conduct in the nonprofit sector, and codes of conduct can vary from one nonprofit to another, the kind of codes we highlight here provides a useful entry point into thinking critically about the extent to which the values of an individualistic ethos that is central to the enlightenment project are reflected in the self-understanding of the nonprofit sector. In other words, is the individualistic thrust of liberalism part and parcel of how nonprofits have come to understand themselves? While such values are not trivial, an uncritical acceptance of them undermines the distinctive role that nonprofits can play in democratic life and civil society, facilitating, intentionally or not, the rationalization and marketization of the sector.

Within all organizations, there are various values competing for priority, often referred to in the literature as the Competing Values Framework (CVF) (Grabowski et al., 2015; Herman & Renz, 1999; Quinn & Rohrbaugh, 1983). As understood within the CVF model, organizations must respond to competing values as articulated by the organization's stakeholders in three dimensions: organizational focus, structural preference, and managerial concern (Quinn & Cameron, 1983; Quinn & Rohrbaugh, 1983). These values correspond quite well with the rationalization of the liberal order with each organization necessarily responding to stakeholder pressures to survive and thrive. However, when applying this framework to voluntary organizations, Grabowski and colleagues identified a fourth dimension perhaps unique to the nonprofit sector: a motivational trait differentiating between the head and the heart. While the three dimensions of the CVF model emphasize problem solving and competition, related to the head, the fourth dimension, that of the heart, puts an emphasis on "behaviors rooted in consciousness and driven by compassion, generosity, and idealism" (Grabowski et al., 2015, 912). Nonprofit organizations with their embrace of the heart and its affect must by necessity deal with the tension between operational needs for rational responses related to organizational survival and its mission rooted in values of compassion and idealism (Grabowski et al., 2015, 917).

The tension between head and heart in today's nonprofit sector has a long historical tradition, particularly in the American case. In part, this is due to what Peter Dobkin Hall describes as the 'deep historical roots' of the "wariness with which organized religion and organized philanthropy regard each other today" (Hall, 1990, 40). The origins of modern philanthropy trace back to the vast side effects of industrialization and urbanization in the late 1800s that rendered existing institutions inadequate to the task of addressing the needs of those incapable of caring for themselves. Hall recounts how Andrew Carnegie's embrace of Darwinist theories "shaped his ideas about philanthropy (that) rested on quantitatively based concepts of efficiency . . . (to determine if individuals) were 'worthy' or 'unworthy,' were they potentially good investment vehicles" (42). The poor became eligible for assistance based on a set of metrics designed to determine their ultimate success as defined by self-sufficiency. Note the similarity between Carnegie's approach toward philanthropy and the values of the head as outlined above in CVF. Clergy at the time, recognizing the "stark confrontation between Christian ideals and the realities of suffering" (51), challenged Carnegie's call for a scientific philanthropy and called for churches to reestablish themselves as a dominant charitable force. The values of religious organizations as understood by religious leaders were much more concerned with values of the heart than were the values of organized philanthropy with its focus on the head, especially when considering What would Jesus do?

Hall concluded that the values of organized philanthropy would never bridge the "chasm between the haves and the have-nots" as this is not within the "capacity of the calculating" (59), urging philanthropy to reconnect with its religious roots of the heart. Nonprofits, therefore, must resist shying away from sustained, critical self-appraisals and instead prioritize identifying and assessing not only its *current* valuational commitments, those of the head, but also the kinds of values that *ought* to inform their functions and roles in democratic and civic life, those of the heart. That goal requires nonprofits to come to terms with and resist the prevailing individualism of modern society (and the extent to which such an individualized ethos and logic may be either explicitly or implicitly held as given by nonprofit managers), replacing such values with relationality and the correlative virtues and practices of the heart, specifically, solidarity rooted in compassion, generosity, and idealism.

Nonprofit codes of conduct: assessing their valuational assumptions

Mapping the proper role and function of nonprofit managers has typically relied on defining what constitutes wrong behavior and the mechanisms to mitigate or deter such behavior. Deborah L. Rhode and Amanda K. Packel, for instance, claim that unethical behavior in nonprofit organizations is often caused by, among other factors, cognitive bias and dissonance, skewed reward or compensation systems, fragmented information across multiple departments and people, and ineffective leadership (Rhode and Packel, 2009, 30–31). In response, they argue that nonprofits do well to take at least two steps: ensure effective codes of conduct and compliance programs, and promote effective financial management (ibid., 34).

The advocacy for and reliance on, in particular, codes of conduct or codes of ethics to guide philanthropic leaders and nonprofit managers, as Margaret Urban Walker might describe, draws on a theoretical-juridical model of ethics. Walker notes its ubiquity in contemporary American life: a "compact set of law-like propositions that 'explain' the moral behavior of a well-formed moral agent" (1998, 7–8). As law-like in character, codes of conduct or ethics are essentially obligation-oriented (e.g., "one shall," "one will"), mapping the boundaries of what constitutes right action or choices within a particular organization.

It is worth noting a concrete example of a theoretical-juridical conception of ethics at play in a nonprofit organization. Consider the eight-point code of ethics of the New York City YWCA (www.ywcanyc.org/code-of-ethics/). Below is a sampling of the codification for one domain of the YWCA's code, fundraising, concerned with the solicitation and efficient administration of funds raised:

1   Provides truthful and current information in our solicitation communications;
2   Does not establish unrealistic donor expectations of what donor gifts will actually accomplish within the limits of our mission and programs;
3   Will not accept donations from organizations or individuals in the knowledge that such donations likely were acquired in violation of applicable laws and regulations or otherwise through actions that would be offensive to the YW's values or in violation of this Code of Ethics;
4   Provides donors access to its most recent annual report and financial statements as approved by the Board of Directors;
5   Assures donors that their gifts will be used for the purposes for which they were given;
6   If in receipt of funds intended to be used for programs or activities that are not part of the organization's present or prospective programs, will either return the funds or, if the intent is in accordance with our mission, treat these as restricted funds and channel them in a manner that honors the donor's intent, after discussing alternate uses with the donor or legal designate, if available; and
7   Ensures that information about donations is handled with respect and confidentiality to the extent provided by law . . .

Agency is restrained by the stipulation that violation of this code may result in disciplinary action or dismissal, in the case of the employee, or removal from the Board of Directors. Such punitive mechanisms reinforce the law-like character of codes of conduct that follow the theoretical-juridical model of ethics. Codes are only as effective as their enforcement provisions, without which these law-like codes would amount to something more akin to general guidelines or recommendations for conduct rather than obligations or requirements.

To think of codes of conduct as theoretical-juridical models of ethics ought not to diminish their value. Rules for shoring up fiduciary responsibilities of managers and donors and upholding institutional transparency are surely essential for a nonprofit agency's integrity, effectiveness, and longevity. Such rules can be an integral part of operationalizing a nonprofit's mission. However, such codes of conduct can also be limited if their primary aim is to establish a set of procedures that minimize legal liability (cf. Dobson 2005 and Wood 2005 in Grobman, 2007, 247). Note the references in the YWCA code of conduct to "in violation to applicable laws" and "to the extent provided by law." When insulating a nonprofit from liability is the normative pull of its code of conduct, then the locus of its code of conduct is *not* about *what makes* a choice right and wrong (this is about moral justification, i.e., which *values* justify the rightness and wrongness of choices or acts). Instead, it is simply about elucidating the question of *which choices* are right and wrong and which ones should be codified into law.

Reducing the ethics of an organization to simply what is legal (in this case through a code of conduct) circumvents larger questions of value, which pertain to questions of "the good." Such questions aim to excavate the larger contexts in which human agency is shaped and operates and not simply on which choices or behaviors are morally and legally right or wrong. Included in such inquiry is assessing what kind, as well as the extent to which, economic, political, or cultural values inform decision-making.

As an expression of the theoretical-juridical model of ethics, codes of conduct such as the one highlighted above from the New York City YWCA tend toward delineating and codifying what is right within pre-existing institutional arrangements and cultural norms or values, the veracity of which may be taken for granted. As such, codes of conduct do little to encourage nonprofit managers to assess whether the very valuational terms or contexts within which codes of conduct are established are themselves morally legitimate. In other words, codes of conduct, as Alistair MacIntyre might put it, do not allow for "criticism [of] the system itself" (1988, 392). While MacIntyre is concerned with the capacity for modern political systems to be self-critical, his concern when applied to the nonprofit sector raises the question of whether a set of rules or codes can adequately define the parameters of the roles and functions of a nonprofit. Instead, the capacity to discern the distinctive roles and functions of a nonprofit requires the capacity to think critically about the codes themselves, that is, the narratives "behind" and "underneath" the codes, or the underlying valuational assumptions or premises of those codes.

The logic and consequences of individualism

What might those valuational assumptions be? And why might it matter to identify and critically assess those values? In other words, what might those values imply about the nature of the work of nonprofits, or how nonprofits conceive of their work? To address these questions, we propose the importance of identifying the conception of human nature or personhood (and its correlative conception of what human persons are capable of knowing) that underlies the theoretical-juridical model of ethics and, accordingly, codes of conduct. This conception of the human person is at its core an individualistic conception, which encourages if not necessitates a legalistic and proceduralistic framework for nonprofit management. While such a framework is conducive to navigating diverse member interests and the complex social realities that nonprofits must navigate, such a framework, we propose, hampers collaborative, collective decision-making that ought to characterize or distinguish the work of nonprofits in democratic life and civil society.

If codes of conduct, following Walker, are best understood as concrete expressions of a theoretical-juridical model of ethics, then such codes, like this model of ethics, take for granted the primacy of the value of individualism. Individualism is, as Mark Roelofs observes, a fundamentally Anglo-American value and ideal. The driving principle of Anglo-American liberalism, according to Roelofs, is "the primacy of personal vocation" which in itself is not necessarily negative, especially in the ways it has, historically speaking, spurred the project of self-improvement. However, that project has also tended toward self-aggrandizement on the one hand and moralism on the other hand (Roelofs, 1976, 5), often devolving further into restrictions of others' freedoms and violations of civil rights. Mitigating those kinds of negative outcomes was one of the preoccupations with enlightenment forebears such as John Locke and Thomas Hobbes. While both diverged in how to resolve politically the problem of inordinate self-interest (which is an inevitable consequence of our natural state as free persons), their search for a political resolution underscored their belief in what Jennifer Herdt refers to as the "unsocial sociability" of human persons: "Being self-interested, human beings come into conflict with one another, but they also have a need for life in society" (2001, 150; see also Schneewind, 1998). In that respect, laws that "secur[ed] peace in human society" were necessary; thus the need for government of some kind (Herdt, 2001, 150).

The desire to mitigate conflict between self-interested individuals eventually meant turning to legalism and proceduralism, which inevitably led to the rise of technical thinking or bureaucratic problem solving. One prominent narrative of that bureaucratic inevitably is offered by MacIntyre who begins with the kind of moral agent the liberal project ultimately produced, a "moral agent [who is able] to stand back from any and every situation in which one is involved, from any and every characteristic that one may possess and to pass judgment on it from a purely universal and abstract point of view that is totally detached from all social particularity" (1981, 31–32). But the freedom of such a socially unsituated self – that is, a self that is independent of any "external" attachments (e.g., family, institutions, traditions, religion) – eventually stood in tension with, among other problems, the need to "limit the anarchy of self-interest," MacIntyre further argues (1981, 35). What he means by the anarchy of self-interest is multifold, but at its root is the way in which the celebration of individualism coincides with a pessimism that we can agree on a common, normative conception of human well-being and the social good. Today, that pessimism has become what David Hollenbach calls the "crisis of humanism," the loss of "confidence in our ability to develop an adequate normative description of what human well-being is, and . . . lost hope in our practical ability to shape a society that enables human beings to develop in that well-being" (2003, 55). Yet, in the absence of a commonly agreed upon account of human well-being and the social good, how are we to adjudicate which choices are the right choices apart from simply saying that whatever an individual person prefers is what makes a choice right? If the rightness of one's decisions and actions are simply a function of her own desires and will, then is it possible to say that one person's account of human well-being is incorrect (or less correct) than another person's account?

These questions underscore a basic problem: the problem of diversity, i.e., of diverse human interests, preferences, and goals. How do we navigate a situation in which there are multiple and competing visions of what constitutes the good life? What is the authoritative standard by which to judge what is truthful and valuable? Pluralism has its benefits, but it has its limits too. One route to bringing order to the "anarchy of self-interest" is turning to the authority and paternalism of bureaucratic expertise, as has been the case for much of modern societies, where "bureaucracy and individualism are partners as well as antagonists," as MacIntyre argues

(1981, 35). The logic of bureaucratic expertise in industrial societies is one of social scientific standards for truth and value (Denhardt, 1981). Another route is the turn to market logics, that is, the reliance on the free market as an essential (or only capable) mechanism to police the pursuit of diverse, individual preferences in a manner that is not centralized, authoritarian, or oppressively judgmental. Irving Kristol's account of the nature of liberal society is a leading example of such faith in the market: "A liberal society is one that is based on a *weak* consensus . . . [no society can be] in a condition of perpetual moral and political chaos. But the liberty of a liberal society derives from a prevalent skepticism as to anyone's ability to know the 'common good' with certainty . . . A liberal society, therefore, will be very tolerant of capitalist transactions between consenting adults because such transactions are for mutual advantage . . . measured by the marketplace" (1996, 137; cf. Hayek, 2001).

If individualism concedes hope in discerning a common, normative conception of the good life – what it means to be a good person, what it means to be a just society in some universally authoritative, binding sense – then legalism and proceduralism constitute an attractive if not obvious moral minimum that free individuals can reasonably assent to for at least the sake of communal order and social peace. The emergence of bureaucratic expertise and paternalism in modern society, as well as a dependence on free-market mechanisms, are both more particularized expressions of this turn to legalism and proceduralism; they are all in response to the moral problematic of the liberal self (i.e., the primacy of individualism and the moral vacuum and crisis of authority that liberal individualism creates).

The moral authority of legalism and proceduralism, emanating from liberal individualism, is evidenced in our earlier discussion of nonprofit codes of conduct, such as the code adopted by the New York City YWCA, in its reliance on prevailing laws, statues, and ordinances, as well as processes that ensure transactional transparency, as the boundaries of permissible and impermissible conduct. However, such a way of settling the question of moral authority is hardly innocuous; it does not necessarily provide any substantive moral guidance other than base-line standards of conduct that would presumably apply to *any person and not just nonprofit managers*. The problem with such a generic account of right and wrong conduct is captured sharply by Russell Connors and Patrick McCormick in their assessment of justice within a culture of individualism:

> As long as we think that we are, first and foremost, individuals, and that our social obligations are weak, secondary ties, then the heart of justice will always be about defending our personal freedoms and punishing those who harm us. But such a stripped down view of either ourselves or the concept of justice . . . can define the minimal standards of individual behavior . . . but it . . . pays insufficient attention to the social systems and structures required for a good community. (1998, 67)

That is the predicament of the nonprofit sector so long as it ignores the moral problematic that the liberal, modern self creates. To be more specific, while, as Stuart C. Mendel argues, "a management-focused model [of nonprofits] is too limiting as a means of understanding the inner workings and the defining characteristics of the modern nonprofit organization," which we referred to previously as the head of the nonprofit organization, what might be the moral framework that allows for adjudication of other models more connected with the heart? Why should we consider, and maybe even prefer, a model of nonprofit management that moves beyond accountability and "performance standards and operational efficiencies" that is typical in business and corporate approaches to management? (Mendel, 2014, 63). These questions are to a degree irrelevant if the nature of nonprofits and their roles and functions are regarded as settled matters. However, as we claimed at the outset, these matters are clearly far from settled and are very much in flow. Whether the work of nonprofits is necessarily advancing human well-being and the social good is of course a more complicated question than it may seem. We also embraced Hall's suggestion that nonprofit organizations embrace values rooted in religious traditions of the heart in order to create a bridge between the haves and the have-nots. In the next section, we focus on how nonprofits as third sector organizations with a focus on social purpose (the heart) differ in their approach from the kinds of services the state or for-profit entities are able to deliver (the head) (Clohesy, 2000). Which methodologies should be adopted to combat the current inadequacy of scientific methods in addressing the needs of the poor and marginalized? Such questions touch on fundamental issues of the good, that is, on the very nature of politics and justice, on what justice ought to be, or what kind of political community and economic arrangements best promote human well-being that go beyond a narrow legalistic and proceduralist account of politics and justice. Those questions further hinge on how the roles and functions of nonprofits ought to be (re)conceived in order to bring to the fore such fundamental questions of the good.

Prioritizing the value of relationality

To reject what Mendel refers to as models of nonprofits that focus on corporatized performance standards and operational efficiencies related to scientific efficiency in favor of other models of nonprofit management (such as those that focus on social purpose) rooted in values of the heart is to engage in a critical analysis of how such models conceive of the function or *telos* of nonprofits and their managers. However, the advocacy of one model over another requires a framework that allows for intelligible moral judgments about each model's account of the ends of the nonprofit enterprise. However, is such a framework possible given how challenging it is to foster moral agreement in a world of diverse interests and visions of the good? Given the seeming intractableness of our disagreements on what constitutes the good life, it is perhaps understandable why nonprofits slide easily into legalistic and proceduralistic ways of thinking about how roles and functions of nonprofit managers ought to be defined (as in codes of professional conduct). That way of conceptualizing roles and functions is the less controversial route than the challenging and potentially contentious task of engaging critical reflection on what constitutes human well-being and the social good and which model of nonprofit management advances, perhaps more genuinely, that conception of the good. Yet, by favoring expediency and pragmatism over critical inquiry, legalistic and proceduralistic approaches to nonprofit management obviate the fact that such approaches inhabit and, as a consequence, reinforce particular social and cultural assumptions, trends, and values. Roseanne Mirabella (2013) has referred to this as the performance mindset of philanthropic giving based on the science of logic models. Foundations provide grants to nonprofit organizations that, in turn, develop goals and objectives to be met during the period of the grant. If the organization achieves its metrics another grant might be forthcoming, if not, the organization might be defunded. This approach "reflects the continued dominance of the rationalist approach to program implementation with its circular or loop system of management" (Mirabella, 2013, 95). The implications of this approach to nonprofit funding is an accountability to the donors rather than accountability to the beneficiaries. That is the paradox of legalism and proceduralism; while their underlying logic is to affirm the diversity of moral visions that individuals pursue (and are entitled to pursue as free individuals), they, at the same time, take for granted particular notions of the good – such as corporatized models of well-being/social responsibility or data-driven, metrics-focused models of truth – as normative. Notions of charity as a gift are outside the frame of this model.

If the roles and functions of nonprofit managers are to avoid simply assuming the givenness of, say, corporatist, market, or bureaucratic premises and logics, then nonprofits do well to move beyond rule making and following to critically addressing the social dynamics at play in modern society. To do so is to approach the question of the roles and functions of nonprofits as a function of ethical discernment *and, ultimately,* judgment (O'Donovan, 2003); that is, as an evaluative task that not only engages in (1) description (what is going on?) but also (2) the appraisal of value (what should we do?). Engaging in the latter question – what should we do? – however, requires moving beyond individualism and its moral limitations (i.e., the ways in which individualism conceptually problematizes moral normativity and the prospects for moral consensus). But how? The concept of virtue, generally construed, hints at a promising path forward.

Consider the Aristotelian emphasis on the virtues as habits of character (i.e., one's moral disposition) which are acquired and supported in community (Aristotle on civic friendship in *Nicomachean Ethics*, Book VIII). Such a conception of the virtues underscores an account of human nature that is relational rather than unbound to anything other than one's own will and preferences (i.e., enlightenment individualism). Such an account of human nature, as Hollenbach observes, underscores "the de facto realities of interaction and interdependence that exist among people" (2003, 50). This emphasis on relationality, however, is not simply a description of contemporary realities in a globalized world, but also a normative statement about human persons as relational beings and how *relationality is the necessary condition for moral discernment and judgment.* Cultivating the conditions for social participation and life together in society (i.e., community) is necessitated by the very fact that human persons are by nature relational or social. And, it is only in community that we are able to understand and address what is significant and insignificant, what kinds of persons we ought to be and what kinds of goals we ought to pursue.

Why is moral deliberation dependent on relationality? What necessitates this interconnection? Moral deliberation is not unlike learning a language (Taylor, 1991, 33). Learning, say, Spanish as a second language requires belonging to a community of sorts, or at least the recognition that one needs to depend on another who is fluent in Spanish. One becomes an independent Spanish speaker only in that dependence. That dependence is not one of servitude, but rather a recognition that one cannot be a certain kind of person (in this case a Spanish speaker) by oneself but only in relationship or community. So too for moral deliberation. As Charles Taylor argues, deliberating about what is significant and insignificant, what we should do and should not do, is made possible by virtue of our dependence on others. This is not to say that we are incapable of individual thoughts, intelligence, and agency, but it is to underscore a conceptual point about the nature of the self and how we think and make choices.

While the legacy of the enlightenment has ingrained in us the idea of subjectivism or the idea that we are capable of making choices as individuals who are unattached to others, or "sources" outside the self, Taylor argues that the choices we make as individuals hardly emerge out of our own inner creative desires and thinking *ex nihilo* (1991, 60–69). More coherent is the position that our desires and thinking are formed constitutively, that is, in necessary and inescapable dialogue with other persons, language systems, cultures, and traditions, both religious and secular. It is only in that dialogic process that a particular self emerges as she questions, tests, assesses, resists, adopts, or revises the values and beliefs she receives or encounters.

Promoting relationality through solidarity

Contrasted with the liberal emphasis on and value for individualistic rationality, agency, and initiative, the Aristotelian concept of virtue brings focus to an alternative value: relationality.

Aristotelian virtue begins with relationality as the *a priori* context that makes moral thinking and doing possible and intelligible. Within this framework of virtue, moral deliberation is necessarily a communal affair, not only in the sense that moral deliberation is dependent upon relationality, but as dependent on relationality, moral deliberation is necessarily aimed at the good of the community, i.e., on the good of those who engage one another in deliberation. As Hollenbach reminds us, a basic Aristotelian insight about the virtues is that they "are finally directed to fuller attainment of the common good" (Hollenbach 2003, 51).

What kind of virtues affirm the value of relationality and foster (or habituate and dispose us to) moral deliberation about the common good? Hollenbach proposes solidarity as a central virtue (Hollenbach 2003, 50). To practice solidarity is to recognize that human life is only possible together and that we have a shared responsibility for one another's well-being. "Everything about us is social" (Maguire, 1980, 58) to a point that "there is no way any one of us can exist apart from everyone else" (Wadell, 2008, 228). That sense of being constitutively related to one another – that our very lives depend on one another – relativizes the sovereignty of individual agency that the enlightenment values so highly. Solidarity necessarily promotes, therefore, what Iris Murdoch would say is the virtue and practice of humility, "the disciplined overcoming of self" (2003, 93). Without humility, solidarity is wanting: "Humility is not a peculiar habit of self-effacement, rather like having an inaudible voice, it is selfless respect for reality and one of the most difficult and central of all virtues" (ibid.).

Solidarity and humility, among other interrelated virtues, are not rubrics that provide immediate and clear-cut guidance and resolutions to moral dilemmas, or to the kind of decisions one needs to make in a given situation, at least not in some obvious and direct way. This has been taken as a significant lacuna of an Aristotelian conception of virtue and can be regarded as one possible challenge to the practical applicability of Aristotelian virtue for nonprofit management. However, that kind of criticism insufficiently appreciates the larger picture that this emphasis on the virtues underscores (e.g., Hursthouse, 1995). The virtue of solidarity (and, correspondingly, humility) *enables and facilitates* moral deliberation about the good. In that sense, solidarity is best regarded as forming the "background of intelligibility" or "horizons against which things take on significance for us" (Taylor, 1991, 37). In other words, solidarity forms the context in which moral deliberations about the values, roles, and functions of nonprofits can take place. "We learn through attending to contexts, vocabulary develops through close attention to objects, and we can only understand others if we can to some extent share their contexts," as Murdoch argues (2003, 31). The context of intelligibility that the practice of solidarity provides is one that identifies the value of persons in their inherent relationality and, as a consequence, the need for social goods to be shared and made available to all in accordance to that inherent relationality. Committing to and practicing the virtue of solidarity, therefore, provides a standard from which to appraise various and competing approaches to nonprofit management. Such a commitment, therefore, asks: to what extent does a particular model of nonprofit management – such as one that relies on market-driven performance standards and operational efficiencies – best support the common good, the value of relationality?

Practicing solidarity cannot be an individual endeavor. That would contravene the value of relational dependence and shared responsibility that solidarity seeks to elevate. As Hollenbach points out, solidarity is "not only a virtue to be enacted by individual persons one at a time. It must also be expressed in the economic, cultural, political, and religious institutions that shape society" (Hollenbach, 2002, 189, as quoted in Wadell, 2008, 229). For nonprofit institutions at least, solidarity is expressed when it cultivates an environment conducive to ongoing, critical self-assessment of themselves as nonprofits. Mirabella has suggested how this might look in practice. For example, we can reframe and challenge authority structures founded on negative freedom "with a positive understanding of freedom that includes engagement with moral considerations, the notion of charity, and concepts of care" (2013, 96) where citizens come together to debate and decide on the common good. Nonprofit organizations are perfect vehicles for these conversations. She also suggests an embrace of democratic feminist theories of management will help us move away from scientific management values towards a care-centered approach to management placing care of beneficiaries clearly at the center of the organization, rather than on the periphery (98), in effect, practicing solidarity with those we serve.

The point here is that nonprofits cannot necessarily assume their roles as settled or obvious. Rather, the guiding principle is the need to be alert to how a nonprofit's assessment of itself – what it ought to be, what it ought to do – is in line not with the latest trends in management such as social enterprise or effective altruism, but rather with the common good; in other words, the value of relationality becomes the defining parameters of a nonprofit's function and roles. Practically speaking, then, the virtue of solidarity (and its underlying value of relationality) disposes and commits nonprofits to fostering an environment in which its constituents or stakeholders do not simply reside in their "domains" and take for granted their prescribed roles. Such segmentation undermines the relationality and sense of shared moral responsibility that solidarity represents. No one division, employee, or stakeholder of an organization can claim itself as the center of gravity for its mission. A nonprofit committed to the advancement of solidarity aims to widen the range of its conversation partners, not limiting itself to simply its priority donors, but to also civic organizations, local religious institutions, and, perhaps most importantly, those whom it serves.

That vision of relational deliberation, motivated and sustained by the virtue of solidarity, calls attention to what Walker calls the expressive-collaborative model of ethics. This model views the "moral life as a continuing negotiation among people ... a socially embodied medium of understanding and adjustment in which people account to each other" (1998, 60). In this model of ethics, the emphasis is less on resolving moral dilemmas or quandaries through reliance on codes and more on fostering those habits that promote moral deliberation that is fundamentally dialogic. Each of the stakeholders within the organization – donors, employees, volunteers, people served and members of the community in which the organization is located – would share their "understandings about who gets to do what to whom and who is supposed to do what for whom" (Walker, 1998, 16). By entering into this dialogue among individuals who acknowledge one another's value and dependence on each other, we modify, alter, or continue practices in various forms. In traditional nonprofit codes of conduct, the intent and wishes of a particular ethos of a particular constituency are most often codified. Resolutions to moral problems or questions in an expressive-collaborative model take place in a larger context of a dialogic deliberation on what the nature of the organization should be and what kinds of choices, processes, and policies best speak to that deliberation. Mirabella suggests accomplishing this through embrace of a collaborative discourse that is open-ended and structured around dialogue and consensus. Unlike the rational scientific approach with its application of definitive outcomes, a collaborative discourse recognizes our inability to control communities and the limitations of depending upon predetermined outcomes (Mirabella, 2013, 99).

Conclusion

We have argued that reliance on codes of conduct in the nonprofit sector is symptomatic of the prevailing hold that the value of individualism has on the nonprofit sector, as well as society as a whole. The uncritical acceptance of individualism particularly in the nonprofit sector too easily invites the marketization and rationalization of the sector's work in society and, thus, corrodes the distinctive role that nonprofits can and ought to play in democratic life and civil society. By prioritizing the value of relationality rather than the value of individualism, the sector will come to rely less on legalistic, corporate-style codes of professional conduct to delineate the roles and functions of nonprofit managers and more on a type of deliberation that is dialogical. Such a vision of deliberation necessarily privileges the role of the nonprofit sector in creating solidarity with communities and advancing the common good. By recognizing the important role of values of the heart, nonprofit organizations can reestablish themselves as central players in civil society, providing spaces for community members to come together in solidarity with each other to deliberate and form consensus on issues of community concern.

References

Clohesy, W. (2000). Altruism and the Endurance of the Good. *Voluntas: International Journal of Voluntary and Nonprofit Organizations 11*(3), 237–253.

Connors, Jr., R.B., & McCormick, P.T. (1998). *Character, Choices and Community: The Three Faces of Christian Ethics*. New York: Paulist Press, 1998.

Denhardt, R. (1981). Toward a Critical Theory of Public Organization. *Public Administration Review* November/December, 628–635.

DiMaggio, P.J., & Anheier, H.K. (1990). The Sociology of Nonprofit Organizations and Sectors. *Annual Review of Sociology, 16*(1), 137–159.

Ebrahim, A., Battilana, J., & Mair, J. (2014). The Governance of Social Enterprises: Mission Drift and Accountability Challenges in Hybrid Organizations. *Research in Organizational Behavior, 34*, 81–100.

Eikenberry, A. M., & Mirabella, R.M. (2018). Extreme Philanthropy: Philanthrocapitalism, Effective Altruism, and the Discourse of Neoliberalism. *PS: Political Science & Politics, 51*(1), 43–47.

Frumkin, P., & Andre-Clark, A. (2000). When Missions, Markets, and Politics Collide: Values and Strategy in the Nonprofit Human Services. *Nonprofit and Voluntary Sector Quarterly 29*(1 suppl), 141–163.

Grabowski, L., Neher, C., Crim, T., & Mathiassen, L. (2015). Competing Values Framework Application to Organizational Effectiveness in Voluntary Organizations: A Case Study. *Nonprofit and Voluntary Sector Quarterly, 44*(5), 908–923.

Grobman, G. (2007). An Analysis of Code of Ethics of Nonprofit, Tax-Exempt Membership Associations: Does Principal Constituency Make a Difference? *Public Integrity 9*(3), 245–263.

Hall, P.D. (1990). The History of Religious Philanthropy in America. In R. Wuthnow & V. Hodgkinson (Eds.), *Faith and Philanthropy in America* (pp. 38–62). San Francisco: Jossey-Bass.

Hayek, F.A. (2001). *Road to Serfdom*. London: Routledge.

Herdt, J. (2001). The Invention of Modern Moral Philosophy: A Review of *The Invention of Autonomy* by J.B. Schneewind, *Journal of Religious Ethics 29*(1), 150.

Herman, R.D., & Renz, D.O. (1999). Theses on Nonprofit Organizational Effectiveness. *Nonprofit and Voluntary Sector Quarterly, 28*(2), 107–126.

Hollenbach, SJ., D. (2002). *The Common Good and Christian Ethics*. Cambridge: Cambridge University Press.

Hollenbach, SJ., D. (2003). *The Global Face of Public Faith: Politics, Human Rights, and Christian Faith*. Washington, DC: Georgetown University Press.

Hursthouse, R. (1995). Applying Virtue Ethics. In R. Hursthouse, G. Lawrence, & W. Quinn (Eds.), *Virtues and Reasons: Essays in Honour of Philippa Foot* (pp. 57–75). Oxford: Clarendon Press.

James, E. (2003). Commercialism and the Mission of Nonprofits. *Society, 40*(4), 29–35.

Kristol, I. (1996). 'Social Justice' and the Poverty of Redistribution. In S. Satris (Ed.), *Taking Sides: Clashing Views on Controversial Moral Issues*, Fifth Edition (pp. 135–140). Guilford, CT: Dushkin.

Maguire, D. C. (1980). *A New American Justice*. Minneapolis, MN: Winston Press.

MacIntyre, A. (1981). *After Virtue*. South Bend, IN: University of Notre Dame Press.

MacIntyre, A. (1988). *Whose Justice? Which Rationality?* South Bend, IN: University of Notre Dame Press.

Mendel, S. (2014). A Field of Its Own. *Stanford Social Innovation Review 12*(1), 61–62.

Mirabella, R. (2013). The Performance Mindset and the "Gift." *Administrative Theory & Praxis 35*(1), 81–105.

Moore, M.H. (2000). Managing for Value: Organizational Strategy in For-profit, Nonprofit, and Governmental Organizations. *Nonprofit and Voluntary Sector Quarterly, 29*(1 suppl), 183–204.

Murdoch, I. (2003). *The Sovereignty of Good*. London: Routledge.

O'Donovan, O. (2003) *The Ways of Judgment*. Grand Rapids, MI: W.B. Eerdmans.

Quinn, R.E., & Cameron, K. (1983). Organizational life cycles and shifting criteria of effectiveness: Some preliminary evidence. *Management science, 29*(1), 33–51.

Quinn, R.E., & Rohrbaugh, J. (1983). A Spatial Model of Effectiveness Criteria: Towards a Competing Values Approach to Organizational Analysis. *Management Science 29*, 363–377.

Rhode, D., & Packel, A. (2009). Ethics and Nonprofits. *Stanford Social Innovation Review* 7(3), 29–35.

Roelofs, H.M. (1976). *Ideology and Myth in American Politics: A Critique of a National Political Mind*. Boston: Little, Brown.

Schneewind, J.B. (1998). *The Invention of Autonomy: A History of Modern Moral Philosophy*. Cambridge: Cambridge University Press.

Taylor, C. (1991). *The Ethics of Authenticity*. Cambridge, MA: Harvard University Press.

Wadell, P.J. (2008). *Happiness and the Christian Moral Life*. Plymouth, UK: Sheed & Ward.

Walker, M.U. (1998). *Moral Understandings: A Feminist Study in Ethics*. New York: Routledge.

Weisbrod, B.A. (1998). The Nonprofit Mission and its Financing: Growing Links between Nonprofits and the Rest of the Economy. In B.A. Weisbrod (Ed.), *To Profit or Not to Profit: The Commercial Transformation of the Nonprofit Sector* (pp. 1–22). New York: Cambridge University Press.

13

STRATEGIC MANAGEMENT

Michael Meyer

PROFESSOR, DEPARTMENT OF MANAGEMENT,
INSTITUTE OF NONPROFIT-MANAGEMENT, WU VIENNA
(VIENNA UNIVERSITY OF ECONOMICS AND BUSINESS), VIENNA, AUSTRIA

Introduction

Organizations of all kinds should benefit from developing strategies. Strategic management has become the supreme discipline of management, both in practice, in research, and in teaching – at least in the eyes of strategists. As strategy is a privilege for the upper hierarchy levels, strategists both in management and in academia claim superiority. Strategy is about long-run capabilities and the investment of resources that should safeguard potentials; it is about positioning, and how markets and environments perceive an organization. Hence strategic management channels decisions in all subject areas such as marketing, finance, and fundraising, and in all organizational units.

Definitions of strategic management date back to the late 1940s (Bracker, 1980: 220). Some scholars played a pivotal role for the development of strategic management, and three of them have coined definitions that emphasize its core dimensions:

1   Strategic management has to assess resources, to analyse and change status quo: "Strategy is analyzing the present situation and changing it if necessary. Incorporated in this is finding out what one's resources are or what they should be" (Drucker, 1955: 17).
2   Strategic management implies a long-term orientation and commensurate resources for reaching long range goals: "Strategy is the determinator of the basic long-term goals of an enterprise, and the adoption of courses of action and the allocation of resources necessary for carrying out these goals" (Chandler, 1962: 13).
3   Strategic management decides about combinations of products and services to achieve an optimal fit between organization and environment: "Strategy is a rule for making decisions determined by product/market scope, growth vector, competitive advantage, and synergy" (Ansoff, 1965: 118). Strategic management has to align the organization and its environment and to develop processes of decision making that consistently deal with the environment (Mintzberg, 1979: 25).

In nonprofit organizations (NPOs), strategic management faces a set of particular challenges as compared to business organizations (Moore, 2000: 189; Magretta, 2012: 37, 89f., 144ff.):

(1) Basically, NPOs do not act in a parallel universe. The belief that the mission and financial objectives are always at odds is fundamentally wrong. In the long run, mission, strategy, and performance are not in conflict.

(2) Though business goals have changed from merely enhancing shareholders' wealth to rather balancing various stakeholders' goals, achieving social missions and yielding a positive impact for direct beneficiaries, other stakeholders, and overall society are still more important for NPOs.

(3) Whereas business revenues stem dominantly from selling products and services, there is a broad range of financial inflows for nonprofits: donations from private givers and foundations, government subsidies, service fees, membership fees, etc.

(4) Whereas the financial bottom line and/or increased equity value are still the core measures of performance in business, in NPOs it is the impact, the effectiveness and efficiency in achieving the mission.

(5) In business organizations, strategic management often aims at finding and exploiting a distinctive capability by positioning it in a market. In NPOs, strategic management should find better ways to achieve missions.

This chapter will not only concentrate on these particularities, but also provide a comprehensive summary of the core concepts and methods of strategic management, and will give an overview of prior research. First, we will briefly relate the history of strategic management and describe alternative approaches. Second, we will outline two complementary approaches to strategic management that are relevant for all organizations, but in particular for NPOs: the resource-based view and the stakeholder view. Third, we will discuss the particularities of NPOs and summarize specific strategic approaches. The emphasis is on the distinction between prescriptive and empirical research on strategy. To conclude, we will briefly change the theoretical perspective and introduce strategic management as the royal road to legitimacy.

Development and approaches of strategic management

Originally, strategy was the art of leading military armies – and was opposed to tactics; in management, this distinction is not always clear. Still, many strategic management thinkers refer so the seminal writings on military strategy by 19th-century Prussian military theorist Carl von Clausewitz and Chinese general and philosopher Sun Tsu who lived around 500 BCE (Stahel, 1981; Maier, 2014). This is not surprising, as military thinking in general and the US commercial–military–political complex in particular have been the offspring of modern management research and business administration (Robert & Gavin, 2008).

Strategic management comprises a set of methods and concepts that should prepare important decisions, i.e., decisions that particularly foster competitive advantages and improve an organization's long-run performance in a way that makes it superior to its competitors. In business management, strategy gained momentum in the early 1960s. It entered into nonprofit management roughly 15 years later. In the late 1970s and early 1980s, triggered by the first oil crisis in 1973, strategic planning became essential in management. In this period, managers of any kind and in all industries had to accept that the future is far from predictable, and planning must not rely on linear growth assumptions. For decades, linear growth had been taken for granted; in the 1970s it was questioned not only by the Club of Rome's "The Limits to Growth" (Meadows et al., 1972).

Organizations had to adapt for sudden and unexpected change, and strategic management pretended to deliver the recipe: By permanently observing their environments and remaining flexible in their structures, processes, and outputs, organizations will gain competitive advantages and survive. The myth of strategy gained ground in the 1970s. "Business school departments fought over who should and could use the term strategic: Management, marketing, finance, human resources, and operations faculty all eagerly appropriated the name" (Barry & Elmes, 1997: 429). Strategy was claimed to prioritize all other decisions, even organizational structure was subject to strategic decisions (Chandler, 1962). Thus, some sort of planning delusion was always characteristic for strategy.

About a decade later, strategic management spread into the nonprofit field. Whereas literature on strategic planning for business started in the 1960s, the first publication on strategy for non-profits turned up in the late 1970s. Diffusion of strategic management into NPOs was not with-out critical refraction: "In the voluntary nonprofit sector there is perhaps a tendency to create a simple caricature of strategic planning or strategic management in the private sector. The history of management fads in the private sector makes that easy to do" (Courtney, 2002).

Meanwhile, strategic management and planning has lost its glamour. The golden age of strategy is bygone (Barry & Elmes, 1997). The planning delusion was challenged by more real-istic and sceptical studies on the limitations of strategic planning and rationality in organizations (e.g., Mintzberg & Waters, 1982; March & Olsen, 1976). Still, strategy remains a privilege for top management positions in organizations. Various approaches to strategic management turned up (Mintzberg et al., 1998). Many of them have sedimented in actual concepts and still shape strategic thinking in organizations.

The *design approach* rests on two pillars: First, an external appraisal of the environment, spot-ting the opportunities and threats that external developments might cause. Second, an internal appraisal of the organization, spotting the strengths and weaknesses of the organization. Based on these analyses, strategies have to be created, evaluated, and selected (Mintzberg et al., 1998: 26). These strategies should then be consistent with the goals and policies, consonant with environmental developments, advantageous for the organization as compared to its competitors, and feasible with the available resources. The design approach offers checklists for external and internal appraisals (Mintzberg et al., 1998: 29f.) and is still influential as it has defined the basic dimensions of strategic management. Yet it neglects the distortion that necessarily happens on the way from thorough analysis to strategy formulation and implementation, and it overestimates the analytical capacity of management.

The *planning approach* suggests external and internal audits, too. It adds a highly differ-entiated cascade of plans that build up on these analyses: short-term, mid-term, and long-term plans; corporate, business, functional, and operational plans; strategic planning, financial control, strategic control, etc. This approach accepted the premises of the design school but prescribed the execution in a highly formalized way (Mintzberg et al., 1998: 57). Still, there is a gap between planning and implementation, and planning itself was overestimated in the 1970s when this approach arose. In addition, Mintzberg (1998: 65f.) lists a couple of sins that happened in strategic planning, amongst them being over-devoted to sophisticated processes, neglecting cultural and organizational restrictions, and being too fascinated by "big" options like mergers and acquisitions, and neglecting the core business. Big investments in planning usually suggest big decisions.

The *positioning approach* arose in the 1980s out of the ashes of the planning delusion. In those years, many big organizations cut expenses for strategic planning. Positioning, which is closely linked with Harvard Professor Michael Porter (1980, 1985, 1986), has emphasized the impor-tance of strategies themselves and added substance as compared to methods and processes. Porter argued that there are only three basic strategies, understood as positions in the marketplace: cost leadership, differentiation, and focus. Furthermore, there are five generic forces that dominate each industry: (1) bargaining power of suppliers, (2) bargaining power of buyers, (3) threat of new entrants, (4) threat of substitutes, and (5) industry rivalry. The constellation of those forces suggests which of the basic strategies is best for an organization. Though all these concepts were primarily developed for business, Porter himself has transferred them to other fields, e.g., to philanthropy (Porter & Kramer, 2002) and nations (Porter, 1990).

The positioning approach provided a fertile soil for *strategy consulting*: Consultants "can arrive cold, with no particular knowledge of a business, analyze the data, juggle a set of generic strategies (basic building blocks) on a chart, write a report, drop an invoice, and leave" (Mintzberg et al., 1998: 94). In a similar vein, the Boston Consulting Group (BCG) became famous with two concepts:

(1) The market-share/market-growth matrix classifies an organization's strategic units. These are bundles of similar products and services. In the BCG matrix, they are either a cash cow (high share, low growth), a star (high share, high growth), a problem child (low share, high growth), or a dog (low share, low growth). According to this position in the portfolio, consultants recommend standard strategies: de-investing and shutting down dogs, investing and nurturing stars, stabilizing cash cows, and selectively dealing with question marks. BCG still recommends its matrix with some modifications: "The matrix also requires a new measure of competitiveness to replace its horizontal axis now that market share is no longer a strong predictor of performance. Finally, the matrix needs to be embedded more deeply into organization behaviour to facilitate its use for strategic experimentation" (Reeves et al., 2014). Portfolio matrices like the BCG share/growth-matrix utilized and simplified the basic dimensions already developed by the design school: organizational strength, measured simply by the market share, and environmental attractiveness, measured by market growth.

(2) The learning curve provides a theoretical rationale for many organizations to expand their activities as it proposes gains in profitability caused by decreasing unit costs. Thus organizations should expand their output and acquire market share in order to gain long-term cost advantage over their competitors. However, the promised benefits of such learning-curve based strategies often failed to materialize, and the concept lost favour during the 1980s (Lieberman, 1987: 441).

The positioning school has been criticized because of its narrow focus on economic forces, its narrow context, its restriction of strategic choice to basically three generic strategies, and its disregard of the process that generates information about the organization and its environment (Mintzberg et al., 1998: 112ff.).

Prescriptive theorizing then shifted its attention from environmental forces to competencies of organizations. This was the birth of the *resource-based view (RBV)*, as opposed to the Michael Porter's market-based view. A second turn tried to specify the environmental side by differentiating specific stakeholders, developing a *stakeholder-based view*. Beyond those prescriptive approaches, Mintzberg et al. (1998) identify approaches that rather explain how organizational strategies unfold: the entrepreneurial school conceives strategy formation as a visionary process, the cognitive school as a mental process, the learning school as an emergent process, the power school as a process of negotiation, the cultural school as a process of collective sense making, the environmental school as a reactive process, and the configuration school as a process of transformation.

The resource-based view

For decades, strategic thinking has oscillated between approaches that emphasize either internal resources or environmental pressures and demands. In the late 1980s, driven by the fashion of lean management and inspired by new institutional economics, in particular transaction cost economics (Jones & Hill, 1988; Williamson, 1989), strategists recommended identifying core competencies of organizations in order to strengthen them (Prahalad & Hamel, 1990). Core processes are distinguished from support processes, which should be rather outsourced under specific conditions. Again, transaction cost economics provides the theoretical backbone for the depth of vertical integration: asset specificity, uncertainty, frequency, and strategic importance (Williamson, 1989, 2002). The more specific competencies and processes, the more uncertain the contractual environment, the more frequent a process is applied, the more important competencies and processes are strategically, the less they are candidates for contracting out.

This notion of core competencies characterizes the early RBV (Hamel & Prahalad, 1994; Prahalad & Hamel, 1990) that was opposed to Michael Porter's market-based view. Core competencies are grounded in collective learning, mainly how to coordinate production skills and integrate technologies, but also communication skills and skills of cooperation across organizational boundaries. Unlike physical assets, those competencies do not deteriorate over time, but are even enhanced when applied and shared. Prahalad and Hamel suggest three criteria to determine whether something is an organization's core competency: (1) it provides potential access not only to one market, but to a broad variety of markets, (2) it makes a significant contribution to customer benefit of the end-product or service, and (3) it is very difficult to imitate because of the complex harmonization of individual technologies and skills. Hamel and Prahalad painted a picture of the corporation as a tree whose roots are its particular competencies. Out of these roots grow the organization's "core products" which, in turn, nourish a number of separate business units. Finally "end products" come out of these business units (Hamel & Prahalad, 1994; Prahalad & Hamel, 1990). The resource-based view relates to the organizational learning literature (Argyris, 1994; Argyris & Schön, 1978, 1996; Fiol & Lyles, 1985; March, 1991), the knowledge-management literature (Argyris, 1993; Nonaka & Hirotaka, 1995), and finally provides a fertile ground for more differentiated concepts.

Likewise, the concept of *dynamic capabilities* partly reintegrates the dynamics of environmental demands. If organizations see their core competencies only as stable capabilities, they might be the reason for today's success, but also for tomorrow's failure. Therefore, dynamic capabilities have to complement competencies to generate new strategies (Eisenhardt & Martin, 2000: 1107). Dynamic capabilities denote an organization's ability to integrate, build, and reconfigure internal and external competencies to address rapidly changing environments and thus reflect an organization's ability to achieve new and innovative forms of competitive advantage given path-dependencies and market positions (Teece et al., 1997: 516). In their interplay with resources, organizational routines, and competencies, core competencies and end products shape the competitive advantage of an organization. Dynamic capabilities are understood as "the firm's processes that use resources – specifically the processes to integrate, reconfigure, gain and release resources – to match or even create market change" (Eisenhardt & Martin, 2000: 1107). Thus, dynamic capabilities are prerequisites for organizational learning (Zollo & Winter, 2002). As meta-routines, they enable organizations to reshape their resource base, and to adequately respond to unexpected events in their environment.

The concept of *ambidexterity* also follows the RBV, as "the ambidextrous organization achieves alignment in its current operations while also adapting effectively to changing environmental demands" (Gibson & Birkinshaw, 2004: 201). Ambidexterity is essential to balance exploitation and exploration, i.e., efficiency and innovation (March, 1991). Refining exploitation more rapidly than exploration would lead to short-term wins, but long-term losses. In literature, different kinds of ambidexterity have been discussed. Structural ambidexterity means to develop structural mechanisms for coping with alignment and adaptability, while contextual ambidexterity suggests not separating units that fulfil those contradictory tasks but rather to build units that encourage members to make use of their autonomy and flexibility (Gibson & Birkinshaw, 2004). Subsequent studies have described organizational structures, behavioural contexts, and leadership processes as promoters of ambidexterity (Raisch & Birkinshaw, 2008: 6; Knight & Paroutis, 2016). As for organizational structure, the findings remain rather vague. They link with former notions of mechanistic vs. organic structures (Burns & Stalker, 1961) and tent vs. palace organizations (Hedberg et al., 1976), stating that ambidextrous organizations combine the best of those two contradictory worlds by spatial separation and parallel structures: e.g., multiple tightly coupled subunits that are themselves loosely coupled with one another (O'Reilly & Tushman, 2004). Meanwhile, ambidexterity has moved beyond the routine–non-routine dichotomy (Lillrank, 2003), e.g., to the tension between morally and instrumental-driven initiatives (Hahn et al., 2015). Both the concepts of dynamic capabilities and organizational ambidexterity focus on the prerequisites of organizations for combining the paradox, namely aligning to current demands and effective adaptation to new challenges.

Hamel & Välikangas (2003) argued that no strategy can last forever and each organization has to permanently be aware of "revolutionary changes" that come in "lightning quick" (Hamel & Välikangas, 2003: 1). *Organizational resilience* has emerged as an answer to the "fallen eagles," the decay of the strong beliefs in strategic planning, optimization, and rational decision-making (Välikangas, 2010: 4). Resilience hereby means the ability of a system to resist major changes and thus endure perturbation without systemic change (Välikangas, 2010: 8), or an organization's ability to sense and correct maladaptive tendencies and to cope positively with unexpected situations (Ortiz-de-Mandojana & Bansal, 2016). Much can be learned about resilience from the study of organizations at and beyond their manifold limits (Farjoun & Starbuck, 2007; Starbuck & Farjoun, 2009). The ingredients of resilience are resourcefulness, robustness, and adaption. As for structural robustness, it can be enforced through loose organizational coupling (Orton & Weick, 1990) and through modularity (D'Adderio & Pollock, 2014). Strategic robustness must face the cognitive, the strategic, the political, and the ideological challenge and it relies on adaptive managerial capabilities. Finally, behavioural robustness builds on idiosyncratic networks that express diverse voices (Välikangas, 2010: 105f.).

Weick and Sutcliffe recommend five principles for strategic resilience (Weick & Sutcliffe, 2011: 45ff.): (1) preoccupation with failure, i.e., a climate of alertness, understanding, and wariness; (2) reluctance to simplify, i.e., avoiding simple explanations for failure using just very few causes; (3) sensitivity to interactions within a complicated and often opaque system; (4) commitment to resilience, i.e., swift adaptation to disturbances, maintenance of core functions and structure, and continuing operations in a degraded form; (5) deference to expertise, which can be treacherous especially after unexpected jolts, and organizations are better off by reorganizing around problems in self-organizing networks. Schemeil (2013), finally, reveals three other factors that contribute to resilience: coupling the technical with the political domain, converting slack into innovation, and setting new challenges while pursuing current activities.

The contributions of the resource-based view to strategic thinking are manifold. It shifted the focus to the internal capabilities of organizations. For NPOs, this specifically addresses human resources, i.e., the competencies of employees and volunteers and the innovative capacities of the organizations. Nonprofits have to develop their resources permanently in order to secure their positions. With its recent shift towards resilience, RBV has finally overcome the criticism that it blinds out environmental developments. On the other hand, strategic recommendations have become rather vague, and it remains widely unclear how organizational structure and strategies become resilient. As environment is primarily seen as a source of jolt and surprise, it has to be complemented with a more differentiated view on environmental forces.

The stakeholder view

This approach was introduced by Freeman (1984), initially intending to offer a pragmatic approach to strategy "that urged organizations to be cognizant of stakeholders to achieve superior performance" (Laplume et al., 2008: 1153). The stakeholder view was a response to at least two strands of strategic thinking that were predominant in the 1980s. First, it proposed an alternative to simple shareholder theories (Blyth et al., 1986). An organization should act in the interest of all its constituents, not only in the interest of shareholders. Second, the stakeholder view also re-established a sociological lens on organizations and their strategies in contrast to pure economic strategy concepts like Michael Porter's positioning approach or to mere contractarian views of organizations (Jensen & Meckling, 1976).

In nonprofit management, the stakeholder approach turned out to be especially attractive and fruitful. Early on, scholars identified an inherent conflict between demand- and supply-side stakeholders in nonprofits: demand-side stakeholders want more quality and quantity for a lower price while supply-side stakeholders want the opposite (Ben-Ner & Van Hoomissen, 1991: 525). "Stakeholder control is a sine qua non for the existence of nonprofit organizations, because it avails the trust required for patronizing the organization, revealing the demand of it, and making donations to it" (Ben-Ner & Van Hoomissen, 1991: 544). As direct control of stakeholders is never complete, governance systems have to permanently enhance stakeholder control, especially of those whose rights are not safeguarded by other legal institutions (e.g., contracts, labour law; see Speckbacher, 2008).

Nonprofit organizations have to identify their priority stakeholders and their demands: donors, influencers, general public, partner organizations, prospects, expert audiences, volunteers, beneficiaries, and corporate partners. Stakeholders can be categorized in terms of power, legitimacy, urgency of their needs, and salience, i.e., the degree to which managers give priority to competing stakeholder claims (Mitchell et al., 1997: 869). In this model, salience is dependent on managers' perception of power, legitimacy, and urgency, yielding eight different types of stakeholders (see Mitchell et al. 1997: 874).

Stakeholder salience will be low when only one of the attributes perceived by managers is present, it will be moderate with two attributes present, and high with all three attributes present (Mitchell et al., 1997). In any case, strategic management must permanently consider stakeholders' interests and carve strategies in order to fulfil their expectations. As nonprofits' effectiveness is a multidimensional construct and a social construction in its core (Dunkel et al., 1997; Herman & Renz, 1999), responsiveness to stakeholders' expectations is a useful overarching criterion for resolving the challenge of differing judgements by different stakeholder groups. Herman and Renz (2008) show that all stakeholder groups rated organizational responsiveness as strongly related to organizational effectiveness.

The stakeholder view contributed two main aspects to strategic management. First, the stakeholder view suggests a finer grained frame to analyse environment. Second, and even more important, it re-linked organizations with society. The purpose of any organization is not to find a promising position in markets to increase their revenues and to safeguard survival, the purpose is to fulfil needs of stakeholders and thus contribute to society.

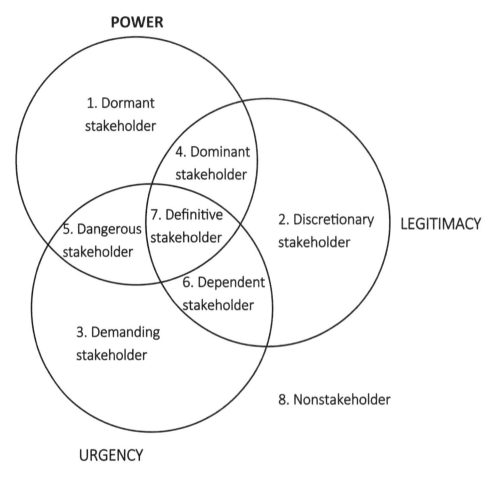

Figure 13.1 Stakeholder typology

Source: Mitchell et al., 1997: 874. Reproduced with permission.

Strategic management in NPOs

Prescriptive concepts and methods

For strategic management and planning in NPOs, there are mainly two conditions that deserve specific consideration: (1) the value produced by nonprofits lies in the achievement of social purposes rather than in gathering revenues, and (2) nonprofits receive revenues from manifold sources other than customer purchases (Moore, 2000: 183). Particularities of nonprofits are their multiple constituencies with partly diverging interests, their non-monetary goals, the non-identity of recipients of services and funders, and a combination of competition and cooperation with other nonprofits, to name but a few. Therefore, approaches that focus on competitive advantages and do not consider multiple constituencies are less useful for nonprofits. The unique resources of an NPO have to result in its capability to yield specific impacts, and the stakeholder portfolios of NPOs are more heterogeneous than in other organizations. Because of these particularities, strategy making in nonprofits is usually more challenging than in business or in public organizations. NPOs that engage in strategic management, however, characterize themselves as more successful (Bryson et al., 2009).

With a considerable time lag, strategic management diffused into NPOs (Kong, 2008). Deriving from the design and planning school, SWOT analyses (strengths, weaknesses, opportunities, threats) were the first methods adopted by NPOs, though the prevailing SWOT analysis has been criticized for its simplicity and generalization. Then the positioning school and Michael Porter's generic strategies appeared on stage, also labelled as the industrial organization (I/O). It took a while until NPOs realized that I/O overemphasized market forces and competition. The pendulum then swung back to internal aspects, focusing on internal resources, core competencies, knowledge and intellectual capital. At that time, many NPOs also adopted the Balanced Scorecard as a method to develop intellectual capital (see Figure 13.2).

Simultaneously with the shift from market to resources, new frameworks for strategy implementation arose in the late 1990s. Amongst them, the *Balanced Scorecard* (BSC) received outstanding prominence especially in nonprofits (Hvenmark, 2013; Kaplan, 2001; Manville, 2006). The model aimed to "translate strategy into action" (Kaplan & Norton, 1996) by suggesting a measurement system of performance indicators in four dimensions: (1) internal processes, (2) finance, (3) learning and growth, (4) customers. Unlike former approaches, BSC gives no recommendation on the process of strategic analysis nor on the content of strategies, but concentrates on the gap between strategy formulation and implementation. "What you measure is what you get" is the core assumption of BSC. In the four dimensions that are crucial for each organization, management should develop a handful of indicators that are easily measurable and thus support strategic control. For NPOs, the four dimensions of BSC have been modified (see Figure 13.3, Balanced Scorecard).

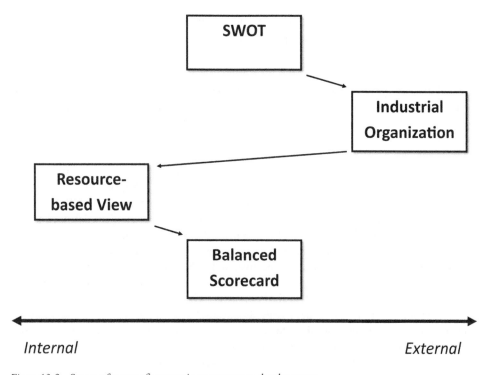

Figure 13.2 Stages of nonprofit strategic management development

Figure 13.3   Core Balanced Scorecard (BSC) questions for NPOs
Source: Niven, 2011: 32. Reproduced with permission.

Based on these perspectives, a manageable number of goals and measures should be developed. Two assumptions underpin the BSC: First, the four goal perspectives are causally interconnected and all contribute to superior strategic goals and the NPO's mission. Second, the four perspectives represent the expectations of major stakeholders: funders, customers, employees, and management.

Again, voices became louder asking whether BSC was an appropriate method for strategic management in NPOs. Despite modifications (see e.g., Niven, 2011; Kaplan, 2001) that explicitly reacted to the critique that the concept of customer does not exist in many NPOs (see the modification from "value for our customer" to "impact for our customers" in Balanced Scorecard, Figure 13.4), other fundamental problems remained unsolved (Kong, 2008: 88). First, there is some concern that the relations among the four perspectives are logical rather than causal. Second, BSC is rather rigid because perspectives and indicators are limited. Third, the environmental perspective is restricted to direct customers or beneficiaries and does not integrate a broader spectrum of stakeholders. Fourth, BSC's major claim "What you measure is what you get" (Kaplan & Norton, 1992: 72) necessarily also means: "You get only that what you measure." Implementing strategies by BSC shifts focus onto the indicators and activities defined in four charts and neglects other areas that arise as equally important but have been overseen in planning. Fifth, and finally, BSC antagonizes financial stakeholders and beneficiaries, not realizing that those perspectives are highly congruent in NPOs as both stakeholder groups are interested

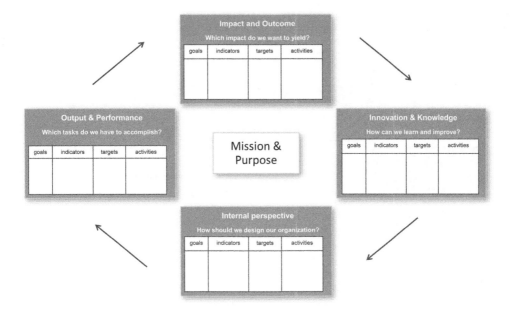

Figure 13.4   Balanced Scorecard (BSC) for NPOs

in the same kind of impact (Kong, 2008: 289). Therefore we argue that NPOs should modify BSCs in a way that does not juxtapose stakeholders but more strongly aligns the perspectives with major strategic impact zones (see e.g., Balanced Scorecard adapted for NPOs, Figure 13.4).

To avoid both planning myopia and planning delusion, NPOs should learn from all the different approaches and views and deploy processes from various perspectives. The design school suggested starting with analysing the environment and the organization, yielding a SWOT analysis. Environment analyses should not only assess political, economic, social, and technological developments, but also the expectations and needs of the NPO's most relevant stakeholders and the dynamics and competition within a particular industry field (e.g., social services, environmentalist advocacy).

For analysing the organization, strategists should not only analyse which products and services the NPO offers in particular markets, but can also apply portfolio analysis for assessing the future potential of the NPO's products facing different market dynamics. In addition, RBV suggests identifying core competencies and dynamic capabilities of the organization, i.e., those strengths that help the NPO to gain a strong position in its field of action. Analyses of environment and the organization that have identified external critical factors and internal core competencies merge in a SWOT (strength, weaknesses, opportunities, threats) analysis (see Figure 13.5).

For deciding the content of strategies, the planning school has suggested differentiating between structural and strategic levels. Organizational structure for example suggests carving concepts for the overall organization, but also for subunits, specific stakeholders, or functions (e.g., funding strategies, marketing strategies, impact strategies). Strategies can also span from the overall mission down to financial issues. Strategists should not differentiate too excessively, as all the sub-strategies must be realigned and communicated within the organization. An ex-ante evaluation of strategies scoring models (Liberatore & Stylianou, 1994) can assess strategies' contribution to superior goal attainment. Scenario technique (Bishop et al., 2007) can help to assess how robust strategies are in alternative environmental settings.

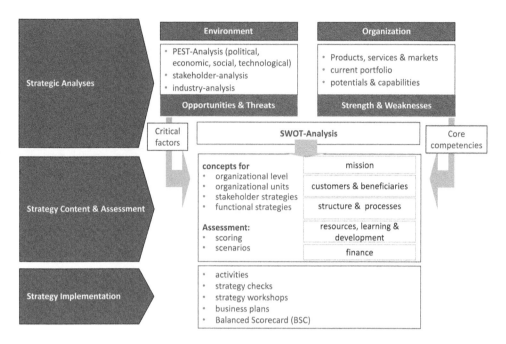

Figure 13.5 A multimethod approach to strategy for NPOs

To this point, strategies are only text documents. After the maybe inspiring process of discussing and drafting strategy documents, the "troubles of the plains" (Bertolt Brecht) start as strategies have to be implemented: Managers must decide on specific activities, they should permanently check whether decisions fit with strategies, and they organize and participate in workshops to communicate strategies within the organization and to adapt them permanently. They also have to cast the strategies in the moulds of business plans and translate it into a BSC.

NPOs are very heterogeneous, hence strategic processes will be quite different and yield different outcomes for different types of NPOs. Though we still miss a shared systematic of the dimensions that differentiate within NPOs, some of those dimensions obviously do affect strategic planning:

(1) *Size* matters, of course. Larger nonprofits are capable to invest more analytical capacity into strategic planning.

(2) The major *field of activities* implies different environmental particularities and different stakeholder structures. In specific fields (e.g., according to the International Classification of Nonprofit Organizations (ICNPO), see Salamon & Anheier, 1996), NPOs will compete with public and business organizations, in others, NPOs are rather amongst themselves. Competition with business organizations, for instance, fosters NPOs' innovativeness (Meyer & Leitner, 2018), but also exerts more pressure on developing strategic positions.

(3) The *functional focus* plays a role as well (e.g., Neumayr et al., 2009). Service providers, advocacy NPOs, and community builders face rather different strategic environments, which, for instance, aggravate SWOT analysis for advocacy NPOs. Defining beneficiaries and clear measures in BSC to proof strategy implementation is much more challenging for advocacy and community building.

(4) The *geographical scope* of NPOs' activities is another aspect with implications for environmental and SWOT analysis, which will differ significantly between NPOs with regional, national, transnational, international, or even global activities. This will also affect mission statements.

(5) *Operational* particularities affect strategic planning, too. Differentiating between (a) programme-based, (b) project-based, and (c) event-based NPOs, we see significant implications for performance measurement and feedback loops to strategic planning. Though clock speed is faster for programme-based NPOs, it will be easier for them to adapt strategies if regular performance feedback is provided. For project-based and event-based NPOs, feedback comes in a more irregular way. For the 'Salzburger Festspiele,' for instance, it takes a year to implement first-order learnings (e.g., Aranda et al., 2017; Argyris & Schön, 1978) and much longer to implement strategic changes. On the other hand, tightening accountability requisites for programme-based NPOs impedes strategic learning (Ebrahim, 2005) and, according to the boiling-frog metaphor (Boyatzis, 2006), it is more difficult for programme-based NPOs to realize the urgency for strategic change.

(6) Finally, NPOs differ significantly regarding their core constituencies and stakeholders. According to those residual claimants or claims (Fama & Jensen, 1983), we distinguish (a) *membership-based NPOs*, e.g., associations and social movement organizations, (b) *asset-based NPOs*, e.g., foundations, and (c) *ownership-based NPOs*, e.g., B-Corps and limited liability corporations. These three types will not only differ in how influential stakeholder groups will be in the process of strategy formation. As these residual claims can also be seen as the origin of resources and legitimacy, they have to be anchored in the mission and somehow mirrored in each strategic objective.

Empirical findings

NPOs face particular barriers to strategic planning. The process requires rational decision-making in a highly charged policy and political environment where balancing interests often predominates, and many nonprofits are short of managerial resources that support strategic planning. Furthermore, nonprofit effectiveness is multidimensional and difficult to measure (Reid et al., 2014; Herman & Renz, 2008). This might explain why NPOs fell behind business organizations for a long time. In 1999, a comprehensive literature review analysed systematically the determinants, the processes applied, and the outcomes and performance in NPOs (Stone et al., 1999). At that time, many NPOs did not use strategic planning at all. Size mattered. Larger NPOs engaged more in strategic planning, and those NPOs that had reached an internal agreement on goals and mission. The single most critical driver was a funding source that required the submission of a strategic plan. Engaging in formal strategic planning also affected power relations in NPOs from boards to managers. The few studies that examined the impact of strategic planning on performance showed that it was associated with organizational growth in terms of funding. Despite rather weak empirical evidence, the authors stated that strategic planning has a quite positive impact on NPOs' performance (Stone et al., 1999: 391). It was mainly the resource environment – funder relations rather than changing demands for services or shifts in clients' needs – that determined strategies' content. Stone et al. (1999) detected a "noticeable absence of attention to internal, organizational determinants of strategy content" in NPOs, indicating that the RBV had not yet arrived in the nonprofit sector at that time.

More than ten years later, Domanski (2011) published another systematic literature review, analysing 50 studies published since 1999. He yielded quite different results. For instance, the RBV had arrived at least in theorizing about NPOs' strategic management, as had the stakeholder view. Whereas organizational age did not play any role until 1999, it does now: Older, better established NPOs engage more in strategic planning. Still, the (business) education of the administrative staff and the level of bureaucracy fosters strategic planning in NPOs. As for the content of strategies, NPOs apply both collaborative and competitive strategies. They are successful when they closely interrelate their strategies, and when they implement both marketing strategies and strategies that improve internal resources. Likewise, the involvement of a broad spectrum of stakeholders in developing mission statements and strategies contributes to better performance (Domanski, 2011: 33).

Both systematic reviews reveal positive impacts of strategic planning on nonprofits' performance. In a more recent study, Horvath et al. (2018) analyse longitudinal data of almost 200 NPOs. Between 2005 and 2015, i.e., during the economic crisis, strategic planning has decreased the likelihood of insolvency whereas a mere orientation toward the needy increased spending, thus threatening the survival of NPOs. These findings, however, also point towards a basic conflict: From the perspective of an organization focused on serving the most needy, "conservation and saving for the future might seem immoral" (Horvath et al., 2018). Strategic planning usually emphasizes the long-run survival of organizations and accepts missing fulfilling beneficiaries' needs in the short run.

On the road to legitimacy

Strategic planning can be seen as an organizational practice that makes NPOs more business-like with all its advantages and drawbacks (Maier et al., 2016). Research suggests that the adoption of corporate management knowledge and practices also leads to change processes, in particular centralization and professionalization, and also institutionalizes the idea that the corporate world provides valid solutions for how to assess and develop NPOs, and creates or widens the divide between internal democratic governance and executive structures (Hvenmark, 2013: 223). Yet managerialism also contributes to legitimacy.

The prescriptive notion of strategic management rests upon a concept of strong organizational rationality with clear imperatives: Define your mission, analyse your environment and your organization, find a strategy that increases your impact and thus contributes to your mission, take activities and decisions that fit with your strategy, check results and readjust goals, strategies, and decisions. These imperatives are outlined above in more detail (e.g., see Figure 13.5). Research that shows how the intensity of strategic management relates to performance apparently supports a core assumption: Strategy helps. The more seriously NPOs engage in strategic management, the better they perform. On the other hand, strong organizational rationality has been contested if not already shot to pieces by various seminal theories and empirical studies (e.g., by March & Olsen, 1976; Meyer & Rowan, 1977; Weick, 1969).

There are two arguments that might resolve this discrepancy. The first one was presented most prominently by Henry Mintzberg (Mintzberg, 1994; Mintzberg et al., 1998; Mintzberg & Waters, 1985). According to him, strategizing in organizations is far from being a clear-cut rational process as described in the prescriptive literature. Some of the strategies have really been intended, planned, and maybe even developed in a thorough process as outline above. However, a significant share of these intended strategies will never be realized. On the other hand, many strategies emerge out of daily decisions and activities. Managers rationalize them *ex-post* in a form of retrospective sense-making (Weick, 1969), cluster them and construct strategic pattern. According to Mintzberg, a majority of realized strategies result from this continuously emerging stream (Mintzberg et al., 1998: 12).

The second argument roots in institutionalist theory. It doubts a direct causality between strategic management and performance and introduces legitimacy. Implementing strategic management, a concept that was designed for business organizations, is one of the major indicators of nonprofits becoming business-like (Dart, 2004; Maier et al., 2016). Thus the diffusion of strategic planning methods into NPOs can be also seen as the result of institutional pressures that force nonprofits towards rationalization (Drori et al., 2006; Hwang & Powell, 2009). From this perspective, strategic management does not directly improve the quality of decisions and make nonprofits act more efficiently and effectively, but first of all contributes to nonprofits' legitimacy (Deephouse & Suchman, 2008; Suchman, 1995). Being considered as a legitimate, professional organization is indispensable for getting resources, e.g., external funding from foundations or public institutions. Due to the institutional pressure towards isomorphism (DiMaggio & Powell, 1983), fewer NPOs can afford not to engage in strategic planning, if only for the records of their funders. This not only explains how strategic management contributes to NPOs' performance; it also explains why and how strategic management conquered the nonprofit sector.

References

Ansoff, Harry Igor. (1965). *Corporate Strategy: An Analytic Approach to Business Strategy for Growth*. New York: McGraw-Hill.

Aranda, Carmen, Arellano, Javier, & Davila, Antonio. (2017). Organizational Learning in Target Setting. *Academy of Management Journal, 60*(3), 1189–1211.

Argyris, C. (1993). *Knowledge for Action*. San Francisco: Jossey Bass.

Argyris, C. (1994). *On Organizational Learning*. Oxford: Blackwell.

Argyris, Chris, & Schön, Donald. (1978). *Organizational Learning I: A Theory of Action Perspective*. Reading, MA: Addison-Wesley.

Argyris, Chris, & Schön, Donald. (1996). *Organizational Learning II: Theory, Method, and Practice*. Reading, MA: Addison-Wesley.

Barry, David, & Elmes, Michael. (1997). Strategy Retold: Toward a Narrative View of Strategic Discourse. *Academy of Management. Academy of Management Review, 22*(2), 429–452.

Ben-Ner, Avner, & Van Hoomissen, Theresa. (1991). Nonprofit Organizations in the Mixed Economy. *Annals of Public and Cooperative Economics, 62*(4), 519–550.

Bishop, Peter, Hines, Andy, & Collins, Terry. (2007). The Current State of Scenario Development: An Overview of Techniques. *Foresight, 9*(1), 5–25.

Blyth, Michael L., Friskey, Elizabeth A., & Rappaport, Alfred. (1986). Implementing the Shareholder Value Approach. *Journal of Business Strategy, 6*(3), 48–58.

Boyatzis, Richard E. (2006). An Overview of Intentional Change from a Complexity Perspective. *Journal of Management Development, 25*(7), 607–623.

Bracker, Jeffrey. (1980). The Historical Development of the Strategic Management Concept. *Academy of Management Review, 5*(2), 219–224. doi: 10.2307/257431

Bryson, John M., Crosby, Barbara C., & Bryson, John K. (2009). Understanding Strategic Planning and the Formulation and Implementation of Strategic Plans as a Way of Knowing: The Contributions of Actor-Network Theory. *International Public Management Journal, 12*(2), 172–207.

Burns, Tom, & Stalker, G.M. (1961). *The Management of Innovation*. London: Tavistock.

Chandler, Alfred D. (1962). *Strategy and Structure: Chapters in the History of Industrial Enterprise*. Boston: MIT.

Courtney, Roger. (2002). *Strategic Managment for Voluntary Nonprofit Organizations*. London: Routledge.

D'Adderio, Luciana, & Pollock, Neil. (2014). Performing Modularity: Competing Rules, Performative Struggles and the Effect of Organizational Theories on the Organization. *Organization Studies, 35*(12), 1813.

Dart, Raymond. (2004). Being "Business-Like" in a Nonprofit Organization: A Grounded and Inductive Typology. *Nonprofit and Voluntary Sector Quarterly, 33*(2), 290–310. doi: 10.1177/0899764004263522

Deephouse, David L., & Suchman, Mark C. (2008). Legitimacy in Organizational Institutionalism. In R. Greenwood, C. Oliver, K. Sahlin, & R. Suddaby (Eds.), *The Sage Handbook of Organizational Institutionalism* (pp. 49–77). London: Sage.

DiMaggio, Paul J., & Powell, Walter W. (1983). The Iron Cage Revisited: Institutional Isomorphism and Collective Rationality in Organizational Fields. *American Sociological Review, 48*, 147–160.

Domanski, Jaroslaw. (2011). The Analysis and Synthesis of Strategic Management Research in the Third Sector from Early 2000 through to Mid-2009. *Foundations of Management, 3*(2), 27. doi: http://dx.doi.org/10.2478/v10238-012-0040-9

Drori, Gili S., Meyer, John W., & Hwang, Hokyu. (2006). *Global Rationalization and "Organization" as Scripted Actorhood*. Paper presented at the 22nd EGOS Colloquium, Sub-Theme 25: Actors, interests and power – their role and relevance in institutional theory, Bergen.

Drucker, Peter F. (1955). *The Practice of Management*. London: Heinemann.

Dunkel, M., Hermann, A., Lindner, D., & Mayrhofer, W. (1997). Auslandseinsätze Aus Sicht Der Unternehmen – Auswertung Strukturierter Interviews Mit Führungskräften Der Bekleidungsindustrie Im Rahmen Des Projektes Personalpolitik 2000. Dresden.

Ebrahim, Alnoor. (2005). Accountability Myopia: Losing Sight of Organizational Learning. *Nonprofit and Voluntary Sector Quarterly, 34*(1), 56–87.

Eisenhardt, K. M., & Martin, J.A. (2000). Dynamic Capabilities: What Are They? *Strategic Management Journal, 21*(10–11), 1105–1121. doi: 10.1002/1097-0266(200010/11)21:10/11<1105::aid-smj133>3.0.co;2-e

Fama, Eugene F., & Jensen, Michael C. (1983). Agency Problems and Residual Claims. *Journal of Law and Economics, 26*(2), 327–349.

Farjoun, Moshe, & Starbuck, William H. (2007). Organizing at and Beyond the Limits. *Organization Studies, 28*(4), 541–566. doi: 10.1177/0170840607076584

Fiol, C. Marlene, & Lyles, Marjorie A. (1985). Organizational Learning. *Academy of Management Review, 10*(4), 803–813.

Freeman, Robert E. (1984). *Strategic Management: A Stakeholder Approach*. Boston: Pitman/Ballinger.

Gibson, Cristina B., & Birkinshaw, Julian. (2004). The Antecedents, Consequences, and Mediating Role of Organizational Ambidexterity. *Academy of Management Journal, 47*(2), 209–226. doi: 10.2307/20159573

Hahn, Tobias, Pinkse, Jonatan, Preuss, Lutz, & Figge, Frank. (2015). Ambidexterity for Corporate Social Performance. *Organization Studies, 37*(2), 213–235. doi: 10.1177/0170840615604506

Hamel, Gary, & Prahalad, Coimbatore K. (1994). *Competing for the Future*. Boston: Harvard Business School.

Hamel, Gary, & Välikangas, Liisa. (2003). The Quest for Resilience. *Harvard Business Review, 81*(9), 52–65.

Hedberg, Bo L.T., Nystrom, Paul C., & Starbuck, William H. (1976). Camping on Seesaws: Prescriptions for a Self-Designing Organization. [1]. *Administrative Science Quarterly, 21*, 41–65.

Herman, D. Robert, & Renz, David O. (1999). Theses on Nonprofit Organization Effectiveness. *Nonprofit and Voluntary Sector Quarterly, 28*(2), 107–126.

Herman, Robert D., & Renz, David O. (2008). Advancing Nonprofit Organizational Effectiveness Research and Theory: Nine Theses. *Nonprofit Management and Leadership, 18*(4), 399–415. doi: 10.1002/nml.195

Horvath, Aaron, Brandtner, Christof, & Powell, Walter W. (2018). Serve or Conserve: Mission, Strategy, and Multi-Level Nonprofit Change During the Great Recession. *Voluntas: International Journal of Voluntary and Nonprofit Organizations*, Online First. doi: 10.1007/s11266-017-9948-8

Hvenmark, Johan. (2013). Business as Usual? On Managerialization and the Adoption of the Balanced Scorecard in a Democratically Governed Civil Society Organization. *Administrative Theory & Praxis, 35*(2), 223–247.

Hwang, Hokyu, & Powell, Walter W. (2009). The Rationalization of Charity: The Influences of Professionalism in the Nonprofit Sector. *Administrative Science Quarterly, 54*, 268–298.

Jensen, Michael C., & Meckling, William H. (1976). Theory of the Firm: Managerial Behavior, Agency Costs and Ownership Structure. [1]. *Journal of Financial Economics* (October), 305–360.

Jones, Gareth R., & Hill, Charles W.L. (1988). Transaction Cost Analysis of Strategy-Structure Choice. [1]. *Strategic Management Journal, 9*, 159–172.

Kaplan, Robert S. (2001). Strategic Performance Measurement and Management in Nonprofit Organizations. *Nonprofit Management and Leadership, 11*(3), 353–370.

Kaplan, Robert S., & Norton, David P. (1992). The Balanced Scorecard – Measures that Drive Performance. *Harvard Business Review, 70*(1), 71–79.

Kaplan, Robert S., & Norton, David P. (1996). *The Balanced Scorecard: Translating Strategy into Action*. Boston: Harvard Business Press.

Knight, Eric, & Paroutis, Sotirios. (2016). Becoming Salient: The TMT Leader's Role in Shaping the Interpretive Context of Paradoxical Tensions. *Organization Studies*. doi: 10.1177/0170840616640844

Kong, Eric. (2008). The Development of Strategic Management in the Non-Profit Context: Intellectual Capital in Social Service Non-Profit Organizations. *International Journal of Management Reviews, 10*(3), 281–299. doi: http://dx.doi.org/10.1111/j.1468-2370.2007.00224.x

Laplume, André O., Sonpar, Karan, & Litz, Reginald A. (2008). Stakeholder Theory: Reviewing a Theory that Moves Us. *Journal of Management, 34*(6), 1152–1189. doi: 10.1177/0149206308324322

Liberatore, Matthew J., & Stylianou, Anthony C. (1994). Using Knowledge-Based Systems for Strategic Market Assessment. *Information & Management, 27*(4), 221–232.

Lieberman, Marvin B. (1987). The Learning Curve, Diffusion, and Competitive Strategy. *Strategic Management Journal, 8*(5), 441–452.

Lillrank, Paul. (2003). The Quality of Standard, Routine and Nonroutine Processes. *Organization Studies, 24*(2), 215–233. doi: 10.1177/0170840603024002344

Magretta, Joan. (2012). *What Management Is*. New York: Free Press.

Maier, Florentine, Meyer, Michael, & Steinbereithner, Martin. (2016). Nonprofit Organizations Becoming Business-Like: A Systematic Review. *Nonprofit and the Voluntary Sector Quarterly, 45*(1), 64–86. doi: 10.1177/0899764014561796

Maier, Gunter. (2014). Management by Strategic Principles Building Social-Strategic-Competence for Leadership. *Academy of Business and Retail Management (ABRM), 4*(4), 397–409.

Manville, Graham. (2006). Implementing a Balanced Scorecard Framework in a Not for Profit SME. *International Journal of Productivity and Performance Management, 56*(2), 162–169.

March, James G. (1991). Exploration and Exploitation in Organizational Learning. *Organization Science, 2*(1), 71–87.

March, James G., & Olsen, Johan P. (1976). *Ambiguity and Choice in Organizations*. Bergen: Universitetsforlaget.

Meadows, Donella H., Meadows, Dennis L., Randers, Jorgen, & Behrens, William W. III. (1972). *The Limits to Growth*. Washington, DC: Potomac Associates and Universe Books.

Meyer, John W., & Rowan, Brian. (1977). Institutionalized Organizations: Formal Structure as Myth and Ceremony. [1]. *American Journal of Sociology, 83*(2), 340–363.

Meyer, Michael, & Leitner, Johannes. (2018). Slack and Innovation: The Role of Human Resources in Nonprofits. *Nonprofit Management and Leadership, 29*(2), 181–201. doi:10.1002/nml.21316

Mintzberg, Henry. (1979). *The Structuring of Organizations: A Synthesis of the Research*. Englewood Cliffs, NJ: Prentice Hall.

Mintzberg, Henry. (1994). The Fall and Rise of Strategic Planning. *Harvard Business Review, 72*(1), 107–114.

Mintzberg, Henry, Ahlstrand, Bruce, & Lampel, Joseph. (1998). *Strategy Safari: A Guided Tour through the Wilds of Strategic Management*. New York: Free Press.

Mintzberg, Henry, & Waters, James A. (1982). Tracking Strategy in an Entrepreneurial Firm. *Academy of Management Journal (pre-1986), 25*(3), 465.

Mintzberg, Henry, & Waters, James A. (1985). Of Strategies, Deliberate and Emergent. [1]. *Strategic Management Journal, 6*, 257–272.

Mitchell, Ronald K., Agle, Bradley R., & Wood, Donna J. (1997). Toward a Theory of Stakeholder Identification and Salience: Defining the Principle of Who and What Really Counts. *Academy of Management Review, 22*(4), 853–886.

Moore, Mark H. (2000). Managing for Value: Organizational Strategy in For-Profit, Non-Profit and Governmental Organizations. *Nonprofit and Voluntary Sector Quarterly, 29*(1), 183–204.

Neumayr, Michaela, Meyer, Michael, Pospíšil, Miroslav, Schneider, Ulrike, & Malý, Ivan. (2009). The Role of Civil Society Organizations in Different Nonprofit Regimes: Evidence from Austria and the Czech Republic. *Comparative Social Research, 26*, 167–196.

Niven, Paul R. (2011). *Balanced Scorecard: Step-by-Step for Government and Nonprofit Agencies*. Hoboken, NJ: John Wiley.

Nonaka, Ikujiro, & Hirotaka, Takeuchi. (1995). *The Knowledge-Creating Company*. New York: Oxford University Press.

O'Reilly, Charles A., & Tushman, Michael L. (2004). The Ambidextrous Organization. *Harvard Business Review, 82*(4), 74–83.

Ortiz-de-Mandojana, Natalia, & Bansal, Pratima. (2016). The Long-Term Benefits of Organizational Resilience through Sustainable Business Practices. *Strategic Management Journal, 37*(8), 1615–1631. doi: http://dx.doi.org/10.1002/smj.2410

Orton, J. Douglas, & Weick, Karl E. (1990). Loosely Coupled Systems: A Reconceptualization. [1]. *Academy of Management Review, 15*(2), 203–223.

Porter, Michael E. (1980). *Competitive Strategy: Techniques for Analyzing Industries and Competitors.* New York: Free Press.

Porter, Michael E. (1985). *Competitive Advantage: Creating and Sustaining Superior Performance.* New York: Free Press.

Porter, Michael E. (Ed.). (1986). *Competition in Global Industries.* Boston: Harvard Business School.

Porter, Michael E. (1990). The Competitive Advantage of Nations. *Harvard Business Review, 68*(2), 73–93.

Porter, Michael E., & Kramer, Mark R. (2002). The Competitive Advantage of Corporate Philanthropy. *Harvard Business Review, 80*(12), 56–67.

Prahalad, Coimbatore K., & Hamel, Gary. (1990). The Core Competence of the Corporation. *Harvard Business Review, 68*(3), 79–91.

Raisch, Sebastian, & Birkinshaw, Julian. (2008). Organizational Ambidexterity: Antecedents, Outcomes, and Moderators. *Journal of Management, 34*(3), 375–409.

Reeves, Martin, Moose, Sandy, & Venema, Thijs. (2014). BCG Classics Revisited: The Growth Share Matrix. Retrieved 2 March 2018 from https://www.bcg.com/de-at/publications/2014/growth-share-matrix-bcg-classics-revisited.aspx

Reid, Margaret F., Brown, Lynne, McNerney, Denise, & Perri, Dominic J. (2014). Time to Raise the Bar on Nonprofit Strategic Planning and Implementation. *Strategy & Leadership, 42*(3), 31–39.

Robert, Westwood, & Gavin, Jack. (2008). The US Commercial-Military-Political Complex and the Emergence of International Business and Management Studies. *Critical Perspectives on International Business, 4*(4), 367–388. doi:10.1108/17422040810915411

Salamon, Lester M., & Anheier, Helmut K. (1996). *The International Classification of Nonprofit Organizations: ICNPO-Revision 1, 1996.* Baltimore, MD: Johns Hopkins University Institute for Policy Studies.

Schemeil, Yves. (2013). Bringing International Organization In: Global Institutions as Adaptive Hybrids. *Organization Studies, 34*(2), 219–252. doi: 10.1177/0170840612473551

Speckbacher, Gerhard. (2008). Nonprofit versus Corporate Governance: An Economic Approach. *Nonprofit Management & Leadership, 18*(3), 295–320.

Stahel, Albert A. (1981). Clausewitz and Sun Tsu: Two Strategies. Upon the Employment of Direct and Indirect Means of War Conduct. [Clausewitz und Sun Tzu: zwei Strategien. Vom Einsatz der direkten und der indirekten Mittel der Kriegsführung]. *Schweizer Monatshefte, 61*(11), 859–872.

Starbuck, William, & Farjoun, Moshe. (2009). *Organization at the Limit: Lessons from the Columbia Disaster.* Malden, MA: John Wiley.

Stone, Melissa M., Bigelow, Barbara, & Crittenden, William. (1999). Research on Strategic Management in Nonprofit Organizations: Synthesis, Analysis, and Future Directions. *Administration & Society, 31*(3), 378–423.

Suchman, Mark C. (1995). Managing Legitimacy: Strategic and Institutional Approaches. *Academy of Management Journal, 20*(3), 571–610.

Teece, David J., Pisano, Gary, & Shuen, Amy. (1997). Dynamic Capabilities and Strategic Management. *Strategic Management Journal, 18*(7), 509–533.

Välikangas, Liisa. (2010). *The Resilient Organization. How Adaptive Cultures Thrive Even When Strategy Fails.* New York: McGraw-Hill.

Weick, Karl E. (1969). *Social Psychology of Organizing.* Reading, MA: Addison-Wesley.

Weick, Karl E., & Sutcliffe, Kathleen M. (2011). *Managing the Unexpected: Resilient Performance in an Age of Uncertainty* (Vol. 8). San Francisco: John Wiley.

Williamson, Oliver E. (1989). Transaction Cost Economics. *Handbook of Industrial Organization, 1*, 135–182.

Williamson, Oliver E. (2002). The Theory of the Firm as Governance Structure: From Choice to Contract. *Journal of Economic Perspectives, 16*(3), 171–195.

Zollo, M., & Winter, S.G. (2002). Deliberate Learning and the Evolution of Dynamic Capabilities. *Organization Science, 13*(3), 339–351. doi: 10.1287/orsc.13.3.339.2780

PART III

Managing internally

14

EVALUATION AND PERFORMANCE MEASUREMENT[1]

Lehn M. Benjamin

ASSOCIATE PROFESSOR, THE LILLY FAMILY SCHOOL OF PHILANTHROPY, INDIANA
UNIVERSITY-PURDUE UNIVERSITY-INDIANAPOLIS, INDIANAPOLIS, IN, USA

David A. Campbell

ASSOCIATE PROFESSOR, DEPARTMENT OF PUBLIC ADMINISTRATION, COLLEGE OF
COMMUNITY AND PUBLIC AFFAIRS, BINGHAMTON UNIVERSITY, BINGHAMTON, NEW YORK, USA

Introduction

Scott Harrison, a former nightclub promoter and Mercy Corps volunteer, started charity:water to provide clean and safe drinking water in developing countries. charity:water works with local partners to build and maintain water wells in areas of greatest need (www.charitywater.org). What is noteworthy about charity:water's model is that it gives donors a way to track their donation and see how their donation contributes to concrete results in a community. charity:water maps all completed projects using a global imaging system that enables donors to literally see the water well that they helped to build and read how this well has changed the lives of local residents. As Scott Harrison tells the story, the charity:water model was a response to a concern he encountered among potential donors in the early stages of starting the organization: they did not trust charities to use their donation effectively. This commitment to reporting results led donors to trust charity:water, even when its initiatives did not turn out exactly as intended (Kristof & WuDunn 2015).

Public opinion surveys seem to confirm Harrison's early experience. For example, a 2015 *Chronicle of Philanthropy* poll found that one-third of those surveyed believe that charities do not do a good job of spending money wisely (Perry 2015). We can see similar concerns motivating the use of social impact bonds and the rising popularity of impact investing and collective impact models. All of these can be seen as evaluative trends, which come on the heels of similar efforts to ensure results in the nonprofit sector, including social return on investing, performance-based contracting and results-based accountability. These efforts seek to address the same critical questions: How can we tell whether these organizations are making a difference? What kinds of evidence will help us distinguish between more effective and less effective nonprofits? Can we better guarantee that these organizations address the pressing problems we see today?

These questions are not new, of course. The desire to ensure that charitable efforts solve social problems, rather than simply alleviate symptoms, was a concern shared by major industrial philanthropists like Carnegie and Rockefeller, who sought to develop scientific approaches to philanthropy at the turn of the 20th century. But as the number of nonprofit organizations increases and communities are more dependent on them to achieve important public policy goals, answering these questions seems more urgent. Consequently, nonprofit leaders today face a funding environment that is more competitive and requires evidence of measurable outcomes. Nonprofit leaders themselves want to know if they are making a difference and what changes they can make to have a bigger impact. With a dizzying array of new evaluative approaches, many nonprofit leaders find themselves wondering what models are appropriate for their organization, what data they can reasonably collect, and what information will shed light on their impact and help them improve their effectiveness.

Finally, it is important to see questions about the results nonprofit organizations produce as an essential challenge to the sector overall, particularly how to distinguish nonprofits from other organizational forms, including for-profit firms and the emergence of new organizational forms like B-Corps. To this point, scholars have identified a range of theoretical perspectives that account for the existence of nonprofit organizations. Most relevant to the discussion of evaluation is an economic argument. The argument suggests that in an environment in which consumers seek to purchase goods or services that are difficult to qualitatively evaluate, such as child care or nursing home services, if given a choice they will choose nonprofits over for-profits because of the non-distribution constraint and the focus on mission over profit. The assumption here is that a focus on mission over profit will generate results that align with a consumer's wishes, essentially mission performance (Weisbrod 2009). Here the non-distribution constraint serves as a proxy for quality. However, with the growing demand for evidence of effectiveness, nonprofits face a real challenge: not only do they need to evaluate products and services which are arguably difficult to evaluate, but also, if they do find a way to meaningfully evaluate, they face competition from other organizational forms, notably for-profit firms.

The goal of this chapter is to advance knowledge about evaluation practice in nonprofit organizations by summarizing the state of management research on this topic, identifying unanswered questions and suggesting future lines of inquiry to advance our understanding. The chapter starts by providing a broad overview of evaluation and defining basic concepts. The second section gives an overview of research on evaluation in the nonprofit sector. The third section takes a closer look at a subset of this research, the research on evaluation practice in nonprofits, and organizes this research around four central questions: (1) Are nonprofits evaluating what they do and if so how? (2) What challenges do nonprofits face as they try to evaluate their work? (3) How is this evaluation activity influencing nonprofits? and (4) What explains these patterns? After summarizing this research, we conclude by suggesting future lines of inquiry.

Overview of evaluation: definitions and development[2]

Evaluation involves the systematic gathering of information about an entity, called an evaluand, to determine its merit or worth, inform decision making and improve policy (Dahler-Larsen 2012; Patton 1997 Scriven & Stokes 1967; Weiss 1998). A few concepts are important in this definition. First, the entity being evaluated or the evaluand can include groups, work processes, program interventions, organizations, organizational networks, fields or sectors. Most evaluations, and evaluation tools, targeted to nonprofits focus on evaluating programs. Second, early evaluators identified two primary purposes of evaluation: formative and summative. *Summative evaluation* provides information to judge merit or worth of the evaluand, while *formative evaluation* provides information to improve implementation practice.[3] Third, the emphasis on the systematic collection of information sets evaluation apart from the evaluative judgments we make every day.

This definition of evaluation seems fairly straightforward, but it elides a confusing array of concepts associated with evaluation evident in the nonprofit sector today. For example, evaluation has become almost synonymous with accountability and transparency. Terms like results, impact and outcomes are also used interchangeably. At the same time, we see the introduction of new evaluative approaches into the nonprofit sector, such as evidence-based practice, collective impact and impact investing. These approaches attempt to respond to the limits of existing evaluation models and to entice new funders to support nonprofits with the promise of more certain results. Table 14.1 provides definitions of common terms associated with evaluation; Table 14.2 provides a list of recent trends in evaluation practice. Understanding why we see this plethora of terms and evaluation approaches in the nonprofit sector requires considering the development of the evaluation field itself. We turn to this task next.

Table 14.1 Terms associated with evaluation

Term	Relationship to evaluation
Accountability	*Accountability* or being accountable requires giving an account of one's actions to some person or body, usually in a position of authority. Accountability is one possible purpose for conducting an evaluation but by no means the only purpose. Other evaluation purposes include supporting learning and generating knowledge.
Effectiveness	*Effectiveness* refers to the extent to which a program or organization has achieved its goals. Effectiveness is one important criterion used to evaluate a program or an organization and is often defined as some level of goal achievement, but other criteria include efficiency, cultural relevance, responsiveness or sustainability.
Impact	Although *impact* is often used colloquially to mean results, more formally impact refers to long-term outcomes or outcomes that can be causally attributed to the intervention.
Logical Frame (Logframe)	*Logical Framework Analysis* is a planning and evaluation tool that has been used primarily in international development since the 1970s.
Monitoring & Evaluation	In international development circles, the ongoing collection of process and outcome data is referred to as *Monitoring and Evaluation* or M&E.
Performance Measurement	*Performance measurement* involves the ongoing collection of evaluative data to inform organizational decision making. This includes the collection of process or output data (i.e., work completed), as well as outcome data or the results of the initiative.
Outcome Measures and Outcome Measurement	*Outcomes* refer to how an individual, family or community is better off as a result of an intervention. *Outcome measurement* is a version of performance measurement that emphasizes the regular collection of outcome data, not simply input and output data.
Output Measures	*Outputs* refer to the work accomplished by a program or organization, such as the number of people served or the number of workshops completed. Measuring outputs is relatively straightforward for most nonprofits and this information is still important for the day-to-day management of the organization, but today the emphasis is on measurable outcomes.

Table 14.2 Trends in evaluation practice

Trend	Description
Collective Impact	*Collective impact* was coined by Kania and Kramer in a 2011 article in the *Stanford Social Innovation Review*. The article articulated a concern that others had pointed to, namely, that expecting individual organizations to affect population level problems (e.g., dropout rates, recidivism, teen pregnancy) was misguided. Tackling these outcomes required all the relevant organizations to work collectively to drive towards the same goal and use the same measurement system (Kania & Kramer 2011).
Impact Investing	*Impact investing* is an evaluative model that considers both the social and financial return of an investment. The idea of using both financial as well as social indicators to assess the value of an intervention is not new. There is a long history of efforts to marry social and financial indicators (Bugg-Levine and Emerson 2011).
Evidence-Based Practice	*Evidence-based practices* are specific techniques or practices that have shown to be effective in repeated studies over time. In assessing the evidence from studies, more weight is given to results from randomized control trials over results from studies employing other evaluation designs, although this has been formally criticized by a number of prominent evaluators (Donaldson, Christie & Mark 2009; Prewitt, Schwandt & Straf 2012; Schwandt 2015).
Social Impact Bonds	Social impact bonds are contracts where the government pays for outcomes. Although previous contracting strategies, such as results-based contracting, also required contractors to deliver outcomes, they paid contractors upfront for results. In contrast with social impact bonds government only pays the agreed amount if outcomes are achieved (Kohli, Besharov & Costa 2012).

The growth and development of the evaluation field

Scriven describes evaluation as a "very young discipline but a very old practice" (1996: 395). Prior to the 1960s, there was no evaluation profession, nor were there specific evaluation models or evaluation theories. And although one can find examples of evaluation throughout history and in diverse societies, descriptions of the evaluation field place its start in the US during the War on Poverty (see Shadish, Cook & Leviton 1991; Stockmann & Meyer 2016; Weiss 1998). The War on Poverty mandated evaluation for the new programs launched under this initiative and by the end of the 1970s evaluation units had been established in most US federal agencies. This development created a demand for this new expertise, and social scientists from a variety of backgrounds – housed in universities and research firms like Rand, Mathematica, and Abt Associates – responded to this call (Shadish et al. 1991; Weiss 1998).

Not long after, Canada, Germany and Sweden started to employ evaluation as a part of their policy processes, but rather than building on earlier European traditions, they followed approaches developed in the US (Furubo 2016: 231). In the US, the practice of evaluation largely focused on assessing incremental levels of change in individual programs. This approach was closely associated with the field of public administration (Dahler-Larsen 2012; Furubo 2016; Stockmann & Meyer 2016).[4] Despite the problems with translating these ideas into other languages and cultures, by the 1990s more countries followed suit, as this approach to evaluation became synonymous with good governance and was integrated into policies of major institutions like the World Bank and the Organization for Economic Cooperation and Development

(OECD) (Furubo 2016; Dahler-Larsen et al. 2017). With the global diffusion and institutional-ization of evaluation, evaluation moved from the province of experts to a general management skill expected of all organizations; something that should be done at all times, regardless of how useful or appropriate it might be (Dahler-Larson 2012: 150–154).

Dahler-Larsen argues that this institutionalization of evaluation is the consequence of the greater uncertainty that characterizes our social world, which has made evaluation more nec-essary but also led to greater skepticism about it (2012). Consequently, to mitigate this uncer-tainty and ensure that evaluation is meaningful we see the proliferation of evaluation approaches that try to address limitations of past models and a growing emphasis on building evaluation capacity, encouraging evaluative thinking and creating an evaluation culture in organizations (Dahler-Larsen 2012). This development is clearly evident in the nonprofit sector, with new models being introduced regularly and with the associated rise of consulting firms, associations, charity rating agencies all dedicated to evaluation and effectiveness of nonprofits. We turn to the consequences of this rise of evaluation in the nonprofit sector next.

Evaluation and nonprofit management

The effectiveness of charitable organizations has long been a concern, but in the 1990s funders and policymakers increasingly began to demand evidence of measurable outcomes from nonprof-its (Easterling 2000; Fowler 1996; United Way of America 1996). This development was partly a response to the growing disillusionment with nonprofits and their ability to address social problems, as well as several high-profile scandals in prominent organizations such as the Wesley Mission in Australia, the Kupat Holim Health Fund in Israel and the United Way of America in the US (Gibelman & Gelman 2001). The focus on outcomes also grew out of a set of public sector management reforms, known as New Public Management, adopted by governments in several countries. These reforms emphasized private sector solutions to address public problems, which on the one hand led to an increasing reliance on private nonprofits and on the other hand emphasized holding organizations accountable for results (e.g., Osborne & Gaebler 1992; Rhodes 1998; Salamon 2002).

In this context, the number of nonprofits increased around the globe as funding began to flow in their direction (Hulme & Edwards 1996). But by the late 1980s, this idealized view of nonprofits started to change. Funders saw the limited capacity of nonprofits to deliver results and their lack of accountability to local communities (Edwards & Hulme 1994; White 1999). The growing skepticism about their effectiveness coupled with these larger public sector reforms meant that nonprofit leaders needed to provide better evidence of results (Light 2000; Najam 1998). Funders, consultants and research firms were ready to help. New tools and templates were created. Trainings helped nonprofit staff develop logic models, identify underlying assumptions of their theories of change and find measures for their program outcomes (Benjamin 2012; Penna & Phillips 2004). Today nonprofits are expected to evaluate, and evaluation has become more institutionalized in the sector (Hwang & Powell 2009; Lynch-Cerullo & Cooney 2011).

Against this backdrop, in the late 1980s and 1990s, as graduate programs and research centers dedicated to the study of nonprofits were emerging, a number of researchers began examining nonprofit effectiveness (Hall 1992; Kanter & Summers 1987). A review of research conducted since then suggests several lines of inquiry that broadly address the topic of evaluation in the non-profit sector. One approach, based in theories of the nonprofit organizational form, considered whether the nonprofits offered some distinct value compared to public and for-profit organi-zations (e.g., Anheier 2004; Kramer 1987; Steinberg 2006). A second line of inquiry addressed performance more narrowly, investigating how best to evaluate nonprofit effectiveness. Here, early researchers drew on organizational sociology and studies of the firm to consider three approaches to evaluating organizations: goal achievement; resource acquisition; and some assessment by multiple constituencies' views of the organization (e.g., Forbes 1998; Herman 1990; Herman & Renz 1997). More recently researchers have proposed multidimensional approaches to understanding nonprofit effectiveness (Anheier 2004; Antadze & Westley 2012; Baruch & Ramalho 2006; Ebrahim & Rangan 2010; Lee & Nowell 2015; Sowa, Selden & Sandfort 2004; Speckbacher 2003; Willems, Boenigk & Jegers 2014). A third line of research has focused on identifying the practices of more or less effective organizations (e.g., Herman & Renz 1998; Smith 1999; Liket & Maas 2015).

Finally, a fourth line of research examined how nonprofits were responding to the demand for evidence of measurable outcomes, including how they were evaluating their work (e.g., Benjamin 2008; Cairns et al. 2005; Carman, Fredericks & Introcaso 2008; Cutt & Murray 2002; Fine, Thayer & Coghlan 2000; Flynn & Hodgkinson 2001; Julian 2001; Lynch-Cerullo & Cooney 2011; Morley, Vinson & Hatry, 2001). This research is closely linked to questions of accountability (Alexander, Brudney & Yang 2010; Benjamin 2008; Bies 2001; Campbell 2002; Cutt & Murray 2002; Ebrahim 2003; Gugerty & Prakash 2010; Kearns 1996). It is this fourth line of research that is most central to understanding evaluation as a management practice in nonprofit organizations and is the focus of the remainder of this chapter. This work has addressed four primary questions: (1) Are nonprofits evaluating what they do, and if so how? (2) What challenges do nonprofits face as they try to evaluate their work? (3) How is evaluation influencing these organizations? and (4) What explains the patterns we see?

Are nonprofit organizations evaluating their work and if so how?

In response to the increased pressure for accountability and results in the nonprofit sector, many studies examined the extent to which nonprofits are evaluating their work, including the kinds of data nonprofits collect, how they collect it and who is responsible for carrying out evaluation for the organization. Although the diverse purposes of the studies we review here, including the unique questions they consider, make it difficult to draw definitive conclusions in response to this question, several themes emerge. First, it appears that in several countries a good portion of formal nonprofits are engaged in evaluation. For example, in a large-scale national survey of 1,965 Canadian nonprofits, 66 percent reported evaluating ongoing programs and services in the last year (Hall et al. 2003: 11). Carman (2007) found a similar result researching North Carolina nonprofits in the US where 65 percent of her sample of 178 reported conducting formal program evaluations. In another study in Santa Catarina, Brazil, 87 percent of the 54 NGOs surveyed reported conducting formal systematic evaluation (Campos et al. 2011). However, in Cambodia, Marshall and Suarez (2014) found that only 32 percent of the 135 nonprofits surveyed nationally used a formal evaluation.

Although almost all the studies reviewed were one-time studies and have not tracked changes in evaluation practice longitudinally, if we compare earlier studies with later studies, it suggests that more nonprofits are evaluating their work or at least reporting that they evaluate their work. For example, an early study in the US found that only 13 percent of the 100 nonprofits surveyed in Cleveland were using measures that would tell them something about their impact (Sheehan 1996). A later study found that 56 percent of 178 nonprofits surveyed nationally collected data on program outcomes, with 45 percent reporting that they had only recently started to measure outcomes (Fine et al. 2000).

In addition to considering the extent to which nonprofits are evaluating their work, studies also look at the methods nonprofits use to evaluate their work. This research suggests that most nonprofits use a combination of evaluation methods but culling data from existing sources is among the most common, and that international NGOs use more sophisticated evaluation designs. For example, Hoefer (2000) found 91 percent of the nonprofits he surveyed in Dallas used agency records, 54 percent used customized instruments, while 34 percent used standardized instruments. Fine et al. (2000) also found that of the 178 US nonprofits they surveyed, 84 percent used program documents in their evaluations, while 66 percent used interviews, 50 percent used observations, 42 percent used focus groups and 19 percent used skill tests. In their study of 1,965 nonprofits in Canada, Hall et al. (2003) found that 83 percent used staff meetings to generate evaluative data, 67 percent used volunteer meetings, 56 percent used surveys, 52 percent used formal evaluations, while 48 percent used interviews, and 45 percent used focus groups. In Brazil, Campos et al. (2011) found that over 50 percent of nonprofits they surveyed conducted impact evaluation, a more sophisticated evaluation design used to assess outcomes, and Kang, Anderson and Finnegan (2012) found 79 percent of the 38 international NGOs conducted outcome evaluation. Other researchers have identified additional methods used by nonprofits such as participant narratives and demographics, and expenditures (Carman 2007); participatory rural appraisal (Kang et al. 2012); and document reviews (Hutchings 2014).

Finally, research indicates that most nonprofits rely on internal staff, not external evaluators, to collect and analyze evaluative data (e.g., Carman 2007; Fine et al. 2000; Hall 2003; Innovation Network 2016). For example, Hall and his colleagues found that 75 percent of the nonprofits they surveyed in Canada relied on internal staff, with only 8 percent using an external evaluator. Similarly, a 2016 national survey in the US found that nonprofit managers and executives were responsible for evaluation, with only 2 percent reporting that they used an outside evaluator and only 6 percent report having internal evaluators, a staff person whose primary role is evaluation (Innovation Network 2016). Others have found similar results (Campos et al. 2011; Carman 2007; Morley et al. 2001). However, those organizations engaged in international development and funded by international donors or multilateral agencies seem to use outside expertise for evaluation, which is consistent with the finding that they are using more sophisticated evaluation designs. Hutchings (2014) describes Oxfam's evaluation practice as a collaboration between regular staff and consultants. In addition, Marshall and Suarez (2014) found that 32 percent of NGOs used a formal evaluation model, and often employed outside evaluators for this purpose (39 percent of their sample received funding from international donors or multilateral agencies). Relying on internal staff to carry out evaluative activities, including designing data collection tools, collecting data and analyzing that data does present challenges. We examine this issue next.

What challenges do nonprofits face as they evaluate their work?

Perhaps because nonprofits rely on internal staff rather than expert evaluators, studies have also uncovered a number of challenges nonprofits face when they evaluate their work. These challenges include lack of expertise, limited time and funding to support evaluation, and funding reporting requirements that are not well aligned with the organization's own evaluation needs. For example, in his study, Hoefer (2000) noted that nonprofits use less rigorous evaluation designs and non-standardized instruments, which are usually created by the nonprofit but have not been tested or validated. This lack of rigor raises concerns about the quality of data nonprofits collect and whether it is possible to use that data for meaningful program evaluation. When looking at the data nonprofits report to funders, one study of 30 South African nonprofits found that for many nonprofits, funders' reporting forms did not make sense. As a result they tended to put a positive spin on the data and the data was inaccurate (Bornstein 2006). Others have found similar issues, noting nonprofits' difficulty in identifying valid measures (Kang et al. 2012;

Moxham & Boaden 2007; Newcomer, Baradei & Garcia 2013) and the poor quality of the eval-uative data nonprofits collect and report to funders (Burger & Owens 2010; Campbell & Lam-bright 2016; Carnochan et al. 2014; Ebrahim 2003). In a contrasting finding, Hall et al. found that the vast majority of the nonprofits they surveyed were satisfied or very satisfied with the quality of their evaluation although, interestingly, funders were somewhat less satisfied (2003: 24).

In addition to capacity and expertise, studies also point to deeper more fundamental problems facing nonprofit managers and practitioners as they attempt to evaluate their work: These evalu-ation models do not seem to adequately capture the non-linear, emergent and relational charac-ter of nonprofit work. For example, Fowler (1996) describes the linear assumptions of evaluation frameworks, most notably the Logframe, intended to capture the results of international devel-opment projects. He contrasts these linear models with the non-linear process of commu-nity change. Others have made similar observations (Antadze & Westley 2012; Benjamin & Campbell 2014; Carnochan et al. 2014; Ebrahim 2003). Furthermore, nonprofit researchers have also suggested that existing program evaluation models used in the sector do not adequately reflect the emergent nature of outcomes, where the outcomes are defined as nonprofits' work in partnership with the communities they serve (e.g., Benjamin 2008; Benjamin & Campbell 2015; Smyth & Schorr 2009; Kang et al. 2012). For example, in their review of evaluation and moni-toring among NGOs in international development, Kang et al. note that the Logical Framework model has been criticized as being inflexible and reflecting a bureaucratic and non-participatory view of the development process (2012: 321). Researchers have also called attention to the signif-icance of relationships – including between nonprofit staff and those they serve – for outcomes, and how outcome measurement models do not give explicit attention to the relational context of the work (e.g., Benjamin 2012; Benjamin & Campbell 2014; Campbell 2010; Carnochan et al. 2014; Ebrahim 2002: 90), including with the more expressive work nonprofits do like the development of social capital and citizenship (Smith 2010).

Finally, researchers have also found that one of the most significant challenges facing non-profits is the sheer volume of data they must collect to meet reporting requirements for different funders. Funders often require their own measures, which are slightly different but are often measuring similar things. Consequently, all of the effort to report data to funders can make eval-uation more difficult, particularly when these reporting requirements are not well aligned with the evaluative data nonprofits need to assess their effectiveness (e.g., Stoecker 2007; Benjamin, Voida and Bopp 2018).

How is evaluation influencing the work of nonprofits?

When outcome measurement was introduced to nonprofits in the 1990s, it was seen as an important change that would give nonprofit leaders the information they needed to improve their effectiveness (*Nonprofit Quarterly* special issue "What we Measure and Why" 1998; Plantz, Greenway & Hendricks 1997). Because outcome measurement and other types of evaluation were often introduced to nonprofits by funders both to ensure nonprofits were accountable and to assess their effectiveness, evaluation has involved inherent tension for nonprofit managers. A tension between using evaluation to learn and to inform decision making, versus using evalu-ation to prove to funders and other stakeholders that the organization is worth supporting. This tension is evident in studies that have examined how evaluation is used by nonprofits and in studies that have looked at how the introduction of evaluation has influenced the sector more broadly.

Studies suggest that nonprofits use evaluation findings to inform decision making about pro-grams and services (Campbell, Lambright & Bronstein 2012; Lee & Clerkin 2017; Newcomer et al. 2013) as well as for organizational learning (Alaimo 2008; Cairns et al. 2005; Kang et al. 2012; Newcomer et al. 2013). Two studies provide more detailed information on the ways in which nonprofits use evaluation information. Hutchings' case study of Oxfam Great Britain noted that the organization was using evaluation information to "to pull out thematic learning, as well as lessons on the design and implementation of interventions" (2014: 6). In addition, Newcomer et al. (2013: 75), in a study of child welfare organizations in Egypt and Colombia, found that the organizations they studied used evaluation data "in the day to day management of programs" and in "strategic management" of the organization. Other studies suggest that nonprofits may not use the data as much as these findings suggest. For example, one study indicated that although 75 percent of nonprofits collect data, only 6 percent report that they feel they are using data effectively (Janus 2018). Campbell and Lambright (2016) also found that providers were dissatisfied with the usefulness of the data they collected.

At the same time, these studies also suggest that nonprofits use evaluation findings to verify to funders they completed work (Campbell et al. 2012); demonstrate responsiveness to funder requirements (Bornstein 2006; Chaplowe & Bamela Engo-Tjega 2007; Kang et al. 2012; Lee & Clerkin 2017); and raise awareness of the results of their work with community members (Campbell et al. 2012; United Way of America 2000). Other studies have identified that nonprofit organizations use evaluation information to signal not only to funders but to stakeholders that they are responsive to their concerns (Bies 2001; Cairns et al. 2005; MacIndoe & Barman 2013) and deserving of resources (Carman 2011; Newcomer et al. 2013; United Way of America 2000).

In addition to questions of use, other studies have looked at the consequences of use for the organizations themselves. LeRoux and Wright (2010), for example, looked not just at whether nonprofits used performance measurement but whether it improved decision making, and they found that the range of performance measures used was positively correlated with self-assessed effectiveness in strategic decision making. Other researchers noted the unintended consequences of evaluation in nonprofit organizations (Tassie et al. 1996). In his study of reporting practice of international NGOs in India, Ebrahim (2003) noted that NGOs' struggle to control the evaluative information they shared with funders inadvertently deterred organizational learning. Benjamin (2008) found that the evaluation framework introduced by one group of funders, coupled with inflexible performance targets, led nonprofits to invest less time building relationships with the communities they served which affected longer term community development efforts. Finally, other researchers found that the introduction of evaluation can reduce opportunities for participation by clients and other stakeholders resulting in more formalized, professionalized and bureaucratic organizations (Hwang & Powell 2006; Smith & Lipsky 1993).

What explains these patterns of evaluation practice?

What is clear from the existing research is that not all nonprofits evaluate their work, collect outcome data or use this data to inform decision making to improve effectiveness. What explains the differences in the patterns that we see? Researchers have provided a range of explanations to account for the variation among nonprofits. The most common explanation is the nonprofit's external environment, as described by resource dependence and new institutional theories (e.g., Carman 2011; Ebrahim 2005; Lynch-Cerullo & Cooney 2011; Thomson 2011). These theories suggest that nonprofits will adopt evaluation practices in response to environmental pressures, most notably the pressure from funders. Several studies seem to confirm funders as the driving force for undertaking evaluation, although there are some mixed findings when it comes to specific types of funders (e.g., Alaimo 2008; Barman & MacIndoe 2012; Campbell et al. 2012; Carman 2009; Marshall & Suarez 2014). For example, although other researchers have found a positive relationship between foundation funding and evaluation practices (Barman & MacIndoe 2012), both Carman (2009) and Marshall & Suarez (2014) found that only government funding was positively associated with the adoption of evaluation practices by nonprofits.

Organizational capacity is also an important determinant of evaluation practice in nonprofit organizations (Barman & MacIndoe 2012; Bornstein 2006; Carnochan et al. 2014; Hall et al. 2003; Hoefer 2000). For example, Barman and MacIndoe (2012) found that organizational capacity mediates how organizations respond to institutional expectations, in this case the adoption of outcome measurement. They found that both administrative and technical capacity help explain the effective implementation of outcome measurement. Further, Thomson's (2011) study of Michigan nonprofits noted that the greater knowledge and technical capacity of larger organizations facilitated their ability to collect and use evaluation data compared to organizations with fewer resources.

Some researchers suggest that organizational culture or leaders' attitudes affect how they approach evaluation. Specifically, whether they see it as a burden and something that is done for funders, or whether they see it as a helpful tool for improving organizational practice (Alaimo 2008; Carman & Fredericks 2010; Carrilio, Packard & Clapp 2003). In his qualitative study of leaders of nonprofit organizations, Alaimo (2008) characterized nonprofit organizations by the extent to which they were systematic in their evaluation approach. He noted that those leaders who approached evaluation systematically tended to characterize evaluation as a tool to measure effectiveness, whereas leaders who approached evaluation in a more ad hoc fashion tended to characterize evaluation as a reporting requirement. Similarly, in a case study of a state-mandated evaluation of a family support program, Carrilio et al. (2003) suggest that the low levels of staff compliance with data collection requirements were the result of managers' philosophical objections to evaluation.

Others have found that the type of organization and perceived purpose of evaluation affect how nonprofits approach evaluation. In one study, Eckerd and Moulton (2011) examined the extent to which the role nonprofits played – service delivery, innovation, social capital, political advocacy, citizenship and funder expression – along with the external environment, affected nonprofits' use of evaluation. While nonprofit roles had little association with the adoption of particular evaluation approaches, the nonprofit role seemed to matter when looking at evaluation use. For example, when nonprofits see their role as building social capital, they are more likely to use evaluation for symbolic purposes while service provision is associated with using evaluation to motivate staff, determine spending priorities and demonstrate program legitimacy. Another study found that the way evaluation is implemented matters:"High participation evaluations were used more than low-participation evaluations in nearly all use categories . . . A category where low participation had slightly higher use was 'to report to a funder'" (Fine et al. 2000: 335).

Evaluation and nonprofit management: future research

Over the last 20 years studies have been conducted in different parts of the world to look at evaluation practice in nonprofit organizations. These studies reveal several dominant themes. To start, a growing number of nonprofits are evaluating the outcomes of their initiatives in response to institutional pressure largely from funders. However, nonprofits often rely on internal staff to cull existing documents and use tailor-made surveys and interview instruments. Consequently, studies have suggested that evaluative data are of inconsistent quality. In addition, the research points to a number of challenges nonprofits face in their evaluation efforts: insufficient capacity; lack of resources and time; limited use of evaluation data by nonprofits; and evaluation approaches that do not account for the emergent, non-linear and relational dimensions of non-profit work. Despite these challenges, nonprofits still use evaluation findings for symbolic as well as instrumental purposes.

Despite the progress that researchers have made, several things are striking when we review this work. Most notably, researchers studying evaluation publish their work in academic journals across a wide range of disciplines and sub-fields, including: international development, public administration, management science, evaluation and nonprofit management. This diversity creates several challenges. For example, disciplinary boundaries may limit researchers' access to or familiarity with work written by scholars in journals outside of their field, inhibiting the process of knowledge development. This may partly explain the number of one-time studies evident in this review, in which researchers use their own instruments with their own terms and questions. The absence of a shared set of terms, definitions and data collection instruments makes it difficult to interpret results across studies. Developing a more robust understanding of evaluation in the sector would require a shared protocol adapted to distinct settings and fields of study. This approach would likely be generative, as scholars learn how evaluation is translated in different settings and what this suggests for the normative context of evaluation. This approach would also make it possible for scholars to share what they find, compare results and repeat studies to deepen understanding of evaluation in nonprofit organizations and strengthen its practice.

Another striking factor in reviewing this research was the reliance on surveys, usually targeted at nonprofit executive directors, to document the extent of institutionalization of evaluation practice in the sector, although these were sometimes coupled with interviews of nonprofit leaders. Most notably, many of the studies we reviewed used surveys to test whether resource dependence and new institutionalism explain the adoption of evaluation practices by nonprofit organizations. Although this research is critical, what we need are detailed ethnographic studies involving all participants in the evaluation process, that help us understand how these evaluation practices are negotiated and interpreted in local settings and the consequences for organizations and communities. These detailed ethnographic studies can help us understand what 'using a logic model' means in an organization in California vs. Copenhagen, Cape Town or Cairo and deepen our understanding of the institutionalization process at the granular level.

Related to the point above, also striking was the extent to which existing research relies heavily on certain theoretical concepts, most notably isomorphism in new institutionalism, to explain patterns of evaluation practice among nonprofits. Although researchers do draw on other perspectives such as resource dependence theory and agency theory, the dangers of relying on one or two concepts to understand organizations is well made by Suddaby:"We lose the variety and complexity of the empirical world of organizations when we begin to view it through a common theoretical lens" (2010: 14). The more recent return of organizational scholars to some of the foundational work that inspired new institutionalism, such as symbolic interactionism and its focus on language and meaning systems, offers up a rich set of theoretical ideas for those studying evaluation practice in nonprofit organizations to consider in the future (e.g., Hallett, Shulman & Fine 2009; Lawrence & Suddaby 2006)

What does all of this suggest for advancing knowledge on this important topic? We see several possibilities for research that would further our understanding of evaluation in the nonprofit sector and inform future practice and policy. To start, we need good descriptive longitudinal data on evaluation practice in the sector. For example, we could develop a basic set of questions or a core survey instrument that could be used in different settings.

At the same time, we need a better understanding of evaluation practice within different countries and cultures. Work in the evaluation field suggests that evaluation terminology and concepts do not translate easily across borders (see Dahler-Larsen et al. 2017). In order to understand how evaluation models and practices are diffused and what the consequences might be for local practice, we need to understand how assessment, reflection and decisions are made in different cultures and countries. For example, what does it mean when an organization in Brazil reports that it conducts impact evaluation compared with when a nonprofit in Cambodia or the UK reports this? We recognize that the impulse to create a standardized instrument to make data comparable across contexts and examine broader patterns of evaluation practice in nonprofits is in tension with this concern about the need to account for how such practices take on different meanings and as a result have different consequences. Therefore, finding a workable balance between the two is important in advancing knowledge.

We also believe that bringing in different interpretive frames might shed new light on this social phenomenon. We have hinted at these above, but nonprofit researchers might consider the work of Goffman, Garfinkel and Hughes along with other sociologists like Burger and Luckman whose work inspired new institutionalism in organizational studies. More specifically, Goffman's concept of a total institution, Garfinkel's notion of accounts and Hughes writings on work provide fruitful starting points for considering evaluation practice in nonprofit organizations. Students of organization have recently turned back to these early roots of new institutionalism to deepen our understanding of organizational life (see Hallett, Shulman & Fine 2009; Hallett & Ventresca 2006; Suddaby 2010).

Finally, although researchers recognize that evaluation can be used both instrumentally as well as symbolically, and that evaluation is a social accomplishment as much as it is an instrumental task, what seems to be missing in the research is an understanding of the evaluation field more broadly: both its historical roots and how it has evolved over time, and what this might suggest for our understanding of evaluation in nonprofits. We offered a small window into the evolution of evaluation as a field of practice earlier in the chapter. However, more attention could be given to understanding evaluation as a field by nonprofit researchers, as this would likely lead to deeper insights about evaluation practice by nonprofit organizations.

Notes

1 We would like to thank Dana Doan and Barbara Duffy for their assistance with this chapter.
2 This description of the evaluation field draws from Shadish, Cook & Leviton's *Foundations of Program Evaluation: Theories of Practices* published by Sage in 1991.
3 As Schwandt has rightly pointed out, this distinction is somewhat problematic because it implies that formative evaluations do not involve judgments of merit or worth. All evaluative activity, such as providing feedback on implementation, involves some assessment of merit or worth (Schwandt 2015).
4 For an overview of evaluation practice in different countries see Furubo, Rist & Sandahl 2002, *International Atlas of Evaluation*.

References

Alaimo, S.P. (2008) Nonprofits and evaluation: Managing expectations from the leader's perspective, *New Directions for Evaluation*, (119), 73–92.

Alexander, J., Brudney, J.L., & Yang, K., (2010) Introduction to the Symposium, *Nonprofit and Voluntary Sector Quarterly, 39*(4), 571–587.

Anheier, H.K. (2004) *Civil society: Measurement, evaluation, policy*, London: CIVICUS Earthscan Publications.

Antadze, N. & Westley, F. (2012) Impact metrics for social innovation: Barriers or bridges to radical change, *Journal of Social Entrepreneurship, 3*(2), 133–150.

Barman, E., & MacIndoe, H. (2012) Institutional pressures and organizational capacity: The case of outcome measurement, *Sociological Forum, 27*, 70–93.

Baruch, Y., & Ramalho, N. (2006) Communalities and distinctions in the measurement of organizational performance and effectiveness across for-profit and nonprofit sectors, *Nonprofit and Voluntary Sector Quarterly*, *35*(1), 39–65.

Benjamin, L.M. (2008) Bearing more risk for results: Performance accountability and nonprofit relational work, *Administration & Society*, *39*(8), 959–983.

Benjamin, L.M. (2012) Nonprofit organizations and outcome measurement: From tracking program activities to focusing on frontline work, *American Journal of Evaluation*, *33*(3), 431–447.

Benjamin, L.M., & Campbell, D. C. (2014) Programs aren't everything, *Stanford Social Innovation Review*, *12*(2), 42–47.

Benjamin, L.M., & Campbell, D. C. (2015) Nonprofit performance: Accounting for the agency of clients, *Nonprofit and Voluntary Sector Quarterly*, *44*(5), 988–1006.

Benjamin, L.M., Voida, A., & Bopp, C. (2018) Policy fields, data systems, and the performance of nonprofit human service organizations, *Human Service Organizations: Management, Leadership & Governance*, *42*(2), 185–204.

Bies, A.L. (2001) Accountability, organizational capacity, and continuous improvement: Findings from Minnesota's nonprofit sector, *New Directions for Philanthropic Fundraising*, (31), 51–80.

Bornstein, L. (2006) Systems of accountability, webs of deceit? Monitoring and evaluation in South African NGOs, *Development*, *49*(2), 52–61.

Bugg-Levine, A., & Emerson, J. (2011) Impact investing: Transforming how we make money while making a difference, *Innovations: Technology, Governance, Globalization*, *6*(3), 9–18.

Burger, R., & Owens, T. (2010) Promoting transparency in the NGO sector: Examining the availability and reliability of self-reported data, *World Development*, *38*(9), 1263–1277.

Cairns, B., Harris, M., Hutchison, R., & Tricker, M. (2005) Improving performance? The adoption and implementation of quality systems in UK nonprofits, *Nonprofit Management and Leadership*, *16*(2), 135–151.

Campbell, D. (2002) Outcomes assessment and the paradox of nonprofit accountability, *Nonprofit Management and Leadership*, *12*(3), 243–259.

Campbell, D. (2010) Is constituency feedback living up to its promise? Provider perceptions of feedback practices in nonprofit human service organizations, *Families in Society*, *91*(3), 313–320.

Campbell, D., Lambright, K., & Bronstein, L. (2012) In the eyes of the beholders: Feedback motivations and practices among nonprofit providers and their funders, *Public Performance and Management Review*, *36*(1), 7–30.

Campbell, D., & Lambright, K. (2016) Program performance and multiple constituency theory, *Nonprofit and Voluntary Sector Quarterly*, *45*(1), 150–171.

Campos, L., Andion, C., Serva, M., Rossetto, A., & Assumpção, J. (2011) Performance evaluation in non-governmental organizations (NGOs): An analysis of evaluation models and their applications in Brazil, *Voluntas: International Journal of Voluntary & Nonprofit Organizations*, *22*(2), 238.

Carman, J.G. (2007) Evaluation practice among community-based organizations: Research into the reality, *American Journal of Evaluation*, *28*(1), 60–75.

Carman, J.G. (2009) Nonprofits, funders, and evaluation: Accountability in action. *American Review of Public Administration*, *39*(4), 374–390.

Carman, J.G. (2011) Understanding evaluation in nonprofit organizations, *Public Performance & Management Review*, *34*(3), 350–377.

Carman, J.G., Fredericks, K.A., & Introcaso, D. (2008) Government and accountability: Paving the way for nonprofits and evaluation, *New Directions for Evaluation*, (119), 5–12.

Carman, J.G., & Fredericks, K.A. (2010) Evaluation capacity and nonprofit organizations: Is the glass half-empty or half-full? *American Journal of Evaluation*, *31*(1), 84–104.

Carnochan, S., Samples, M., Myers, M., & Austin, M.J. (2014) Performance measurement challenges in nonprofit human service organizations, *Nonprofit and Voluntary Sector Quarterly*, *43*(6), 1014–1032.

Carrilio, T., Packard, T., & Clapp, J. (2003) Nothing in – nothing out – Barriers to use of performance data in social service programs, *Administration in Social Work*, *27*(4), 61–75.

Chaplowe, S., & Bamela Engo-Tjega, R. (2007) Civil society organizations and evaluation: Lessons from Africa, *Evaluation*, *13*(2), 257–274.

Cutt, J., & Murray, V.V. (2002) *Accountability and effectiveness evaluation in non-profit organizations*, London: Routledge.

Dahler-Larsen, P. (2012) *The evaluation society*, Stanford, CA: Stanford University Press.

Dahler-Larsen, P., Abma, T., Bustelo, M., et al. (2017) Evaluation, language and untranslatables, *American Journal of Evaluation, 38*(1), 114–125.

Donaldson, S.I., Christie, C.A., & Mark, M.M. (2009) *What counts as credible evidence in applied research and evaluation practice?* Thousand Oaks, CA: Sage.

Easterling, D. (2000) Using outcome evaluation to guide grantmaking: Theory, reality, and possibilities, *Nonprofit and Voluntary Sector Quarterly, 29*(3), 482–486.

Ebrahim, A. (2002) Information struggles: The role of information in the reproduction of NGO–funder relationships, *Nonprofit and Voluntary Sector Quarterly, 31*(1), 84–114.

Ebrahim, A. (2003) Accountability in practice: Mechanisms for NGOs, *World Development, 31*(5), 813–829.

Ebrahim, A. (2005) Accountability myopia: Losing sight of organizational learning, *Nonprofit and Voluntary Sector Quarterly, 34*(1), 56–87.

Ebrahim, A.S., & Rangan, V.K. (2010) *The limits of nonprofit impact: A contingency framework for measuring social performance,* Working Paper 10-099. Harvard Business School.

Eckerd, A., & Moulton, S. (2011) Heterogeneous roles and heterogeneous practices: Understanding the adoption and uses of nonprofit performance evaluations, *American Journal of Evaluation, 32*(1), 98–117.

Edwards, M., & Hulme, D. (1994) *NGOs and development: Performance and accountability in the "new world order,"* London: Save the Children Fund-UK.

Fine, A.H., Thayer, C.E., & Coghlan, A. (2000) Program evaluation practice in the nonprofit sector, *Nonprofit Management and Leadership, 10*(3), 331–339.

Flynn, P., & Hodgkinson, V.A. (Eds.) (2001) *Measuring the impact of the nonprofit sector,* New York: Kluwer Academic/Plenum.

Forbes, D.P. (1998) Measuring the unmeasurable: Empirical studies of nonprofit organization effectiveness from 1977 to 1997, *Nonprofit and Voluntary Sector Quarterly, 27*(2), 183–202.

Fowler, A. (1996) Demonstrating NGO performance: Problems and possibilities, *Development in Practice, 6*(1), 58–65.

Furubo, J.-E. (2016) Evaluation, its heritage and its future. In Stockmann R., & Meyer W. (Eds.), *The future of evaluation* (pp. 228–237), London: Palgrave Macmillan.

Furubo, J.-E., Rist, R.C., & Sandahl, R. (2002) *International atlas of evaluation,* New Brunswick, NJ: Transaction Publishers.

Gibelman, M., & Gelman, S.R. (2001) Very public scandals: Nongovernmental organizations in trouble, *Voluntas: International Journal of Voluntary and Nonprofit Organizations, 12*(1), 49–66.

Gugerty, M.K., & Prakash, A. (2010) *Voluntary regulation of NGOs and nonprofits: An accountability club framework,* Cambridge: Cambridge University Press.

Hall, M.H., Phillips, S.D., Meillat, C., & Pickering, D. (2003) *Assessing performance: Evaluation practices and perspectives in Canada's voluntary sector,* Canadian Centre for Philanthropy and the Centre for Voluntary Sector Research and Development, Ontario.

Hall, P.D. (1992) *Inventing the nonprofit sector and other essays on philanthropy, voluntarism, and nonprofit organizations,* Baltimore, MD: Johns Hopkins University Press.

Hallett, T., & Ventresca, M.J. (2006) Inhabited institutions: Social interactions and organizational forms in Gouldner's Patterns of Industrial Bureaucracy, *Theory and Society, 35*(2), 213–236.

Hallett, T., Shulman, D., & Fine, G.A. (2009) Peopling organizations: The promise of classic symbolic interactionism for an inhabited institutionalism. In Adler, P.S. (Ed.), *The Oxford handbook of sociology and organization studies: Classical foundations* (pp. 486–510). Oxford: Oxford University Press.

Herman, R.D. (1990) Methodological issues in studying the effectiveness of nongovernmental and nonprofit organizations, *Nonprofit and Voluntary Sector Quarterly, 19*(3), 293–306.

Herman, R.D., & Renz, D.O. (1997) Multiple constituencies and the social construction of nonprofit organization effectiveness. *Nonprofit and Voluntary Sector Quarterly, 26*(2), 185–206.

Herman, R.D., & Renz, D.O. (1998) Nonprofit organizational effectiveness: Contrasts between especially effective and less effective organizations, *Nonprofit Management and Leadership, 9*(1), 23–38.

Herman, R.D., & Renz, D.O. (1999) Theses on nonprofit organizational effectiveness, *Nonprofit and Voluntary Sector Quarterly, 28*(2), 107–126.

Hoefer, R. (2000) Accountability in action? Program evaluation in nonprofit human service agencies, *Nonprofit Management and Leadership, 11*(2), 167–177.

Hulme, D., & Edwards, M. (1996) *Beyond the magic bullet: NGO performance and accountability in the post–Cold War world,* Bloomfield, CT: Kumarian Press.

Hutchings, C. (2014) Balancing accountability and learning: A review of Oxfam GB's global performance framework, *Journal of Development Effectiveness, 6*(4), 425–435.

Hwang, H., & Powell, W.W. (2009) The rationalization of charity: The influences of professionalism in the nonprofit sector, *Administrative Science Quarterly*, *54*(2), 268–298.

Innovation Network (2016) *State of evaluation 2016: Evaluation practice and capacity in the nonprofit sector.*

Janus, K.K. (2018) Creating a data culture, *Stanford Social Innovation Review,* March 2.

Julian, D.A. (2001) A case study of the implementation of outcomes-based funding within a local United Way system: Some implications for practicing community psychology, *American Journal of Community Psychology*, *29*(6), 851–874.

Kang, J., Anderson, S.G., & Finnegan, D. (2012) The evaluation practices of US international NGOs, *Development in Practice*, *22*(3), 317–333.

Kania, J., & Kramer, M. (2011) Collective impact, *Stanford Social Innovation Review*, *9*(1), 36–41.

Kanter, R.M., & Summers, D.V. (1987) Doing well by doing good: Dilemmas of performance measurement in nonprofit organisations and the need for a multiple constituency approach. In W.W. Powell (Ed.), *The nonprofit sector: A research handbook*, New Haven, CT: Yale University Press.

Kearns, K.P. (1996) *Managing for accountability: Preserving the public trust in public and nonprofit organizations*, San Francisco: Jossey-Bass.

Kohli, J., Besharov, D.J., & Costa, K. (2012) *What are social impact bonds? An innovative new financing tool for social programs*, Center for American Progress.

Kramer, R.M. (1987) Voluntary agencies and the personal social services. In W.W. Powell (Ed.), *The nonprofit sector: A research handbook*, New Haven, CT: Yale University Press.

Kristof, N.D., & WuDunn, S. (2015) *A path appears: Transforming lives, creating opportunity*, New York: Vintage.

Lawrence, T.B., & Suddaby, R. (2006) Institutions and institutional work. In R. Stuart, C. Clegg, B. Hardy, & W.R. Nord (Eds.), *The Sage handbook of organization studies* (2nd ed., pp. 215–254). London: Sage.

Lee, C., & Nowell, B. (2015) A framework for assessing the performance of nonprofit organizations, *American Journal of Evaluation*, *36*(3), 299–319.

Lee, C. & Clerkin, R. (2017) Exploring the use of outcome measures in human service nonprofits: Combining agency, institutional and organizational capacity perspectives, *Public Performance and Management Review*, *40*(3), 601–624.

LeRoux, K., & Wright, N.S. (2010) Does performance measurement improve strategic decision making? Findings from a national survey of nonprofit social service agencies, *Nonprofit and Voluntary Sector Quarterly*, *39*(4), 571–587.

Light, P.C. (2000) *Making nonprofits work: a report on the tides of nonprofit management reform*, Washington, DC: Aspen Institute, Brookings Institution Press.

Liket, K.C., & Maas, K. (2015). Nonprofit organizational effectiveness: Analysis of best practices. *Nonprofit and Voluntary Sector Quarterly*, *44*(2), 268–296.

Lynch-Cerullo, K. & Cooney, K. (2011) Moving from outputs to outcomes: A review of the evolution of performance measurement in the nonprofit human services sector, *Administration in Social Work, 35*, 364–388.

MacIndoe, H., & Barman, E. (2013) How organizational stakeholders shape performance measurement in nonprofits: Exploring a multidimensional measure, *Nonprofit and Voluntary Sector Quarterly*, *42*(4), 716–738.

Marshall, J.H., & Suarez, D. (2014) The flow of management practices: An analysis of NGO monitoring and evaluation dynamics, *Nonprofit and Voluntary Sector Quarterly*, *43*(6), 1033–1051.

Morley, E., Vinson, E., & Hatry, H. (2001) *Outcome measurement in nonprofit organisations: Current practices and recommendations,* Independent Sector.

Moxham, C., & Boaden, R. (2007) The impact of performance measurement in the voluntary sector: Identification of contextual and processual factors, *International Journal of Operations & Production Management*, *27*(8), 826–845.

Najam, A. (1998) Searching for NGO effectiveness, *Development Policy Review*, *16*(3), 305–310.

Newcomer, K., Baradei, L.E., & Garcia, S. (2013) Expectations and capacity of performance measurement in NGOs in the development context, *Public Administration and Development*, *33*(1), 62–79.

Osborne, D., & Gaebler, T. (1992) *Reinventing government: How the entrepreneurial spirit is transforming government*, Reading, MA: Addison Wesley.

Patton, M.Q. (1997) *Utilization-focused evaluation: The new century text*, Thousand Oaks, CA: Sage.

Penna, R.M., & Phillips, W.J. (2004) *Outcome frameworks: An overview for practitioners*, Center for Outcomes, Rensselaerville Institute.

Perry, S. (2015) 1 in 3 Americans lacks faith in charities, Chronicle poll finds, *The Chronicle of Philanthropy*, October 5. Retrieved from https://www.philanthropy.com/article/1-in-3-Americans-Lacks-Faith/233613/

Plantz, M.C., Greenway, M.T., & Hendricks, M. (1997) Outcome measurement: Showing results in the nonprofit sector, *New Directions for Evaluation*, (75), 15–30.

Prewitt, K., Schwandt, T.A., & Straf, M.L. (2012) *Using science as evidence in public policy*, Committee on the Use of Social Science Knowledge in Public Policy, Division of Behavioral and Social Sciences and Education, National Research Council, Washington, DC: National Academies Press.

Rhodes, M. (1998) Globalization, labour markets and welfare states: A future of 'competitive corporatism'? In *The future of European welfare* (pp. 178–203), London: Palgrave Macmillan.

Salamon, L.M. (Ed.). (2002) *The state of nonprofit America*, Washington, DC: Brookings Institution Press.

Schwandt, T. (2015) *Evaluation foundations revisited: Cultivating a life of the mind for practice*, Stanford, CA: Stanford University Press.

Scriven, M. (1996) Reflections. In *Evaluation roots, tracing theories, views and influences* (pp. 183–195), Thousand Oaks, CA: Sage.

Scriven, M.S., & Stokes, R.E. (1967) The methodology of evaluation. In *Perspectives of curriculum evaluation*, Chicago: Rand McNally.

Shadish, W.R., Cook, T.D., & Leviton, L.C. (1991) *Foundations of program evaluation: Theories of practice*, Newbury Park, CA: Sage.

Sheehan Jr., R.M. (1996) Mission accomplishment as philanthropic organization effectiveness: Key findings from the excellence in philanthropy project, *Nonprofit and Voluntary Sector Quarterly*, *25*(1), 110–123.

Smith, D.H. (1999) The effective grassroots association II: Organizational factors that produce external impact, *Nonprofit Management and Leadership*, *10*(1), 103–116.

Smith, S.R. (2010) Nonprofits and public administration: Reconciling performance management and citizen engagement, *American Review of Public Administration*, *40*(2), 129–152.

Smith, S.R., & Lipsky, M. (1993) *Nonprofits for hire: The welfare state in the age of contracting*, Cambridge, MA: Harvard University Press.

Smyth, K.F., & Schorr, L.B. (2009) A lot to lose: A call to rethink what constitutes "evidence" in finding social interventions that work, Working Paper, Malcolm Weiner Center for Social Policy, Harvard Kennedy School.

Sowa, J.E., Selden, S.C., & Sandfort, J.R. (2004) No longer unmeasurable? A multidimensional integrated model of nonprofit organizational effectiveness, *Nonprofit and Voluntary Sector Quarterly*, *33*(4), 711–728.

Speckbacher, G. (2003) The economics of performance management in nonprofit organizations, *Nonprofit Management and Leadership*, *13*(3), 267–281.

Steinberg, R. (2006) Economic theories of nonprofit organizations. In W.W. Powell & R. Steinberg (Eds.), *The nonprofit sector: A research handbook* (2nd ed., pp. 117–139), New Haven, CT: Yale University Press.

Stockmann, R., & Meyer, W. (2016) The future of evaluation: Global trends, new challenges and shared perspectives. In Stockmann R., & Meyer W. (Eds.), *The future of evaluation* (pp. 9–19), London: Palgrave Macmillan.

Stoecker, R. (2007) Research practices and needs of non-profit organizations in an urban center, *Journal of Sociology & Social Welfare*, *34*, 97.

Suddaby, R. (2010) Challenges for institutional theory, *Journal of Management Inquiry*, *19*(1), 14–20.

Tassie, B., Murray, V., Cutt, J., & Bragg, D. (1996) Rationality and politics: What really goes on when funders evaluate the performance of fundees? *Nonprofit and Voluntary Sector Quarterly*, *25*(3), 347–363.

Thomson, D.E. (2011) The role of funders in driving nonprofit performance measurement and use in strategic management, *Public Performance & Management Review*, *35*(1), 54–78.

United Way of America (1996) *Measuring program outcomes: A practical approach*, Alexandria, VA: United Way of America.

United Way of America (2000) *Agency experiences with outcome measurement*, Alexandria, VA: United Way of America.

Weisbrod, B.A. (2009). *The nonprofit economy*, Cambridge, MA: Harvard University Press.

Weiss, C.H. (1998) *Methods for studying programs and policies*, London: Prentice Hall.

What we measure and why [Special issue] (1998) *New England Nonprofit Quarterly*, *5*(3).

White, S.C. (1999) NGOs, civil society, and the state in Bangladesh: The politics of representing the poor, *Development and Change*, *30*(2), 307–326.

Willems, J., Boenigk, S., & Jegers, M. (2014) Seven trade-offs in measuring nonprofit performance and effectiveness, *Voluntas: International Journal of Voluntary and Nonprofit Organizations*, *25*(6), 1648–1670.

15

BUDGETING AND FINANCIAL MANAGEMENT

A multi-year budgeting approach

Marcus Lam

ASSISTANT PROFESSOR, UNIVERSITY OF SAN DIEGO, SCHOOL OF LEADERSHIP AND
EDUCATION SCIENCES, DEPARTMENT OF LEADERSHIP STUDIES, SAN DIEGO, CA, USA

Bob Beatty

ADJUNCT FACULTY, UNIVERSITY OF SAN DIEGO, SCHOOL OF LEADERSHIP AND
EDUCATION SCIENCES, DEPARTMENT OF LEADERSHIP STUDIES, SAN DIEGO, CA, USA

Introduction

A budget is a monetary expression of a nonprofit organization's mission. It commonly takes the form of an annual plan that projects how much an organization will receive in revenue in the upcoming fiscal year and how the organization will spend that revenue. A simple budget plan consists of various line-items of anticipated income sources along with line-items of anticipated expenses, with total projected expenses not to exceed total projected revenue. The budget plan, along with the strategic and operational plans, make up the three prongs of an organization's Management Control System (Hansen et al., 2003; Anthony and Young, 2003). In this chapter, we will review the budgeting literature in the context of general Management Control Systems (MCS) research. We focus first on the traditional line-item budget, discuss is components and possible reasons for its ubiquity and prevalence among nonprofits. Next, we will draw from contingency-based studies to discuss possible contextual or "situational factors" that correlate with certain components of the MCS, such as participative or top-down, hierarchical budgeting models. We will then offer one possible alternative to the traditional line-item budget, the multi-year (MY) budget, and demonstrate, through a case study, how a multi-year budgeting model may work in a nonprofit setting. Next, we will briefly discuss research on budgeting among international nonprofits; and finally, we will conclude with a discussion about areas for further research on MCS and budgeting in the nonprofit field.

The line-item budget

Budgeting is one of the most important but also – if done well – one of the most resource-intensive processes in nonprofit financial management. To date, many nonprofits, regardless of size or sub-sector, utilize the traditional line-item budget model. Despite its ubiquity, the traditional line-item budget can often lead to inefficiencies that impede an organization from achieving its long-term strategic goals. This leads to many complaints about the budgeting process. From a process perspective, the traditional line-item budget fosters a tendency to charge expenses to budget line-items which have available budget balances, instead of the appropriate line-item. As future budgets are typically based on prior actuals, the miscoding of expenses is built into future budgets.

With respect to organizational outcomes, the line-item budget model generally leads to several negative outcomes, such as meaningless year-to-date budget variances, misallocation of staff resources by focusing on being "within budget," or being "penny-wise and pound foolish" rather than allocating resources to accomplishing mission outcomes. Finally, from a practitioner perspective, complaints of the line-item budget include, "at the line level, we give our input, but then decisions are made by one or two people so it doesn't matter what information you provide"; or from the board level, "there is no connection between the programs we discuss at Board meetings and the approved budget"; or from the executive director level, "as long as I come in under budget on expenses and over budget on fundraising, the Board doesn't understand about other budget functions."[1]

In short, instead of the traditional budgeting models, typically the line-item budget, being a plan that will be modified as required to fit a future reality, it becomes a straitjacket not allowing the organization to effectively adapt to said future realities.

One possible explanation for the inefficiencies of traditional budgeting models that has been put forth by management accounting scholars is that traditional budgeting overemphasizes control, transparency, and accountability, to the detriment of strategic and operational planning, as part of the overall management control system. For nonprofits, budgeting, with this emphasis on control, transparency, and accountability, has been "de-coupled" from program effectiveness.

The management control system and line-item budget

We follow Covaleski et al. (2007) and define budgeting as both the budget document and the process of arriving at the budget document. Budgeting is one of three prongs of an organization's overall "Management Control System" (MCS) (Hansen et al., 2003; Anthony and Young, 2003). The other two prongs are strategic planning and operational planning. As Anthony and Young (2003) argue, all three are vital to an organization's overall effectiveness. However, as it has evolved and utilized across all organizations, the MCS has become synonymous with budgeting, and budgeting has become synonymous with control – all to the detriment of strategic and operational planning. This "de-coupling" from the other two vital components of the MCS may explain the numerous complaints from practitioners about the inefficiencies and limitations of budgeting (Hansen et al., 2003).

There are several reasons for this development. According to Hansen et al. (2003), budgeting has become synonymous with the MCS because it represents universal processes of accounting which are common to all organizations. Operational planning, on the other hand, is idiosyncratic and based on specific technologies, differing across organizations. Similarly, strategic planning is carried out on an irregular basis and only involves upper management, often without input from lower front-line workers and therefore also differs across organizations (Hansen et al., 2003). Thus, budgeting has become viewed as a universal means of control and removed from the strategic planning and operational planning components of the overall management control system. This is to the detriment of overall organizational effectiveness and may account for the dissatisfaction and inefficiencies that practitioners experience with the budgeting process. How, then, can we link budgeting back to strategic and operational planning as part of the overall MCS?

First, let's examine the idea of budgeting as a means of control by focusing on the traditional line-item operating budget and its core components. The traditional line-time budget document is calculated either on a cash or accrual basis, and its constituent parts are as follows: line-items of expenses and revenue by departmental units (the larger the organization and the more departments, the more line-items); a focus on inputs (rather than outputs or outcomes); projected on an annual basis (rather than a multi-year basis); incremental (changes from year to year are not drastic and often not comprehensive); and most importantly, balanced, or ensuring that projected revenues cover projected expenses.

The budget process in creating the line-time budget document is generally a top-down, hierarchical approach in which management allocates funds to departmental units with some input from, and negotiations with, various departmental units regarding expenses, costs, and revenue; the final adoption of the budget document being contingent on approval by the board of directors (Wildavsky, 1978; Dropkin et al., 2007). Depending on the size of the organization or agency, the process of budget negotiations usually starts three to six months prior to the start of the next fiscal year.

Table 15.1 illustrates a traditional line-item budget. Revenue line-items are grouped together at the top of the budget document followed by the expenses. By putting revenue line-items at the top, emphasis is placed on income-generating activities rather than program outcomes. Thus, it is unclear, from this traditional line-item budget document, what the organization hopes to accomplish.

Wildavsky (1978) suggests that the traditional line-item budget persists because, "it has the virtue of its defects" (p. 508). That is, it is functional without being disruptive and does not cause agencies to question core assumptions about revenues or expenses. For example, the traditional line-item budget is incremental, tacking on minor percentage increases in revenue or expenses, rather than comprehensive, reviewing program objectives and starting from scratch if expenses do not meet program objectives. Incremental budgeting, in short, is not too disruptive or resource intensive. The traditional line-item budget is backwards looking because it is easier to base the current year on what is known, rather than future forecasts that may involve unpredictable events. It is therefore less disruptive to plan based on annual projections rather than multi-year projections. Similarly, because budgets are projected out only on an annual basis, the traditional line-item budget is constructed on a cash basis rather than a volume basis as volume budgeting entails greater uncertainty (Wildavsky, 1978).

But above all, the traditional line-item budget has the virtue of "apparent" transparency, an important consideration for both government agencies and nonprofit organizations, as fiduciaries of public resources. What this implies is that the traditional line-item budget, as used in nonprofit agencies, serves primarily as a means of control over resource allocation and spending; and this, simultaneously, signals accountability and transparency to external stakeholders. This control function is particularly important for nonprofit and public agencies who have no ownership rights to organizational revenues and assets and are thus beholden to the general public for the spending of those assets and resources. Thus, nonprofits use budgeting to foster and maintain legitimacy – an important precursor for raising further revenue and long-term sustainability. With this in mind, the traditional line-item budget, with its inherent limitations, fills the control and legitimacy roles, albeit imperfectly but adequately.[2,3]

Table 15.1 Line-item operating budget

	Current year	Next year	Change
Revenues, Gains, and Other Support			
Total grants and contracts	19,266,143	21,715,832	2,449,689
Total service fees	2,856,404	3,018,932	162,528
Total contributions/gifts	381,000	381,000	–
Total other	2,787	2,787	–
Total Revenues, Gains, and Other Support	22,506,335	25,118,551	2,612,217
Expenses			
Total personnel, consultants, and related	16,501,205	18,184,296	1,683,091
Total occupancy & telephone	2,958,106	3,050,622	92,516
Total food & program materials	931,720	997,439	65,719
Total subcontractors & program fees	1,661,746	1,669,872	8,126
Total equipment, software, vehicles, furniture	511,908	511,908	–
Total all other	257,170	257,170	–
Total Expenses	22,821,854	24,671,307	1,849,453
Difference between receipts and expenses:	(315,519)	447,244	762,764
Cash adjustments to operating expenses & receipts:			
Depreciation/amortization	147,134	147,134	–
Transfers to Board Advisory Fund	–	–	–
Debt repayment	(30,000)	(30,000)	–
Total non-operating	117,134	117,134	–
Net cash impact from operations:	(198,386)	564,378	762,764
Cash in reserve – beginning of year	**1,074,899**	**876,513**	
Cash in reserve – end of year	**876,513**	**1,440,891**	
Change in cash reserves	**(198,386)**	**564,378**	

Budgeting in context

The inefficiencies and inadequacies of the annual line-item budget can perhaps be understood by examining the contextual or environmental factors related to the MCS. Through what are broadly known as "contingency-based" research studies, scholars have identified contextual or environmental variables that are predictive of specific budgeting models, or MCS, and further, how these budget models and MCS may interact with contextual variables to impact organizational or employee performance (Chenhall, 2003; Otley, 2016; Merchant, 1985, 1981).

While most of these studies focus primarily on the for-profit sector, we draw selectively from these studies to discuss findings or contextual variables relevant to the nonprofit context.[4] Specifically, we focus on two contextual variables that may be predictive of specific MCS: the external environment and technology[5] (Chenhall, 2003; Otley, 2016; Covaleski et al. 2007). We will briefly define and discuss these contextual variables and follow with a reflection on the contingency framework's implications for budgeting in nonprofit organizations.

First, the external environment focuses on measures of uncertainty. Variables used by researchers to operationalize uncertainty include the following: turbulence, hostility, diversity, and complexity (Chenhall, 2003). Turbulence and hostility refer to general aspects of the environment. Specifically, turbulent environments are ones that are unpredictable, fluctuating, ambiguous, and risky. Hostile environments are ones that are dominating, restrictive, and stressful (Ibid.). Diversity and complexity, on the other hand, refer to more specific aspects of the environment. Diversity can refer to variety in products/services, inputs, or customers. Complexity refers to the speed at which the technology – used by the organization in generating its products or services – changes and develops (Ibid.).

Thus, external environments that are highly uncertain (turbulent, hostile, diverse, and complex) will require MCS that are more open and less focused on internal controls. For budgeting, this means less focus on traditional budgets that have tight control over departmental units. However, Chenhall (2003) also suggests that when "tight financial controls" are used by organizations operating in uncertain environments, this should be accompanied by "flexible, interpersonal interactions" between departmental units as well as management and front-line workers (p. 138).

Nonprofits operate in highly uncertain environments. The elements of the external environment that may create the greatest amount of uncertainty include: diversity (of customers, inputs, or services); turbulence (of funding streams, regulations, expectations of donors and funders); or complexity (specifically for industries that utilize relatively rapidly changing machine technologies as such as those in the health sector; the issue of rapid change in technology may be less relevant for nonprofits that provide more traditional service programs such as homeless prevention or job training). The implication, therefore, is that traditional budgeting models such as the line-item budget may be a poor fit for nonprofits operating in highly uncertain environments. Greater uncertainty and technological complexity may warrant more open and flexible budgeting models, perhaps ones that build in more budgetary slack (Merchant, 1985).

However, one specific element of the external environment that is arguably more relevant to nonprofits (compared to for-profit businesses) is the need for accountability to external stakeholders (Ahmed, 2014). In highly turbulent environments, in particular for nonprofits operating outside of the US where donors may exert greater influence over nonprofit operations, the need for accountability may outweigh the diversity and complexity elements, so that nonprofits impose tighter controls through traditional budgeting approaches even if evidence supports the effectiveness of more flexible and open budgeting models. In short, one element of the environment (accountability to stake holders due to turbulence) outweighs the other elements.

The next important contextual variable is technology, defined as, "how the organization's work processes operate (the way tasks transform inputs into outputs) including hardware (such as machines and tools), materials, people, software and knowledge" (Chenhall, 2003, p. 139). Technology can further be conceptualized along three dimensions: *complexity* refers to the degree that work process can be standardized and products created through mass production; task *uncertainty* refers to the "variability" of the tasks and the "analyzability" of methods of performing the tasks, as well as "predictability in measuring outputs"; and *interdependence* refers to the dependence of using one technology to complete a task before moving on to the next task.[6] With respect to budgeting, Chenhall (2003) proposes that traditional budgets and formal control processes are associated with technologies characterized by standardized and automated processes, less task uncertainty, and less task interdependence.

However, given that nonprofits are more service oriented and thus "people-processing organizations" (Hasenfeld, 2010), their technology generally refers to the programs or interventions developed to change specific client behaviors. As such, this form of technology is not characterized by standardized or automated processes, but rather highly individualized treatment plans based on the needs of the clients. Thus, they are more distinctive and personalized. Programs and intervention technologies may also be characterized by interdependence among work units with outcomes often not precisely measured (i.e., technological uncertainty).

Given the high complexity, interdependence, and uncertainty with which to measure outcomes that characterizes many of the technologies employed by nonprofits, the transparency and accountability of programmatic and operational processes become even more important (Ahmed, 2014). As we see with the external environment, traditional budgeting models are employed in nonprofit organizations despite their technological complexity and uncertainty because transparency and accountability to donors may outweigh other considerations; and the traditional line-item budget allows for control, transparency, and accountability.

To summarize, the contingency-based studies have suggested that specific management control structures, such as formal and traditional budgeting with tight financial controls, are correlated with specific elements of the environment or context. Specifically, environmental variables that are associated with traditional and formal budgets include external environments characterized by less uncertainty, and technology that is characterized by standardized and automated processes with low task interdependence. Yet, nonprofits operate in external environments with greater uncertainty and utilize technology that is less automated, less interdependent, and more personalized.

In the next section, we outline an alternative approach to the traditional line-item budget, the multi-year (MY) budgeting approach, that may address the limitations of the traditional line-item budget. In short, as we will discuss, the MY approach is focused on outcomes and forces the organization to engage with stakeholders (both internal and external) and thus is "outward-in," rather than cost-centric and "bottom-up," as is the case with the traditional line-item budget. A focus on outcomes, rather than costs, therefore, necessitates a multi-year approach. As such, the MY budgeting approach has the potential to "link" back the strategic and operational planning aspects of the overall MCS that were lost with the traditional line-item budget's overemphasis on control and transparency.

The multi-year budget

The community problems being solved by nonprofit organizations require years of planning, implementation, and data gathering. However, nonprofits typically budget in single-year intervals. The result is a financial strategy that is "de-coupled" – and is often misaligned – with programmatic and fundraising strategies.

Multi-year budgeting can increase integration and alignment. Further, a well-constructed multi-year budget supports the ability to perform "what-if" scenario planning (such as fundraising declines or program changes), metrics management, and the ability to target changes in balance sheet items such as reserves. It also requires the nonprofit staff and Board to continually update their strategy.

Format

In the best-of-all scenarios, an organization has a clearly defined mission to produce specified measurable outcomes by some future date, as well as expected interim year targets. The rationale for the number of outcomes, the quality of the outcomes, the strategic priority of supporting projects, and definition of outcomes, is documented in a separate document. Rather than starting with annual revenue at the top of the document, the multi-year budget contains the following components:

1   The number of outcomes is the starting point (and at the top section of the budget).
2   The expense required each year to produce the outcomes is then specified (staffing, materials, rent, etc.). This is essentially the program budget required to produce the outcomes. If administrative and overhead costs are not included in the program budget, then they should be included on the next line.
3   Administrative and overhead costs (salary, materials, rent, etc.) should be included next.
4   The funding plan by year (fundraising costs and projected results) is next.
5   The resulting funding surplus/ deficit, if any, is the difference between program, administrative, and fundraising costs.
6   Other sources and uses of funding can be included in the funding plan section or separated and included here if appropriate. The result is the net funding surplus/ gap.
7   Below the net funding surplus or gap is any targeted balance sheet items, such as additional or minimum reserves required, and any resulting impact on the funding surplus or gap. (See Table 15.2.)

Once the basic format is set, it is a simple matter to add and embed calculations of the resulting metrics, such as cost of staff per outcome, fundraising cost per dollar of revenue, and administrative cost per outcome or other measure. As the metrics change over the multi-year period, decision makers can assess whether the changes are appropriate and acceptable, or if further changes to costs or number of outcomes are appropriate.

Additionally, the structure of the model can be modified to support "what-if" scenarios (such as changes in revenues or costs) and the resulting impact on budgeted surpluses, deficits, and reserves. For instance, if salary expense is anticipated to increase over the period, and no change in the number or quality of the outcomes occurs, the metrics for salary cost per outcome will deteriorate. "What-if" scenario planning allows management and decision makers to identify changes necessary in the budgeted outcomes and/or expenses to make the metrics improve to targeted levels over the budget period. Similarly, if reserves are expected to increase to a certain level (either fixed dollar amount or a multiple of monthly expenses), the what-if scenario can identify the additional funding or reduced expenses required.

Process

Creating multi-year budgets requires a high level of engagement from key budget managers, a common agreement of mission outcomes, and a degree of technical competence to build, update, and maintain the budget model itself.

Timing: The process should begin six months before the annual approval date, which is often sometime during the last month of the current fiscal year. At the front end, the program team will identify the outcomes targeted time periods (3–5 years). These numbers are likely to change as specific budgets are produced and funding surpluses or deficits are identified. Specific budgets by budget managers should be updated and submitted at least monthly. The process usually involves a monthly roll-up which identifies the funding surplus or deficit as well as the underlying resulting metrics. At each version, key decision makers are involved to indicate to budget managers needed changes in the individual budgets. A near final version should be reviewed in detail by key decision makers (CEO and Board) in the second month before the annual approval date. The final version should only involve minor changes in expense items and finalization of key numbers such as year-to-date actual revenue or year-to-date actual expense.

Model and data development: Generally, the model relies on multiple individual or departmental budgets, which "roll up" to the above outlined format. The model is typically developed by finance staff, as it is based on and needs to fit with accounting system data structure. Each budget manager is provided a format, usually with year-to-date actual results, and possibly with projections for the balance of the fiscal year. The more detailed and standardized the format, the better.

If possible, the model should enable managers to build future year budgets based on underlying metrics, instead of the most recent year plus or minus a percentage. For instance, if the program staff today require one full-time equivalent (FTE) per target outcome, and in future years intend to improve the staff efficiency by, say, 5 percent per year, then in years 2 through 5 of the model, managers should be able to enter that metric (1.05 outcomes per FTE in year 2, 1.1 per FTE in year 3, 1.16 in year 4, and 1.21 in year 5). The resulting FTE requirement should be the result of the targeted number of outcomes in each year times the efficiency metric. Similar to fundraising metrics, the salary cost per dollar raised should be able to drive the revenue projections. In all such cases, this allows budget managers to be proactive in managing their department metrics. If the results are "unacceptable," this opens the budget conversation to how to increase effectiveness while managing efficiency. By doing so, managers can produce budgets that reflect a multi-year strategy and anticipate objections from key decision makers (i.e., the CEO and Board).

With each iteration of the rolled-up budget, the issues should become clearer and the dissonance between financial strategy, program strategy, and fundraising strategy is forced to become aligned. As an example, if an unacceptable funding deficit exists and the fundraising strategy has been vetted, then the number of outcomes to be targeted may need to be reduced to produce an acceptable funding surplus. However, in that discussion, new commitments or fundraising strategies may be made by key decision makers to close the funding gap (instead of reducing outcomes). Further, it may be that the fundraising strategy relies on a certain level of outcomes; reducing outcomes may result in lower fundraising results. The iterative and integrated process results in aligning the strategies and clarifying the interaction between functions. Without a multi-year time frame, the metrics and integration are not available to other managers and key decision makers.

If the core strategy does not change from year to year, the annual process to update the budget is fairly simple. If the strategy changes, then the effort required from budget managers and decision makers will increase accordingly. Next, an illustrative case study of a large multi-service human service agency will be provided to demonstrate the format and process of a multi-year budgeting approach.

Multi-year budget case study

After years of thoughtful strategy discussions and planning, Client "A" changed its mission from primarily a fundraising/fund-distributing organization toward a fundraising/backbone infrastructure partner for the nonprofit community. Over the next two to three years, the mission evolved to include a substantial portion of actual direct service in addition to backbone support. During this period, operating reserves declined below the minimums allowed in the reserves policy. The decline in reserves was a surprise to the Board, and raised several issues including the following:

1   While the programmatic mission aspects were changed, the financial strategy aspects were not included directly as part of the discussion; the result was that the financial management proved a poor fit with the requirements of the "new" organization. A wide gap developed between the capacity of the finance team and the needs of the organization. The failure to plan for the shortfall in reserves was merely the tip of the iceberg.
2   The existing reserves policy had been developed – and was appropriate for – the original mission. The change in mission, however, required a rethinking of the role of reserves given the new mission, instead of a simplistic replacement to get to the standards of the existing policy.

New financial management was brought into the organization and worked with the Board to clarify and understand these issues. The Board quickly reached consensus that the previous changes to the mission involved a shift from a short-term operating strategy to a long-term operating strategy – a truly fundamental shift in the organizational culture and operations.

The Board recognized that a key difference of the new mission was that it was now outcome-focused and required a multi-year commitment to fund program efforts and third-party stakeholders; a longer-term and higher-risk profile than the previous mission. This resulted in a Board mandate to rethink the reserves policy in a way that reflected the new mission.

A new policy on reserves was developed. Its key provision was a requirement that reserves (liquid net assets) must be able to ensure funding of five years of mission impact efforts and funding commitments, to mitigate the risk of not achieving program outcomes due to unanticipated cost increases or declines in donor funds. Specifically, liquid net assets would be equal to or greater than the net cash required in a downside scenario of the five-year budget. The new policy required the establishment of a consolidated, rolling five-year budget for program, fundraising, and operations (the expected scenario; see Table 15.2, lines 64–68), and included a predetermined worst-case scenario based on the 2008 economic crash (the downside scenario; see Table 15.2, lines 70–77). Other requirements were that the expected case must be cash positive or self-funding (i.e., no reserves would be used to fund the expected scenario); thus, reserves would only be used to ensure five-year efforts in a downside scenario. In the event that the five-year expected case was not cash positive, then no funding commitments beyond the current year could be made. Commitments included grants to other community partners, contractors, lease agreements, and staffing.

Table 15.2 illustrates a simplified version of the MY budget. Lines 2–3 are the total program costs. Total costs for "community impact" (line 2) is based on extensive discussion between management, program units, and front-line service providers. The exact process and formulas for determining "number of community impact efforts" (line 14) is beyond the scope of this illustrative case study and may differ among nonprofits. As one can imagine, the community impact measures are unique and based on the individual programs and services provided by an organization.[7]

For this illustrative case, community impact measures involved a process of moving community partners from individual agency goals and programs to a single cohesive agreement on goals and methods for measurement. Results were classified on a development continuum from "early stage" to "late stage." The results of these extensive "community impact" discussions are summarized in lines 14–18 of Table 15.2. It is also good practice to have an "average stage of community impact efforts" (line 15) and "success score" (line 18) as these enable the

Table 15.2 Funding requirements to produce community impact outcomes for the next five years

		(Illustrative case study of a multi-year budget)					
Line #		5-year period	2015/16	2016/17	2017/18	2018/19	2019/20
1	**Program costs & outcomes**						
2	Community Impact	5,535,705	904,922	920,867	1,054,793	1,239,147	1,415,976
3	Grant Writing	874,932	172,746	131,972	128,056	218,081	224,077
4	Operating Budgets for Program work (lines 2+3)	6,410,637	1,077,668	1,052,839	1,182,849	1,457,228	1,640,053
5							
6	Special allocations, grants, & other distributions	8,006,010	1,689,010	1,453,500	1,104,500	1,704,500	2,054,500
7	**Gross money needed for Program work (lines: 4+6)**	14,416,647	2,766,678	2,506,339	2,287,349	3,161,728	3,694,553
8							
9	Funding from PY revenues other carry forward offsets	(1,033,571)	(744,420)	(289,151)			
10	Offsetting grant revenue	(5,106,453)	(1,556,253)	(1,389,300)	(600,300)	(780,300)	(780,300)
11							
12	**Net Total money needed for Program work (lines: 7+9+10)**	**8,276,623**	**466,005**	**827,888**	**1,687,049**	**2,381,428**	**2,914,253**
13							
14	# of community impact efforts (a)	15	9	11	14	20	23
15	Average stage of community impact efforts (b)	3.0	2.4	2.8	3.1	3.1	3.6
16	Program cost per effort (from Community Impact tab)	191,785	318,411	162,713	163,203	154,073	160,524
17	Outcomes (# of efforts ★ average stage) (c)	48	22	31	43	61	82
18	Success score (weighted scale of efforts, cost, stage) (d)	73	46	67	76	80	95
19	Program FTE	14.4	10.6	11.3	14.0	17.0	19.0
20							

Line		(1)	(2)	(3)	(4)	(5)	(6)
21	Fundraising & Marketing costs						
22	Total FTE FR & Mktg	21.8	22.0	21.75	21.75	21.75	21.75
23							
24	Total money needed for Fundraising & Marketing (e)	11,021,900	2,089,336	2,155,941	2,213,010	2,258,354	2,305,259
25							
26	$ expected, net of pledge loss	28,909,783	5,306,058	5,370,805	5,642,893	5,935,473	6,654,554
27	$ transferred to next year operations	(28,909,783)	(5,306,058)	(5,370,805)	(5,642,893)	(5,935,473)	(6,654,554)
28	$ transferred from prior year revenues	27,388,098	5,132,868	5,306,058	5,370,805	5,642,893	5,935,473
29	FR & Mktg Cost per $	0.38	0.39	0.40	0.39	0.38	0.35
30	FR & Marketing FTE	21.8	22.0	21.8	21.8	21.8	21.8
31							
32	**Cash needed / (remaining) after FR & Marketing costs (lines: 12+24–28)**	(8,089,575)	(2,577,527)	(2,322,229)	(1,470,746)	(1,003,111)	(715,962)
33							
34	Admin costs						
35	Average FTE	54.1	50.3	51.0	53.8	56.8	58.8
36	Average Admin Cost per Total FTE	42,362	44,720	43,136	42,521	41,036	40,398
37	Admin FTE	17.9	17.7	18.0	18.0	18.0	18.0
38	Estimated OH rate		16.9%	16.9%	19.3%	18.9%	18.9%
39							
40	Total money needed for Admin costs	11,436,686	2,249,057	2,199,954	2,285,511	2,328,792	2,373,371
41							
42	**Cash needed / (remaining) after Admin costs (lines: 32+40)**	3,347,111	(328,470)	(122,275)	814,766	1,325,681	1,657,409
43							
44	Other uses of cash						
45	Cash funding	1,547,426	313,033	271,795	320,866	320,866	320,866

(Continued)

Table 15.2 (Continued)

Line #		5-year period	2015/16	2016/17	2017/18	2018/19	2019/20
	(Illustrative case study of a multi-year budget)						
46	Claim on undesignated revenues	267,838	53,568	53,568	53,568	53,568	53,568
47	(Redacted cost)	250,000	50,000	50,000	50,000	50,000	50,000
48	Capital expenses greater than/ (less than) depreciation	(53,139)	(23,291)	(29,848)	–	–	–
49	Total other uses of cash (primarily funding) (lines: 45+46+47+48)	2,012,124	393,309	345,514	424,434	424,434	424,434
50							
51	**Cash needed / (remaining) after Other uses of cash (lines: 42+49)**	**5,359,235**	**64,839**	**223,239**	**1,239,199**	**1,750,115**	**2,081,843**
52							
53	Other sources of cash						
54	Rent from tenants	256,585	51,317	51,317	51,317	51,317	51,317
55	Distributions from "endowment fund"	1,295,189	255,470	259,930	259,930	259,930	259,930
56	Distributions from "endowment fund"	125,000	25,000	25,000	25,000	25,000	25,000
57	Reimbursements	113,453	61,035	52,418			
58	Total other sources of cash (primarily endowment fund distribution) (lines: 54+55+56+57)	1,790,227	392,822	388,665	336,247	336,247	336,247
59							
60	Net cash needed / (remaining) after other sources & uses of cash (lines: 51–58)	3,569,008	(327,983)	(165,425)	902,953	1,413,868	1,745,596
61	*FDP carry over funding from PY variances*			(327,983)	(493,408)	409,544	1,823,412
62	**Net Cash needed / (remaining) – Cumulative (lines: 60+61)**	**3,569,008**	**(327,983)**	**(493,408)**	**409,544**	**1,823,412**	**3,569,008**
63							

		Total					
64	**Expected Scenario**						
65	Total costs (lines: 7+24+40+49)	38,887,357	7,498,381	7,207,749	7,210,304	8,173,308	8,797,616
66	Total cash expected in (lines: −9−10+30+60)	35,318,349	7,826,363	7,373,174	6,307,352	6,759,440	7,052,020
67	Net cash needed / (remaining) – Each year (lines: 65–66)	3,569,008	(327,983)	(165,425)	902,953	1,413,868	1,745,596
68	Net cash needed / (remaining) – Cumulative (lines: 65–61+66)	3,569,008	(327,983)	(493,408)	409,544	1,823,412	3,569,008
69							
70	**Downside Scenario**						
71	Revenue $ below expected		90%	90%	90%	90%	90%
72	Costs higher than expected		110%	110%	110%	110%	110%
73	Pledge loss worse than expected		10%	10%	10%	10%	10%
74	Endowment assets less than expected		80%				
75	Total costs (lines: 65 * 72)	42,776,093	8,248,219	7,928,524	7,931,335	8,990,638	9,677,378
76	Total cash expected	27,793,848	5,155,636	5,295,292	5,386,528	5,656,884	6,299,509
77	Net cash needed / (remaining) (lines: 75–76)	14,982,245	3,092,583	2,633,231	2,544,807	3,333,755	3,377,869
78							
79	Reserves as of (date omitted)						
80	(as defined by reserve policy and includes "endowment")	5,117,828					
81	In downside scenario	4,078,108					
82							

(Continued)

Table 15.2 (Continued)

(Illustrative case study of a multi-year budget)

Line #		5-year period	2015/16	2016/17	2017/18	2018/19	2019/20
83	In the expected case, are reserves needed? s/b "No" (f)	Yes					
84	Are "endowment" balances more than the proposed Operating budget? s/b "Yes" (g)	Yes					
85	In the Downside case, are reserves greater than the cash needed? s/b "Yes" (h)	No					

Notes

This is a simplified example of a multi-year budget for case study purposes. The real multi-year budget comprises 150+ spreadsheet tabs which are not presented here. As such, many of the values in this table refer to sub-tables in the external tabs and therefore may not correspond exactly with each other due to rounding, etc. The most complex calculations are quantifying efforts to produce outcomes as summarized in lines (14–18, 21).

(a) The process of determining community impact efforts is resource intensive and requires detailed bottom-up budgeting for each period in the budget including prioritization of each effort.

(b) Average stage of community impact efforts refers to a continuum from early to late stage and includes criteria for measurability, determination, and delivery of results.

(c) This formula is important because it defines "outcomes" as the product of quantity and quality

(d) Success score is defined as a function of stage, cost, and volume of efforts. It is calculated based on respective weighting of 50%, 35%, and 15%, which indicates the organization's priority on creating later stage lower cost efforts over high numbers of efforts.

(e) Based on annual total budgeted cost of the fundraising and marketing departments / divided by the full-time equivalent staff in the departments. The costs include staff & consulting expense as well as advertising, travel, and other expense.

(f) Difference is $3,569,008

(g) Difference is $163,076

(h) Difference is ($10,904,136)

In black fill – funding gap

In grey fill – funding surplus

organization to understand when and at what level the overall organization is performing in relation to the funding involved. The net total cost required to produce program outcomes (line 12) is the difference between "gross money for program work" (line 7) and carry-overs from previous year as well as any offsetting grant revenue (lines 9–10). The net cash remaining, after fundraising and marketing costs, is summarized on line 32. Similarly, the net cash remaining, after administrative costs and "other uses of cash," is summarized on lines 42 and 51 respectively. The final "net cash" needed (line 62) is the cash remaining after costs (fundraising, marketing, administrative, and others) as well as "other sources of cash" (line 60) are considered.

The "expected scenario" (lines 64–68) is simply a summary of the total costs, total cash expected, and the cash needed or remaining after considering any carry-overs from the prior year. The final "net cash needed/remaining" in the "expected scenario" (line 68) is equal to the "net cash needed/remaining" for the overall programs (line 62). Finally, as illustrated in Table 15.2, one unique aspect of this MY budgeting approach is the ability to forecast a "what-if" downside scenario (lines 70–77). A final summary of the budget (lines 79–85) indicates if the expected or downside scenarios result in a funding gap or surplus (lines 83–85).

In brief, the Board determined that solving long-term community problems should not be subject to short-term fluctuations in donor funding. Through the use of multi-year budgeting and downside scenario planning, they could mitigate the risk of over-committing funds.

With the new policy in place, finance staff led the development of the model and outlined the deliverables for each budget manager in the organization. An initial key to success was program management who understood the rationale and benefits from planning for outcomes. The downside scenario (from the expected case) was based on the 2008 economic crash and included a simultaneous 10 percent reduction in revenue, 10 percent increase in operating costs, 10 percent increase in pledge loss, and a 20 percent decline in market value of investments (see Table 15.2, lines 71–74).

After developing the initial draft, management presented updated versions to the Board each month and worked through questions and improvements in the model. A startling revelation came to light in the process: there was a funding gap of $3.5M if the desired outcomes were to be produced, which would have a significant impact on reserves (see Table 15.2, line 83). As a result, three things happened:

1   Management (financial and program) developed a scalable correlation tool within the model that allowed what-if assumptions for the quantity and quality of outcomes to be achieved and the resulting funding gap. This required very specific measurements and ratings for definitions of outcomes quality and cost and how each activity contributed to the outcomes quality and quantity. The tool allowed the Board to make a proactive decision of whether to reduce the funding gap to zero by reducing the quality/quantity of outcomes, or to maintain the current quality/quantity of outcomes and put a strategy in place to close the funding gap. The tool allowed the funding gap or the outcomes to be reduced from the expected case to zero, and anywhere in between (to find the optimal tradeoff).

2   Management was directed to find other cost-cutting that would produce the same level of outcomes while reducing the cost involved. This provided clarity to management and staff as to why the cost-cutting was needed (which aligned well with staff and created an open dialogue about expenses and contributions toward success). Priorities became clear and cost reductions were narrowly targeted toward expenses that did not support the outcomes.

3   The Board used the information itself in two ways. First, to explore and target their fund-raising efforts to close the gap. For instance, a new fundraising theme was developed along the lines of "we need your help to ensure that these outcomes will be achieved." Second, the Board was in the process of hiring a new CEO and the candidates were asked to create a plan to close the funding gap. A new CEO was ultimately selected who had a very clear plan for how to close the funding gap as well as a clear direction for the job requirements and performance expectations from the Board (the CEO's "boss").

Multi-year budgeting in context

Finally, it is instructive to keep in mind some contextual variables when implementing a MY budget framework. Drawing from the previous discussion, we suggest that the external variables that may be important to consider include: the composition of revenue sources and expectation of various funders (turbulence); the number and diversity of programs and services offered; the diversity of its clientele; and the degree to which technology (programs and service interventions) are "interdependent and automated" or "independent and personalized."

Organizations with revenue dominated by government or foundation funders may be pressured to be more transparent and to articulate outcomes. In this case, the MY budget approach may be a good fit as it is outcomes focused. However, nonprofits may need to be more transparent with how outcomes are quantified and involve the funders directly in outcome discussions. The more funders, the more stakeholders with which the nonprofit must engage. Nonprofits with revenue portfolios dominated by fee for service income may have less of an incentive to quantify or measure outcomes and thus require more time and negotiations to convince stakeholders (board of directors, staff, etc.) of the value of a MY budget approach.

Organizations that operate a breadth of diverse programs and services, and thus serve more diverse groups of clientele, may require higher coordination and planning when implementing a MY budget. However, in many ways, it is even more important that such organizations do the MY integrated budgeting. Larger, multi-service organizations may tend to lose sense of a unified mission and result in "mini-companies," similar to a conglomerate, with no real rationale for being in business. Investing the resources upfront to develop a MY budget with an "outcomes scoring model" may allow multi-service organizations to identify the programs that are the most cost effective in producing outcomes. The organization can then rank programs and decide how to improve program effectiveness, delete or "spin off" less effective programs, or consider adding only programs that are above current "average" effectiveness.

For organizations that employ complex technologies, a MY budget, with its focus on outcomes, may also be more appropriate. Technological complexity is defined as the high interdependence of individual tasks in order to produce the final product or service. This interdependence of tasks characterizes many of the technologies (i.e., program interventions) employed by nonprofit human service organizations. For example, program interventions that aim to change behavior or develop skills are often delivered in stages and clients cannot advance until completion of an earlier stage of the program (i.e., job skills training, substance recovery programs, etc.). Thus, outcomes are operationalized at the end stage of the intervention, while intermediate stages are operationalized by outputs. A traditional line-item budget is more likely to emphasize outputs via expense line-items (see Table 15.1) and is thus more appropriate for organizations with lower technological complexity. Whereas, a MY budget will induce organizations to articulate outcomes, and thus is more appropriate for organizations with high technological complexity (see Table 15.2).

While the multi-year budgeting process requires time, leadership from management, and commitment from line-workers, we argue that it can be utilized to some degree by nonprofits of all sizes and not just large, well-resourced ones. Given these considerations, the multi-year budgeting approach fits with Ahmed's (2014) argument that nonprofit MCS should manage both internal and external interdependencies and serve three roles: symbolic, behavioral, and exchange. Behaviorally, concrete outcomes clearly linked to the organization's long-term mission can serve as a high and positive motivator for staff at all levels of the organization.[8] The exchange role is addressed by linking revenue to outcomes and planning for "self-funding" budgets as well as incorporating a downside, "what-if" scenario planning.[9] Finally, and like the behavioral role, a focus on outcomes can serve a powerful symbolic role to link organizational values with community and client level values.[10]

Budgeting in the international context

In the international context, Ahmed (2014) points out that, "control mechanisms used by Western organizations are not easily transferable to developing countries because their socio-political contexts are different" (p. 264). Thus, while it may be difficult to draw "best practices" for international NGOs, we highlight in this section factors that may influence the MCS and, hence, budgeting models used by international NGOs.

Chenhall's (2003) discussion of the impact of "national culture" on MCS is also instructive here. "National culture" is commonly conceptualized along the following dimensions: "power distance (acceptance of unequal distribution of power); individualism vs. collectivism (placing self-interest ahead of the group); uncertainty avoidance (preference to avoid uncertainty and rely on rules and structures); masculinity vs. femininity (achievement, assertiveness and material success vs. modesty and preference for quality of life); and, subsequently, Confucian dynamism (status, respect for tradition, protecting one's face)" (Hofestede, 1984 as cited by Chenhall, 2003, p. 153). While findings from studies are mixed, some patterns regarding national culture's impact on MCS do emerge. For example, the positive relationship between accounting performance measures and job satisfaction among companies in Asian countries may be attributed to acceptance of higher unequal distribution of power (Chenhall, 2003).

Ahmed (2014) points out further that NGOs in developing countries operate in more uncertain environments and therefore the need for accountability is greater. Thus, NGOs are more sensitive to funder expectations and pressures and more likely to use traditional budget models that focus on control and transparency. As such, the MCS may serve to manage external interdependencies over internal interdependencies and thus play a more "exchange" role (documenting resources for efficiencies and reporting this to stakeholders) rather than a "behavioral" role (establishing goals and objectives to motivate employee behavior) (Ahmed, 2014). Further, it is also more difficult for MCS to manage internal interdependencies and play a "behavioral" role because control mechanisms may be costlier. Workers in developing countries may be drawn to careers in NGOs for professional and monetary reasons rather than a strong commitment to the organization's mission; and as Ahmed (2014) suggests, "employees who are highly committed to their organization's goals ... reduces other control problems, such as lack of direction or poor motivation" (p. 262).

Similarities do exist, however, particularly among NGOs operating in Western countries. For example, Amans et al. (2015) and Ezzamel et al. (2012) in studies of NGOs in France and the UK, respectively, point out the influence of the institutional environment on budgeting processes. Amans et al. (2015) highlight the competing institutional logics that French performing arts nonprofits must contend with and how this may impact budgeting processes.

Specifically, the three competing logics in their institutional environment are: artistic, managerial, and political. Artistic logics are characterized by "high sensitivity, imagination, and inspiration; creativity; originality; and taste" and organizations guided primarily by this logic tend to use budgets as a planning and monitoring tool to keep artistic expenses in line with budgeted costs (Amans et al., 2015, p. 58).

Managerial logics are characterized by an emphasis on "efficiency, control, regularity and predictability, and calculation and measurement," and organizations guided primarily by this logic tend to use the budget as a forecasting and planning tool with a focus on results rather than cost monitoring (Amans et al., 2015, p. 60). Budgets are also used as a basis for corrective action in organizations guided by managerial logics.

Finally, given that performing arts nonprofits in France are publicly funded, they also face a political logic, defined as the pressure to conform to government funder expectations with a focus towards establishing legitimacy. Thus, organizations guided primarily by a political logic are characterized by high board control with the budgeting process being more centralized and hierarchical with little input or debate from staff. The budget is also used primarily as an informative tool to pass along information rather than a negotiating tool. With regards to the funding environment, organizations with a low number of funders and low funding uncertainty are characterized by budgeting processes that are more bureaucratic, less democratic, and more "informative" in nature. Whereas organizations with a high number of funders and high funding uncertainty are characterized by budgeting processes that are less bureaucratic, with strong interpersonal relationships between internal and external actors, and more democratic with the budget used as an "implicative" or negotiating tool (Amens et al., 2015).

Arguably, nonprofits operating in the US also need to contend with institutional logics that are often competing and that create tensions among various budgeting models and processes. How nonprofits respond may differ from those in other developed countries and depend on the contingencies mentioned previously; however, this remains an area rich for research. It is perhaps not surprising that nonprofits in the US are more akin to those in developed countries because they may experience similar external pressures, and thus use similar budgeting models to address these situational factors compared to their counterparts in developing countries. As such, the MY budgeting framework may be more accessible to NGOs in developed countries versus developing countries.

Conclusion

Looking forward, there are numerous areas for research on management control systems, budgeting, and financial management in nonprofit organizations. To date, most of the research on MCS has been in the for-profit business field. With the exception of a few studies, there has been little empirical research conducted in the nonprofit literature on contingency-based perspectives and how it may impact MCS or the relationship between MCS and firm, employee, or client level outcomes. Further, while multi-year budgeting processes have been examined in the public administration field, no empirical studies on the MY budgeting approach have been conducted in the nonprofit field, as far as we know.[11] Using MY budget models as a predictor for important outcome variables at the employee, programmatic, organizational levels are all rich areas for research. Similarly, given the MY budget's focus on outcomes and its longitudinal approach, there are rich opportunities to incorporate geographical informational systems (GIS) and spatial modeling methods to examine how MY budget approaches may contribute to long-term positive community impacts or more efficient and effective coordination of nonprofit activities.[12]

For practice, the shift from traditional budgeting models, with its focus on control and accountability, to a multi-year approach, that focuses on outcomes, may seem like a difficult and daunting transition. We argue, however, that the complexity and challenge is not with the MY budgeting tool, but with the broader organizational context, such as convincing all stakeholders of the value of an outcomes approach. Other chapters in this volume offer insights into addressing these broader organizational management challenges. Development of a MY budget plan simply requires a discussion of how to articulate and quantify outcomes (even crudely measured outcomes are preferable to no outcomes). While the illustrative case study in this chapter focuses on a large, multi-service and multi-million-dollar agency, the MY tool can be applied just as effectively in small, single-program agencies.

In this chapter, we have offered an argument that management control systems, as used in nonprofits, overemphasize budgeting and control through use of the traditional line-item budget. This focus on the line-item budget is limiting and results in inefficiencies that may not further the organization's mission or impact. We also offered an alternative method, the multi-year budget, a more holistic approach that brings back the strategic and operational planning components of the MCS. We demonstrated how a MY model may be implemented through an illustrative case study, as well as discussed relevant contingencies that may impact MCS and the implementation of MY budgeting in nonprofits. While the MY budgeting approach involves upfront investment in time and resources by the organization, the long-term benefits on this investment will reach beyond the organization to funders, stakeholders, and, most importantly, to the clients and community whom the organization serves.

Notes

1   The general criticism about the budgeting process is not limited to nonprofits. For further studies and discussion about budgeting and its limitations in the for-profit business literature, see for example: Hope and Fraser, 2003a, 2003b; Libby and Lindsay, 2010; Libby and Lindsey, 2003a, 2003b.
2   Ahmed (2014) has argued that management control systems (MCS) in nonprofits must consider both internal and external interdependencies and serve three roles: symbolic, behavioral, and exchange. Thus, the traditional line-item budget, with its focus on control, emphasizes the exchange role to the detriment of the behavioral and symbolic roles.
3   Institutional pressure from funders (both government and philanthropic) to demonstrate transparency, accountability, and control of resources may also explain the wide diffusion of the annual line-item budget. As a result, this "one-size" fits all approach may not consider the appropriateness of the line-item budget model or its effectiveness in the nonprofit setting.
4   See Tucker (2010) or Tucker and Parker (2013) for nonprofit examples. These authors examined the relationship between MCS, strategy formulation and apply the contingency approach to understanding performance. Amans et al. (2015) and Ezzamel et al. (2012) are notable examples in the international context and will be discussed below.
5   Chenhall (2003) also identifies structure, strategy, size, and national culture in the contingency-based approach. We focus less on structure and strategy as they are embedded in the external environment and technology. Chenhall (2003) points out that strategy, "is the means whereby managers can influence the nature of the external environment, the technologies of the organization, the structural arrangements and the control culture and the MCS" (p. 150). The impact of national culture will be discussed briefly in the section Budgeting in the international context. For organizational size, research suggests that larger organizations are diverse in their operations with more sub-units and a divisionalized organizational structure; formalized operating procedures; and specialized functions. This leads to more formal and sophisticated MCS systems with participative budgeting processes (Chenhall, 2003). However, nonprofits are small (in terms of revenue and paid employees) and generally have a difficult time growing or "scaling up" their programs (Ahmed, 2014). Nonprofits may also lack the "managerial capacities" to coordinate and implement diverse programs or manage resources regardless of organizational size (Ahmed, 2014). Thus, nonprofits may be less likely to implement a highly complex MCS.

6 Interdependence can further be either "pooled (no direct relationship between adjacent processes), to sequential (one-way interdependencies), to reciprocal (two-way interdependencies)" (Chenhall, 2003, p. 139).

7 For further discussion on operationalizing outcomes and linking outcomes to the finances of an organization, the Balance Score Card may be a good approach. See for example: Kaplan and Norton (1996); Niven (2008).

8 The behavioral role refers to, "the understanding and control of organisational members' behaviour through establishing goals, objectives and standards" (Ansari and Bell, 1991 as cited by Ahmed, 2014, p. 262).

9 The exchange role refers to, "efficient resource allocation to satisfy the organisation's stakeholders" (Ansari and Bell, 1991 as cited by Ahmed, 2014, p. 262).

10 The symbolic role refers to, "identifying and creating a community, understanding its values and beliefs and translating these into relevant organisational actions" (Ansari and Bell, 1991 as cited by Ahmed, 2014, p. 262).

11 For examples of studies of multi-year budgeting in the public administration field, see Blomand and Guajardo, 2000; Boex et al., 2000; and Hou, 2006.

12 For examples of the integration of geographic and financial variables, see: Lam & McDougle, 2016; Paarlberg et al., 2018.

References

Z.U. Ahmed. (2014). "Management control issues in Non-Governmental Organisations (NGOs): An evaluation of contingency factors and potential for future research." *International Journal of Managerial and Financial Accounting*: 6(3), 251–271.

P. Amans, A. Mazars-Chapelon, and F. Villesèque-Dubus. (2015). "Budgeting in institutional complexity: The case of performing arts organizations." *Management Accounting Research*: 27, 47–66.

R.N. Anthony and D.W. Young. (2003). *Management Control in Nonprofit Organizations*, 7th Ed. New York: McGraw-Hill.

B. Blomand and S. Guajardo. (2000). "Multi-year budgeting: A primer for finance officers." *Government Finance Review:* February, 39–43.

L.F.J. Boex, J. Martinez-Vazquez, and R.M. McNab. (2000). "Multi-year budgeting: A review of international practices and lessons for developing and transitional economies." *Public Budgeting and Finance:* 20(2), Summer, 91–112.

R.H. Chenhall. (2003). "Management control systems design within its organizational context: Findings from contingency-based research and directions for the future." *Accounting, Organizations and Society*: 28, 127–168.

M. Covaleski, J.H.Evans III, J. Luft, and M.D. Shields. (2007). "Budgeting research: Three theoretical perspectives and criteria for selective integration." *Handbook of Management Accounting Research* Volume 2, 587–624. Oxford: Elsevier.

M. Dropkin, J. Halpin, and B. La Touche. (2007). *The Budget-Building Book for Nonprofits*, 2nd Ed. San Francisco: Jossey-Bass.

M. Ezzamel, K. Robson, and P. Stapleton. (2012). "The logics of budgeting: Theorization and practice variation in the educational field." *Accounting, Organizations and Society:* 37, 281–303.

S.C. Hansen, D.T. Otley, and W.A. Van der Stede. (2003). "Practice developments in budgeting: An overview and research perspective." *Journal of Management Accounting Research*: 15, 95–116.

Y. Hasenfeld. (2010). *Human Services as Complex Organizations,* 2nd Ed. Los Angeles: Sage.

J. Hope and R. Fraser. (2003a). "Who needs budgets?" *Harvard Business Review*: 81(2), 108–115.

J. Hope and R. Fraser. (2003b). "Beyond budgeting: How managers can break free from the annual performance trap." Boston: Harvard Business School Press.

Y. Hou. (2006). "Budgeting for fiscal stability over the business cycle: A countercyclical fiscal policy and the multiyear perspective on budgeting." *Public Administration Review:* 66(5), 730–741.

R.S. Kaplan and D.P. Norton. (1996). "The Balanced Scorecard." Boston: Harvard Business School Press.

M. Lam and L.M. McDougle. (2016). "Community variation in the financial health of nonprofit human service organizations: An examination of organizational and contextual effects." *Nonprofit and Voluntary Sector Quarterly:* 45(3), 500–525.

T. Libby and R. Murray Lindsay. (2003a). "Budgeting – an unnecessary evil, Part 1." *CMA Management*: 32, March, 30–33.

T. Libby and R. Murray Lindsay. (2003b). "Budgeting – an unnecessary evil, Part 2." *CMA Management*: 32, April, 28–31.

T. Libby and R. Murray Lindsay. (2010). "Beyond budgeting or budgeting reconsidered? A survey of North-American budgeting practice." *Management Accounting Research*: 21, 56–75.

K.A. Merchant. (1981). "The design of the corporate budgeting system: Influences on managerial behavior and performance." *Accounting Review*: 56(4), 813–829.

K.A. Merchant. (1985). "Budgeting and the propensity to create budgetary slack." *Accounting, Organizations and Society*: 10(2), 201–210.

P.R. Niven. (2008). *Balance Scorecard Step-by-Step for Government and Nonprofit Agencies,* 2nd Ed. Hoboken, NJ: Wiley.

D. Otley. (2016). "The contingency theory of management accounting and control: 1980–2014." *Management Accounting Research*: 31, 45–62.

L.E. Paarlberg, S.H. An, R. Nesbit, R.K. Christensen, and J. Bullock. (2018). "A field too crowded? How measures of market structure shape nonprofit fiscal health." *Nonprofit and Voluntary Sector Quarterly*: 47(3), 453–473.

B.P. Tucker. (2010). "Through which lens? Contingency and institutional approaches to conceptualising organisational performance in the not-for-profit sector." *Journal of Applied Management Accounting Research*: 8(1), 17–33.

B.P. Tucker, and L.D. Parker. (2013). "Out of control? Strategy in the NFP sector: The implications for management control." *Accounting, Auditing & Accountability Journal*: 26(2), 234–266.

A. Wildavsky. (1978). "A budget for all seasons? Why the traditional budget lasts." *Public Administration Review*: 38(6), 501–509.

16

THE ESSENTIAL NATURE OF INTERNAL CONTROLS

Nathan J. Grasse

ASSOCIATE PROFESSOR, SCHOOL OF PUBLIC POLICY AND ADMINISTRATION,
CARLETON UNIVERSITY, OTTAWA, ON, CANADA

Daniel Gordon Neely

ASSOCIATE PROFESSOR, SHELDON B. LUBAR SCHOOL OF BUSINESS, UNIVERSITY
OF WISCONSIN-MILWAUKEE, MILWAUKEE, WI, USA

Introduction

The nonprofit sector is built on a foundation of trust and charitable works. Nonprofits themselves exist to provide a public benefit, whether that be through the arts, health services, education, or some other societal need. Typically, nonprofit organizations are provided concessions from the government in exchange for providing public benefits. For example, in the United States, under certain conditions, charities can forgo paying taxes on the income that they generate. To ensure that nonprofit organizations are providing public benefit and not misdirecting valuable resources, regulators and stakeholders demand accountability from nonprofit organizations. In the United States, many charities are required to file a Form 990 informational tax return with the Internal Revenue Service (IRS) disclosing their financial statements as well as providing responses to important questions such as the components of their governance structure and the level of compensation they pay officers. Beyond regulators, stakeholders also demand that charities that receive their support in the form of grants and donations demonstrate they are allocating resources in the intended fashion. One way nonprofits can ensure they meet the demands for accountability is through a robust set of internal controls within their organization.

Internal controls are defined as "a system or plan of accounting and financial organization within a business comprising all the methods and measures necessary for safeguarding its assets, checking the accuracy of its accounting data or otherwise substantiating its financial statements, and policing previously adopted rules, procedures and policies as to compliance and effectiveness" (Merriam-Webster 2017). Internal controls include preventive controls, such as segregation of duties to ensure no one person has complete control over financial transactions, and detective controls such as review of the financial statements by the board of directors and committees of the board. Failure to have robust internal controls in place can lead to lapses in oversight of operations, reporting and/or compliance, as well as financial or reputational harm to the nonprofit organization.

Most employees in the nonprofit sector hold themselves up to the highest ethical standard and are passionate about the mission of the nonprofit organization for which they work. However, a lack of sound internal controls can lead to important errors in operations and reporting. In the extreme, poor internal controls can facilitate fraud. While errors undermine an organization's ability to fulfill their mission, fraud has the potential to have long-term and sweeping effects, as the salience of these incidents can gain media attention and undermine public confidence in the organization and the sector. Greenlee et al. (2007) document 58 cases of fraud at nonprofit organizations and note that the median financial loss was one hundred thousand dollars. In their sample, over 97 percent of the reported frauds that occurred were considered asset misappropriations (e.g. the stealing of cash or other assets). In general, fraud is more likely to occur when the perpetrator is a trusted employee. Consistent with this notion, Greenlee et al. (2007) find that the perpetrators of the frauds in their sample had spent an average of over seven years at the nonprofit organization.

In order to ensure sound operations and prevent outright fraud, every nonprofit should have a robust system of internal controls in place. The purpose of this chapter is to provide an overview of contemporary thinking on control frameworks. We will start with a background of key regulatory measures that have been taken to ensure sound compliance with financial reporting, as well as laws and regulations. We will then review widely accepted internal control and information technology (IT) control frameworks, and look to examples of control failures to illustrate the impact of key elements of control.

Developing regulatory frameworks and the role of external auditors

As early as 1910, in the United States, committees were formed to consider cases of charity fraud, waste, and abuse (Renz 2016). In 1942, the federal government required charities to file an annual information return which has evolved to the current requirement for most charities to file a version of the Form 990 (Fremont-Smith 2009). Starting in the late 1950s, states began to require charities to register and file annual financial reports (Fremont-Smith 2009). In the mid-1990s, the federal government significantly expanded their regulatory role over charitable organizations by among other things creating intermediate sanctions on excess benefits (Fremont-Smith 2009).

More recently, as a result of several high-profile frauds in the for-profit sector, in 2002 congress passed the Sarbanes–Oxley Act (SOX) (Nezhina and Brudney 2012). While SOX was intended to curb frauds in the for-profit sector, two provisions of SOX directly impacted nonprofit organizations: protection of whistleblowers and document retention (Saxton and Neely 2019). The first, whistleblower protection, requires organizations to protect individuals who are assisting federal investigations of fraud, while the second, document retention, prohibits the alteration or destruction of documents to impede a federal investigation. To address these SOX requirements, nonprofit organizations have adopted policies protecting whistleblowers and ensuring documentation is appropriately retained. Saxton and Neely (2019) find that for a sample of 7,129 nonprofit organizations rated by Charity Navigator, 91 percent had a written whistleblower protection policy, and 90 percent had a records retention policy.

Beyond the direct requirements of SOX, there has been a noted "spill-over" effect where nonprofit organizations have adopted best practices influenced by SOX. For example, a survey of 304 nonprofit organizations revealed that almost half of nonprofits had adopted at least one SOX provision they were not required to follow (Nezhina and Brudney 2012). In addition, recent evidence finds that most nonprofits have adopted a conflict of interest policy which is not a SOX provision that nonprofits are required to follow (Saxton and Neely 2019).

In addition, states have included regulatory requirements designed to increase accountability among nonprofit organizations. Perhaps most notably, on the heels of SOX, California enacted the Nonprofit Integrity Act of 2004 (NIA). The NIA required nonprofits to have an external audit and an audit committee. In addition, the Act required the board of directors to approve the compensation of the chief executive officer (CEO) and the chief financial officer (CFO) to ensure the compensation was just and reasonable (Neely 2011). More recently, New York enacted the Nonprofit Revitalization Act of 2013 (NRA). The NRA requires New York charities to have a conflict of interest policy, and requires directors to disclose potential conflicts on an annual basis.

The federal government also plays a role in nonprofit oversight primarily through requiring nonprofit organizations to file a Form 990 on an annual basis. The Form 990 was revised in 2008 to include questions pertaining to key control elements such as whether the organization has a written policy covering whistleblower protections, and document retention. While the IRS does not require such policies to be in place, many view the requirement to disclose such policies as an inducement to ensure the organization has such policies in place (Boland et al. 2018).

Many nonprofit organizations hire an accounting firm to audit their financial records. As a part of performing their audit, the accounting firm is required to obtain reasonable assurance that the financial statements are free from material misstatements due to errors or fraud (AICPA 2017). However, the external auditor's focus on obtaining only *reasonable assurance* that there are no *material misstatements*, makes it unlikely the auditor will detect frauds of relatively small amounts, and/or frauds that involve collusion. In fact, a recent survey of the Association of Certified Fraud Examiners (ACFE) finds that in less than 4 percent of fraud cases the external auditor is the first to discover the fraud (ACFE 2018). In a majority of the cases, the fraud is detected either by a tip, or the internal audit function. Encouraging open communication throughout the organization can be one of the most powerful controls within a nonprofit.

The COSO framework

The Committee of Sponsoring Organizations of the Treadway Commission (COSO) is the preeminent influence on internal controls in the United States. COSO is an independent private sector body jointly sponsored by five major professional organizations: the American Accounting Association, the American Institute of Certified Public Accountants, Financial Executives International, the Institute of Internal Auditors, and the Institute of Management Accountants (COSO 2017). COSO is charged with studying the causes of fraudulent financial reporting with the objective of reducing or eliminating instances of fraudulent financial reporting (COSO 2017). To that end, COSO has created a framework to assess the effectiveness of internal controls. The framework is used by auditors when expressing an opinion on the effectiveness of internal controls over financial reporting for publicly traded companies. In addition, the COSO framework is widely used by nonprofit organizations to ensure a sufficient internal control structure (AICPA 2015).

The COSO framework has three main objectives: operations, reporting, and compliance. The purpose of the operations objective is to ensure the efficiency and effectiveness of the organization's operations. In addition to meeting financial and performance goals, the COSO framework is designed to ensure assets are safeguarded against loss. The reporting objective is designed to ensure the external and internal financial reporting is free of material error, is timely and transparent, and meets the standards of regulators and other stakeholders. Finally, the compliance objective ensures that the entity follows all laws and regulations.

The COSO framework has five integrated components designed to meet the three objectives: control environment, risk assessment, control activities, information and communication, and monitoring activities. Imbedded within the five components are 17 guiding principles.

Control environment

The first component, control environment, incorporates the environment of the whole organization and assesses whether the organization has structures and processes in place to ensure the integrity and ethical values of the organization are not compromised. There are five principles within the control environment component: (1) the organization demonstrates a commitment to integrity and ethical values; (2) the board of directors demonstrates independence from management and exercises oversight of the development and performance of internal control; (3) management establishes, with board oversight, structures, reporting lines, and appropriate authorities and responsibilities in the pursuit of objectives; (4) the organization demonstrates a commitment to attract, develop, and retain competent individuals in alignment with objectives; (5) the organization holds individuals accountable for their internal control responsibilities in the pursuit of objectives. Overall, an appropriate "tone at the top" must be set by the board and executives of the nonprofit organization to ensure a high level of ethics and integrity within the organization.

An example of a lax control environment and a poor "tone at the top" occurred at the Vietnow National Headquarters, Inc. Vietnow's mission was to help veterans (veterans helping veterans) and to help raise community awareness of the difficulties veterans face. As reported by the *Chicago Tribune* ("Vietnam veterans charity dissolved after 'egregious fraud'") on November 6, 2017, Vietnow raised over fifteen million dollars over a 10-year period to further their mission. However, more than 80 percent of the funds went to professional fundraisers, while most of the rest went to cover administrative expenses. According to the attorney for Vietnow, the charity officers' motives were "altruistic. Unfortunately, they relied upon professional fundraisers to raise money and to assist them in complying with the necessary financial regulations" (Jackson and Marx 2017). Further, one of the charity's officers noted they had failed to provide proper oversight of its finances. While none of the officers received compensation, the fundamental lack of oversight culminated in a poor control environment, ultimately leading to the dissolution of Vietnow.

Risk assessment

The second integrated component, risk assessment, covers the processes used to monitor and control risk throughout the organization. The risk assessment component contains four guiding principles, that the organization: (1) specifies objectives with sufficient clarity to enable the identification and assessment of risks relating to objectives; (2) identifies risks to the achievement of its objectives across the entity and analyzes risks as a basis for determining how the risks should be managed; (3) considers the potential for fraud in assessing risks to the achievement of objectives; (4) identifies and assesses changes that could significantly impact the system of internal control. Risk assessment requires a continuous monitoring of areas deemed high risk, and an overall evaluation of risks on a periodic basis. The focus is on proactive intervention to minimize risks and ultimately minimize the chance of an internal control failure.

Assessing risks to the organization and responding timely is key to the organization's health and survival, as is demonstrated by the case of the Center for Building Hope. The Center for Building Hope's mission was to offer free resources and support to cancer patients and their family members. As reported by the *Bradenton Herald* on July 8, 2016 ("Center for Building

Hope facility attracting attention from potential buyers"), the Center for Building Hope had been running deficits for several years and had defaulted on a more than two million dollar mortgage (Jones 2016). A contributing factor to the financial problems was the acquisition of Brides Against Breast Cancer. Brides Against Breast Cancer contributed two-thirds of the overall revenue, but led to much higher expenses including almost tripling the CEO's compensation over a three-year period (from $125,000 to $335,000) and paying exorbitant credit card transaction processing fees to a company controlled by the CEO. Proper assessment of risk would have led the board to scrutinize the acquisition of Brides Against Breast Cancer in much greater detail and perhaps resulted in a conclusion to not take on such a large acquisition.

Control activities

The third integrated component, control activities, involves the policies and procedures put in place to minimize the risks to the organization. Control activities can be either preventive or detective in nature. Preventive activities, such as a conflict of interest policy, are designed to ensure no new control failure surfaces. Detective controls, such as bank reconciliations, are designed to catch errors that have already occurred. The control activities component is guided by three principles: (1) the organization selects and develops control activities that contribute to the mitigation of risks to the achievement of objectives to acceptable levels; (2) the organization selects and develops general control activities over technology to support the achievement of objectives; (3) the organization deploys control activities through policies that establish what is expected and procedures that put policies into action. Overall, deciding which control activities to put in place is best viewed through a cost-benefit lens. While, ideally, organizations would have a robust control environment that eliminates all risks to the organization, practically, organizations must choose among a set of cost-effective controls that minimize risk to a tolerable level.

The presence of key control activities can play an important role in preventing occupational fraud. For example, Saxton and Neely (2019) find that the presence of a whistleblower policy, conflict of interest policy, and/or a document retention policy is associated with a reduced likelihood of receiving a donor advisory from Charity Navigator. Further they find the more of these policies the organization has, the lower the likelihood of receiving a donor advisory. Similarly, Harris et al. (2017) find that the presence of a conflict of interest policy and/or a whistleblower policy is associated with a reduced likelihood of incurring a significant asset diversion. However, the effective implementation of the policies is crucial to ensure accountability within the organization. For example, in 2016 the CFO of Mental Health Systems was placed on paid leave (his employment was terminated a few months later) the same week he raised concerns about improper billing by the organization's senior executives to San Diego County officials. Ultimately, San Diego County required Mental Health Systems to correct the $300,000 billing error or risk losing its $35 million grant. While Mental Health Systems reported having a whistleblower policy on their Form 990, failure to protect whistleblowers can have a chilling effect on the willingness of other employees to speak up in the future.

Information and communication

The fourth integrated component, information and communication, involves communicating to necessary individuals their responsibilities in maintaining an effective control environment. For example, for a code of conduct to be relevant it is necessary not only to have a written code of conduct policy, but also effectively to communicate the code of conduct expectations to all employees. The information and communication component has three guiding principles: (1) the organization obtains or generates and uses relevant, quality information to support the functioning of internal control; (2) the organization internally communicates information, including objectives and responsibilities for internal control, necessary to support the functioning of internal control; (3) the organization communicates with external parties regarding matters affecting the functioning of internal control. It is important that all stakeholders of the organization (e.g. the board, vendors, employees, clients, etc.) be apprised of relevant control information to ensure controls in place are effectively executed.

An example of failing to communicate the importance of internal control polices is found in the case of the Tennessee Coalition to End Domestic and Sexual Violence, in which the Tennessee Comptroller found the organization deficient in monitoring pay and the appropriate use of grant funds (Tennessee Comptroller of the Treasury 2017). Additionally, the Comptroller indicated that the organization failed to require board members to sign a "Board Member Agreement Form," which includes board members' responsibilities to avoid violations of the organization's conflicts of interest policy. The organization failed to communicate other important aspects of internal control as well; for example, board members were not required to annually disclose conflicts of interest (p. 7).

Monitoring activities

The final integrated component, monitoring activities, involves the periodic evaluation of the system of controls in place. Any identified deficiencies in controls should be promptly corrected, with significant deficiencies communicated to the top levels of the organization. The monitoring activities component has two guiding principles: (1) the organization selects, develops, and performs ongoing and/or separate evaluations to ascertain whether the components of internal control are present and functioning; (2) the organization evaluates and communicates internal control deficiencies in a timely manner to those parties responsible for taking corrective action, including senior management and the board of directors, as appropriate.

Failure to monitor control systems can lead organizations to systemic failure. This almost happened in the case of the Milwaukee Public Museum, where a public auditor found the board lax in oversight activity. This contributed to a deteriorating financial position and the misallocation of donor restricted funds. Fundamental oversight of the actions of board committees would have provided notice of problems in the control system; in this case, even a simple system such as monitoring attendance might have called attention to insufficient oversight. This lack of monitoring facilitated a failure to separate responsibility for important duties in the areas of financial reporting and reviewing investments. Ultimately, endowment funds were used to cover operating deficits (Milwaukee County Director of Audit: Committee on Finance and Audit 2005), and although the organization has recovered, its future was imperiled by these failures.

Overall, abiding by the 17 principles of COSO will help to ensure that nonprofit organizations have a sufficiently robust internal control structure in order to minimize risks to the organization.

The case of the Newark Water Conservation and Development Corporation

Cases can often help to demonstrate the potential severity of internal control failures. The case of the Newark Water Conservation and Development Corporation (NWCDC) demonstrates the potential implications of inadequate internal controls. This case illustrates problems related to at least four elements of the COSO framework: this includes lax attitudes toward integrity and ethical values, a lack of active monitoring at the trustee level, insufficient communication mechanisms, little evidence of any monitoring of the internal controls system within the organization, and insufficient policies and systems to provide information to decision makers. In this case, private inurement by the executive director and others, risky decision making, and inappropriate oversight contributed to the waste of millions of dollars of public funds (State of New Jersey: Office of the State Comptroller 2014).

The NWCDC had managed conservation, development, and the property management of real estate on behalf of the city of Newark since 1973, expanding to water treatment and storage in 1998 (State of New Jersey: Office of the State Comptroller 2014). The NWCDC received funds for both real estate and water functions from the city, which constituted the vast majority of revenue received over the organization's history. Created to serve a very clear public service and acting as an agent of the municipal government, the NWCDC ultimately was dissolved due to a failure to act responsibly in the public's interest.

Numerous problems arose in the NWCDC, including the approval of a generous severance package for the executive director on the day of the organization's dissolution. This severance was not indicative of the organization's performance or seemingly appropriate given the conditions of employment (State of New Jersey: Office of the State Comptroller 2014). The executive director also received an additional $800K in compensation from the period of January 2006 to March 2013, over 72 percent more than was approved by the board during this period (State of New Jersey: Office of the State Comptroller 2014). Problems extended to the area of procurement, where the NWCDC failed to award contracts in a manner consistent with local law, despite the fact that legal compliance was required by the organization's articles of incorporation. For example, the NWCDC awarded no-bid contacts. Some awards were made to individuals with direct connections to officers of the organization and without documentation that would be required in normal circumstances.

Problems extended to financial oversight and reporting. For example, the executive director operated an investment account without appropriate oversight and the organization operated without an investment policy for some time. This contributed to investment losses. Additionally, unauthorized loans were made to other organizations, with terms disproportionately in their interest. Petty cash was mismanaged, with large expenditures over time funded with petty cash. The comptroller determined that reporting was inadequate, with expenditures omitted from the general ledger. Record keeping was also inadequate, with expenditures recorded as "miscellaneous" despite the presence of information sufficient to their categorization.

Ultimately, the New Jersey State Comptroller found the board of the NWCDC failed to demonstrate due care in governance, acted with inappropriate intent in some instances, failed to exercise appropriate oversight in others, and exacerbated harm by failing to enact or enforce policies that would have prevented misbehavior in areas such as contracting and expenditures. Overall, the failure to react to or detect system weaknesses and misbehavior demonstrates inappropriate intent or a tremendous dereliction of the duties of monitoring and evaluation at the board level. At best, the board was unconcerned with the exercise of the internal controls necessary to manage risk in the organization. Below the board, actors violated organizational policy, failed to provide the board with information, and did not exercise reasonable business judgment when carrying out responsibilities.

We can examine some failures in greater detail in order to determine how an appropriate control orientation would have prevented problems in the NWCDC. Most importantly, it is reasonable to assume that a commitment to ethics at the top of the organization coupled with the exercise of appropriate oversight would have led the board to change its own decisions and to question other actions in the organization. It would also have created an environment with appropriate concern for ethics and control. In the case of the NWCDC, we can see direct results of this failure on the organization's 990 form, which indicates no requirement to disclose conflicts of interest, no monitoring or enforcement of the written conflict of interest policy, no whistleblower policy, and no policy on the retention or destruction of written documents.

A severance package awarded to the executive director provides an example of a board failing to exercise due care or reasonable judgment, as this severance should not have been awarded on the day of dissolution. This is clear given the widespread problems in the organization, as well as compensation awarded despite the lack of a legal obligation to offer severance, except in the case of dismissal without cause (State of New Jersey: Office of the State Comptroller 2014).

Generous contracts awarded to those close to the organization also should have been prevented by a basic commitment to ethics. As one recipient was the parent of a trustee, members of the board should clearly have been aware of a violation of the organization's policies in this area. A commitment to ethics also would have caused the board to act in response to other contracts that violated the organization's policies, including no-bid contracts, contracts paid in advance, and contracts (also no-bid) that were awarded to former employees (State of New Jersey: Office of the State Comptroller 2014).

The board failed to exercise reasonable judgment regarding investments, trustees did not inquire about major investment losses; although this may have been exacerbated by the failure of the executive director and outside auditor to highlight these losses, it does not excuse the boards' negligence.

The proper creation, monitoring, and enforcement of organizational policy by the board also would have prevented some abuses. This included financial matters (p. 29, State of New Jersey: Office of the State Comptroller 2014), where the Board Treasurer was formally responsible for oversight. The board failed to create an investment policy and directly contravened its own articles of incorporation by acting with fewer trustees than required (p. 31, State of New Jersey: Office of the State Comptroller 2014).

Assuming a commitment to ethics, other elements of an appropriate control policy would have further reduced risk for the NWCDC. For example, the division of responsibilities among the organization's staff could have prevented issues with investments and compensation. The investment account was managed exclusively by the executive director and without any internal oversight (albeit with contention about the degree of oversight provided by an external auditor). While the board raised questions about the organization's finances, they relied too heavily on a single individual for information in this area. In this way, even an intent to engage in timely and active oversight would have been undermined by relying on the information provided. Appropriate separation of duties would have required at least two individuals to oversee important financial matters and made misrepresentation more difficult. The executive director's actions to self-award excessive pay were facilitated by an inadequate division of responsibilities, with the executive director formally able to issue payroll checks to herself until at least 2011, and practically able to do so even after the creation of a policy dividing responsibilities in this area (State of New Jersey: Office of the State Comptroller 2014).

Proper documentation and monitoring may have eliminated some abuses. For example, receipts labeled as "miscellaneous" may have masked inappropriate nonbusiness expenses, whereas adequately categorizing expenses facilitates the detection of abnormal activity. The oversight of petty cash was so insufficient as to allow for a cash reimbursement of $3,900 for receipts totaling $1,100 and for the executive director to use petty cash to compensate an individual over $23,000 for part-time labor (2014, p. 28). Inappropriate documentation and monitoring undermine the integrity of financial information in the organization, contributing to financial documents that do not accurately convey information to those inside or outside of the organization. Just as important, failure in these areas contributes to a sense that the organization is not acting to prevent inappropriate behavior, creating the perception that such misconduct is less likely to be detected and encouraging abuses.

The case of Birmingham Health Care – when internal controls will struggle to prevent abuse

The case of Birmingham Health Care (BHC) represents another abuse of the public trust. The former executive director of the organization was indicted for conspiracy, wire fraud, bank fraud, and money laundering and ultimately convicted of a material diversion of over $13 million through BHC and other agencies; with the chief financial officer pleading guilty to wire fraud, bank fraud, and money laundering. Perhaps most dramatically, this included a CFO convicted of charges that she falsified a death certificate with the intent of collecting life insurance benefits and "sent drugs and other items through the mail in an attempt to intimidate a witness and the families of a prosecutor and FBI agent investigating the health care fraud case" (Faulk 2016).

Ultimately, this case became one of the examples used to illustrate fraud by the Internal Revenue Service (IRS 2017), including the presence of irregular real estate transactions, inappropriate contracts, the diversion of assets in the form of medication, and misappropriation; as well as money laundering and conspiracy (Faulk 2016).

Without speaking to the presence of a control system in the BHC, collusion among officers with key responsibilities in an organization creates a tremendous obstacle for appropriate control. The separation of duties, so critical to detection and reporting fraud or abuse, often relies on relatively few employees with expertise in financial management, or who can access the systems that support appropriate financial management. Separation of duties should reduce risk by allowing these employees to evaluate activities and signal error or abuse. Collusion eliminates this natural check and cripples control systems. In the case of Birmingham Health Care, the collusion between the executive director and chief financial officer removes two key positions with oversight responsibility, control over information, and that serve to convey critical signals to other actors fundamental to control. The only potential remedy in such cases, an informed and active governing board, remains an aspiration for many charitable organizations, which highlights the need for board training and development to include internal control issues.

The case of American Veterans Foundation – lack of organizational policies

The American Veterans Foundation (AVF) is a Sarasota Florida based charitable organization with a mission to assist veterans who are homeless or in jeopardy of becoming homeless, providing patients in veteran's homes with toiletries, clothing, books, games and other items; providing comfort and "we care" packages to deployed troops. The Michigan Attorney General issued a notice of intended action and cease and desist order against AVF for deceptive solicitations and diversions of funds raised to other purposes. From 2014 to 2016, AVF raised more than four million dollars in contributions nationwide but spent only 1 percent of these funds on programs. In 2014, AVF made only one grant that went directly to a homeless veteran totaling $1,565. Most of the annual expenses were for professional fundraising fees. A review of the Form 990 shows that common governance measures, such as a whistleblower policy, a written document retention and destruction policy, and a conflict of interest policy, were absent at the organization.

International approaches to internal controls

Examining the COSO framework and cases of failure illustrate the general principles of internal control. While the COSO framework originated in the US and much of the research on internal controls focuses on charities and nonprofits in the United States, the principles represented in COSO are reflected internationally. Examining the expectations of regulators regarding the use of and reporting necessary on issues related to internal controls demonstrates the similar perspectives on the principles of control, but also that the implementation of these principles varies widely. We look to a few countries to demonstrate these approaches to internal controls in different contexts. We provide a brief summary of expectations regarding internal financial controls in a few countries. While this list is far from comprehensive, we hope it might provide a starting point for scholars interested in a comparative analysis of control frameworks.

Australia

The Australian Charities and Not-for-profits Commission (ACNC) does not directly assess the internal controls of Australian charities, but does recommend internal financial controls in its governance standards, with a focus on financial reporting, monitoring, and separation of duties (ACNC 2013). The CPA Australia provides guidance on the control environment, risk assessment, segregation of duties, monitoring for fraud, and internal financial controls (CPA Australia 2011).

Canada

The COSO framework is used for internal control in Canada, but more attention on internal controls would benefit Canadian charities. One positive in Canada arises from the primary national regulator, the Charities Directorate of the Canadian Revenue Agency (CRA). Although the Directorate does not provide specific guidance on internal control mechanisms, it does sometimes evaluate the internal controls of charitable organizations. This includes an accounting of the individuals responsible for financial and other functions such as receiving mail and fundraising for the organization, as well as the systems used. These financial functions divided into revenues, expenses, and records.

Revenue functions include responsibility for hand-delivered payments, those received by mail, bank deposits, processing donation receipts, signing receipts, reconciliation of receipts, and appraising gift-in-kind donations. The choice between manual and electronic receipting is also recorded.

In the area of expenses, responsibilities evaluated include preparing checks, authorizing payment of invoices, authorization for signing checks; as well as the policy issue of the threshold at which a dual signature is required. Organizations are also asked about the storage of physical records and the storage of donation receipts.

While the CRA assessment covers some aspects of the risk and control components of the COSO framework, the scope of this evaluation could widen. Specifically, assessing the systems utilized by charities and the degree of active monitoring in the organization might indicate whether the climate of the organization supports appropriate internal controls. Providing additional guidance to charities on internal controls also might help to signal their importance to Canadian charities.

England and Wales

The Charity Commission for England and Wales also provides guidance on internal financial controls, including both legal requirements and suggestions for good practice (Charity

Commission for England and Wales 2012). This guidance is based on the principles set forth in Financial Reporting Council guidance for corporations (Financial Reporting Council 2014).

Delineating the legal requirements of trustees in the areas of maintaining accounting systems, risk management, fundraising, tainted donations (made and refunded to improve the donor's tax position), wage, salary, and pension systems, and endowment management; the Charity Commission also references the acting legislation in many areas and provides additional guidance for charities.

Suggested best practice is provided in other areas, including general advice on segregation of duties and monitoring, as well as specific guidance in the areas of income; purchases, payments and loans; and assets and investments.

Ireland

In Ireland, the Charities Regulator is empowered to evaluate organizations' internal controls and provides guidance on internal financial controls. While organizations can tailor their internal control policies, they must be prepared to justify deviations from the guidelines (Charities Regulatory Authority 2017).

The Charities Regulator guidelines cover income, expenditure, banking, assets and investments, and monitoring. These cover process issues, staffing, record keeping and specific monitoring in each area; and questions that provide guidance to charities. The specificity of guidance is impressive, including seven revenue categories, four types of expenditures, five areas regarding banking, and three asset categories. For example, the questions below provide guidance in the area of donations:

a) Does the charity maximize the allowable tax relief on donations?
b) Are the applicable "Enduring Certificates (CHY3 Cert)" or "Annual Certificates (CHY4 Cert)" obtained from donors?
c) Are regular checks made to ensure all eligible tax repayments are obtained?
d) Does the charity keep the records of the eligible tax repayments claimed?

Overall, the Charities Regulator conveys the importance of internal controls to Irish charities, as well as high quality information, a commendable level of support.

COBIT, IT, and internal controls

While organizations in many countries have access to accountability frameworks, there is one aspect of the organization that many organizations ignore in their control frameworks – information technology. When organizations rely on systems to martial information resources, considering information technology is essential to minimize risk. Despite this fact, we posit that information asymmetries between those responsible for the organization on the whole, those managing internal controls, and those responsible for information and technology is likely to lead many nonprofits to fail to integrate IT into the organization's control framework.

Appropriate information technology practices have been demonstrated to support risk management in for-profit organizations (Rubino and Vitolla 2014a). Scholars have identified the potential for nonprofits to utilize IT, but also deficits in IT practices (Hackler and Saxton 2007). As nonprofit organizations become more reliant on technology, they should engage in deliberate consideration of IT control systems as part of their overall internal control framework.

Information technology systems are critically important to appropriate control in many organizations producing information, as the information needed for auditing is generated by these systems (Rubino and Vitolla 2014b; Geerts et al. 2013), but it should be considered even for organizations that do not have staff dedicated to information systems (IS) or IT functions.

Research from the for-profit sector supports the need to integrate IT into control systems. IT plays a critical role in internal control and minimizing material weakness, including maintaining the integrity of financial data, managing resources, general controls for IT assurance and application-specific controls to monitor transactions and store data (Rubino and Vitolla 2014b).

While this chapter cannot address these issues comprehensively, we want to introduce IT governance and management as an essential dimension of organizations' control systems. As failure in this area can introduce risk independent of other elements of the control framework, charitable and nonprofit organizations should not overlook information technology. A brief description of one framework, cases demonstrating failures to apply these principles, a comparative look at a few other approaches to control frameworks, and links to some of the references available for organizations focusing on IT control issues is provided below to frame IT governance and control for charitable and nonprofit organizations.

While larger nonprofits may have considered the issue of IT control, we expect many charities and nonprofits have not considered the issue at all. For these organizations, the Control Objectives for Information and Related Technology (COBIT) framework (www.isaca.org/COBIT), developed by the Information Systems Audit and Control Association (ISACA), provides guidance on the appropriate governance of IT systems. Originally focused specifically on audit and control, it has evolved into the most widely recognized IT governance framework.

COBIT identifies three levels of need related to IT, organizational information requirements, resources requirements, and process requirements. It also establishes goals related to each level (Rubino and Vitolla 2014b). The following five process areas relate to these goals, and these are supported by 37 principles (COBIT 2012):

1   Evaluate, Direct and Monitor
2   Align, Plan and Organize
3   Build, Acquire and Implement
4   Deliver, Service and Support
5   Monitor and Evaluate.

Fundamentally, these areas and the supporting principles guide organizations' IT strategy, policy and practice, including consideration of their governance framework, managing and using information in the face of increasing information demands, integrating IT and IT decision making into the organization, ensuring IT compliance, risk optimization and management, and monitoring for effectiveness.

While not designed to be prescriptive, COBIT has been identified as important to financial reporting in for-profit firms (Kerr and Murthy 2013) and consistent with the assessment of IT auditors in this sector (Tuttle and Vandervelde 2007). This suggests nonprofit organizations could consider the framework to guide their own IT governance. Furthermore, COBIT incorporates a balanced scorecard approach to assessment, which makes it more accessible to nonprofit practitioners (Martello et al. 2008).

Although not focused on nonprofit organizations, Rubino and Vitolla (2014b) map COBIT processes onto the components of the COSO framework, providing a useful introduction to the utility of COBIT for internal control. They connect each of the 37 process principles of COBIT onto the five COSO components, demonstrating the essential connection between information technology and internal control.[1] Charities and nonprofits should consider this aspect of internal control in order to ensure appropriate governance, as failure to address IT may serve to inject unnecessary risk into operations.

A lack of IT controls can result in substantial losses for the nonprofit organization. The case of Community of Caring in Erie, PA, is telling (O'Neill 2017). As reported in 2015, this social service agency had 71 client identities stolen by an employee (US Attorney's Office: Western District of Pennsylvania 2015). The employee, reportedly working as a chef, accessed clients' identities and, unbeknownst to them, filed fraudulent tax returns on their behalf. The employee and a co-defendant were able to secure over $100,000 in fraudulent tax refunds, a cautionary tale for the importance of maintaining IT controls in the form of secure client records.

Concluding remarks

Outside of the regulatory framework, and COSO, best practices for appropriate controls have been set up by leading independent associations such as the National Council of Nonprofits. Charities have access to information on internal controls and, given their public missions and tax-exempt status, cannot be excused for neglecting this critical aspect of the organization. Nonprofit management curriculum also must be sure to incorporate instruction in this area.[2]

In addition to the cases of fraud stemming from the failure to implement effective controls, we can also understand the importance of internal controls by looking to associations between internal controls and other variables. Scholarship indicates that following best practice for establishing strong internal controls is associated with notable benefits for the nonprofit organization. For example, Petrovits et al. (2011) find that weaknesses in internal controls are associated with lower donations and government grants. Similarly, Harris et al. (2015) find that the presence of a stronger control environment, as measured by seven factors including having formal written policies and reviewing and approving executive compensation, is associated with higher levels of contributions and government grants. In addition to enhancing funding, strong controls can minimize the risk of fraudulent activity within the organization. Harris et al. (2017) find that strong controls, such as board monitoring and tone at the top, are associated with a reduced probability of suffering an asset diversion. Saxton and Neely (2019) focus on the three SOX-inspired policies – whistleblower policy, conflict of interest policy, and document retention policy – and find that the presence of these policies is associated with a reduced likelihood of receiving a donor advisory from Charity Navigator. Overall, empirical evidence consistently supports associations between strong internal controls and additional funding, as well as protection from fraudulent activity.

Given the unusual governance structures of charitable organizations, in which the self-selected board may serve as the only formal check on management authority, internal controls are critical to maintaining the organization's intended public benefit. While those responsible for governing and managing the organization cannot be expected to be expert in every aspect of the organization or its operations, they certainly must be aware of their oversight responsibility and the essential nature of internal controls to maintaining the organization.

Notes

1   We would direct scholars interested in research in this area and practitioners to examine their work and the COBIT standards for a more comprehensive introduction to IT and internal control.
2   For example, see Nonprofit Academic Council Curricular Guidelines, https://static1.squarespace.com/static/569409d24bf11844ad28ed01/t/56bbdff1b654f965b7c93e1b/1455153140726/NACC_Curricular_Guidelines_100615.pdf

Bibliography

American Institute of Certified Public Accountants (AICPA). (2015). *The AICPA Audit Committee Tool Kit Not-For-Profit Entities,* 3rd Edition. New York: AICPA.

American Institute of Certified Public Accountants (AICPA). (2017). AU-C Section 240. Consideration of Fraud in a Financial Statement Audit. Retrieved from https://www.aicpa.org/Research/Standards/AuditAttest/DownloadableDocuments/AU-C-00240.pdf

Association of Certified Fraud Examiners (ACFE). (2018). Report to the Nations on Occupational Fraud and Abuse. Accessed February 12, 2018 at: www.acfe.com/rttn2016/detection.aspx

Australian Charities and Not-for-profits Commission (ACNC). (2013). *Protect Your Charity from Fraud: The ACNC's Guide to Fraud Prevention.* Melbourne: ACNC.

Boland, C., Johnson, M.F., & Hogan, C. (2018). Motivating Compliance: Firm Response to Mandatory Existence Disclosure Policies. *Accounting Horizon, 32*(2): 103–119.

Burks, J.J. (2015). Accounting Errors in Nonprofit Organizations. *Accounting Horizons, 29*(2): 341–361.

Burks, J.J. (2016). Reactions of Nonprofit Monitors to Financial Reporting Problems. *Social Sciences Research Network.* Available at: http://dx.doi.org/10.2139/ssrn.2471138

Charities Regulatory Authority (2017). Internal Financial Controls Guidelines for Charities.

Charity Commission for England and Wales. (2012). Internal Financial Controls for Charities (CC8).

Chartered Professional Accountants, Australia. (2011). Internal Controls for Not-for-profit Organisations. Southbank, VIC: CPA Australia.

COBIT 5: A Business Framework for the Governance and Management of Enterprise IT. ISACA, 2012.

Coe, C.K., & Ellis, C. (1991). Internal Controls in State, Local, and Nonprofit Agencies. *Public Budgeting & Finance, 11*(3): 43–55.

Committee of Sponsoring Organizations of the Treadway Commission. (COSO). (2017). About Us. Accessed September 18, 2017 at: https://www.coso.org/Pages/aboutus.aspx

Duncan, J.B., Flesher, D.L., & Stocks, M.H. (1999). Internal Control Systems in US Churches: An Examination of the Effects of Church Size and Denomination on Systems of Internal Control. *Accounting, Auditing & Accountability Journal, 12*(2): 142–164.

Fama, E.F., & Jensen, M.C. (1983). Separation of Ownership and Control. *Journal of Law and Economics, 26*(2): 301–325.

Faulk, K. (2016). Former Birmingham Health Care CFO Sentenced in $11 Million Fraud. Accessed October 19, 2017 at: www.al.com/news/birmingham/index.ssf/2016/08/former_birmingham_health_care_5.html

Financial Reporting Council. (2014). Guidance on Risk Management, Internal Control and Related Financial and Business Reporting. London: FRC.

Fremont-Smith, M.R. (2009). *Governing Nonprofit Organizations: Federal and State Law and Regulation.* Cambridge: Harvard University Press.

Gallagher, M., & Radcliffe, V.S. (2002). Internal Controls in Nonprofit Organizations: The Case of the American Cancer Society, Ohio Division. *Nonprofit Management and Leadership, 12*(3): 313–325.

Geerts, G.L., Graham, L.E., Mauldin, E.G., McCarthy, W.E., & Richardson, V.J. (2013). Integrating Information Technology into Accounting Research and Practice. *Accounting Horizons American Accounting Association, 27*(4): 815–840.

Greenlee, J., Fischer, M., Gordon, T., & Keating, E. (2007). An Investigation of Fraud in Nonprofit Organizations: Occurrences and Deterrents. *Nonprofit and Voluntary Sector Quarterly, 36*(4): 676–694.

Hackler, D., & Saxton, G.D. (2007). The Strategic Use of Information Technology by Nonprofit Organizations: Increasing Capacity and Untapped Potential. *Public Administration Review, 67*(3): 474–487.

Hall, P.D., (2016). Historical Perspectives on Nonprofits in the United States. In Renz, D.O. (Ed.). *The Jossey-Bass Handbook of Nonprofit Leadership and Management,* 4th ed. Hoboken, NJ: John Wiley, 3–42.

Harris, E., Petrovits, C.M., & Yetman, M.H. (2015). The Effect of Nonprofit Governance on Donations: Evidence from the Revised Form 990. *Accounting Review, 90*(2): 579–610.

Harris, E., Petrovits, C., & Yetman, M.H. (2017). Why Bad Things Happen to Good Organizations: The Link Between Governance and Asset Diversions in Public Charities. *Journal of Business Ethics, 146*(1): 1–18.

Internal Revenue Service (IRS). (2017). Examples of Money Laundering in 2017. https://www.irs.gov/compliance/criminal-investigation/examples-of-money-laundering-investigations-for-fiscal-year-2017

Jackson, D., & Marx, G. (2017). Vietnam Veterans Charity Dissolved after "Egregious Fraud." *Chicago Tribune.* Accessed on March 20, 2018 at: www.chicagotribune.com/news/watchdog/ct-vietnow-met-20171106-story.html

Jones Jr., James A. (2016). Center for Building Hope Attracting Attention from Buyers. *Bradenton Herald*. Accessed on March 20, 2018 from: www.bradenton.com/news/local/article88539117.html

Kerr, D.S., & Murthy, U. S. (2013). The Importance of the COBIT Framework IT Processes for Effective Internal Control over Financial Reporting in Organizations: An International Survey. *Information & Management, 50*(7): 590–597.

Martello, M., Watson, J.G., & Fischer, M.J. (2008). Implementing a Balanced Scorecard in a Not-For-Profit Organization. *Journal of Business and Economics Research, 6*(9): 67–80.

McDonald, Jeff. (2016). CFO Who Blew Whistle on Charity is Terminated. *San Diego Union-Tribune*. Accessed March 20, 2018 at: www.sandiegouniontribune.com/news/watchdog/sdut-hawkey-fired-2016may16-story.html

Merriam-Webster. (2017). Definition of Internal Control. Dictionary. Accessed September 26, 2017 at: https://www.merriam-webster.com/dictionary/internal%20control

Milwaukee County Director of Audit: Committee on Finance and Audit. (2005). An audit of the Milwaukee Public Museum, Inc.: 2005 Financial Crisis Final Report.

Neely, D.G. (2011). The Impact of Regulation on the US Nonprofit Sector: Initial Evidence from the Nonprofit Integrity Act of 2004. *Accounting Horizons, 25*(1): 107–125.

Nezhina, T.G., & Brudney, J.L. (2012). Unintended? The Effects of Adoption of the Sarbanes–Oxley Act on Nonprofit Organizations. *Nonprofit Management and Leadership, 22*(3): 321–346.

Oliver, M. (2015). Former Nonprofit CEO Arrested, Charged in $14 Million Health Care Fraud Case. AL.COM. Accessed October 19, 2017 at: www.al.com/news/index.ssf/2015/02/former_ceo_of_nonprofits_to_ai.html

O'Neil, Madeleine. (2017). Man Pleads Guilty in Erie Identity Theft Case. GoErie.com. Accessed on March 20, 2018 at: www.goerie.com/news/20171003/man-pleads-guilty-in-erie-identity-theft-case

Petrovits, C., Shakespeare, C., & Shih, A. (2011). The Causes and Consequences of Internal Control Problems in Nonprofit Organizations. *Accounting Review, 86*(1): 325–357.

Renz, D.O. (Ed.). (2016). *The Jossey-Bass Handbook of Nonprofit Leadership and Management,* 4th ed. Hoboken, NJ: John Wiley.

Rubino, M., & Vitolla, F. (2014a). Corporate Governance and the Information System. How a Framework for IT Governance Supports ERM. *Corporate Governance, 14*(3): 320–338.

Rubino, M., & Vitolla, F. (2014b). Internal Control over Financial Reporting: Opportunities Using the COBIT Framework. *Managerial Auditing Journal, 29*(8): 736–771.

Saxton, G., & Neely, D. G. (2019). The Relationship Between Sarbanes–Oxley Policies and Donor Advisories in Nonprofit Organizations. *Journal of Business Ethics*, 158(2), 333–351.

State of New Jersey: Office of the State Comptroller. (2014). Investigative Report: Newark Watershed Conservation and Development Corporation.

Tennessee Comptroller of the Treasury. (2017). Tennessee Coalition to End Domestic and Sexual Violence: Comptroller's Investigative Report.

Tuttle, B., & Vandervelde, S.D. (2007). An Empirical Examination of COBIT as an Internal Control Framework for Information Technology. *International Journal of Accounting Information Systems, 8*(4): 240–263.

United States Attorney's Office: Northern District of Alabama. (2015). Former Non-Profit Health Clinics CEO Arrested on 112-Count Indictment.

United States Attorney's Office: Western District of Pennsylvania. (2015). Erie Woman Sentenced to Prison for Identity Theft Scheme.

17

INFORMATION AND COMMUNICATIONS TECHNOLOGY MANAGEMENT

John McNutt

PROFESSOR, THE JOSEPH R. BIDEN, JR. SCHOOL OF PUBLIC
POLICY AND ADMINISTRATION, UNIVERSITY OF DELAWARE,
NEWARK, DE 19716, USA

Technology and mission: How nonprofits use technology in support of their mission

Information and Communication Technology (ICT) supports the mission of nonprofits by allowing them to make the best use of the time and talents of their workers and volunteers. Information and communication technology generally refers to those technologies that support computing and data processing as well as communications. This is a transition from the label *information technology* that affirms the use of technology to facilitate communications at all levels.

In the past, technology often had a bad reputation in the nonprofit sector with complaints that it dehumanizes the organization and detracts from the mission. In reality, it allows organizations to expand their operations, reaching more of those in need and creating stronger and healthier communities. Like any other tool at the disposal of nonprofit managers, technology can potentially have undesirable side effects, but in part, the resistance against technology is often based on lack of familiarity, doubts about the ability to use it effectively and usually unrealistic fears.

Nonprofits are founded by and staffed by people who care deeply about a problem or issue, be that children, art, theater, historic homes, the list goes on. While nonprofit professionals are passionate about their organization's missions, unfortunately, very few are moved by the more technical aspects of nonprofit management. A tireless advocate for abused and neglected children may feel afraid and intimated by financial management and budgeting, technology and statistics. This puts them at a disadvantage in managing their organization. The professionalization of nonprofit management has eased this issue to some extent, but many nonprofit managers will still need help and support to navigate the management of their organizations. Using technology wisely requires learning new skills, perspectives and vocabulary. This can be stressful and often expensive. The point is that while there is resistance to technology, the rewards of using technology far outstrip the barriers that we encounter.

The ICT that nonprofits deploy spans a wide range. Some technology was created for specific nonprofit needs. Fundraising technology is a good example of this type of application. On

249

balance, however, most technology that nonprofit organizations use was developed for other purposes and contexts. Developing nonprofit ICT capacity therefore often involves repurposing or reengineering technologies through the creation of a set of processes. This is often difficult and accounts for the lag between when a technology is created and when it is adopted by nonprofit organizations.

There has long been a discussion of the relative level of technology sophistication of nonprofits vs organizations in the public and commercial sectors (Cortes & Rafter, 2007; McNutt, Guo, Goldkind & An, 2018). Early studies suggested that there were differences and that the nonprofit sector trailed behind (Burt & Taylor, 2000; 2003; Princeton Survey Associates, 2001). Later studies raised questions about this contention (see Geller, Abramson & de Leon, 2010; Finn, Maher & Forster, 2006). Currently there are few national studies of nonprofit technology and many of those are dependent on large purposive samples such as the Nonprofit Technology Network/M+R's Annual Survey (2017). Some small nonprofits are very well wired and others lack even basic technology. This is probably true of many small businesses and smaller government agencies. This organizational digital divide may be a question of scale and resources rather than resistance. A decade ago, a different conclusion might have been the correct one. As new generations have entered the sector's workforce, they brought with them an understanding of and a familiarity with technology.

Another development is that for many types of nonprofits, technology is becoming part of service delivery. Online psychotherapy, technology-led psychosocial interventions, telemedicine and other technology are part of many nonprofit health and human services agencies (McNutt, Guo, Goldkind & An, 2018; Oldenburg, Taylor, O'Neil, Cocker & Cameron, 2015; Bennett & Glasgow, 2009). Theater, music, museums and arts organizations make use of technology as a driving force in their programs (Toepler & Wyszomirski, 2012). Hospitals and universities need better research technology if they are to remain competitive. In addition, universities have created online programs that allow undergraduate and graduate programs to be offered regardless of distance. The growth of Massive Open Online Courses (MOOCs) has the potential to substantially democratize education.

Technology adoption is becoming more widespread among both organizations and individuals. Along with a growing number of users of the Internet, social media/Web 2.0 and other technology in the general population, there is now an expectation among their stakeholders that nonprofits will be technology friendly. The expectation is that the user experience at a nonprofit will be similar to that at an online retailer.

Finally, the push from the policy system and other sectors is an important force. The ability to work with state agencies and insurance companies made upgrading technology important. Federal rules on medical records pushed hospitals to make changes in their technology. Because technology changes so quickly, the adequacy of an organization's technology is a moving target. Smartphones are much more capable than many computers a few decades ago and new dimensions of technology are emerging daily.

The evolution of nonprofit technology

The development and use of information and communication technology has a long history and some of the early computers were created and housed in nonprofit organizations (McNutt, Guo, Goldkind & An, 2018). This included research centers, medical facilities and universities.

Functional early computers were called mainframe or legacy computers. These were giant systems that took up floors or even entire buildings. They required substantial professional maintenance and were extremely expensive. Large commercial organizations, government organizations, hospitals and research universities employed these technologies. Supercomputers are a special case of mainframe computers. While mainframe and legacy technology have come down in size, the technology is still too large and too expensive for many nonprofit organizations. The development of minicomputers in the 1970s brought more nonprofit organizations into computing. Even smaller computers (microcomputers or personal computers) entered the marketplace soon after and made computer ownership far more likely. Early small computers were not very capable by today's standards. Eventually, personal technology became smaller, more portable and more capable. Today's tablets and smartphones are faster and more able than desktop computers of a few decades ago. Smaller and smaller technology is developed every day.

At this point networking began to emerge as a way to connect computers locally (Local Area Networks or LANS) and over wider distances. The Internet began as a military project sponsored by the Defense Advanced Research Projects Agency (DARPA) to connect defense related computers throughout the nation (Hafner & Lyon, 1996). Other networks (such as UseNet and Bitnet) also developed and there were nonprofit efforts to provide network access including the community technology movement, community technology centers and activist-oriented networking efforts like PeaceNet and Earthnet (Schuler, 1996; Downing, 1989). Commercial entities, such as America Online (AOL), were also active and there were a number of other efforts to support connectivity. The early face of networking, even as the Internet emerged, was primitive and largely text based. The development of the World Wide Web in the 1990s represented a real move forward in making the Internet accessible. Combined with commercialization, Internet usage exploded. While there was some interactivity, it was still a one-way form of communications and is often referred to as Web 1.0. Nonprofits began to employ email, websites, discussion lists and so forth. Even before the century turned, new technology began to emerge in force. These new technologies, often called Web 2.0 or social media, were Internet-based software that allowed more interactivity and user-generated content and the sharing of collective intelligence (O'Reilly, 2005, 2007; Kanter & Fine, 2010). These included blogging, social networking sites (such as Facebook), Microblogging (Twitter), Wikis, video and image sharing and many other related systems. Social media has revolutionized many aspects of nonprofit communications, marketing, member and volunteer engagement and fundraising. It is a key part of nonprofit efforts toward advocacy and policymaking. It has not replaced many older forms of technology in communication (McNutt & Barlow, 2012) and it seems unlikely that it will. Email and discussion list software (such as Listserv) are products of the 1970s and 1980s. While a lot of effort has been devoted to measuring social media/Web 2.0 output, it is still unclear how that affects actual nonprofit outcomes.

Social media/Web 2.0 is also technology that is mainstream and well understood. It is certainly not new or unusual. Most of the base technology is over a decade old and some (like Blogging) was used widely in the 1990s. It enjoys extensive use in the general population. According to the Pew Internet and American Life Project (Greenwood, Perrin & Duggan, 2016, n.p.), "Nearly eight-in-ten *online* Americans (79%) now use Facebook, more than double the share that uses Twitter (24%), Pinterest (31%), Instagram (32%) or LinkedIn (29%)" (Greenwood et al., 2016). While Web 2.0 will continue to evolve, Internet-based technology has moved to Web 3.0, the Semantic Web.

In Web 3.0, the structure is different and a network of data becomes more critical (Hendler, 2009). This is a move away from the document-based architecture that characterized earlier forms of the Internet. Web 3.0 is data-centric as opposed to document-centric.

The centrality of nonprofit data will likely fuel the next evolution in nonprofit technology. There are currently many discussions about the data informed nonprofit organization. This, in turn, will be supported by the Internet of Things (IoT), data science and evidence-based management and policy and open government. The movement toward nonprofit metrics will also make data collection, storage and visualization key capacities for nonprofits.

How technology is organized in a nonprofit

While technology can help nonprofit organizations to perform the activities necessary to pursue their mission, the same technology may lead to changes in the way that organizations are structured. Having new capacity means that work can be done in a different manner and that leads to changes in how work is organized (Cascio & Montealegre, 2016). Nonprofit technology specialists often speak of the differences between pre-technology nonprofits and technology-enhanced or enabled nonprofits.

One of the most obvious implications is span of control, the number of people that a supervisor can control. Technology can greatly expand a manager's ability to supervise. Collaborative technologies make coordinating activities far easier and technologies such as project management software make monitoring and evaluation possible. The impact of all of these technologies means that more people and more activities can be managed by fewer supervisors. This leads, eventually, to flatter organizations. It also means that supervisory positions can be repurposed which might result in smaller organizations.

Virtual organizations are relatively new structures for nonprofits but have been used in the commercial sector for decades. A virtual organization is one that coordinates many independent units via technology. The creation of virtual organizations or virtual associations is dependent on technology that can facilitate coordination. These technologies allow remote work to be conducted in a nonprofit organization and lower the transaction costs of a synchronization of effort. This means that it is possible to expand activities by combining individuals and other organizations into a larger overall effort. While some virtual organizations have a bricks and mortar (physical) presence, others do not. Organizations, like Anonymous (Massa, 2016), exists only online. Anonymous is a group that advocates for social justice and social causes online and uses Internet tools to disrupt their opponents.

Another example of a virtual nonprofit is the Katrina People Finder Project, which coordinated the efforts of virtual volunteers to locate people who were displaced after being evacuated from the hurricanes in the Gulf Coast. A completely virtual organization, they identified many missing people and posted their names and locations to a Wiki-based website (McNutt, Adler, Jones & Menon, 2006).

Finally, there is the emergence of leaderless organizations (see Chapter 11 by Ruth Simsa) that are technologically enabled. These are face-to-face efforts that are coordinated via technology (Brainard, Boland & McNutt, 2012; Earl & Kimport, 2011; McNutt, 2018). Examples include the Tea Party, Occupy Wall Street and the Arab Spring movements. This corresponds to discussions in many fields about self-organization, which refers to organizing without organizers or spontaneously developed organizations. While this was always possible, technology facilitates the process.

The potential impact of technology on what a nonprofit is and what the nonprofit sector will be in the future is an interesting topic for exploration. As we continue to move into the information society, the role of nonprofit organizations remains uncertain in this respect (McNutt, Brainard, Zeng & Kovacic, 2016).

Technology and internal operations

The fundamental purpose that technology serves in almost any type of organization is to provide managers and other decision makers with the type of information that is necessary to make reasonable and informed decisions. This often includes a range information from various areas of management (human resources (HR), programs, financial management, fundraising and so forth) that are ideally keyed to the level of organization (place in the hierarchy or organizational structure) or job function that the user is addressing. Senior managers need different information to do their jobs than do lower level administrators or staff. This type of system has always been referred to a Management Information System (MIS) but, in recent years, a number of related terms have begun to emerge, such as Enterprise Resource Management and customer relationship management systems. At their heart, all of these approaches depend on well-developed and well-maintained databases.

Why data is king

While other aspects of technology may be more attention-getting, the database is the workhorse of nonprofit technology. Simple databases are ubiquitous in the nonprofit sector and many agencies have multiple databases. Databases are critical components of fundraising and advocacy software. Larger organizations use data warehouses or data marts that allow storage of many more pieces of information. Even larger storage is provided by datacenters and cloud-based data storage systems that permit organizations to store their data in external sites. One of the more vexing problems is how to integrate all of the data from multiple sources so that it can be used appropriately.

Nonprofit data comes from a number of sources. Financial data, program data, HR data, fundraising data and so forth come from administrative systems, which may be stand-alone systems or integrated into a larger system. Some of the data might come from information systems outside of the organization (for example, data from a bank or brokerage house). More and more data comes from technology itself, including online metrics and social media (Boland & McNutt, 2013). In recent years, data systems have had to integrate unstructured data along with traditional structured data. Finally, many organizations actively collect their own data and conduct their own research. McNutt, Justice and Carter (2014) found that the majority of nonprofit advocacy organizations that they studied in Delaware conducted their own research.

The information from these databases must be presented in such a way the data can inform relevant decisions, meaning the right information at the right level of detail. This data is often presented in a dashboard that allows decision makers to make the best use of the available data. Data visualization is an emerging field and the potential of software that can effectively present even complex relationships will make understanding more likely.

Data science techniques have begun to move into the sector, especially in larger organizations and those with more substantial research capacity. The use of large datasets, advanced analytical and visualization techniques, new data sources and other new forms of data involved practice are beginning to emerge in some nonprofits (McNutt, Justice & Barlow, 2017; McNutt & Barlow, 2019). The Data for Good (data4good) movement has created relationships between data scientists in other fields and social change organizations that can make use of their skills. These partnerships have addressed some of the world's most important challenges (Mann & Sahuguet, 2018). Collaborative and participatory data collection is a feature of many data for good efforts (Bishop, 2010). Finally, the growth of data philanthropy (making corporate data available to nonprofits as part of their philanthropy programs) promises to fuel the growth of nonprofit data science (McKeever, Greene, MacDonald, Tatian & Jones, 2018).

Nonprofit data is a primary asset of any organization. It includes information on financial situations, HR, client and programs and so forth. This information is mission critical for planning and decision making. It also carries with it the threat of liability if it is compromised. Security from various threats is and will continue to be a major concern of nonprofit managers (see Hoy & Phelps, 2009; Imboden, Phillips, Seib & Fiorentino, 2013).

Knowledge management is another function that aims to preserve organizational data and other intellectual assets (Hurley & Green, 2005). Knowledge management systems secure and curate an organization's knowledge assets. This includes organizational data and other examples of intellectual assets such as processes and technologies. A dedicated set of technologies power knowledge management efforts and allow organizations to identify the critical assets and formulate strategies to curate and preserve them.

Other internal operations

Financial management is very probably the part of nonprofit organizations that most resembles technology in the other sectors (although the accounting is different). While spreadsheet programs are ubiquitous, many organizations use dedicated accounting packages and technology that tracks inventory and activity. For more specific financial tasks (like evaluating investments or calculating benefit payments), there are dedicated packages that only deal with these issues.

Human resources records and reporting: Many nonprofits are service organizations that spend most of their revenue on staff. Proper record keeping and analysis is therefore crucially important. Technology can facilitate recruiting and onboarding. Recruiting can be conducted through the organization's website or social media presence and can use online job boards. Checking a potential employee's background through various Internet resources, as well as tools like email and Skype can speed the process. A potentially tricky situation is whether a potential employee's social media posts should be considered in the employment decision (Drouin, O'Connor, Schmidt & Miller, 2015). A number of noteworthy situations have been seen in the media where posts on Facebook have resulted in denial of employment. Most nonprofit organizations will find it useful to create and implement a social media policy for their employees.

Another issue within the HR realm is telework (Fay, 2017) and virtual teamwork (Kirkman, Gibson & Kim, 2012.). Technology facilitates a variety of alternative locations for nonprofit employees. This can create employee compliance, morale and productivity issues, as well as a range of legal and ethical issues.

Given the range of compliance issues that today's nonprofits deal with, well-developed records can make it easier to deal with requests from government. In addition, education and staff development can be facilitated and improved with an entire range of e-learning technologies such as learning management systems, interactive video, learn on demand systems and so forth. Technology also makes it easier to track learning outcomes.

Communication: Very probably, communications is the most important capacity that technology brings to nonprofit organizations. Technology can facilitate internal communication including the sharing of documents and images. Face-to-face meetings can be conducted over distance with a number of teleconferencing systems.

Board support: Technology that supports board functioning is still emergent but many of the management technologies discussed previously could be used here. Virtual board meetings are an easy fit for web conferencing technology. Harrison & Murray (2015) have examined the possibility of technology-based board assessment.

Strategic planning: Planning and project management software have become important tools for strategic planners. This is another area where data is of major importance. Doing organizational analysis and environmental assessment depends on some data and more of the right data makes the process stronger and the findings more robust.

Technology and external operations

These internal technology uses correspond to an entire range of externally facing systems. Nonprofit organizations constantly interact with their environments and the area of marketing and promotion, advocacy, fundraising and volunteer recruitment and management.

Marketing

Marketing is a major function of management; it deals with handling interaction between the organization and other actors (Grau, 2013). This includes marketing research, segmentation, developing a marketing mix, branding, promotion and advertising. Technology has added much to the research and segmentation arena. Large pre-collected datasets allow research on potential consumers and supporters at a minute level. Branding and promotion use many types of technology, including email, social networking, video, image sharing and so forth (see Chapter 25 by Jane Hudson, this volume; Fletcher & Lee, 2012; Kanter & Fine, 2010). All of the Web 1.0 Internet technologies (websites, email) are useful in this regard.

The relationship features of social media/Web 2.0 technologies have come into their own in nonprofit marketing, providing a range of effective tools to engage constituencies (see Guo & Saxton, 2018; Dumont, 2013a, 2013b; Kanter & Fine, 2010). Many nonprofit organizations have Facebook and Twitter accounts and some have multiple accounts. Instagram and YouTube are popular in the sector and are often integrated with other parts of the social media arsenal.

This capacity often comes at a cost of message control for nonprofit administrators (Wright & Hinson, 2008; Kanter & Fine, 2010). Allowing people to participate on your organization's website can be risky. The extensive use of social media by citizen groups (McNutt, 2018) and individuals is a nightmare for many organizations and nonprofits are no exception (Crijns, Cauberghe, Hudders & Claeys, 2017; Jordan, Upright & Tice-Owens, 2016). Reputation is an important asset and public trust can be destroyed by a tweet, post or video that raises questions about a nonprofit's worth. This requires a plan for crisis management in the event that such an attack occurs.

The actual effects of social media on relevant nonprofit metrics are still soft. Social media metrics provide a great deal of information about impacts in the social media space but less in how that relates to things like community support and trust. What "Likes" actually translate into in terms of tangible effects remains unsettled in the literature.

Advocacy

Advocacy is a central function of the nonprofit sector, both to defend the sector and to advocate for those who cannot defend themselves (McNutt & Goldkind, 2018; McNutt, 2018). Advocacy is also an area where technology has made and will continue to make considerable contributions. Advocacy is hard work and the results are not always certain. In the 1980s, advocates began to turn to technology to help in their work (Wittig & Schmitz, 1996; Yerxa & Moll, 1994).

These were basic technologies with pre-Internet networking. This changed with the development of the Internet and more capable technology. Advocates began to use websites and online videos in their advocacy work and political campaign technology became infused into nonprofit advocacy work. The development of Web 2.0 signaled a sea change in nonprofit advocacy efforts in specific and political campaigning in general (Guo & Saxton, 2014). Howard Dean's run for the Democratic presidential nomination in 2004 demonstrated that a political campaign that used technology and allowed considerable participation and a lack of message control could be workable (Teachout & Streeter, 2008). Prior to 2004, it was assumed that the campaign would control the message and that deviations to the message, even by the candidate, were not allowed. That is incompatible with the use of Web 2.0 technology. Dean's campaign manager, Joe Trippi (2004) designed a campaign that violated the assumption of message control. While Dean eventually lost, his innovations changed not only electoral campaigns but also issue advocacy campaigns as well. Most modern advocacy campaigns use social media/Web 2.0 tools like Facebook, Twitter and YouTube. Many use a comprehensive advocacy system. Wireless apps are also popular. These are applications that work with a mobile telephone and provide information or some other capacity to support a political process such as Getting Out the Vote. In addition, a lot of older technology is used. Email is still very popular as are static websites. All of this is integrated with the organization's traditional advocacy techniques. Technology often supports traditional organizing and lobbying.

This is another area where use of data becomes important (McNutt & Goldkind, 2018). Information is a key to advocacy success (especially lobbying) and many advocacy organizations conduct their own research (McNutt, Justice & Carter, 2014). Emerging data science tools (McNutt, Justice & Barlow, 2017) and technologies like Geographic Information Systems (Bishop, 2010) interface well with the needs of advocates. The rise of political microtargeting allows individual constituent wants and needs to be understood at very granular level. This allows very specific messages based on a person's interests or needs. The controversy over the role of Cambridge Analytica in the 2016 election is an aspect of the political campaign's quest for data.

Fundraising

Few will deny that fundraising is crucial to nonprofit organizations and managers. Fundraising includes major gifts, federation fundraising, special events, grassroots fundraising, planned giving, grants and contracts and a variety of other solicitation techniques. Technology can greatly assist the conduct of all these processes. The Internet has added a number of online techniques that are proving their worth (Adler & Carpenter, 2015; Castillo, Petrie & Wardell, 2014; Mansfield, 2014; Saxton & Wang, 2014; Shier & Handy, 2012; Davis & Moscato, 2018).

Fundamentally, what technology does in support of fundraising falls into three areas. First, it provides information for traditional fundraising tools. The technology-backed fundraising tools that make grant research and prospect research possible are an example. They not only automate a time-intensive process; they allow for the extension of traditional sources of information far beyond what was previously available. Any nonprofit professional who has done this type of research the manual way will appreciate how much easier these new tools make their work. The vast amount of additional online data can create databases on prospects that were impossible to obtain in the past. Along this vein, we can understand the impact of our efforts more clearly by the data that we extract from the process. This is an area where data science is beginning to make substantial contributions and the potential for development is considerable (Nandeshwar & Devine, 2018).

Second, they can automate the interactive aspects of fundraising. Mundane technology such as project management software, databases, social networking sites, online calendars and even the lowly email can make fundraising easier and more successful. This means changing very little in traditional methods but reaping the benefits of new tools.

Third, there are the tools that rely on technology (Grobman, 2006). This seems to have developed in three stages, although earlier technologies are still successful. Early approaches used website-based donation systems, online wish lists (where the organization advertised for traditional donations of needed items) and email-based fundraising. These are still popular tools today. Next, charity malls and shop-for-a-cause systems emerged. *Charity malls* are websites that include appeals from many organizations and *Shop for a Cause* allows charities to advertise supporting merchants and obtain a donation for everyone who clicks through to the vendor's e-commerce site. The developing relationship between e-commerce and fundraising is fascinating and can yield some exciting developments. The last stage occurs when Web 2.0 technologies emerged on the scene (Saxton & Wang, 2014). Most of the social networking sites allow for donations and there are a number of nonprofit-related sites that provide dedicated fundraising services. Crowdfunding systems are a growing force in nonprofit funding, especially for international and domestic emergencies (Stiver, Barroca, Minocha, Richards & Roberts, 2015). Text-to-give or SMS-based fundraising has grown substantially and there are a number of mobile apps that facilitate fundraising. Peer-to-peer fundraising is another promising area that is likely to grow (Adler & Carpenter, 2015).

Fundraising is an activity that is based on trust and transparency (Lee & Joseph, 2013; Dumont, 2013a). Online systems such as Candid, formerly Guidestar (www.guidestar.org), and Charity Navigator (www.charitynavigator.org/) allow donors to validate the claims on charities before they give. These sites provide a substantial amount of information about nonprofit organizations seeking funding. To the extent that fear and uncertainty are discouraging giving, this type of system is immediately valuable.

Volunteer recruitment and management

Many nonprofit organizations depend on volunteers for everything from menial tasks to board members. Those organizations that are serious about using volunteers intelligently will find technology a useful friend. Volunteer recruiting can be conducted on the organization's own website or on third party sites like volunteermatch.org. The use of virtual volunteers (Liu, Harrison, Lai, Chikoto & Jones-Lungo, 2016) and episodic volunteers is made possible by technology (Cravens, 2006). These types of volunteers have been used in efforts throughout the world. Finally, technology tools can make the management of volunteers more successful. It might also help in committing volunteers to an organization (Emrich & Pierdzioch, 2016).

Technology has made great strides in managing nonprofit organizations. The contributions are undeniable and few serious managers will doubt its importance. The next section will examine how technology itself is managed.

Managing, selecting and implementing technology

In order to be successful, technology must be properly managed. This requires planning, budgeting, handling resistance, creating a change strategy, staffing the technology and evaluating and monitoring the results. While this needs to be integrated with the organization's overall work, part of it should be dedicated to the technology effort.

Planning and budgeting

Planning is part of good management and it makes having a successful program more certain (Podolsky, 2003). Having a dedicated technology plan and a dedicated technology budget is thought to lead to better technology outcomes. In most organizations, technology is seen as a supplement to the main activity which can lead to the organization ignoring its technology needs when funds are tight. Having a separate plan and a separate budget means that the organization will at least acknowledge technology's stake in the overall enterprise.

Resistance to technology and the change strategy

Not everyone is likely to embrace technology fully. Resistance can occur for an entire range of reasons, some of them rational and others not. Popular reasons for resisting technology include skill anxiety, time constraints, feelings that technology leads to depersonalization, job loss worry, costs and so forth. In order to overcome this resistance, a change strategy is needed. One popular strategy is Diffusion of Innovation (DOI) theory (Rogers, 2003; Robinson, Swan & Newell, 1996; Strang & Soule, 1998). In DOI theory, an innovation is introduced by a change agent into a system. The innovation is communicated via networks to various population groups. In Rogers' (2003) formulation, the population groups (ordered by ease of adoption) are innovators, early adopters, early majority, late majority and laggards. Each successive group brings in the next group. Different innovation characteristics determine if and how quickly an innovation is adopted. These characteristics include compatibility, complexity, trialability, comparative advantage and observability. Rogers (2003) also talks about opinion leaders who support and encourage the adoption of the innovations. Adoption rates start out slow until they reach critical mass, and after reaching critical mass the process accelerates. This process is called the S curve. Diffusion of Innovation theory is amply supported by social science findings, but it does have its detractors as well.

Staffing technology

Training and technical support are essential elements of a workable technology enterprise. If workers cannot use technology or it does not work, it is useless to the organization. Most organizations will staff their technology needs with their own employees. Some are trained for the work and others are "accidental techies." Consultants and volunteers can also provide assistance. Efforts like Code for America (www.codeforamerica.org) can provide organizations, whether governmental or nonprofit, with a trained technologist. In some cases, technology help is provided by third parties. Early on, there was a group of nonprofit technology consultants called circuit riders (McInerney, 2007) who provided technology help to nonprofits. Additionally, Application Service Providers (ASP) provide a means for nonprofits to outsource their entire technology systems. Finally, civic hacking and civic hackathons (McNutt & Justice, 2016) can provide organizations with some of the technology help that they need. Organizations must realize that training and technical support should be major parts of their technology budget.

Evaluating technology

Evaluation assures that technology is working, meeting the needs of the organization and its constituencies. Different techniques can assure that the proper information is collected and that the analysis informs management.

Managing technology in a nonprofit organization is critical to a well-functioning organization. Planning, budgeting, a sensible change strategy, proper staffing and ongoing evaluation are important aspects of technology management.

What is ahead for nonprofit technology?

Exciting things are happening in the technology world of nonprofits and more can be expected in the future. There are three major streams in this future: the technology, the social constructs surrounding the technology and the emerging nonprofit technology partnership. There is little question that technology will become more capable. It will also become more diverse and many of the things that will become possible will seem like magic. The growth of smaller and more friendly technology units is also inevitable.

The social constructions that surround technology will change. The Open Civic Data and Civic Technology movements (McNutt et al., 2016) will provide new models for how nonprofits can work with the community and the other sectors through technology. Innovations like civic hacking and the growth of civic hackathons (McNutt & Justice, 2016) will be great assets for the sector both in terms of instrumental assistance for individual nonprofits and creating opportunities for serving communities.

Finally, more and more nonprofits will find the virtual form optimal. They will be able to use new tools to pursue their mission without the burden (and costs) of bricks and mortar facilities. Having a physical space has many consequences that often push the organization away from its mission. The times are changing. Technology will be part of a nonprofit renaissance. New tools and newer capacities will make it possible, but nonprofits need to fully embrace it.

Bibliography

Adler, S., & Carpenter, H. (2015). Peer-to-peer fundraising success: Paws with a Cause®. In *Cases on Strategic Social Media Utilization in the Nonprofit Sector* (pp. 24–64). Hershey, PA: IGI Global.

Bennett, G.G., & Glasgow, R.E. (2009). The delivery of public health interventions via the Internet: Actualizing their potential. *Annual Review of Public Health, 30*, 273–292.

Bishop, S.W. (2010). Building programmatic capacity at the grassroots level: The reactions of local nonprofit organizations to public participation geographic information systems. *Nonprofit and Voluntary Sector Quarterly, 39*(6), 991–1013.

Boland, K.M., & McNutt, J.G. (2013). Assessing e-government success strategies using Internet search data. In Gil Garcia, R. (Ed.), *E-Government Success Factors and Measures: Theories, Concepts, and Methodologies.* Harrisburg, PA: IGI Books.

Brainard, L., Boland, K., & McNutt, J.G. (2012). The advent of technology enhanced leaderless transnational social movement organizations: Implications for transnational advocacy. Paper read at the ARNOVA Meeting, Indianapolis, IN, November 15–17.

Burt, E., & Taylor, J.A. (2000). Information and communication technologies: Reshaping voluntary organizations? *Nonprofit Management and Leadership, 11*(2), 131–143.

Burt, E., & Taylor, J. (2003). New technologies, embedded values, and strategic change: Evidence from the UK voluntary sector. *Nonprofit and Voluntary Sector Quarterly, 32*(1), 115–127.

Cascio, W.F., & Montealegre, R. (2016). How technology is changing work and organizations. *Annual Review of Organizational Psychology and Organizational Behavior, 3*, 349–375.

Castillo, M., Petrie, R., & Wardell, C. (2014). Fundraising through online social networks: A field experiment on peer-to-peer solicitation. *Journal of Public Economics, 114*, 29–35.

Cortes, M., & Rafter, K (Eds.). (2007). *Information Technology Adoption in the Nonprofit Sector.* Chicago: Lyceum Books.

Cravens, J. (2006). Involving international online volunteers: Factors for success, organizational benefits, and new views of community. *International Journal of Volunteer Administration, 24*(1), 15–23.

Crijns, H., Cauberghe, V., Hudders, L., & Claeys, A.S. (2017). How to deal with online consumer comments during a crisis? The impact of personalized organizational responses on organizational reputation. *Computers in Human Behavior, 75*, 619–631.

Davis, D.Z., & Moscato, D. (2018). The philanthropic avatar: An analysis of fundraising in virtual worlds through the lens of social capital. *International Journal of Strategic Communication*, 1–19.

Drouin, M., O'Connor, K.W., Schmidt, G.B., & Miller, D.A. (2015). Facebook fired: Legal perspectives and young adults' opinions on the use of social media in hiring and firing decisions. *Computers in Human Behavior, 46*, 123–128.

Downing, J.D. (1989). Computers for political change: PeaceNet and public data access. *Journal of Communication, 39*(3), 154–162.

Dumont, G.E. (2013a). Nonprofit virtual accountability an index and its application. *Nonprofit and Voluntary Sector Quarterly, 42*(5), 1049–1067.

Dumont, G.E. (2013b). Transparency or accountability? The purpose of online technologies for nonprofits. *International Review of Public Administration, 18*(3), 7–29.

Earl, J., & Kimport, K. (2011). *Digitally Enabled Social Change.* Cambridge, MA: MIT Press.

Emrich, E., & Pierdzioch, C. (2016). The Internet and the commitment of volunteers: Empirical evidence for the Red Cross. *Nonprofit and Voluntary Sector Quarterly, 45*(5), 1013–1030.

Fay, M.J. (2017). Telework. In Scott, C.R. et al. (Eds.), *The International Encyclopedia of Organizational Communication.* New York: Wiley.

Finn, S., Maher, J.K., & Forster, J. (2006). Indicators of information and communication technology adoption in the nonprofit sector: Changes between 2000 and 2004. *Nonprofit Management and Leadership, 16*(3), 277–295.

Fletcher, A., & Lee, M.J. (2012). Current social media uses and evaluations in American museums. *Museum Management and Curatorship, 27*(5), 505–521.

Geller, S.L., Abramson, A.J., & de Leon, E. (2010). *The Nonprofit Technology Gap – Myth or Reality.* Listening Post Project, 20.

Goldkind, L. & McNutt, J.G. (2014). Social media & social change: Nonprofits and using social media strategies to meet advocacy goals. In A.M. Lucia-Casademunt & J.A. Ariza-Montes (Eds.), *Information Communication Technologies (ICT) Management in Non-profit Organization.* Hershey, PA: IGI Global.

Grau, S. (2013). *Marketing for Nonprofit Organizations: Insights and Innovation.* Chicago: Lyceum Books

Greenwood, S., Perrin, A. & Duggan, M. (2016). Social media update 2016: Facebook usage and engagement is on the rise, while adoption of other platforms holds steady. Washington, DC: Pew Internet and American Life Project. www.pewinternet.org/2016/11/11/social-media-update-2016/

Grobman, G. (2006). *Fundraising Online: Using the Internet to Raise Serious Money for Your Nonprofit Organization.* Harrisburg, PA: White Hat Communications.

Guo, C., & Saxton, G.D. (2014). Tweeting social change: How social media are changing nonprofit advocacy. *Nonprofit and Voluntary Sector Quarterly, 43* (1), 57–79. 0899764012471585.

Guo, C., & Saxton, G.D. (2018). Speaking and being heard: How nonprofit advocacy organizations gain attention on social media. *Nonprofit and Voluntary Sector Quarterly, 47*, 1.

Hafner, K. & Lyon, M. (1996). *Where Wizards Stay Up Late: The Origins of the Internet.* New York: Simon & Schuster.

Hamann, D.J., & Bezboruah, K.C. (2013). Utilization of technology by long-term care providers: Comparisons between for-profit and nonprofit institutions. *Journal of Aging and Health, 25*(4), 535–554.

Hendler, J. (2009). Web 3.0 emerging. *Computer, 42*(1), 111–113.

Harrison, Y.D., & Murray, V. (2015). The effect of an online self-assessment tool on nonprofit board performance. *Nonprofit and Voluntary Sector Quarterly, 44*(6), 1129–1151.

Hoy, M.G., & Phelps, J. (2009). Online privacy and security practices of the 100 largest US nonprofit organizations. *International Journal of Nonprofit and Voluntary Sector Marketing, 14*(1), 71–82.

Hurley, T.A., & Green, C.W. (2005). Knowledge management and the nonprofit industry: A within and between approach. *Journal of Knowledge Management Practice, 6*(1), 1–10.

Imboden, T.R., Phillips, J.N., Seib, J.D., & Fiorentino, S.R. (2013). How are nonprofit organizations influenced to create and adopt information security policies. *Issues in Information Systems, 14*(2), 166–173.

Jordan, T.A., Upright, P., & Tice-Owens, K. (2016). Crisis management in nonprofit organizations: A case study of crisis communication and planning. *Journal of Nonprofit Education and Leadership, 6*(2).

Kanter, B., & Fine, A. (2010). *The Networked Nonprofit: Connecting with Social Media to Drive Change.* San Francisco: John Wiley.

Kirkman, B.L., Gibson, C.B., & Kim, K. (2012). Across borders and technologies: Advancements in virtual teams research. In *The Oxford Handbook of Organizational Psychology, Volume 2.* Edited by Steve W.J. Kozlowski. New York: Oxford University Press.

Krueger, J.C., & Haytko, D.L. (2015). Nonprofit adaptation to Web 2.0 and digital marketing strategies. *Journal of Technology Research, 6*, 1.

Lee, R.L., & Joseph, R.C. (2013). An examination of web disclosure and organizational transparency. *Computers in Human Behavior, 29*(6), 2218–2224.

Liu, H.K., Harrison, Y.D., Lai, J.J., Chikoto, G.L., & Jones-Lungo, K. (2016). Online and virtual volunteering. In Smith, D.H., Stebbins, R., & Grotz, J. (Eds.), *The Palgrave Handbook of Volunteering, Civic Participation, and Nonprofit Associations* (pp. 290–310). London: Palgrave Macmillan.

Mann, G., & Sahuguet, A. (2018). With great data comes great responsibility: How data science can be applied to solve public interest problems without losing its soul. *Journal of Technology in Human Services, 36*(1), 1–7.

Mansfield, H. (2014). *Mobile for Good: A How-To Fundraising Guide for Nonprofits*. McGraw Hill Professional.

Massa, F.G. (2016). Guardians of the Internet: Building and sustaining the anonymous online community. *Organization Studies, 38*, 7.

McInerney, P.B. (2007). Geeks for good: Technology evangelism and the role of circuit riders in IT adoption among nonprofits. *Nonprofits and technology: Emerging research for usable knowledge,* 148–162.

McKeever, B., Greene, S., MacDonald, G., Tatian, P. & Jones, D. (2018). *Data Philanthropy: Unlocking the Power of Private Data for Public Good*. Washington, DC: Urban Institute.

McNutt, J.G. (Ed.). (2018). *Technology, Activism and Social Justice*. London: Oxford University Press.

McNutt, J.G., Adler, G., Jones, J. & Menon, G.M. (2006). The cyber commons responds to a major disaster: A study of on-line volunteers in the face of a natural disaster. Paper presented at the 35th Annual ARNOVA Conference, Chicago, IL, November.

McNutt, J.G. & Menon, G.M. (2008). Cyberactivism and progressive human services. *Families and Society, 89* (1), 33–38.

McNutt, J.G. & Barlow, J. (2012). A longitudinal study of political technology use by nonprofit child advocacy organizations. In Manoharan, A. & Holtzer, M. (Eds.), *E-Governance and Civic Engagement: Factors and Determinants of E-Democracy*. Harrisburg, PA: IGI Books.

McNutt, J.G., Justice, J. & Carter, D. (2014). Examining intersections between open government and nonprofit advocacy: Theoretical and empirical perspectives about an emerging relationship. Paper read at International Research Society for Public Management Conference, Ottawa, Canada.

McNutt, J.G., Brainard, L., Zeng, Y., & Kovacic, P. (2016). Information and technology for associations. In Smith, D.H., Stebbins, R., & Grotz, J. (Eds.), *Palgrave Handbook of Volunteering, Civic Participation, and Nonprofit Associations*. London: Palgrave Macmillan.

McNutt, J.G. & Justice, J.B. (2016). Predicting civic hackathons in local communities: Perspectives from social capital and creative class theory. Paper read at the 12th International Society for Third Sector Research Conference, Ersta Skondal University College, Stockholm, Sweden, June 28–July 1.

McNutt, J.G., Justice, J.B., Melitski, M.J., Ahn, M.J., Siddiqui, S., Carter, D.T., & Kline, A.D. (2016). The diffusion of civic technology and open government in the United States. *Information Polity 21*: 153–170.

McNutt, J.G., Justice, J.B., & Barlow, J. (2017). Fun with numbers: Data in the service of political action and advocacy in smart communities. Presentation for the Eighth annual Northeast Conference on Public Administration (NECoPA), Public Administration, Policy and Community Development: Managing a Changing Landscape. University of Vermont, Burlington, VT November.

McNutt, J.G., & Goldkind, L. (2018). E-activism: Development and growth. In Mehdi Khosrow-Pour (Ed.), *Encyclopedia of Information Science and Technology* (4th Ed.). Hershey, PA: IGI Global. DOI: 10.4018/978-1-5225-2255-3.ch310

McNutt, J.G., Guo, C., Goldkind, L., & An, S. (2018). Technology in nonprofit organizations and voluntary action. *Voluntaristics Review, 3*(1) 1–63.

McNutt, J.G., & Barlow, J. (2019). Data Science use by state level child advocacy organizations. Paper read at 48th Annual ARNOVA Conference: Nonprofits and Philanthropy in a Polarized World: Speaking Truth to Power and Using Power to Speak Truth, San Diego, CA, November.

Miller, P.B. (2013). *From the digital divide to digital inclusion and beyond: Update on telecentres and community technology centers* (CTCs). Available at SSRN 2241167.

M+R (2017). *Benchmarks 2017*. Washington, DC: Author http://mrbenchmarks.com/

Nandeshwar, A.R., & Devine, R. (2018). *Data Science for Fundraising: Build Data-Driven Solutions Using R*. Las Vegas: Data Insight Partners.

Oldenburg, B., Taylor, C.B., O'Neil, A., Cocker, F., & Cameron, L.D. (2015). Using new technologies to improve the prevention and management of chronic conditions in populations. *Annual Review of Public Health, 36*, 483–505.

O'Reilly, T. (2005). *Web 2.0: Compact definition?* Message posted to http://radar.oreilly.com/2005/10/web-20-compact-definition.html

O'Reilly, T. (2007). What is Web 2.0: Design patterns and business models for the next generation of software. *Communications and Strategies, 65*(1), 17–37.

Podolsky, J. (2003). *Wired for Good: Strategic Technology Planning for Nonprofits.* New York: John Wiley.

Princeton Survey Research Associates (2001). *Wired, Willing and Ready: Nonprofit Human Services Organizations' Adoption of Information Technology.* Washington, DC: Independent Sector & Cisco Systems.

Reddick, C.G., & Ponomariov, B. (2013). The effect of individuals' organization affiliation on their Internet donations. *Nonprofit and Voluntary Sector Quarterly, 42*(6), 1197–1223.

Robinson, M., Swan, J., & Newell, S. (1996). The role of networks in the diffusion of technological innovation. *Journal of Management Studies, 33*(3), 333–359.

Rogers, E. (2003). *Diffusion of Innovations* (5th Edition). New York: Free Press.

Saxton, G.D., & Wang, L. (2014). The social network effect: The determinants of giving through social media. *Nonprofit and Voluntary Sector Quarterly, 43*(5), 850–868.

Schuler, D. (1996). *New Community Networks: Wired for Change.* Reading, MA: Addison-Wesley.

Shier, M.L., & Handy, F. (2012). Understanding online donor behavior: The role of donor characteristics, perceptions of the Internet, website and program, and influence from social networks. *International Journal of Nonprofit and Voluntary Sector Marketing, 17*(3), 219–230.

Smith, A., Schlozman, K., Verba, S., & Brady, H. (2009). *The Internet and Civic Engagement.* Washington, DC. PEW Internet and American Life Projects. Retrieved from www.pewinternet.org/Reports/2009/15--The-Internet-and-Civic-Engagement.aspx

Stiver, A., Barroca, L., Minocha, S., Richards, M., & Roberts, D. (2015). Civic crowdfunding research: Challenges, opportunities, and future agenda. *New Media & Society, 17*(2), 249–271.

Strang, D., & Soule, S.A. (1998). Diffusion in organizations and social movements: From hybrid corn to poison pills. *Annual Review of Sociology, 22*(1), 265–291.

Teachout, Z., & Streeter, T. (Eds.). (2008). *Mousepads, Shoeleather and Hope.* Boulder, CO: Paradigm Publishers.

Toepler, S., & Wyszomirski, M. (2012). Arts and culture. In Salamon, L. *The State of Nonprofit America.* 2nd ed. (pp. 229–265). Washington, DC: Brookings Institution Press.

Trippi, J. (2004). *The Revolution Will Not Be Televised: Democracy, the Internet and the Overthrow of Everything.* New York: Reagan Book/Harper Collins.

Wittig, M.A., & Schmitz, J. (1996). Electronic grassroots organizing. *Journal of Social Issues, 52*(1), 53–69.

Wright, D.K., & Hinson, M.D. (2008). How blogs and social media are changing public relations and the way it is practiced. *Public Relations Journal, 2*(2), 1–21.

Yerxa, S.W., & Moll, M. (1994). Notes from the grassroots: On-line lobbying in Canada. *Internet Research, 4*(4), 9–19.

18

NONPROFIT HUMAN RESOURCE MANAGEMENT

Allison R. Russell

POSTDOCTORAL FELLOW, SCHOOL OF SOCIAL POLICY AND PRACTICE, UNIVERSITY
OF PENNSYLVANIA, PHILADELPHIA, PA, USA

Marlene Walk

ASSISTANT PROFESSOR, PAUL H. O'NEILL SCHOOL OF PUBLIC AND ENVIRONMENTAL
AFFAIRS, INDIANA UNIVERSITY-PURDUE UNIVERSITY, INDIANAPOLIS, IN, USA

Femida Handy

PROFESSOR AND DIRECTOR, PHD PROGRAM IN SOCIAL WELFARE, SCHOOL OF SOCIAL
POLICY AND PRACTICE, UNIVERSITY OF PENNSYLVANIA, PHILADELPHIA, PA, USA

Introduction

Human resource management (HRM) once referred solely to the management of paid staff in for-profit organizations. However, with the growth of the nonprofit sector around the world, HRM is now widely applied to nonprofit organizations as well, where their unique organizational characteristics often challenge traditional assumptions and make the direct application of "best practices" from the for-profit world difficult, if not impossible.

Nevertheless, as both for-profit and nonprofit employees need to be recruited, compensated, motivated, engaged, and retained to meet organizational goals, nonprofit HRM has borrowed from the classical HRM literature in the for-profit context. Hence, the nonprofit literature on managing its paid and unpaid workers has addressed the uniqueness of (1) the organizational form (mission-driven with multiple funding sources and subject to a non-distribution constraint) and (2) its workers (particularly, the unpaid workers who cannot be incentivized by wages – see Chapter 19 by Hager and Renfro in this volume).

For example, HR practices of nonprofit organizations, unlike those of their for-profit counterparts, often involve a partnership between paid staff and volunteers. This partnership is referred to as co-production (Brudney 1990; Brudney & England 1983; see Chapter 20 by Brandsen, Steen & Verschuere in this volume) and has been investigated in both the public and nonprofit sector contexts (e.g., Verschuere, Brandsen & Pestoff 2012; Paarlberg & Gen 2009). The managerial challenges involved with co-production include resolving incompatible priorities of paid and unpaid workers and instituting different measures for quality control and risk management. Depending on the specific structure of volunteer and paid employee work tasks, as well as the degree of interchangeability between paid and unpaid workers (e.g., Handy,

Mook & Quarter 2008), HR management of paid staff and volunteers will either overlap or be distinct when tasks are not easily exchanged. In large organizations, such as hospitals, the management of paid and unpaid workers is differentiated by having two separate departments (Handy & Srinivasan 2005). Managing paid and unpaid workers in the same organization can be harmonious or discordant, depending on the nature of the tasks subject to interchange between the two, the frequency of interchange, and employee perceptions. Combined with the mission-driven nature of nonprofits and the reality that people are often the nonprofit's only organizational resource, these characteristics of nonprofit organizations often challenge many assumptions derived from traditional HRM.

Undoubtedly, HRM is a broad and complex subject, in which the "best answers" to questions about managing personnel and resources will vary from organization to organization, especially given the diversity of the nonprofit sector. In an effort to provide a survey of the subject as it relates to the nonprofit context, we focus the present chapter on two broad aspects of nonprofit HRM: emerging research trends and unique challenges. We have already introduced one of the biggest challenges of nonprofit HRM: the composition of the nonprofit workforce (for more extensive coverage on the topic of volunteer management, please see Chapter 19 by Hager and Renfro, this volume). We next move to a discussion of recent trends in nonprofit HRM research, with a focus on recent nonprofit HRM research in non-western and international contexts.

In the next section, we cover the unique challenges of HRM in nonprofits. We first explore how potential job-seekers choose the sector for employment. If nonprofit workers exercise sector choice in seeking employment with mission-driven organizations whose values align with their own, then the creation and implementation of nonprofit HR policies will be significantly different than in other sectors. While governance and HRM are different categories, we briefly examine how an all-volunteer board creates HRM policies and what role it plays in HRM decisions. We also examine the impact of the recent call in the nonprofit sector for greater accountability on the formation of codes of ethics and on the relationship between ethical considerations and HRM. Finally, we conclude with the future of nonprofit HRM research, including a brief word on the intriguing challenge HRM faces with the aging out of volunteers.

Trends in nonprofit HRM research

Strategic HRM

As the nonprofit sector grows in size and importance, scholars continue to explore if public and private sector HRM can be effectively applied to the nonprofit context. One promising direction is strategic HRM (SHRM). According to Guo and colleagues (2011), "Strategic HRM integrates HRM practices with the strategic purposes of the organization" (249). Guo et al. (2011: 256) developed a list of 13 SHRM practices, which includes providing competitive compensation packages and opportunities for professional development; using targeted recruitment strategies; and seeking employees whose values align with those of the organization and its mission. Unlike other HRM approaches, SHRM produces HR practices that can be applied to questions of organizational strategy and long-term goals, providing a link between the organization's mission and its performance (Akingbola 2013). With its strong emphasis on employee performance and strategic development (Ridder, Piening & Baluch 2012), SHRM has emerged as an attractive option for many nonprofits looking to develop or improve their HRM practices.

Because nonprofits are able to attract employees who are drawn to the mission of the organization (Handy & Katz 1998; Hansmann 1980), nonprofit employees have a high level of commitment to achieving the goals of the organization (Kim 2005; Light 2002). This commitment emphasizes the social and psychological contract between an employee and a nonprofit. Based on this assumption, Akingbola (2013) presents a model for the determinants of strategic HRM in nonprofits, noting that the implementation of SHRM depends on the number of external funders and related financial constraints, competencies of employees and managers, and other factors. According to Akingbola (2013), the underlying focus of SHRM is how the nonprofit "manages the effects of the interactions and processes between social mission, multiple institutional relationships and social legitimacy with internal operational efficiency" (77). Because of the degree of diversity among different organizations in the sector, Akingbola (2013) does not present a one-size-fits-all definition for SHRM, but instead illustrates how SHRM may emerge and evolve in nonprofit organizations, given a variety of different contexts and characteristics.

Despite the promise of SHRM for nonprofit organizations, many factors influence their ability to implement such strategies effectively. For instance, Guo and colleagues (2011) found that the size of the nonprofit, its affiliation with a national organization, its dependence on contractors, and the extent to which the information technologies have been implemented all impact organizations' adoption of SHRM practices. In terms of paid and unpaid workers, the authors found that organizations with more paid staff tended to adopt SHRM strategies to a greater extent, while organizations with a greater level of dependence on volunteer labor had a different approach to SHRM (Guo et al., 2011). Akinlade and Shalack (2016) also highlight the importance of volunteer labor in the SHRM equation, arguing that SHRM practices should be linked to strategies of volunteer retention and recruitment to maximize effectiveness. Similarly, Rogers, Jiang, Rogers, and Intindola (2016) characterize various well-known volunteer management practices as important components of SHRM, especially in organizations with large, institutionalized volunteer programs (e.g., hospitals). Finally, Walk, Schinnenburg, and Handy (2014) note the importance of seeking employee perspectives on strategic HR practices, a critical but at times underutilized facet of strategic HRM for nonprofits. All in all, nonprofit organizations looking to implement SHRM should consider not only their organization's size and available resources but also the composition of their workforce and the perceptions of their workers, as all of these factors can influence the suitability, form, and long-term effectiveness of SHRM strategies.

Nonprofit HRM in international contexts

Despite the growth of the nonprofit sector around the world, much of the literature on nonprofit human resource management is based in the United States or other Western contexts (Bartram, Cavanagh & Hoye 2017). While journals like the *International Journal of Human Resource Management* and *Human Resource Development International* broadly highlight international trends in HRM, there is a need for researchers and practitioners alike to focus more explicitly on HRM in the international nonprofit and nongovernmental sector. Increasingly, HRM research explores development and implementation of HR practices at not only locally based nonprofit organizations in many countries but also in international NGOs (INGOs), that may be based in one country but do work in one or more other countries. In the latter case in particular, the challenges around managing both paid staff and volunteers are often amplified by cultural and linguistic differences.

Thus, the exploration of international trends in this area is particularly important because the unique social and cultural elements of different countries and regions will impact the design and implementation of HRM practices. Below we highlight some recent findings from research on nonprofit HRM in international contexts, looking particularly at research on HRM in non-western countries in which the local nonprofit sectors are emerging and developing.

Middle East

The nonprofit sector remains small in the Middle East, but it has been characterized as "emerging" by civil society theorists and nonprofit scholars (e.g., Casey 2016). As the sector continues to develop in this region, we can expect an increase in the number of research studies on nonprofit HRM in Middle Eastern nations, as scholars and practitioners begin to address HRM challenges of developing nonprofits.

One recent paper by Yassine and Zein (2016) points to the dearth of research on nonprofit HRM in the Middle East and identifies discrepancies in HRM practices and effectiveness between the fledgling nonprofit sector and the more established public and private sectors. Using survey data from 510 Lebanese employees, the authors compare employee development, job satisfaction, and retention between workers in the private and nonprofit sectors. Their findings indicate higher scores on these three measures among the private sector employees as compared to their nonprofit sector counterparts, suggesting that a greater emphasis on development and implementation of HR practices, tailored specifically to nonprofit sector employees, is needed. An examination of the role of volunteers or the interaction of volunteers and paid staff within nonprofit organizations was beyond the scope of this study.

In examining the impact of inter-organizational collaboration on HR capacity in Lebanese nonprofits, AbouAssi and Jo (2017) investigate one possible means of addressing the shortcomings of HRM in the Middle Eastern context. They find that "partnerships generally may enhance an organization's human resource capacity" (696). Thus, engagement with other organizations, both within and outside the nonprofit sector, may lead to increased HR capacity, including ability to hire more paid staff and to provide better opportunities for professional development of staff. However, the authors caution that collaboration alone, without a strong commitment to HRM, may lead to greater costs, especially those associated with managing new partnerships that nonprofits are not equipped to handle. Unlike Yassine and Zein (2016), AbouAssi and Jo (2017) expand the scope of their work to include not only paid staff but also volunteers, who represent a critical component of HR capacity in many nonprofits.

Asia

Despite the growth of the nonprofit sector in Asia, HRM research continues to focus on public and private organizations, whereas articles examining HRM practices in locally based nonprofits appear far less frequently. Two recent articles on HRM in Asian nonprofits, Chang and colleagues (2015) and Park and Kim (2016), simultaneously highlight the lack of formalized HRM strategies in small, local nonprofits in Asia and the importance of addressing this challenge. Both studies focus on HRM as it pertains to paid staff through such mechanisms as employee training opportunities, performance, and motivations.

Chang and colleagues (2015) investigate employee training programs in Taiwanese nonprofit organizations. According to the authors, in the emerging Taiwanese nonprofit sector, the vast majority of nonprofit organizations have only 10 employees or fewer, creating an environment in which more formalized HRM strategies may not be possible or practical. The authors find that the small Taiwanese nonprofits included in their study utilize several strategies for overcoming size and resource limitations, including increased use of on-the-job approaches to employee training and greater employee autonomy in devising and undertaking new learning opportunities. The authors conclude by noting that more flexible employee training and learning approaches may be better suited to small, developing nonprofits than the more traditional, formalized approaches espoused in the broader HRM literature.

Park and Kim (2016) examine the role of HRM in utilizing and encouraging public service motivation (PSM) in Korean nonprofit organizations. For instance, they find that both human resource development and performance management systems can positively influence perceptions of person–organization fit, which in turn leads to enhanced nonprofit PSM, i.e., employees' intrinsic motivations in the workplace. They also report that higher levels of nonprofit PSM were associated with improved accountability among employees, ultimately suggesting that HRM strategies can foster not only greater intrinsic motivation but also improved accountability. As in Chang and colleagues (2015), the authors emphasize the importance of these findings in the context of small, developing nonprofit organizations.

Human resource management in INGOs

Because of their complexity and size, INGOs face unique HRM challenges. INGOs often are headquartered in one country but complete projects and conduct operations in one or more other countries around the world. As such, they typically have a large number of employees, both in their home countries and around the world, including paid and unpaid workers with a wide range of skills and backgrounds (Oelberger, Fechter & McWha-Hermann 2017). In the realm of international HRM, we would expect INGO practices to differ quite a lot from the small, developing, locally based nonprofit organizations described by the authors cited previously.

Again, the study of international HRM remains largely rooted in the context of private sector organizations, or multinational corporations/enterprises, rather than in the context of INGOs, but many have called for greater consideration of INGOs and the organizational factors that set them apart from private sector organizations (e.g., Khallouk & Robert 2017; De Cieri & Dowling 2006). Oelberger and colleagues (2017) highlight many of these important differences, including the incredible diversity of INGO workers in terms of their nationalities, unique skills, tasks, and, consequently, levels of status within the organization. Notably, the authors note the way in which volunteers and "locals" tend to fall to the bottom of the organizational hierarchy (Oelberger et al. 2017: 291).

Working through these complex social structures both internal and external to INGOs is a crucial part of – and sometimes barrier to – their development of HRM strategies. For example, in a study of Australian INGO workers based in Vietnam, Fee, Heizmann, and Gray (2015) found that "shared trust" between expatriate workers and their host-country counterparts was key to successful capacity-building strategies (19). While these authors note the importance of various elements of HRM, such as skills development and mutual learning, these elements alone will not be sufficient to nurture shared trust if extreme discrepancies in expatriate and local workers' pay remain a point of contention within the organization, as illustrated by the Kenyan case (see Republic of Kenya, 2016). In addition to the challenge of fostering shared trust among employees, O'Sullivan (2010) notes that comparatively greater levels of accountability to various external stakeholders in INGOs, especially with regard to spending decisions, acts as a barrier to development of HRM strategies. Furthermore, HRM in INGOs could be the difference between achieving or failing to achieve an urgent response to humanitarian crises. For example, Merlot and De Cieri's (2012) study of INGOs responding to the 2004 Indian Ocean tsunami led the authors to conclude that "the quality of human resources and the human resource systems . . . form crucial aspects of an organization's disaster management" (1303).

Challenges of nonprofit HRM: Understanding the nonprofit context

Who works for nonprofits: Sector choice theory and HRM

To practice HRM successfully in nonprofit organizations, we must consider who works for nonprofit organizations, and whether these individuals are different from workers in other sectors. If the answer is positive, then clearly policies designed for public sector or for-profit workers may not apply without due consideration. The literature to date has given us ample evidence that employees self-select themselves into particular sectors, and this selection is neither random nor simply driven by availability of employment. Thus, understanding some general characteristics of those likely to be working and attracted to work in the nonprofit sector is of fundamental importance to the study of HRM in nonprofits.

Earlier research that examined differences of wages in the nonprofit sector as compared to the other sectors (Ballard 2005; Leete 2000; Roomkin & Weisbrod 1999; Preston 1989; Weisbrod 1983) reveals that wage differentials occurred in some subsectors and mostly in certain levels of employment, largely in managerial levels and up. Handy and Katz (1998) have argued that the offer of lower wages by nonprofits creates a self-sorting of applicants to the nonprofit sector whereby nonprofits are able to attract the kinds of employees who value working for mission-driven organizations whose values align with their own. Thus, such mission-motivated individuals are willing to take a wage penalty to work for the nonprofit of their choice. The argument is two-fold: the individuals in the study saw lost monetary wages as a donation to the nonprofit, and, subsequently, the satisfaction of working for an organization whose mission aligned with their own values compensated them for the wages lost. Handy and Katz (1998) characterize these perspectives of nonprofit workers as a form of non-monetary benefits. Further research has supported these findings: executive directors of Canadian nonprofits perceived that their wages were significantly lower than what they might have received for comparable work in the for-profit sector yet they chose to continue to work for their nonprofits for reasons that are values-based and that they found certain job features attractive (Handy et al. 2007). Word and Park's (2015) study of nonprofit managers in the United States suggests that individuals change employment and move to the nonprofit sector because of their wish to serve others. These findings continue to lend support to the notion that workers in nonprofits are indeed different than workers in other sectors in their valuation and appreciation of their choice of work to be in the service to others (Word & Park 2009; Light 2002).

While individual characteristics, such as mission-related motivations, explains sector choice, nonprofits must pay attention to the many characteristics of the jobs they offer to keep employees, who are so intrinsically motivated, engaged, and productive. Several theories of motivational job design such as the 'Job Characteristics Model' emphasize how certain job characteristics, such as task significance or the extent to which a job affects the lives of others, impact worker motivation (Hackman & Oldham 1980). Such job characteristics also intensify the meaningfulness of work tasks, often resulting in higher work performance. Thus, because the mission of the organization attracts intrinsically motivated employees, job design is crucial in retaining nonprofit employees and reducing turnover when expectations are not met (Walk et al. 2013a). Other perceived characteristics of nonprofits often contribute to employee satisfaction and motivation, such as having less hierarchical organizational structures (Devaro & Brookshire 2007); relatively less gender-based wage discrimination, with the male–female pay gap around 8 percentage points smaller in the nonprofit sector as compared to the for-profit sector (Faulk et al. 2013; Leete 2000); greater workplace commitment to diversity, work–life issues (Pitt-Catsouphes et al. 2004), and fringe benefits (Handy & Katz 1998); and greater freedom and control in job functions and work schedules (LeRoux & Feeney 2013).

An analytical framework for HRM in nonprofits suggested by Ridder and McCandless (2010) underscores the following: as the workers in nonprofits are often driven by different needs and motivations rather than by financial rewards (Theuvsen 2004), attention should be paid to HR practices that ensure workers have meaningful tasks, an ongoing understanding of the impact of their work, a certain level of independence, and responsibility. Thus, HRM should be strategic and aligned with reinforcing both mission-attachment and the values fit between workers' motivations and organizational goals (Ridder et al. 2012; Pynes 1997). This helps to ensure that highly motivated workers, the most important resource for nonprofits, continue to be attracted to and satisfied by their work.

Furthermore, as many nonprofits function under funding pressures and tight budget constraints, their financial vulnerability can have an impact on worker morale as well as job satisfaction and organizational commitment (Cunningham 2005; Alatrista & Arrowsmith 2004; Mirvis 1992; Schnitzer & Leutner 1997). In addition, the multiple stakeholders for whom nonprofits are responsible (such as boards, funders, clients, workers, and community) have substantially diverse interests, creating an environment in which HRM strategies such as a simple pay-for-performance incentive to reduce financial vulnerability and increase efficiency often backfire against the intrinsic motivation (Deckop & Cirka 2000). Thus, retaining workers requires HRM to invest in training that would help the nonprofit accomplish its goals, which in turn increases workers' sense of commitment to the organization and its mission. A values-driven HRM also recognizes the role of worker collaboration in designing new procedures and systems for staff recruitment and retention (Ridder and McCandless 2010).

Governance and accountability as key aspects of nonprofit HRM

Maximization of profits is the bottom line in private firms. HRM, and especially strategic HRM with its goals-oriented focus, exists to enable firms to achieve this bottom line. In nonprofit organizations, however, the centrality of a social mission and the number of stakeholders to whom the organization may be accountable (including clients, dues paying members, donors, government, and others) add complexity to the formation and function of HR practices. In this subsection, we cover the role of the board of directors, accountability, and ethical considerations as they relate to nonprofit HRM. We start with boards of directors.

The role of the board in nonprofit HRM

What is the role of the board in HRM? While the board has an exclusive role in governance, its role in management and HRM in particular is less clear. While the board has fiduciary responsibility for the nonprofit and as such approves all financial disbursements, should the board approve all salaries, or just that of the chief executive? What are the best practices for boards when it comes to matters HRM? According to Sidney Abrams (2014), the board has legal responsibilities to the nonprofit in six main areas: hiring, workplace policies, compensation, evaluation, grievances/whistleblowing, and layoffs. These responsibilities are echoed by the Standards for Excellence Institute (2014), which emphasizes the board's role in maintaining public trust, an ongoing effort that can be accomplished in part through the establishment and maintenance of sound organizational policies with regard to HRM. While this touches many of the HR practices and policies, most boards relegate these with minimal supervision to the HR staff in those nonprofits where HRM is done by professionals. There are indeed no strict rules for how boards engage in HRM, and in smaller nonprofits, boards may be more hands-on and deeply involved with HR matters.

Regardless of how board roles are fashioned, governance and management are separate functions, with the separation to ensure that board members can hold their managers accountable for the functioning of the nonprofit. However, in their review of the literature, Ostrower and Stone (2006) find that, in practice, the balance of power between board members and managers is heterogeneous and depends on several factors, such as the individual personalities and characteristics of board members and managers, the size and age of the organization, the degree of bureaucracy and professionalization, the financial stability of the organization, and its dependence on the board members.

Additionally, a study of UK nonprofits noted that many nonprofits have started adopting for-profit practices, which has raised a concern that nonprofit boards would use monetary incentives for their chief executives. This was not borne out by the evidence; HR practices continue to show a pattern consistent with promoting intrinsic motivations (Jobome 2006). The implication of HRM for nonprofit boards involved in setting salaries and benefits is to eschew monetary incentives and focus relatively more on intrinsic incentives. In promoting intrinsic motivations, boards may find creative ways to reward paid executives by opening up a range of fringe benefits that both appeal to their senior executives and are tied with the organizational mission and values. These strategies might include offering opportunities for executives to upgrade their knowledge through training and conferences or subsidizing related education endeavors by offering tuition assistance. Additionally, boards can recognize the impact of their senior leadership in promoting the mission of the nonprofit by nominating their leaders to prestigious awards and fellowships. Such awards are often much more meaningful than a prize or cash bonus, and do not crowd out the intrinsic motivations of employees (Frey 2007).

Accountability and ethical considerations

Another important piece of HRM is establishing standards for ethical behavior for all employees and, if necessary, a disciplinary process in the event of misconduct. In nonprofits, a strong and clear code of ethics can provide guidelines for not only representing the organization and its mission in a professional and principled manner but also ensuring that there is an appropriate channel for reporting observed misconduct, even if (and especially when) that misconduct occurs above one's pay grade. According to Grobman (2007), codes of ethics can provide individuals with guidelines for how to act with other employees, interface with the public, identify unethical behavior when it arises, and navigate difficult situations where multiple stakeholders have competing interests or conflicting opinions about the "right" course of action. Similarly, written codes of ethics can act as signals of a nonprofit's "ethical climate," demonstrating to external stakeholders the organization's expectations of its employees, as well as its broader values (Malloy & Agarwal 2010; Laratta 2009). Thus, both the employee-focused aspects of codes of ethics and these other functions are critical for nonprofits whose employees and volunteers frequently interface with multiple stakeholders to whom the organization is accountable.

In the past two decades, several high-profile scandals have rocked the nonprofit world, including the well-known examples of the American Red Cross and United Way. In response to these scandals and to growing public concerns, the US Senate Finance Committee initiated a series of discussions and hearings to examine transparency and accountability in the charitable sector, leading to the creation of Independent Sector's Panel on the Nonprofit Sector (Independent Sector 2005). Many scholars have since characterized the rising interest in codes of ethics as a common response to this increasing public scrutiny of the nonprofit sector as a whole and an example of "self-regulation" on the part of individual organizations (Bromley & Orchard 2015: 351). A 2007 National Nonprofit Ethics Survey, conducted by the Ethics Resource Center, found that nearly 50 percent of employees had observed at least one act of misconduct in the previous year. Interestingly, 32 percent of employees indicated that their organization not only has an ethics and compliance program in place, but also that the program is well implemented, and only 11 percent indicated their organization had a strong ethical culture (Ethics Resource Center 2007). This leaves many organizations without an ethics and compliance program in place or its useful implementation. Many ethical breaches happen in areas of employee misbehavior (conflict of interest, fraud, compensation, nepotism, etc.).

In a 2015 survey of nonprofit board members, more than two out three members of boards said that their nonprofit had faced one or more serious governance-related problem in the last 10 years (Lacker, Donatiello, Meehan & Tayan 2015). Furthermore, nearly one in four respondents had asked their executive director to leave or had to respond to an unexpected resignation. These findings, while not pointing directly to misconduct in the nonprofits, are nevertheless suggestive of problems that continue to brew with respect to governance and leadership issues (Lacker et al. 2015). Undoubtedly, there is still much work to be done in establishing good governance practices, a goal that is intimately connected with the establishment of sound HRM strategies.

The literature on nonprofit governance notes that "written rules shape organizational dynamics and the awareness of written policies on ethical behavior affects members' conduct" (Lee 2016: 97). However, Rhode and Packel (2009) note that written codes of ethics are not effective without sufficient employee buy-in and, ultimately, awareness and understanding. Reflecting the dialectical nature of ethics more broadly (Hamilton & Slatten 2013), this hurdle can be overcome by ensuring that employee input is received and incorporated throughout the process of creating and establishing a code of ethics – a process that for many organizations should include integral volunteer workers as well as paid staff. Involving volunteers in this process can help to clarify the organization's expectations for them in a proactive rather than reactive way, and also help them to feel more integrated with the organization's mission, goals, and values.

Without a written code of ethics, all HR practices and policies, however well intended or crafted, will have little or no impact in nonprofits that largely deal with a mission-motivated labor force. Mission-driven employees who have made sacrifices in terms of wages and incentives to be a part of a nonprofit are likely to be intolerant of misdemeanors and unethical behaviors in a nonprofit whose mission they espouse. Thus, nonprofits cannot afford to leave discussions of ethical conduct until after a scandal occurs; instead, they need to make training and updates on ethical conduct, guided by an actionable and clear code of ethics, a part of their HRM strategies at all levels of the organization.

Future directions of nonprofit HRM research

HRM in the nonprofit context utilizes theories and constructs from the for-profit context, including SHRM, that emphasize the notion of internal fit and bundling between the five main HR practices of recruitment and selection, retention, training and development, performance management, and pay and benefits, as well as the external fit between HR practices and the organizational mission (Lengnick-Hall et al. 2009; Devanna et al. 1984). Whereas the core principles of these theories and practices generally apply to the nonprofit context as we have discussed, further adaptation is necessary given the specific motivations of paid staff to self-select into nonprofit employment (Word & Park 2009; Light 2002; Handy & Katz 1998); the non-contractual relationship that volunteers have with the nonprofit organizations (Tilly & Tilly 1994); the heterogeneous stakeholders including board members, clients, and staff (Herman & Renz 1997); and the resource constraints of nonprofit organizations (Froelich 1999). Both conceptual and empirical work have been done in the past few years to further our understanding of the content of these adaptations (Walk et al. 2014, 2013a; Akingbola 2013; Ridder et al. 2012; Ridder & McCandless 2010; Guo et al. 2011). Only recently, the first textbook on the nonprofit-specific aspects of HRM was published (Sowa & Word 2017). In light of these great developments, we now turn to the question, "What is next for nonprofit HRM?" When looking to the for-profit literature for guidance, as we oftentimes do, two promising themes arise that could inform future nonprofit HRM research and practice: proactive workplace behavior and talent management.

First, the literature around proactive workplace behavior has been flourishing in the past few decades, and scholars have investigated its benefits (and at times challenges). Proactive workplace behavior has been defined as "anticipatory action that employees take to impact themselves and/or their environments" (Grant & Ashford 2008: 4). Even though the impact of proactive work-place behavior on organizational performance is still unclear, scholars point to the importance of proactive employees in an increasing volatile environment (Tummers, Kruyen, Vijverberg & Voesenek 2015; Grant & Ashford 2008).

One of these behaviors is job crafting, defined as the changes that individuals make in the task, relational, and cognitive boundaries of their work (Wrzesniewski & Dutton 2001), with the aim of making their work more meaningful. Job crafting as such is an unsolicited behav-ior in the workplace that employees engage in, oftentimes unbeknownst to the organization. Job crafting is positively related to individual-level outcomes such as psychological well-being (Berg, Wrzesniewski & Dutton 2010) and work engagement (Bakker, Tims & Derks 2012), as well as commitment, performance, and job satisfaction (Leana, Appelbaum & Shevchuk 2009). Research has identified certain antecedents of proactivity such as autonomy (Grant & Ashford 2008; Hackman & Oldham 1980), participation in decision making, and teamwork (Tummers et al. 2015). HRM, therefore, has a unique role in enabling proactive workplace behaviors. As such, nonprofit HRM in the design of jobs can be cognizant about allowing for more autonomy, teamwork, and participation.

Research on proactive workplace behaviors in the nonprofit context is rare; for instance, we do not yet know if it happens to the same or a similar extent as it does in the for-profit context. If nonprofit employees are motivated differently, do they also differ in their proac-tive workplace engagement? Since many nonprofits are small, informal, and generally under-resourced, employees often do whatever needs to get done – despite what is in their formal job description. Can this behavior be considered proactive or rather reactive to the circumstances? Since nonprofit work tends to be client-centric, other possible questions include, who is the target of proactive workplace behavior? Is proactive workplace behavior restricted to colleagues, or does it extend to clients and other stakeholders? And, what are potential situations in which proactivity might be negative? Future research is needed to address these important inquiries in the context of nonprofit HRM.

A second fruitful theme is talent management. Talent management is defined as a system-atic process to identify key positions that contribute to the strategic goals of the organization, the strategic development of a pool of talents to fill these roles, and an effective HR system to facilitate the process of filling these positions (Collings & Mellahi 2009). The emphasis on tal-ent management has emerged since the late 1990s and was especially important for companies competing on a global scale for talents (Walk, Schinnenburg & Handy 2013a; Tarique & Schuler

2010). The basic premise, however, applies to a broader spectrum of organizations, in which the main focus is to maximize "the competitive advantage of an organization's human capital" (Collings & Mellahi 2009: 304). Since nonprofit organizations increasingly compete for qualified personnel, talent management is another avenue for future research and practice.

To date, not much research has been done on talent management in nonprofit organizations (see Carpenter 2017 for an exception). Nonprofit employees, however, frequently complain about the lack of career trajectories within their organizations (Walk, Schinnenburg & Handy 2013b). Likewise, recent findings suggest that millennial nonprofit workers are more sector-agnostic than previous generations, and therefore may be less inclined to self-select into nonprofit work or to remain with a nonprofit organization if opportunities for growth and continuous development are not present (Johnson & Ng 2015). These findings become even more concerning for the sector in the context of baby boomer retirement from many nonprofit leadership and management roles (Tierney 2006). As such, talent management strategies, which may include succession planning to develop "homegrown leaders" (Landles-Cobb, Kramer & Milway 2015), might provide nonprofit HR managers with valuable tools to recruit the right personnel, especially when clear career trajectories can be offered.

Finally, we cannot conclude without a brief note on an important and emerging aspect of volunteer management that has critical implications for HRM: the aging out of volunteers. As the population ages, scholars have become increasingly interested in the topic of productive aging, or the ways in which adults in retirement engage fruitfully with their communities (Einolf 2009). A common activity for retired adults looking to remain active community members is volunteering, and evidence suggests that older volunteers contribute more time to their volunteering than younger age cohorts (Choi & Chou 2010; Mutchler, Burr & Caro 2003). Although the literature has demonstrated substantial quantitative evidence for the link between volunteering and improved health and well-being on the part of older volunteers (e.g., Piliavin & Siegl 2015), little is known about the impact of withdrawing from volunteering when health issues and other concerns contribute to older volunteers' decisions to "retire" from their volunteering. However, we argue that this second retirement of sorts is a critical and emerging topic in the field of both gerontology and nonprofit management, with several important implications for nonprofit HRM, especially in organizations relying heavily on volunteer workers and tending to recruit volunteers from among retirees. Future research examining this transition and its impact on not only nonprofit organizations but also the well-being of volunteers is needed.

This chapter has focused on the emerging trends and sector-specific challenges of nonprofit HRM. Although the literature on the for-profit side of HRM is extensive, uncertainties remain around the efficacy of its direct application to the nonprofit sector, with its diverse range of stakeholders, social mission, and unique workforce composition. As we have discussed, many scholars have begun to take up this question in their research, but as this section on future directions shows, much exciting work remains to be done. Ultimately, nonprofit practitioners and researchers alike should be heartened rather than discouraged by the context-specific nature of nonprofit HRM, as the complexity of the sector offers us the opportunity to incorporate multiple perspectives and strategies into the development and implementation of effective HR strategies in innovative, creative, and human-centered ways.

References

AbouAssi, K & Jo, S 2017, 'Partnerships among Lebanese nonprofit organizations: Assessing the impact on human resource capacity', *American Review of Public Administration*, vol. 47, no. 6, pp. 687–698.

Abrams, S 2014, 'The board's role in human resource management', *BoardSource*. Available from: https://www.nonprofithr.com/wp-content/uploads/2014/10/The-Boards-Role-in-HR-Management.pdfc.

Akingbola, K 2013, 'A model of strategic nonprofit human resource management', *Voluntas,* vol. 24, pp. 214–240.

Akingbola, K 2012, 'Context and nonprofit human resource management', *Administration & Society*, vol. 45, no. 8, pp. 974–1004.

Akinlade, D & Shalack, R 2016, 'Strategic human resource management in nonprofit organizations: A case for mission-driven human resource practices', *Proceedings of the Academy of Organizational Culture, Communications, and Conflict,* vol. 21, no. 1.

Alatrista, J & Arrowsmith, J 2004, 'Managing employee commitment in the not-for-profit sector', *Personnel Review*, vol. 33, no. 5, pp. 536–548.

Bakker, AB, Tims, M & Derks, D 2012, 'Proactive personality and job performance: The role of job crafting and work engagement', *Human Relations,* vol. 65, no. 10, pp. 1359–1378.

Ballard, A 2005, *Understanding the Next Generation of Nonprofit Employees: The Impact of Educational Debt*, Goldman School of Public Policy, University of California at Berkeley.

Bartram, T, Cavanagh, J & Hoye, R 2017, 'The growing importance of human resource management in the NGO, volunteer and not-for-profit sectors' [Introduction to the special issue on nonprofit HRM], *International Journal of Human Resource Management*, vol. 28, no. 14, pp. 1901–1911.

Berg, J, Wrzesniewski, A & Dutton, JE 2010, 'Perceiving and responding to challenges in job crafting at different ranks: When proactivity requires adaptivity', *Journal of Organizational Behavior,* vol. 31, no. 2–3, pp. 158–186.

Bromley, P & Orchard, CD 2016, 'Managed morality: The rise of professional codes of conduct in the U.S. nonprofit sector', *Nonprofit and Voluntary Sector Quarterly*, vol. 45, no. 2, pp. 351–374.

Brudney, JL 1990, *Fostering Volunteer Programs in the Public Sector: Planning, Initiating, and Managing Voluntary Activities*, Jossey-Bass, San Francisco.

Brudney, JL & England, RE 1983, 'Toward a definition of the coproduction concept', *Public Administration Review*, vol. 43, no. 1, pp. 59–65.

Carpenter, H 2017, 'Talent management', in Sowa, J & Word, J (Eds), *The Nonprofit Human Resource Management Handbook: From Theory to Practice*. Routledge, New York.

Casey, J 2016, 'Comparing nonprofit sectors around the world: What do we know and how do we know it?', *Journal of Nonprofit Education and Leadership*, Available from: http://dx.doi.org/10.18666/JNEL-2016-V6-I3-7583.

Chang, WW, Chun-Mam, H & Kuo, YC 2015, 'Design of employee training in Taiwanese nonprofits', *Nonprofit and Voluntary Sector Quarterly*, vol. 44, no. 1, pp. 25–46.

Choi, NG & Chou, RJ-A 2010, 'Time and money volunteering among older adults: The relationship between past and current volunteering and correlates of change and stability', *Ageing and Society*, vol. 30, no. 4, pp. 559–581.

Collings, DG & Mellahi, K 2009, 'Strategic talent management: A review and research agenda', *Human Resource Management Review,* vol. 19, no. 4, pp. 304–313.

Cunningham, I 2005, 'Struggling to care: Employee attitudes to work at the sharp end of service provision in the voluntary sector', Paper presented at the Annual Labour Process Conference, Glasgow.

Deckop, JR & Cirka, CC 2000, 'The risk and reward of a double-edged sword: Effects of a merit pay program on intrinsic motivation', *Nonprofit and Voluntary Sector Quarterly,* vol. 29, no. 3, pp. 400–418.

Devanna, MA et al. 1984, 'A framework for strategic human resource management', in *Strategic Human Resource Management*, pp. 33–55. Wiley, New York.

Devaro, J & Brookshire, D 2007, 'Promotions and incentives in nonprofit and for-profit organizations', *Industrial and Labor Relations (ILR) Review*, vol. 60, no. 3, pp. 311–339.

De Cieri, H & Dowling, PJ 2006, 'Strategic human resource management in multinational enterprises', in Stahl, GK & Bjorkman, I (Eds), *Handbook of Research in International Human Resource Management*, pp. 15–35. Edward Elgar, Northampton, MA.

Einolf, CJ 2009, 'Will the boomers volunteer during retirement? Comparing the Baby Boom, Silent, and Long Civic cohorts', *Nonprofit and Voluntary Sector Quarterly*, vol. 38, no. 2, pp. 181–199.

Ethics Resource Center 2007, *National Nonprofit Ethics Survey: An Inside View of Nonprofit Sector Ethics*. Retrieved from http://community.corporatecompliance.org/HigherLogic/System/DownloadDocumentFile.ashx?DocumentFileKey=8625367f-2c62-4c82-ae5f-293bc6eded03

Faulk, L, Edwards, LH, Lewis, GB & McGinnis, J 2013, 'An analysis of gender pay disparity in the nonprofit sector: An outcome of labor motivation or gendered jobs?', *Nonprofit and Voluntary Sector Quarterly*, vol. 42, no. 6, pp. 1268–1287.

Fee, A, Heizmann, H & Gray, SJ 2015, 'Towards a theory of effective cross-cultural capacity development: The experiences of Australian international NGO expatriates in Vietnam', *International Journal of Human Resource Management*, doi: 10.1080/09585192.2015.1093015

Frey, BS 2007, 'Awards as compensation', *European Management Review*, vol. 4, no. 1, pp. 6–14.

Froelich, KA 1999, 'Diversification of revenue strategies: Evolving resource dependence in nonprofit organizations', *Nonprofit and Voluntary Sector Quarterly*, vol. 28, no. 3, pp. 246–268.

Grant, A & Ashford, SJ 2008, 'The dynamics of proactivity at work', *Research in Organizational Behavior*, vol. 28, no. 1, pp. 3–34.

Grobman, GM 2007, 'An analysis of codes of ethics of nonprofit, tax-exempt membership associations', *Public Integrity*, vol. 9, no. 3, pp. 245–263.

Guo, C, Brown, WA, Ashcraft, RF, Yoshioka, CF & Dong, HKD 2011, 'Strategic human resources management in nonprofit organizations', *Review of Public Personnel Administration*, vol. 31, no. 3, pp. 248–269.

Hackman, JR & Oldham, GR 1980, *Work Redesign*, Addison-Wesley, Reading, MA.

Hamilton, JB & Slatten, LAD 2013, 'A nonprofit's practical guide to resolving ethical questions', *Journal of Applied Management and Entrepreneurship*, vol. 18, no. 2, pp. 39–58.

Handy, F & Katz, E 1998, 'The wage differential between nonprofit institutions and corporations: Getting more by paying less?' *Journal of Comparative Economics*, vol. 26, no. 2, pp. 246–261.

Handy, F, Mook, L & Quarter, J 2008, 'The interchangeability of paid staff and volunteers in nonprofit organizations', *Nonprofit and Voluntary Sector Quarterly*, vol. 37, no. 1, pp. 76–92.

Handy, F, Mook, L, Ginieniewicz, J & Quarter, J 2007, 'The moral high ground: Perceptions of wage differentials among executive directors of Canadian nonprofits', *Philanthropist*, vol. 21, no. 2, pp. 109–127.

Handy, F & Srinivasan, N 2005, 'The demand for volunteer labor: A study of hospital volunteers', *Nonprofit and Voluntary Sector Quarterly*, vol. 34, no. 4, pp. 491–509.

Hansmann, H 1980, 'The role of nonprofit enterprise', *Yale Law Journal*, vol. 89, no. 5, pp. 835–902.

Herman, RD & Renz, DO 1997, 'Multiple constituencies and the social construction of nonprofit organization effectiveness', *Nonprofit and Voluntary Sector Quarterly*, vol. 26, no. 2, pp. 185–206.

Independent Sector 2005, *Panel on the Nonprofit Sector: Strengthening Transparency, Governance, Accountability of Charitable Organizations*. Retrieved from http://www.iupui.edu/~spea1/V525/Hay-summer/Modules/02/Panel%20on%20the%20NP%20Sector%20-%20Govt%20Regulation%20and%20Ethical%20Concerns.pdf

Jobome, GO 2006, 'Management pay, governance and performance: The case of large UK nonprofits', *Financial Accountability & Management*, vol. 22, no. 4, pp. 331–358.

Johnson, JM & Ng, ES 2015, 'Money talks or millennials walk: The effect of compensation on nonprofit millennial workers sector-switching intentions', *Review of Public Personnel Administration*, 0734371X15587980.

Khallouk, M & Robert, M 2017, 'Obstacles to management innovation in nonprofit organizations: The case of an international nongovernmental organization', *Journal of Innovation Economics and Management* [Online first version.]

Kim, SE 2005, 'Balancing competing accountability requirements: Challenges in performance improvement of the nonprofit human services agency', *Public Performance and Management Review*, vol. 29, no. 2, pp. 145–163.

Lacker, DF, Donatiello, NE, Meehan, B & Tayan, B 2015, '2015 survey on board of directors of nonprofit organizations', *Stanford Business Review*. Retrieved from https://www.gsb.stanford.edu/faculty-research/publications/2015-survey-board-directors-nonprofit-organizations

Landles-Cobb, L, Kramer, K & Milway, KS 2015, October 22, 'The nonprofit leadership development deficit', *Stanford Social Innovation Review*. Retrieved from https://ssir.org/articles/entry/the_nonprofit_leadership_development_deficit

Laratta, R 2009, 'Ethical climate in nonprofit organizations: A comparative study', *International Journal of Sociology and Social Policy*, vol. 29, no. 7/8, pp 358–371.

Leana, C, Appelbaum, E & Shevchuk, I 2009, 'Work process and quality of care in early childhood education: The role of job crafting', *Academy of Management Journal*, vol. 52, no. 6, pp. 1169–1192.

Lee, Y 2016, 'What encourages nonprofits' adoption of good governance policies?', *Nonprofit Management & Leadership*, vol. 27, no. 1, pp. 95–112.

Leete, L 2006, 'Work in the nonprofit sector', in Powell, WW & Steinberg, R (Eds), *The Nonprofit Sector: A Research Handbook*, 2nd edn, pp. 159–179, Yale University Press, New Haven, CT.

Leete, L 2000, 'Wage equity and employee motivation in nonprofit and for-profit organizations', *Journal of Economic Behavior & Organization*, vol. 43, no. 4, pp. 423–446.

Lengnick-Hall, ML et al. 2009, 'Strategic human resource management: The evolution of the field', *Human Resource Management Review*, vol. 19, no. 2, pp. 64–85.

LeRoux, K & Feeney, MK 2013, 'Factors attracting individuals to nonprofit management over public and private sector management', *Nonprofit Management and Leadership*, vol. 24, no. 1, pp. 43–62.

Light, PC 2002, 'The content of their character: The state of the nonprofit workforce', *Nonprofit Quarterly*, pp. 6–16.

Malloy, DC & Agarwal, J 2008, 'Ethical climate in government and nonprofit sectors: Public policy implications for service delivery', *Journal of Business Ethics*, vol. 94, pp. 3–21.

Merlot, ES & De Cieri, H 2012, 'The challenges of the 2004 Indian Ocean tsunami for strategic international human resource management in multinational nonprofit enterprises', *International Journal of Human Resource Management*, vol. 23, no. 7, pp. 1303–1319.

Mirvis, PH 1992, 'The quality of employment in the nonprofit sector: An update on employee attitudes in nonprofits versus business and government', *Nonprofit Management and Leadership*, vol. 3, no. 1, pp. 23–41.

Mutchler, JE, Burr, JA & Caro, FG 2003, 'From paid worker to volunteer: Leaving the paid workforce and volunteering in later life', *Social Forces*, vol. 81, no. 4, pp. 1267–1293.

Oelberger, CR, Fechter, AM & McWha-Hermann, I 2017, 'Managing human resources in international NGOs', in Sowa, J & Word, J (Eds), *The Nonprofit Human Resource Management Handbook: From Theory to Practice*, pp. 285–303, Routledge, New York.

Ostrower, F & Stone, MM 2006, 'Governance: Research trends, gaps, and future prospects', in Powell, WW & Steinberg, R (Eds), *The Nonprofit Sector: A Research Handbook*, 2nd edn, pp. 612–628, Yale University Press, New Haven, CT.

O'Sullivan, SL 2010, 'International human resource management challenges in Canadian development INGOs', *European Management Journal*, vol. 28, pp. 421–440.

Paarlberg, LE & Gen, S 2009, 'Exploring the determinants of nonprofit coproduction of public service delivery: The case of k-12 public education', *American Review of Public Administration*, vol. 39, no. 4, pp. 391–408.

Park, SM & Kim, MY 2016, 'Antecedents and outcomes of non-profit public service motivation in Korean NPOs', *International Journal of Manpower*, vol. 37, no. 5, pp. 777–803.

Piliavin, JA & Siegl, E 2015, 'Health and well-being consequences of formal volunteering', in Schroeder, DA & Graziano, WG (Eds), *Oxford Handbook of Prosocial Behavior*, Oxford University Press, Oxford.

Pitt-Catsouphes, M, Swanberg, JE, Bond, JT & Galinsky, E 2004, 'Work–life policies and programs: Comparing the responsiveness of nonprofit and for-profit organizations', *Nonprofit Management and Leadership*, vol. 14, no. 3, pp. 291–312.

Preston, AE 1989, 'The nonprofit worker in a for-profit world', *Journal for Labor Economics*, vol. 7, no. 4, pp. 438–463.

Pynes, JE 1997, *Human Resources Management for Public and Nonprofit Organizations*, Wiley, Hoboken, NJ.

Republic of Kenya 2016, April 21, Circular no. NGOB2904/2016/ED. Retrieved from http://www.ngobureau.or.ke/?wpdmpro=circular-number-ngob29042016ed

Rhode, DL & Packel, AK 2009, 'Ethics and nonprofits', *Stanford Social Innovation Review*, vol. 7, no. 3, pp. 29–35.

Ridder, HG & McCandless, A 2010, 'Influences on the architecture of human resource management in nonprofit organizations: An analytical framework', *Nonprofit and Voluntary Sector Quarterly*, vol. 39, no. 1, pp. 124–141.

Ridder, HG, Piening, EP & Baluch, AM 2012, 'The third way reconfigured: How and why nonprofit organizations are shifting their human resource management', *Voluntas*, vol. 23, pp. 605–635.

Rogers, SE, Jiang, K, Rogers, CM & Intindola, M 2016, 'Strategic human resource management of volunteers and the link to hospital patient satisfaction', *Nonprofit and Voluntary Sector Quarterly*, vol. 45, no. 2, pp. 409–424.

Roomkin, M & Weisbrod, B 1999, 'Managerial compensation and incentives in for-profit and nonprofit hospitals', *Journal of Law Economics and Organization*, vol. 15, pp. 750–781.

Schlosser, FK & Zinni, DM 2011, 'Transitioning ageing workers from paid to unpaid work in non-profits', *Human Resource Management Journal*, vol. 21, no. 2, pp. 156–170.

Schnitzer, H & Leutner, E 1997, 'Austrian association for the disabled: Specific characteristics of HRM in NPOs and their consequences for organizational culture', in Buber, R & Meyer, M (Eds), *Nonprofit Management Case Studies*, pp. 323–345. Schaffer-Poeschel, Stuttgart, Germany.

Sowa, J & Word, J (Eds) 2017, *The Nonprofit Human Resource Management Handbook: From Theory to Practice*, Routledge, New York.

Standards for Excellence Institute 2014, *An Ethics and Accountability Code for the Nonprofit Sector*. Retrieved from https://standardsforexcellence.org/Home-2/codeTarique, I & Schuler, RS 2010, 'Global talent management: Literature review, integrative framework, and suggestions for further research', *Journal of World Business*, vol. 45, pp. 122–133.

Theuvsen, L 2004, 'Doing better while doing good: Motivational aspects of pay-for-performance effectiveness in nonprofit organizations', *Voluntas*, vol. 15, no. 2, pp. 117–136.

Tierney, TJ 2006, March, *The Nonprofit Sector's Leadership Deficit*, The Bridgespan Group. Retrieved from http://imap.wildforeverfuture.org/downloads/Leadership_Deficit_White_Paper.pdf

Tilly, C & Tilly, C 1994, 'Capitalist work and labor markets', in Smelser, N & Swedberg, R (Eds), *Handbook of Economic Sociology*, pp. 283–313, Princeton University Press, Princeton, NJ.

Tummers, L, Kruyen, PM, Vijverberg, DM & Voesenek, TJ 2015, 'Connecting HRM and change management: The importance of proactivity and vitality', *Journal of Organizational Change Management*, vol. 28, no. 4, pp. 627–640.

Verschuere, B, Brandsen, T & Pestoff, V 2012, 'Co-production: The state of the art in research and the future agenda', *Voluntas*, vol. 23, no. 4, pp. 1083–1101.

Walk, M, Schinnenburg, H & Handy, F 2014, 'Missing in action: Strategic human resource management in German nonprofits', *Voluntas*, vol. 25, pp. 991–1021.

Walk, M, Handy, F & Schinnenburg, H 2013a, 'Expectations and experiences of young employees: The case of German nonprofits', *Administration in Social Work*, vol. 37, no. 2, pp. 133–146.

Walk, M, Schinnenburg, H & Handy, F 2013b, 'What do talents want? Work expectations in India, China, and Germany', *German Journal of Research in Human Resource Management*, vol. 27, no. 3, pp. 251–278. doi:10.1688/1862-0000_ZfP_2013_03_Walk

Weisbrod, BA 1983, 'Nonprofit and proprietary sector behavior: Wage differentials among lawyers', *Journal for Labor Economics*, vol. 1, no. 3, pp. 246–263.

Word, J & Park, SM 2015, 'The new public service? Empirical research on job choice motivation in the nonprofit sector', *Personnel Review*, vol. 44, no. 1, pp. 91–118.

Word, J & Park, SM 2009, 'Working across the divide: Job involvement in the public and nonprofit sectors', *Review of Public Personnel Administration*, vol. 29, no. 2, pp. 103–133.

Wrzesniewski, A & Dutton, JE 2001, 'Crafting a job: Revisioning employees as active crafters of their work', *Academy of Management Review*, vol. 26, no. 2, pp. 179–201.

Yassine, N & Zein, R 2016, 'Human resource management in the Middle East: Lebanese HR practices in NGOs and the private sector', *S.A.M. Advanced Management Journal*, vol. 81, no. 1, pp. 34–40.

19

VOLUNTEER MANAGEMENT AND THE PSYCHOLOGICAL CONTRACT

Mark A. Hager

ASSOCIATE PROFESSOR, SCHOOL OF COMMUNITY RESOURCES & DEVELOPMENT,
ARIZONA STATE UNIVERSITY, PHOENIX, AZ, USA

Kathy T. Renfro

DOCTORAL STUDENT, SCHOOL OF COMMUNITY RESOURCES & DEVELOPMENT,
ARIZONA STATE UNIVERSITY, PHOENIX, AZ, USA

Volunteer management or *volunteer administration* denotes the organizational function or program responsible for attracting and engaging volunteers in advancing the missions of nonprofit organizations, informal associations, government, and even some for-profit service organizations. This function is often overlooked and under-resourced: since volunteers are "free," how much should an organization put into managing and supporting them? Many executives and boards think of volunteers and volunteer administration as a sideshow, and they do not invest in the volunteer program. The consequence is predictable: volunteers leave, and the ones who stay are not as happy or productive as they could be (Moreno-Jimenez & Villodres, 2010; O'Donohue, Martin & Torugsa, 2015; Allen & Mueller, 2013). On the other hand, some excellent organizations put time, attention, and financial resources into volunteer management and reap substantial benefits. *Retention* of volunteers is central to both the practice and academic literatures on volunteer administration, and much of volunteer administration is geared to this goal (Hager & Brudney, 2004). Certainly, the broader organization and its various programs might be most interested in what volunteers can add to the mission, but the volunteer management team has a particular interest in attracting and keeping those volunteers.

Organizations run the spectrum from those that provide a poor experience to those that provide a great experience for volunteers. Some fall across the middle range of that spectrum, but the two camps on either end are pretty stark and easy to identify. The thesis motivating this chapter is that *the positive experience and productivity of a volunteer is determined almost exclusively by the alignment between what the organization provides to the volunteer and what the volunteer expects of the organization.* Effective volunteer management, then, is the facilitation of this alignment. A great volunteer administrator is someone who marries the needs of the organization with the needs of a given volunteer. This leaves little room for the middle ground: organizations either provide mutually productive experiences for their volunteers, or they do not.

Although we are not the first to describe effective volunteer engagement in this way, this chapter introduces some new ideas (or, at least, new combinations of ideas) on the topic. The idea that animates this particular perspective on volunteer management is that people (individual prospective volunteers) are constantly evaluating whether the social conditions they face justify any actions they might take, including joining, continuing to engage, or leaving the organizations that need them. This idea has been represented in the social sciences as the *psychological contract* perspective. The main purpose of this chapter is to introduce the reader to the state of the art in practice and research in volunteer administration, but we do so with regular reference to and integration of this perspective. We invite the reader to look at volunteer management through the lens of the psychological contract that volunteers make with organizations.

The psychological contract

The idea that our social relationships are the result of informal 'contracts' goes back some 400 years. Thomas Hobbes, among others like John Locke and Jean-Jacques Rousseau, theorized how human communities and institutions emerged from an original state of isolated individuals (Hampton, 1988; Locke, Hume, & Rousseau, 1960). That is, before these isolated individuals agreed (through an informal 'social contract') not to kill each other whenever they crossed paths, their lives were "solitary, poor, nasty, brutish, and short" (Hobbes, 2010; *Leviathan* originally published in 1651). Once the basic contract was established, we made regular assessments and tradeoffs about what kinds of social associations improved our lives, resulting in villages and governments. This still goes on today, every day. For example, we propose that this same kind of individual calculation takes place when individuals are faced with the prospect of trading their smartphone solitaire, internet surfing, Netflix bingeing, or even neighborhood socializing for some form of higher community engagement. One prominent way that people get involved in communities is by spending time and effort working with community organizations as volunteers. Whether or not such volunteerism becomes the activity that captures their time and effort is determined by the *psychological contract* they establish with such community organizations. If the contract is established and then "breached," volunteers find another place to volunteer, or go back to their Netflix.

Over the past half-century or so, in uneven fits and starts, theorists and some empiricists have investigated this informal contracting idea in the workplace context (Conway & Briner, 2009; Anderson & Schalk, 1998; Coyle-Shapiro & Kessler, 2000; Shore & Tetrick, 1994; Guest, 2004). Of course, people employed for pay in modern workplaces are subjected to formal legal contracts, or at least some form of *transactional* contract that spells out what kinds of benefits (especially salary) will be meted out for what kinds of work. Even some formal volunteer programs employ written agreements that outline the conditions of exchange. These are not the kinds of contracts we are focused on here. Rather, much (probably most) of what happens in workplaces is governed by informal or *relational* "contracts" that are important in worker decisions about where and how hard they work, but are not written down (Thompson & Bunderson, 2003; Alfes, Shantz, & Saksida, 2015; Vantilborgh, et al., 2014). For example, a Gen X manager and her new Boomer employee might have an unspoken agreement that he will be paid more than the new Millennial employee is paid, due to longer work history. If the manager breaches this relational contract, the new Boomer employee may feel justified in leaving his job or doing inferior work. Every smile has the potential to reinforce this relational contract, while every slight has the potential to break it down.

This idea that workers are influenced by informal expectations and adherence to unstated obligations has mostly been explored and tested in studies of employees in for-profit business organizations. Whereas Jean-Jacques Rousseau is prominently associated with social contract theory, his modern namesake Denise Rousseau (1989, 1990, 1995; Rousseau & Tijoriwal, 1998; Rousseau, Hansen, & Tomprou, 2018) is something of a marking point for research on the force of the psychological contract in workplaces, or the evolution of modern thinking on the psychological contract. Rousseau popularized and catalyzed research on the psychological contract, much of which was more narrow, prescriptive, and quantitative (the better for publishing in the reputable business journals) than the earlier conceptual treatments. Indeed, in his review on the state of scholarly attention to the idea of the psychological contract, Nichols (2013) describes the flow of scholarly thinking on the psychological contract as "pre-Rousseau" vs. "post-Rousseau," with his accolades focused on the earlier period. We like to think that our conception of the psychological contract is at least indicative of the pre-Rousseau version. Nichols characterizes the pre-Rousseau psychological contract lens as "a social constructionist view of reality and epistemological position that qualitative research can provide valid knowledge" (2013, p. 990). He is thereby critical of the evolution of psychological contract theory over the past several decades ("post-Rousseau"). The post-Rousseau turn is grounded too firmly in employee relationships, rather than in decisions to volunteer. It has focused too much on quantitative empirical measurements of discrete states, rather than recognizing that our social arrangements are constantly negotiated and reconsidered. It has tended to study only the view of workers, rather than the *bilateral* relationship between workers and organizations. Nichols believes that psychological contract theory deserves a renaissance, a return to its social constructionist roots. We agree.

A variety of published articles attempt to transplant psychological contract theory from the paid worker case to the volunteer case, but much of this work is carried out in the post-Rousseau tradition. This is unfortunate, since the idea that workers make decisions on *relational* contract grounds probably has more potential for fostering our understanding of volunteers than it does in fostering our understanding of employees. Thompson and Bunderson stand as an exemplar of the state of post-Rousseau psychological contract theory when they advance the idea (in a top-notch business journal) that employees might make engagement decisions based on *ideological* rewards, grounded in "the promotion of a cause they highly value" (2003, p. 571). Well, of course they do: this conception is basic to our understanding of why many people work in nonprofit organizations, and is key to understanding why many people volunteer. That the business literature has to specifically call out *ideology* and *values* as dimensions of the psychological contract is indicative of how little the modern stream of psychological contract theory speaks to the nonprofit case. Human resource management principles developed in the business sphere do not often translate seamlessly to nonprofits (Studer, 2016). Nonprofit scholars should take the lead in advancing this perspective due to its great potential for increased understanding of the relationship between the motivations, ideologies, and values of volunteers and the needs of community organizations.

In this chapter, we refer to a psychological contract "lens" or perspective that scholars or practitioners might employ to better understand why volunteers might choose to engage with or disengage from community organizations or programs. Our lens is the social constructionist, pre-Rousseau lens that characterizes individual choices as multifaceted and complex. At its root, the idea is simple: match the needs and expectations of the volunteer with the vision and handiwork of the organization, from first contact to every one thereafter. Mismatch results in breach of the contract and inevitable exit of volunteers. However, as with all social constructionist lenses, complications threaten the easy application of these ideas. In the sections that follow, we describe both complications among volunteers and complications among organizations that observers must consider in utilizing this lens to understand and predict volunteer behavior.

Complications on the volunteer side

Beginning a quarter-century ago and unfolding over a decade, Gil Clary and his colleagues published an assortment of research papers geared toward understanding the motivations of volunteers (see especially Clary, Snyder, Ridge, Copeland, Stukas, Haugen, & Miene, 1998). Our thesis echoes theirs: they wanted to tie the psychology of volunteers to effective management strategies of volunteer administrators (Clary, Snyder, & Ridge, 1992). Central to their research is an enduring contribution to the field, their *Volunteer Functions Inventory*. A primary contribution (and vital complication in the enduring quest to engage volunteers in thoughtful and productive ways) is the assertion that people choose to spend their time working with community organizations *for a variety of reasons*.

Clary and colleagues measured and validated six such reasons: *values* (people volunteer for causes that concern or inspire them); *understanding* (people volunteer to gain new knowledge and skills); *social* (people volunteer to be with friends, meet new people, or to be identified with a favorable activity); *career* (people volunteer to improve their job skills and chances); *protective* (people volunteer to escape guilt or assuage personal problems); and *enhancement* (people volunteer to enhance their own affect and outlook). Esmond and Dunlop's (2004) formulation has 10 categories. Other researchers frequently refer more simply to *intrinsic* versus *extrinsic*, volunteer motivations. Still others frame these motivations as *altruistic* versus *egoistic*. The underlying point in each is the same: volunteers choose to act for a variety of reasons. What's more, volunteers may face multiple interlaced motivations at once. Moreover, motivations change over time. This diversity of interrelated motivations challenges simple statements about or applications of the psychological contract lens. Indeed, a poor volunteer–organization relationship that might breach the psychological contract for a volunteer with a deep dedication to a cause might be tolerable to another volunteer who is seeking job skills rather than social change. The strength and value of the psychological contract varies with the motivations of the volunteer.

A second complication is the assortment of engagement opportunities available to volunteers, and the reported shifting in task and mode preferences over the past several decades. An apparent decline in long-term commitments is the most glaring example. McCurley and Lynch (2011) outline volunteer management principles geared toward what they call the *super-volunteer*, or the long-term volunteer who regularly dedicates large blocks of time to their chosen organization, usually related to service delivery. Describing the dimensions of the psychological contract for the super-volunteer might (maybe) be straightforward, but it would overlook the fact that volunteer preferences come in many flavors. Young people are not inclined to this super-volunteer status. Working adults usually do not have this option, since their time blocks are otherwise occupied. Retirees best fit the bill. However, volunteers of all stripes have forced the field to recognize the need for more *episodic* assignments. Macduff (2005) describes episodic assignments as those that comprise loosely connected episodes, are of short duration, are temporary, or only happen occasionally. *Episodic* is the antithesis of the super-volunteer, and volunteer management practice has been slow to adapt to it. The dynamics of the psychological contract are also more difficult to specify in these situations, where volunteer commitment may be lower, since engagement is more shallow or sporadic. The proliferation of the internet and smartphones has both broadened and reinforced episodic assignments, which suggests that they are here to stay – or at least a harbinger of a different future. The choice of how much, how long, or how intensively a volunteer wants to engage a community organization is another dimension of the psychological contract that smart volunteer administrators have to consider in their quest to recruit and retain their volunteers.

Complications on the organization side

Volunteer motivations and preferences may be diverse, but so are the needs and offerings of nonprofit organizations. McCurley and Lynch's (2011) super-volunteer calls to mind what Macduff, Netting, and O'Connor (2009) label the *traditional volunteer program* and its canon of best practices (Hager, 2013). In the traditional program, volunteers resemble employees and may even be managed by human resource (HR) professionals. If you imagine volunteers as regularly scheduled, carrying out prescribed tasks organized by program staff, you are imagining the traditional program. In this case, again, the application of our psychological contract lens is relatively straightforward. However, Macduff and colleagues remind us that not all nonprofits provide services, and not all volunteers engage organizations in that *traditional* mold.

One prominent counter-example is the *social change* nonprofit (think social movement organizations) whose 'volunteers' might better be thought of as passionate change agents, ready to march, write, call, and even fight (if necessary) at a moment's notice. For these individuals, the dynamics of the psychological contract are strongly at work, but the ways that nonprofits 'manage' them are not usually covered in the volunteer management canon. Macduff and colleagues also describe the *serendipitous* volunteer program, which emphasizes coordination and consensus building over 'management'; and the *entrepreneurial* volunteer program that provides opportunity and support to creative mavericks with unique skills. We call out this diversity to guard against the inclination to oversimplify that might result from focusing exclusively on the traditional volunteer program. If the psychological contract lens has utility in facilitating the relationship between volunteers and organizations, it has to be flexible enough to cover a diversity of real-world situations. A social constructionist view of the psychological contract helps.

A second complication is perhaps more basic. That is, due to the under-investment of organizations in volunteer administration, too much management happens by accident, or not at all (Alfes, Shantz, & Bailey, 2016). In an (aging) national snapshot of volunteer administration programs, the Urban Institute (2004) reported that less than two-thirds of nonprofits that worked with volunteers had a staff member responsible for volunteer administration, and most of those staff members spent more than half of their time on job responsibilities *unrelated to volunteer administration*. Consequently, any call for volunteer administrators to peer through a psychological contract lens to improve their retention of volunteers will run squarely into a capacity problem. That is, most volunteer administrators may not have the training, time, or professional inclination to optimize their programs. In our introduction, we described two camps of nonprofit organizations: one that provides good experiences for its volunteers and one that does not. Those that have the processes and culture in place to provide good experiences might benefit more from the psychological contract lens, if they are not already practicing it. Those that struggle to provide good experiences for their volunteers might aspire to a more productive path. Otherwise, they will continue to struggle mightily, churning through volunteers and other resources with little to show for it.

Core processes in volunteer administration

Volunteer management capacity is a phrase coined by Hager and Brudney (2010) to specifically refer to the extent to which an organization has adopted a range of 'best practices' in volunteer administration. These practices can be found across both the practice (Ellis, 2010) and scholarly literatures in volunteer management, including identification of roles, recruitment, selection, placement, orientation, training, supervision, recognition, and evaluation of volunteers. Connors (2012) describes most of these elements in what he calls the "volunteer management process" and sums them up as "the fundamental management model" (xxii). In 2015, the Council for Certification in Volunteer and Administration (CCVA) published its *Body of Knowledge and Competency Framework*. This framework outlines 67 competencies in seven broad categories reminiscent of the traditional canon. Subsequently, Hager and Brudney (2016) asserted that many elements of the framework could be conceptualized as stages of organizational engagement with volunteers whose primary purpose and outcome is *retention* of those volunteers. These stages run from planning, to recruitment, to orientation, to 'go-time,' to recognition. The new wrinkle we are suggesting in this current chapter is that volunteers form and constantly evaluate their psychological contract with nonprofit organizations as they move through these stages. This psychological contract perspective reformulates some of the traditional wisdom and scholarly orientation to the field.

Planning stage

On the organizational side, managers assess their needs; articulate objectives for incorporating volunteers into operations; lay down policies, procedures, and tools for productively working with volunteers; and consider how to evaluate and mitigate risk from volunteers. Before volunteers get in the door, smart organizations lay the groundwork for productive relationships with their volunteers.

As constant social constructionists, volunteers plan, too. "Social construction" cannot be done individually, in isolation. Social construction is inherently about joint construction of understandings of the social world (Berger & Luckman, 1966). Organizations project a public version of themselves, and volunteers use whatever information is available to them to decide whether they want to associate with that organization or not. Boezeman and Ellemers (2008, 2014) argue that volunteers build personal *social identity* through decisions about which organizations they should engage. These scholars assert that prospective volunteers look for two things in this identity construction process: pride and respect. *Pride* is largely a function of the reputation of the organization: If the community organization has a positive brand, volunteers reinforce positive self-identity by associating with that brand. *Respect* is reflected in the degree to which individuals feel that organizations will support their needs as a volunteer. Evidence that the organization has indeed laid down its groundwork for productively working with volunteers factors into the calculations of prospective volunteers.

This idea that volunteers monitor *respect* in their pre-volunteering decisions sheds light on a particular finding in the Hager and Brudney (2011) research. Their national study showed a relationship between organizations with a weak volunteer culture (lacked funds in supporting volunteers, had staff that were indifferent to or resisted volunteers, or did not dedicate sufficient staff time to train and supervise volunteers) and *problems recruiting volunteers*. Quandary: How would volunteers know about this weak culture if they have not volunteered yet? Boezeman and Ellemer's formulation suggests that prospective volunteers monitor from the outside (observe social media, parse solicitation verbiage, watch body language) and make volunteer decisions accordingly. More recently, Kappelides, Cuskelly, and Hoye (2019) conclude that "volunteers begin to develop a psychological contract with their respective organizations based on the perceived expectations they form … from the very first stages of being recruited." Organizations attentive to impending psychological contracts put out signals and information that reflect respect for volunteers. However, organizations less prepared to provide positive engagements for volunteers broadcast other signals that volunteers interpret as disrespectful to their time and attention. Volunteers at this stage do not even need to breach a psychological contract: they simply elect not to pursue one at all.

Because they were not looking through a psychological contract lens, Hager and Brudney (2016) overlooked the CCVA *Body of Knowledge and Competency Framework* section on "Advocacy for Volunteer Involvement," dismissing it as tangential to retention of volunteers. Practices in this section of the framework include designing a communications plan for volunteer services, informing stakeholders of volunteer service opportunities, and developing volunteers as advocates. When viewed through a psychological contract perspective, however, such advocacy becomes more central as potential signals of respect for volunteers. That is, cultivation of the volunteer program propagates the *respect* that underlies the earliest stage of engaging volunteers, which lays the foundation for a long relationship.

Recruitment stage

Once the groundwork is laid, recruitment is a mostly mechanical process of passively alerting people that the organization is open to engaging volunteers, or more actively reaching out to a likely pool of interested individuals. Personal asks can be golden. Kappelides and colleagues (2019) characterize recruitment as the first point of formation of the volunteer's psychological contract with a community organization. Smart organizations have shaped volunteer positions, and maybe even crafted "job descriptions" for each position; these position descriptions are sometimes the basis for transactional contracts and formal performance evaluations. Savvy volunteer administrators know where and how best to recruit, since scattershot recruiting methods waste time and money (Hager & Brudney, 2011). The individuals who responded to recruitment efforts have decided that the organization is at least worth a look. Whether it is worth more than that requires greater establishment and evolution of the psychological contract.

Organizations that think they are doing people a favor by offering them the opportunity to volunteer do so at their peril. On the first date, the organization is under as much scrutiny as the volunteer, if not more. The organization needs volunteers more than volunteers need organizations: volunteers can walk away any time and find a better use for their time and interests. Nonetheless, volunteer management capacity and the traditional management model puts the onus of interviewing, screening volunteers, and matching them to appropriate assignments on the organization alone (Ward & McKillop, 2010). Interviewing and screening are particularly important to volunteer programs that have specific tasks for designated volunteers to perform, but apply less to non-traditional settings. When the goal is finding the right volunteers for at least semi-long-term engagements, then both sides benefit from a match. Organizations need volunteers with the disposition and skills to do productive work, and volunteers need assignments that match well with their motivations. Part of the value of the interview is that either side can swipe left and curtail further engagement.

The suggestion that volunteer administrators should cater to the particular needs and motivations of volunteers is fairly common in the literature (e.g. Snyder & Omoto, 2008; Caldwell, Farmer, & Fedor, 2008; Sundeen, Raskoff, & Garcia, 2007). The reason for investing effort and resources into this screening and matching to assignments is clear when considered through the psychological contract lens. Volunteers make long-term or concerted investments in organizations when conditions meet their expectations and needs. An assignment that does not meet a volunteer's needs (be they values, understanding, social, career, protective, or enhancement needs) may immediately compromise or inevitably wear away at the volunteer's decision to sustain his or her association with the organization (Stukas, Hoye, Nicholson, Brown, & Aisbett,

2016; Aranda, Hurtado, & Topa, 2018). When organization and volunteer needs are misaligned at the interview, screening, and matching phase, the psychological contract will likely trend toward a breach (Walker, Accadia, & Costa, 2016).

Orientation or onboarding stage

On the other hand, when organization and volunteer needs are aligned, the psychological contract is reinforced. Volunteers make at least an initial commitment to working with the organization. The literature traditionally refers to the best practice of 'orienting' volunteers to the organization and their assignments, but the fashionable term these days is 'onboarding,' a term that seems to be bleeding from general HR usage into volunteer administration. In the words of Kolar, Skilton, and Judge (2016, p. 6), "[p]roper management of any workforce includes a system of legal compliance, job analysis and design, recruitment, selection, onboarding, training, and performance management practices in supervision, and this same approach must be extended to volunteers." We welcome this shift in language, especially to the extent that it reinforces a focus on socializing volunteers to culture, tasks, and work spaces. In the traditional mold, orientation involves talking at volunteers, plying them with information as if they are vessels that can be filled with an orientation video, a welcome from the director, a read through a policy manual, a walk through the back offices, and a quick chat with a staff member who will be guiding their work. This approach to orientation likely fails to reinforce the budding psychological contract.

Although some might use "orientation" and "onboarding" interchangeably, we conceive *onboarding* as more volunteer-centric than the traditional orientation process. Cable, Gino, and Staats (2013) discuss employee onboarding as "personal-identity socialization," which squares nicely with our psychological contract lens. According to these researchers, this variety of onboarding "involves encouraging newcomers to express their unique perspectives and strengths on the job from the very beginning and inviting them to frame their work as a platform for doing what they do best" (24). Cable and colleagues suggest four principles of onboarding: (1) give new workers an opportunity to express their best selves; (2) help them identify their unique strengths; (3) focus on introductions and interactions with other team members; and (4) invite newcomers to reflect on how their strengths intersect with prospective tasks and responsibilities. Done right, we suggest that such onboarding can begin to connect volunteers to organizational culture and mission, which will reinforce their motivations for volunteering. Anything else slows acculturation, or even erodes enthusiasm for engagement.

Go-time stage

In the CCVA Competency Framework, several different organizational processes make up what we call *go-time*. Collectively, go-time refers to the routine engagement of the volunteer with the work of the organization, but comprises the preparation of organizational representatives to work with volunteers as well as the supervision of volunteers and communication with them about their task engagements.

People unfamiliar with volunteer administration sometimes think that the volunteer administrator or volunteer management program is responsible for monitoring and fostering the work of volunteers, but this is not the case in most mature volunteer programs. Once volunteers move into go-time, the volunteer management program hands volunteers off to relevant programs and program staff, and may have very little to do with supervision and integration of the volunteer into the organization's workflow. Rather, the volunteer management team works with staff (or experienced volunteers in supervisory roles) to define volunteer tasks and ensure that these supervisors are prepared to work with volunteers in productive ways (Macduff, 2012; Dickin, Dollahite, & Habicht, 2010). When staff are trained and prepared in this way, they are readied to welcome volunteers into their unit cultures and tasks. When staff do not participate in defining volunteer roles and are not trained in working with volunteers, working with volunteers becomes a chore rather than a joy, and socialization of volunteers is left to chance. All too often, staff members are left feeling threatened that volunteers are coming for their jobs (Rimes, Nesbit, Christensen, & Brudney, 2017). Volunteers are left feeling like their work units are not ready for them. The psychological contract is breached, and volunteers start imagining better uses of their time and talents.

Supervision of volunteers can cut both ways: the right level and kind of supervision can reinforce a volunteer's commitment to his or her tasks, while the wrong kind can breach the psychological contract. McCurley and Lynch (2011, Chapter 8) describe the need to gauge an appropriate *level of control* over the work of volunteers. Level 1: Some volunteers have the experience and expertise that calls for self-assignment to tasks without apprising other organizational representatives. Level 2: Others might be trusted to self-assign, but should check progress with supervisors. Level 3: Others might only be prepared to recommend self-assignment, with supervisors making all decisions. Level 4: Other volunteers might have no authority for self-assignment at all, with supervisors spelling out all tasks. Any of these levels of control might be appropriate for a given volunteer or situation, but mismatching control can cause a volunteer to feel either adrift or overly controlled. Hager and Brudney's (2015) nonprofits that report strong supervision of and communication with volunteers also face greater problems retaining volunteers. That troublesome relationship is particularly pronounced among nonprofits that rely on younger volunteers. While the *reason* for this relationship is not clear, we suspect it has to do with the failure to match supervision and communication to the needs and expectations of volunteers.

Recognition

Like most other processes we have described so far, recognition matters for reinforcing the psychological contract and thereby retaining volunteers – but recognition has value only when it is matched to the psychological demands of the volunteer. The chestnut that you should "Thank Your Volunteers!" runs deep in the culture of practice, and, to be sure, thanking volunteers is never a bad idea. Many organizations hold volunteer recognition events, or make sure that volunteers get personal recognition on milestone dates. Whether this practice reinforces the psychological contract, and thereby the retention of volunteers, is an open question. People who are motivated to volunteer for *social* reasons, or to *enhance* their own affect and outlook, might particularly appreciate overt recognition. Others might bristle at it.

Spending time with people who are dying requires an especially dedicated volunteer. Claxton-Oldfield and Jones (2012) designed a Volunteer Retention Questionnaire and asked hospice volunteers the extent to which a variety of forces influence their decision to keep volunteering. For these volunteers, recognition fell pretty far down the list of incentives. High on the list of incentives are such items as *enjoying what I do*, *learning from patients*, and *believing in the philosophy of hospice care*. We might say that these are the conditions that reinforce the psychological contract. Among the lowest on the list of incentives are *receiving special calls or cards from volunteer manager on your birthday*, *being recognized in the newsletter*, and *being formally recognized for your volunteer work with a pin for years of service*. Although well intended, these kinds of recognition do not reinforce the reasons why most people volunteer, or at least not these hospice volunteers.

This theme is also reflected in Smith and Grove's (2017) research on the satisfactions and dissatisfactions of disaster response volunteers. The committed volunteers they studied reported some desire for recognition, but it was recognition from the community rather than from volunteer managers or other staff that kept them going. They quote one of their respondents: "people came running out to our vehicle when we were in the community and they would bring their kids out to the emergency vehicle to thank us. . . . It's the little things like that" (360). Both the hospice and the disaster response examples underline our thesis that volunteer managers must match the motivations of volunteers with appropriate ways of supporting them. Recognition must be authentic, and on the terms deemed appropriate by the volunteers. A 'thank you' banquet might not produce the returns that volunteer managers hope for.

A few take-aways

Our thesis in this chapter has been that *the positive experience and productivity of a volunteer is determined largely by the alignment between what the organization provides to the volunteer and what the volunteer expects of the organization.* The psychological contract lens we have emphasized focuses on the constant calculations that volunteers make to determine whether they should engage or continue to engage the community organizations that need them. Volunteer administration is about reinforcing that psychological contract every step of the way.

Getting inside the heads of these volunteers is not easy. Volunteer managers have to be psychologists, but they have to be sociologists, too. That is, race, class, and gender almost certainly play large roles in the expectations that volunteers have of their volunteer assignments. Demographic shifts require volunteer managers to recruit a more diverse volunteer base. No "one size fits all" recruitment program will capture the interest of volunteers from diverse backgrounds. The psychological contract begins at the recruitment stage, or when volunteers begin to form impressions of organization brands and reputations. Carefully planned advertising enhances organizational attractiveness. However, different people absorb those messages in different ways. For example, Avery and McKay (2006) found that women and people from minority populations were less responsive to recruitment messages delivered by white males, and were less likely to view the organization favorably than did white male applicants. Potential volunteers hear different messages. Shields (2009) suggests that organizations make strategic decisions about the volunteers they want to attract, and market the organization to highlight benefits a specific group wants most.

At its core, the psychological contract perspective gives easy advice for attracting and retaining happy and productive volunteers: just be what they need. However, discerning and meeting needs is a daunting task, especially when organizations do not put time and money into developing the capacity to provide excellent experiences for their volunteers. As we note in the introduction of the chapter, too many executive directors and board members give short shrift to volunteer administration, assuming that volunteers will flock to volunteer assignments after a Facebook post and stick with it regardless of how much thought the organization has put into the tasks and assignments. They won't. They will not show up, or they will leave. These organizations need to take a close look at organizations in the other camp, those that invest in people and processes necessary to create a culture and conditions conducive to volunteer engagement. These organizations and their professional volunteer management team make psychological contracts with volunteers and honor them, every day.

References

Alfes, K., Shantz, A., and Saksida, T. (2015). Committed to whom: Unraveling how relational job design influences volunteers' turnover intentions and time spent volunteering. *Voluntas, 26*, pp. 2479–2499.

Alfes, K., Shantz, A., and Bailey, C. (2016). Enhancing volunteer engagement to achieve desirable outcomes: What can nonprofit employers do? *Voluntas 27*, pp. 595–617.

Allen, J., and Mueller, S. (2013). The revolving door: A closer look at major factors in volunteers' intention to quit. *Journal of Community Psychology, 41*(2), pp. 139–155.

Anderson, N., and Schalk, R. (1998). The psychological contract in retrospect and prospect. *Journal of Organizational Behavior, 19*, pp. 637–647.

Aranda, M., Hurtado, M.D., and Topa, G. (2018). Breach of psychological contract and organizational citizenship behaviors in volunteerism: The mediator role of affect and the moderation of volunteers' age. *Voluntas, 29*, pp. 59–70.

Avery, D., and McKay, P. (2006). Target practice: An organizational impression management approach to attracting minority and female job applicants. *Personnel Psychology, 59*, pp. 157–187.

Berger, P.L., and Luckman, T. (1966). *The Social Construction of Reality: A Treatise in the Sociology of Knowledge*, Garden City, NY: Anchor Books.

Boezeman, E., and Ellemers, N. (2008). Volunteer recruitment: The role of organizational support and anticipated respect in non-volunteers' attraction to charitable volunteer organizations. *Journal of Applied Psychology, 93*(5), pp. 1013–1026.

Boezeman, E., and Ellemers, N. (2014). Volunteer recruitment. In *The Oxford Handbook of Recruitment* (pp. 73–87), edited by K.Y.T Yu and D.M. Cable. New York: Oxford University Press.

Cable, D.M., Gino, F., and Staats, B.R. (2013). Reinventing employee onboarding. *MIT Sloan Management Review*, Spring, pp. 23–28.

Caldwell, S.D., Farmer, S.M., and Fedor, D.B. (2008). The influence of age on volunteer contributions in a nonprofit organization. *Journal of Organizational Behavior, 29*(3), pp. 311–333.

Clary, E.G., Snyder, M., and Ridge, R. (1992). Volunteers' motivations: A functional strategy for the recruitment, placement, and retention of volunteers. *Nonprofit Management & Leadership, 2*(4), pp. 333–350.

Clary, E.G., Snyder, M., Ridge, R.D., Copeland, J., Stukas, A.A., Haugen, J., and Miene, P. (1998). Understanding and assessing the motivations of volunteers: A functional approach. *Journal of Personality and Social Psychology, 74*(6), pp. 1516.

Claxton-Oldfield, S., and Jones, R. (2012). Holding on to what you have got: Keeping hospice palliative care volunteers volunteering. *American Journal of Hospice & Palliative Medicine, 30*(5), pp. 467–472.

Connors, T.D. (2012). Preface. In *The Volunteer Management Handbook: Leadership Strategies for Success* (2nd ed., pp. xiii–xliii), edited by T.D. Connors. Hoboken, NJ: Wiley.

Conway, N., and Briner, R., (2009). Fifty years of psychological contract research: What do we know and what are the main challenges? *International Review of Industrial and Organizational Psychology, 21*, pp. 71–131.

Council for Certification in Volunteer Administration. (2015). *CCVA Body of Knowledge and Competency Framework*. Accessed April 24, 2019 at http://cvacert.org/wp-content/uploads/2015/09/2015-CVA-Competency-Framework-FINAL-2015-Sep-03.pdf

Coyle-Shapiro, J., and Kessler, I. (2000). Consequences of the psychological contract for the employment relationship: A large scale survey. *Journal of Management Studies, 37*(7), pp. 903–930.

Dickin, K.L., Dollahite, J.S., and Habicht, J. (2010). Job satisfaction and retention of community nutrition educators: The importance of perceived value of the program, consultative supervision, and work relationships. *Journal of Nutrition Education and Behavior, 42*(5), pp. 337–344.

Ellis, S. (2010). *From the Top Down: The Executive Role in Successful Volunteer Involvement* (3rd edn). Jacksonville, FL: Energize, Inc.

Esmond, J., and Dunlop, P. (2004). *Developing the volunteer motivation inventory to assess the underlying motivational drives of volunteers in Western Australia.* Community Link and Network (CLAN) WA, Inc.

Guest, D.E. (2004). The psychology of the employment relationship: An analysis based on the psychological contract. *Applied Psychology, 53*(4), pp. 541–555.

Hager, M. (2013). Toward emergent strategy in volunteer administration. *International Journal of Volunteer Administration, 29*(3), pp. 13–22.

Hager, M., and Brudney, J. (2004). *Volunteer Management Practices and Retention of Volunteers.* Washington, DC: The Urban Institute.

Hager, M., and Brudney, J. (2010). Sustaining volunteer involvement. In *Volunteer Administration: Professional Practice* (1st edn, pp. 215–248), edited by K. Seel. Ontario, Canada: LexisNexis Canada and the Council for Certification in Volunteer Administration.

Hager M., and Brudney, J. (2011). Problems recruiting volunteers: Nature versus nurture. *Nonprofit Management & Leadership, 22*(2), pp. 137–157.

Hager, M., and Brudney, J. (2015). In search of strategy: Universalistic, contingent, and configurational adoption of volunteer management practices. *Nonprofit Management & Leadership, 25*(3), pp. 235–254.

Hager, M., and Brudney, J. (2016). Sustaining volunteer involvement. In *Volunteer Administration: Professional Practice* (3rd edn, pp. 225–247), edited by K. Seel. Ontario, Canada: LexisNexis Canada and the Council for Certification in Volunteer Administration.

Hampton, J. (1988). *Hobbes and the Social Contract Tradition.* Cambridge: Cambridge University Press.

Hobbes, T. (2010). *Leviathan.* Revised edition, edited by A.P. Martinich and B. Battiste. Ontario, Broadview Press. Leviathan originally published in 1651.

Kappelides, P., Cuskelly, G., and Hoye, R. (2019). The influence of volunteer recruitment practices and expectations on the development of volunteers' psychological contracts. *Voluntas, 30*(1), pp. 259–271.

Kolar, D., Skilton, S., and Judge, L.W. (2016). Human resource management with a volunteer workforce. *Journal of Facility Planning, Design, and Management, 4*(1), pp. 5–12.

Locke, J., Hume, D., and Rousseau, J. (1960). *Social Contract: Essays by Locke, Hume, and Rousseau* (Vol. 511). Oxford: Oxford University Press.

Macduff, N. (2005). Societal changes and the rise of the episodic volunteer. *Emerging Areas of Volunteering, 1*(2), pp. 49–61.

Macduff, N. (2012). Volunteer and staff relations. In *The Volunteer Management Handbook: Leadership Strategies for Success* (2nd edn, pp. 255–271), edited by T.D. Connors. Hoboken, NJ: John Wiley.

Macduff, N., Netting, F.E., and O'Connor, M.K. (2009). Multiple ways of coordinating volunteers with differing styles of service. *Journal of Community Practice, 17*(4), pp. 400–423.

McCurley, S., and Lynch, R. (2011). *Volunteer Management: Mobilizing All the Resources of the Community* (3rd edn). Plattsburgh, NY: Interpub Group.

Moreno-Jimenez, M., and Villodres, M. (2010). Prediction of burnout in volunteers. *Journal of Applied Social Psychology, 40*(7), pp. 1798–1818.

Nichols, G. (2013). The psychological contract of volunteers: A new research agenda. *Voluntas, 24*, pp. 986–1005.

O'Donohue, W., Martin, A., and Torugsa, N. (2015). Understanding individual responses to failure by the organization to fulfil its obligations: Examining the influence of psychological capital and psychological contract type. *Human Resource Management Journal, 25*(1), pp. 131–147.

Rimes, H., Nesbit, R., Christensen, R.K., and Brudney, J.L. (2017). Exploring the dynamics of volunteer and staff interactions. *Nonprofit Management & Leadership, 28*(2), pp. 195–213.

Rousseau, D.M. (1989) Psychological and implied contracts in organizations. *Employee Responsibilities and Rights Journal, 2*(2), pp. 121–139.

Rousseau, D.M. (1990). New hire perceptions of their own and their employer's obligations: A study of psychological contracts. *Journal of Organizational Behavior, 11*, pp. 389–400.

Rousseau, D.M. (1995). *Psychological Contracts in Organizations: Understanding Written and Unwritten Agreements.* Thousand Oaks, CA: Sage Publications.

Rousseau, D.M., and Tijoriwala, S.A. (1998). Assessing psychological contracts: Issues, alternatives and measures. *Journal of Organizational Behavior, 19*, pp. 679–695.

Rousseau, D.M., Hansen, S.D., and Tomprou, M. (2018). A dynamic phase model of psychological contract processes. *Journal of Organizational Behavior, 39*(9), pp. 1081–1098.

Shields, P. (2009). Young adult volunteers: Recruitment appeals and other marketing strategies. *Journal of Nonprofit & Public Sector Marketing, 21*, pp. 139–159.

Shore, L.M., and Tetrick, L.E. (1994). The psychological contract as an explanatory framework in the employment relationship. *Journal of Organizational Behavior (1986–1998)*, 91.

Smith, S.L., and Grove, C.J. (2017). Bittersweet and paradoxical: Disaster response volunteering with the American Red Cross. *Nonprofit Management & Leadership, 27*(3), pp. 353–369.

Snyder, M., and Omoto, A.M. (2008). Volunteerism: Social issues perspectives and social policy implications. *Social Issues and Policy Review, 2*(1), pp. 1–36.

Studer, S. (2016). Volunteer management: Responding to the uniqueness of volunteers. *Nonprofit and Volunteer Sector Quarterly, 45*(4), pp. 688–714.

Stukas, A.A., Hoye, R., Nicholson, M., Brown, K.M., and Aisbett, L. (2016). Motivations to volunteer and their associations with volunteers' well-being. *Nonprofit and Voluntary Sector Quarterly, 45*(1), pp. 112–132.

Sundeen, R.A., Raskoff, S.A., and Garcia, M.C. (2007). Differences in perceived barriers to volunteering to formal organizations: Lack of time versus lack of interest. *Nonprofit Management & Leadership, 17*(3), pp. 279–300.

Thompson, J., and Bunderson, S. (2003). Violations of principle: Ideological currency in the psychological contract. *Academy of Management Review, 28*, pp. 571–586.

Urban Institute. (2004). *Volunteer Management Capacity in America's Charities and Congregations: A Briefing Report*. Washington, DC: The Urban Institute.

Vantilborgh, T., Bidee, J., Pepermans, R., Willems, J., Huybrechts, G., and Jegers, M. (2014). Effects of ideological and relational psychological contract breach and fulfilment on volunteers' work effort. *European Journal of Work and Organizational Psychology, 23*(2), pp. 217–230.

Walker, A., Accadia, R., and Costa, B. (2016). Volunteer retention: The importance of organizational support and psychological contract breach. *Journal of Community Psychology, 44*(8), pp. 1059–1069.

Ward, A.M., and McKillop, D.G. (2010). Profiling: A strategy for successful volunteer recruitment in credit unions. *Financial Accountability & Management, 26*(4), pp. 367–391.

20

CO-PRODUCTION

Taco Brandsen

PROFESSOR, INSTITUTE FOR MANAGEMENT RESEARCH,
RADBOUD UNIVERSITY, NIJMEGEN, THE NETHERLANDS

Trui Steen

PROFESSOR, KU LEUVEN PUBLIC GOVERNANCE INSTITUTE,
KU LEUVEN, LEUVEN, BELGIUM

Bram Verschuere

ASSOCIATE PROFESSOR, DEPARTMENT OF PUBLIC
GOVERNANCE AND MANAGEMENT, GHENT UNIVERSITY, GHENT, BELGIUM

Introduction

Co-production is a specific kind of citizen participation in which citizens take an active and direct role in the delivery of services. Although it occurs in all kinds of commercial services, we will here focus on services delivered by public and nonprofit organizations, where it is still a more novel concept. Examples of such co-production are patients designing their treatments in collaboration with medical personnel; citizens contributing to public safety through community watches; students working with teachers to design their lessons; or residents engaging in community development projects alongside social workers.

This is a marked departure both from classic participation in public services, which focuses on strategic consultations with representatives of citizens, and from volunteering outside a professional context. Co-production is a hands-on approach that involves citizens more concretely, in organized activities that affect them directly and personally. In a sense, it weds the areas of public management and civil society; and this is indeed visible in the diverse backgrounds of the scholars its study attracts.

The chapter will describe how co-production has increasingly entered the agenda of academics and policymakers, as interest in citizen participation has more generally soared. Expectations are high. Co-production is regarded as a possible solution to the public sector's decreased legitimacy and dwindling resources, by accessing more of society's resources. In addition, it is seen as part of a more general drive to reinvigorate voluntary participation and strengthen social cohesion in an increasingly fragmented and individualized society (Brudney & England, 1983; Pestoff, 1998; Alford, 2002; Bovaird, 2007).

The popularity has come at the price of great confusion over what the concept means. In the chapter, we will show how to demarcate its meaning more precisely, to prevent it from becoming just another catch-all term. We will explain how research has progressed, moving from agenda-setting towards methodologically more diverse approaches and a sounder evidence base. Finally, we will discuss some of the major issues in current research on the topic, such as whether co-production overcomes the elitist tendencies of classical participation.

The revival of interest in co-production[1]

It is easy to forget, now that the participation of citizens is fashionable, that it was for long considered undesirable or unimportant; often, it still is. After Elinor Ostrom (1975) published the first work on co-production in the 1970s, there was an initial surge of interest in the topic, which died down in the 1980s. It is clear to see why: it was simply not in tune with the times. Ostrom had not only pointed out that many public services were already delivered by different public and private actors, but also that the service delivery additionally depended on the efforts of the citizens and clients who consumed them (Pestoff et al., 2012). Although there remained widespread support for more choice in public services, this took the shape of market-inspired reforms, in which citizens were cast as consumers. Although there is room for co-production within such a perspective, it is different from one fostered in a paradigm of participation and collaboration. After market-inspired reforms fell out of grace academically (although in practice they are still very much alive), interest in co-production gradually revived (Nabatchi et al., 2017). In public discourse, co-production at the individual level still remains relatively insignificant compared to classical types of individual participation and to partnerships between government and civil society. However, this may change as the former become more viable and the limits of the latter become more apparent.

Advances in technology and cultural changes have made co-production far easier to implement. In Elinor Ostrom's time, communication was a practical problem that made co-production time-intensive and costly. Simply getting people's personal contact details could require major effort. Now it is far easier for public employees to interact with citizens, both collectively and individually. As more sophisticated technologies become available, services that were hitherto dominated by professionals leave more room for individual input and choice. For instance, it has become easier for people to assess their own health, to an extent that was until recently considered impossible. By implication, this changes their interactions with medical professionals.

Simultaneously, cultural shifts have created an environment in which co-production has become more feasible and in which the potential of new technologies could be realized. Generally, individualization and the decline of traditional authority have changed the position of professionals in society. It has become more accepted for citizens as non-experts (or, as others argue, experts on themselves) to take more responsibility for the services they or their dependents receive. Likewise, there is now more recognition among governments that citizens need to be involved in the design and implementation of policies. However, the actual extent of citizen involvement still differs strongly between types of services, organizations and cultural contexts. If there is a movement towards a new type of service delivery, it is a slow and chequered one, even if the public discourse suggests a rapid transformation.

At the same time, it has become evident that participation is not in itself a panacea. It has been believed that new types of participation would help solve the so-called democratic deficit. Yet attempts by governments to engage citizens have often been dogged by lack of interest, mutual frustration and limited representation. The reasons for this are various. The fact that policymakers and professionals are not prepared or able to follow up on the input of citizens certainly plays a part. Citizens may have unrealistic expectations of what governments can achieve. But the shape of participation also determines its effectiveness. If alternatives to representative democracy resemble the institutions of representative democracy, then they will also mirror its ills. Many types of participation copy the features of policy and politics: in their emphasis on certain (official) settings, a specialized discourse, the need for certain skills. Citizens without the necessary skills or resources are still likely to be excluded, even if the format is partially changed. This realization has encouraged the search for more radical alternatives, which include self-organization and co-production. Yet whether these alternatives function better, and under what conditions, still remains to be seen.

Defining co-production[2]

What is co-production exactly? There are various definitions around, but the essentials are the following:

- Co-production is a relationship between the employees of an organization and (groups of) individual citizens.
- It requires direct and active inputs from these citizens to the work of the organization.
- The professional is a paid employee of the organization, whereas the citizen receives compensation below market value or no compensation at all.

In other words, co-production will be defined as "a relationship between a paid employee of an organization and (groups of) individual citizens that requires a direct and active contribution from these citizens to the work of the organization" (Brandsen & Honingh, 2016). This implies a number of choices, which set co-production apart from participation and volunteering more generally. The definition is not meant to set a barbed-wire fence around the concept and grey areas will always exist. However, terminological confusion has marred the intellectual progress of the field, a point to which we will return later. If it is to be a meaningful concept, it is important to be more precise about what it is, and more especially about what it is not.

To begin with, an explicit element of the definition is that co-production is about collaboration between organizations (e.g. public agencies and nonprofit organizations) and citizens. Whether the latter refers to citizens individually (as in Ostrom's definition) or individually as well as collectively (as suggested by Parks et al., 1981, 1999) remains open, but it excludes inter-organizational collaboration, which Pestoff and Brandsen (2008) have referred to as "co-management" or "co-governance." Indeed, where the term "co-production" has been used with reference to inter-organizational links, this appears to have originated in a different tradition of research and the terminological similarity appears to be accidental, although some scholars have merged the different approaches and used co-production as a more encompassing label.

The requirement for active input by individual citizens in services they receive distinguishes co-production from passive consumerism: it is not enough simply to use a product or receive a service. In that sense, co-production can be seen as a specific variety of volunteering. The citizens in question can be direct recipients of a service, but need not necessarily be so. For instance, the participation of family members of children in child care has been an oft-studied topic (e.g. Vamstad 2012).

Finally, co-production is primarily linked to the provision of services. In the literature we are referring to, these are usually nonprofit services. Some scholarship includes participation through advocacy (for example, on representative councils) or inputs by citizens that occur outside an organizational context (for example, citizens contributing to public safety by keeping an eye on their neighbours' houses). However, these are problematic. Should we include advocacy or inputs outside an organization, co-production becomes virtually synonymous with any type of participation. The public value of such contributions by citizens is undeniable, but as an academic concept, co-production has little value unless it is clearly demarcated. Another consideration is that the activities, experiences and skills involved in advocacy differ quite strongly from those involved in the direct production of a service. For instance, if mental health care clients consult with their therapists to jointly shape their personal treatment, this requires other skills than the representation of mental health care clients on the boards of treatments centres. This is not to say that advocacy cannot be co-produced, as Abramson et al. (2015) show, in a case study of a service-oriented nonprofit organization that provides assistance to HIV-AIDS patients. Professionals and clients together started engaging in advocacy, as a strategy to ensure organizational survival in a context of governmental budget cuts.

In other words, this does not include all inputs by citizens that may affect the overall design and delivery of a service, but the focus is on the direct input of citizens on the individual design and delivery of a service during the production phase. "Direct" here means that the input by a citizen affects the service individually provided to her or him. This need not be restricted to face-to-face contacts. Indeed, some interesting developments in co-production are through the Internet (for example, guided online self-treatment in mental health care). However, it does exclude advocacy (voice) or the shift to an alternative provider (exit), both of which rely on indirect mechanisms to affect the services provided to the individual in question and only at a future point.

Let us illustrate these choices using the example of housing (Brandsen & Helderman, 2012):

- If individual tenants or groups of tenants work with the staff of the tenant association, this is co-production. If the association collaborates with a local council, it is not.
- If tenants actively collaborate in the maintenance or design of the housing, it is co-production. If they only passively receive what they pay for, it is not.
- If tenants actively collaborate in the maintenance or design of their own housing, collectively or individually, it is co-production. If they sit on a representative council, it is not.

Different types of co-production

Co-production practices can differ markedly in terms of scope and purpose. Previous work (Brandsen & Honingh, 2016) has distinguished two dimensions by which they can be categorized as: (1) the extent to which citizens design services delivered to them and (2) the proximity of co-production to the primary process.

The type of voluntary input

Various authors have argued that co-production must be voluntary in nature. But there are different ways to interpret this. If we understand it as freely given or withheld, it implies a rational choice on the part of the citizen to co-produce or not. Yet some authors have pointed out that co-production is an inherent part of the delivery of certain services and therefore not a question of choice. This is more than saying that co-production is necessary for effective service delivery because producer and citizen inputs are interdependent; rather, that it is impossible to have a situation without co-production (Osborne & Strokosch, 2013). "From a service-dominant approach, there is no way to avoid the coproduction of public services because it is an inalienable element of such services. The question thus is not how to 'add-in' coproduction to public services but rather how to manage and work with its implications for effective public service delivery" (p. 146). This clearly demonstrates how the study of co-production has become more multidisciplinary: the assumption of free, rational choice central to the economic perspective is here challenged by insights from disciplines such as psychology, sociology and the services management literature. If services have inherent co-production, then free will does not enter into it: to make use of the service is to co-produce. This distinction between chosen and non-chosen co-production is a source of variation in the processes of co-production, which makes it a highly relevant variable in studying the phenomenon, but not a suitable element for a basic definition.

This means that, even if co-production is inherent, citizens can design services with different degrees of active input. As Porter (2012, p. 38) has noted:

> There are two different usages of the concept here. In the first, co-production is associated with a specific good or service where inputs from both producer and consumer are combined (and) in which if co-production is omitted the service will not be created. Inputs from the consumer producer are required to create a public service in the first usage, but in the second usage, inputs from consumers may be contingently added to enhance qualities and quantities of a public service.

The challenge is therefore to separate those elements that are inherent from those which are merely possible or desirable. Following this distinction, the question is whether a contribution to co-production must always be voluntary in the sense of freely given. If co-production is an inherent part of the production relationship, one could imagine situations where co-production is not freely given (Fledderus et al., 2015). By extension, even though most co-production practices are a specific type of volunteering, it is possible to coerce citizens to co-produce, even if that feels counterintuitive. Consider the example of a high school class: students may not have chosen to be physically present, but they determine the nature of the lessons nonetheless, even if they freely choose to withhold their attention. Although learning is essential to an effective lesson (Porter, 2012) it is possible to design lessons in any number of ways. Pupils can sit back and listen to a talk, with learning a one-way street; the teacher can prepare questions and exercises to encourage interaction; or she or he can actively engage students in designing the lesson, jointly choosing what to address and how to shape the interaction. Which is the best method from a didactic perspective is a question for the experts, but the point for co-production research is that the lessons have both an inherent and a chosen element. One can have the former without the latter.

The example shows that, in addition to inherent technical qualities of a service that compel users to co-produce, there may be regulatory mechanisms to force it. Students under a certain age are obliged to take part in classes and absence is sanctioned. Yet even within such a system of obligations, different approaches to co-production will coexist, as teachers and students will always have at least some leeway to shape the nature of their interaction. The variety in types of co-production becomes even greater when we compare different public services, since the extent to which co-production is inherent differs along with the type of activity (for instance, in healing a broken leg as compared to supervising an undergraduate student).

This implies that, in cases such as teaching, the extent of co-production is the result of a combination of technical characteristics, legal rules and voluntary choices (which, to add to the complexity, may be shaped both at the individual, group and organizational level).

Summing up, the extent to which citizens are allowed to design the production of the service delivered to them is a dimension along which to distinguish different types.

Core and complementary tasks

Earlier we noted (1) that co-production concerns the joint production of public services; and (2) that co-production concerns the interaction between citizens and employees of the organization

Table 20.1 Different types of co-production

	Implementation	*Design and implementation*
Complementary task	Complementary co-production in implementation	Complementary co-production in service design and implementation
Core task	Co-production in the implementation of core services	Co-production in the design and implementation of core services

in the production of services. Yet it is possible that the co-production in question does not directly produce public services, but does contribute inputs to an organization that supports the production process indirectly. This is more than a theoretical possibility, because various activities described in the co-production literature arguably do not relate directly to the organization's core services, even if they undoubtedly contribute to them. When university alumni give a guest lecture as part of a regular course, they directly contribute to the teaching process. When they speak at a publicity event for a university's programs, this ultimately contributes to the goals of the organization, but it is not a direct contribution to teaching. It does involve a joint process with the organization's employees, but it is not part of the core (primary) process, which makes it co-production of a different sort. Of course, the question what is the core process of an organization is open to different interpretations, which may shift over time. It cannot be determined a priori and should be clearly defined on a case-by-case basis.

In other words, there is variation in the extent to which co-production involves tasks that are part of the organization's core services. Accordingly, the proximity to core services will become a second dimension for distinguishing different types of co-production.

Varieties of co-production

Summing up, in addition to basic elements of co-production, we have now identified the following variable elements:

- The extent to which citizens are involved, not only in the implementation, but also in the design of professionally produced services.
- The proximity of the tasks that citizens perform to the core services of the organization.

The combination of these dimensions then leads to four various potential types of co-production, visualized in Table 20.1.

> *Complementary co-production in service design and implementation* occurs when citizens are engaged in co-production, but in tasks that are complementary to the core process rather than part of it. This happens, for instance, when parents help plan and organize extracurricular activities like school excursions or design and plant a school garden. These activities are part of the professional organization's mission, but they do not directly involve citizens in the core activities of teaching.
>
> *Complementary co-production in service implementation* occurs when citizens are actively engaged in the implementation, but not the design, of a complementary task. Examples are students assisting the university in organizing welcome days or parents helping to prepare school plays: they are undoubtedly necessary and important, but they do not directly contribute to the core activity of teaching and they usually do not have the opportunity to design or redesign the events.

Co-production in the design and implementation of core services is a situation where citizens are directly involved in producing core services of an organization and are directly involved in both the design and implementation of the individual service provided to them. Examples are postgraduate training modules where entrants, together with instructors, define their own learning objectives and learning activities; participative building projects in which (future) tenants of a housing cooperative work with architects and builders in the design, construction and maintenance of their homes; or patients working with dietitians to modify their lifestyle.

Co-production in the implementation of core services occurs when citizens are actively engaged in the implementation, but not the design, of an individual service that is at the core of the organization. For instance, as discussed earlier, co-production may be inherent to the production process ("inherent" meaning that active engagement by the client is essential to its successful implementation), but institutionally designed so that citizens do not have direct influence on how it is designed in their individual case. Examples are children's education during which students follow strictly defined lessons, yet their input is still crucial to effective learning; or enforced services, such as mandatory employment reintegration. Alternatively, co-production may not be inherent, but deliberately included as part of the design.

The state of the art in research

The reason to re-think the nature of co-production is that its use, both in research and practice, has grown considerably over the past decade. This was certainly not a given and, indeed, for a long time the topic received only marginal attention.

Following first steps by Nobel Prize winner Elinor Ostrom and her associates, research on co-production consisted of early explorations of co-production in public services – particularly associated with the work of Brudney and England (1983), Pestoff (1998), Alford (2002) and Bovaird (2007). In subsequent years, these were accompanied by a number of mostly small and qualitative cases demonstrating the relevance and potential benefits of this type of participation (for instance, those bundled in Pestoff et al., 2012). More recently, there were efforts to make research in this area more systematic and rigorous. One of the explanations is that the research community has also become much more coherent, with the emergence of stable platforms for research on these topics (e.g., through the European Group for Public Administration (EGPA), International Institute of Administrative Sciences (IIAS), International Research Society for Public Management (IRSPM) networks).

To a certain extent, research into co-production has moved from agenda-setting to fact-finding. The data that are collected by researchers have improved in quality and a number of methodologically more diverse and critical studies emerged examining specific aspects of co-production. This has begun to open up areas that were until recently black boxes. These include the motives for citizens to engage in co-production (Van Eijk et al., 2017), the role of professionals in co-production (Tuurnas, 2015), or its effects, for instance on trust (Fledderus, 2015) and inclusiveness (Vanleene et al., 2018). We now thus have more research that is providing first answers to the key questions of why, how and with what effects co-production takes place (or not). But we also observe more attention to the uneasy and critical questions about the dark side of co-production: although many practitioners still see participation as something that is mainly good practice, research also increasingly discusses and shows (potential) pitfalls and drawbacks in terms of unequal participation opportunities, quality of services and unequal benefits of co-produced public services (Steen et al., 2018).

The methods, traditionally single case studies, have further expanded to cross-national comparative case studies (e.g., Voorberg et al., 2015; Bovaird et al., 2016; Van Eijk et al., 2017), experiments (e.g., Jakobsen, 2013) and longitudinal studies (e.g., Fledderus, 2015). Although case study research with mainly qualitative data is still dominant in the field, we observe an increasing amount of research that applies quantitative and even experimental methods.

Finally, given the potential of increased citizen participation to mitigate the effects of the big societal issues of our time (e.g., climate and environment, poverty, migration), researchers increasingly recognize that relying only on public administration paradigms and theories will not suffice to understand the benefits and risks of co-production of public services for and with people who suffer from the effects of these issues. The challenge of providing access to safe drinking water and water sanitation services, for example, shows the need to combine insights on the governance conditions for citizen co-production with an understanding of the socio-economic and the physical (technical, spatial and environmental) context at hand (Moretto & Ranzato, 2017). Multi- and interdisciplinary approaches in which public administration scholars cooperate with scholars from other disciplines will need to be developed further.

Despite these recent advancements in the field, there are still challenges to tackle as a research community. Most pressingly, the diverse uses of the term co-production, combined with the prevalence of highly particular case studies, have hindered meaningful comparisons between different studies. In terms of scope and dynamics, individual participation in health care is quite different from the collaboration between local nonprofit organizations and municipalities, yet the co-production label has been used to cover all. Also, there were studies in which the term has been stretched to cover any individual action directly or indirectly contributing to the effectiveness of public services. Anyone watching over their property might be regarded as co-producing public safety. Although individual contributions to the public good are undeniably essential, extending co-production to cover all of them makes the term useless as an academic concept. However, attempts to develop new and more precise definitions – even if they are quite different – have vastly increased the cumulative potential of research in this area.

Conclusion: Current discussions

The methodologically diverse approaches to co-production have started to open up some areas that were until recently black boxes. We conclude by flagging some of the more salient topics that have concerned scholars in recent years.

One of the most intriguing issues in co-production is whether it is more inclusive than classical types of participation in public services. It has often been argued that the latter replicates existing patterns of inequality, because they rely strongly on deliberation and this favours highly educated citizens, with high levels of cultural and social capital. Is co-production different? There is some evidence to suggest this. For instance, research by Clark et al. (2013) and Bovaird et al. (2015) has shown only limited effects of socio-economic differences, at least for services with low thresholds. Moreover, there is potential for co-production particularly in initiatives directed towards vulnerable populations such as projects aimed at de-isolating elderly persons, reactivating the long-term unemployed or empowering residents of derelict neighbourhoods. But much more research will be needed to determine when co-production makes a difference.

Another important issue is how public policies can encourage co-production. Potentially they could do so in several different ways, but usually they aim to give citizens more control over the design of the services they personally receive, based on the reasoning that organizational resistance must and can be reduced through top-down intervention. An example is legislation to protect patients' autonomy and provide for informed consent to medical interventions. Also, policies are more likely to be directed at core services, since these are the most likely to trigger interventions and to enhance service quality. But there are also policies meant to encourage complementary co-production, for instance, by giving parents a greater role in after-school programmes. Depending on the extent to which they can shape these after-school activities, this involves design and/or implementation.

Notes

1   This section is based on the introduction to Brandsen, Steen and Verschuere (2018).
2   This section is based on Brandsen and Honingh (2016).

References

Abramson, A., Benjamin, L. & Toepler, S. (2015). Metro TeenAIDS: Serve and Advocate. In R. Cnaan & D. Vinokur-Kaplan (Eds.), *Cases in Innovative Nonprofits: Organizations that Make a Difference* (pp. 229–242). Thousand Oaks, CA: Sage.

Alford, J. (2002). Why do Public Sector Clients Co-Produce? Towards a Contingency Theory, *Administration & Society*, 34(1): 32–56.

Bovaird, T. (2007). Beyond Engagement & Participation: User & Community Co-Production of Public Services, *Public Administration Review*, 67(5): 846–860.

Bovaird, T., Van Ryzin, G., Loeffler, E. & Parrado, S. (2015). Activating Citizens to Participate in Collective Co-Production of Public Services, *Journal of Social Policy*, 44: 1–23.

Bovaird, T., Stoker, G., Loeffler, E., Jones, T. & Pinilla Roncancio, M. (2016). Activating Collective Coprodution for Public Services: Influencing Citizens to Participate in Complex Governance Mechanisms, *International Review of Administrative Sciences*, 82(1): 47–68.

Brandsen, T. & Helderman, J.K. (2012). The Trade-Off Between Capital and Community: The Conditions for Successful Co-Production in Housing, *Voluntas*, 23: 1139–1155.

Brandsen, T. & Honingh, M. (2016). Distinguishing Different Types of Co-production: A Conceptual Analysis Based on the Classical Definitions, *Public Administration Review*, 76(3): 427–435.

Brandsen, T., Steen, T. & Verschuere, B. (Eds.). (2018). *Co-Production and Co-Creation: Engaging Citizens in Public Services*. London: Routledge.

Brudney, J. & England, E. (1983). Toward a Definition of the Coproduction Concept, *Public Administration Review*, 43(1): 59–65.

Clark, B.Y., Brudney, J.L. & Jang, S.G. (2013). Coproduction of Government Services and the New Information Technology: Investigating the Distributional Biases, *Public Administration Review*, 73(5): 687–701.

Fledderus, J. (2015). Building Trust through Public Service Co-production, *International Journal of Public Sector Management*, 28(7): 550–565.

Fledderus, J., Brandsen, T. & Honingh, M.E. (2015). User Co-production of Public Service Delivery: An Uncertainty Approach, *Public Policy and Administration*, 30(2): 145–164.

Jakobsen, M. (2013). Can Government Initiatives Increase Citizen Coproduction? Results of a Randomized Field Experiment, *Journal of Public Administration Research and Theory*, 23(1): 27–54.

Moretto, L. & Ranzato, M. (2017). A Socio-natural Standpoint to Understand Coproduction of Water, Energy and Waste Services, *Urban Research and Practice*, 10(1): 1–21.

Nabatchi, T., Sancino, A. & Sicilia, M. (2017). Varieties of Participation in Public Services: The Who, When, and What of Coproduction, *Public Administration Review*, 77(5): 766–776.

Osborne, S.P. & Strokosch, K. (2013). It Takes Two to Tango? Understanding the Co-production of Public Services by Integrating the Services Management and Public Administration Perspectives, *British Journal of Management*, 24: 31–47.

Ostrom, E. (1975). *The Delivery of Urban Services: Outcomes of Change*. Beverly Hills, CA: Sage.

Parks, R.B., et al. (1981). Consumers as Co-producers of Public Services: Some Economic and Institutional Considerations, *Policy Studies Journal*, 9(7): 1001–1011.

Parks, R.B., et al. (1999). Consumers as Co-producers of Public Services. Some Institutional and Economic Considerations. Polycentric Governance and Development. In M.D. McGinnes (Ed.), *Reading from the Workshop in Political Theory and Policy Analysis*. Ann Arbor, MI: University of Michigan Press.

Pestoff, V. (1998). *Beyond the Market and State. Civil Democracy & Social Enterprises in a Welfare Society*. Aldershot: Ashgate.

Pestoff, V. & Brandsen, T. (Eds.). (2008). *Co-Production, the Third Sector and the Delivery of Public Services.* Abingdon: Routledge.

Pestoff, V., Brandsen, T. & Verschuere, B. (Eds.). (2012). *New Public Governance, the Third Sector and Co-Production.* Abingdon: Routledge.

Porter, D.O. 2012. Co-production and Network Structures in Public Education. In V. Pestoff, T. Brandsen, & B. Verschuere (Eds.), *New Public Governance, the Third Sector and Co-production* (pp. 145–168). New York: Routledge.

Steen, T., Brandsen, T. & Verschuere, B. (2018). The Dark Side of Co-creation and Co-production: Seven Evils. In T. Brandsen, T. Steen, & B. Verschuere (Eds.), *Co-production and Co-creation: Engaging Citizens in Public Services* (pp. 9–17). London: Routledge.

Tuurnas, S. (2015). Learning to Co-produce? The Perspective of Public Service Professionals, *International Journal of Public Sector Management*, 28(7): 583–598.

Vamstad, J. (2012). Co-production and Service Quality: A New Perspective for the Swedish Welfare State. In V. Pestoff, T. Brandsen, & B. Verschuere (Eds.), *New Public Governance, the Third Sector and Co-production.* New York: Routledge.

Van Eijk, C., Steen, T. & Verschuere, B. (2017). Co-Producing Safety in the Local Community: A Q-methodology Study on the Incentives of Belgian and Dutch Members of Neighbourhood Watch Schemes, *Local Government Studies*, 43(3:, 323–343.

Vanleene, D., Voets, J. & Verschuere, B. (2018). The Co-production of a Community: Engaging Citizens in Derelict Neighbourhoods, *Voluntas*, 29(1): 201–221.

Voorberg, W., Bekkers, V. & Tummers, L. (2015). A Systematic Review of Co-creation and Co-production: Embarking on the Social Innovation Journey, *Public Management Review*, 17(9): 1333–1357.

21

ASSOCIATION AND MEMBERSHIP MANAGEMENT

Mary Tschirhart

DIRECTOR AND PROFESSOR, THE TRACHTENBERG SCHOOL OF PUBLIC POLICY
AND PUBLIC ADMINISTRATION, THE GEORGE WASHINGTON UNIVERSITY,
WASHINGTON, DC, USA

A membership association serves member interests as a component of its core mission and honors member rights as an obligation. Knoke (1986:2) defines it as a "formally organized named group, most of whose members – whether persons or organizations – are not financially recompensed for their participation." The legal structure of the country where a membership association resides suggests its focus and its regulatory constraints (Johnson, 2014). In some countries, membership associations are the dominant form of civil society organization and have a charitable mission that serves a broad public as the driving force. In other countries, such as the United States, the membership association label fits several categories for nonprofit organizations that are mutual benefit organizations. They serve their members as their primary audience, and perhaps the broader public as a secondary audience. Examples of associations include professional and trade associations, labor unions, religious sects, recreational and service clubs, communes, social movement organizations, cooperatives, chambers of commerce, and fraternal organizations. A shared characteristic is that, no matter the country where established, its leaders may be engaged in strategic management.

This chapter focuses on membership management variations and issues connected to four decision domains relevant to membership associations. The decision domains are how to strategize and manage:

- *Membership involvement* (initial, development, maintenance, and separation stages)
- *Membership roles* (volunteer, donor, and decision-maker)
- *Membership size* (as relates to mission and benefits offered to members)
- *Financial foundation* (dues, tariffs, and other revenue).

After discussing each decision domain, the chapter closes with a list of practical implications for the strategic management of associations. In addition, it provides research questions to pursue to advance understanding of membership dynamics and provoke new implications.

Membership involvement

Traditional strategic human resource management for employees and volunteers follows a cycle of involvement which also is applicable to members in associations. The stages of the cycle are initial involvement, development, maintenance, and separation (Tschirhart and Bielefeld, 2012).

The outcomes of these stages may foster a membership that is more or less homogeneous in member views, needs, and interests. The following subsections discuss issues related to member types organized by stages in the cycle of involvement.

Cycle of Involvement: Initial Involvement of Members. In the initial involvement stage, individuals are attracted to participating in an organization. Those inside the organization may screen and select individuals to join the organization through a formal or informal recruitment process. For membership associations, this may take the form of a candidate demonstrating alignment with membership requirements, engaging in pledge activities, completing apprenticeship periods, and having existing members vote for a candidate's inclusion in the association. In some associations there may be little screening of new members, for example in a credit union typically the only qualification is to have the funds to set up an account. In other associations, being able to pay dues is sufficient to be a member.

Who is qualified to be a member relates to whom the association exists to serve. For associations focusing on serving individual members and the member collectivity, selection may be dependent on a decision that the candidate's interests sufficiently match those of existing members so as not to be harmful to existing members having their interests met. For example a labor union may allow only the employees they are representing to be members to help ensure that the employees' interests remain the priority in negotiations. Associations with very large organizations as members may keep out small organizations that, because of their size, have different needs and interests (Solebello, Tschirhart and Leiter, 2016). For associations which focus more on serving the broader public than their members, the decision consideration may be whether or not the prospective member can contribute to the broad public service mission and if the value of involving the new member outweighs the costs.

In addition to the mission of the association and economic considerations, there may be other factors affecting initial involvement activities. Institutionalized practices can influence perceptions of which types of members are desirable to recruit. These may emerge from coercive laws and bylaws that restrict or mandate discrimination, historical legacies, copying of practices, cultural norms, and other factors. For example, in some countries, fair housing laws restrict homeowners' associations from housing discrimination though continued complaints suggest it still may exist (Trifun, 2009). Changing old practices and norms in membership associations to foster diversity and inclusion at any stage of member involvement can be challenging, requiring focused efforts and diversity champions (AbouAssi, 2017; Solebello et al., 2016).

Cycle of Involvement: Development of Members (may include progression of members through association levels). In the development stage, socialization occurs. Explicit and implicit (psychological) contracts (Epitropaki, 2013) activate and violations may occur if expectations and contracted obligations are unmet. New members brought into an association begin to understand the organization and their fellow members and may or may not feel like they belong. Association leaders may identify members' learning needs and, perhaps, act to address them. Members in the development stage may experiment and determine if they can free-load and still obtain the benefits they seek from their membership. Olson (1965) argues that to avoid member freeriding activity, leaders use incentives and disincentives to get members to contribute to the collective good of the membership.

In this stage, commitment to an association and conformity to its values and norms may deepen as a member moves through categories of membership. Some associations have levels of membership based on tenure and achievements within the association. These associations, including craft guilds and fraternal organizations that are part of Freemasonry, provide benefits to their members based on their level (e.g., apprentice, journeyman, fellow). This type of system may encourage members to continue to develop their membership qualifications in order to obtain stature and influence in the association. Other associations demonstrate little attention to differentiating the developmental needs of members, offering a "one-size fits all" involvement approach. Typically in these associations, if members need to gain knowledge in order to optimize access to association benefits, it is up to them to figure out how to do this.

Cycle of Involvement: Maintenance of Members (retention of members). In the maintenance stage, members in an association receive incentives to foster their continued participation. The rewards for remaining in a membership association and participating in its activities may be extrinsic or intrinsic. For example, it may come with access to information and events, networking opportunities, discounts on goods and services, reputational advantages, and other benefits unavailable to non-members. There is some evidence that the more diverse the membership and the more members are connected to multiple associations, the greater the networking and resource-exchange benefits that may lead to members using what they learn to inspire new entrepreneurial activities (Teckchandani, 2014).

In the maintenance stage, an association may keep records on members' involvement and track performance and satisfaction. In some associations, members have a code of ethics and may be subject to probation or dismissal if they violate the code. There may be rules and standards to reward members for performance. The European Union serves as an example (Schimmelfennig, 2016) of an association with different membership levels based on a performance grading system based on its standards for governance practices. As in other associations, a potential member may decide its standards are different than those used by the association and decide not to participate. There may be grievance procedures available to existing members to appeal an association's determination that requirements for continued membership are unmet.

Cycle of Involvement: Separation of Members (exit from the association). In the separation stage of the cycle of involvement, either the member or the association decides to end the relationship or, in rarer cases, transform it. At any stage of the cycle of involvement, it is useful to maintain a positive relationship with former members. Former members may help in attracting new members, providing referrals to the association and its members, giving feedback to improve member development and other association activities, and advancing a positive internal image and external reputation for the association.

Associations that struggle to retain members may find that members do not feel rewarded for their involvement or that the perceived costs of obtaining benefits through membership outweigh their perceived value. Some benefits may go to non-members as well as members, which may make members question why they should continue to invest in the association. Also, the member may have received the desired benefits from the association and feel the association is no longer useful. For example, once an association of mobile food vendors legitimized the industry and kept vendors from engaging in destructive self-interests (Esparza, Walker and Rossman, 2014), members needed to recognize other benefits of participating in order to continue their membership.

Both external and internal factors may affect renewal/continuance decisions of members. As an example, there are three key external factors used to explain the decline in membership of the American Psychological Association (Robiner, Fossum and Hong, 2015). The association suffers from competition from other associations that provide more specialized benefits. Resources once only offered through the association became available through other means. The third key factor is generational shifts in priorities of potential members. In a health care professional association, Ki (2018) finds that key predictors of not renewing membership are perceptions of the membership dues value and attitude toward the association.

Membership associations may have a range of categories for members, some of which are for those who no longer can or wish to be active or may have a hardship in paying the standard dues. For members who are retirees or others who otherwise might separate from the association, a category allowing continuation of at least some of the member benefits may maintain a relationship that otherwise would end. One of the hardest types of members to retain are student members who joined with reduced rates. Retaining members after they no longer qualify as students and have to pay higher fees or fulfill stricter membership requirements may be challenging. Examples of retirees and students demonstrate that the cycle of involvement can be a circle rather than a line. As retirees and students separate from one class of membership, they may enter into a different membership classification, thus starting the initial involvement stage for the new classification.

Membership roles

The roles that members fulfill within an association depend on their capacity and interests as well as those of the association. Members likely understand if the association primarily exists to serve them, the membership as a whole, or a broader public. As rational actors, and if their membership is truly voluntary, they participate in associations in ways that they hope will fulfill their needs or those of the institutions or domains they are representing. In political interest groups, for example, if a member joins an association as a designated representative of another entity, they are more likely to behave in ways to support the pursuit of collective goods than to pursue a personal agenda (King and Walker, 1992). Within an association, members may fulfill a variety of roles. Incentives and supports offered by associations may affect members' interests and ability to serve in these roles. Discussed below are common member roles of volunteer, donor, and decision-maker.

Roles: Members as volunteers. In some associations, a benefit for members is being able to assist in the association's activities as a volunteer. Through this voluntary (not required) participation, members may meet new people, learn new skills, mentor the next generation, and shape their environment. They may get career benefits, help others, and create a better society. Still, it is problematic to generalize about members' motivations for volunteering. Hager (2014) found that members' valuing of incentives to volunteer differs across associations. There also are likely to be differences in motivations and the effectiveness of incentives for volunteering within an association.

Not all associations effectively engage their members who wish to volunteer. There are associations that fail to provide meaningful experiences for their member volunteers (Gazley and Dignam, 2008). Effective volunteer engagement includes thanking members who are volunteering, facilitating their volunteering through training, organizing the scheduling of volunteer work, offering clear volunteer roles, providing adequate resources, giving developmental feedback, and engaging in other practices we know are part of effective human resource management.

Members who are highly committed may not be able to participate in their association as a volunteer due to their own limitations or barriers erected by other members who wish to exclude them (e.g., Lake, 2013; Nathaus, 2010). Not only does discrimination occur when candidates are screened for membership, it can occur formally and informally when members are or are not offered opportunities to participate as a volunteer. Associations can have systems in place to ensure a fair and transparent volunteer program. Leaders can ensure that all members have access to training, resources, and volunteer opportunities appropriate to diverse members' abilities and interests.

Roles: Members as donors. In addition to paying any required dues, members may donate to their association. The donations may support association initiatives, subsidize other members' dues, or be passed to other organizations or individuals for charitable or advocacy purposes. Members of professional associations donate to their associations for many of the same reasons they give to other types of nonprofits: someone they trusted asked them and they believed in the cause supported by donations (Gazley and Dignam, 2010; Wang and Ashcraft, 2014). A further element is that they are more likely to give if they are satisfied with their membership in the association (Gazley and Dignam, 2010).

There is variation in the incentives for donating offered by associations and how much members value these incentives (Hager, 2014). Common incentives are recognition and access to opportunities. Hoolwerf and Schuyt (2010) claim that many members support global philanthropic causes through their membership association and this form of philanthropy has not yet reached its potential. Associations can focus and facilitate individual and organization members' philanthropic desires. As Kou et al. (2014) find, there can be association chapter-level effects on giving that complement individual characteristics influencing giving behaviors.

Roles: Members as decision-makers. Members may participate in their associations in internal decision-making and even governance (e.g., association board) roles. There are a variety of frameworks for looking at governance structures that apply to membership associations (e.g., Bradshaw, 2009; von Schnurbein 2009). Members may have more or less power depending on which form is used. Outside of these governance structures, members can exert influence as operational volunteers and even whistleblowers. The type of structure in which members operate can be key to their influence in pushing member interests as the top priority of the association. Take the case of credit unions which typically have a one vote per member governance structure. This works well when there is only one membership group but when there are multiple groups, management tends to pay itself more instead of putting the funds towards direct member benefits (Leggett and Strand, 2002). In associations that have chapters, local units may have varying levels of autonomy and ability to regulate a national office (Young, Bania and Bailey, 1996). More centralized associations tend to give more resources to local units but retain more control over them (Young, 1989). Agency problems exist in membership associations and the distribution of decision authority and input among the membership collective, committees, the governance board, and the executive director influences the form these problems take (AbouAssi, Tschirhart and Makhlouf, 2017). Section representatives, delegate assemblies, and other structural mechanisms may allow members to voice their opinions, even if they do not have direct voting privileges (Leroy, 1997).

Membership size

Association leaders should consider what membership size is optimal to fulfill their association's purpose. Size of the membership may affect the types of members and the roles they have in an association. Size may depend on the business model of the association. Economic calculations can show the fixed and marginal cost of serving one more member of a specific type. To further elaborate considerations for membership size, the next sections briefly touch on the connection between association size and the association's mission and benefit offerings.

Membership size and mission. For some associations, size depends on the maximum and minimum number of member participation positions to fulfill the mission. Take the example of a sports club within a league. Once a sports club has attracted the correct number for a team, a new member will not have a place on the team unless a rotation or apprentice system is established, or multiple teams can exist within the club. Size also may be restricted by the pool of potential membership candidates as defined by the mission. Membership may be limited to only those specified in the mission statement as having certain demographic, geographic, employment, need, or other characteristics. In some associations, such as professional associations focused on a minority segment of a profession, the association may invest in efforts to increase the pool of potential members, for example, by offering programs for female students to increase their interest and preparation for science and engineering professions. The development of the future membership pool may be an important part of the association's mission.

Membership size and nature of benefits. The value of some benefits offered by associations stays the same, no matter the number of users. The value of a benefit may even increase with greater membership size, for instance when member discounts for commercial goods and services are larger if the membership is larger. Another example would be in a service club devoted to fund-raising and grant-making, members may benefit from the social comradery and good feelings from their philanthropy. The more members, potentially the more funds to give away and more opportunity for social engagement. The benefits of comradery and good feelings are relatively cost-free to the association, intangible, and not depleted when consumed. This makes it easier to consider adding new members than if adding a new member takes away what existing members receive or costs to the association increase with volume. However, even with intangible goods, at some point, adding more members may reduce the value individual members get from a benefit. For example, in the service club noted above, as size grows, there may be a loss of intimacy needed for the benefit of the feeling of comradery and worthwhile involvement.

Restrictions in the benefit pie may influence strategies and goals for association membership size. Steinberg (2007) suggests that membership size should reflect the available member benefits with price of membership equilibrating the supply and demand of those benefits. If benefits are sliced too thin so that all members can get a share, the slices may have little value. This can be the case in associations that market themselves as serving an elite group. If anyone can join, it is difficult to defend a claim that membership is prestigious. The benefit is reduced when more are consuming it.

As mentioned earlier, in some associations, a certain number of participants is required. For example, a member of a sports team cannot enjoy a victory or a community orchestra member cannot perform if the membership is too small. When active participation produces the key benefit of being in an association, having an optimal size likely will bring the highest member satisfaction. A participation requirement can serve a gatekeeping function controlling access to a limited resource, but it also can ensure that a benefit is available.

Financial foundation

Membership associations vary in the size and diversity of their revenue streams. Pratt (2005) categorizes membership associations in general as having a revenue profile with medium reliability and high autonomy. He suggests that this revenue archetype brings management challenges of high expectations for transparency, member engagement, interactive communications, leadership development, collection of dues, and member politics. Discussed next are financial features relevant to membership associations: member dues, entry and exit tariffs, and other revenue.

Financial Foundation: Member dues. A unique feature of membership associations is the potential use of member dues for all or part of their revenues. Dues are the annual financial obligation of members (Bowman, 2017). If dues-paying members do not have rights in the organization then the dues are donations (Steinberg, 2007). For the purposes of this chapter, we are assuming that members' payment of dues designates them as active members who can partake of benefits exclusive to members. However, not all membership associations charge dues and some treat dues payments as voluntary. Dues may be set on a tiered system with some members paying more than others. If members perceive this dues system as transparent and fair, dues rates may increase with little fear of losing membership renewals (Steinberg, 2007); there is decreased elasticity in the demand for membership. However, if there are substitutes for the goods or services available through other means, or membership is not a necessity nor a luxury, it is likely to be more elastic (Bowman, 2017). Who pays the dues may influence demand elasticity. Not all members pay their own dues. For example, employers may pay for their employees' dues and sponsors may pay student dues. Also, associations may subsidize their dues using other revenue sources (Bowman, 2017). Economic theory suggests that association leaders should understand their competition, membership numbers, and member perception of benefits and set dues accordingly.

Dues revenue tends to be more predictable than program revenue. The more an association is dependent on dues, the less its financial risk (Bowman, 2017). To encourage new memberships and renewals, and even out the flow of revenues and reduce risks, membership associations may offer dues options that involve paying a one-time membership fee for life, multi-year payment arrangements, and package deals to sponsors, employers, and other entities who are willing to cover multiple memberships for a set period of time. Financial management systems can facilitate reminder notices for payment of dues and otherwise help support the flow of dues revenue.

Financial Foundation: Member entry and exit tariffs. Some associations may charge members entry and exit tariffs (Bowman, 2017). Entry tariffs for members are initiation fees. As part of joining an association, there may be a one-time charge. The rationales for initiation fees could be additional administrative costs to set up the membership, provide training, equip the member with supplies, and increase the capacity of the association to handle the extra burden and increased congestion of members caused by the new participant. Bowman gives the example of a golf club which may have to deal with extra waiting times on the golf course or sharing of lockers by members. Exit tariffs may be required for a member to exit the association. These fees may help the association recover from the loss of resources the member had been providing.

Willingness to pay entry and exit tariffs may help to screen for commitment of potential members. This screen may be particularly useful when membership is limited and members bring unique assets to the association. The loss of any one member may cause other members to suffer.

Financial Foundation: Other revenue. In addition to dues and tariffs as a source of revenue, membership associations may have income from other sources such as sales of products and services, subscription fees, investments, grants, royalties, endowments, and gifts. Bowman (2017) found that large associations tended to have more revenue from program services while small to medium-sized associations had more from dues. Conference and event registrations can be a significant source of revenue, particularly for associations that offer benefits requiring member interaction. When participation in these types of events is restricted to those who are members or offered at a significant discount to members, it is difficult to disentangle the incentives for paying membership dues from the incentives for paying event fees. Purchases of membership and registration may be simultaneous. This is the case for many professional and trade associations with an annual conference.

Concluding thoughts including ideas for research and practice

There is still much to learn to guide strategic management for membership associations (Tschirhart and Gazley, 2014; Tschirhart, 2006). The research needs noted in my and my co-author's review in 2014 are still relevant today. We have a base of knowledge but need more research to understand complexities and new realities. The guidance available for association leaders draws much from business and nonprofit management scholarship as well as psychology, sociology, economics, and other disciplines. The fundamentals of human and social behavior are relevant to membership associations just as they are to any formalized organization. What needs more study are decision domains unique to associations which includes those related to membership variations and issues.

I suggest more scholarly research and association leader attention to all the topics outlined in this chapter. For each topic, I offer leaders a practical implication(s) and scholars an idea(s) for future research. While the list below is limited in depth and breadth, my hope is that it can inspire thoughts and debate on what we may assume about associations and what more we should learn.

Membership Involvement: Initial Involvement

- *Practical Implication:* Existing research identifies many motives for joining an association as well as barriers for engagement. Associations that are responsive to the potential variation in potential, new, and long-standing members' interests and capacity for participation will likely be more effective with member recruitment and retention. Association leaders can design the initial involvement stage to reduce barriers for member candidates whose motives for joining align well with the association's mission and capacity to provide benefits.
- *Research Ideas:* Scholars know more about why individuals join associations than about how associations develop policies and manage the process of member selection and initial participation. Research on organizational factors affecting the policies and processes, and the outcomes of these policies and practices, could inform questions about membership trends, discriminatory and inclusionary practices, and data analytics for membership management.

Membership Involvement: Development of Members

- *Practical Implication:* There are often varied opportunities for learning in associations with targeting of specific opportunities to member subgroups. Still, it is likely that much of the learning that occurs in associations is not structured by the association, but rather informal, passed from member to member. The use of membership categories designating developmental level, mentoring programs, and membership surveys can be helpful in determining which members may share developmental needs and interests. These also may surface sources of expertise and other developmental supports. This information could help leaders create structured and informal developmental opportunities.
- *Research Ideas:* Involvement in an association can be transformative for members. Norms, values, attitudes, and behaviors of members can change with immersion in an association. We know more about how socialization affects individual participants

and less about how this socialization affects organizational members. Research on how organizational members become more similar through involvement in an association may shed light on knowledge transfer across organizations, institutionalization, and industry-level changes.

Membership Involvement: Maintenance of Members

- *Practical Implication:* In the maintenance stage of the cycle of involvement, there are standard tasks such as managing provision of benefits, recognizing and rewarding performance, facilitating safe and productive activities, and keeping records. Effectively and ethically carrying out these tasks can help ensure that members feel appropriately supported during their engagement with the association. Leaders may find that a careful review of maintenance tasks within their association can reveal ways to secure and protect their members' rights and the resources provided by and to members.
- *Research Ideas:* We know little about what affects current and former members' loyalty to an association and the outcomes of this loyalty, beyond longevity of membership. While there are some studies of influences on member satisfaction, this is different than understanding influences on loyalty. Are some types of involvement activities more conducive to producing loyalty than others? Are individuals who hold multiple association memberships more likely to be loyal? Does loyalty have negative effects such as close-mindedness? Research on loyalty in associations may reveal connections to innovativeness and advocacy efforts of associations, specific benefit offerings such as certification supports, diversity of membership, member philanthropic generosity, as well as membership retention.

Membership Involvement: Separation of Members

- *Practical Implication:* Members leave associations for a variety of reasons. The exit may be voluntary or involuntary, desired or not. I believe associations have an ethical responsibility to treat members fairly at all stages of the cycle of involvement. Examining reasons for exit may reveal equity and other concerns connected to involvement stages that association leaders can work to address. Managing the separation stage well can positively influence how former members engage with the association in the future and may help in moving members into different categories of membership, such as emeritus for those who are no longer directly engaged in forwarding the mission of the association.
- *Research Ideas:* We know little about competition and collaboration among associations for members. More research on this topic may inform our understanding of why associations occasionally emerge from other associations, for example, to serve a specific subgroup of members who are dissatisfied with the original association or want to supplement its offerings. We also may learn if competition and collaboration among associations produces some of the same outcomes that we find in the for-profit sector. It may also reveal strategies for recruiting members from other associations and encouraging members recruited by others to stay in an association.

Membership Roles: Volunteer

- *Practical Implication:* Associations vary in their emphasis on and expertise in offering volunteer opportunities for members. The general guidance for any volunteer program applies to associations. To add to these guidelines, association leaders should consider how members perceive volunteer opportunities and how the association may be influencing these perceptions. Perhaps, members feel they are paying enough dues so that there should be no need for them to volunteer to ensure they get the promised benefits from their membership. On the other hand, they may perceive that their membership is what gives them access to the volunteer opportunities that they see as beneficial.

- *Research Ideas:* We are only beginning to understand variations in volunteer structures and cultures within associations. It is likely that there are volunteer program archetypes found across associations, each with their own advantages and disadvantages. There may be predictable patterns in use of these archetypes by associations. Research on the landscape of volunteer programs within associations may suggest more specific advice for associations than the general volunteer literature can provide.

Membership Roles: Donor

- *Practical Implication:* Not all associations offer philanthropic opportunities to members. When they do, they may be limited to funding assistance to other members of the association rather than or in addition to recipients outside the association. Basic principles of fund development apply in membership associations, though they may not be as well tested in these settings. Like in other settings, if members receive appreciation and hear about the positive impact of their donations, they are more likely to give again and be satisfied with their experience as a donor. There are a range of motivations and incentives for giving that associations can tap. Associations may choose to set up an affiliated foundation to handle the solicitation process and steward gifts. In this case, donations may have greater tax advantages for members. In addition, the foundation may offer members additional volunteering and leadership opportunities.

- *Research Ideas:* The relationship between associations and affiliated foundations needs more study in order to inform policies and practice, as well as theory. Further research on members' philanthropic behaviors may bring useful insights. Are members more likely to give to help association insiders or outsiders and why? Is the frequency and amount of members' donations linked to dues levels? Are their predictable differences between members who give and those that do not that suggest new strategies for fund development? How closely linked to the association's mission are philanthropic activities by members and does perception by members of this closeness affect donation behavior? By learning more about philanthropic structures and processes used by associations and the philanthropy of their members, we may uncover additional ways that associations add value to the communities they serve.

Membership Roles: Decision-maker

- *Practical Implication:* Associations vary in the degree that members, in general, are empowered and who within the membership has the most and least power in particular decision domains like operations or policy. We now know more about how to encourage shared leadership within and across nonprofit organizations. Association leaders may find that incorporating members into shared leadership teams makes sense for mission fulfillment, association growth, and financial health. Member involvement in decision-making may lead to innovative ideas and greater member commitment. Also, accountability for the work of the association may be better spread across the association.

- *Research Ideas:* Much of the literature on governance structures in associations is old, only descriptive, and applies to complex, structured organizations and not to more informal grassroots associations. We know little about how new technologies may affect member engagement in decision-making and the transparency of decision processes. While there are some case studies that illuminate less well-researched approaches to member decision-making, they are not easy to find in the general governance literature for the nonprofit sector. A fresh look at this topic may bring findings that can improve accountability in associations.

Membership Size

- *Practical Implication:* This chapter has noted how an association's mission and the nature of the benefits it offers can affect what is the optimal size for the association. Purely economic calculations on costs and revenues can offer only one lens on what it may mean to bring in more members or lose members. Association leaders have options for goals and strategies for membership size and should choose wisely. Being too large or too small may undermine the benefits that members bring to and receive from an association.
- *Research Ideas:* Many scholars have tracked trends in the number of associations and the memberships individuals hold. Less research is available on trends in the size of associations' memberships. It is unclear if there are more or less choices of associations to join and whether competition for members affects membership size. We also do not know if and when there are general limits to how large an association grows before there is likely to be splintering or a need for subgroups within the association to keep members satisfied. Perhaps given changes in communication tools, any size limitations have changed. A study identifying factors affecting association size now and in the past, and the outcomes linked to size, may reveal findings to inform strategic management.

Financial Foundation: Dues, Tariffs, and Other Revenue

- *Practical Implication:* Associations have a range of options for bringing in revenue. Some associations appear to be more entrepreneurial than others in bringing in earned income and philanthropic dollars. Leaders whose associations are struggling financially may find that attracting new members is not the only and may not even be the best answer to financial woes. Building financial models for the current membership size, a decline in size, and a growth in size may be useful in revealing the range of strategies available. Complicating matters may be the step of incorporating membership categories and the revenues and costs associated with each into analyses. Adding this complexity to financial planning is useful, especially if members change from one category to another. Financial projections should take into account membership category progressions.
- *Research Ideas:* Due to a flurry of recent research, we now know more about associations' financial structures. Analyses of financial models have revealed weaknesses and strengths in membership associations. Still, there is more to learn. One area that seems promising is to look at how associations handle dues payment lapses and the outcomes of their approaches. Does forgiveness of dues debt, allowing some members not to pay dues, and carrying members who are late in their dues payments for a specified period of time have different advantages and disadvantages to an association depending on circumstances? How resilient does an association have to be to maintain financial

stability given the level of unpredictability of their dues revenue? What are sources of financial resiliency for an association, e.g., reserve funds, endowments, and reliable income streams? Better understanding of dues as a revenue source may reveal useful financial strategies.

The association label is a broad umbrella. Many different types of organizations exist under it. This chapter illustrates some of the unique features of being member-based that distinguish membership associations from other types of civil society organizations. The chapter also emphasizes the variety of options that leaders have for the design, operations, and governance of their association. I would be remiss if the chapter did not also discuss the need for more research on membership-related aspects of associations. Associations influence all of us whether or not we belong to one. This chapter offers ideas for readers interested in learning more about associations.

References

AbouAssi, Khaldoun and An, S.H. (2017) Gender representation and organizational size: Examining opportunities for members' involvement in membership organizations. *Public Management Review* 19(10): 1437–1454.

AbouAssi, Khaldoun, Tschirhart, Mary and Makhlouf, Nadeen H. (2017) *Nonprofit Management and Leadership* 28(2): 237–247.

Bowman, H. Woods (2017) Toward a theory of membership association finance. *Nonprofit and Voluntary Sector Quarterly* 46(4): 772–793.

Bradshaw, Patricia (2009) A contingency approach to nonprofit governance. *Nonprofit Management and Leadership* 20(1): 61–81.

Epitropaki, Olga (2013) A multi-level investigation of psychological contract breach and organizational identification through the lens of perceived organizational membership: Testing a moderated-mediated model. *Journal of Organizational Behavior* 34(1): 65–86.

Esparza, N., Walker, E.T., and Rossman, G. (2014) Trade associations and the legitimation of entrepreneurial movements: Mobile food vendors' associations in the emerging gourmet food truck industry. *Nonprofit and Voluntary Sector Quarterly* 43(2): 143S–162S.

Gazley, Beth and Dignam, Monica (2010) *The Decision to Give: What Motivates Individuals to Support Professional Associations*. Washington, DC: ASAE & The Center for Association Leadership.

Gazley, Beth and Dignam, Monica (2008) *The Decision to Volunteer: Why People Give Their Time and How You Can Engage Them*. Washington, DC: ASAE & The Center for Association Leadership.

Hager, M.A. (2014) Engagement motivations in professional associations. *Nonprofit and Voluntary Sector Quarterly* 43(2): 39S–60S.

Hoolwerf, B., and Schuyt, T. (2010, March) Service clubs: Serving communities? Data from a national research (Philanthropic Studies Working Paper Series). Amsterdam, The Netherlands: VU University Amsterdam.

Johnson, E.W. (2014) Toward international comparative research on associational activity: Variation in the form and focus of voluntary associations in four nations. *Nonprofit and Voluntary Sector Quarterly* 43(2): 163S–181S.

Ki, Eyun-Jung (2018) Determinants of health care professional association members' intention to renew and recommend membership to others. *International Journal of Nonprofit and Voluntary Sector Marketing*.

King, David C. and Walker, Jack L. (1992) The provision of benefits by interest groups in the United States. *Journal of Politics* 54(2): 394–426.

Knoke, David (1986) Associations and interest groups. *Annual Review of Sociology* 12: 1–21.

Kou, X., Hayat, A. D., Mesch, D., and Osili, U. (2014) The global dynamics of gender and philanthropy: A study of charitable giving by Lions Clubs International members. *Nonprofit and Voluntary Sector Quarterly* 43(2): 18S–38S.

Lake, R.J. (2013) They treat me like I'm scum: Social exclusion and established-outsider relations in a British tennis club. *International Review for the Sociology of Sport* 48: 112–128.

Leggett, Keith J. and Strand, Robert W. (2002) Membership growth, multiple membership groups and agency control at credit unions. *Review of Financial Economics* 11(1): 37–46.

Leroy, Wayne E. (1997) Association governance and structure. In John B. Cox (Ed.) *Professional Practices in Association Management*, pp. 1–10. Washington, DC: ASAE.

Nathaus, K. (2010) Leisure clubs and social integration of workers in Germany, 1860–1914, with a comparative glance at the British case. *Geschichte Und Gesellschaft* 36: 37–65.

Olson, M. (1965) *The Logic of Collective Action*. Cambridge, MA: Harvard University Press.

Pratt, Jon (2005) Analyzing the dynamics of funding: Reliability and autonomy. *Nonprofit Quarterly* Winter: 74–79.

Robiner, William N., Fossum, Thyra A. and Hong, Barry A. (2015) Bowling alone: The decline of social engagement and other challenges for the American Psychological Association and its divisions. *Clinical Psychology: Science and Practice* 22(4): 366–383.

Schimmelfennig, Frank (2016) Good governance and differentiated integration: Graded membership in the European Union. *European Journal of Political Research* 55(4): 789–810.

Solebello, Nicholas, Tschirhart, Mary and Leiter, Jeffrey (2016) The paradox of inclusion and exclusion in membership associations. *Human Relations* 69(2): 439–460.

Steinberg, Richard (2007) Membership income. In D.R. Young (Ed.) *Financing Nonprofits: Putting Theory into Practice* (pp. 121–155). Latham, MD: National Center on Nonprofit Enterprise.

Teckchandani, A. (2014) Do membership associations affect entrepreneurship? The effect of type, composition and engagement. *Nonprofit and Voluntary Sector Quarterly* 43(2): 84S–104S.

Trifun, Natasha (2009) Residential segregation after the Fair Housing Act. *Human Rights* 36(4): 14–19.

Tschirhart, Mary (2006) Membership associations. In W.W. Powell and R. Steinberg (Eds.) *The Non-Profit Sector: A Research Handbook*, 2nd Edition (pp. 523–541). London: Yale University Press.

Tschirhart, Mary and Gazley, Beth (2014) Advancing scholarship on membership associations: New research and next steps. *Nonprofit and Voluntary sector Quarterly* 43(2): 3S–17S.

Tschirhart, Mary and Bielefeld, Wolfgang (2012) *Managing Nonprofit Organizations*. San Francisco: Jossey-Bass.

Von Schnurbein, G. (2009) Patterns of governance structures in trade associations and unions. *Nonprofit Management and Leadership* 20(1): 97–115.

Wang, Lili and Ashcraft, Robert F. (2014) Organizational commitment and involvement: Explaining the decision to give to associations. *Nonprofit and Voluntary Sector Quarterly* 43(2): 61S–83S.

Young, Dennis R. (1989) Local autonomy in a franchise age. *Nonprofit and Voluntary Sector Quarterly* 19: 101–117.

Young, Dennis R., Bania, N. and Bailey, D. (1996) Structure and accountability: A study of national nonprofit organizations. *Nonprofit Management and Leadership* 6: 347–365.

PART IV

Managing externally

22

COLLABORATIONS AND NETWORKS[1]

David Suárez

ASSOCIATE PROFESSOR, EVANS SCHOOL OF PUBLIC POLICY AND GOVERNANCE,
UNIVERSITY OF WASHINGTON, SEATTLE, WA, USA

Hokyu Hwang

ASSOCIATE PROFESSOR, UNSW BUSINESS SCHOOL, UNSW SYDNEY, SYDNEY, AUSTRALIA

Introduction

Interorganizational collaborations and networks have existed for quite some time in the United States and elsewhere, yet over the last few decades there has been a dramatic increase in these types of relationships – both within and across sectors (Galaskiewicz 1985; Gray 1989; Powell 1990; Oliver and Ebers 1998; Austin 2000; Selsky and Parker 2005; Bryson, Crosby, and Stone 2006, 2015; McGuire 2006; Ansell and Gash 2008; Emerson, Nabatchi, and Balogh 2012; Parmigiani and Rivera-Santos 2011). Scholarship on the topic has paralleled the growing prevalence of collaboration and networks, leading to an extensive but fragmented body of research. Some scholarship has emphasized relationships within a specific sector, while other work investigates dyadic cross-sector collaboration. Yet another body of research considers multi-sector networks (Huxham and Vangen 2004; Galaskiewicz and Sinclair Colman 2006; Milward and Provan 2006; Thomson and Perry 2006; Agranoff 2006, 2007; Provan and Kenis 2008; Austin and Seitanidi 2012a, 2012b).

Drawing on the sprawling literature on interorganizational relationships in this chapter, we focus on collaborations and networks involving nonprofit organizations (Varda, Shoup, and Miller 2012; Gazley and Guo 2015). Though we provide a concise and current review, our primary contribution is to offer a novel organizing framework for studying nonprofit collaborations and networks. Rather than attempt to identify new skills or activities that have been overlooked in prior research or critical practices or strategies that potentially could generate collaborative advantage consistently across contexts, we take a broader view of the topic (Huxham and Vangen 2005). In order to identify gaps in the literature, we explore nonprofit collaborations and networks in relation to two key dimensions: (1) the sector of the nonprofit partner and (2) the defining purpose or mission of a focal nonprofit. We privilege these two axes because they constitute longstanding identifiers or markers for organizations and yet both are in flux.

Over the last few decades the boundaries between sectors have become much more porous, diminishing the sharp distinctions between public, nonprofit, and for-profit (business) organizations (Battilana and Lee 2014; Battilana, Besharov, and Mitzninneck 2017; Bromley and

Meyer 2017). Social entrepreneurship and the monetization of social impact have gained traction in the nonprofit sector, many for-profit organizations now commit to corporate social responsibility (CSR; see Chapter 29 by Roza and Meijs) and have started to embrace impact investing, public agencies have adopted a variety of practices or tools associated with the business sector, and a new organizational form that defies easy sectoral classification is starting to emerge (low-profit limited liability corporations (LC3s), B-corporations, for-benefit corporations – see Chapter 35 by Abramson and Billings). Sectors nevertheless still have some distinguishing characteristics and supposedly have unique strengths that can be leveraged through collaboration, raising many questions about how sectors matter with respect to partnerships with nonprofit organizations.

Like the blurring of sectoral boundaries, distinctions within the nonprofit sector are eroding. Service provision and advocacy constitute the two core roles of nonprofit organizations, which produce functional differentiation (Frumkin 2002). Service-providing nonprofits are prohibited from engaging in electioneering, and lobbying cannot be a substantial component of their work. Although these are the only legal restrictions they face on advocating for social change, service-providing organizations historically have incorporated social change activity into their repertoire only rarely (Berry 2005; Suárez and Hwang 2008). The women's rights movement and the broader civil rights movement began to alter this pattern, as advocacy organizations began to deliver services as a strategy for organizational survival (Clemens 1993; Minkoff 1994). Public sector reform and the growth of public sector contracting also politicized nonprofits and spurred engagement in advocacy (Marwell 2004; Mosley 2012).

These transformations across societal sectors and within the nonprofit sector have not been addressed much in relation to nonprofit collaboration and networks. In an effort to surface new or underexplored research questions, we explore nonprofit relationships with other organizations in relation to partner sector (nonprofit, philanthropic, public, and mixed) and nonprofit purpose or function (services, advocacy, and hybrid). We, first, examine the institutional conditions driving the growing prevalence of collaboration over time (Meyer and Rowan 1977; DiMaggio and Powell 1983; Drori, Meyer, and Hwang 2006; Bromley and Meyer 2015). In order to establish a common understanding of collaboration, we document the diverse forms and purposes of interorganizational relationships and summarize research on the antecedents, processes, and structures that influence collaborative performance. We then introduce our framework and conclude with an agenda for future research.

Institutional change, interorganizational collaboration, and networks

Collaboration is a defining feature of nonprofit organizations and the nonprofit sector. Internally, nonprofits are often the outcome of concerted efforts among collaborating citizens. Externally, nonprofits are structurally located between the beneficiaries of their services and the broader world from which they draw resources to support their causes. In this sense, the success of nonprofits depends often on their relationships to the field-level processes (Marwell 2009, p. 11). From raising philanthropic and government grants and generating commercial revenues to collecting necessary information and to procuring needed expert and professional help, nonprofits develop extra-local relationships so that much-needed resources can flow to the communities they support. The external embeddedness of nonprofits in broader fields, institutions, and relationships helps nonprofits access and mobilize resources for their causes. While extensive collaborations and networks in the nonprofit sector consequently are not surprising, the growing frequency of these interorganizational relationships reveals the importance of the institutional context for nonprofits.

Several changes in the nonprofit sector and its institutional environment have, in recent years, facilitated the proliferation of collaboration and have diversified the types of collective endeavors (Salamon 1987, 1994; Kettl 1997). Internally, the sector's professionalization and formalization have made nonprofit organizations more receptive to working across organizational and sectoral boundaries. The sector's professionalization has meant the influx of managerial expertise into the sector and the adoption of managerial practices, which, in turn, decreases cultural distance between sectors and opens up organizations to a diverse set of organizational practices including (cross-sector) collaboration and other types of partnerships (Suárez and Hwang 2013). The rationalization of the nonprofit sector has meant that nonprofits have become more goal-oriented and are more likely to entertain a variety of organizational and management tools to achieve their mission (Hwang and Powell 2009; Hwang and Bromley 2015).

The devolution of the state, including the retrenchment of the welfare state and the distribution of funding for social services through market mechanisms, while creating heightened competition by introducing new players, has rendered partnership and collaboration across sectoral boundaries more relevant, as organizations, nonprofit or otherwise, seek public–private partnerships in order to put together the most competitive coalition (Clemens and Guthrie 2010, p. 13). For instance, in the area of low-income housing development, the legislation of the Low-Income Housing Tax Credit (LIHTC) in the US introduced nonprofit intermediaries and created incentives for collaboration with banks and corporations, private developers as well as other nonprofits in urban low-income housing development projects (Guthrie and McQuarrie 2008; McQuarrie 2010).

There has also been a growing perception that many of society's ills – such as climate change, sustainability, poverty, inequality – are complex, wicked problems that require combined efforts of organizations across sectors (Goldsmith and Eggers 2004; Osborne 2006; Bryson et al. 2015). The impetus for (cross-sector) collaboration is easily reinforced in a culture where, often, governments and foundations insist that funding recipients collaborate, even if they have little evidence that it will work (Bryson et al. 2006, p. 45). Moreover, with the institutionalization of corporate social responsibilities, corporations recognize the benefits of engaging nonprofit organizations, that bring to collaboration complementary knowledge and networks as well as legitimacy (Den Hond, de Bakker, and Doh 2015). The retreat of the state and the rise of soft law and private regulation, especially in the transnational arena, have meant that nongovernmental organizations directly engage corporations. While anticorporate campaigns like naming and shaming and boycotts are confrontational and antagonistic, nonprofits' interactions with corporations sometimes can involve more joint efforts at developing private regulatory systems like certification and standards (King and Pearce 2010).

The nonprofit sector and interorganizational relationships

Social theory aids in explaining the growing prevalence of interorganizational relationships, yet operational definitions of collaborations differ markedly. Encompassing definitions emphasize some degree of interdependence and resource exchange. For example, according to a widely cited article, collaboration is a process in which autonomous actors interact through formal and informal negotiation, jointly creating rules and structures governing their relationships and ways to act or decide on the issues that brought them together; it is a process involving shared norms and mutually beneficial interactions (Thomson and Perry 2006, p. 23). Another frequently cited article on cross-sector collaboration defines the activity as: The linking or sharing of information, resources, activities, and capabilities by organizations in two or more sectors to achieve jointly an outcome that could not be achieved by organizations in one sector separately (Bryson et al. 2006, p. 44).

While these definitions establish boundaries for broad phenomena, they leave substantial room for variation in the depth, breadth, forms, and purposes of those relationships. Interorganizational relationships for instance refer to alliances, joint ventures, partnerships, and coalitions. Enough commonality exists among them to be considered collaborations, but the specific labels usually characterize distinctive forms (Oliver and Ebers 1998; Parmigiani and Rivera-Santos 2011). The depth and breadth of collaborations vary across these collaborative forms as well. The ties that constitute collaborations can be formal or informal (some partnerships utilize contracts and some do not, some specify clearly defined roles for staff while others do not), and some collaborations involve both extensive and intensive contacts between organizations while others entail more limited, trivial ties (de Souza 2003; Guo and Acar 2005; Gazley 2008).

The purposes of partnerships and the motivations for organizations to reach out are quite varied. Some hope to learn from partners, seek legitimacy, gain resources, and/or share (financial) risk, while others partner to shape policy. Perhaps because collaborations vary so extensively, the organizational theories utilized to understand them draw from several disciplines and frequently offer competing hypotheses (for useful summaries of theories commonly utilized in research on interorganizational ties see Galaskiewicz 1985; Oliver 1990; Powell et al. 2005; Barringer and Harrison 2000; Van Slyke 2006; and Scott and Davis 2007). Besides the differences identified so far, a key feature of networks is the participation of three or more organizations, yet the definitions for collaboration listed above are as applicable for ties among multiple organizations as they are for ties between two organizations (Podolny and Page 1998; Agranoff and McGuire 2003; Milward and Provan 2006).

The concept of collaboration thus serves as a very broad umbrella term for an assortment of relationships that involve two or more organizations. Because empirical research does not draw on a common, clearly specified definition of collaboration, making generalizable inferences about best practices for management poses considerable challenges. Nevertheless, in the following section we build on prior reviews of the salient determinants of collaborative performance, emphasizing antecedents, processes, and structures.

Antecedents, processes and structures that shape collaborative outcomes

Despite considerable differences in depth, breadth, forms and purposes, research on collaboration has identified key contingencies or factors that shape outcomes. To begin with, collaborative performance can be influenced by exogenous environmental or contextual factors such as geography, time (historical period), political and economic dynamics (sectoral interdependence, complexity, turbulence, competition), and the specific field or policy domain involved (i.e., environment, education). Collaborations also are sensitive to more immediate contextual conditions such as the nature and complexity of the problem to be addressed, the availability of resources, the incentives for participation, the presence of committed leaders (sponsors/champions), and the prior histories and collaborative capacities of participants (Wood and Gray 1991; Huxham and Vangen 2004; Stone and Sandfort 2009; Bryson et al. 2006, 2015; Thomson and Perry 2006; Emerson et al. 2012; Ansell and Gash 2008; Agranoff 2012; Cornforth, Hayes, and Vangen 2014; Suárez and Esparza 2017).

While to some extent these aspects of interorganizational relationships may be beyond management influence, leaders have control over the initial conditions in many instances – they may be able to frame the problem or agenda, convene stakeholders, delimit participation, structure deliberation, and set the strategic direction (Gray 1989; Wood and Gray 1991). Leaders are not always able to control the initial conditions, however. The levers they can manipulate most easily to produce desired outcomes often involve collaborative processes and structures associated with implementation. Whether or not leaders can specify the criteria for member-ship in a collaboration, for example, they can manage the commitment and motivation of the players involved. Moreover, leaders can work to achieve diverse participation, develop shared understandings, and forge agreements with the participating organizations regardless of the ini-tial conditions they encounter (Bryson et al. 2006, 2015).

Other common management tasks involve designing processes to build trust and legitimacy, distribute resources, facilitate communication, align goals, resolve conflicts, insure accounta-bility, collect and evaluate data, and tackle power imbalances or competing logics (Huxham and Vangen 2005; Bryson et al. 2006, 2015; Thomson and Perry 2006; Ansell and Gash 2008; Emerson et al. 2012; Varda et al. 2012). Though these management tasks contribute to collab-orative performance, they sometimes can be in tension with one another, and how they are handled or prioritized can have significant structural consequences (Thomson and Perry 2006; Bryson et al. 2015). Should flexibility or stability be prioritized? Control or trust? Autonomy or interdependence? Inclusivity or efficiency? Earlier we highlighted that collaborations differ in terms of depth, breadth, form, and purpose, and some of the variation results from the processes and structures that leaders intentionally put into place.

Determining the governance structure for a collaboration is yet another important manage-ment task, particularly for networks (Milward and Provan 2006; Cornforth et al. 2014). Some service-provision networks have no formal or official governance structure, some assign the role to a lead organization that is internal to the network, and yet others designate an administra-tive organization that is external to the network – which also may act as backbone support for data analysis and evaluation (Provan and Kenis 2008; Kania and Kramer 2011). Capturing the dynamic interplay between structure and process in the management of collaborations, a recent review of research on public health networks concludes: Networks that are structured in par-ticular ways (e.g., centralized vs decentralized, formal vs informal, temporary vs long term) likely lend themselves to different management strategies (e.g., hierarchical vs vertical, majority rule vs consensus, strategic vs bureaucratic), which when maximized may strengthen the capacity of a network to produce clear and valid outcomes (Varda et al. 2012, p. 569).

As noted above, aligning processes and structures to maximize performance is no easy task, and a final source of complexity associated with collaboration involves the outcomes themselves (Provan and Milward 1995, 2001; Sagawa and Segal 2000; Herranz 2008). The diverse and sometimes ill-defined goals that collaborations seek to achieve vary widely and the time required for results to become evident can depend on the outcome, making comparisons of performance across cases problematic. Some collaborations may require considerable time before a valid assessment might even be possible (if improvements are expected to occur in stepwise manner), for instance, while others could be assessed after a short period. Moreover, collaborations can be assessed at the level of the organization, the partnership, and the network – and collaborations presumably can succeed at some levels while failing at others. Participants can benefit unevenly from a collaboration, for instance, with some organizations bearing considerably more costs than others, or a collaboration could benefit organizations involved while failing to achieve its main goals for clients or customers.

The performance of collaborations is beginning to be evaluated in relation to the public value they create for society as well, and especially with regard to outcomes that extend beyond the immediate, narrow goals of a partnership or network (Innes and Booher 1999; Gray 2000; Bryson et al. 2006, 2015; Provan, Fish, and Sydow 2007; Bryson, Crosby, and Bloomberg 2014; Emerson and Nabatchi 2015; Page et al. 2015). Because of (a) the lack of a standardized defi-nition of collaboration, (b) the breadth of antecedents, processes, and structures that shape collaborations, and (c) the diversity of outcomes and levels of analysis involved with assessing collaborative performance, we are reluctant to make strong claims about implications for practice. Like several other studies that summarize research on collaboration, the main generalization we can offer is that collaborating is difficult, context-sensitive, time consuming, and tends to require the investment of considerable economic, social, and cultural resources (de Souza 2003; Huxham and Vangen 2005; Bryson et al. 2006, 2015). We also echo Huxham and Vangen (2004, p. 200) who concluded that unless potential for real collaborative advantage is clear, it is generally best, if there is a choice, to avoid collaboration.

Even though there is widespread recognition that interorganizational collaboration is challenging, and even though there is no systematic evidence that collaboration is more effective as a strategy for achieving social outcomes than independent work by multiple organizations, demands for collaboration only seem to be growing (Goldsmith and Eggers 2004; Osborne 2006; Bryson et al. 2006, 2015). Our review clarifies the main topics and issues that have been explored, but research has focused much more extensively on some areas than others. In order to surface new research questions and draw attention to underexplored aspects of collaboration, in the next section we map nonprofit collaboration research by sector and purpose.

Mapping nonprofit collaboration research by sector and purpose

In a parsimonious overview of the nonprofit sector, Frumkin (2002) posited that nonprofit organizations have expressive and instrumental functions – or purposes – and that those functions can be divided into supply-side and demand-side orientations. The instrumental function attends to service delivery and social entrepreneurship, and the expressive function attends to civic and political engagement as well as to values and faith. This representation highlights the core role or mission of a given nonprofit organization. Mapping research by the primary purpose of a focal nonprofit helps clarify if research on collaboration is more prevalent in relation to service-providing nonprofits than in relation to advocacy nonprofits and shows the extent to which research on service-providing nonprofits and advocacy nonprofits is in dialogue. Because some nonprofits now combine these two primary purposes, we add a blended category to this first dimension for mapping nonprofit research (Minkoff 2002; Hwang and Suárez 2019).

Not only do nonprofits have purposes that could be consequential for collaboration, nonprofits form partnerships with nonprofits and with organizations from other sectors. Just as collaborations may differ depending on the primary function of a focal nonprofit, collaboration may vary by the sector of the organization with whom the focal nonprofit establishes a tie. Thus, the second dimension incorporates the sector of partner organizations: nonprofit, foundation (philanthropic), government, business, and mixed (nonprofit, government, foundation, business). Foundations, while part of the nonprofit sector, differ markedly from typical nonprofits that provide services or engage in advocacy. With the mixed category, multi-sector partnerships may not involve organizations from all four of the sectors captured in Table 22.1, but for parsimony we include all possible permutations.

Table 22.1 summarizes our framework for mapping research on nonprofit collaboration by intersecting nonprofit purpose (from the perspective of a focal actor) and the sector of the collaborative partner(s). The 15 cells in the table have three potential colors (blank, light, dark) representing the extensiveness of research on collaboration (low, medium, and high, respectively). In addition, some of the cells have labels that attempt to describe collaborations in a given purpose–sector combination (i.e., services–government, advocacy–foundation). We elaborate the table in detail below, organizing the sections in relation to the sector of the nonprofit partner. Starting with nonprofit partnerships with other nonprofits, we consider research in relation

Table 22.1 Mapping nonprofit collaboration research by sector and purpose

		Focal Nonprofit Purpose / Function		
		Services	*Advocacy*	*Services & Advocacy*
Sector of Focal Nonprofit Partner	Nonprofit (NPO)	Conventional Partnership	Coalition; Social Movement; Transnational Network	
	Foundation (Phil)	Patronage; Service Network	Patronage; Social Movement	Strategic Philanthropy; Philanthro-Capitalism
	Government (Gov't)	Third-Party Government; Service Network	Policy Formation	Politicization; Machine Politics
	Business (FPO)	Social Venture / Alliance; Cause-Related Marketing; Corporate Social Responsibility		
	FPO / Gov't / Phil	Service Network; Collective Impact; Collaborative Governance; Philanthropic Coproduction		

Note: Darker shading indicates more extensive research (low, medium, high)

to core nonprofit purpose (services, advocacy, blended services and advocacy) and then repeat this presentation style with partnerships involving other sectors – moving from left to right in a row and then proceeding to the next row. The framework comprehensively captures all theoretically possible combinations of collaboration involving nonprofit organizations. At the same time, empty or sparsely populated cells point to the limits of cross-sectoral collaboration involving some sectors and to the areas in which scholarly labor simply has not caught up with the changes in the empirical world.

Nonprofit–nonprofit

The first row of Table 22.1 refers to nonprofit collaborations and networks involving organizations from the same sector. While service-providing nonprofits can partner with nonprofits that have a different purpose or mission, for conceptual clarity we emphasize ties between service-providing nonprofits in the top-left cell. We label these collaborations as conventional partnerships because they are common and very diverse. These relationships can be informal or formal, with informal collaborations sometimes involving little more than information exchange or client referrals and formal collaborations sometimes involving joint programming or joint ventures (Guo and Acar 2005; Proulx, Hager, and Klein 2014; Gazley and Guo 2015). As common as they are, our review suggests that ties involving only service-providing nonprofits have not been studied very extensively. The cell consequently is shaded lightly to indicate that much more research could be conducted to clarify if and how within-sector collaborations and networks are distinctive.

Nonprofits with advocacy as a primary function or purpose, the middle cell in the top row, also collaborate frequently with other nonprofit organizations. Collaborations in this cell overlap somewhat with other partnerships in this row, but for ease of presentation we focus on partnerships among advocacy organizations. Much of the extant research on this topic emphasizes coalitions of organizations working together for social change, whether as part of domestic or transnational social movements, though advocacy organizations also partner with just one organization at a time (McAdam, McCarthy, and Zald 1996; Keck and Sikkink 1998; Davis et al. 2005; Baumgartner et al. 2009; Prakash and Gugerty 2010). Since extensive research exists on ties among advocacy organizations, the cell has a dark shade. Novel avenues of research nevertheless exist for comparing advocacy collaborations to service-provision collaborations – and for investigating collaborations between advocacy nonprofits and nonprofits with blended purposes.

The final cell in the first row refers to collaborations between nonprofits that combine services with advocacy and other nonprofits. Early research on hybrid organizations emphasized identity-based social movement organizations for racial minorities and women's rights groups (Clemens 1993; Minkoff 1994, 1999, 2002; Minkoff, Aisenbrey, and Agnone 2008). A growing body of research indicates that this pattern is not limited to identity-based organizations as many nonprofits now integrate these two purposes (Suárez 2009; Mosley 2011). With the rise of rights-based approaches to development, many humanitarian and international development nonprofits (or NGOs) also have been blending these once-distinctive activities (Schmitz and Mitchell 2016). Despite the growth of hybrids, the cell is blank (no color) because little research seems to exist on collaboration or networks involving these nonprofits (Fyall and McGuire 2015).

Taken together, our review suggests that research on collaborations between nonprofit organizations is much less extensive than might be expected. Considerable research exists on collaboration between advocacy nonprofits, but the same cannot be said for research on collaborations between service-providing nonprofits or hybrids. Moreover, little research explores how collaborations between nonprofits with the same purpose or function differ from collaborations between nonprofits with different purposes.

Nonprofit–foundation (philanthropy)

The second row of Table 22.1 refers to collaborative ties between philanthropic organizations and nonprofits. Continuing with the pattern of moving from left to right for each row in the table, the main role that foundations play is that of grant maker – primarily for service-providing nonprofits. What constitutes a collaboration between a service-providing nonprofit and a foundation is not entirely clear. Such collaborations likely are more formal (thus less diverse in range) than nonprofit–nonprofit collaborations. Collaborations presumably entail financial ties like a foundation grant, for instance, even though grants do not necessarily equate with collaborations. Research indicates that many foundations are beginning to require grant recipients to collaborate and that they support service-provision networks, yet the cell is lightly shaded because a gap exists in the literature on foundations as partners to nonprofits (Bryson et al. 2006; Ostrower 2005).

Foundation support for advocacy nonprofits has been limited, and when provided, philanthropic grants to nonprofits tend to channel grant recipients away from contentious tactics and into more professionalized social change activity (Jenkins 1998; Frumkin 1998). Foundations nevertheless have served as a key source of support for advocacy groups, contributing to the success of some social movements (Goss 2007; Suárez and Lee 2011; Suárez 2012). Perhaps because foundation support for social change activity is scarce, grants to advocacy nonprofits often are characterized as patronage – suggesting stewardship and collaboration (Jenkins 2006). Like the cell for collaborations between foundations and service-providing nonprofits, this cell is lightly shaded because few studies delineate distinctive aspects of collaboration between foundations and advocacy nonprofits or address relationships besides formal grants (Ferris 2009).

Until recently, research on advocacy and social movements has treated foundations as relevant primarily in relation to resource mobilization – not as actors directly working to shape policy (Jenkins 2006; McAdam et al. 1996). With the emergence of a New Gilded Age of philanthropy – the dramatic growth of very wealthy, engaged philanthropists associated with technology entrepreneurship – foundations have started to embrace advocacy as a tool or tactic for achieving mission (Frumkin 2006; Bishop and Green 2008; Reckhow 2013, 2016; Goss 2016; Tompkins-Stange 2016; Callahan 2017). This transformation is relevant for collaboration with nonprofits regardless of purpose but perhaps especially for those with a blended purpose – because foundations can develop multifaceted ties by simultaneously supporting services and promoting (or even participating in) advocacy activity. Since these aspects of strategic philanthropy are relatively new, the cell is lightly shaded to indicate modest research output involving foundation collaborations with blended purpose nonprofits, though the topic deserves more scholarly attention.

Our review of collaboration between nonprofits and foundations suggests that considerable work remains to be done, not only to assess the distinctiveness of these partnerships but also to understand how they might differ across nonprofit purpose. At the same time, mapping the landscape of nonprofit collaborations with foundations suggest that ties are likely to become more dynamic or multiplex over time. With the emergence of strategic philanthropy and venture philanthropy, the repertoire of foundation ties is extending well beyond patronage through grantmaking.

Nonprofit–government

The third row of Table 22.1 attends to collaboration with government. Unlike intra-sector collaboration (nonprofit to nonprofit or to foundation), an extensive literature exists on non-profit collaboration with public agencies. Early research on this topic drew attention to the role of nonprofits as partners in public service (Salamon 1987, 1994). The use of nonprofits for government program implementation accelerated in the 1960s and remains common today (Smith and Lipsky 1993). Some studies distinguish contracting from collaborating, highlighting the difference between principal–agent ties and stewardship ties, and many studies also attend to informal ties that are beyond the contract (Van Slyke 2006; Gazley and Brudney 2007; Gazley 2008; Suárez 2011).

Research on collaboration between service-providing nonprofits and public agencies is not limited to dyadic ties – a considerable body of research continues to explore service provision networks (Stone 2000; Herranz 2008; Isett et al. 2011; Kania and Kramer 2011; Lecy, Mergel and Schmitz 2014). Collaboration is relevant to this particular work but is somewhat limited because public sector organizations tend to be assumed as network leaders (Milward and Provan 2006; Rethemeyer and Hatmaker 2008). Networks in which public agencies are the lead organization – and the principal for all principal–agent ties in the network – may be the most common, but alternatives certainly exist. Despite some gaps in what is addressed in research on collaboration between nonprofits and public agencies, this cell has a dark shade because it is one of the types of collaboration that has received the most scholarly attention.

Considerable research also has investigated the role of advocacy nonprofits in shaping government policy, but situates organizations from these two sectors in an antagonistic relationship (Andrews and Edwards 2004; Jenkins 2006; Baumgartner et al. 2009). Studies on collaboration between advocacy nonprofits and government agencies tend to emphasize policy formation, and this line of work is not in close dialogue with research on collaborations for service provision (Lecy et al. 2014; Weible and Carter 2017). Summarizing distinctions between research on policy networks and service networks, Rethemeyer and Hatmaker (2008, p. 620) state: Policy network scholars have generally focused on decisions with less interest in implementation, whereas scholars of collaborative networks have plowed ahead with analysis of what works without questioning how choices about service provision feed back into the system of decision.

The cell for research on collaboration between advocacy nonprofits and government agencies nevertheless is lightly shaded because the policy implementation literature recognizes that advocacy nonprofits can and sometimes do work in concert with public agencies (Rosenau 2000; Leach, Pelkey and Sabatier 2002). Advocacy nonprofits can be critical sources of information in the formulation of public policy, and many studies – especially those drawing on the advocacy coalition framework (ACF) – identify other avenues for collaboration (Weible and Carter 2017). Moving from collaborations between government and advocacy nonprofits, the last cell in the row considers collaboration between government and nonprofits with a blended purpose. The separation between service-providing nonprofits and advocacy nonprofits has softened, and this transformation has many implications for collaboration in relation to third-party government (LeRoux and Goerdel 2009; Mosley 2011, 2012; Fyall and McGuire 2015; Fyall 2017).

Not all nonprofits that blend services and advocacy have a collaborative relationship with government, and not all nonprofits that receive government revenue to provide public services engage in advocacy. The growth of third-party government nevertheless has contributed to the politicization of service provision, generating collaborative ties between nonprofits and government that can be reminiscent of machine or patronage politics (Marwell 2004; Levine 2016). In modest forms, nonprofits may leverage collaboration to advocate successfully for new or continued government funding. In more questionable forms, legislators may collaborate with nonprofits by directing government resources to them in exchange for access to, and perhaps even votes from, local constituents. This cell is lightly shaded because this line of research is just beginning to flourish, but our general finding is that research on nonprofit collaboration with government has a great deal of depth and breadth.

Nonprofit–business

Some of the biggest gaps in research on nonprofit collaboration become apparent when considering ties to for-profit businesses. Many different types of relationships (and labels for them) constitute collaborations between service-providing nonprofits and businesses, including licensing agreements, sponsorships, social ventures, social alliances, cause-related marketing campaigns, and activities associated with corporate social responsibility initiatives such as in-kind giving and employee volunteering (Austin 2000; Berger, Cunningham, and Drumwright 2004; Galaskiewicz and Sinclair Colman 2006; Austin and Seitanidi 2012a, 2012b; Suárez and Hwang 2013). Some of these collaborative activities are more philanthropic than others, and some are transactional while others entail extensive interaction and resource exchange. We give this cell a dark shade because many different types of relationships have been studied. Much of this work approaches the topic from the perspective of the business, and considerable opportunity exists for novel research on how service-providing nonprofits interact with businesses.

While a large literature exists on the role of advocacy nonprofits in pressuring businesses to change practices or policies, research on collaboration between advocacy nonprofits and businesses is far less common and examples of collaborative initiatives are quite rare in the research literature (Rondinelli and London 2003; Argenti 2004). The relationship between corporations and advocacy nonprofits tends to be adversarial because corporations, along with the state, are the main targets of advocacy organizations' activities. However, the relationship can transform into a more collaborative one when both parties can benefit from doing so. For instance, the negative publicity generated by protest activities mobilized by advocacy organizations may have tangible effects on the targeted corporations' bottom line and social legitimacy, and those corporations can show their commitment to improving their behavior by developing ties with their adversaries (King and Soule 2007; King and Pearce 2010).

For advocacy organizations, the efficacy of collaborating with corporations may outweigh that of relying on more confrontational tactics, especially when they can participate in the development of industry standards or certification systems or other types of soft law and private regulation (Yaziji and Doh 2009). Given the growing importance of private regulation and soft law, especially in the regulation of corporate behavior, we expect this area to attract more scholarly attention. The guiding questions would be: under what situations would businesses and advocacy groups share common interest in social change? What are the issue domains where business and advocacy nonprofits are likely to form partnerships? Furthermore, what would these collaborations look like, especially when compared to more typical business–nonprofit collaborations in service delivery? The cell nevertheless is blank (no color) to indicate a lack of scholarly attention to this type of tie.

Research on collaboration between businesses and nonprofits that blend services and advocacy seems to be just as rare as research on businesses that collaborate with advocacy nonprofits. The cell for research on collaboration between corporations and blended-purpose nonprofits consequently is blank, though we expect opportunities to explore this type of tie will increase over time. Taken together, the most obvious finding from our literature review is that scholarship on ties between corporations and service-providing nonprofits is much more prevalent than studies of ties between corporations and nonprofits with other purposes. Research on the determinants of business collaboration with nonprofits that engage in advocacy is greatly needed, as is theorization regarding how these partnerships might be distinctive and what might shape their prevalence over time. Our map of the landscape of research on collaboration also suggests that research comparing nonprofit collaboration with businesses to nonprofit collaborations with other types of organizations might yield insightful findings.

Mixed networks: nonprofit–business–government–philanthropy

Research on networks of organizations involving just one or two total sectors is discussed along with other types of collaborations in the rows above, but that by no means exhausts the range of potential networks in which a nonprofit can become involved. This final row thus considers networks with a nonprofit and participants from at least two other sectors (foundation, business, government). Beginning with collaborations involving a service-providing nonprofit (as the focal actor) and a mix of organizations from other sectors, extensive research exists under the labels of collaborative governance and service networks (Selsky and Parker 2005; Rethemeyer and Hatmaker 2008; Isett et al. 2011; Lecy et al. 2014). This line of work overlaps a great deal with the section above on government collaboration with service-providing nonprofits because in most studies public agencies are the principal actor – the primary funder, convener, and network manager.

What distinguishes this body of work from research on collaborations between government and service nonprofits is the presence of a foundation or a business in the network. Though many networks for collaborative governance and service implementation involve foundations and/or businesses – not just as stakeholders but also as members – how the presence of these organizations shape those networks has not been studied extensively. How networks involving public agencies and service-provision nonprofits differ from those involving a broader range of organizational players merits more research attention as well. For instance, some studies exist on philanthropic coproduction, when foundations and nonprofits collaborate to support a public agency, but this type of research remains uncommon (Brecher and Wise 2008; Suárez 2015; Suárez and Esparza 2017). Despite the limited breadth of questions addressed by research in this cell, owing to its extensiveness we give it a dark shade.

Like research on collaboration involving an advocacy nonprofit and organizations from just one additional sector, studies of networks involving an advocacy nonprofit and organizations representing multiple sectors are quite limited. Since the extant research in this area tends to focus on policy formation, moreover, it overlaps considerably with studies on collaboration between advocacy nonprofits and government (Leach et al. 2002; Weible and Carter 2017; Rethemeyer and Hatmaker 2008; Isett et al. 2011; Lecy et al. 2014). How the involvement of foundations and businesses shape policy formation networks has not received scholarly attention, and how the dynamics of collaboration in policy formation networks differ from those of service implementation networks is no more common. Though the cell above on collaboration between advocacy nonprofits and government has a light shade, we give this cell no color (blank) to reflect just how much work remains to be done to elucidate the consequences of business and foundation involvement.

The final cell in our table aligns with nonprofits that have a blended purpose (services and advocacy) and collaborate with organizations from more than one additional sector. As mentioned above, even though plenty of studies exist on partnerships in public service and service implementation networks, for the most part the literature is just beginning to consider these relationships in the context of politicized third-party government (Marwell 2004; LeRoux and Goerdel 2009; Mosley 2012; Fyall 2017; Levine 2016). While studies recognize that many service-providing nonprofits now engage in advocacy as a strategy or tactic for achieving mission, how this trend alters or shapes networks that involve public agencies and other types of organizations is especially novel research territory. This cell has no color to reflect the lack of depth and breadth of scholarship in this area, and overall our mapping of research on multi-sector collaboration suggests that new insights could be gleaned by expanding beyond conventional service-provision networks.

Discussion and conclusion

Not only are interorganizational relationships becoming more ubiquitous, collaborations and networks routinely are encouraged or even mandated as the optimal approach for addressing complex social problems. Changes in the nonprofit sector and in its broader environment have contributed to the perceived need and efficacy of collaboration. However, a broad overview of the literature spanning several disciplinary boundaries reveals that collaboration consists of diverse forms of interactions and relationships involving organizations from multiple sectors. Even after limiting the scope of the phenomena to the ties involving nonprofits, there exists a dizzying array of intra- and cross-sector collaborations purposed for a wide variety of ends. This sprawling proliferation presents a challenge for scholars interested in the topic. In order to force specificity and identify aspects of collaboration that have received insufficient attention, we have offered a novel framework for mapping the research literature.

In particular, we focus on two crucial dimensions of collaborative relationships: (1) the purpose or function of the focal nonprofit organizations (service-provision, advocacy, and blended or hybrid) and (2) the sector of the partner organization (nonprofit, foundation, government, and for-profit). The framework distinguishes nonprofit organizations based on their function, incorporating the changing landscape of the nonprofit sector by taking into consideration the growing presence of hybrid nonprofits that blend service delivery and advocacy. Further, as one of the main drivers of the proliferation of collaboration stems from the shifting motivations of organizations in other sectors precipitated by the changes in the wider institutional environment, we explore the breadth and depth of research on collaboration in relation to sector. Our approach consequently serves to identify types of collaborative ties that have been overlooked or underappreciated.

An additional benefit of our framework for mapping the research literature is that it establishes a benchmark of sorts for understanding longitudinal patterns. It is not clear whether the increase in interorganizational interactions replicates simply the collaboration patterns of the past, signals the growing popularity of certain types of ties, or indicates an emergence of new types of collaboration. Our framework therefore provides a way to categorize and capture collaborations at a fine-grained level and follow their shifting prevalence. That is, the myriad possibilities at the intersection of the focal nonprofit's purpose and the partnering organization's sector shed light on the variety of motivations giving rise to collaborations of different types. The framework also enables researchers to identify how the distribution of collaborations and partnerships shifts over time as changing contexts shape the disposition of nonprofit organizations and their potential partners for collaborations.

Finally, whether the issue is partnerships of two organizations or multi-organizational networks, the optimistic belief in the power and promise of combined efforts usually outweighs the potential perils and pitfalls of collaboration. Although often overlooked, the challenges associated with designing, implementing, and managing collaborations are clear and may vary across the types of collaborations identified in our framework. The types of uncertainty and contingency that beset collaborations also may depend on the types of organizations involved in collaboration. Moreover, the outcomes or goals that collaborations seek to bring about may set the parameters of collaborative endeavors. For instance, the concreteness of service delivery and the diffuseness (and transformational ambition) of advocacy may have different implications for the design, implementation, and management of collaboration. By providing an overview of prior research on the determinants of collaborative performance and then presenting our framework based on nonprofit purpose and partner sector, we reveal many new avenues for comparative studies.

Note

1   This work was supported by the Ministry of Education of the Republic of Korea and the National Research Foundation of Korea (NRF-2016S1A3A2925085).

Bibliography

Agranoff, R. (2006) Inside collaborative networks: Ten lessons for public managers. *Public Administration Review* 66(s1): 56–65.

Agranoff, R. (2007) *Managing within networks: Adding value to public organizations.* Washington, DC: Georgetown University Press.

Agranoff, R. (2012) *Collaborating to manage: A primer for the public sector.* Washington, DC: Georgetown University Press.

Agranoff, R. and McGuire, M. (2003) *Collaborative public management: New strategies for local governments.* Washington, DC: Georgetown University Press.

Andrews, K. and Edwards, B. (2004) Advocacy organizations in the U.S. political process. *Annual Review of Sociology* 30:479–506.

Ansell, C. and Gash, A. (2008) Collaborative governance in theory and practice. *Journal of Public Administration Research and Theory* 18(4): 543–571.

Argenti, P. (2004) Collaborating with activists: How Starbucks works with NGOs. *California Management Review* 47(1): 91–116.

Austin, J. (2000) Strategic collaboration between nonprofits and business. *Nonprofit and Voluntary Sector Quarterly* 29(1): 69–97.

Austin, J. and Seitanidi, M. (2012a) A review of partnering between nonprofits and businesses: Part I. *Nonprofit and Voluntary Sector Quarterly* 41(5): 726–758.

Austin, J. and Seitanidi, M. (2012b) A review of partnering between nonprofits and businesses: Part II. *Nonprofit and Voluntary Sector Quarterly* 41(6): 929–968.

Battilana, J. and Lee, M. (2014) Advancing research on hybrid organizing – insights from the study of social enterprises. *Academy of Management Annals* 8(1): 397–441.

Battilana, J., Besharov, M. and Mitzinnneck, B. (2017) On hybrids and hybrid organizing: A review and roadmap for future research. In Royston Greenwood et al. (eds.), *The SAGE handbook of organizational institutionalism*. Thousand Oaks, CA: Sage, 128–162

Barringer, B. and Harrison, J. (2000) Walking a tightrope: Creating value through interorganizational relationships. *Journal of Management* 26(3): 367–403.

Baumgartner, F., Berry, J., Hojnacki, M., Kimball, D.C. and Leech, B. (2009) *Lobbying and policy change: Who wins, who loses, and why*. Chicago. University of Chicago Press.

Berger, I., Cunningham, P. and Drumwright, M. (2004) Social alliances: Company/nonprofit collaboration. *California Management Review* 47(1): 58–90.

Berry, J. (2005) Nonprofits and civic engagement. *Public Administration Review* 65(5): 568–578.

Bishop, M. and Green, M. (2008) *Philanthrocapitalism: How the rich can save the world*. New York: Bloomsbury Press.

Brecher, C. and Wise, O. (2008) Looking a gift horse in the mouth: Challenges in managing philanthropic support for public services. *Public Administration Review* 68(s1): 146–161.

Bromley, P. and Meyer, J. (2015) *Hyper-organization: Global organizational expansion*. Oxford: Oxford University Press.

Bromley, P. and Meyer, J. (2017) 'They are all organizations': The cultural roots of blurring between the nonprofit, business, and government sectors. *Administration & Society* 49(7): 939–966.

Bryson, J., Crosby, B. and Stone, M. (2006) The design and implementation of cross-sector collaborations: Propositions from the literature. *Public Administration Review* 66(s1): 44–55.

Bryson, J., Crosby, B. and Bloomberg, L. (2014) Public value governance: Moving beyond traditional public administration and the New Public Management. *Public Administration Review* 74(4): 445–456.

Bryson, J., Crosby, B. and Stone, M. (2015) Designing and implementing cross-sector collaborations: Needed and challenging. *Public Administration Review* 75(5): 647–663.

Callahan, D. (2017) *The givers: Wealth, power, and philanthropy in a new gilded age*. New York: Knopf.

Clemens, E. (1993) Organizational repertoires and institutional change: Women's groups and the transformation of U.S. politics, 1890–1920. *American Journal of Sociology* 98(4): 755–798.

Clemens, E. and Guthrie, D., eds. (2010) *Politics and partnerships: The role of associations in America's political past and present*. Chicago: University of Chicago Press.

Cornforth, C., Hayes, J. and Vangen, S. (2014) Nonprofit–public collaborations: Understanding governance dynamics. *Nonprofit and Voluntary Sector Quarterly* 44(4): 775–795.

Davis, G., McAdam, D. Scott, W. and Zald, M. (2005) *Social movements and organization theory*. New York: Cambridge University Press.

de Souza, X. (2003) *Perfect fit or shotgun marriage? Understanding the power and pitfalls in partnerships*. Cambridge, MA: The Community Problem-Solving Project @ MIT.

Den Hond, F. and de Bakker, F. (2007) Ideologically motivated activism: How activist groups influence corporate social change activities. *Academy of Management Review* 32(3): 901–924.

Den Hond, F., de Bakker, F. and Doh, J. (2015) What prompts companies to collaboration with NGOs? Recent evidence from the Netherlands. *Business & Society* 54(2): 187–228.

DiMaggio, P. and Powell, W. (1983) The iron cage revisited: Institutional isomorphism and collective rationality in organizational fields. *American Sociological Review* 48(2): 147–160.

Donahue, J. and Zeckhauser, R. (2011) *Collaborative governance*. Princeton, NJ: Princeton University Press.

Drori, G., Meyer, J. and Hwang, H., eds. (2006) *Globalization and organization: World society and organizational change*. Oxford: Oxford University Press.

Emerson, K. and Nabatchi, T. (2015) Evaluating the productivity of collaborative governance regimes: A performance matrix. *Public Performance & Management Review* 38: 717–747.

Emerson, K., Nabatchi, T. and Balogh, S. (2012) An integrative framework for collaborative governance. *Journal of Public Administration Research and Theory* 22(1): 1–29

Ferris, J., ed. (2009) *Foundations and public policy*. Washington, DC: Foundation Center.

Frumkin, P. (1998) The long recoil from regulation: Private philanthropic foundations and the Tax Reform Act of 1969. *American Review of Public Administration* 28(3): 266–286.

Frumkin, P. (2002) *On being nonprofit: A conceptual and policy primer*. Cambridge, MA: Harvard University Press.

Frumkin, P. (2006) *Strategic giving*. Chicago: University of Chicago Press.

Fyall, R. (2017) Nonprofits as advocates and providers: A conceptual framework. *Policy Studies Journal* 45(1): 121–143.

Fyall, R. and McGuire, M. (2015) Advocating for policy change in nonprofit coalitions. *Nonprofit and Voluntary Sector Quarterly* 44(6): 1274–1291.

Galaskiewicz, J. (1985) Interorganizational relations. *Annual Review of Sociology* 11: 281–304.

Galaskiewicz, J. and Bielefeld, W. (1998) *Nonprofit organizations in an age of uncertainty: A study of organizational change*. Hawthorne, NY: Adline.

Galaskiewicz, J. and Sinclair Colman, M. (2006) Collaboration between corporations and nonprofit organizations. In W. Powell and R. Steinberg (eds.), *The Nonprofit Sector: A Research Handbook*. New Haven, CT: Yale University Press, 180–206.

Gazley, B. (2008) Beyond the contract: The scope and nature of informal government–nonprofit partnerships. *Public Administration Review* 68(1): 141–154.

Gazley, B. and Brudney, J. (2007) The purpose (and perils) of government–nonprofit partnership. *Nonprofit and Voluntary Sector Quarterly* 36(3): 389–415.

Gazley, B. and Guo, C. (2015) What do we know about nonprofit collaboration? A comprehensive systematic review of the literature. *Academy of Management Proceedings* 15409 (doi: 10.5465/AMBPP.2015.303).

Goldsmith, S. and Eggers, W. (2004) *Governing by network: The new shape of the public sector*. Washington, DC: Brookings Institute

Goss, K. (2007) Foundations of feminism: How philanthropic patrons shaped gender politics. *Social Science Quarterly* 88(5): 1174–1191.

Goss, K. (2016) Policy plutocrats: How America's wealthy seek to influence governance. *PS: Political Science & Politics* 49(3): 442–448.

Gray, B. (1989) *Collaborating: Finding common ground for multiparty problems*. San Francisco: Jossey-Bass.

Gray, B. (2000) Assessing inter-organizational collaboration: Multiple conceptions and multiple methods. In D. Faulkner and M. de Rond (eds.), *Perspectives on Collaboration*. New York: Oxford University Press, 243–260.

Guo, C. and Acar, M. (2005) Understanding collaboration among nonprofit organizations: Combining resource dependency, institutional, and network perspectives. *Nonprofit and Voluntary Sector Quarterly* 34(3): 340–361.

Guthrie, D. and McQuarrie, M. (2008) Providing for the public good: Corporate–Community relations in the era of the receding welfare state. *City and Community* 7(2): 113–139.

Herranz, J. (2008) The multisector trilemma of network management. *Journal of Public Administration Research and Theory* 18(1): 1–32.

Huxham, C. and Vangen, S. (2004) Doing things collaboratively: Realizing the advantage or succumbing to inertia? *Organizational Dynamics* 33(2): 190–201.

Huxham, C. and Vangen, S. (2005) *Managing to collaborate: The theory and practice of collaborative advantage*. New York: Routledge.

Hwang, H. and Bromley, P. (2015) Internal and external determinants of formal plans in the nonprofit sector. *International Public Management Journal* 18(4): 568–588.

Hwang, H. and Powell, W. (2009) The rationalization of charity: The influences of professionalism in the nonprofit sector. *Administrative Science Quarterly* 54(2): 268–298.

Hwang, H. and Suárez, D. (2019). Beyond service provision: Advocacy and the construction of nonprofits as organizational actors. *Research in the Sociology of Organizations* 58: 87–109.

Innes, J. and Booher, D. (1999) Consensus building and complex adaptive systems: A framework for evaluating collaborative planning. *Journal of the American Planning Association* 65(4): 412–423.

Isett, K., Mergel, I., LeRoux, K., Mischen, P. and Rethemeyer, R. (2011) Networks in public administration scholarship: Understanding where we are and where we need to go. *Journal of Public Administration Research and Theory* 21(s1): 157–173.

Jenkins, J.C. (1998) Channeling social protest. In W. Powell and E. Clemens (eds.), *Private action and the public good*. New Haven, CT: Yale University Press, 206–216.

Jenkins, J.C. (2006) Nonprofit organizations and political advocacy. In W. Powell and R. Steinberg (eds.), *The nonprofit sector: A research handbook*. New Haven, CT: Yale University Press, 307–332.

Kania, J. and Kramer, M. (2011) Collective impact. *Stanford Social Innovation Review* (Winter): 36–41.

Keck, M. and Sikkink, K. (1998) *Activists beyond borders*. Ithaca, NY: Cornell University Press.

Kettl, D. (1997) The global revolution in public management: Driving themes, missing links. *Journal of Policy Analysis and Management* 16(3): 446–462.

King, B. and Soule, S. (2007) Social movements as extra-institutional entrepreneurs: The effect of protests on stock price returns. *Administrative Science Quarterly* 52(3): 413–442.

King, B. and Pearce, N. (2010) The contentiousness of markets: Politics, social movements, and institutional change in markets. *Annual Review of Sociology* 36(1): 249–267.

Leach, W., Pelkey, N. and Sabatier, P. (2002) Stakeholder partnerships as collaborative policymaking. *Journal of Policy Analysis and Management* 21(4): 645–670.

Lecy, J., Mergel, I. and Schmitz, H.P. (2014) Networks in public administration: Current scholarship in review. *Public Management Review* 16(5): 643–665.

LeRoux, K. and Goerdel, H. (2009) Political advocacy by nonprofit organizations. *Public Performance & Management Review* 32(4): 514–536.

Levine, J. (2016) The privatization of political representation: Community-based organizations as nonelected community representatives. *American Sociological Review* 81(6): 1251–1275.

Marwell, N. (2004) Privatizing the welfare state: Nonprofit community-based organizations as political actors. *American Sociological Review* 69: 265–291.

Marwell, N. (2009) *Bargaining for Brooklyn: Community organizations in the entrepreneurial city*. Chicago: University of Chicago Press.

McAdam, D., McCarthy, J. and Zald, M.N. eds., (1996) *Comparative perspectives on social movements: Political opportunities, mobilizing structures, and cultural framings*. Cambridge: Cambridge University Press.

McGuire, M. (2006) Collaborative public management: Assessing what we know and how we know it. *Public Administration Review* 66(S1): 33–43.

McQuarrie, M. (2010) Nonprofits and the reconstruction of urban governance: Housing production and community development in Cleveland, 1975–2005. In E. Clemens and D. Guthrie (eds.), *Politics and partnerships*. Chicago: University of Chicago Press, 237–268.

Meyer, J. and Rowan, B. (1977) Institutionalized organizations: Formal structure as myth and ceremony. *American Journal of Sociology* 83(2): 340–363.

Milward, B. and Provan, K. (2006) *A manager's guide to choosing and using collaborative networks*. Washington, DC: IBM Center for the Business of Government.

Minkoff, D. (1994) From service provision to institutional advocacy: The shifting legitimacy of organizational forms. *Social Forces* 72: 943–969.

Minkoff, D. (1999) Bending with the wind: Organizational change in American women's and minority organizations. *American Journal of Sociology* 104: 1666–1673.

Minkoff, D. (2002) The emergence of hybrid organizational forms: Combining identity-based service provision and political action. *Nonprofit and Voluntary Sector Quarterly* 31(3): 377–401.

Minkoff, D., Aisenbrey, S. and Agnone, J. (2008) Organizational diversity in the US advocacy sector. *Social Problems* 55(4): 525–548.

Mosley, J. (2011) Institutionalization, privatization, and political opportunity: What tactical choices reveal about the policy advocacy of human services nonprofits. *Nonprofit and Voluntary Sector Quarterly* 40: 435–457.

Mosley, J. (2012) Keeping the lights on: How government funding concerns drive the advocacy agendas of nonprofit homeless service providers. *Journal of Public Administration Research and Theory* 22: 841–866.

Oliver, A. and Ebers, M. (1998) Networking network studies: An analysis of conceptual configurations in the study of inter-organizational relationships. *Organization Studies* 19(4): 549–583.

Oliver, C. (1990) Determinants of interorganizational relationships: Integration and future directions. *Academy of Management Review* 15(2): 241–265.

Osborne, S. (2006) The new public governance? *Public Management Review* 8(3): 377–387.

Ostrower, F. (2005) The reality underneath the buzz of partnerships: The potentials and pitfalls of partnering. *Stanford Social Innovation Review* 3(1): 34–41.

Page, S., Stone, M., Bryson, J. and Crosby, B. (2015) Public value creation by cross-sector collaborations: A framework and challenges of assessment. *Public Administration* 93(3): 715–732.

Parmigiani, A. and Rivera-Santos, M. (2011) Clearing a path through the forest: A meta-review of inter-organizational relationships. *Journal of Management* 37(4): 1108–1136.

Pfeffer, J. and Salancik, G. (1978) *The external control of organizations: A resource dependence perspective*. New York: Harper and Row.

Podolny, J. and Page, K. (1998) Network forms of organization. *Annual Review of Sociology* 24: 57–76.

Powell, W.W. (1990) Neither market nor hierarchy: Network forms of organization. *Research in Organizational Behavior* 12: 295–336.

Powell, W., Koput, K. and Smith-Doerr, L. (1996) Interorganizational collaboration and the locus of innovation: Networks of learning in biotechnology. *Administrative Science Quarterly* 41: 116–146.

Powell, W., White, D., Koput, K. and Owen-Smith, J. (2005) Network dynamics and field evolution: The growth of interorganizational collaboration in the life sciences. *American Journal of Sociology* 110(4): 1132–1205.

Prakash, A. and Gugerty. M.K., eds. (2010) *Advocacy organizations and collective action*. Cambridge: Cambridge University Press.

Proulx, K., Hager, M. and Klein, K. (2014) Models of collaboration between nonprofit organizations. *International Journal of Productivity and Performance Management* 63(6): 746–765.

Provan, K. and Milward, B. (1995) A preliminary theory of interorganizational effectiveness: A comparative study of four community mental health systems. *Administrative Science Quarterly* 40(1): 1–33.

Provan, K. and Milward, B. (2001) Do networks really work? A framework for evaluating public-sector organizational networks. *Public Administration Review* 61(4): 414–423.

Provan, K., Fish, A. and Sydow, J. (2007) Interorganizational networks at the network level: A review of the empirical literature on whole networks. *Journal of Management* 33(3): 479–516.

Provan, K. and Kenis, P. (2008) Modes of network governance: Structure, management, and effectiveness. *Journal of Public Administration Research and Theory* 18(2): 229–252.

Reckhow, S. (2013) *Follow the money: How foundation dollars change public school politics*. New York: Oxford University Press.

Reckhow, S. (2016) More than patrons: How foundations fuel policy change and backlash. *PS: Political Science & Politics* 49(3): 449–454.

Rethemeyer, R.K. and Hatmaker, D. (2008) Network management reconsidered: An inquiry into management of network structures in public sector service provision. *Journal of Public Administration Research and Theory* 18(4): 617–646.

Rondinelli, D. and London, T. (2003) How corporations and environmental groups cooperate: Assessing cross-sector alliances and collaborations. *Academy of Management Executive* 17(1): 61–76.

Rosenau, P. (2000) *Public–private policy partnerships*. Cambridge, MA: MIT Press.

Sagawa, S. and Segal, E. (2000) Common interest, common good: Creating value through business and social sector. *California Management Review* 42(2): 105–122.

Salamon, L. (1987) Partners in public service: The scope and theory of government–nonprofit relations. In W. Powell (ed.), *The nonprofit sector: A research handbook*. New Haven, CT: Yale University Press, 99–117.

Salamon, L. (1994) The rise of the nonprofit sector. *Foreign Affairs* 73(3): 111–124.

Schmitz, H.P. and Mitchell, G. (2016) The other side of the coin: NGOs, rights-based approaches, and public administration. *Public Administration Review* 76(2): 252–262.

Scott, W.R. and Davis, G. (2007) *Organizations and organizing*. Upper Saddle River, NJ: Pearson Education.

Selsky, J.W. and Parker, B. (2005) Cross-sector partnerships to address social issues: Challenges to theory and practice. *Journal of Management* 31(6): 849–873.

Smith, S. and Lipsky, M. (1993) *Nonprofits for hire: The welfare state in the age of contracting*. First Edition. Cambridge, MA: Harvard University Press.

Stone, M. (2000) Exploring the effects of collaborations on member organizations: Washington County's welfare-to-work partnership. *Nonprofit and Voluntary Sector Quarterly* 29(s1): 98–119.

Stone, M. and Sandfort, J. (2009) Building a policy fields framework to inform research on nonprofit organizations. *Nonprofit and Voluntary Sector Quarterly* 38(6): 1054–1075.

Suárez, D. (2009) Nonprofit advocacy and civic engagement on the Internet. *Administration & Society* 41(3): 267–289.

Suárez, D. (2011) Collaboration and professionalization: The contours of public sector funding for nonprofits. *Journal of Public Administration Research and Theory* 21(2): 307–326.

Suárez, D. (2012) Grantmaking as advocacy: The emergence of social justice philanthropy. *Nonprofit Management and Leadership* 22(3): 259–280.

Suárez, D. (2015) Creating public value through collaboration: The restoration and preservation of Crissy Field. In J. Bryson and B. Crosby (eds.), *Creating public value in practice*. Boca Raton, FL: Taylor & Francis, 293–310.

Suárez, D. and Hwang, H. (2008) Civic engagement and nonprofit lobbying in California. *Nonprofit and Voluntary Sector Quarterly* 37(1): 92–112.

Suárez, D. and Lee, Y. (2011) Participation and policy: Foundation support for civic engagement and community organizing in the United States. *Public Management Review* 13(8): 1117–1138.

Suárez, D. and Hwang, H. (2013) Resource constraints or cultural conformity? Nonprofit relationships with businesses. *Voluntas: International Journal of Voluntary and Nonprofit Organizations* 24(3): 581–605.

Suárez, D. and Esparza, N. (2017) Institutional change and management in public–nonprofit partnerships. *American Review of Public Administration* 47(6): 648–660.

Thomson, A.M. and Perry, J. (2006) Collaboration processes: Inside the black box. *Public Administration Review* 66(1): 19–32.

Tompkins-Stange, M. (2016) *Policy patrons: Philanthropy, education reform, and the politics of influence*. Cambridge, MA: Harvard Education Press.

Van Slyke, D. (2006) Agents or stewards: Using theory to understand the government–nonprofit social service contracting relationship. *Journal of Public Administration Research and Theory* 12(2): 157–187.

Varda, D., Shoup, J.A. and Miller, S. (2012) A systematic review of collaboration and network research in the public affairs literature: Implications for public health practice and research. *American Journal of Public Health* 102(3): 564–571.

Weible, C. and Carter, D. (2017) Advancing policy process research at its overlap with public management scholarship. *Policy Studies Journal* 45(1): 22–49.

Wood, D.J. and Gray, B. (1991) Toward a comprehensive theory of collaboration. *Journal of Applied Behavioral Science* 27(2): 139–162.

Yaziji, M. and Doh, J. (2009) *NGOs and corporations: Conflict and collaboration*. Cambridge: Cambridge University Press.

23

ADVOCACY AND LOBBYING

Jennifer E. Mosley

ASSOCIATE PROFESSOR, SCHOOL OF SOCIAL SERVICE ADMINISTRATION,
UNIVERSITY OF CHICAGO, CHICAGO, IL, USA

Tadeo Weiner-Davis

DOCTORAL STUDENT, SCHOOL OF SOCIAL SERVICE ADMINISTRATION,
UNIVERSITY OF CHICAGO, CHICAGO, IL, USA

Theresa Anasti

ASSISTANT PROFESSOR, DEPARTMENT OF SOCIOLOGY, ANTHROPOLOGY,
SOCIAL WORK, AND CRIMINAL JUSTICE, OAKLAND UNIVERSITY, ROCHESTER, MI, USA

Introduction

One of the strengths of the nonprofit sector lies in its ability to create spaces for individuals to come together to promote their vision of the common good. The position of the nonprofit sector in civil society – outside of the family, the state, and the market – makes it a key space for dialogue, formation of preferences, and collective action. In this way, the nonprofit sector has long played an important role in advocacy and civic engagement. Advocacy can help organizations achieve their mission, improve the lives of vulnerable or underrepresented clients or constituents, and protect civil and human rights (Boris & Krehely, 2002; Andrews & Edwards, 2004; Berry & Arons, 2003; Jenkins, 1987, 2006; Fyall, 2016). For these and other reasons, advocacy is often considered a core function of the nonprofit sector.

In this chapter, we begin by defining advocacy and lobbying in the nonprofit sector. We review what is known about the types of nonprofits that are most involved in advocacy and what shape that advocacy takes, noting cross-national variations. We then point out current issues and trends in the study of nonprofit advocacy, specifically the importance of collaboration for nonprofits that wish to be engaged in advocacy, and the distinctions between top-down vs bottom-up models of advocating. In this discussion, we consider ways to reduce the barriers that may preclude some nonprofits from advocating. We then step back to consider the contributions of nonprofit advocacy to advancing civil society and democracy and the shape advocacy currently takes in more authoritarian contexts, particularly Russia and China. We conclude with questions of accountability in international advocacy, specifically from the global North to the global South.

What is advocacy and what does it include?

Advocacy is a broad term without a single or legal definition. It has been defined variously as "any attempt to influence the decisions of any institutional elite on behalf of a collective interest"

(Jenkins, 1987, p. 297); "a wide range of individual and collective expression or action on a cause, idea, or policy" (Reid, 2000, p. 1); "an act of organizing the strategic use of information to democratize unequal power relations" (Jordan & van Tuijl, 2000, p. 2052); and "the attempt to influence public policy, either directly or indirectly" (Pekkanen & Smith, 2014, p. 47). Common nonprofit advocacy activities include, but are not limited to, voter registration drives, discussions with government officials, protests, creating petition letters, public awareness campaigns, testifying at legislative hearings, writing public education reports, and lobbying, among other activities.

Lobbying is a subtype of advocacy that, in the United States, is defined and regulated by the Internal Revenue Service (IRS). It is defined as supporting the adoption or rejection of legislation, or contacting legislative officials to propose, support, or oppose legislation (IRS, 2018). Contrary to popular perception, 501(c)(3) nonprofits can legally lobby legislative officials, but are regulated by what is referred to as the "substantial part test" meaning that "no substantial part of the activities" may be for "carrying on propaganda, or otherwise attempting to influence legislation" (26 U.S.C. § 501). Because there are no official guidelines on what constitutes "substantial," US nonprofits that choose to engage in more substantial lobbying have the option of filing IRS form 5768 (also known as the H election). The election clarifies what percent of annual financial expenditures may be comprised of lobbying expenditures. However, most nonprofits are unaware of the existence of the H election, and the number of nonprofits that take the election remains small (Berry & Arons, 2003; Manny 2012).

Confusion over what is and is not allowed in advocacy is common among managers in the nonprofit sector. Because of this, some scholars have suggested that the IRS restrictions around advocacy and lobbying may cause many 501(c)(3) nonprofits to shy away from political activity altogether for fear of losing their IRS status designation or seeming too political (e.g., Berry & Arons, 2003; Jenkins, 1987). However, other research indicates that not all managers fall prey to this fear. Suarez and Hwang (2008) found that knowledge around IRS restrictions increased the likelihood of nonprofit lobbying and Mosley (2014) found that despite the limited knowledge that managers had around IRS regulations, many homeless service nonprofits still engaged in lobbying.

Degree of advocacy engagement

Nonprofit organizations vary in their level of engagement in advocacy. Some nonprofits, like interest group and social movement organizations, engage almost exclusively in advocacy (see Andrews & Edwards, 2004, for a discussion of the differences between these groups). Other nonprofits engage in advocacy as a way of fulfilling a mission – their advocacy participation may wax and wane both over time and in intensity.

Rates of advocacy involvement vary across studies, from lows of around 25% of the population of nonprofits to highs of around 75%, depending on the methodology and definition of advocacy used. For example, Child and Gronbjerg (2007) found that only 27% of their Indiana sample were involved in advocacy and most were involved at a minimal level, relying on volunteer labor to advocate and devoting only minimal staff and financial resources to it. On the other hand, Salamon and Geller with Lorentz (2008) found that three out of every four (73%) of their nationwide respondents engaged in some advocacy or lobbying over the previous year. Similarly, Bass, Arons, Guinane, and Carter (2007) found in a different large national sample that 75% engaged in some kind of advocacy activity. Of those, three out of five carried out these activities at least once a month, but 85% of respondents allocated less than 2% of their budget to advocacy. More recently, Pekkanen and Smith (2014) found that about 40% of the nonprofits in their Seattle sample were engaged in advocacy.

In regards to how advocacy engagement might vary by field, Child and Gronbjerg (2007) find that environmental, animal-related, and health organizations were more likely to advocate than other organizational fields. Salamon and Geller (2008) reported the following rates by organizational field: children and family services (80%), elderly housing and services (89%), community and economic development (69%), museums (46%), and theaters (59%). Pekkanen and Smith (2014) report that the five organizational fields they found most involved in advocacy were labor (89%), political (73%), environmental (59%), professional (49%), and business (44%).[1] Some studies have found much higher rates in some areas: Mosley (2014) found that 93% of homeless service providers in Chicago participated in some form of advocacy, while Kim and Mason (2018) found 83% of arts and culture organizations participated in advocacy. However, both of the aforementioned studies noted that the overall levels of advocacy at these organizations were low. Other studies concur that time spent on advocacy is generally low even when nonprofits do engage in some type of advocacy (Bass et al., 2007; Donaldson, 2007). Overall, while it appears that many organizations do not provide substantial resources to advocacy activities, most are engaged at some level.

Since not all nonprofits engage in advocacy, what prevents or predicts such involvement? Likewise, what organizational characteristics are associated with increased involvement? The most commonly cited barriers stem from lack of resources, expertise, and funding. When asked what held them back from advocacy, non-advocating respondents to the Salamon and Geller survey (2008) reported the following barriers: lack of staff time (70%), lack of staff skills (45%), no need because coalitions engage in advocacy on their behalf (36%), and finding advocacy irrelevant to the organizational mission (30%). In terms of what facilitates organizational involvement in advocacy, factors surrounding funding, leadership, and professional norms seem to matter the most. Mosley (2010) found that greater organizational size, government funding, professional leadership, and greater collaborative ties all were associated with advocacy involvement. Pekkanen and Smith (2014) also found that more funding, including more funding from the government, increased the likelihood of advocating. LeRoux and Goerdel (2009) found that increased dependence on government funding, collaborative networking, and having a registered lobbyist on the board increased likelihood of advocacy.

It is not hard to understand why well-resourced organizations are better positioned to afford advocacy engagement. Advocacy takes money and staff time that many small organizations simply don't have. In many organizations there is no staff person whose job it is to engage in advocacy. As such, an agency executive director might be the only person involved, and most of their time is already well booked. These staffing issues also contribute to barriers having to do with perceived experience or expertise to be able to advocate on an issue. This could entail anything between knowing how to run a social media advocacy campaign to having the necessary relationships in a statehouse to push a vote one way or the other.

In regards to government funding in particular, while there is research in non-US contexts that government funding deters participation in advocacy (see Schmid, Bar, & Nirel 2008 on the Israeli case) in the US context the preponderance of the evidence indicates that government funding either encourages or at least does not suppress advocacy among nonprofits (Chaves, Stephens, & Galaskiewicz, 2004; LeRoux & Goerdel 2009; Mosley 2010). This finding was initially surprising to many researchers – wouldn't organizations with government funding be afraid of retribution if they were thought to be creating difficulties for lawmakers? This finding is now generally explained through the notion of resource dependence: nonprofits that are more dependent on government funding are incentivized to advocate in order to ensure the stability of those funding streams. For example, Mosley (2012) found that homeless service providers that receive government funding engage in advocacy largely to maintain or improve funding relationships. In addition, the receipt of government grants often involves a process that requires a lot of relationship-building with a counterpart in a public agency. As a nonprofit manager, it is likely that you would want to maintain well-established lines of communications with policymakers to share your successes, your struggles, and future needs; all of these things can be interpreted broadly as advocacy.

Tactics and targets of nonprofit advocacy

As indicated previously, nonprofit advocacy includes a wide range of activities. Those activities are commonly broken down by choice of *tactics* and *targets*. Advocacy tactics speak to *how* nonprofits attempt to influence; advocacy *targets* are those to whom the tactics are aimed. In other words, the target is the person, organization, or institution that is the intended recipient of advocacy tactics.

Advocacy tactics are generally broken down into two categories: *insider* and *indirect* (including *outsider*) (Gais & Walker, 1991; Gormley & Cymrot, 2006; Mosley, 2011). Insider tactics involve working within policy systems, often through direct relationships with decision-makers. Common examples of insider tactics include lobbying policymakers, testifying in hearings, and participating on governmental committees. These activities put the nonprofit in direct relationship with the target of the advocacy, working within the system to foster social change and policy practice.

In contrast, indirect tactics take place outside of the formal political system. These tactics range from activities that are intended to raise public awareness or change thinking on a specific issue (such as media engagement or releasing policy reports). Outsider activities are intended to disrupt business as usual and include activities like protests or boycotts. The primary targets for indirect tactics vary; they include the general public, but may also include policymakers, corporations, and other institutions.

While some organizations may rely more heavily on one type of tactic or another, organizations typically utilize a range of tactics in their advocacy work. For instance, it is entirely plausible that a nonprofit manager may sit on a government task force or committee at the same time that the organization is putting together a policy report to be released to the public and helping to organize a public rally. In general, insider tactics are more likely to be used when an organization's advocacy goals are dependent on action being taken by decision-makers (for example, when legislators are to vote on proposed legislation or when a department is deciding how to implement a program). It is important to note, however, that insider tactics require professional expertise and direct access to policymakers (Gormley & Cymriot, 2006; Mosley, 2011) – something that not all nonprofits have. Indirect tactics may be more accessible to those nonprofits that lack preexisting relationships with policymakers.

While many nonprofits do engage in both insider and indirect tactics, most surveys indicate that outsider tactics are relatively uncommon (Donaldson, 2007; Gormley & Cymriot, 2006; Mosley, 2011; Salamon & Geller, 2008). For example, Buffardi, Pekkanen, and Smith (2017) found that only 3% of their US-based nonprofit sample was involved in strikes and demonstrations. Some scholars have posed that increased government funding of nonprofits encourages the use of insider tactics in order to increase or maintain organizational funding (Marwell, 2004; Mosley, 2012). However, effective outsider tactics may create inroads for the use of more insider tactics. Scott, Deschenes, Hopkins, Newman, and McLaughlin (2006) found that some programs initiated through outsider tactics eventually became establishment programs, a transition which they described as from the "streets" to the "suites" (p. 704). Similarly, Anasti (2017) found that an all-volunteer sex worker rights organization used outsider tactics to initially promote their agenda, the success of which led to talks and partnerships with more mainstream nonprofit and government agencies. Meanwhile, Fyall and McGuire (2015) question the distinction between insider and outsider tactics: they found that almost all of the nonprofit managers in their study indicated that their organization participated in both, noting that there are different purposes for each tactical activity. However, while the managers they interviewed thought that some outsider tactics were essential, they did not believe "that it alone could influence policy" (p. 1284).

Collaboration in an advocacy context

Nonprofits often advocate as part of wider networks, coalitions, and collaborations at the state, national, and international levels. In fact, one of the most commonly reported advocacy tactics by nonprofit organizations is participation in and through coalitions or collaborations (Bass et al., 2007; Mosley, 2011; Chen, 2018; Fyall & McGuire, 2015). Collaboration is defined as "what occurs when different nonprofit organizations work together to address problems through joint effort, resources and decision making and share ownership of the final product or service" (Guo and Acar, 2005, pp. 342–343). Coalitions are relatively formal collaborations between two or more organizations in order to jointly carry out an advocacy campaign. Involvement in coalitions of various kinds is widespread enough that Fyall and McGuire (2015) argue that researchers' focus on single organizations and their involvement in advocacy actually obscures the way that most advocacy is done – through networks of actors – and may result in an underreporting of advocacy.

There are many reasons to carry out advocacy by working in coalition. Importantly, it is thought to be effective because it may help organizations have a larger voice and consolidate resources (Gamson, 1975; Staggenborg, 1986). Fyall & McGuire (2015) found that many of the nonprofit advocates they studied believed that participation in coalitions was the only way to achieve policy change. For organizations that can spare few resources, this is also an efficient way that they can speak up for issues they deem important. Working in a group can help organizations stay involved in issues over time and respond in a coordinated fashion to external threats (Chen, 2018). It can also help organizations situate individual case advocacy into a more policy-oriented agenda (Chin, 2018) and help organizations improve and signal their political legitimacy (Anasti, 2017).

When organizational actors take part in a coalition, they not only engage in advocacy activities but also maximize and exchange resources in other ways. In a study of 24 nonprofit organizations in Australia, for example, 67% indicated that they engage in advocacy via "coordination," which included joint advocacy projects, membership arrangements, and partnerships (Onyx et al., 2010). The coordinated activities varied in formality from the sharing of trainings and workshops to the development of more sophisticated advocacy efforts. Sandfort (2014) similarly found that, in working as a network, organizations could better retain and process the historical experiences behind their advocacy. These organizations did not come together to simply state their opinion on a policy as part of a group; they additionally shared knowledge, resources, and other information that would transform each member of the coalition into a more robust advocate and contributor to the network. Most importantly, network advocacy can foment a level of solidarity and camaraderie that can help organizations through tough campaigns.

Use of social media and its relationship to top-down and bottom-up models of advocacy

As new technology and modes of communication (e.g., Facebook, Twitter, etc.) come to the fore, the manner in which nonprofits and concerned citizens come together to advocate is changing (Guo & Saxton, 2014). Social media provides new ways for nonprofit organizations to interface with clients, donors, and advocacy allies. Research shows that organizations are increasingly utilizing social media sites to engage the public. In a study of 188 advocacy organizations, for example, 93% utilized at least one social media tool (87% using Facebook, 80% using Twitter, and 72% using YouTube) (Guo & Saxton, 2014). Similarly, Obar, Zube, and Lampe (2012) found that all of the nonprofit advocacy organizations in their sample used some form of social media almost every day. This frequent usage may have considerable implications for how nonprofits promote their advocacy, as Lovejoy and Saxton (2012) note that nonprofits are actually better at engaging with their constituency using Twitter than they are with traditional websites.

Social media platforms are versatile in the type of advocacy that can be conducted (e.g., public education, petitions, direct lobbying, administrative lobbying, media advocacy). At the same time, they provide an extremely decentralized medium through which "followers" may join or leave with a minimal degree of social interaction. While some scholars and activists are fairly pessimistic about the possibilities of the new communication platforms – arguing that "clicks" and "likes" cannot replace face-to-face interaction – others contend that these offer opportunities for engagement that are different in degree, but not in nature, from offline modes of communication (Karpf, 2010).

The phenomenon of social media also offers a potential bridge between traditional top-down and bottom-up models of advocacy. As the labels suggest, top-down advocacy in the nonprofit sector rests on the involvement of organizational leadership and professional expertise when it comes to advocacy. Bottom-up advocacy, also known as "grassroots," relies more heavily on the involvement of constituents, patrons, and service-users. The definitional distinction does not mean that in practice they are mutually exclusive, however. One can imagine a scenario in which a nonprofit organization consults its constituents heavily (bottom-up) before the executive director sits down with a government official (top-down). This distinction is relevant to social media use because social media offers up new communication lines between professional leaders and engaged constituents. By allowing for easy feedback, polling, and calls to action, it may enable nonprofits to be more engaged with and informed regarding constituents' preferences, potentially leading to more democratic advocacy outcomes.

Cross-national advocacy

The potential for open, vocal advocacy by nonprofit organizations is partly mediated by the cultural and political histories of nation-states (Salamon & Anheier, 1998; Kabalo, 2009). Much commonality exists among the nonprofit sectors in Western countries (Salamon & Sokolowski, 2016). This includes, for example, a similar path of professionalization with increasingly formal structures and staff, reasonably secure sources of funding (e.g., philanthropic and government grants), and increasingly sophisticated marketing capabilities (Han, 2017). As demonstrated elsewhere in this chapter, increased organizational size and additional funding have also been associated with a higher likelihood of advocating.

This is not to say that all contexts are the same. For example, research points to differences in regards to the effect of government funding on nonprofit advocacy across nations. Schmid et al. (2008) found that amongst Israeli nonprofits, the higher the dependence on nonprofit funding, the lower the advocacy activity, which is contradictory to what is found in most US-based studies. The evidence from other countries is mixed: Maddison & Denniss (2005) found that government funding obstructed the advocacy efforts of nonprofit organizations in Australia, but Neumayr, Schneider, and Meyer (2015) found that, in Austria, it does not.

Other differences arise from the presence of transnational governmental entities (such as the European Union – EU), static electoral systems, and the rise of new bureaucratic cultures (such as New Public Management). For example, the global reach of the European Union and other international entities has resulted in opportunities for a more international- and transnational-focused set of actors to emerge and advocate at various levels (Cullen, 2015).

The presence of a transnational entity such as the EU forces organizations to focus on international as well as domestic issues as these become more intimately connected. For example, nonprofits, including unions, may advocate for global as well as local labor standards. These nonprofits can monitor, research, and advocate around policies that may affect labor and wages. Because such policies are affected by actors as disparate as the EU, the Organization for Economic Cooperation and Development (OECD), the World Bank, and the International Monetary Fund, advocacy led by professionalized experts is essential (Fransen & Burgoon, 2015). A related effect of such transnational entities is an increase in opportunities for organizations to advocate around civic and governmental integration. For example, by bringing together Central and Eastern European countries, the EU "facilitated citizen participation indirectly by changing opportunity structures for civil society" (Guasti, 2016, p. 229). Because some of these efforts were partly funded by the EU, new nonprofit funding structures allowed for new types of advocacy to emerge.

Differences in electoral configurations also influence the role of nonprofit advocacy. For example, Wales has had single-party dominance for the past 150 years. Such an uninterrupted political configuration has significant effects on the relationship between government and the third sector, primarily because there is increased blurring between political party and the state (Chaney, 2015). An overly close relationship between the state and nonprofits can be self-perpetuating, as "diminishing engagement and criticality from third sector organizations may further strengthen the dominant party" (p. 1480).

The wax and wane of bureaucratic cultures also influences the ability of nonprofits to advocate. As Australian government actors came to embrace New Public Management ideology starting in the 1980s, by the late 1990s Australian attitudes toward nonprofit advocacy and nonprofit involvement in the democratic process were dim. Some scholars have termed it an ideology of "democratic constraint" wherein nonprofits were discouraged from advocacy participation (Maddison & Denniss, 2005; Phillips, 2006).

These highlights demonstrate that the emergence and occurrence of nonprofit advocacy across Western nations is not monolithic. In order to appreciate the role of nonprofit advocacy, it is important to understand the historical, political, and cultural contexts of the region from whence it emerges.

Contributions of nonprofit advocacy to democracy

There are different interpretations of the overall effect of the nonprofit advocacy on democratic policy systems. In the US, these arguments generally fall under two camps: Madisonian (named after the fourth president of the United States) and Tocquevillian (named after the 19th-century French diplomat and thinker) (Jenkins, 2006).

Madisonian arguments express worries of excessive and distorted interest advocacy. According to these views, nonprofits' involvement in the policy process might act to undermine democratic functioning by overloading the political system or misrepresenting communities. The cacophony of input into the political process might make it difficult for government officials to make decisions and some groups – likely those with more power – will inevitably end up having more access to government actors than others, potentially leading to deepening inequities.

In the other camp, Tocquevillian arguments are concerned with access for those underrepresented in politics and see nonprofits as potentially boosting their interests. This argument generally holds that, without nonprofit advocacy, the political voice of powerful individuals and groups would go unchecked. In this view, the advocacy field can be seen as a failed or manipulated market where some aggregate voices are, by design, more easily heard (Berry & Arons, 2003, p. 34). In order to counter the tilted nature of the advocacy scales, nonprofits emerge to raise the voices of marginalized individuals. One example of the latter is the massive 2006 mobilization of immigrants in the United States in response to anti-immigrant federal legislation. Cordero-Guzmán, Martin, Quiroz-Becerra, and Theodore (2008) find that the unexpectedly large turnout was only possible through the mobilization work of immigrant-serving nonprofit organizations. What's more, the marches gave voice to a population that is not only marginalized but, in many cases, legally unable to vote.

Implicit to both arguments is the notion that the nonprofit sector creates opportunities for citizens to come together to apply pressure on government. Many have argued that the space the nonprofit sector creates for citizen engagement facilitates relationship building and information sharing, which are building blocks for a vibrant civil society (Frumkin, 2002; Boris & Krehely, 2002). In the case of the immigrant mobilization mentioned above, in addition to the importance of the advocacy objectives, the process by which immigrants and allies came together to talk and take action built the connections "to transform the energy of the protests into an enduring political base that can translate into electoral power" (Cordero-Guzmán et al., 2008, p. 614).

That said, perceptions of the role of nonprofit advocacy varies significantly across countries, as important distinctions exist in regards to degree of openness to advocacy, types of organizations that engage, legal restrictions, and legitimacy concerns. In the following section we present findings on how advocacy engagement differs in less open regimes, such as in Russia and China, from the developed democracies discussed previously. We also address the special case of advocates working cross-nationally, particularly in regards to the accountability concerns that arise when NGOs based in developed nations advocate in emerging ones.

Advocacy in authoritarian regimes

The difference in nonprofit advocacy between developed democracies and more authoritarian regimes such as China and Russia is stark. In the case of Russia, the end of the USSR precipitated a drastic reorganization of government services and social dynamics (Cerami, 2009). Whereas civil society was highly regulated and institutionalized under Soviet rule, the transition to the new Russian Federation resulted in a much more amorphous and undefined civil space between citizens and their government (Crotty, 2009). Since the fall of the USSR, the Russian government has increasingly sought to control NGO activity of various forms. This trend continued in the passage of what is colloquially known as the "NGO Law" in 2006, which, along with subsequent amendments, created stricter regulations on the use of funding for nonprofits, classified organizations deemed politically active and receiving foreign funding as "foreign agents," and imposed large fines for "unofficial demonstrations." The overall effect has been to inhibit NGO activity, especially advocacy for human rights in favor of state-aligned nonprofits (Crotty, Hall, & Ljubownikow, 2014; Krasnopolskaya, Skokova, & Pape, 2015).

That said, while the Russian brand of democratic governance curtails many activities commonly associated with nonprofit advocacy in the West, advocacy still occurs. For example, the environmental advocacy movement has grown largely due to the involvement of nonprofit organizations. Crotty (2009) found, at the time of her study, 15 separate organizations advocating on environmental issues in Samara Oblast. The majority used non-confrontational, indirect tactics to advocate (e.g. roundtables and publications) but there were a few who relied on direct-action tactics (mostly those with overseas funding). Similarly, research has documented health and education nonprofits in Perm, Yekaterinburg, and Samara using insider tactics to advocate around issues of organizational maintenance (Ljubownikow & Crotty, 2016). Overall, while these cases don't provide evidence of robust advocacy engagement among Russia's nonprofit sector, it demonstrates the potential for future action.

The political context surrounding nonprofit advocacy in China shares many similarities with the Russian case. After the 1949 victory of Mao's Communist Party of China, all social welfare services were placed under the domain of the party-state, and civil society organizations were generally seen as a threat (Hsu, Hsu, & Hasmath, 2017). This began to change starting in 1978 when the Chinese Communist Party decided to pursue major reforms leading to a milestone: the 1984 Decision on Reform of the Economic Structure (Whiting, 1991). Unfortunately, any hint of a flourishing nonprofit-led civil society was eliminated after the 1989 Tiananmen protests (Hsu et al., 2017). In the following decades, Chinese law made it difficult for NGOs to develop. Organizations, for example, have to establish ties with a governmental supervisory agency and undergo a complicated application process in addition to various other hurdles (Hsu et al., 2017). As a result, a voluntary NGO culture is foreign to many Chinese citizens and securing funding and volunteers is difficult. While there has been significant growth in the number of nonprofit organizations in China in the past two decades, most of these are government-organized nongovernmental organizations (GONGOs) that are direct creations of government agencies and therefore less likely to engage in the type of advocacy we see in the West (Spires, Tao, & Chan, 2014).

Although the authoritarian Chinese state makes it difficult for NGOs to function and speak up, evidence exists of advocacy activity. Similar to the Russian case, environment-focused advocacy organizations have been able to engage with elected officials to address concerns (Li, Lo, & Tang, 2017). Environment-related advocacy may be more possible than advocacy on other topics, however, because environmental concerns are officially recognized by the Chinese government. There is evidence, however, of more public-education focused advocacy efforts taking place around disability access and domestic violence (Zhang, 2017; Bräuer, 2016). Although advocacy under authoritarian China is still difficult, signs of a growing nonprofit sector show promise for future citizen engagement, perhaps more so than in the Russian case.

Accountability concerns brought about by transnational advocacy

Another cross-national advocacy related issue is the degree to which transnational advocacy is different than domestically focused advocacy. At an international level, advocacy often takes place in transnational NGO networks or "sets of relationships between NGOs and other organizations that simultaneously pursue activities in different political arenas to challenge the status quo" (Jordan & van Tuijl, 2000, p. 2053). These networks engage in global campaigns focusing on issues such as pollution, human rights, and human trafficking, among others. Transnational nonprofit advocacy takes place for many of the same reasons outlined above: to contribute to a vibrant civil society, include the voices of less represented communities, and change policy to improve the lives of people.

Accountability concerns arise when cross-border advocacy is promulgated by individuals and organizations that are external to a particular community and lack strong connections to citizens on the ground. International advocacy inherently introduces inequalities into the advocacy process: asymmetries of resources, knowledge, decision-making power, and expertise arise among organizations from the global North and South (Jordan & van Tuijl, 2000). As a result, many scholars have called for increased accountability to affected communities (not just to funders) and for increased attention to democratic legitimacy (Hudson, 2000). Political responsibility "is a commitment to embrace not only goals in a campaign but to conduct the campaign with democratic principles foremost in the process" (Jordan & van Tuijl, 2000, p. 2053) so that local knowledge and experience can be fully incorporated into social and policy change.

In practice, international advocacy is not as democratic or effective as many would hope. In a study of 40 civil society organizations in Pakistan, international aid was correlated with an inability to mobilize citizens, material aspirations among NGO leaders, and lower general organizational performance (Bano, 2008). Similarly, NGOs funded internationally in Nicaragua were more professionalized but less connected to their constituencies leading to a "demobilization and depoliticization of civil society" in the country (Chahim & Prakash, 2014, p. 508). While NGO managers identify beneficiaries as important constituents, "accountability practices rarely include mechanisms to make such voices heard" (Schmitz, Raggo, & Vijfeijken, 2012, p. 1189).

Conclusion

In this chapter, we have established that nonprofit advocacy is not a fringe activity, but rather a core function of the nonprofit sector. Nonprofit managers should look at advocacy as an activity that will help ensure their organization's survival as well as help express the preferences of constituents and potentially make policy more equitable. Because advocacy consists of a multitude of activities, ranging from meeting with legislators to political protests, the tactics chosen largely depend on advocacy goals; nonprofit organizations can and do utilize both insider and outsider tactics in their work towards policy change.

Advocacy can be engaged in by organizations of all sizes and capabilities. While the percentage of nonprofits that meaningfully engage in advocacy varies significantly depending upon the nonprofit field, there is a significant concern that many nonprofits perceive significant barriers in engaging in political activity. Overall it appears that the main reasons organizations do not participate in advocacy is lack of funding, lack of expertise, and fear of political retribution, depending on country context. Considering the wide range of types of nonprofit organizations, it is difficult to state definitively what may lead nonprofits to increase their advocacy efforts but there are several important strategies that nonprofits may use to overcome those barriers and start or increase their engagement in advocacy.

In particular, collaboration with other nonprofits and social media use are advocacy tools that are accessible to all nonprofits, regardless of size, and may be particularly useful for under-resourced organizations, those that lack relationships with policymakers, or those who are working to build a constituency or advocacy skills. First, social media use can expand reach and is easily accessible and low cost. It can also be a useful tool for connecting a nonprofit with its constituents, promulgating a more "bottom-up" approach to the policy process. That said, it is unclear the degree to which online engagement translates into more sustained political participation and it does require skill and time. Second, association with a coalition can increase visibility and legitimacy, as well as help educate nonprofits just beginning to be involved in advocacy on how to better accomplish advocacy activities. Coalition involvement may particularly help organizations that may be fearful about participation in advocacy, as the coalition can decide to divvy up political tasks among organizations with varying levels of advocacy experience and can provide cover for those who worry about political exposure. Both of these tools are recommended to help get more nonprofit organizations engaged in advocacy.

Much of the research on nonprofit advocacy has been focused on the US context. This is understandable, considering the dominant role of nonprofit organizations in the delivery of US human services, and the prominent role of civil society in the US. However, growing research on nonprofit advocacy in other Western countries has revealed that while there are similarities between advocacy in countries, political context plays an important role in the degree to which nonprofits are emboldened to advocate and the types of issues they focus on.

Moreover, there is a growing realization of the role that advocacy can play even in authoritarian contexts, where participation in advocacy contains more risk. This literature shows that nonprofits in Russia do engage in advocacy, although they largely focus on non-confrontational tactics, such as policy roundtables. Nonprofit organizations in China also engage in advocacy, although much of their work focuses on issues recognized by the government as important, such as environmental protection. This indicates that nonprofit advocacy around controversial issues is still a difficult process. Although nonprofit advocacy is still in a nascent stage in these authoritarian contexts, the efforts of nonprofits to engage in advocacy is encouraging and indicates progression towards a more visible civil society.

The case of international advocacy raises concerns with effectiveness and accountability when advocating cross-nationally. Many NGOs are led by individuals who are external to the affected community, and fail to include mechanisms through which constituents' voices can be heard. This may be the result of the "West is Best" approach, wherein advocacy organizations from wealthy nations enter under-resourced countries with good intentions, yet a lack of understanding of the local culture. This leads to a disjuncture between the organization and the issue the nonprofit is trying to address. More awareness needs to be cultivated by nonprofits engaging in advocacy internationally in order to improve representation, and include more affected voices in the political process.

This advice can be usefully applied to nonprofits advocating domestically as well. Nonprofit advocacy is often held up as an important bulwark against authoritarianism and elite control of the political process. Nonprofits can and should amplify the voices of those they represent. But in order to fulfill those important civil society functions, advocacy must be carried out democratically and in relationship to affected constituencies. Given the barriers to being involved in advocacy and the low rates of involvement by many in the sector, helping to ensure that small nonprofits and those without a history of advocacy engagement are involved is an important advocacy goal as well.

Note

1 We exclude the "advocacy field" organizations from this list since, by definition, all they do is advocate.

References

Anasti, T. (2017). Radical professionals? Sex worker rights activists and collaboration with human service nonprofits. *Human Service Organizations: Management, Leadership and Governance, 4*(41), 416–437.

Andrews, K., & Edwards, B. (2004). Advocacy organizations in the US political process. *Annual Review of Sociology, 30*, 479–506.

Bano, M. (2008). Dangerous correlations: AID's impact on NGOs' performance and ability to mobilize members in Pakistan. *World Development, 36*(11), 2297–2313. https://doi.org/10.1016/j.worlddev.2007.11.001

Bass, G. D., Arons, D. F., Guinane, K., & Carter, M. F. (2007). *Seen but Not Heard: Strengthening Nonprofit Advocacy*. Washington, DC: Aspen Institute.

Berry, J. M., & Arons, D. F. (2003). *A Voice for Nonprofits*. Washington, DC: Brookings Institution Press.

Boris, E. T., & Krehely, J. (2002). Civic participation and advocacy. In L. M. Salamon (Ed.), *The State of Nonprofit America* (pp. 299–330). Washington, DC: Brookings Institution.

Bräuer, S. (2016). Becoming public: Tactical innovation in the Beijing anti-domestic violence movement. *VOLUNTAS: International Journal of Voluntary and Nonprofit Organizations*, *27*(5), 2106–2130. https://doi. org/10.1007/s11266-015-9610-2

Buffardi, A. L., Pekkanen, R. J., & Smith, S. R. (2017). Protective or proactive? Dimensions of and advocacy activities associated with reported policy change by nonprofit organizations. *VOLUNTAS: International Journal of Voluntary and Nonprofit Organizations*, *28*(3), 1226–1248. https://doi.org/10.1007/s11266-017-9849-x

Cerami, A. (2009). Welfare state developments in the Russian Federation: Oil-led social policy and 'The Russian Miracle.' *Social Policy & Administration*, *43*(2), 105–120. https://doi.org/10.1111/j.1467-9515. 2009.00650.x

Chahim, D., & Prakash, A. (2014). NGOization, foreign funding, and the Nicaraguan civil society. *VOLUNTAS: International Journal of Voluntary & Nonprofit Organizations*, *25*(2), 487–513. https://doi. org/10.1007/s11266-012-9348-z

Chaney, P. (2015). Exploring the pathologies of one-party-dominance on third sector public policy engagement in liberal democracies: Evidence from meso-government in the UK. *VOLUNTAS: International Journal of Voluntary & Nonprofit Organizations*, *26*(4), 1460–1484. https://doi.org/10.1007/s112 66-014-9493-7

Chaves, M., Stephens, L., & Galaskiewicz, J. (2004). Does government funding suppress nonprofits' political activity? *American Sociological Review*, *69*, 292–316.

Chen, K. K. (2018). Interorganizational advocacy among nonprofit organizations in strategic action fields: Exogenous shocks and local responses. *Nonprofit and Voluntary Sector Quarterly*, *0*(0), 1–22. https://doi. org/10.1177/0899764017753319

Child, C. D., & Gronbjerg, K. A. (2007). Nonprofit advocacy organizations: Their characteristics and activities. *Social Science Quarterly*, *88*(1), 259–281. https://doi.org/10.1111/%28ISSN%291540-6237/ issues

Chin, J. J. (2018). Service-providing nonprofits working in coalition to advocacy for policy change. *Nonprofit and Voluntary Sector Quarterly*, *47*(1), 27–48.

Cordero-Guzmán, H., Martin, N., Quiroz-Becerra, V., & Theodore, N. (2008). Voting with their feet: Nonprofit organizations and immigrant mobilization. *American Behavioral Scientist*, *52*(4), 598–617. https://doi.org/10.1177/0002764208324609

Crotty, J. (2009). Making a difference? NGOs and civil society development in Russia. *Europe-Asia Studies*, (1), 85. https://doi.org/10.1080/09668130802532936

Crotty, J., Hall, S. M., & Ljubownikow, S. (2014). Post-Soviet civil society development in the Russian Federation: The impact of the NGO Law. *Europe-Asia Studies*, *66*(8), 1253–1269. https://doi.org/10.1080/ 09668136.2014.941697

Cullen, P. (2015). European Union non-governmental organizational coalitions as professional social movement communities. *Journal of Civil Society*, *11*(2), 201–225.

Donaldson, L. (2007). Advocacy by nonprofit human service agencies: Organizational factors as correlates to advocacy behavior. *Journal of Community Practice*, *15*(3), 139–158.

Fransen, L., & Burgoon, B. (2015). Global labour-standards advocacy by European civil society organizations: Trends and developments. *British Journal of Industrial Relations*, *53*(2), 204–230. https://doi. org/10.1111/bjir.12017

Frumkin, P. (2002). *On Being Nonprofit: A Conceptual Policy Primer*. Cambridge, MA: Harvard University Press.

Fyall, R. (2016). The power of nonprofits: Mechanisms for nonprofit policy influence. *Public Administration Review*, *76*(6), 938–948. https://doi.org/10.1111/puar.12550

Fyall, R., & McGuire, M. (2015). Advocating for policy change in nonprofit coalitions. *Nonprofit and Voluntary Sector Quarterly*, *44*(6), 1274–1291.

Gais, T. L., & Walker, J. L. (1991). Pathways to influence in American politics. In J. L. Walker (Ed.), *Mobilizing Interest Groups in America* (pp. 103–122). Ann Arbor, MI: University of Michigan Press.

Gamson, W. A. (1975). *The Strategy of Social Protest*. Homewood, IL: Dorsey Press.

Gormley, W. T., & Cymrot, H. (2006). The strategic choice of child advocacy groups. *Nonprofit and Voluntary Sector Quarterly*, *35*(1), 102–122.

Guasti, P. (2016). Development of citizen participation in Central and Eastern Europe after the EU enlargement and economic crises. *Communist and Post-Communist Studies*, *49*(3), 219–231.

Guo, C., & Acar, M. (2005). Understanding collaboration among nonprofit organizations: Combining resource dependency, institutional, and network perspectives. *Nonprofit and Voluntary Sector Quarterly, 34*(3), 340–361. https://doi.org/10.1177/0899764005275411

Guo, C., & Saxton, G.D. (2014). Tweeting social change: How social media are changing nonprofit advocacy. *Nonprofit and Voluntary Sector Quarterly, 43*(1), 57–79. https://doi.org/10.1177/0899764012471585

Han, J. (2017). Social marketisation and policy influence of third sector organisations: Evidence from the UK. *VOLUNTAS: International Journal of Voluntary and Nonprofit Organizations, 28*(3), 1209–1225. https://doi.org/10.1007/s11266-017-9853-1

Hsu, J.Y.J., Hsu, C.L., & Hasmath, R. (2017). NGO strategies in an authoritarian context, and their implications for citizenship: The case of the People's Republic of China. *VOLUNTAS: International Journal of Voluntary and Nonprofit Organizations, 28*(3), 1157–1179. https://doi.org/10.1007/s11266-016-9806-0

Hudson, A. (2000). Making the connection: Legitimacy claims, legitimacy chains and northern NGOs' international advocacy. In D. Lewis & T. Wallace (Eds.), *New Roles and Relevance: Development NGOs and the Challenge of Change* (pp. 89–97). Bloomfield, CT: Kumarian Press.

Internal Revenue Code. 26 U.S.C. § 501(c)(3).

Internal Revenue Service (IRS). (2018). *Lobbying.* U.S. Department of the Treasury. Retrieved from: https://www.irs.gov/charities-non-profits/lobbying

Jenkins, C. (1987). Nonprofit organizations and policy advocacy. In W.W. Powell (Ed.), *The Nonprofit Sector: A Research Handbook.* New Haven, CT: Yale University Press.

Jenkins, C. (2006). Nonprofit organizations and political advocacy. In W.W. Powell & R. Steinberg (Eds.), *The Nonprofit Sector: A Research Handbook* (2nd ed.). New Haven, CT: Yale University Press.

Jordan, L., & van Tuijl, P. (2000). Political responsibility in transnational NGO advocacy. *World Development, 28*(12), 2051–2065. https://doi.org/10.1016/S0305-750X(00)00078-4

Kabalo, P. (2009). A fifth nonprofit regime?: Revisiting social origins theory using Jewish associational life as a new state model. *Nonprofit and Voluntary Sector Quarterly, 38*(4), 627–642. https://doi.org/10.1177/0899764009333333

Karpf, D. (2010). Online political mobilization from the advocacy group's perspective: Looking beyond clicktivism. *Policy & Internet, 2*(4), 7–41. https://doi.org/10.2202/1944-2866.1098

Kim, M. & Mason, D.P. (2018). Representation and diversity, advocacy, and nonprofit arts organizations. *Nonprofit and Voluntary Sector Quarterly, 47*(1), 49–71. https://doi.org/10.1177/0899764017728364

Krasnopolskaya, I., Skokova, Y., & Pape, U. (2015). Government–nonprofit relations in Russia's regions: An exploratory analysis. *VOLUNTAS: International Journal of Voluntary and Nonprofit Organizations, 26*(6), 2238–2266. https://doi.org/10.1007/s11266-015-9654-3

LeRoux, K. & Goerdel, H.T. (2009). Political advocacy by nonprofit organizations: A strategic management explanation. *Public Performance and Management Review, 32*(4), 514–536.

Li, H., Lo, C.W.-H., & Tang, S.-Y. (2017). Nonprofit policy advocacy under authoritarianism. *Public Administration Review, 77*(1), 103–117. https://doi.org/10.1111/%28ISSN%291540-6210/issues

Ljubownikow, S., & Crotty, J. (2016). Nonprofit influence on public policy: Exploring nonprofit advocacy in Russia. *Nonprofit and Voluntary Sector Quarterly, 45*(2), 314–332.

Lovejoy, K., & Saxton, G. (2012). Information, community and action: How nonprofits use social media. *Journal of Computer-Mediated Communication, 17*(3), 337–353.

Maddison, S., & Denniss, R. (2005). Democratic constraint and embrace: Implications for progressive non-government advocacy organizations in Australia. *Australian Journal of Political Science, 40*(3), 373–389.

Manny, J.S. (2012). Nonprofit legislative speech: Aligning policy, law and reality. *Case Western Reserve Law Review, 62*(3), 757–799.

Marwell, N. (2004). Privatizing the welfare state: Nonprofit community-based organizations as political actors. *American Sociological Review, (2), 265.

Mosley, J.E. (2010). Organizational resources and environmental incentives: Understanding the policy advocacy involvement of human service nonprofits. *Social Service Review, 84*(1), 57–76.

Mosley, J.E. (2011). Institutionalization, privatization, and political opportunity: What tactical choices reveal about the policy advocacy of human service nonprofits. *Nonprofit and Voluntary Sector Quarterly, 40*(3), 435–457.

Mosley, J.E. (2012). Keeping the lights on: How government funding concerns drive the advocacy agendas of nonprofit homeless service providers. *Journal of Public Administration Research and Theory, 22*(4), 841–866. https://doi.org/10.1093/jopart/mus003

Mosley, J. (2014). From skid row to the statehouse: How nonprofit homeless service providers overcome barriers to policy advocacy involvement. In R. Pekkanen, S. Smith, & Y. Tsujinaka (Eds.), *Nonprofits & Advocacy*. Baltimore, MD: Johns Hopkins University Press.

Neumayr, M., Schneider, U., & Meyer, M. (2015). Public funding and its impact on nonprofit advocacy. *Nonprofit and Voluntary Sector Quarterly, 44*(2), 297–318.

Obar, J. A., Zube, P., & Lampe, C. (2012). Advocacy 2.0: An analysis of how advocacy groups in the United States perceive and use social media as tools for facilitating civic engagement and collective action. *Journal of Information Policy, 2*, 1–25.

Onyx, J., Armitage, L., Dalton, B., Melville, R., Casey, J., & Banks, R. (2010). Advocacy with gloves on: The "manners" of strategy used by some third sector organizations undertaking advocacy in NSW and Queensland. *VOLUNTAS, International Journal of Voluntary and Nonprofit Organizations, 21*(1), 41–61. https://doi.org/10.1007/s11266-009-9106-z

Pekkanen, R., & Smith, S. (2014). Nonprofit advocacy in Seattle and Washington, DC. In R. Pekkanen, S. Smith, & Y. Tsujinaka (Eds.), *Nonprofits & Advocacy*. Baltimore, MD: Johns Hopkins University Press.

Phillips, R. (2006). The role of nonprofit advocacy organizations in Australian democracy and policy governance. *VOLUNTAS: International Journal of Voluntary and Nonprofit Organizations, 17*(1), 57–73. https://doi.org/10.1007/s11266-005-9004-y

Reid, E. (2000). Understanding the word "advocacy." In *Nonprofit Advocacy and the Policy Process* (Vol. 1, pp. 1–8). Washington, DC: Urban Institute Press.

Salamon, L. M., & Anheier, H. K. (1998). Social origins of civil society: Explaining the nonprofit sector cross-nationally. *VOLUNTAS: International Journal of Voluntary and Nonprofit Organizations, 9*(3), 213–248. https://doi.org/10.1023/A:1022058200985

Salamon, L. M., & Sokolowski, S. W. (2016). Beyond nonprofits: Re-conceptualizing the third sector. *VOLUNTAS: International Journal of Voluntary and Nonprofit Organizations, 27*(4), 1515–1545. https://doi.org/10.1007/s11266-016-9726-z

Salamon, Lester M., & Geller, S. L., with Lorentz, S. C. (2008). *Nonprofit America: A force for democracy?* Listening Post Project Communique no. 9. Baltimore, MD: Johns Hopkins University.

Sandfort, J. (2014). Analyzing the practice of nonprofit advocacy comparing two human service networks. In R. Pekkanen, S. Smith, & Y. Tsujinaka (Eds.), *Nonprofits & Advocacy*. Baltimore, MD: Johns Hopkins University Press.

Schmid, H., Bar, M., & Nirel, R. (2008). Advocacy activities in nonprofit human service organizations: Implications for policy. *Nonprofit and Voluntary Sector Quarterly, 37*(4), 581–602.

Schmitz, H. P., Raggo, P., & Vijfeijken, T. B. (2012). Accountability of transnational NGOs: Aspirations vs. practice. *Nonprofit and Voluntary Sector Quarterly, 41*(6), 1175–1194. https://doi.org/10.1177/0899764011431165

Scott, W. R., Deschenes, S., Hopkins, K., Newman, A., & McLaughlin, M. (2006). Advocacy organizations and the field of youth services: Ongoing efforts to restructure a field. *Nonprofit and Voluntary Sector Quarterly, 35*(4), 691–714.

Spires, A., Tao, L., & Chan, K. (2014). Societal support for China's grass-roots NGOs: Evidence from Yunnan, Guangdong and Beijing. *China Journal, 71*.

Staggenborg, S. (1986). Coalition work in the pro-choice movement: Organizational and environmental opportunities and obstacles. *Social Problems, 33*(5), 374–390.

Suarez, D. F., & Hwang, H. (2008). Civic engagement and nonprofit lobbying in California, 1998–2003. *Nonprofit and Voluntary Sector Quarterly, 37*(1), 93–112.

Whiting, S. (1991). The politics of NGO development in China. *VOLUNTAS: International Journal of Voluntary and Nonprofit Organizations, 2*(2), 16–48.

Zhang, C. (2017). 'Nothing about us without us': The emerging disability movement and advocacy in China. *Disability & Society, 32*(7), 1096–1101. https://doi.org/10.1080/09687599.2017.1321229

24

NONPROFITS AND POLITICAL PARTICIPATION

Kelly LeRoux

PROFESSOR, DEPARTMENT OF PUBLIC ADMINISTRATION, COLLEGE OF URBAN
PLANNING AND PUBLIC AFFAIRS, UNIVERSITY OF ILLINOIS AT CHICAGO, CHICAGO, IL, USA

Mary K. Feeney

PROFESSOR AND LINCOLN PROFESSOR OF ETHICS IN PUBLIC AFFAIRS, SCHOOL OF
PUBLIC ADMINISTRATION, ARIZONA STATE UNIVERSITY, PHOENIX, AZ, USA

Introduction

In a variety of forms ranging from public charities and civic organizations to advocacy groups, nonprofit and civil society organizations have long acted as foundational institutions for promoting civic engagement and furthering democratic ideals (Skocpol 1997; Putnam 2000). Nonprofits serve as outlets for citizens to financially support social causes, provide political education and increase public awareness of salient issues, link citizens to political actors and institutions, and mobilize people for action in the policy and political arena. These actions also occur between and among groups of citizens outside the sphere of formally incorporated, registered nonprofit organizations, through informal collective action efforts and as expressions of civil society. The result of these activities is that nonprofits and civil society groups play a critical role in shaping politics and political participation at all levels of government.

Much of the scholarly attention related to this topic has been focused on the advocacy and lobbying efforts of formally registered organizations (see Chapter 23 by Mosley et al.), viewing nonprofits from the perspective of interest groups that exist "to speak for, act for, look after the interests of their respective groups" (Pitkin 1972: 117). While indeed these efforts are important and represent a critical role for nonprofits in shaping public policies, this chapter departs from the notion of nonprofits as interest groups, instead focusing on ways that nonprofits and civil society groups mobilize citizens for direct action. Whereas advocacy primarily serves a political *representation* function, this chapter centers on the political *mobilization* roles of nonprofits and civil society groups and their efforts to increase *direct participation* in the political process.

In this chapter, we examine three specific mechanisms for nonprofit and civil society groups to increase individual political participation and to make democracy more inclusive. First, we examine protest politics and social movements, highlighting some specific global movements and the lessons they reveal for organizations and individual organizers. Second, we examine the roles of nonprofit and civil society groups in expanding voter participation in democratic societies. Finally, we examine some ways that nonprofits build civic and political leadership.

Protest politics and social movements

Demonstrations and protests have long been a mechanism for groups and collections of people to articulate political discontent and demands for social reform. Protests take the form of large, organized groups of people who gather to march, rally in a particular meeting place, or hear speakers. Protests are a distinct form of political participation in that they are intended to be disruptive to the mainstream and to attract the attention of the media and broader community. Participation in mass protests is one way that individuals who lack the resources for more conventional forms of political influence (money) can exert political power by disrupting normal routines. We are witnessing growth in the number and size of these protests in the United States and beyond. Numerous social, political, and economic factors have shaped the rise of protests, including the growth of income inequality, increased heterogeneity in society, escalating environmental concerns including the accelerating pace of climate change, widespread availability and use of information communication technologies, and a global wave of populism that has ushered in controversial policies, particularly with regard to trade, immigration, and terrorism.

Once considered an "unconventional" form of political activity, protests have attracted an increasing number of participants in recent years, and are a popular form of political expression among Millennials who, when compared to older Americans, are more likely to participate in protests and report beliefs that protests are an effective form of political action (Ruiz-Grossman 2017). Social media have played a key role in helping nonprofit organizations tap previously unconnected individuals, adding more points of contact and enabling the recruitment of previously unaffiliated individuals to protests (Goldstein 2017). While only 4 percent of the US adult population participated in an organized protest in 2008 (Smith et al. 2009), political expressions including rallies, protests, boycotts, and "die-ins" have escalated in popularity in recent years (Stuster 2013). Internationally, we have seen mass protests as part of the Arab Spring, in response to elections and border conflicts (e.g., Crimea), as counter demonstrations against populist leaders (e.g., Erdogan in Turkey, Trump in the US), in opposition to alt-right and fascist movements (e.g., Charlottesville, Virginia, US, in 2017), and in defense of human rights. Across the globe, countries are experiencing a robust period of activity for protests, some of which are highly organized, systematic components of broader social movements, while others are more isolated events.

Social movements are emergent collections of discontented individuals and are often characterized by informal collective action with a focus on a specific political, social, or economic issue (McAdam 1982). Three modern social movements, Occupy, Black Lives Matter, and Women's March offer useful examples of social movements that rely on mass protests as a key strategy for political organizing. The Occupy movement is an international movement against economic and social inequality. The movement initiated as a loosely organized response to the Great Recession, primarily focusing on protests and sit-ins to occupy public spaces. The first occupation was of Zuccotti Park at Wall Street in New York City in September 2011. By October 2011, with the help of social media, the movement grew to include people occupying spaces in more than 951 cities in 82 countries across the world (Thompson 2011; Adam 2011). The movement used technology and participatory democracy techniques to mobilize, spread information, raise funds, and maintain momentum. The primary theme that emerged from the Occupy movement is the political slogan "we are the 99%" in reference to the concentration of wealth among the top 1 percent of income earners (Whoriskey 2011).

The Occupy movement has been widely criticized for failing to formalize its mission, a lack of leadership, unclear messaging, and poor organization (Gibson 2013). At its core, the movement rejected the notion of hierarchy, power, and control, and embraced a belief in direct democracy, relying on a consensus-based approach to decision making. With such a vast number of participants and a lack of leadership, the movement failed to identify a set of specific policy objectives. Without coalescing into a formal structure or organization, the movement was also unable to sustain its momentum. Still, others point to the ways in which the protests, online information sharing, and sit-ins had global impact by sparking conversations that became part of the mainstream rhetoric of subsequent policies, political agendas, and popular dialogue (Levitin 2015). For instance, in his US presidential campaign, Bernie Sanders regularly referred to the 99 percent and a need to tackle income inequality through new public policies. The movement also drew attention to the need for regulation on unfair banking practices and legislation protecting college students from predatory lending. Moreover, Occupy set the stage for subsequent spin-off movements related to economic inequality, such as the Fight for $15 campaign.

The Fight for $15 is an organized effort to increase the minimum wage to $15. Fight for $15 describes itself as a global movement in over 300 cities on six continents.[1] This modern-day labor movement pits masses of low-wage workers against the wealthy CEOs and shareholders of major fast food chains and retailers, such as McDonald's and Walmart. The Fight for $15 has been especially active in the US, coordinating and carrying out protests, strikes, and boycotts in 220 US cities (Greenhouse and Kasperkevic 2015). While the specific objectives vary from place to place, the movement generally seeks a higher federal minimum wage, puts pressure on corporate CEOs to raise wages, and calls for workers' right to unionize without retaliation. Participation in the movement has expanded beyond fast food and retail employees to include workers in other low-wage industries, such as childcare and home health. Protest efforts have yielded substantive results in many cases, compelling Seattle, San Francisco, Los Angeles, and New York to adopt a $15 minimum wage, and Chicago and Kansas City a $13 wage (Greenhouse 2015). Similarly, citizen-driven ballot proposals have increased the minimum wage to $12 in Arizona, Colorado, and Maine, and compelled employers to offer paid sick leave in Arizona and Washington (Wyatt 2016).

The Black Lives Matter (BLM) movement is another example of a social change movement that relies heavily on social media presence and protest and demonstration tactics to raise public awareness, galvanize support, and to overtly challenge elite power structures. BLM finds its roots in a call to action after a US case in which George Zimmerman fatally shot Trayvon Martin. BLM became an international social force following the fatal police shooting of Michael Brown and choking death of Eric Garner at police hands. Using online and in-person organizing, BLM has mobilized masses of individuals, community organizations, and online resources in protests about law enforcement, racial profiling, the militarization of police, and racial inequality in the justice system. They have also organized conferences, sit-ins, and raised funds. BLM, similar to Occupy, started as a decentralized network with no formal hierarchy or structure and has evolved into an international activist movement led by its founders Patrisse Cullors, Alicia Garza, and Opel Tometi. BLM has local chapters dedicated to Black self-determination and a large presence on social media, with more than 300,000 Twitter followers.[2] BLM leadership met with President Obama and presidential candidates Hillary Clinton and Bernie Sanders and spoke at the 2016 Democratic National Convention. BLM has been instrumental in pushing US state legislatures and politicians to remove Confederate monuments and flags from public spaces.

Women's March represents another recent global protest movement that has breathed new life into the decades-old quest for gender equality and women's rights. This movement was largely propelled by the election of Donald Trump to the US Presidency in 2016. Trump campaigned on policies that threaten to diminish women's rights in the areas of reproductive freedoms, LGBTQ protections, and to reverse the Obama administration's policy steps toward equal pay in the workplace, equitable women's health care coverage, and protections for victims of sexual assault. Throughout the campaign, Trump maintained a hostile stance toward his female political opponent, displaying aggressive behavior on national television. After Clinton won the popular vote, many nonprofits serving women's interests such as Planned Parenthood, American Civil Liberties Union, American Teachers Federation, NARAL-ProChoice America, Human Rights Campaign, and many others joined forces to stage a protest in the nation's capital of Washington, DC, the day after Trump's inauguration. Due to the coordinated efforts of these organizations and their online mobilization efforts, Women's March 2017 quickly scaled into a global phenomenon, with marches staged in 673 cities across 60 countries, and an estimated number of over 4.5 million participants, making Women's March the largest coordinated protest in US history and one of the largest ever in world history (www.womensmarch.com).

Having adapted from the missteps of earlier movements such as Occupy, Women's March launched with a far more strategic approach than other recent movement of its magnitude. In addition to attracting the endorsements and funding of numerous nonprofit corporate "brands," it has formed a board of directors and is working to build sustained organizing capacity by hiring an appointed leader and paid staff to develop and carry out policy objectives. The movement is still in its formative stages, but has organized a Women's Convention and set the stage for the #metoo online movement, which brings awareness to the pervasiveness of sexual harassment. Women's Movement appears to be positioning itself for the sustained pursuit of policies that benefit women's interests, and for the ongoing mobilization of citizens toward these ends.

Protest politics vary widely in their impact on the political system, depending in large part on the degree of formality in their organization. Protest efforts can be citizen-driven, spontaneous, ad hoc, and motivated by emotion, without a clear objective underlying the activity. Protest activities may also be sustained, highly coordinated efforts, linked in service to a particular policy goal, or set of goals, as BLM has achieved via local chapters, fundraising, and strong social media coordination efforts. When the approach tends more toward the latter, nonprofits and civil society groups can play important roles in advancing social movements.

Not all sustained protest activity or protest movements will develop into formally incorporated, registered associations or organizations and some may be co-opted by powerful nonprofits. There are mixed opinions about whether formally incorporated nonprofits should play any role at all in social movements (LeRoux and Feeney, 2015). On the one hand, institutionalized organizations and their bureaucratic features can inhibit true social change by watering down the radical elements of more spontaneous collective action or through co-optation of protest leaders by elites (Piven and Cloward, 1977). For example, many involved with the BLM movement contend that more traditional civil rights organizations such as the National Association for the Advancement of Colored People (NAACP) have institutionalized elite interests at the expense of real social change. On the other hand, social movements relying solely on voluntary activism generally lack the leadership, capacity, and resources needed for sustained effort and meaningful long-term change, as evidenced by the slowdown of the Occupy movement.[3] Although it is early, Women's March appears to be positioning itself to have the organizational infrastructure to sustain a long-term investment in achieving its policy goals. Still, Women's March runs the risk of being perceived as serving elite women's interests, and has been criticized for its lack of attention to intersectionality of women and to issues that are unique to women of color.

While Occupy, Black Lives Matter, and Women's March arise from different sources of discontent and seek different ends, they share in common their use of protest as an expression of civic engagement and the demand for economic, social, and political change. Protest politics and social movements represent a key mechanism for mobilizing the public, civil society groups, and formal nonprofit organizations for political action. These movements have used varying types of organizing structures and ties to formal nonprofits to bring together civil society groups and in some cases create new groups and organizations to mobilize for political action. Their differences present trade-offs. Balancing the role of civil society groups and formal nonprofit organizations, more or less resources, exclusive or expansive membership, and broad mission or narrow policy focus, will result in more or less flexibility and political impact. Having an awareness of these trade-offs is important for both those working to build movements from the bottom up, as well as those working from the top down to consolidate power by forging partnerships and alliances across existing nonprofit organizations and groups.

Expanding voter participation

Another important way that nonprofit organizations promote political participation is through voter mobilization efforts. Nonprofit and civil society groups in numerous countries work to get out the vote and help to ensure transparency and integrity of the election process. As one approach to dealing with the problem of "hollowed out" democracy, Anheier (2015) calls for greater NGO involvement in eliciting participation of the electorate. For example, numerous civil society groups in Scotland, such as the Third Sector for Yes campaign, helped to produce an unprecedented rate of voter turnout in the 2014 referendum election on Scottish independence. A large share of the turnout was comprised of young and newly enfranchised voters who were specific targets of the groups' mobilization efforts (Civicus 2015). In response to a government that had grown increasingly suppressive of protest activity, in 2013 voluntary activists in Turkey mobilized via personal social networks and technology to form the Vote and Beyond Initiative. This civil society group provides training for volunteers to act as independent election observers. In their inaugural attempt at election oversight in March 2014, more than 26,000 volunteers participated in the initiative, providing oversight of almost 95 percent of the votes cast, and the Vote and Beyond Initiative now acts as a registered organization with plans for monitoring future elections (Civicus 2015). In the US, nonprofit organizations not only work to mobilize prospective voters, but act as an extension of the state by helping to register voters.

Within the US, voter participation rates remain low relative to other western democracies, ranking 26th among developed countries (Desilver 2018). Voter turnout in the US reaches its highest rates during presidential election years, when just over half of eligible voters cast ballots; for example, voter turnout was 61.4 percent in the 2016 presidential election (File 2017). As with all other forms of political participation, income has a direct linear relationship with voting (Brady, Verba, and Schlozman 1995; Rosenstone and Hansen 1993). While nonprofit groups of all types register and mobilize prospective voters, nonprofits may be particularly well suited to increasing voter participation among younger and low-income citizens.

Nonprofit organizations in the US became legally empowered to carry out nonpartisan voter registration efforts through the National Voter Registration Act (NVRA), also known as the "Motor Voter" law, supported by the Clinton administration and enacted into law by Congress in 1993. The goal of the legislation was to ameliorate historic disparities in voter turnout rates that fall along lines of race, income, age, and disability (Piven and Cloward 1996). To this end, the law called for making voter registration opportunities available across all public social service agencies, including health, housing, welfare, and unemployment agencies (Piven and Cloward 1988), and by extension, nonprofit organizations that act as agents of the state in delivering government-funded social welfare services via contracts and grants (Salamon 1995). The Motor Voter Act requires all offices of state-funded programs, including nonprofits, that provide services to persons with disabilities to offer voter registration assistance on-site at the service agency. While the law carries a *mandate* for state-funded service providers to make voter registration available on-site for clients, the law is explicit in encouraging all other "nongovernmental entities" to offer nonpartisan voter registration opportunities as well.

Despite the expansion of voter registration opportunities through the 1993 NVRA, registration rates remained disproportionately lower among low-income citizens (U.S. Census 2016). Many factors play a role in the lower voter participation rates of lower income citizens, including state voter identity laws, information barriers related to voter registration deadlines, processes, polling locations, and frequent address changes and failure to update registration information. Of course, apathy and lack of interest in politics and policy also account for part of the reason that people do not vote. Nonprofits are uniquely positioned to address challenges of access and apathy to help remedy the voter participation gap. Community-based nonprofits not only have frequent and sustained contact with low-probability voters, communities often view them as more trustworthy institutions than government agencies or officials. One study of voter registration among racial minorities in Florida demonstrated that black, Hispanic, and citizens from Spanish-speaking households were more than twice as likely to register to vote via third-party nonprofit groups as white citizens and those from English-speaking households (Donovan 2011).

Human service organizations are not alone in their efforts to engage voters. Other types of nonprofits such as the League of Women Voters, Voto Latino, and Nonprofit Vote have missions dedicated entirely to voter engagement. Additionally, nonprofits, civic groups, ethnic and immigrant service organizations, and community organizing groups have started taking advantage of mass protests as a venue for promoting voter registration, for example registering voters at pro-immigration rallies and BLM protests.

In addition to providing on-site voter registration, nonprofits can also increase the likelihood of voting among their communities through various nonpartisan Get Out the Vote (GOTV) efforts, including voting reminders in person, by phone, mail, or social media, as well as providing transportation to the polls on election day. As part of their voter engagement efforts, many nonprofits also provide various forms of voter education. Authorized nonpartisan voter education activities by human service nonprofits include sharing information on: voter registration deadlines, candidates, ballot measures, finding polling locations, filling out a sample ballot, and any other nonpartisan education intended to increase the likelihood of voting or making informed political choices. Providing voter education through forums (e.g., candidate debates or candidate positions on issues, and voting records) are permissible for all public charities so long as the organization's message is designed to encourage democratic participation rather than promote a specific candidate. Other types of nonprofits, such as those registered as lobbying groups and certain categories of trade associations, are permitted to take a more explicit stance in supporting and endorsing candidates and their platforms.

There is strong evidence that nonpartisan voter registration and GOTV efforts by nonprofits are effective. Evidence from numerous field experiments carried out with nonprofit groups engaged in nonpartisan canvassing have revealed increased turnout rates ranging anywhere from 6 to 12 percentage points (Gerber and Green 1999, 2000a, 2000b; Green, Gerber, and Nickerson 2003). Additional research has shown that *'agency-based'* voter engagement, those done *on-site* at community centers or human service offices, are even more effective, increasing turnout by 11 percentage points for each additional voting-related contact (LeRoux and Krawczyk 2014). Moreover, the impact of nonprofits' voter engagement efforts may extend well beyond those directly mobilized. One study revealed that for each voting-related contact a client receives from a service agency, the likelihood of *encouraging family and friends to vote* increases by 4.5 percentage points (Nonprofit Vote 2011). Perhaps the most important actions that nonprofits take in their voter engagement work is to register non-voters and help them become first-time voters. Voting in one election substantially increases the likelihood of voting in future elections by as much as 46 percent (Gerber, Green, and Shachar 2003).

Given the effectiveness of these voter engagement efforts, the nonprofit sector has been referred to as the "sleeping giant of democracy" (Rongitsch 2008). There is untapped potential of the sector to increase voter participation. Currently, less than one-third of all nonprofit human service organizations in the US engage in voter mobilization activities (LeRoux 2011). If these activities were implemented on a more widespread basis as the NVRA sought to accomplish, nonprofits could have a substantial impact on elections.

Building civic and political leadership

Finally, nonprofits play an important political role by cultivating civic leadership and educating the public about government and the political process. Many types of nonprofits perform these roles. Here, we limit our discussion to community organizing groups, electoral capacity-building groups, and community-based organizations. Although these three types of organizations target different individuals and use different methods, they all work to build civic capacity among individuals and communities that are under-represented in politics and policy including youth, low-income persons, people of color, and women.

Community organizing nonprofits emphasize the importance of "cultivating indigenous leadership" (Dreier 1996; Gittell and Vidal 1998). In addition to pressing for legislative change and social reform using some of the approaches described earlier in this chapter, community organizing groups seek to empower community members and promote the general well-being of entire communities rather than specific interest groups. They accomplish these objectives by identifying and training community leaders to become activists, facilitating coalitions, mobilizing community members to vote, pressuring local lawmakers and government administrators for reforms that will benefit the community, developing issue campaigns, and organizing protest activities if conventional strategies fail to bring about the desired social change.

One example of a well-established community organizing network is People Improving Communities through Organizing National Network (PICO). PICO is a federated system of faith-based community organizing efforts that works to create social change in low-income communities throughout the United States. Typical of other community organizing groups, PICO uses the strategy of empowering community members through leadership training and civic capacity-building so that they may pursue needed local political reforms related to housing, health care, economic security, school improvement, youth development, and immigration reform.

Electoral capacity-building groups are another type of nonprofit that helps to build civic leadership. These organizations are varied in their nonprofit status (e.g., public charities, social welfare organizations) and have grown in number, particularly after the 2016 US Presidential election and the 2017 Women's Marches, and include groups such as VoteRunLead, Emily's List, and She Should Run. These organizations aim to increase representation of under-represented groups in elected office. She Should Run is a public charity with a mission of getting 250,000 women running for office by 2030. VoteRunLead aims to leverage technology to train and accelerate the number of women in civic and political leadership. Run For Something is a similar capacity-building organization, but aimed specifically at Millennials and "getting people under 35 on the ballot everywhere." Still other electoral capacity-building organizations aim to increase representation of specific expertise in government. For example, leaders in science, technology, engineering, and mathematics fields founded 314 Action to promote and encourage scientists to run for political office noting that "like Pi, science is all around us."

Community-based nonprofit organizations are uniquely suited for building civic capacity and promoting civic engagement among those who are most likely to eschew political participation. Community-based organizations, including those that provide social services, have "built-in" mechanisms for teaching and encouraging political participation skills. For example, nonprofits help to develop civic participation and leadership skills by including clients and community members on nonprofit governing boards, organizational advisory boards, committees, and event planning committees. Clarke (2000) emphasized the importance of institutionalizing activities within nonprofits for shaping the political identities of individuals and groups. Drawing on the work of March and Olsen (1995) and Jones (1994), Clarke (2000) notes that nonprofits create "communities of interest" that promote political identities among clients and encourage them to act as democratic citizens.

Evidence suggests these types of experiences can enhance the political efficacy of social services clients and help to transfer knowledge and skills to other settings (Soss 1999). For example, nonprofit clients and community members can apply what they have learned within their "community of interest" by engaging in other civic activities and means of political expression in the wider community including voting, following and participating in local politics and policy decisions. Community-based organizations help service users and their community members to develop the personal resources needed to effect change in their cities and neighborhoods.

What's next?

Nonprofit organizations, civil society groups, and protest movements have been instrumental in influencing politics and policies across time, levels of government, and national contexts, and play increasingly important roles in shaping the civic and political actions of individual citizens and groups. Through their roles in protest politics and social movements, expanding voter participation, and building civic and political leadership, nonprofits and civil society groups are particularly well suited to increase political participation, in particular among those whose perspectives are marginalized or under-represented.

This contemporary era of rapidly expanding technology, increased heterogeneity in society, and heightened political awareness and activism presents both opportunities and challenges for individuals, nonprofits, and civil society groups. A new generation of young people is seeking ways to have an impact on policy issues and policymakers. If they are thoughtful, clear, and strategic in their efforts, nonprofit and civil society groups can capitalize on this opportunity to engage new groups in politics and policy issues. Individuals face unprecedented demands on their time and must make choices about where to invest their energies. Nonprofits and civil society groups, including protest movements, can enhance their prospects of attracting and sustaining energy when they have legitimate leadership, clarity of objective, and deploy their resources strategically.

Leadership is necessary for articulating and carrying forward the vision and values of any nonprofit or civil society organization that sets out to achieve social change. What constitutes good leadership is the subject of great debate, but for the purposes of our discussion, long-term and committed effective leadership requires someone serving in a paid position. Leadership is often defined by followership, and the credibility accorded to the leader by others engaged in the pursuit of a common goal or interest. In formally established nonprofit organizations, leadership is often coterminous with formal authority and thus the ability to delegate and carry out political activities is more straightforward, whether they involve coordinating agency activities with local protest movements, voter mobilization, or identifying and encouraging people into pipelines for civic leadership positions. However, within protest movements that are built from the ground up, leadership may be more ephemeral or eschewed altogether. Yet, movements must be managed if they are to achieve long-term impact, and participants must arrive at a place of sufficient trust in delegating discretion to a leader or leadership team. An ideal leader will listen to diverse perspectives and forge consensus, plan, coordinate, and execute actions of members, sustain the interest of followers, and secure resources. Civic and political capacity-building organizations, whether electoral groups like She Should Run or community-based organizations such as Scouts or Parent Teacher Organization (PTO), should work to identify potential leaders from among their members who have the skills or ability to evolve into nonprofit or voluntary activist leaders.

Nonprofits and civil society groups also stand a greater chance for success in mobilization when they can clarify their objectives and message effectively about them. When it comes to objectives, it is better to be realistic than to overreach. The US-based grassroots movement, Moms Demand Action, was formed in response to mass shootings in the US, but established a set of objectives based on common-sense reforms, a.k.a. "gun sense" rather than "gun control" or attempts to restrict second amendment rights. The movement's leader was realistic about political feasibility and set forth objectives focused on achievable reforms including background checks for gun buyers, laws to prevent gun purchases by those with domestic assault convictions, and campaigns to discourage businesses from permitting open carry. Moms Demand Action has met with a good deal of success in enacting these reforms in various US states. In clarifying their objectives, nonprofits, civil society, and protest movement groups must also establish reasonable targets by which to measure their own success. Whether it is to register 10 new voters or 1,000, whether it is to identify 1 new person to run for office or serve on a citizen advisory board or 100, groups need to make a plan and set goals to know whether they are making progress.

While resources are important, *how* they are used may be far more important. Nonprofits, civil society groups, and protest movements need action plans that rely on whatever resources they have, however limited. Leaders must be able to delegate and get things done. Many nonprofits that engage in protest organizing and voter mobilization rely on volunteers to map out logistics, coordinate other helpers and leaders, and carry out activities. Technology, and social media especially, must be used strategically to advance movements and organizational memberships. There is clear evidence that social media have changed the protest and political organizing environment, including how many people show up and the types of people that show up (Tufekci and Wilson 2012). Online organizing has implications for nonprofits and protest movements. For nonprofit organizations, social media offer additional mechanisms for recruiting people to events and mission. Traditionally, social movements recruit people through friends, family, and social networks. Social media activate those same relationships at a faster speed, offering organizations more channels to reach people, including those who were previously unconnected to the organization (Goldstein 2017). Nonprofit organizations can use technology to tap previously unaffiliated members and resources. For online movements (those without formal nonprofit organizations), movement entrepreneurs are key to success, decision-making is more discretionary, the focus on leadership declines, and organizational form is less important. For online movements, ideological and internet-related concerns can be more important than leadership and organizational form (Earl and Schussman 2003). Nonprofit organizations will need to anticipate and manage the various changes that technology brings, including the opportunity for expanding reach and recruitment while at the same time encountering new forms of organizing. With leadership, clarity of mission, and a focus on best deployment of resources, including this new technological and social frontier, nonprofit organizations, civil society groups, and protest movements will continue to respond to and shape the political environment through active participation.

Notes

1 http://fightfor15.org/about-us/. Date accessed September 28, 2017.
2 As of September 2018, @blklivesmatter
3 LeRoux and Feeney 2015.

References

Adam, K. (2011) Occupy Wall Street Protests Go Global. *Washington Post.* October 15. https://www. washingtonpost.com/world/europe/occupy-wall-street-protests-go-global/2011/10/15/gIQAp7 kimL_story.html?utm_term=.f632d5ce8ac2 [Accessed 18 September 2017].

Anheier, H. (2015) How to Rule the Void? Policy Responses to a "Hollowing Out" of Democracy. *Global Policy*, 6(1).

Brady, H.E., Verba, S. and Schlozman, K.L. (1995) Beyond SES: A Resource Model of Political Participation. *American Political Science Review*, 89(2): 271–294.

Clarke, S.E. (2000) Governance Tasks and Nonprofit Organizations. In *Nonprofits in Urban America*, eds. Hula, R.C. and Jackson-Elmoore, C., 199–221, Westport, CT: Quorum Books.

Civicus. (2015) The State of Civil Society Report. www.civicus.org/images/StateOfCivilSocietyFull Report2015.pdf [Accessed 19 September 2017].

Desilver, D. (2018) U.S. Trails Most Developed Countries in Voter Turnout. https://www.pewresearch. org/fact-tank/2018/05/21/u-s-voter-turnout-trails-most-developed-countries/ [Accessed 17 December 2019].

Donovan, M.K. (2011) *States Move to Restrict Voting: What Nonprofits Can Do to Defend the Right to Vote.* Webinar given by the Fair Elections Legal Network, October 27.

Dreier, P. (1996) Community Empowerment Strategies: The Limits and Potential of Community Organizing in Urban Neighborhoods. *Cityscape*, 2(2), 121–159.

Earl, J. and Schussman, A. (2003) The New Site of Activism: On-line Organizations, Movement Entrepreneurs, and the Changing Location of Social Movement Decision Making. *Research in Social Movements, Conflicts and Change*, 24: 155–187.

File, T. (2017) Voting in America: A Look at the 2016 Presidential Election. *U.S. Census Bureau*, May 10.

Gerber, A.S. and Green, D.P. (1999) Does Canvassing Increase Voter Turnout? A Field Experiment. *National Academy of Sciences*, 96(19): 10939–10942.

Gerber, A.S. and Green, D.P. (2000a) The Effect of a Nonpartisan Get-Out-the-Vote Drive: An Experimental Study of Leafleting. *Journal of Politics*, 62(3): 846–857.

Gerber, A.S. and Green, D.P. (2000b) The Effects of Canvassing, Telephone Calls, and Direct Mail on Voter Turnout: A Field Experiment. *American Political Science Review*, 94(3): 653–663.

Gerber, A.S., Green, D.P. and Shachar, R. (2003) Voting May Be Habit-Forming: Evidence from a Randomized Field Experiment. *American Journal of Political Science*, 47(3): 540–550.

Gibson, M.R. (2013) The Anarchism of the Occupy Movement. *Australian Journal of Political Science*, 48(3): 335–348. DOI: 10.1080/10361146.2013.820687

Gittell, R. and Vidal, A. (1998) *Community Organizing: Building Social Capital as a Development Strategy.* Thousand Oaks, CA: Sage.

Goldstein, S. (2017) How Effective Is Social Media in Leading to True Change? KJZZ radio. Published: Tuesday, October 17, 3:24pm. Available at https://kjzz.org/content/552729/how-effective-social-me dia-leading-true-change [Accessed 29 October 2017].

Green, Donald P., Gerber, A.S. and Nickerson, D.W. (2003) Getting Out the Vote in Local Elections: Results from Six Door-to-Door Canvassing Experiments. *Journal of Politics*, 65(4): 1083–1096.

Greenhouse, S. (2015) How to Get Low-Wage Workers into the Middle Class. *The Atlantic,* August 19.

Greenhouse, S. and Kasperkevic, J. (2015) Fight for $15 Swells into Largest Protest by Low-Wage Workers in US History. *The Guardian,* April 15.

Jones, B.D. (1994) *Reconceiving Decision Making in Democratic Politics.* Chicago: University of Chicago Press.

LeRoux, K. (2011) Examining Implementation of the National Voter Registration Act by Nonprofit Organizations: An Institutional Explanation. *Policy Studies Journal,* 39(4): 565–589.

LeRoux, K. and Krawczyk, K. (2014) Can Nonprofit Organizations Increase Voter Turnout? Findings from an Agency-Based Voter Mobilization Experiment. *Nonprofit and Voluntary Sector Quarterly,* 43(2): 272–292.

LeRoux, K. and Feeney, M.K. (2015) *Nonprofit Organizations and Civil Society in the United States.* New York: Routledge.

Levitin, M. (2015) The Triumph of Occupy Wall Street. *The Atlantic.* June 10. https://www.theatlantic. com/politics/archive/2015/06/the-triumph-of-occupy-wall-street/395408/ [Accessed 18 September 2017].

March, J.G. and Olsen, J.P. (1995) *Democratic Governance.* New York: Free Press.

McAdam, D. (1982) *Political Process and the Development of Black Insurgency, 1930–1970.* Chicago: University of Chicago Press.

Nonprofit Vote. (2011) Nonprofits Increase Voting: Findings from a Nonprofit Voter Mobilization Experiment. May. Boston, MA.

Pitkin, H.F. (1972) *The Concept of Representation.* Berkley, CA: University of California Press.

Piven, F.F. and Cloward, R.A. (1977) *Poor People's Movements: Why They Succeed, How They Fail.* New York: Random House.

Piven, F.F. and Cloward, R.A. (1988) National Voter Registration Reform: How it Might be Won. *P.S. Political Science and Politics*, 21(4): 868–875.

Piven, F.F. and Cloward, R.A. (1996) Northern Bourbons: A Preliminary Report on the National Voter Registration Act. *PS: Political Science and Politics,* 29(1): 39–42.

Putnam, R.D. (2000) *Bowling Alone: The Collapse and Revival of Community in America.* New York: Simon and Schuster.

Rongitsch, B. (2008) Election 2008: More Nonprofits Engaging More Voters. *The Nonprofit Quarterly,* Spring.

Rosenstone, S.J. and Hansen, J.M. (1993) *Mobilization, Participation, and Democracy in America.* New York: Macmillan.

Ruiz-Grossman, S. (2017) Millennials Are the Foot Soldiers of the Resistance. IMPACT February 23. https://www.huffingtonpost.com/entry/trump-protest-poll_us_58addc16e4b0d0a6ef47517e [Accessed 26 August 2018].

Salamon, L.M. (1995) *Partners in Public Service: Government–Nonprofit Relations in the Modern Welfare State.* Baltimore, MD: Johns Hopkins University Press.

Skocpol, T. (1997) America's Voluntary Groups Thrive in a National Network. *The Brookings Review,* 15(4): 15–19.

Smith, A., Lehman-Schlozman, K., Verba, S. and Brady, H. (2009) The Current State of Civic Engagement in America. *Pew Research Center,* September 1. www.pewinternet.org/2009/09/01/the-current-state-of-civic-engagement-in-america/ [Accessed 18 September 2017].

Soss, J. (1999) Lessons of Welfare: Policy Design, Political Learning, and Political Action. *American Political Science Review,* 93(2): 363–380.

Stuster, J.D. (2013) Mapped, Every Protest on the Planet Since 1979: From Cairo, to Wall Street to the West Bank, Plotting a World of Upheaval. *Foreign Policy,* August 23. http://foreignpolicy.com/2013/08/23/mapped-every-protest-on-the-planet-since-1979/ [Accessed 18 September 2017].

Thompson, D. (2011) Occupy the World: The '99 Percent' Movement Goes Global. *The Atlantic.* October 15. https://www.theatlantic.com/business/archive/2011/10/occupy-the-world-the-99-percent-movement-goes-global/246757/ [Accessed 18 September 2017].

Tufekci, Z. and Wilson, C. (2012) Social Media and the Decision to Participate in Political Protest: Observations from Tahrir Square. *Journal of Communication,* 62(2): 363–379.

U.S. Census. (2016) Voting and Registration in the Election of November 2016. https://www.census.gov/data/tables/time-series/demo/voting-and-registration/p20-580.html [Accessed 17 December 2019].

Whoriskey, P. (2011) CBO: Incomes of Top Earners Grow at a Pace Far Faster than Everyone Else's. *Washington Post*, October 26. https://www.washingtonpost.com/business/economy/cbo-incomes-of-top-earners-grow-at-a-pace-far-faster-than-everyone-elses/2011/10/26/gIQAHlVFKM_story.html?utm_term=.b9e4d12068ab [Accessed 18 September 2017].

Wyatt, K. (2016) Five More States Vote on Minimum Wage as Federal Wage Stalls. Associated Press. October 16. www.pbs.org/newshour/rundown/minimum-wage-five-states-vote/ [Accessed 18 September 2017].

25

NONPROFIT MARKETING
AND BRANDING

Jane Hudson

LECTURER IN MARKETING, PLYMOUTH BUSINESS SCHOOL,
UNIVERSITY OF PLYMOUTH, PLYMOUTH, UK

Introduction

Kotler and Levy (1969) are widely credited as bringing the academic debate of the relevance of marketing theory and application to nonprofit organizations (see for example Sargeant & Wymer 2008). They defined marketing as "serving human wants and needs sensitively" (1969: 15) and argued that marketing had been regarded as a narrow business function for far too long. At that time such a definition was controversial. However, by the late 1970s the debate had 'fizzled out' as marketers became more preoccupied with other key constituents of the marketing discipline such as services marketing (Lovelock & Weinberg 1990). In the last five decades the acceptance of marketing theory, application, and tools within the nonprofit domain has been widespread. Most notable was the *Journal of Marketing*'s 1971 special issue with a focus on marketing's social and environmental role. In the 1980s the first generic nonprofit marketing textbooks were developed (for example see Kotler & Andreasen 1982) and were then followed by a number of more specialized nonprofit marketing texts in the fields of healthcare (see Kotler & Clarke 1986), the arts (Mokwa, Prieve, & Dawson 1980), social marketing (Manoff 1985), and fundraising (Sargeant & Jay 2004).

In the scholarly journal field there has been the notable development of generic marketing journals devoted to the academic and practical understanding of marketing theory in the context of nonprofits, charities, voluntary organizations, and the public sector (see for example the *International Journal of Nonprofit and Voluntary Sector Marketing* or the *Journal of Nonprofit & Public Sector Marketing*). Furthermore, there has been the development of more niche sector-specific journals such as the *Journal of Educational Advancement*, the *Journal of Marketing for Higher Education*, *Health Marketing Quarterly*, the *Journal of Health Care Marketing* and the *Social Marketing Quarterly*.

This chapter will present a succinct overview of the key elements of nonprofit marketing to date and it is intended to be a starting point for the reader. It has been argued that academic knowledge of nonprofit marketing is fragmented and biased towards applied research (Wymer 2013). This bias towards applied research has, to a certain extent, limited the generalizability of nonprofit marketing theory. However, we can confidently state that many marketing ideas, models, and frameworks have as much relevance to the nonprofit as the for-profit domain. It is also fair to state that the adoption of marketing ideas in the nonprofit sector is no longer controversial and many nonprofits now employ marketing personnel to address marketing issues.

It is also worth noting that whilst for most for-profit organizations their marketing function primarily considers their customers, the nonprofits have two constituencies to consider – service beneficiaries and funders. Thus nonprofit marketing has to consider two distinct markets, the market for resource attraction and the market for resource allocation. Given the constraints of a single book chapter there is the need for brevity and I will focus on only a few key issues and identify the differences between for-profit and nonprofit marketing. More specifically we will discuss the nonprofit marketing concept, orientation, strategy, and branding in the context of this so-called digital age. We begin by defining the nonprofit marketing concept.

Defining the nonprofit marketing concept

The marketing concept was first defined by Drucker (1954) as a business philosophy that focuses on the customer as being central to the organizations' strategy and operations (Padanyi 2008). Furthermore, understanding the marketplace (customer, competitors, and environment) in which they operate is key to success and growth, so there is the need to be outward-looking and develop market orientation (Warnaby & Finney 2005; Chad, Kyriazis, & Motion 2013). This has led to the growth of market orientation where commercial organizations focus on the various complexities of their consumer and customer in the context of environmental forces.

Unlike marketing in the commercial domain, there is currently no consensus of how to define or conceptualize the nonprofit marketing concept (Wymer, Boenigk, & Möhlmann 2015). The notion of extending the marketing concept to include non-commercial organizations has been widely accredited to Kotler and Levy (1969) who argued that marketing activities are necessary regardless of whether an organization is profit seeking or not. Similarly, it has been argued that nonprofits seek surplus revenues to enable them to continue with their valuable work (Hay 1990). Other authors have pointed out that nonprofits operate in the same environment with similar demands (Anthony & Young 1990), constraints, and competition (Tuckman 1998). Undeniably there are some similarities between commercial and nonprofit organizations, but there are key differences for nonprofits such as:

- The objective is for short, medium, and long-term societal benefit;
- Nonprofits are often resource poor with high degrees of accountability of expenditure;
- Performance is measured by beneficiaries/clients served, their satisfaction, and the propensity for repeat donation;
- The product offered can be physical, services, information, and behavioural change with large fluctuations in demand;
- The workforce can be both paid and volunteers;
- Governance is by trustees or a voluntary board of directors.

(Adapted from Chad et al. 2013)

Historically, and rather controversially, nonprofit organizations have thus utilized the most pertinent commercial marketing tools and tactics (Sargeant & Wymer 2008). This application of commercial marketing tools and tactics to the nonprofit setting has also been mirrored in academia with researchers applying the concept of market orientation to nonprofits (see for example Brady, Brace-Govan, Brennan, & Conduit 2011).

This notion of transferring the commercial marketing concept, without some adjustment to account for the specific needs of nonprofit organizations, has been problematic. Marketing concepts were conceptualized for national, multinational, and global businesses and largely ignored the needs of wider society, focusing instead on satisfying the customer where profitable.

It was the focus on society that was missing from the commercial marketing concept and it was the wider needs of society that nonprofit organizations seek to serve. Thus the term Societal Orientation was coined in the early millennium and proffered as better serving the nonprofit organizational needs (Zuluaga & Schneider 2008). More recently Wymer et al. (2015) argue that neither market orientation nor societal orientation is adequate in order to operationalize marketing in nonprofits. They suggest that this domain is under-researched in nonprofits and develop the term nonprofit market orientation (122). Furthermore, their qualitative research suggests that there are four key concepts that comprise nonprofit marketing orientation (126):

1 *Brand Orientation* – brand as the organization's image through important audiences' lens. The image is implemented through various forms of communication;
2 *Supporters Orientation* – marketing as a means to recruit supporters, develop relationships with supporters, and/or attract resources to the organizations;
3 *Commercial Orientation* – the use of business terminology and metaphors;
4 *Service Orientation* – the engagement with service provision and service quality.

Clearly there are some parallels to be drawn between commercial and nonprofit marketing, but the contrast is vast and the research into this critical area is, at best, underdeveloped. Until consensus is reached there will continue to be a fragmented field of research and practice.

Marketing strategy

Whilst we have established that there are some overlaps and differences between commercial and nonprofit marketing, the success of the nonprofit organization depends on developing strategies that deliver its mission and facilitate it achieving its goals (Krug & Weinberg 2008). In a for-profit context the marketing function is concerned with developing goods and services, which will then be sold to customers. The marketing function in the commercial context considers the most efficient and effective marketing mix, more commonly known as the 4Ps – product, price, place, and promotion – to ensure the optimal return on their investment. This will generate revenue which can, in turn, be used to purchase the raw materials necessary to produce the next generation of goods and services – and so on. In short there is only one primary constituency that needs to be targeted by the marketing function, namely the customers of the organization.

Strategic planning in the context of nonprofits is arguably more complex than in commercial markets, as they do not necessarily operate within the traditional marketing mix. They need to consider the target market for both resource allocation (beneficiaries) and resource attraction (volunteers and donors) rather than targeting customers for the sale of a traditional product or service. It is argued that there are three target markets to consider: beneficiaries, volunteers, and donors or funders (Pope, Sterrett Isely, & Asamoa-Tutu 2009). Furthermore, the target markets are often distinct (for example they might only supporter a particular cause such as cancer care) and likely to respond differently to the organization's marketing mix depending on their interest in the cause and their resources (Andreasen & Kotler 2008). To add to this complexity the benefits sought from each target group are often not financially or transaction based, thus making it more challenging for nonprofits to communicate distinct benefits to each target market. For example, the benefits sought for those who receive cancer care from a nonprofit (the beneficiary target market) will be relief from their suffering, medication, support for them and their loved ones, etc. In contrast those that give financial support and volunteer for a cancer relief nonprofit (donors and volunteers) seek a wide variety of intrinsic and extrinsic benefits such as increased self-esteem, psychological well-being, public recognition, etc. (for further reading please see Bekkers & Weipking 2011). We will now examine each of the three main target markets:

Beneficiaries

Most nonprofit organizations' primary purpose is to provide services for those in society when (a) commercial organizations will not provide (as there is no profit to be made) and (b) the state does not or cannot provide (due to appropriateness or lack of funds). For example, the UK's Royal Society for the Prevention of Cruelty to Animals (RSPCA) is a good example of where it would not be commercially viable to offer animal welfare and protection services to mistreated and neglected animals and the state, despite offering some basic animal welfare legislation, cannot provide. When targeting these consumers of services, or beneficiaries as they are referred to in the nonprofit sector, the nonprofit should consider both the internal appropriateness and external attractiveness of the services offered. Unfortunately, whilst some activities and services may be highly relevant to the organization's mission and desired by the beneficiary (internally appropriate), they may be more difficult to fund than others that are perhaps more tangential, as they lack external attractiveness and thus will not attract funding. For example, a homeless shelter offering drug and alcohol addiction treatment may be internally appropriate to the nonprofit as it will help those with these addictions find their way off the streets. To funders, however, it may be seen as tangential to the core mission of helping the homeless as those with addictions may be thought of as being responsible for their plight. This makes the management of an appropriate portfolio of activities and services much more complex than would be the case in the for-profit environment.

To date the existing academic research into nonprofit beneficiaries largely focuses on targeting those that use arts organizations (see for example Hume & Mort 2008; Kemp 2015). This may be due to the more socially acceptable outcomes and that it may be easier to obtain access to these beneficiaries as there is very little published research into other types of beneficiaries. More often both practitioner and academic articles referring to nonprofit 'customers' are actually examining donors, as opposed to the beneficiaries who are in receipt of the services provided by the nonprofit. This leaves a significant gap in our current understanding of this nonprofit customer.

Volunteers

Volunteers are a crucial resource and part of most nonprofit operations. However, nonprofits often encounter difficulty recruiting and retaining good volunteers (Taghian, D'Souza, & Polonsky 2012). As the nonprofit sector becomes more competitive and an increasing number of organizations seek to recruit volunteers, potential volunteers can be more selective in their choices (Randle & Dolnicar 2009). Although the academic literature acknowledges that the motivation to volunteer is a complex phenomenon (Taghian et al. 2012), nonprofit organizations need to include it in their marketing strategy. Motives to volunteer have been examined extensively in the academic literature from a variety of perspectives, such as life stages (Black & Jirovic 1999), egoistic-instrumental motives and altruistic–ideological motives (Frish & Gerrard 1981). Furthermore it is argued that there are six primary needs or motive functions that volunteering serves in the long term: (1) an expression of personally held values; (2) increasing one's understanding of the world; (3) developing and strengthening of one's social relationships and benefiting from social reward; (4) self-enhancement by growing psychologically; and (5) protecting oneself by addressing personal problems and reducing negative feelings (Guntert, Neufeind, & Wehner 2015; Clary et al. 1998). In the short term volunteering research suggests that there are some further motivational functions, for example in the domain of event volunteering it has been suggested that good citizenship (one's identification with the event location) and excitement (the desire to experience something special and exciting) are important (Guntert et al. 2015). Alternatively, in the case of volunteering during an emergency the notion of social solidarity and in particular community-oriented motivations are prominent (Kulick 2017).

The challenge, however, is how to identify the right consumer (people most likely to volunteer), target them (get your organization into the repertoire of nonprofit choices), attract them (get them started volunteering), and keep them loyal (continue volunteering for as long as possible) (Randle & Dolnicar 2012). There have been numerous research studies that have examined volunteering recruitment and retention for a variety of causes. For example Devaney et al. (2015) identify some key nonprofit characteristics that play an important part in the recruitment of volunteers:

- The high positive profile of the recruiting nonprofit organization;
- Organizational support for induction, training, and ongoing inclusivity;
- The organization's flexibility towards volunteer availability and time commitment.

As the volunteer marketplace continues to evolve in these challenging economic times each nonprofit needs to understand the mechanisms by which they can recruit the 'right' type of support. This requires an understanding of how to market to this target audience, which in turn requires the prerequisite of understanding volunteer motives and what precisely attracts them. In the digital environment nonprofits have numerous ways to potentially recruit volunteers. For example in the UK there are a variety of websites that will match organizations and volunteers depending on the requirements of the role and skills and availability of the potential volunteer (see for example *https://volunteeringmatters.org.uk*).

Donors

Nonprofits typically derive their voluntary income from one of three sources: individual donors, corporate donors, or trusts/foundations. Government funds also form a significant source of income for the sector, but this is frequently in the form of a contractual relationship for the provision of specific goods or services and therefore not regarded as a 'voluntary' contribution. Gifts from living individuals form the majority of a typical organization's voluntary income and are typically solicited through marketing channels by fundraising campaigns. In the US, for example, total giving to the nonprofit sector in 2016 stood at $390 billion. A staggering 90 per cent of Americans offered donations to nonprofits with people giving on average 2 per cent of their income and contributing 72 per cent of the total income accruing to the sector; the balance coming from corporations, foundations, and bequests (Giving USA 2017). In the UK the picture is slightly less rosy with £9.7 billion given to charities by individuals and only 61 per cent of the UK population donating charity in 2016 (CAF UK Giving 2017). Furthermore, on average the cost of fundraising is around 10 per cent of the total income (Charity Financials 2018).

Fundraising is the main function for stimulating individual donations and often uses an integrated marketing communications (IMC) approach to deliver fundraising campaign objectives. For example, Greenpeace campaigned in 2018 to end the production of non-sustainable palm oil through their 'Save Rang-tan' campaign (Greenpeace.org.uk). This is an IMC campaign to create awareness of the issue, encourage collective action to pressure commercial organizations to operate in more sustainable ways through petitions, engage with existing supporters and recruit new supporters to raise funds. The communication to individuals was achieved through a variety of mediums, for example Greenpeace worked with the commercial retailer Iceland to develop a Christmas advert that focused on the plight of orang-utans. This achieved over 30 million views despite never appearing on television and was supported by their website, social media, public relations (through traditional media there were over 100 TV and radio clips and over 30 UK print newspaper articles), and telephone fundraising. The impact of this campaign was tangible with over 1.2 million supporters signing the petition to stop the use of non-sustainable palm oil.

In academe it has been recognized that in order to fundraise successfully, we must understand the motivations of individuals to give gifts. Therefore, it has been the focus of much research, with contributions stemming from the fields of economics, clinical psychology, social psychology, anthropology, and sociology. A key contribution from the discipline of nonprofit marketing has been the development of composite models of helping behaviour whose goal has been to explain the donation of money, time, and even body parts (see for example Burnett & Wood 1988; Guy & Patton 1989; Bendapudi, Singh, & Bendapudi 1996; Sargeant 1999). The extant literature has recognized a variety of motives for individual giving; these vary from simply being asked to give, to being stimulated by more complex psychological and social motives such as enhanced self-image and positive reputational benefits (Bekkers and Weipking 2011).

Whilst it is important to understand the audiences that nonprofits need to target to gain resources, we also need to consider the key assets that a nonprofit has at its marketing and fundraising teams' disposal – the brand. This review will now consider one of a nonprofit organization's key assets, that of the brand.

Nonprofit branding

The brand has long been recognized as central to an organization's success and arguably it is no different for nonprofit organizations. Nonprofit branding has come of age in the twenty-first century with brands and brand management of increasing interest to practitioners and academics alike (Hudson 2008). It has been argued that a strong brand is a facet of charities that plays an important strategic role (Chapleo 2013). The unique emotional elements of a brand that communicate their philosophies and values offer critical benefits such as sustainable competitive advantage (Harris and de Chernatony 2001) and differentiation from competition (Hankinson 2001). Decisions regarding nonprofit support are largely based upon individual perceptions of the work that organizations do. Branding helps individuals form these perceptions.

Furthermore, there is a wealth of evidence that branding can impact an organization's ability to successfully raise funds. As Tapp (1996: 335) notes, while "charities do not describe much of what they do as 'branding', organizations have long been concerned with maintaining a consistent style and tone of voice and conducting periodic reviews of both policies and actions to ensure that a consistent personality is projected." In his view, such practices are at the heart of brand management.

What is a brand?

The American Marketing Association (AMA) in 1960 defined a brand as: "A name, term, sign, symbol, or design, or a combination of them, intended to identify the good or services of one seller or group of sellers and to differentiate them from those of competitors."

This definition has been widely criticized for being overly simplistic and it fails to recognize just how much brands have evolved in the past 60 years (Hudson 2008; Conejo & Wooliscroft

2015). Brands have evolved into potentially rich symbols that signify associative meanings and feelings to consumers (Danesi 2004; Oswald 2012). As such most contemporary brand definitions move beyond considering only the tangible functional elements of the brand to considering the intangible, emotional, symbolic, and representational elements of the brand (see for example de Chernatony & Harris 2000). Furthermore, it is argued that a brand not only stands for the benefits of profit and driving consumer product or service choice but for self-expressive, emotive, and social benefits (Aaker 2012). Additionally, it has been posited that brands, due to their symbolic attributes, are co-created especially within the service domain (Brodie et al. 2006). Given the changing nature of brands and how their meaning has changed Conejo and Wooliscroft (2015: 297) suggest the following definition:

> Brands are re-defined as complex multidimensional constructs with varying degrees of meaning, independence, co-creation and scope. Brands are semiotic marketing systems that generate value for direct and indirect participants, society, and the broader environment, through the exchange of co-created meaning.

Whilst comprehensive, we could ask if the brand has the same definition in the nonprofit context. In stark contrast to Conejo and Wooliscroft's (2015) complex definition, the UK National Society for the Prevention of Cruelty to Children (NSPCC) defines its brand more simply and holistically as "everything we are, everything we say, everything we do" (Hudson 2008: 66).

Why brand?

A brand is powerful for an organization and transforms the consumer's experience with that organization, leading to customer loyalty, continued business, trust, and satisfaction. Thus, a brand is an asset to an organization or service that drives the organizational strategy and performance. Simply expressed branding should be a critical issue for nonprofits because it has been shown to positively impact income generation (see for example Kennedy 1998; Grounds & Harkness 1998). A strong brand that clearly and symbolically conveys the values and beliefs of the nonprofit organization to potential donors and the wider stakeholders suggests very powerful reasons why it may be worthy of support (Hudson 2008; Groza & Gordon 2016). This is significant as where donors lack knowledge of a charity and its image they may either ignore or 'distort' their communications messages to justify not giving a gift (Bendapudi et al. 1996). It is argued there are distinct advantages to branding in the nonprofit sector, which are as follows:

1   The brand is an aid to learning and can be used to progressively educate stakeholders about the valuable work undertaken;
2   Branding differentiates one nonprofit from another in this increasingly competitive marketplace;
3   The brand reduces risk for donors as the nonprofit acts as their agents in disbursing funds (see 'Agency theory' for further explanation);
4   Branding provides reputation insurance, donors are more likely to forgive a trusted and well-understood brand that has a short-term crisis;
5   Brands provide a focus for the supporter relationship.

(Hudson 2008: 67)

There are clearly benefits to branding in the nonprofit sector but how does a nonprofit build a brand? The definitions of brands clearly indicate that there are functional and emotional components of brand. The functional components are more tangible in that it should be relatively easy to communicate to the stakeholders the good work that the organization achieves (for example how many animals a Cats and Dogs shelter may save from destruction). However, the emotional and symbolic components of brand are more complex and not so easily communicated or understood. Brand personality has been explored in the academic literature to attempt to understand how nonprofits can communicate and develop relationships with their supporters in an expressive and symbolic manner (Groza & Gordon 2016).

Brand personality

The notion of brand personality is not a recent phenomenon. In the commercial domain the idea is familiar and accepted by both practitioners and academics alike (see for example Ghantous 2016). Brand personality can be defined as a "set of human characteristics associated with a brand" (Aaker 1997: 347). Consumers thus view brands as having human characteristics despite being inanimate objects (Aaker 1997; Aaker et al. 2001; Sargeant, Ford, & Hudson 2008; Groza & Gordon 2016). Brand personality offers an expressive, symbolic approach to how a brand represents itself and affects brand choice by consumers. Conversely a brand personality enables the consumer to express their notion of self as they are drawn to a brand because of a congruence they develop with the brand's personality associations (Geuens, Weijters, & de Wulf 2009). Expressed simply, consumers identify with the human characteristics of a brand that are similar to their self-concept or how they aspire to be. This requires the brand personality and values portrayed to be distinct.

In the nonprofit sector brand personality has received some attention in the last decade. It is suggested that successful charity brands enable donors to express their personalities, messages, and emotions to others through their association with the brand (Stride & Lee 2007). However, Sargeant et al. (2008) argue that achieving a distinct personality is considerably more difficult in the charity context than in the commercial sector, since many facets of charity personality are in fact shared by the sector as a whole. Charities are generally regarded, for example, as being caring, sympathetic, and compassionate. Donors and supporters appear to start from this assumption unless evidence appears to the contrary. Only values and characteristics linked to 'emotional stimulation,' 'service,' 'voice,' and 'tradition' are capable of distinguishing between organizations. Organizations perceived as distinctive command a higher share of a donor's charitable wallet than those lacking such differentiation. Furthermore, the donor's self-concept is impacted by the nonprofit's brand personality thus increasing an individual's giving intentions (Hou, Du, & Tian 2009). Further research by Groza and Gordon (2016) explored which brand personality traits in the nonprofit context facilitated relationship building. They suggest that highlighting the personality dimensions of nurturance, ruggedness, and sophistication when seeking to engage with potential donors, volunteers, and clients (126). They also reinforce the notion that if potential donors perceive the nonprofit's brand personality to be congruent with their own personality they will show increased levels of support whether financial or volunteering.

Having explored the role of branding in nonprofit marketing we now turn to examine the digital context and its impact on nonprofit marketing.

The digital era

Much has been written in the commercial marketing domain about the development and impact of digital technology on marketing activities. There are currently in excess of 3.58 billion internet users, and as such the importance of online websites as a communication tool cannot be underestimated (Statista 2018). Digital marketing has evolved from a term that specifically describes the process of using digital technologies – such as websites – to acquire new customers, build preferences, retain customers, build and promote brands, and increase sales. Furthermore, it can be defined as "an adaptive, technology-enabled process by which firms collaborate with customers and partners to jointly create, communicate, deliver, and sustain value for all stakeholders" (Kannan & Li 2017: 23).

Given that there is rapid technological change within the global environment it is hardly surprising that nonprofits, with their financial constraints, face challenges when it comes to the adoption and use of such innovative technology (see Chapter 17 by McNutt, this volume). In fact it has been argued that nonprofits are 'laggards' when it comes to adopting new technology (Waters 2014). The evidence from the United States, based on a survey of 133 nonprofits across a variety of causes, suggests that some are starting to reap the benefits of using the internet for their online marketing, advocacy, and fundraising with:

i growth in traffic to nonprofit websites;
ii 10% growth in nonprofit email lists in 2016 to nearly 50 million subscribers;
iii 10% growth in email volume to 3.6 billion emails sent;
iv social media audiences grew with a 50% growth on Twitter, 23% growth on Facebook, and 101% on Instagram;
v online revenue grew by 14% to $535.6 million;
vi there were 7.2 million advocacy actions.

(M+R Benchmark Study 2017)

Whilst it is interesting to note that there has been growth in the US, in the UK the evidence is rather mixed. In 2013 UK registered charities spent just 2 per cent of their £394 million advertising budget on internet advertising (Saxton 2014) and this rose to only 5 per cent in 2016 (Kay 2017). This has led one industry researcher, Joe Saxton, to state "Charities are either unwilling or unable to use the internet as effectively as the corporate world does. This either is due to the innate cautiousness of charities, or a failure to find techniques that really work" (Kay 2017). Anecdotal evidence suggests that most UK and US charities have an online presence, but currently there is little research to indicate the efficacy of these digital tools.

To date academic research into the nonprofit sector digital use has also largely been based in the US and the UK and has focused on how nonprofits use the Web (Burger 2015), how they use social media to engage with stakeholders (Saxton & Guo 2014), adopt social media within organizations (Waters & Jones 2011), or to fundraise (Lucas 2017). Websites are considered particularly attractive to inform and persuade target audiences as they have desirable characteristics such as content richness, design flexibility, interactivity, and are relatively low cost (van Noort, Voorveld, & van Reijmersdal 2012). For nonprofit organizations, their website can offer new ways to reach their target audiences as it:

a enables nonprofits to actually interact with their stakeholders;
b actively engages them with the content; and
c even motivates them to donate online.

(Cugelman, Thelwall, & Dawes 2011)

In order to reach their target audiences commercial and nonprofit organizations alike need to consider the various different marketing mixes that may be used. In particular that the marketing mix has been adapted to reflect the change in the technological and social environment that marketing operates in.

Digital marketing mix

The marketing mix can be defined as "the marketing manager's set of key tools that can be adjusted, improved or changed in order to match the needs of the marketplace, to gain competitive advantage and to maximize long-term profits" (Jackson & Ahuja 2016: 171). Probably the most well known and taught is McCarthy's marketing mix, which consists of the highly memorable '4Ps' – product, price, place, and promotion (McCarthy 1960). Since then the marketing environment has changed and the marketing mix has evolved to match these technological and societal changes. The first major change was the development of the concept of 'integrated marketing communications' (IMC) that includes media advertising, sales promotion, public relations, package design, personal selling, and direct marketing. Subsequent changes in technology have facilitated the rapid expansion of cyberspace that is changing consumers' lifestyles and this has been accelerated by the introduction of 'Web 2.0' (Jackson & Ahuja 2016). Within this evolving and emerging virtual domain, corporate blogs, online communities, social networks, and wikis have changed the lives of individuals. Furthermore, this has arguably changed the way people relate to information, brands, other people, and even their own self-identity.

The marketing mix in the twenty-first century needs to include online activities, such as the role of blogs, online communities, smartphone adoption, co-creation (the involvement of consumer in new product development, see for example Lego life, https://www.lego.com/en-gb/life), influencer marketing (such as vloggers and bloggers), digitalized personal communication, and multiple communication platforms (for example emails, instant messaging, and banner advertising). In the nonprofit context the organization should certainly consider the digital communications mix, as shown in Figure 25.1. This model clearly depicts how online tools, such as social media, can be used to complement more traditional offline forms of communications, such as direct mail. Sargeant and Shattuck (2017) present clear guidance on how nonprofits can best utilize the digital environment both in the context of fundraising and gaining vital advocacy.

Whilst most of us are familiar with the use of online channels to promote a product or cause there has been a particular rise in the use of social media platforms within nonprofits.

Social media

Social media first appeared in the mid- to late 2000s and are distinct from other forms of new media in that they encourage interactivity and two-way communication through the sharing of updates, photographs, and messages (Saxton & Wang 2014). Due to their interactivity social media platforms dominate discussions of online advocacy because of their ease of use and abilities to utilize peer-to-peer networks to spread advocacy messages (Goldkind & McNutt 2014; Guo & Saxton 2013). Extant studies have demonstrated social media's efficacy for, among other purposes, stakeholder discourse (Waters, Burnett, Lamm, & Lucas 2009), community-building (Briones, Kuch, Liu, & Jin 2011; Lovejoy & Saxton 2012), and advocacy work (Guo & Saxton 2013). These studies suggest that social media allow organizations to connect with and mobilize the public, as well as the more standard use of sending and receiving information (Lovejoy, Waters, & Saxton 2012). This is apparent in nonprofit organizations' increasing use of Facebook, Twitter, GoFundMe, Crowdrise, and other social media applications for their fundraising activities. Furthermore, it has been argued that social networking applications such as Facebook,

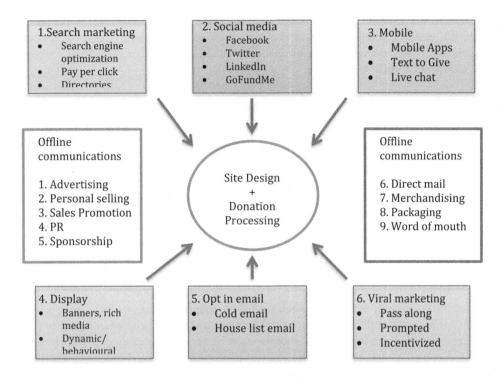

Figure 25.1 Digital communications mix (adapted from Sargeant & Shattuck 2017: 318)

Twitter, and Crowdrise offer new ways for nonprofits to engage the wider community in fundraising efforts (Saxton & Wang 2014).

Twitter and Facebook, in particular, have acquired significant attention from nonprofit organizations as innovative communication tools that both supplement and replace the traditional website (Nonprofit Technology Network 2012). However, marketers and fundraisers need to be careful not to employ only one-way communication strategies where they use social media merely to disseminate pertinent information (McCorkingdale, Distaso, & Sisco 2013). The audiences' engagement and interaction is key to developing support and longer-term relationships.

In terms of fundraising it has been argued that social media holds three key advantages over traditional media:

a   nonprofits can use crowdfunding which enables them to reach a larger, more geographically dispersed audience that are willing to support the cause either through donation or by sharing and publicizing the cause;

b   potential donors are solicited by a member of their social network and thus has pre-established connections and relationships with them – arguably making them more trustworthy;

c   the potential donor's response to the solicitation is highly visible to their social network peer group.

(Saxton & Wang 2014)

Practically speaking there are some notable examples of successful nonprofit social media campaigns. In the UK Comic Relief, for example, reportedly raised more than £37 million on

Facebook and Twitter in 2011 (Taylor 2011). More recently, the Ice Bucket Challenge meme in the UK increased Macmillan Cancer Support's fundraised income by a reported £3 million (Townsend 2014). Facebook in particular has received some attention from academic researchers and practitioners.

Facebook

Facebook has over 1.8 billion active users worldwide, of which around 543 million users accessed the site through their mobile (Statista 2018). In the UK, there are over 31 million active users, and over half of them use the site every day. There has been some debate surrounding the value of Facebook to fundraising in particular, with UNICEF Sweden warning that Facebook "likes" are not enough to pay for life-saving polio vaccines for children (Khazan 2013). Moylan (2013) calls this a form of "passive activism" and states that it is useless unless it is supported with more tangible and meaningful activity such as donation. In 2011, Facebook channelled around 1 million individual donors to JustGiving, who collectively gave £22 million (£1 million of this was donated through the mobile version of Facebook). By May 2012, 32 per cent of donations on the JustGiving platform came from Facebook, a 130 per cent year-on-year growth (Waddington 2013). Whilst there is some debate surrounding the efficacy of Facebook to garner donations, Lucas (2017) suggests that Facebook is primarily used to strengthen relationships with supporters, mainly via humanizing the brand, fostering obligations, and encouraging social interaction (2). Furthermore, it is interesting to note that the most likely outcome of a nonprofit Facebook page or fundraising campaign is the public or social sharing of the Facebook page. This poses an interesting challenge for nonprofits, how do you move supporters from being advocates to financial donors?

Conclusion

This chapter has discussed a select few of the key tenets that are pertinent to nonprofit marketing. In doing so there are many areas that have been excluded, such as the different types of nonprofit marketing applications (social marketing, arts marketing, health marketing, and higher education marketing to name but a few), all of which have their own body of academic knowledge.

This review of the literature clearly indicates that the nonprofit marketing discipline has much to learn and understand. For example, we still lack an adequate and universally acceptable definition of the nonprofit marketing concept and its orientation. Research tells us that the nonprofit sector shares some characteristics with the for-profit market, but there are some key distinctions. For example, in nonprofit marketing we have three distinct audiences to target, the beneficiaries, the volunteer, and the donor.

As part of conducting this review we have identified some key areas where more research is required in order to progress the field. These can be divided into four areas, which are as follows:

1 The need to develop a clear definition of the nonprofit marketing concept and how this then relates to the nonprofit marketing orientation;
2 Understanding of nonprofit beneficiaries and their set of needs. To date research has largely focused on donors and what attracts and satisfies them rather than understanding the very reason for the nonprofits' existence. For example, we understand little about the beneficiaries of some of the less glamorous nonprofit causes such as HIV sufferers or narcotics addicts, precisely what their needs are and how we can best service those needs other than in a functional way;

3   Develop a greater understanding of how marketing can be used to attract appropriate and sustainable volunteering in a competitive marketplace. This is particularly important in the UK where the government is rapidly withdrawing services within the community and the vulnerable public relies on volunteers to help meet their basic needs;

4   Examine how nonprofit supporters interact with online platforms and social networking. Furthermore, understand whether advocacy is connected to financial support through donation. This is particularly pertinent given the digital-savvy Millennial generation who are keen advocates and volunteers but largely fail to make financial donations.

It is also fair to state that the majority of the existing research is geographically located in the US and UK. Whilst some of the marketing principles and tools are globally applicable, cultural norms are very likely to play their part in nonprofit organizations and their ability to serve their beneficiaries. Therefore, as always there must be more research to understand this vitally important field.

References

Aaker, D. (2012) Win the brand relevance battle and then build competitor barriers. *California Management Review*, 54(2).

Aaker, J.L. (1997) Dimensions of brand personality. *Journal of Marketing Research*, 34(1): 347–356.

Aaker, J.L., Benet-Martínez, V. & Garolera, J. (2001) Consumption symbols as carriers of culture: A study of Japanese and Spanish brand personality constructs. *Journal of Personality and Social Psychology*, 81(3): 492–508.

Andreasen, A.R. & Kotler, P. (2008) *Strategic Marketing for Nonprofit Organizations* (7th ed.). Upper Saddle River, NJ: Pearson Prentice Hall.

Anthony, R. & Young, D. (1990) Characteristics of nonprofit organizations. In Gies, D., Ott, S. & Shafritz, J. (Eds.), *The Organization: Essential Readings*. Pacific Grove, CA: Brooks/Cole Publishing.

Bekkers, R. & Weipking, P. (2011) A literature review of empirical studies of philanthropy: Eight mechanisms that drive charitable giving. *Nonprofit and Voluntary Sector Quarterly*, 40(5): 924–973

Bendapudi, N., Singh, S.N. & Bendapudi, V. (1996) Enhancing helping behavior: An integrative framework for promotion planning. *Journal of Marketing*, 60(3): 33–54.

Black, B. & Jirovic, R.L. (1999) Age differences in volunteer participation. *Journal of Volunteer Administration*, 17: 38–47.

Brady, E., Brace-Govan, J., Brennan, L. & Conduit, J. (2011) Market orientation and marketing in nonprofit organizations. Indications for fundraising from Victoria. *International Journal of Nonprofit and Voluntary Sector Marketing*, 16: 84–98.

Briones, R.L., Kuch, B., Liu, B. & Jin, Y. (2011) Keeping up with the digital age: How the American Red Cross uses social media to build relationships. *Public Relations Review*, 37: 37–43.

Brodie, Roderick J., Glynn, M.S. & Little, V. (2006) The service brand and the service dominant logic: Missing fundamental premise or the need for stronger theory. *Marketing Theory*, 6(3): 363–379.

Burger, T. (2015) Use of digital advocacy by German nonprofit foundations on Facebook. *Public Relations Review*, 41: 523–525.

Burnett, J.J. & Wood. V.R. (1988) A proposed model of the donation decision process. *Research in Consumer Behavior*, 3: 1–47.

CAF UK Giving. (2017) An overview of charitable giving in the UK. Charities Aid Foundation. Retrieved from: https://www.cafonline.org/docs/default-source/about-us-publications/caf-uk-giving-web.pdf?sfvrsn=8 [accessed 20 February 2018].

Chad, P., Kyriazis, E. & Motion, J. (2013) Development of a market orientation research agenda for the nonprofit sector. *Journal of Nonprofit & Public Sector Marketing*, 25(1): 1–27.

Chapleo, C. (2013) Brand "infrastructure" in nonprofit organisations: Challenges to successful brand building? *Journal of Marketing Communications*, 21(3): 199–209.

Charity Financials. (2018) Charity Financials top 100 fundraisers spotlight. Annual Report. https://secure.charityfinancials.com/library/?pitem=charity-financials-top-100-fundraisers-spotlight-2018&_ga=2.34879522.2013720049.1545387304-1652300736.1545387300 [Accessed 20 December 2018].

Clary, E.G., Snyder, M., Ridge, R., Copeland, J., Stukas, A.A., Haugen, J. & Miene, P. (1998) Understanding and assessing the motivations of volunteers: A functional approach. *Journal of Personality and Social Psychology,* 74: 1516–1530.

Conejo, F. & Wooliscroft, B. (2015) Brands defined as semiotic marketing systems. *Journal of Macromarketing,* 35(3): 287–301.

Cugelman, B., Thelwall, M. & Dawes, P. (2011) Online interventions for social marketing health behavior change campaigns: A meta-analysis of psychological architectures and adherence factors. *Journal of Medical Internet Research,* 13(1): 17.

Danesi, M. (2004) *Messages, Signs and Meanings: A Basic Textbook in Semiotics and Communication.* Toronto, Canada: Canadian Scholars.

de Chernatony, L. & Harris, F. (2000) Developing corporate brands Through considering internal and external stakeholders. *Corporate Reputation Review,* 3: 268.

Devaney, C., Kearns, N., Fives, A., Canavan, J., Lyons R. & Eaton, P. (2015) Recruiting and retaining older adult volunteers: Implications for practice. *Journal of Nonprofit & Public Sector Marketing,* 27(4): 331–350, DOI: 10.1080/10495142.2015.1015373

Drucker, P. (1954) *The Practice of Management.* New York: Harper.

Frish, M.B. and Gerrard, M. (1981) Natural helping systems: A survey of Red Cross volunteers. *American Journal of Community Psychology,* 9: 567–579.

Geuens, M., Weijters, B. & De Wulf, K. (2009) A new measure of brand personality. International Journal of Research in Marketing, 26(2): 97–107.

Ghantous, N. (2016) The impact of services brand personality on consumer–brand relationship quality. *Services Marketing Quarterly,* 37(3): 185–199.

Giving USA. (2017) Giving USA 2017: The Annual Report on Philanthropy for the Year 2016. Retrieved from; https://givingusa.org/wp-content/uploads/2017/06/Giving-USA-2017-Infographic.jpg [accessed 12 February 2018].

Goldkind, L. & McNutt, J.G. (2014) Social media and social change: Nonprofits and using social media strategies to meet advocacy goals. In A.-M. José Antonio & L.-C. Ana María (Eds.), *ICT Management in Non-Profit Organizations* (pp. 56–72). Hershey, PA: IGI Global.

Grounds, J. & Harkness, J. (1998) Developing a brand from within: Involving employees and volunteers when developing a new brand position. *Journal of Nonprofit and Voluntary Sector Marketing,* 3(2): 179–184.

Groza, M.P. & Gordon, G.L. (2016) The effects of nonprofit brand personality and self-brand congruity on brand relationships. *Marketing Management Journal,* 26(2): 117–129.

Guntert, S.T., Neufeind, M. & Wehner, T. (2015) Motives for event volunteering: Extending the functional approach. *Nonprofit and Voluntary Sector Quarterly,* 44(4): 686–707.

Guo, C. & Saxton, G.D. (2013) Tweeting social change: How social media are changing nonprofit advocacy. *Nonprofit and Voluntary Sector Quarterly,* 43(1): 57–79.

Guy, B.S. & Patton, W.E. (1989) The marketing of altruistic causes: Understanding why people help. *Journal of Services Marketing,* 2(1): 5–16.

Hankinson, P. (2001) Brand orientation in the charity sector: A framework for discussion and research. *International Journal of Nonprofit and Voluntary Sector Marketing,* 6: 231–242.

Harris, F. & de Chernatony, L. (2001) Corporate branding and corporate brand performance. *European Journal of Marketing,* 35: 441–456.

Hay, R. (1990) *Strategic Management in Non-profit Organizations.* New York: Quorum Books.

Hou, J., Du, L. & Tian, Z. (2009) The effects of nonprofit brand equity on individual giving intention: Mediating by the self concept of individual donor. *International Journal of Nonprofit and Voluntary Sector Marketing,* 14(3): 215–229.

Hudson, J. (2008) The branding of charities. In Sargeant, A. & Wymer, W. (Eds.), *The Routledge Companion to Nonprofit Marketing* (pp. 65–74). Abingdon: Routledge.

Hume, M. & Mort, G.S. (2008) Satisfaction in performing arts: The role of value?. *European Journal of Marketing,* 42: 311–326.

Jackson, G. & Ahuja, V. (2016), Dawn of the digital age and the evolution of the marketing mix. *Journal of Direct, Data and Digital Marketing Practice,* 17: 170–186.

Kannan, P. & Lee, A. (2017) Digital marketing: A framework, review and research agenda. *International Journal of Research in Marketing,* 34: 22–45.

Kay, L. (2017) Charities failing to use internet effectively for advertising, research shows. Third Sector online: https://www.thirdsector.co.uk/charities-failing-use-internet-effectively-advertising-research-shows/communications/article/1446602 [accessed 12 February 2018].

Kemp, E. (2015) Engaging consumers in esthetic offerings: Conceptualizing and developing a measure for arts engagement. *International Journal of Nonprofit and Voluntary Sector Marketing*, 20(2): 137–148.

Kennedy, S. (1998) The power of positioning: A case history from the Children's Society. *Journal of Nonprofit and Voluntary Sector Marketing*, 3(3): 324–330.

Khazan, O. (2013) UNICEF tells slacktivists: Give money, not Facebook likes. *The Atlantic* [Online]. Retrieved from: www.theatlantic.com [accessed 10 February 2018].

Kotler, P. & Andreasen, A. (1982) *Strategic Marketing for Nonprofit Organizations*. Englewood Cliffs, NJ: Prentice-Hall.

Kotler, P. & Clarke, R.N. (1986) *Marketing for Health Care Organizations*. Englewood Cliffs, NJ: Prentice Hall.

Kotler, P. & Levy, S. (1969) Broadening the concept of marketing. *Journal of Marketing*, 33(1): 10–15.

Krug, K. & Weinberg, C. (2008) Marketing strategies and portfolio analysis. In Sargeant, A. & Wymer, W. (Eds.), *The Routledge Companion to Nonprofit Marketing* (pp. 75–91). Abingdon: Routledge.

Kulik, L. (2017) Volunteering during an emergency: A life stage perspective. *Nonprofit and Voluntary Sector Quarterly*, 46(2): 419–441.

Lovejoy, K. & Saxton, G.D. (2012) Information, community, and action: How nonprofit organizations use social media. *Journal of Computer-Mediated Communication*, 17: 337–353.

Lovejoy, K., Waters, R.D. & Saxton, G.D. (2012) Engaging stakeholders through Twitter: How nonprofit organizations are getting more out of 140 characters or less. *Public Relations Review*, 38: 313–318.

Lovelock, C.H. & Weinberg, C.B. (1990) Public and non profit marketing: Themes and issues for the 1990s. In C.H. Lovelock & C.B. Weinberg (Eds.), *Public and Non Profit Marketing* (2nd Ed.). San Francisco: Scientific Press.

Lucas, E. (2017) Reinventing the rattling tin: How UK charities use Facebook in fundraising. *International Journal of Nonprofit Voluntary Sector Marketing*, 22.

Manoff, R.K. (1985) *Social Marketing: New Imperative for Public Health*. New York: Praeger.

McCarthy, E.J. (1960) *Basic Marketing: A Managerial Approach*. Homewood, IL: Richard D. Irwin.

McCorkingdale, T., Distaso, M. & Sisco, H. (2013) How Millennials are engaging and building relationships with organizations on Facebook. *Journal of Social Media in Society*, 2, 1. Retrieved from: www.thejsms.org/tsmri/index.php/TSMRI/article/view/15 [accessed 21 December 2017].

Mokwa, M.P., Prieve, A. & Dawson, W.M. (1980) *Marketing the Arts*. Westport, CT: Praeger.

Moylan, B. (2013) The red marriage equality sign on your Facebook profile is completely useless. Vice [Online]. Retrieved from https://www.vice.Com. [accessed 20 December 2017].

M+R Benchmark Study (2017) available at: https://mrbenchmarks.com [accessed 20 December 2017].

Nonprofit Technology Network. (2012) Nonprofit social network benchmark report. Available at: www.NonprofitSocialNetworkSurvey.com

Oswald, Laura R. (2012) *Marketing Semiotics: Signs, Strategies, and Brand Value*. Oxford: Oxford University Press.

Padanyi, P. (2008) Operationalizing the marketing concept: Achieving market orientation in the nonprofit context. In A. Sargeant & W. Wymer (Eds.), *The Routledge Companion to Nonprofit Marketing* (pp. 11–27). Abingdon: Routledge.

Penner, L.A. (2002) Dispositional and organisational influences on sustained volunteerism: An interactionist perspective. *Journal of Social Issues*, 58: 447–467.

Pope, J., Sterrett Isely, E. & Asamoa-Tutu, F. (2009) Developing a marketing strategy for nonprofit organisations: An exploratory study. *Journal of Nonprofit & Public Sector Marketing*, 21(2): 184–201.

Randle, M. & Dolnicar, S. (2009) Does cultural background affect volunteering behaviour? *Journal of Nonprofit & Public Sector Marketing*, 21(2): 225–247.

Randle, M. & Dolnicar, S. (2012) Attracting volunteers in highly multicultural societies: A marketing challenge. *Journal of Nonprofit & Public Sector Marketing*, 24(4): 351–369.

Sargeant, A. (1999) *Marketing Management for Nonprofit Organizations*. Oxford: Oxford University Press.

Sargeant, A. & Jay, E. (2004) *Fundraising Management: Analysis, Planning and Practice*. London: Routledge.

Sargeant, A. & Wymer, W. (2008) *The Routledge Companion to Nonprofit Marketing*. Abingdon: Routledge.

Sargeant, A., Ford, J.B. & Hudson, J. (2008) Charity brand personality: The relationship with giving behavior. *Nonprofit and Voluntary Sector Quarterly*, 37(3): 468–491.

Sargeant, A. & Shattuck, S. (2017) Digital fundraising. In A. Sargeant, Jen Shang & Associates (Eds.), *Fundraising Principles and Practice* (2nd ed., pp. 318–359). Hoboken, NJ: John Wiley.

Saxton, G. & Guo, C. (2014) Online stakeholder targeting and the acquisition of social media capital. *International Journal of No-profit and Voluntary Sector Marketing*, 19: 286–300.

Saxton, G. & Wang, L. (2014) The social network effect: The determinants of giving through social media. *Nonprofit and Voluntary Sector Quarterly*, 43(5): 850–868.

Saxton, J. (2014) UK charities spend bulk of near £400m advertising budget on direct mail. Civil Society, https://www.civilsociety.co.uk/news/uk-charities-spend-bulk-of-near--400m-advertising-budget-on-direct-mail.html#sthash.HIllZAw1.dpuf [accessed 21 February 2018].

Statista. (2018) Number of internet users worldwide from 2005 to 2017. Statistica, The Statistic Portal. https://www.statista.com/statistics/273018/number-of-internet-users-worldwide/ [accessed 20 February].

Stride, H. & S. Lee. (2007) No logo? No way. Branding in the non-profit sector. *Journal of Marketing Management,* 23(1–2): 107–122.

Taghian, M., D'Souza, C. & Polonsky, M. (2012) A study of older Australians' volunteering and quality of life: Empirical evidence and policy implications. *Journal of Nonprofit & Public Sector Marketing,* 24(2): 101–122.

Tapp, A. (1996) Charity brands: A qualitative study of current practice. *Journal of Nonprofit and Voluntary Sector Marketing,* 1(4): 327–336.

Taylor, R. (2011) How Comic Relief has benefited from social media. [Weblog]. Retrieved from: www.redcmarketing.net/blog/onlinemarketing/how-comic-relief-has-benefited-from-social-media/ [accessed 22 February 2018].

Townsend, L. (2014) How much has the ice bucket challenge achieved? BBC News Magazine [online]. Retrieved from: www.bbc.co.uk/news/magazine-29013707 [accessed 20 February 2018].

Tuckman, H. (1998) Competition, commercialization, and the evolution of non-profit organizational structures. *Journal of Policy Analysis and Management,* 17(2): 175–194.

van Noort, G., Voorveld, H.A. & van Reijmersdal, E.A. (2012) Interactivity in brand web sites: Cognitive, affective, and behavioral responses explained by consumers' online flow experience. *Journal of Interactive Marketing,* 26: 223–234.

Waddington, J. (2013) The future of Facebook fundraising. *International Journal of Nonprofit and Voluntary Sector Marketing,* 18: 187–191.

Warnaby, G. & Finney, J. (2005) Creating customer value in the not-for-profit sector: A case study of the British Library. *International Journal of Nonprofit and Voluntary Sector Marketing,* 10(3): 183–195.

Waters, R. (2014) Overcoming nonprofit sector challenges through improved communication. *International Journal of Nonprofit and Voluntary Sector Marketing,* 19: 221–223.

Waters, R., Burnett, E., Lamm, A. & Lucas, J. (2009) Engaging stakeholders through social networking: How nonprofit organizations are using Facebook. *Public Relations Review,* 35: 102–106.

Waters, R. & Jones, P. (2011) Using video to build an organization's identity and brand: A content analysis of nonprofit organisations' YouTube videos. *Journal of Nonprofit & Public Sector Marketing,* 23(3).

Wymer, W. (2013) The influence of marketing scholarship's legacy on nonprofit marketing. *International Journal of Financial Studies,* 1: 102–118.

Wymer, W., Boenigk, S. & Möhlmann, M. (2015) The conceptualization of nonprofit marketing orientation: A critical reflection and contributions toward closing the practice–theory gap. *Journal of Nonprofit & Public Sector Marketing,* 27(2).

Zuluaga, L. & Schneider, U. (2008) Market orientation and organisational performance in the non-profit context: Exploring both concepts and the relationship between them. *Journal of Nonprofit & Public Sector Marketing,* 19(2).

26

RELATIONSHIP FUNDRAISING 2.0

Lessons from social psychology

Adrian Sargeant

DIRECTOR, INSTITUTE FOR SUSTAINABLE PHILANTHROPY, PLYMOUTH, UK

Ian MacQuillin

DIRECTOR, ROGARE: THE FUNDRAISING THINK TANK, LONDON, UK

Introduction

The concept of relationship fundraising has been around since the early 1990s. It was first mooted by British fundraiser Ken Burnett in 1992. The related concept of relationship marketing, by contrast, dates back to the 1970s where early marketing scholars realized that in business to business scenarios, price appeared to have much less significance in the securing of contracts than they imagined. Rather, buyers preferred suppliers that they had had past dealings with, since they knew how those firms operated and could presumably trust them to deliver. Early service researchers also got to that point, recognizing that in their domain service customers did not simply evaluate individual transactions but considered the experience from previous interactions too. It seemed in aggregate that the quality of supplier relationships was much more important than the cost of the product or service per se and they thus sought to explain exchange by reference to relationship variables (e.g., Anderson and Narus 1990; Berry 1983; Hakansson 1982).

Fundraisers equating relationship fundraising with relationship marketing therefore need to understand that the concept they are adopting was originally developed, not in a parallel form of consumer marketing, but rather in the business to business domain where buyers and sellers were both genuinely active in the establishment of the relationship and both believed that the partnership with the other party was genuinely important (Ford 1980; Turnbull 1979; Zeithaml, Parasuraman and Berry 1983).

It wasn't until the late 1980s when Dwyer, Schurr and Oh (1987, p.12) proposed that consumer markets might also benefit from "attention to conditions that foster relational bonds leading to reliable repeat business." It was suggested that the tools and techniques of direct marketing could facilitate such relationships but in reality they were hampered by the technology available at that time (Goldberg 1988). It wasn't until the 1990s when massive improvements in database technologies took place and barriers to access (such as price) began to lower making it possible for many businesses to maintain better records and begin to personalize interactions with their customers (Blattberg and Deighton 1991; Treacy and Wiererma 1993). New technology also made it possible to identify the most important customers on a database, calculate their lifetime

Table 26.1 Comparison of transactional and relational approaches

	Transactional	Relational
Focus	Single sales	Customer retention
Key measures	Immediate ROI, revenue, response rate	Lifetime value
Timescale	Short term	Long term
Orientation	Purchase	Relationship
Customer service	Little emphasis	Major emphasis

value (LTV) and identify and exploit potential cross-sell or up-sell opportunities (e.g., Reichheld and Sasser 1990). In short, much of consumer marketing began to undergo a transformation away from a focus on transactions to a focus on relationships, as Table 26.1 indicates.

Thus, at around the time that Ken Burnett (1992) was writing his now seminal *Relationship Fundraising* text, a similar transition towards a focus on relationships was being articulated in business to consumer marketing. Marketers and fundraisers alike were all looking for an approach to revenue generation based on a shared sense of relationship, connection, trust and commitment. For Burnett (1992, p. 25):

> [Relationship Fundraising's] overriding consideration is to care for and develop that bond [between supporter and nonprofit] and to do nothing that might damage or jeopardise it. Every activity is therefore geared toward making sure donors know they are important, valued and considered, which has the effect of maximising funds per donor in the long term.

Although a burgeoning literature now offers advice in how best to conduct relationship marketing there has been rather less interest in how to conduct relationship fundraising (Sargeant 2016); many fundraisers use the term, but there is barely any agreement on what it might actually involve (MacQuillin 2016). However, some core commonalities of what fundraisers consider to be a 'donorcentric' approach, or the donorcentric process, do exist. Research among fundraising practitioners conducted by our fundraising Think Tank Rogare in 2016 revealed the donorcentric process to be that (ibid.):

1   Fundraisers need to understand donors . . .
2   . . . so they can connect them to a cause . . .
3   . . . by focusing on the cause not the organization . . .
4   . . . and build deeper relationships with them . . .
5   . . . by using two-way communications.

Authors have of course sought to draw in ideas from the domain of relationship marketing (Sargeant and Jay 2014; Ahern and Joyaux 2012), but there has been surprisingly little interest in whether there might be additional learning from the domain of psychology, and in particular how human beings forge relationships that could offer utility for fundraisers. This seems a particular oversight since fundraising practitioners consider a core part of the donorcentric or relationship fundraising approach to donors to be to build 'deeper relationships' with them, for which social psychology would appear to provide the most suitable explanatory framework.

In this chapter, therefore, we seek to address that gap and offer insights for fundraising from the domain of social psychology that could, and perhaps should, be informing our fundraising practice.

Why do donors need relationships?

In a general sense the social psychology literature suggests that the kind of relationships we should be building with our donors are those that contribute to their sense of human wellbeing.

Psychologists, such as Ryff (1989), have in turn specified six elements that are commonly used to measure wellbeing. They are: 1. Need to make a difference; 2. Autonomy; 3. Positive relations with others; 4. Growth; 5. Purpose in life; and 6. Self-acceptance. We will elaborate on each below.

Competence: Defined as the competence to choose or create environments best suited to an individual's needs/values and where they are capable of making a desirable difference. In the context of fundraising, for example, if donors to the American Cancer Society perceive they can make a difference in finding a cure for cancer, they will experience high psychological wellbeing along this dimension. Similarly, if a disability charity's donors feel they can make a tangible difference in another human being's life by participating in a gala dinner they will experience high psychological wellbeing.

Autonomy: Defined as a sense of self-determination and the ability to resist social pressures to think and act in certain ways. An individual would experience a high degree of autonomy if they perceive that they have selected a new and innovative form of giving to participate in. They will also experience higher autonomy if they are in some sense in control of their own experience and in the context of fundraising from their peers have options around who to ask and how.

Connectedness: Defined as the need that people have for warm, satisfying and trusting relationships with others (Deci and Ryan 2011). These others might be charity personnel, volunteers, beneficiaries or other donors. The greater the sense of connection that one might engender the higher the psychological wellbeing along this dimension.

Growth: Defined as a feeling of continued development, realizing one's own potential, seeing oneself as growing and expanding, seeing improvement in self and behavior over time, being open to new experiences, and changing in ways that reflect more self-knowledge and effectiveness. Many different kinds of events have a clear potential to contribute to an individual's growth as individuals master a new level of fitness, for example, or wrestle with one of the world's great causes or issues.

Purpose in life: Defined as having goals for the future of one's life and a strong sense of direction. Research indicates that the clearer one's life purpose is the higher one experiences psychological wellbeing (e.g., Reker, Peacock and Wong 1987; Ryff 1989; Ryff and Keyes 1995). A relationship with a nonprofit can help define or fulfill an individual's purpose (or express it). Our research suggests that the more inclusive one's life purpose becomes of the needs of others (and ideally humanity) the greater will be the experience of wellbeing (Shang and Sargeant 2017).

Self-acceptance: Defined as the ability to experience positive feelings about their sense of self in the past. Looking back, can we accept the selves we have been? The more integrated our sense of self is of all our life experiences; the higher self-acceptance we will experience (Ryff and Essex 1992). Fundraising might thus encourage the sharing of life stories, or telling of stories that a donor may be able to identify with, because they too may have had similar experiences. Sharing how others have accepted their sense of self might potentially prompt others to do likewise.

Fundraisers tend to focus on the needs of the beneficiary and so the materials they produce tend to communicate those beneficiary needs to individuals who might be willing to give to support them (MacQuillin, Sargeant and Shang 2016; Shang and Sargeant 2017). This may be a smart approach in the context of new donor acquisition where the focus in the relationship is on the relationship target (be it the beneficiary, the organization, the cause, the mission). But while individuals' working models of others are more salient during initial attraction, their own working model of self is more salient during relationship building (Holmes and Johnson 2009). Once a charity has delivered a satisfying first gift experience, social psychology research predicts that they will begin to transition their focus of attention in deriving satisfaction in the relationship from "how attractive the nonprofit is" to "what needs this relationship can fulfill for them." In short, they will experience higher satisfaction in longer-term relationships if the needs we outline above are met.

So fundraisers need to choose their relationship target carefully, beginning with the first contact. It needs to be chosen such that that relationship has the biggest potential for deepening, is most likely to consistently meet the donors' most important needs over the longest period and has the lowest cost to maintain.

Building commitment

However, satisfaction alone does not fully explain why people would want to remain in or build a relationship. Caryl Rusbult (Rusbult, Agnew and Arriaga 2011, p. 5) found two more factors determining the strength and quality of romantic relationships (ibid., p. 3): size of past investment and absence of alternatives or the existence of only poor quality alternatives.

Size of past investment, in a relationship context, refers to the value of sunk costs put into the relationship – the amount of tangible and intangible resources (in a romantic context this might include time, effort, mutual friends, reputation) that a person has contributed to the relationship and therefore stands to lose or have diminished in value if the relationship breaks down (Rusbult et al. 2011, p. 22). Investments are defined as: "The magnitude and importance of the resources that are attached to a relationship – resources that would decline in value or be lost if the relationship were to end" (Rusbult, Martz and Agnew 1998, p. 359).

In making the first gift, it is not only the amount of money that people give (tangible investment) that matters, it is also how people feel towards the beneficiaries or about the case for support (an intangible) that would be factored into one's calculation of 'investment.' So the stronger the case for the support, the more intangible investment donors would have made into their relationship from the outset.

The theory suggests that people may remain committed to an unsatisfactory relationship (i.e., low satisfaction levels) that they would prefer to leave, because leaving would incur "unacceptably high costs" (ibid.) – for example, mental trauma to any children involved in an acrimonious divorce. Similarly, happy relationships (i.e., high levels of satisfaction) are not always stable and long-lasting (Crisp and Turner 2014, p. 417) because they could potentially be too costly to maintain.

Need-to-Belong theory posits that humans do not only have the need to form relationships, but they also have the need to maintain them (Baumeister and Leary 1995). So once people have made a donation to a charity, stopping giving could be experienced as a loss for them psychologically. So once fundraisers secure the first gift, securing the second gift could be understood as a process of "preventing" a sense of loss for donors. The higher the monetary and emotional investment donors put into their first gift, the bigger a loss of sunk cost their second gift has to save.

Absence or poor quality of alternatives, in a relationship context refers to the availability of alternatives if a person should leave the relationship – in other words, could higher levels of satisfaction be obtained from alternative relationship partners. These need not be new romantic partners; it could mean only hanging out with friends rather than going home (or indeed having no relationship at all) (Rusbult et al. 1998): "The more compelling the alternatives are viewed, the less committed one will be to the current partner. If alternatives are not perceived as particularly attractive, one will be more committed to the current partner" (Agnew 2009, p. 246).

In the context of romantic relationships, what this means is that feeling satisfied with only the focal relationship is not sufficient for someone to stay in or build that relationship. In deciding if one is satisfied *enough* to stay with a current romantic partner, an individual will compare all the outcomes from the current relationship against all the outcomes and interactions received in previous romantic relationships or other concurrent relationships (like friendships). If current outcomes exceed those of past or current experiences, that person will be satisfied with their relationship; if they fall short of past outcomes, he/she will be dissatisfied (Agnew 2009, p. 246). Past relationship experiences thus create expectations for a given domain of relationship behavior (ibid.). So creating a high satisfaction in one focal charity is not good enough, the focal charity must provide the most satisfied experience that a donor is currently receiving.

The three factors of satisfaction, investment size and alternative availability have been widely empirically validated (Agnew, Arriaga and Wilson 2008, p. 153). Collectively, they account for an average of 61.2 percent of the variance in commitment (Le and Agnew 2003). This means if fundraisers can take care of donors' satisfaction, secure the highest tangible and intangible investment from the individual, and ensure they are the best alternative amongst donors' entire choice set, then they would have secured 60 percent of all the potential for these donors to commit to a relationship with them. This 'commitment level' (Rusbult et al. 1998, p. 359) is defined as "The intent to persist in a relationship, including long-term orientation toward the involvement as well as feelings of psychological attachment."

A recent study extended the concept of investment from past investment to future investments. Goodfriend and Agnew (2008) came up with four types of investments:

- Past tangible investment (such as shared debts, pets, jointly purchased items);
- Past intangible investment (such as self-disclosures, effort and time);
- Planned tangible investment;
- Planned intangible investment.

It showed that both types of intangible investment were much stronger predictors of commitment than past tangible investments, and planned tangible investments had their own significant effect to predict commitment. Second, the study found that both forms of planned investment were significant predictors of commitment above and beyond past tangible but not past intangible investments (ibid., p. 1646).

If all types of investments are taken into account and the most important people (e.g., their family and friends) in our donors' lives agree with our donors' perception, the overall model accounts for more than 75 percent of the variance in commitment (Agnew et al. 2008, p. 161; Rusbult et al. 2011, p. 20). This is an additional 15 percent increase in comparison to the 61.2 percent variance accounted for by the three elements of satisfaction, past investment and alternatives (Le and Agnew 2003). This means if fundraisers can encourage donors to reflect on how much they would like to contribute to the charity in the future (planned future investment) and how much making a potential impact with their gifts mean to them (emotional investment), then they have the potential to increase their donors' commitment beyond the level determined by donors' past satisfaction, past investment and available alternatives. This learning is powerful because fundraisers cannot change what happened in the past and cannot change what others do, but they can engage their donors in planning for the future and hopefully help them feel good about it when they do.

If fundraisers can consistently make donors feel that this future planning meets their need to be a competent person to act in their love for others, and if they are the only relationship that the donors have in order to feel this way, then donors will become dependent on them to meet these needs. The same longing after the first gift can thus be strengthened through every follow-up interaction created for them. When this happens, psychologists predict that donors will then seek more interactions (Rusbult et al. 2011, p. 4) (e.g., look up your event notices, sign up on your Facebook, follow your tweets) and commit even more to this relationship (Thibaut and Kelley 1959; Rusbult et al. 1998, p. 359).

How do people know when their needs are met by a relationship?

All the above theories seem to assume that donors know when a particular need is met. Similarly, they assume that donors know which relationship is meeting which one of their needs, how dependable these relationships are in meeting these needs and how committed they should therefore be to maintaining and/or building these relationships.

It turns out that people are better at telling when their lower levels needs are met, such as detecting when they are full versus when they are hungry, when they are sheltered versus when they are sleeping in the rain, when they feel safe or unsafe at home. People are not as good at articulating what their higher level needs are and determining when they are fulfilled. These needs include the ones we articulated above. When people are unsure about what is important they look into their closest relationships for insights. Charities could potentially become a source of insight that donors might rely on.

Deepening the relationship

Self-verification theory (Swann 1983, 1999) says that people can always feel better if others important to them see them in the same way they see themselves. That is they would like to experience consistency in their lives, and the role of others in close relationships with them is simply to confirm what they know already about themselves.

This could be one reason why a vast literature has identified that people are generally attracted to others who are similar to them (Brewer, Brewer and De Paul 1968): Actual similarity between partners is correlated with how attached people actually feel to the partner. In addition, research indicates how ideally similar one would like to be with another has additional predictive power on how they will eventually feel about the relationship. This ideal will then in turn influence how people behave towards others, by, for example, increasing the frequency of their communication, applying more effort to get to know someone, or selectively rehearsing and thus remembering the good contacts they have had in the past with their partner and forgetting about the bad ones (Gagné and Lydon 2004).

So if physical attractions give us the chance for a gift and satisfaction/commitment is key in maintaining and building a relationship, intimacy in an interpersonal relationship context allows *two people to validate all components of personal worth* (Sullivan 1953, p. 246). It is a "collaboration" in which "both partners reveal themselves, and seek and express validation of each other's attributes" (Reis and Shaver 1988, p. 369). Reis and Shaver (1988) developed a model of intimacy that argued that the most intimate relationships are those that are caring, understood and involve validation.

When partners sense that they mutually foster these three factors, they become more aware that their relationship is intimate and become more committed to it (ibid., p. 385). Intimate partners are also more likely to develop a sense of "we-ness," first because of a sense of "mutuality" in that each partner shares the other's experiences and, second, because they recognize that there are common assumptions and understandings about the relationship (ibid., p. 384). Intimate relationships are also typically more reciprocal (ibid.).

Self-disclosure has been called the "central defining attribute" of an intimate relationship (Waring et al. 1980), including:

- cognitive self-disclosure – the revelation of private thoughts and ideas (Chelune et al. 1984);
- affective self-disclosure – the revelation of feelings (Stern 1997, p. 10).

The constraints that communication costs impose on fundraising activities dictate that historically mass and largely one-way communication has been the dominant paradigm. What the relationship literature tells us is that we should develop two-way communication opportunities – which relationship fundraising practitioners identified as the way to 'deepen' relationships with donors in the donorcentric process (MacQuillin 2016) – personalize our communications with our donors, prioritize what we ask our donors to disclose and identify the best personal responses to such disclosures.

When facing a limited budget, we may choose between asking for cognitive disclosure (as in many donor surveys) versus asking for affective disclosure (currently rarely done except for telemarketing calls especially in those made for legacies). Both are necessary in building intimacy. One could choose for each communication to focus on only one type of disclosure or both. We would recommend that fundraisers choose based on how they intend to personalize the responses. When asked for cognitive disclosure, donors need to know they are heard and understood; when asked for affective disclosure, donors need to know their feelings are cared for. Unless one can effectively and efficiently make donors feel both, one might be better off focusing on one type of disclosure at a time.

If one were to go down the route of cognitive disclosure, one may choose to ask questions in the way suggested by Social Penetration Theory (Altman and Taylor 1973). It describes how the process of self-disclosure increases intimacy in a close relationship through a process of feedback: if, when a person reveals information about themselves, this is received positively, it encourages them to self-disclose more intimate details over time (Baack, Fogliasso and Harris 2000, pp. 39–40). The process is enhanced if both parties feel positively about the relationship, with the relational partner 'matching' the other's disclosures and the result is a "greater willingness to reveal items closer to the central core of one's personality" (ibid., p. 40). As time goes on, people disclose ever more intimate (deeper) information about themselves, from matters such as dress style at the most superficial level to their innermost fears and self-concept at the deepest level of disclosure (ibid.). As disclosure is a matter of going through ever-deeper layers, Social Penetration Theory is often referred to as the 'onion theory of personality' (ibid.).

Willingness to disclose is influenced by three factors (ibid., pp. 40–42):

- Personal characteristics
- Assessment of rewards and costs
- Situational context.

Personal characteristics. The broad topics individuals might disclose information about – e.g., politics, sport, religion, personal ethics, etc. – are known as 'breadth categories.' Each breadth category has a depth associated with it, indicating how far into the 'onion' a person is prepared to disclose about this subject.

Rewards and costs. As is common to social exchange theories, relational partners review anticipated costs and rewards before disclosing. Disclosure, and greater intimacy, results if the rewards are perceived to outweigh the costs.

Situational context. The breadth and depth of disclosure depends on the relationship stage. The theory states that social penetration moves most quickly at the early stages of a relationship, with shallow depth penetration of the outer layers, but after that it slows considerably.

What this suggests is that if one were to conduct donor surveys, the earlier they could be conducted, the greater the value that could be derived from the disclosure. Questions can be posed in such a way that extend on either breadth or depth.

Research has shown that intimacy increases in the early stages of a relationship, as disclosure increases (e.g., Laurenceau, Barrett and Pietromonaco 1998). However, too much information disclosed too quickly at the start of a relationship can scare off a potential partner, causing them to emotionally withdraw from the developing relationship if they are not ready to reciprocate or match the level of disclosure (Crisp and Turner 2014, p. 399).

The way to structure one's questions at early stages is thus to focus on breadth building questions, because we know people will not feel the need to withdraw from disclosure when we are not "looking" too deep. So we maximize the utility of breadth disclosure. We then have very few depth questions at the end, but donors are not "forced" to respond to them. If they choose to do so, then we build the connection with them, and if not, we have ended their disclosure at a level that they are comfortable with. When donors choose to end their disclosure, the information could then be used as a segmentation variable to help us design future communications with our donors.

Once a certain level of intimacy is reached, self-disclosure plateaus during the middle phase of the relationship and decreases (depenetration) as the relationship comes to an end (ibid.).

Many fundraisers feel uncomfortable about asking donors for their personal views on things, especially when such personal views are highly emotional or perceived as being too personal (deep). We would encourage fundraisers to reflect on who the relationship partner is that makes the ask, the environment in which the question is asked, who the fundraiser is asking it from and what stage they have reached in their relationship.

The role of similarity

"Similarity-attraction" is the second most robust finding in attraction research (Tidwell, Eastwick and Finkel 2013). To take a fundraising example, similarity attraction could be one of the many reasons why in the domain of major gifts, major gifts are usually solicited by peers who are like their donors. The additional insights that we can gain by looking more deeply at the different types of similarities may help us structure such encounters. Surface level similarity (such as gender, age, ethnicity) leads one to infer deeper level similarity during the initial encounter (Harrison, Price and Bell 1998). In the long run however, it is deep level similarity that determines performance outcomes (ibid.). Surface level similarities can increase the quality of experience during initial encounters, because it increases initial attraction. What fundraisers need to do to deepen the relationship is to find individuals to interact with the donor who are similar to him/her at deep levels in their beliefs, values, and meanings in life.

Similarity is also important in direct response relationships e.g., relationships conducted by mail or email. The impact of similarity in domains including moral, political, religious, social and philosophic issues, which have been thought to reflect one's core attitudes and values, have been thoroughly tested in the 1980s (Jamieson, Lydon and Zanna 1987). This work highlights that donors have to agree with what you believe in, but if one wants to deepen their feeling of perceived similarity one might also talk about activities that the organization (and possibly other stakeholders) might share with the donor that fundamentally express those beliefs. One might even invent activities that allow the donor to see the depth of the similarity in those beliefs.

To take a further fundraising example, while acquisition events (initiating relationships) aim to create the right arousal level to increase initial attraction, development events should aim to create the opportunities necessary to deepen perceived similarity, build deeper intimacy and increase how satisfied supporters are in experiencing a fulfilled life.

The limitation of self-verification theory to fulfill higher level needs for human fulfillment is that similarity (be it surface level or deep level) does not allow sufficient room for creative growth, or growth beyond the individual's own imagination. Similar individuals end up in the same social groups of similar others. Even when individuals find others with similar ideals to them, they are limiting their growth potential to those with the same ideals.

Self-enhancement theory (Murray, Holmes and Griffin 1996; Morling and Epstein 1997) tells us that people seek partners who view them as favorably as possible. Now, the growth potential expands to anything imaginable by others that might connect with us in life. So can charities help individuals stretch their potential? If so, what kind of potential is most productive for fundraising purposes?

Katz and Beach (2000) tell us that people are most likely to seek partners who give them both verification and enhancement, and that in the absence of the latter, they seek the former. That is they would only actively look for others who see themselves in the same way they do, when they cannot find those who see them as favorably as possible. If charities constantly inspire their donors to become the very best they can, they will become their best source for living a more fulfilled life.

Thus a key question in development communications becomes how fundraisers can stretch their donors' imagination about just how good a human being they can be?

Conclusions

Everything we know about how to build a good relationship as a parent or a friend, we can apply to relationship fundraising. When we build our fundraising relationships in the same way we build all other relationships, we are more likely to succeed. This chapter has highlighted a number of approaches that might offer utility for fundraisers:

1   Donor relationships should be engineered to offer the greatest value for supporters. From the science of human wellbeing we highlight the idea that fundraisers can enhance feelings of wellbeing through their fundraising activity. Notable here are the needs donors have for competence, autonomy, connectedness and growth. In simple terms how we make our donors feel should be as critical an issue in fundraising as the impact we have on our beneficiaries.

2   Fundraisers also need to give greater consideration to the focus of the relationship. Is the primary relationship with other donors, the organization itself or its beneficiaries? Clarity in this respect allows fundraisers to focus on developing the sense of connectedness the donor

might feel with the focal other. Relationships are only experienced as fulfilling if this sense of connectedness is provided.

3   In seeking to build commitment donors should be encouraged to reflect not only on the contributions they have made in the past but also on the contributions they might wish to make in the future. While fundraisers cannot change what has happened in the past to shape a donor's relationship, they can help shape how a donor sees their relationship developing in the future. This can significantly increase commitment.

4   As they reflect on how they might want to support the organization in the future it would seem similarly smart to have them reflect on how this will build their personal competence to act in their love of others. If the nonprofit can assist individuals in developing that competence, theory suggests that the donor will come to rely on the nonprofit to fulfill, that basic need and stay supporting as a consequence.

5   Fundraisers must be cognizant of how the drivers of satisfaction change by relationship stage. Lower and then higher order needs are important as the relationship progresses. This suggests a variable that might be used for the purposes of segmentation.

6   It should be noted, however, that individuals only exhibit competence in detecting when their lower order needs are met. As a consequence individuals in longer term relationships need not only to have their higher level needs met, but communications can also assist donors in reflecting on what those higher level needs might be and how well they are doing in each respect.

7   The concept of intimacy is also a fertile area for fundraising thought and innovation. The sector does work on soliciting 'disclosures', typically about the work of the organization and the significance of the needs of its beneficiaries or (in enlightened) organizations, donors. Encouraging donors to participate in affective self-disclosure and responding appropriately when this takes place would significantly impact retention.

8   If intimacy is pursued as a strategy, it would seem wise to be mindful of the stage of the relationship a given individual might be in and to structure survey approaches to reflect this dimension, balancing the dimensions we identified earlier of breadth and depth.

9   Perceived similarity is also a core issue in retention. In seeking to build loyalty, charities should reflect on how the donor can be encouraged to see similarities between themselves and the focal other (the beneficiary, the organization, another donor, etc.). Our review suggests that merely exposing donors to the values of the organization is not enough. They need to be encouraged to participate in activities that allow them to experience the similar beliefs and values being applied. Words alone may be insufficient.

10 Self-enhancement theory also suggests that similarity, while powerful, is not enough. Rather than merely reflecting who a donor is in our communications we should be reflecting equally on who that donor could be, stretching their sense of who they might need to be to live a fulfilled life.

Relationship fundraising will only succeed as a strategy when nonprofits are clear about the nature of the exchange and the role that they can play in allowing their donors to lead a fulfilled life. Echoing an earlier point, as a sector we need to care at least as much about how we impact the lives of our supporters as we do about how we impact the lives of our beneficiaries.

References

Agnew, Christopher. (2009) Commitment, theories and typologies. In H. Reis & S. Sprecher (Eds.), *Encyclopedia of Human Relationships* (pp. 246–249). Thousand Oaks, CA: Sage. doi: http://dx.doi.org/10.4135/9781412958479.n83

Agnew, C.R., Arriaga, X.B., & Wilson, J.E. (2008) Committed to what? Using the bases of relational commitment model to understand continuity and changes in social relationships. In J.P. Forgas & J. Fitness (Eds.), *Social Relationships: Cognitive, Affective and Motivational Processes* (pp.147–164). New York: Psychology Press.

Ahern, T., & Joyaux, S. (2012) *Keep Your Donors: The Guide to Better Communications & Stronger Relationships*. New York: Wiley.

Altman, I., & Taylor, D.A. (1973) *Social Penetration: The Development of Interpersonal Relationships*. New York: Holt, Rinehart & Winston.

Anderson, J.C., & Narus, J.A. (1990) A model of distributor firm and manufacturing firm working partnerships. *Journal of Marketing*, 54, 42–58.

Baack, D., Fogliasso, C., & Harris, J. (2000) The personal impact of ethical decisions: A social penetration theory. *Journal of Business Ethics*, 24(1), 39–49.

Baumeister, Roy F., & Leary, Mark R. (1995) The need to belong: Desire for interpersonal attachments as a fundamental human motivation. *Psychological Bulletin*, 117(3), 497–529.

Berry, L.L. (1983) Relationship marketing. In L.L. Berry, G.L. Shostack, & Upah, G.D. (Eds.), *Emerging Perspectives on Services Marketing* (pp. 25–28). Chicago: American Marketing Association.

Blattberg, R.C., & Deighton, J. (1991) Interactive marketing: Exploiting the age of addressability. *Sloan Management Review*, Fall, 5–14.

Brewer, Robert E., Brewer, Marilynn B., & De Paul, U. (1968) Attraction and accuracy of perception in Dyads. *Journal of Personality and Social Psychology*, 8(2), 188–193.

Burnett, K. (1992) *Relationship Fundraising*. London: White Lion Press.

Chelune, Gordon J., Robison, Joan T., & Kommor, Martin J. (1984) A cognitive interactional model of intimate relationships. In Valerian J. Derlega (Ed.), *Communicating, Intimacy, and Close Relationships* (pp. 11–40). Orlando, FL: Academic Press.

Crisp, Richard J., & Turner, Rhiannon N. (2014) *Essential Social Psychology*, 3rd Edition. London: Sage.

Deci, E.L., & Ryan, R.M. (2011) Self-determination theory. In P. van Lange, A. Kruglanski, & E. Tory Higgins (Eds.), *Handbook of Theories of Social Psychology: Volume One* (pp. 416–437). London: Sage.

Dwyer, F., Schurr, P., & Oh, S. (1987) Developing buyer–seller relationships. *Journal of Marketing*, 51(2), 11–27.

Ford, D. (1980) *Understanding Business Markets: Interaction, Relationships, Networks*. London: Harcourt Brace.

Gagné, Faby M., & Lydon, John E. (2004) Bias and accuracy in close relationships: An integrative review. *Personality and Social Psychology Review*, 6(4), 322–338.

Goldberg, B. (1988) Relationship marketing. *Direct Marketing*, 51(6), 103–105.

Goodfriend, W., & Agnew, C.R. (2008) Sunken costs and desired plans: Examining different types of investments in close relationships. *Personality and Social Psychology Bulletin*, 34, 1639–1652.

Hakansson, H. (1982) *International Marketing and Purchasing of Industrial Goods: An Interaction Approach*. Chichester: John Wiley.

Harrison, David A., Price Kenneth, H., & Bell, Myrtle. (1998) Beyond relational demography: Time and the effects of surface- and deep-level diversity on work group cohesion. *Academy of Management Journal*, 41(1), 96–107.

Holmes, Bjarne M., & Johnson, Kimberly R. (2009) Adult attachment and romantic partner preference: A review. *Journal of Social and Personal Relationships*, 26(6–7), 833–852.

Jamieson, David W., Lydon, John E., & Zanna, Mark P. (1987) Attitude and activity preference similarity: Differential bases of interpersonal attraction for low and high self-monitors. *Journal of Personality and Social Psychology*, 53(6), 1052–1060.

Katz, Jennifer & Beach, Steven R.H. (2000) Looking for Love? Self-verification and self-enhancement effects on initial romantic attraction. *Personality and Social Psychology Bulletin*, 26(12), 1526–1539.

Laurenceau, J.P., Barrett, L.F., & Pietromonaco, P.R. (1998) Intimacy as an interpersonal process: The importance of self-disclosure, partner disclosure, and perceived partner responsiveness in interpersonal exchanges. *Journal of Personality and Social Psychology*, 74(5), 1238.

Le, B., & Agnew, C.R. (2003) Commitment and its theorized determinants: A meta-analysis of the Investment Model. *Personal Relationships*, 10, 37–57.

MacQuillin, I. (2016) *Relationship Fundraising: Where Do We Go from Here? Vol. 3 – Trends and challenges identified by practitioners*. Plymouth: Hartsook Centre for Sustainable Philanthropy, Plymouth University.

MacQuillin, I., Sargeant, A., & Shang, J. (2016) *Relationship Fundraising: Where Do We Go from Here? Volume 2 – Review of theory from social psychology*. Plymouth: Centre for Sustainable Philanthropy, Plymouth University.

Morling, Beth & Symour, Epstein. (1997) Compromises produced by the dialectic between self-verification and self-enhancement. *Journal of Personality and Social Psychology*, 73(6), 1268–1283.

Murray, S.L., Holmes, J.G., & Griffin, D.W. (1996) The self-fulfilling nature of positive illusions in romantic relationships: Love is not blind, but prescient. *Journal of Personality and Social Psychology*, 71, 1155–1180.

Reichheld, F.F., & Sasser, W.E. (1990) Zero defections: Quality comes to services. *Harvard Business Review*, Sept.–Oct., 105–111.

Reis, H.T., & Shaver, P. (1988) Intimacy as an interpersonal process. In Steve Duck et al. (Eds.), *Handbook of Personal Relationships* (pp. 367–389). Chichester: John Wiley.

Reker, G.T. Peacock, E.J., & Wong, P.T. (1987) Meaning and purpose in life and wellbeing: A life-span perspective. *Journal of Gerontology*, 42, 44–49.

Rusbult, Caryl E., Agnew, Christopher, & Arriaga, Ximena. (2011) The Investment Model of Commitment Processes. Purdue University, Department of Psychological Sciences Faculty Publications. Paper 26. http://docs.lib.purdue.edu/psychpubs/26

Rusbult, C.E., Martz, J.M., & Agnew, C.R. (1998) The Investment Model Scale: Measuring commitment level, satisfaction level, quality of alternatives, and investment size. *Personal Relationships*, 5, 357–391.

Ryff, C.D. (1989) Happiness is everything, or is it? Explorations on the meaning of psychological wellbeing. *Journal of Personality and Social Psychology*, 57(6),1069–1081.

Ryff, C.D., & Essex, M.J. (1992) Psychological well-being in adulthood and old age: Descriptive markers and explanatory processes. In K.W. Schaie & M.P. Lawton (Eds.), *Annual Review of Gerontology and Geriatrics* (Vol. 11, pp. 144–171). New York: Springer.

Ryff, C.D., & Keyes, C.L.M. (1995) The structure of psychological wellbeing revisited. *Journal of Personality and Social Psychology*, 69(4), 719–727.

Sargeant, A. (2016) *Relationship Fundraising: Where Do We Go from Here? Vol 1 – Review of theory from relationship marketing.* Plymouth: Hartsook Centre for Sustainable Philanthropy, Plymouth University.

Sargeant, A., & Jay, E. (2014) *Fundraising Management* (3rd Edition). London: Routledge.

Shang, J., & Sargeant, A. (2017) *Tomorrow's Philanthropy.* London: Resource Alliance.

Stern, B.B. (1997) Advertising intimacy: Relationship marketing and the services consumer. *Journal of Advertising*, 26(4), 7–19.

Sullivan, H.S. (1953) The Interpersonal Theory of Psychiatry. New York: Norton.

Swann, W.B., Jr. (1983) Self-verification: Bringing social reality into harmony with the self. In J. Suls & A.G. Greenwald (Eds.), *Psychological Perspectives on the Self* (Vol. 2, pp. 33–66). Hillsdale, NJ: Erlbaum.

Swann, W. Jr. (1999) *Resilient Identities: Self, Relationships, and the Construction of Social Reality.* New York: Basic Books.

Thibaut, J.W., & Kelley, H.H. (1959) *The Social Psychology of Groups.* New York: Wiley.

Tidwell, Natasha D., Eastwick, Paul W., & Finkel, Eli J. (2013) Perceived, not actual, similarity predicts initial attraction in a live romantic context: Evidence from the speed-dating paradigm. *Personal Relationships*, 20(2), 199–215.

Treacy, M., & Wieserma, F. (1993) Customer intimacy and other value disciplines. *Harvard Business Review*, 71(1), 84–93.

Turnbull, P.W. (1979) Roles of personal contacts in industrial export marketing. *Scandinavian Journal of Management*, 7, 325–339.

Waring, E.M., Tillman, M.P., Frelick, L., Russell, L., & Weisz, G. (1980) Concepts of intimacy in the general population. *Journal of Nervous and Mental Disease*, 168 (August), 471–474.

Zeithaml, V.H., Parasuraman, A., & Berry, L.L. (1983) Problems and strategies in services marketing. *Journal of Marketing*, 49 (Spring), 33–46.

PART V

Funding sources

27

INDIVIDUAL GIVING AND PHILANTHROPY

Beth Breeze

DIRECTOR, CENTRE FOR PHILANTHROPY, UNIVERSITY OF KENT, CANTERBURY, UK

Introduction

Philanthropic giving by individuals, which includes small donations as well as major gifts, is of considerable interest to managers of nonprofit organizations. It is typically viewed as a greatly desired yet elusive source of income. Most major nonprofits employ specialist fundraising staff to foster and facilitate philanthropic support from individuals, and many smaller nonprofits commit some time and energy, even if no dedicated staff and little budget is available for this undertaking.

This chapter will begin by reflecting on the importance of individual philanthropy and considering our contemporary awareness and understanding within a historical context. It then moves on to discuss definitional issues, examining how individual philanthropy differs from institutionalized philanthropy, as well as from closely related concepts such as charity and volunteering. Data on the global scale and contribution of individual philanthropic acts will then be presented, followed by a summary of what is known about donor motivation and how this knowledge is operationalized by fundraisers who seek to encourage and facilitate individual philanthropy. This chapter ends with a discussion of the changing nature of individual philanthropists, and highlights the lack of consistency in how nonprofits and donors view individual philanthropy.

The importance of individual philanthropy

The degree of interest and aspiration invested in achieving success with this funding stream is understandable. In those countries in which private philanthropy is identified as the primary source of funding for the nonprofit sector (Salamon and Anheier, 1998) the vast majority of that private giving comes from individual donors rather than from institutional donors, which includes charitable trusts and foundations, as well as corporations. For example in the US, 80 per cent of total donated income comes from individuals (a combination of 72 per cent from living individuals and 8 per cent from charitable bequests), whereas only 15 per cent of annual total charitable giving comes from charitable foundations and just 5 per cent is from corporations (all figures from Giving USA Foundation, 2017). This is even more remarkable when we consider the extent of public and media interest in certain institutional donors such as the Bill and Melinda Gates Foundation, yet in 2017 that foundation spent around $9 billion, compared to $282 billion donated collectively by individuals in the US, meaning that the mass of people gave $31 for every $1 spent by the world's biggest – and arguably most highly scrutinized – grant-making foundation.

Yet it is not only the *quantities* of individual philanthropy that matter, but also its *qualities* are highly valued. Unlike government contracts and corporate sponsorship, where the recipient charity must deliver specific outputs as stipulated in the agreement, there has traditionally been more flexibility in the use of income from individual donors. Therefore this funding stream is particularly valued as a means of securing general revenue to pay for core costs such as rent, utilities and salaries. Furthermore, income from philanthropic donations is often a key source of funding available for innovative and riskier work (Starr, 2011; Acs, 2013). Such 'unrestricted' income is thus highly valued by nonprofit organizations, to the extent that charities have been found to value funds they can spend as they deem appropriate, twice as much as they value restricted funds (nfpSynergy, 2018). However, some individual donors – especially those making major gifts – may also prefer to earmark their contribution for specific projects and programmes. The current dominant fundraising paradigm of 'relationship fundraising' advocates gift designation (i.e. assigning donations for specific expenditures) because it is thought to be more appealing to donors and more likely to result in repeat gifts (Burk, 2003: 86–87; Mohan and Breeze, 2016: 106).

Awareness and understanding of individual philanthropy over time

Individual philanthropic acts have been present in all historical eras and in every geographical region, and are encouraged by every major religion (Ilchman et al., 1998) as well as being a core component of secular humanitarianism. Philanthropy is a long-standing and essential aspect of human life that touches most people's lives at some point because,

> societies rely on philanthropy to address some of their most vexing social problems, to do some of their most urgent public work, and to express some of their most heartfelt beliefs and values.
>
> *(Moody and Breeze, 2016: xi)*

The first decades of the 21st century have seen an increasing profile for philanthropy worldwide (Phillips and Jung, 2016), as well as the emergence of new actors and new tools that are described as re-shaping global philanthropy (Dietel, 2014; Salamon, 2014). Not all of these developments relate solely to the individuals involved in philanthropy, as the so-called "new frontiers of philanthropy" also refer to changes occurring amongst institutional donors, as well as a shift towards collaborations between the philanthropy, public and private sectors (Salamon, 2014; futureagenda, 2018). Yet individuals continue to be the most obvious 'face' of philanthropy, and public awareness is focused on individual donors rather than their institutional, or cross-sectoral, counterparts. For example, in 2006 *Time* magazine named three philanthropists as its "Persons of the Year": the Irish rock star Bono plus Microsoft founder Bill Gates and his wife Melinda. To claim that philanthropists – rather than politicians, industrialists or international statesmen – best fulfilled the criteria of having "done the most to influence the events of the year", was a defining moment in attracting attention to the activities and personalities of philanthropists. Later that same year, in June 2006, the world's then-second richest man, Warren Buffett, announced he was donating almost all of his $40 billion fortune to the philanthropic foundation run by the world's richest man, Bill Gates, who had recently declared his intention to retire from business to focus on philanthropy. These acts sealed the perception that the philanthropic tradition had been "revived and reinvented" and led some to suggest that philanthropy has become an integral part of being rich in the 21st century (Bishop and Green, 2008: 3, 46). Relatedly, it is noteworthy that discussions of international politics and global business issues now routinely incorporate consideration of the role of philanthropy, for example it is now common for major philanthropists to feature on panels at the annual World Economic Forum held in Davos, Switzerland.

The current important role of philanthropy is best described as a 'reinvention' because philanthropic activity has been more important than state action for most of human history. Individual donors provided the primary response to problems such as poverty and illness, as well as meeting the need for education, culture and the betterment of society, until at least the 17th century (see, for example, Owen, 1965; Prochaska, 1990; Cunningham and Innes, 1998). A confounding factor in achieving a meaningful understanding of the remit and impact of individual philanthropy over time is that it has encompassed such a wide range of disparate activity, from giving a small coin to a beggar to founding an expensive institution such as a hospital (see, for example, Andrews, 1950: 19). Capturing a comprehensive account of the scope and scale of historic individual philanthropy is riven with difficulty because no records exist of informal almsgiving. Even for those donations where a paper trail exists such as charitable legacies, as used in a study of historic English philanthropy (Jordan, 1959), we must contend with vague and unquantifiable directions in wills including items of unknown economic value donated to unknown others with subjective motivations, such as "a sheep" given "for the pleasure of almighty god" (as described in Goose, 2006). Thus we must tread carefully when claiming that any particular period represents a 'golden age' in individual philanthropy – be it during the Victorian period in England, early 20th-century US or contemporary 21st-century society.

Rather than grapple with historical unknowns, we move instead to consider how individual philanthropy differs from institutionalized philanthropy, as well as from closely related concepts such as charity and volunteering.

Definitions and closely related concepts

Whilst it is relatively easy to point to long-standing evidence of philanthropic activity, from the enormous – and enormously expensive – cathedrals built across northern Europe during the Middle Ages, to the recent expansion of food banks across many countries pursuing austerity policies, it is more difficult to provide a precise definition of either 'philanthropy' or 'philanthropist'. It has been suggested that being philanthropic is innate or part of the *a priori* human experience (Payton, 1984; Gurin and Til, 1990: 4) because philanthropy has existed in every historical period and been a feature of every culture (Ilchman et al., 1998: ix), thus it is "as old as humanity itself; we can safely consider it universal" (Payton and Moody, 2008: 14). Yet the suggestion that philanthropy is somehow immanent sits uneasily with modern sensibilities, underscored by the discipline of social science, that view human knowledge and behaviours as socially derived (Durkheim, 1897, 1915; Morris, 1987: 115). Furthermore, studies of philanthropy in Antiquity and early Christianity conclude that the apparent continuity from pagan benevolence to Christian charity to modern philanthropy may be due to erroneous assumptions that its meaning has remained constant over time (Andrews, 1950: 31), leading Davis to warn against assuming that "our contemporary vocabulary is sufficiently supple to capture the arguments and presumptions of our precursors" (Davis, 1996: 4).

The fact that philanthropy varies in different eras and in different countries is evident in the frequency with which both Victorian and American philanthropy are contrasted with contemporary UK philanthropy, in an exercise which usually highlights the inadequacy of the latter (for example Prochaska, 1990; McCarthy, 2005; Handy, 2006: 2; McCully, 2008). Differences relate to how the activity is viewed, as well as the enthusiasm with which it is undertaken. For example, one comparative transatlantic study points out that whilst 'philanthropy' is a popular term in the US, "for many in Britain it still carries disparaging connotations of Victorian 'do-gooderism' and is often seen as elitist, patronising, morally judgmental and ineffective" (Wright, 2002: 7). Given this variation across time and place, any study of philanthropy must take account of the context in which it occurs because,

> each culture develops a distinctive philanthropic tradition that reflects other aspects of that society . . . To understand philanthropy in any culture, we have to understand the sources of the philanthropic tradition, both ancient and modern, and how these influenced philanthropic actions and meaning over time.
>
> *(Payton and Moody, 2008: 131)*

Yet to claim that philanthropy is a socially and culturally embedded concept does little to advance the task of defining this key term, so we turn instead to etymology and dictionary definitions.

Etymology and dictionary definitions

The roots of the word 'philanthropy' are from the Greek, with 'philo' meaning 'love of', and 'anthropos' meaning 'man'. There is no etymological reason for 'philanthropy' to involve financial transactions because 'love of mankind' can clearly be demonstrated in many non-monetary ways, but in practice the word is usually applied to donations of money.

The dictionary defines 'philanthropy' as primarily an emotional disposition: "love of humankind" with a more concrete secondary definition: "practical benevolence". Despite the positive connotations of these official definitions, more negative interpretations abound. For example, philanthropy is said to involve, "people getting credit for giving back what their ancestors should never have taken in the first place" (Panas, 1984: 49) and the philanthropist is said to be, "fuzzy-minded, self-indulgent, too preoccupied with his own emotional satisfactions" (Nightingale, 1973: 111). Derogatory definitions and embodiments also appear widely in popular culture, such as the foolishly philanthropic Mrs Jellyby in Charles Dickens' *Bleak House* who is blind to the needs in her own household, or Mrs Cheveley in Oscar Wilde's *An Ideal Husband* who complains that "philanthropy seems to have become simply the refuge of people who wish to annoy their fellow creatures". Clearly, neither etymology nor dictionary definitions satisfactorily accommodate the meaning of 'philanthropy' in its common usage. This is because it is a loaded term and a contested concept (Daly, 2012) that evokes ideological reactions (DiMaggio and Anheier, 1990: 153), and because its meaning changes and develops over time as a result of being embedded in specific circumstances, including historical, political, economic and social contexts.

The multidisciplinary study of philanthropy, including economics, psychology and sociology, also impacts on our understanding of philanthropy as different disciplines bring their own theories and concepts to bear (Moody and Breeze, 2016: 5). For all these reasons, it may not be possible to develop a generally accepted definition of philanthropy (Gurin and Van Til, 1990).

Philanthropy in relation to similar concepts

The task of defining philanthropy is aggravated by the existence of similar terms and concepts that are used in a variety of overlapping and interlocking ways (Morris, 2004: 139). There is, therefore, a need to differentiate 'philanthropy' from closely related concepts including 'benevolence' (Ditchfield, 1998: 194; Andreoni, 2001: 11,369), 'giving' (McCarthy, 2001: 1) and 'sharing' (Ilchman et al., 1998: ix), but most often it is 'charity' that is confused and contrasted with 'philanthropy'. A common proposition is that 'philanthropy' is the broad concept referring to all types of giving and helping that improves the quality of life for all, whilst 'charity' is the subset of help given to the indigent (Bremner, 1988: 3; Wolpert, 1989: 380; Gurin and Til, 1990: 4; Ostrower, 1995: 4). The most frequently cited version of this formulation is Jencks' suggestion that, "it seems best to use the term 'philanthropy' to describe gifts in general, and to reserve the word 'charity' for those gifts that are specifically aimed at the poor or the needy" (Jencks, 1987: 322).

Others reject the notion that 'charity' is a subset of 'philanthropy', perceiving them to be qualitatively different. For example, philanthropy is said to have a secular orientation in contrast to the religious inspiration and purpose of charity (Cunningham and Innes, 1998: 2), alternatively charity is said to be aimed at individuals whilst philanthropy is an organized effort to improve the socioeconomic conditions of a whole community (Hewa and Stapleton, 2006: 4). Payton's definition of philanthropy as "the prudent sister of charity" (Payton, 1988: 32) reflects a typically American preference for the word 'philanthropy' over 'charity' which, in that country, invokes notions of amateur and random almsgiving.

A common point of differentiation between 'charity' and 'philanthropy' suggests that charity exists to alleviate suffering whilst philanthropy is preventative (Andrews, 1950: 21; Frumkin, 2006: 5–6). In support of this position Frumkin cites two people widely considered to be 'fathers of modern philanthropy': Andrew Carnegie whose 'Gospel of Wealth' argues that philanthropy should "provide ladders for the aspiring to rise" (Carnegie, 1899) and John D. Rockefeller who wrote that, "if people can be educated to help themselves, we strike at the root of many evils of the world" (cited in Frumkin, 2006: 8). Thus both Carnegie and Rockefeller appear to suggest that philanthropy is about preventing, rather than ameliorating the symptoms of, poverty.

The difficulties in drawing boundaries between related concepts such as charity, voluntarism, altruism and generosity lead some to conclude that it is "futile" to seek a precise definition of philanthropy (Martin, 1994: 8) because it is "difficult or more probably incapable of strict definition" (Gray, 1905: viii), and "many leading scholars in the field doubt that one can be developed" (Gurin and Til, 1990: 3).

Amongst those prepared to offer definitions, the most widely cited is Payton's simple formulation that philanthropy is 'private action for the public good' (Payton, 1988). Less elegantly phrased, though more substantive, suggestions include "the voluntary transfer of economic goods or resources to an organization or another individual" (Knapp and Kendall, 1991: 1), "the voluntary social relation of care by which donors respond directly to others in need" (Havens et al., 2006: 1) and the advancement of society, "by providing necessary social, cultural and educational services which are not provided by the state or the market" (Adam, 2004: 4).

Academics and practitioners continue struggling to pin down a precise definition of 'individual philanthropy', and the task becomes more complicated as the serious study of philanthropy takes root in a more diverse set of countries and regions, including, for example, in Africa where the language of 'gifting' appears to be more acceptable than that of 'philanthropy' (Fowler and Wilkinson-Maposo, 2013). The most satisfactory position to date is to agree that 'philanthropy' is a contested concept, and will likely remain so, because the concept changes according to the culture, climate and needs of each time, so cannot be definitively defined.

The lack of an agreed definition is compounded by the arguably more serious lack of accurate data about philanthropy, to which we now turn.

The scale and contribution of individual philanthropy across the world

Despite the heightened awareness of philanthropy and the growing prominence of individual philanthropists, there is minimal robust data available to help us understand its scale and contribution. This is a result of two factors: the fairly embryonic state of philanthropic studies research across the world (see, for example, Keidan et al., 2014) and the fact – discussed above – that the extent, nature and local understanding of philanthropy differs across the world (Wiepking and Handy, 2015).

Despite profound problems in comparability, two studies have attempted to capture data on individual philanthropy across the world: the World Giving Index (CAF, 2017) and a study of philanthropy in 26 countries (Wiepking and Handy, 2015).

Since 2005, the Gallup World Poll, which now collects data from individuals in 140 countries, has included the following question: 'In the past month, have you donated money to a charity?'. The results are reported in the World Giving Index (WGI) published by the UK Charities Aid Foundation. This question only asks whether or not people give, with no further scrutiny of how much is given, how often, or to what cause, all of which are arguably more useful data points for

Table 27.1 Countries reporting over half of their population donated to charity in the last month

Country	Percentage of population who donated to charity in last month
Myanmar	91
Indonesia	79
Malta	73
Iceland	68
Thailand	68
New Zealand	65
Netherlands	64
United Kingdom	64
Australia	63
Canada	61
Ireland	60
Singapore	58
USA	56
Germany	55
Norway	55
Sweden	55
United Arab Emirates	55
Denmark	54
Israel	53
Kenya	52
Hong Kong	51
Switzerland	51

Source: CAF, 2017: 40.

Table 27.2 Countries reporting less than 10% of their population donated to charity in the last month (%)

Country	Percentage of population who donated to charity in last month
El Salvador	9
Madagascar	8
China	8
Botswana	7
Mauritania	6
Georgia	6
Yemen	3
Morocco	2

Source: CAF, 2017: 41.

nonprofit managers. Nonetheless, in the absence of other global comparative data on individual philanthropy, the most recent results (CAF, 2017) usefully demonstrate that private giving is commonplace – with a majority of the population donating to charity in the past month in 22 countries (as listed in Table 27.1), and only 8 countries reporting that less than 10 per cent of their population donated to charity in the past month (as listed in Table 27.2). Thus the contemporary ubiquitous nature of individual philanthropy is confirmed.

Deeper insights are provided in the second study, which seeks to explain levels and variation in individual philanthropy across 26 countries, in order to explore how the contexts in which people live affects their willingness to give (Wiepking and Handy, 2015: 5). This approach is in line with Adloff's (2016) social theory perspective on philanthropy which insists that explanations of private giving must take account not only of the characteristics of individuals (what he terms the 'micro level') but also the intermediary structures that influence donors (the 'meso level') and how wider society influences individual giving (the 'macro level').

The top-level data on annual individual philanthropic contributions reported in Wiepking and Handy's study, summarized in Figure 27.1, is provided by experts in 19 of the 26 countries, where representative national-level survey data is available.

In addition to this top-level data on amounts given, this study – and the Individual International Philanthropy Database (IIPD) which was created as a result of combining this data – contains further detail on the amounts and destination of individual philanthropy across 26 countries, including variables such as percentage of the population that donates, total amounts given and average size of donations. The study also highlights global variation in the destination of individual philanthropic donations, demonstrating that chosen causes vary as a result of micro-, meso- and macro-factors. Focusing on the UK, we can exemplify each of these factors in turn: the widespread popular affection for pets in the UK means that animal welfare charities enjoy substantial support from individual donors (illustrating the importance of individual/ micro-level factors); as many of the world's best-known international aid charities began in the UK, that sector is well organized and capable of fundraising large sums (illustrating the importance of structural/meso-level factors); and as the state funds public service broadcasting in the UK, there is currently no need to raise philanthropic funds for this service (illustrating the importance of wider society/macro-level factors).

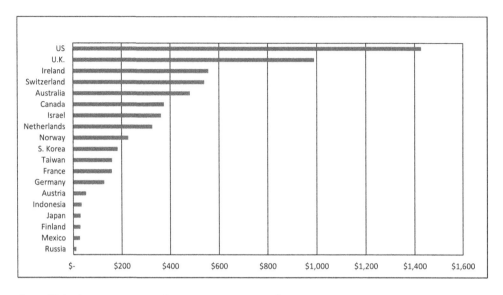

Figure 27.1 Average per capita donation in 2012, US Dollars, various countries

Source: Based on Wiepking and Handy (2016), drawing on the Individual International Philanthropy Database (IIPD).

In addition to geographic considerations, variation in chosen cause areas correlate with other factors such as religiosity and income levels. Clotfelter's study of 'who benefits' from charity in the US finds the distribution of gifts of the most affluent households is quite different from those of lower- and middle-income households, for example amongst people with a higher income, giving to colleges, universities and cultural institutions becomes much more prominent (Clotfelter, 1992: 15).

Wiepking and Handy identify eight contextual factors that are most useful in explaining variations in why people give across the 26 countries in their study: (1) the presence of a 'culture of philanthropy' in that country; (2) higher levels of public trust; (3) the existence of regulatory and legislative frameworks; (4) fiscal incentives for charitable giving; (5) the state of the nonprofit sector; (6) political and economic stability or growth; (7) population changes; and (8) international giving. Notwithstanding the empirical evidence for the influence of these eight contextual factors, Wiepking and Handy also argue that individual values and beliefs, such as altruistic propensities, continue to be "an important and indispensable motivating factor" (2015: 618). The next section looks more deeply at this question of the intrinsic and extrinsic motivations that influence individual philanthropy.

Motivations: Push and pull factors behind individual philanthropy

Since the early 1970s there has been a growing body of research studying the motivations that drive individual philanthropic behaviours. These studies have been carried out by academics working in many different disciplines including economics, psychology, sociology and business studies. Some studies focus on the micro- or individual-level factors (such as gender, age and personality) that are most closely associated with being philanthropic, whilst others are concerned with the social, cultural and political contexts that are more or less likely to encourage individual philanthropy at the meso- and macro-levels.

A systematic study of this cross-disciplinary literature on philanthropy, conducted by Dutch academics René Bekkers and Pamala Wiepking, reviewed the findings of over 500 articles that contain empirical analyses of philanthropic behaviour by adult individuals and households – their study excludes papers containing theoretical analyses, and empiricist accounts of giving by children or by organizations, such as corporation or charitable trusts and foundations. As a result, eight overarching mechanisms that drive individual philanthropic giving are identified, as shown in Table 27.3.

Applying general mechanisms to specific causes

It is a central tenet of fundraising best practice that every organization seeking philanthropic funding should have its own unique 'case for support' that clearly and succinctly explains the organization's purpose and why it needs donations (see, for example, Sargeant and Jay, 2014: 111–116;

Table 27.3 The eight mechanisms that drive charitable giving

Mechanism	Explanation
Awareness of need	People give when they are aware that an organization needs funds – this awareness is raised through the media and word of mouth as well as through the charities' own efforts in fundraising and communication.
Solicitation	Most giving is prompted by an 'ask', so actively soliciting donations is more effective than passively presenting opportunities to give.
Costs/Benefits	Donors are incentivized when the 'price of giving' is lowered by tax breaks and matched funding, and by receipt of benefits such as invitations to events and access to interesting relationships and unusual experiences.
Altruism	Caring about the beneficiaries, and a belief that donations will have a positive effect on their welfare, is a driver of giving.
Reputation	Donations are more likely when giving is viewed as a positive thing to do, and donors are rewarded socially by public approval and an enhanced reputation.
Psychological benefits	In addition to social benefits, donors seek psychological benefits. These include feeling good, alleviating guilt, opportunity to express gratitude and avoiding the cognitive dissonance that occurs when values and actions are not aligned.
Values	When personal values (such as belief in the value of heritage) align with organizational values (such as a charity that exists to protect heritage) there is a greater probability of a donation occurring.
Efficacy	Donors want their contribution to make a meaningful difference. Demonstrating efficacy to the donor can be formal (e.g., through evaluation reports and financial information) or informal (e.g., through anecdotes in charity communications, participating in a 'seeing is believing' trip, and modelling by high status people whose actions are emulated).

Source: Based on Bekkers and Wiepking, 2011.

Seiler, 2016). Successful fundraising organizations will also have a detailed strategy that sets out how resources can best be used to maximize voluntary income (see, for example, Joyaux, 2011; Worth, 2016: 117–146). Both the case for support and the strategy should be understood and supported by trustees, staff and volunteers, and these documents should be regularly reviewed and adjusted as necessary in response to changes in the internal and external environment. Understanding the eight mechanisms, and how they apply to any specific charity and its potential donors, is a useful part of this planning and review process. Table 27.4 offers an example of how this academic knowledge can be utilized by nonprofit managers, by applying the 'eight mechanisms' framework to the subsector of heritage organizations.

The next section continues to focus on the application of academic knowledge to the practice of seeking and securing individual philanthropic support.

Table 27.4 How the 'eight mechanisms' model applies to fundraising for endowments by heritage organizations

Mechanism	Example in relation to heritage organizations
Need	The needs served by heritage organizations are often less obvious than many charities, such as those providing food and shelter. So every opportunity and communications channel must be taken to explain the importance of heritage and to remind people that the organization is seeking funds.
Solicitation	Proactive fundraising is essential for every type of charity. Heritage organizations need to invest in the fundraising function, and recruit and train fundraisers with the skills and the confidence to "make the ask".
Costs/Benefits	Heritage organizations need to highlight how the value of donations can be enhanced through charitable tax breaks and matched funding schemes, so that donors can enjoy seeing their money go further. Coming up with imaginative benefits (with no/low material value to comply with Gift Aid rules) such as 'behind the scenes' tours and access to expert staff, is a key part of successful fundraising.
Altruism	Articulating who will benefit from heritage organizations is a necessary precondition to trigger donors' sense of care and compassion for those served by the charity.
Reputation	Finding meaningful ways to celebrate and recognize donors, including appropriate naming opportunities, seeking positive press coverage and membership of exclusive 'friends' and 'giving groups', can promote giving.
Psychological rewards	Investing in providing excellent donor care so that supporters know they are appreciated will enable people to experience the 'joy of giving' and feel good about themselves and their decision to donate.
Values	Fundraising efforts are best focused on people who believe in the value and importance of heritage in general and are supportive of the specific mission of the charity. Those who are members, visit the heritage site and/or have given to similar charities are all likely to be 'good prospects'.
Efficacy	Producing information that demonstrates your successful outcomes and positive impact, and making efforts to spread the word and harness the power of role models will enhance the confidence of potential donors.

Source: Breeze and Lipscomb, 2017, drawing on Bekkers and Wiepking, 2011.

Fundraising from individual philanthropists

A key premise behind fundraising from individual philanthropists is that donations must be *asked for*, as well as *donated*. This premise reflects what is known as the social-organizational approach to altruism, which was originally set out by Richard Titmuss in his study of blood donation schemes in the UK and US (Titmuss, 1970). Titmuss demonstrated that the quantity and quality of collection schemes influences the amount of blood that is donated, thus underlining the point, discussed previously, that gifts are shaped by meso- and macro-factors as well as by individual-level characteristics.

Later studies have confirmed and built upon Titmuss' pioneering research, for example Healy has shown that,

> altruism is structured, promoted, and made logistically possible by organizations and institutions with a strong interest in producing it . . . most of the altruism we observe in modern societies is more likely than not to have a strongly institutionalized aspect, with staffed organisations working to produce contexts in which it can happen.
>
> *(Healy, 2004: 387–90)*

The growing importance of the 'demand-side' of asking to encourage the 'supply-side' of giving has been described as a quintessential feature of modern philanthropy (Zunz, 2011). Since the start of the 20th century there has been a growth in the mobilization of donations across the globe (Norton, 2007; Cagney and Ross, 2013) in order to fund the work of the expanding non-profit sector. Yet despite the emergence of the fundraising profession over the last hundred years or so, most research attention has been focused on giving and donors, whilst asking and askers have as yet failed to secure serious scholarly attention. This academic neglect is surprising given the importance of fundraised income to most nonprofit organizations and good causes. Studies demonstrate that being asked is "the single biggest determinant of charitable giving" (Barman, 2017: 279). Yet philanthropy research as it currently exists in all disciplines is donor-centric, focused on the supply of donations at the expense of paying attention to the demand-side that consists of paid and volunteer askers.

One reason for overlooking fundraisers is a preference to interpret generosity as entirely innate, viewing it as a personal and private decision to respond to needs that exist in society (Breeze, 2017: 6). Instinctive kindness, and gifts that appear to be freely given, are far more highly culturally valued than reacting to a request (Derrida, 1992; Osteen, 2002; Komter, 2005). Yet the inconvenient truth is that individuals do not, on the whole, make spontaneous charitable donations: almost all gifts are prompted and facilitated to some degree (Bryant et al., 2003; Bekkers, 2005; Adloff, 2016: 60). The common wisdom that "if you don't ask, you won't get" has been confirmed by studies demonstrating that people are more likely to give, and also tend to donate more, when they are asked (Andreoni, 2006). Experimental studies confirm the positive effect of asking in securing donations (Okten and Weisbrod, 2000: 271; Yörük, 2009; Oppenheimer and Olivola, 2011) and conclude that "giving is rare without fundraising" (Meer, 2016: 5). As already noted, the major overview of research on determinants of charitable giving confirmed that solicitation is one of the eight key mechanisms that drive philanthropy (Bekkers and Wiepking, 2011) and, furthermore, most people say their main reason for *not* giving is because they were not asked (Piliavin and Charng, 1990: 35; Duronio and Tempel, 1997: 173).

One aspect of this topic that has received some attention is the impact on those being asked, who sometimes report feelings of discomfort, particularly when asked by paid fundraisers. Asking for money – even if it is on behalf of others – can be viewed as a form of begging (Breeze and Scaife, 2015: 571), 'rather squalid' (Allford, 1993: 105) and 'an odious activity' (Bloland and Tempel, 2004: 16). Whilst some hostility to fundraising is expressed with reference to specific methods and techniques (such as receiving 'excessive' direct mail, or dislike of being approached in the street or on one's doorstep), the source of antipathy likely relates to the essential nature of the act. Money and morals are viewed as deeply private matters (Zelizer, 2005), which means that any sort of request for donations can offend deeply held values regarding privacy (Harrah-Conforth and Borsos, 1991: 28–29). Fundraisers can be perceived as exhibiting moral superiority, and hence exposed to the "do-gooder derogation" experienced by those whose existence threatens the self-worth of those who feel "judged and found wanting" by moral minorities (Minson and Monin, 2011: 205).

Despite widespread antipathy to fundraisers, their role remains essential in encouraging individual philanthropy, and has been found to comprise three interrelated tasks (Breeze, 2017:139):

1 *Fostering* a philanthropic culture – both within the charity and in wider society.
2 *Framing* needs – to establish the legitimacy of the cause and educate potential donors about the existence of credible voluntary solutions.
3 *Facilitating* donations – provide a trusted and, where possible, enjoyable way for donors to respond to needs.

The key implication for nonprofit managers is that the job of fundraising involves a far wider remit than simply 'raising funds'. The vast majority of fundraisers' time must be spent creating conducive contexts in which philanthropy can thrive, inspiring and educating both colleagues and potential donors, and setting the stage for successful asking and effective giving.

The changing face of individual philanthropy

Whilst individual-level characteristics are not the sole factor that explains the incidence and quantities of individual philanthropy, as discussed above, they remain a matter of considerable interest to nonprofit managers who seek a better understanding of the types of people who do, and who could, provide private financial support. This section begins by describing the rise of the 'new philanthropist' and then explores what is known about developments in relation to donors' age and gender.

New philanthropists

Towards the end of the 20th century the phrase 'new philanthropist' emerged to refer to those making large donations who are distinctive in three ways (Breeze, 2011). Firstly, they are said to have a different demographic profile to their predecessors, being younger, richer, more likely to be self-made and living a cosmopolitan lifestyle. Secondly, they are alleged to support new types of causes, including emerging issues such as global health problems and the environmental crisis. Thirdly, these new philanthropists are said to conduct their giving in new ways by setting up their own foundations and projects instead of funding existing charities: they aspire to be catalysts for change and try to use their power to leverage money from other funders (especially the government) and claim to pay far greater attention to how their money is spent, by demanding targets, performance indicators and measurable outcomes. It is these latter aspects of the 'new philanthropy' that lies behind the synonymous label of 'philanthrocapitalism' (as defined by Bishop and Green, 2008), which refers to the application of businesslike skills to the charity sector.

Not everyone concurs with the proposition that contemporary major donors are distinctively new, noting that historically many self-made entrepreneurs began giving before retirement, such as Andrew Carnegie and John D. Rockefeller, who both took a 'hands-on' approach to distributing their philanthropic funds. The rise of 'scientific philanthropy' in the late 18th century demonstrates that new approaches have arisen throughout the history of philanthropic activity, and one of the standard historical explanations of Victorian philanthropy is that it offered an opportunity for 'new money' to buy the status required to be integrated into the elite. Thus:

> Philanthropy has undergone continual processes of change and has appeared "new" at many points in its history. The role of the philanthropist is continually being reinvented to reflect contemporary needs, dominant values, available wealth, technological developments and the broader socio-political context. Philanthropy is now, as it always has been, a product of its time.
>
> *(Breeze, 2011: 192)*

Whether or not contemporary donors uniquely deserve the epithet of 'new', we turn now to other studies that highlight some interesting changes in the key demographic characteristics of today's individual philanthropists.

Age

Many research studies demonstrate that the age of individual philanthropists is correlated with giving: there is a positive relationship between age and income because people tend to earn more as they get older and they tend to have less demands on that income as they age, particularly at the point at which they pay off their mortgage. The implications for nonprofit organizations are illustrated by a UK study which found that more than half of all donations to charity are from the over-60s, and that this older group are also twice as likely to give to charity as those aged under 30: in 2010, 32 per cent of over-60s had donated in the past fortnight, compared to 16 per cent of the under-30s (Smith, 2012). Whilst these figures might understandably trouble nonprofit leaders concerned about the future sustainability of their organization, it is important to bear in mind that the standard methods used by charity fundraisers – such as direct mail and gala events – might be more suitable for reaching older donors, and that fundraising using technology, such as online and text giving, generates a more enthusiastic response amongst younger people (CAF, 2017: 14). Therefore nonprofit leaders can seek to 'future proof' their philanthropic income by embracing new methods to reach new generations of donors.

Amongst major donors there also appears to be some notable differences between younger and older philanthropists. A UK study found this manifested in relation to their preferred causes (for example the older group were found to be five times as likely to support religious causes), spread of donations (with younger donors more likely to concentrate their giving on a smaller number of recipient organizations) and approaches to giving (with younger donors more likely to seek philanthropic advice and to prioritize giving during their lifetime over leaving a charitable legacy) (all data in Breeze and Lloyd, 2013).

An in-depth study of generational attitudes to giving conducted in the US argues that the younger generation are primarily defined by their desire for impact and their intention to "disrupt giving strategies" by focusing on a smaller number of causes, pursuing systematic change and using more diverse tools, including impact investing, micro-loans, collaborative giving and working through for-profit as well as nonprofit structures (Goldseker and Moody, 2017: 10–11). Citing evidence on the growing wealth concentration and the forthcoming intergenerational transfer of wealth, the authors of this study counsel nonprofit leaders to act soon to avoid losing support in the future:

> Don't wait! Gen X and Millennial major donors are eager to jumpstart their Impact Revolution . . . They might not be the biggest donors this year, or even for 5 or 10 years to come, but eventually they will be, and then they will dominate major giving for decades to come. Those organizations . . . that can figure out how best to engage next gen donors will gain loyal and active supporters for a very long time.
>
> *(Goldseker and Moody, 2017: 276)*

Gender

There is a general fascination with gender differences in giving, evidenced by the number of media articles and conference sessions exploring if and how men and women give differently. At the forefront of this body of work is the Women's Philanthropy Institute, based in the Lilly Family School of Philanthropy at Indiana University in the US, which published a literature review summarizing the existing academic research on women, gender and philanthropy (Mesch et al., 2015). This overview challenges many of the broad generalizations regarding gender, and finds that marital status also matters: not only do single women give more than single men, but getting married has a positive influence on giving levels, especially for the male partner, and married couples tend to make giving decisions jointly. Lessons for nonprofit managers are summarized thus:

> it is clear that women play a distinct and powerful role in philanthropy. Nonprofit organizations can use the findings from academic research to develop methods of identifying and cultivating female donors.
>
> *(Mesch et al., 2015: 5)*

Another, less-noted, aspect of gender and philanthropy is that fundraising is "gendered female" in important ways that often fail to be acknowledged by researchers and practitioners alike (Dale, 2017). The feminization of the fundraising profession has implications for nonprofit leaders not only in terms of how solicitation occurs, but also in how those tasked with raising philanthropic income are treated, as Dale notes:

> the day-to-day work of fundraisers, and its similarity to stereotypically female work, place women at a systematic disadvantage in the profession and enable men to maintain a disproportionate share of the most financially lucrative and executive-level positions.
>
> *(Dale, 2017: 7)*

Conclusions on individual philanthropy

This chapter began by noting that, despite its ubiquity and ongoing significance in contemporary society, and despite recent efforts to attain greater empirical and theoretical understanding, there is still much we do not know about individual philanthropy. More research is needed to plug the gaps in our knowledge about how individual philanthropy has changed over time, how best to define it, and how it varies across nations, as well as across generations and genders.

We do know that when a nonprofit organization becomes interested in individual philanthropy, it usually means it is looking for a new or expanded income source, despite the etymological meaning of philanthropy being 'the love of mankind'. The gap between these two definitions – cash versus caritas – may cast a useful light on some of the problems encountered when nonprofit organizations try to engage with individual philanthropists. Qualitative research on contemporary philanthropy demonstrates clearly that, from the donors' perspective, it is not just a financial transaction because it is about much more than money (see, for example, Ostrower, 1995; Schervish, 2005, 2007; Breeze and Lloyd, 2013). In particular, being philanthropic has transformative potential for donors as it can contribute to their identity work, help to rewrite their moral biographies, shape their personal legacy and enable their pursuit of modern standards of success, notably significance, influence and authenticity.

Since the turn of the millennium many claims have been made regarding the "revival and reinvention" (Bishop and Green, 2008: 2) of individual philanthropy. The belief in a new age of philanthropy has gained widespread credence and a breed of 'new philanthropists' are contrasted with the allegedly more local, limited and less discriminating ambitions of their philanthropic predecessors. Today's individual donors are also engaging in novel ways of organizing their philanthropy and social investing by developing new tools to mobilize and leverage a wider array of private resources (as detailed in Salamon, 2014). There has also been substantial growth recorded in philanthropy conducted via collective methods such as giving circles (Eikenberry, 2009) and through methods that bypass existing charities to establish new kinds of philanthropic organizations that can be controlled without the distributional and regulatory constraints imposed on traditional charitable entities – a notable example being the Chan Zuckerberg Initiative, founded in 2015, which takes the form of a limited liability company.

Whilst the terminology and organizational forms may be somewhat novel, the practice and purpose of individual philanthropy is both long-standing and constantly changing over time in order to reflect contemporary needs, dominant values, available wealth, technological developments and the broader socio-political, economic and cultural context. In sum: individual philanthropy continues to be a crucial income stream for funding nonprofit activity, that is constantly being re-imagined by donors, and therefore requires keen ongoing attention by nonprofit managers.

References

Acs, Z. J. (2013) *Why Philanthropy Matters: How the wealthy give, and what it means for our economic well-being*, Princeton, NJ: Princeton University Press.

Adam, T. (2004) *Philanthropy, Patronage and Civil Society: Experiences from Germany, Great Britain and North America*, Bloomington: Indiana University Press.

Adloff, F. (2016) Approaching Philanthropy from a Social Theory Perspective, in T. Jung, S. Phillips and J. Harrow (Eds.) *The Routledge Companion to Philanthropy*, London: Routledge.

Allford, M. (1993) *Charity Appeals: The complete guide to success*, London: J M Dent.

Andreoni, J. (2001) Economics of Philanthropy, in N. Smeltser and P. Baltes (Eds.) *International Encyclopedia of the Social and Behavioural Sciences*, Oxford: Elsevier.

Andreoni, J. (2006) Philanthropy, in S. Kolm and J.M. Ythier (Eds.) *Handbook of the Economics of Giving, Altruism and Reciprocity,* North-Holland: Elsevier.

Andrews, F.E. (1950) *Philanthropic Giving,* New York: Russell Sage Foundation.

Barman, E. (2017) The social bases of philanthropy, *Annual Review of Sociology,* 43: 271–290.

Bekkers, R. (2005) It's Not All in the Ask: Effects and effectiveness of recruitment strategies used by non-profits in the Netherlands, Paper presented at the 34th annual ARNOVA conference, Washington, DC.

Bekkers, R. and Wiepking, P. (2011) A literature review of empirical studies of philanthropy: Eight mechanisms that drive charitable giving, *Nonprofit and Voluntary Sector Quarterly,* 40(5): 924–973.

Bishop, M. and Green, M. (2008) *Philanthrocapitalism: How the rich can save the world,* New York: Bloomsburg Press.

Bloland, H.G. and Tempel, E.R. (2004) Measuring professionalism, *New Directions for Philanthropic Fundraising,* 43: 5–20.

Breeze, B. (2011) Is there a "New Philanthropy"?, in C. Rochester, G. Campbell Gosling, A. Penn and M. Zimmeck (Eds.) *Understanding Roots of Voluntary Action: Historical perspectives on current social policy,* Brighton: Sussex Academic Press.

Breeze, B. (2017) *The New Fundraisers: Who organizes charitable giving in contemporary society?* Bristol: Policy Press.

Breeze, B. and Lipscomb, L. (2017) Evaluation of the Catalyst: Endowment grant Programme, a report written for the Heritage Lottery Fund, available online https://www.kent.ac.uk/sspssr/philanthropy/publications/documents/endowments_evaluation_report.pdf [Accessed 12/8/18].

Breeze, B. and Lloyd, T. (2013) *Richer Lives: Why rich people give,* London: Directory of Social Change.

Breeze, B. and Scaife, W. (2015) Encouraging Generosity: The practice and organization of fund-raising across nations, in P. Wiepking and F. Handy (Eds.) *The Palgrave Handbook of Global Philanthropy,* Basingstoke: Palgrave Macmillan.

Bremner, R. (1988) *American Philanthropy,* second edition. Chicago: University of Chicago Press.

Bryant, W.K., Slaughter, H.J., Kang, H. and Tax, A. (2003) Participating in philanthropic activities: Donating money and time, *Journal of Consumer Policy,* 26: 43–73.

Burk, P. (2003) *Donor-Centred Fundraising,* Chicago: Burk and Associates Ltd.

CAF (2017) *UK Giving 2017: An overview of charitable giving in the UK during 2017,* West Malling: Charities Aid Foundation.

Cagney, P. and Ross, B. (2013) *Global Fundraising: How the world is changing the rules of philanthropy,* Hoboken, NJ: John Wiley.

Carnegie, A. (1889). Wealth, *North American Review,* 148(391): 653–665.

Clotfelter, C.T. (Ed.) (1992) *Who Benefits from the Nonprofit Sector?* Chicago: Chicago University Press

Cunningham, H. and Innes, J. (Eds.) (1998) *Charity, Philanthropy and Reform: From the 1690s to 1850,* Basingstoke: Macmillan.

Dale, E. (2017) Fundraising as women's work? Examining the profession with a gender lens, *International Journal of Nonprofit and Voluntary Sector Marketing,* 22(4).

Daly, S. (2012) Philanthropy as an essentially contested concept, *Voluntas,* 23(3): 535–557.

Davis, S. (1996) Philanthropy as a Virtue in Late Antiquity, in J.B. Schneewind (Ed.) *Giving: Western ideas of philanthropy,* Bloomington: Indiana University Press.

Derrida, J. (1992) *Given Time: 1. Counterfeit money,* Chicago: University of Chicago Press.

Dietel, W. (2014) Foreword, in L. Salamon (Ed.) *New Frontiers of Philanthropy: A guide to the new tools and actors reshaping global philanthropy and social investing,* Oxford: Oxford University Press.

DiMaggio, P.J. and Anheier, H.K. (1990) The sociology of nonprofit organisations, *Annual Review of Sociology,* 16: 137–159.

Ditchfield, G.M. (1998) English Rational Dissent and Philanthropy, in H. Cunningham and J. Innes (Eds.) *Charity, Philanthropy and Reform: From the 1690s to 1850,* Basingstoke: Macmillan.

Durkheim, E. (1982 [1897]) *Suicide,* Basingstoke: Macmillan.

Durkheim, E. (1915) *The Elementary Forms of the Religious Life,* London: Allen & Unwin.

Duronio, M.A. and Tempel, E.R. (1997) *Fund Raisers: Their careers, stories, concerns and accomplishments,* San Francisco: Jossey Bass.

Eikenberry, A.M. (2009) (2009) *Giving Circles: Philanthropy, voluntary association, and democracy,* Bloomington: Indiana University Press.

Fowler, A. and Wilkinson-Maposo, S. (2013) Horizontal Philanthropy among the Poor in Southern Africa: Grounded perspectives in social capital and civic association, in T.A.A.B. Moyo (Ed.) *Giving to Help: Helping to Give: The context and politics of African philanthropy,* Senegal: Amalion Publishing.

Frumkin, P. (2006) *Strategic Giving: The art and science of philanthropy*, Chicago: University of Chicago Press.

Futureagenda. (2018) *Future of Philanthropy: Insights from multiple expert discussions around the world*, London: Future Agenda.

Giving USA Foundation. (2017) *Giving USA 2017: The Annual Report on Philanthropy for the Year 2016*, researched and written by the Indiana University Lilly Family School of Philanthropy. Available online at www.givingusa.org

Goldseker, S. and Moody, M. (2017) *Generation Impact: How next gen donors are revolutionizing giving*, Hoboken, NJ: John Wiley.

Goose, N. (2006) The rise and decline of philanthropy in early modern Colchester: The unacceptable face of mercantilism? *Social History*, 31(4): 469–487.

Gray, B. K. (1905) *A History of Philanthropy: From the dissolution of the monasteries to the taking of the first census*, London: Frank Cass.

Gurin, M. G. and Til, J. V. (1990) Philanthropy in its Historical Context, in J. V. Til (Ed.) *Critical Issues in American Philanthropy: Strengthening theory and practice*, San Francisco: Jossey-Bass.

Handy, C. (2006) *The New Philanthropists*, London: William Heinemann.

Harrah-Conforth, J. and Borsos, J. (1991) The Evolution of Professional Fund Raising 1890–1990, in D. F. Burlingame and L. J. Hulse (Eds.) *Taking Fund Raising Seriously: Advancing the profession and practice of raising money*, San Francisco: Jossey-Bass.

Havens, J. J., O'Herlihy, M. A. and Schervish, P. (2006) Charitable Giving: How much, by whom, to what, and how? In W. W. Powell and R. Steinberg (Eds.) *The Non-Profit Sector: A research handbook*, New Haven, CT: Yale University Press.

Healy, K. (2004) Altruism as an organizational problem: The case of organ procurement, *American Sociological Review*, 69(3): 387–404.

Hewa, S. and Stapleton, D. H. (Eds.) (2006) *Globalization, Philanthropy and Civil Society: Toward a new political culture in the twenty-first century*, New York: Springer.

Ilchman, W. F., Katz, S. N. and Queen II, E. L. (Eds.) (1998) *Philanthropy in the World's Traditions*, Bloomington: Indiana University Press.

Jencks, C. (1987) Who Gives to What? In W. Powell (Ed.) *The NonProfit Sector: A research handbook*, New Haven, CT: Yale University Press.

Jordan, W. K. (1959) *Philanthropy in England 1480–1660: A Study of the changing pattern of English social aspirations*, London: George Allen & Unwin.

Joyaux, S. (2011) *Strategic Fund Development: Building profitable relationships that last*, 3rd edition. Hoboken: NJ: John Wiley.

Keidan, C., Jung, T. and Pharoah, C. (2014) *Philanthropy education in the UK and continental Europe: Current provision, perceptions and opportunities*, London: Centre for Giving and Philanthropy.

Knapp, M. and Kendall, J. (1991) Barriers to Giving. *Personal Social Services Research Unit Discussion Papers*, University of Kent at Canterbury.

Komter, A. (2005) *Social Solidarity and The Gift*, Cambridge: Cambridge University Press.

Martin, M. W. (1994) *Virtuous Giving: Philanthropy, voluntary service and caring*, Bloomington: Indiana University Press.

McCarthy, K. D. (Ed.) (2001) *Women, Philanthropy and Civil Society*, Bloomington: Indiana University Press.

McCarthy, K. D. (2005) *American Creed: Philanthropy and the rise of civil society 1700–1865*, Chicago: Chicago University Press.

McCully, G. (2008) *Philanthropy Reconsidered: Private initiatives, public good, quality of life*, Bloomington: AuthorHouse.

Meer, J. (2016) Does Fundraising Create New Giving? Working Paper 22033, National Bureau of Economic Research, Cambridge, MA: NBER.

Mesch, D., Osili, U., Ackerman, J. and Dale, E. (2015) *How and Why Women Give: Current and future directions for research on women's philanthropy*, Indianapolis, IN: Lilly Family School of Philanthropy.

Minson, J. A. and Monin, B. (2011) Do-gooder derogation: Putting down morally motivated others to defuse implicit moral reproach, *Social Psychological and Personality Science*, 3(2): 200–207.

Mohan, J. and Breeze, B. (2016) *The Logic of Charity: Great expectations in hard times*, Basingstoke: Palgrave Macmillan.

Moody, M. and Breeze, B. (2016) *The Philanthropy Reader*, London: Routledge.

Morris, B. (1987) *Anthropological Studies of Religion*, Cambridge: Cambridge University Press.

Morris, S. (2004) Changing Perceptions of Philanthropy in the Voluntary Housing Field in Nineteenth and Early Twentieth Century London, in T. Adam (Ed.) *Philanthropy, Patronage and Civil Society: Experiences from Germany, Great Britain and North America.* Bloomington: Indiana University Press.

nfpSynergy. (2018) *Taking nothing for granted survey 2018*, London. Available online https://nfpsynergy.net/press-release/what-do-charities-think-about-grant-makers-and-grant-applications#downloads [Accessed July 30, 2018].

Nightingale, B. (1973) *Charities*, London: Allen Lane.

Norton, M. (2007) *Need to Know? Fundraising*, London: HarperCollins.

Okten, C. and Weisbrod, B. (2000) Determinants of donations in private nonprofit markets, *Journal of Public Economics,* 75(2): 255–272.

Oppenheimer, D.M. and Olivola, C.Y. (2011) *The Science of Giving: Experimental approaches to the study of charity*, New York: Psychology Press.

Osteen, M. (Ed.) (2002) *The Question of the Gift: Essays across disciplines*, London: Routledge.

Ostrower, F. (1995) *Why the Wealthy Give: The culture of elite philanthropy*, Princeton, NJ: Princeton University Press.

Owen, D. (1965) *English Philanthropy 1660–1960*, London: Oxford University Press.

Panas, Jerold (1984) *Mega Gifts: Who gives them, who gets them?* Chicago: Bonus Books.

Payton, R. (1984) *Major Challenges to Philanthropy*, Washington, DC: Independent Sector.

Payton, R.L. (1988) *Philanthropy: Voluntary action for the public good*, New York: American Council on Education/Macmillan.

Payton, R.L. and Moody, M.P. (2008) *Understanding Philanthropy: Its meaning and mission*, Bloomington: Indiana University Press.

Phillips, S. and Jung, T. (2016) A New 'New' Philanthropy, in T. Jung, S. Phillips and J. Harrow (Eds.) *The Routledge Companion to Philanthropy*, Abingdon, Oxon: Routledge.

Piliavin, J.A. and Charng, H.-W. (1990) Altruism: A review of recent theory and research, *Annual Review of Sociology,* 16: 27–65.

Prochaska, F. (1990) Philanthropy, in F.M.L. Thompson (Ed.) *The Cambridge Social History of Britain 1750–1950,* Cambridge: Cambridge University Press.

Salamon, L. (Ed.) (2014) *New Frontiers of Philanthropy: A guide to the new tools and actors reshaping global philanthropy and social investing*, Oxford: Oxford University Press.

Salamon, L. and Anheier, H. (1998) Social origins of civil society: Explaining the nonprofit sector cross-nationally, *Voluntas,* 9(3): 213–248.

Sargeant, A. and Jay, E. (2014) *Fundraising Management: Analysis, planning and practice*, 3rd edition. New York: Routledge.

Schervish, P. (2005) Major donors, major motives: The people and purposes behind major gifts, *New Directions for Philanthropic Fundraising,* 47: 59–87.

Schervish, P. (2007) Why the Wealthy Give: Factors which mobilise philanthropy among high net worth individuals, in A. Sargeant and W. Wymer Jr. (Eds.) *The Routledge Companion to Nonprofit Marketing*, London: Routledge.

Seiler, T.L. (2016) Developing and Articulating a Case for Support, in E.R. Tempel, T.L. Seiler and D.F. Burlingame (Eds.) *Achieving Excellence in Fundraising*, 4th edition. Hoboken, NJ: John Wiley.

Smith, S. (2012) Mind the Gap: The growing generational divide in charitable giving: a research paper, Tunbridge Wells: Charities Aid Foundation.

Starr, K. (2011) Just give 'em the money: The power and pleasure of unrestricted funding, *Stanford Social Innovation Review*, 3 August.

Titmuss, R.M. (1970) *The Gift Relationship: From human blood to social policy*, London: George Allen & Unwin.

Wiepking, P. and Handy, F. (Eds.) (2015) *The Palgrave Handbook of Global Philanthropy*, Basingstoke: Palgrave Macmillan.

Wiepking, P. and Handy, F. (2016) Global Philanthropy: How institutional factors enable philanthropic giving, paper presented at 45th ARNOVA international conference, Washington, DC, 17–19 November.

Wolpert, J. (1989) Key Indicators of Generosity in Communities, in V. Hodgkinson and R.W. Lyman (Eds.) *The Future of the NonProfit Sector: Challenges, changes and policy considerations*, San Francisco: Jossey-Bass.

Worth, M. (2016) *Fundraising: Principles and practice*, Thousand Oaks, CA: Sage.

Wright, K. (2002) Generosity versus Altruism: Philanthropy and charity in the US and UK, *Civil Society Working Paper 17*, London: London School of Economics.

Yörük, B. (2009) How responsive are charitable donors to requests to give?, *Journal of Public Economics*, 93(9): 1111–1117.

Zelizer, V. (2005) *The Purchase of Intimacy*, Princeton, NJ: Princeton University Press.

Zunz, O. (2011) *Philanthropy in America: A History*, Princeton, NJ: Princeton University Press.

28

THE NONPROFIT SECTOR'S 'RICH RELATIONS'?

Foundations and their grantmaking activities

Tobias Jung

PROFESSOR OF MANAGEMENT AND DIRECTOR, CENTRE FOR THE STUDY
OF PHILANTHROPY & PUBLIC GOOD, SCHOOL OF MANAGEMENT, UNIVERSITY
OF ST. ANDREWS, ST. ANDREWS, SCOTLAND, UK

Introduction

As the number and resources of foundations, as well as their socio-political and economic importance, continue to grow globally (Johnson, 2018; Toepler, 2018b), this chapter outlines and critically discusses the grantmaking foundation arena. The chapter highlights foundations' characteristics, raises questions about the nature and portrayal of foundations' grantmaking activities, considers the social and moral acceptability of their resources, and points to wider issues relating to the roles, purposes, and legitimacy of foundations. All of this, however, comes with a caveat. Namely, that the sphere of philanthropic foundations frequently appears akin to treacle: uncrystallized, partly refined, sickly sweet, sticky, slow-moving, messy.

The foundation arena seems uncrystallized in that it is a potpourri of ideas. Even foundations' own associations and umbrella bodies acknowledge that "the term foundation has no precise meaning" (Association of Charitable Foundations, 2018; Council on Foundations, 2018). Confusions and imprecisions are commonplace. The area is only partly refined in that while there is a large body of work on foundations from within the US, nuanced international understanding remains emergent. Here, the erroneous application and replication of US foundation labels (themselves tax law distinctions) across international contexts, as well as an overemphasis on a relatively small set of foundations that tend to be outliers rather than the norm – in relation to their resources, behaviour, and/or practices – have not been helpful. The field can appear both sweet and sickly in that reflective discourse has tended to be limited. Pleasantries and paranoia about foundations, glorifying and hypercritical perspectives, tend to go hand in hand (Jung & Harrow, 2019). Foundation discourse also appears somewhat sticky in that, historically, ideas seem to linger (Cunningham, 2016). The result is twofold. On the one hand, a diversity of labels can mask the same idea. Thus, the conceptual differences between scientific (Carnegie, 1901), strategic (Brown, 1979), high-impact (Grace & Wendroff, 2000), and entrepreneurial philanthropy (Gordon, Harvey, Shaw, & Maclean, 2016) are debatable. On the other hand, the same labels seem to be repeatedly applied in reference to different ideas. Examples include the use and casting of "creative philanthropy" (Anheier & Leat, 2006 vs. Murphy, 1976), "pragmatic philanthropy"

(Shapiro, Mirchandani, & Jang, 2018 vs. Thümler, 2017), and "venture philanthropy" (Katz, 2005 vs. Stone, 1975). Finally, the field's velocity: while foundations are frequently seen as amongst the oldest institutional forms in the world, comparative and integrative research on foundations is a relatively recent area, and only a slowly advancing one (Anheier, 2018; Toepler, 2018b). Bearing all of this in mind, how can we start to understand the idea of a foundation?

What is a foundation?

Essentially, a foundation is an independent entity to which a donor transfers assets. This entity is then required to use those assets, and any associated returns, in pursuit of one or more defined purposes (Anheier & Toepler, 1999; Goldsworth, 2016). In civil law systems, such as Germany, it is usually the case that such an entity is a specific, codified, legal structure. However, in common law systems, such as the UK, it is customary to use the foundation label in an uncodified manner to point to an entity's specific activities or to the public benefits it provides. Beyond this, things get conceptually and practically messy.

A foundation's donor can be an individual, a group, or a body from the private, public, or non-profit sector, or even a combination thereof. Assets can be of a financial or non-financial form, as well as permanent or transient. Depending on country-specific contexts, foundation purposes can be either of a public or a private nature (European Foundation Centre, 2015). A variety of approaches can be used to achieve a foundation's purpose. These include those that are perceived as traditional and mainstream – such as operating or grantmaking – but, increasingly, can also include social finance or the provision of prizes and awards (Frumkin, 2014; Salamon, 2014). While the latter are sometimes cast as representing the "new frontiers" of philanthropy (Salamon, 2014), the extent to which they are indeed novel developments warrants further exploration. Their underlying ideas, principles, and practices, as well as the challenges they present, appear relatively ancient with strong historical roots and precedents (e.g. Brealey, 2013; Schoon, 2015). Taken together, these diverse options and possible combinations mean that a multiplicity of ways in which foundations can be clustered, classified, and categorized can be found in the literature (see Jung, Harrow, & Leat, 2018).

Operators and grantmakers

Public, policy and academic debates are often dominated by the image of foundations as grant-makers, with grantmaking widely considered to be "the core business of charitable foundations" (Orosz, 2004, p. 204). Both historically and contemporaneously, however, grantmaking foundations constitute a global minority. Operating foundations – those that design and carry out their own projects instead of funding others – have tended to prevail (Johnson, 2018; Toepler, 1999). Given that some of the most established foundation brands in the world – such as Carnegie and Rockefeller – originally favoured and began with an operating model, the question arises as to why the grantmaking approach gained prominence (Leat, 2016).

Firstly, the emphasis on foundations' grantmaking appears to be an "accident of history" (Leat, 2016, p. 299). While the operating approach offers the advantage of maintaining control over and ownership of a foundation's activities, it is also more costly, slower, and inflexible compared to the grantmaking one (Frumkin, 2006). Following the emergence of the big US foundations at the beginning of the 20th century, such considerations gained importance; the growth of these foundations occurred alongside growing socio-economic needs and urgent political pressures for foundations to step up and assist with addressing these needs (Leat, 2016). With US foundations also taking on increasingly prominent roles in shaping pre- and post-World War I and II policies and practices at national and international levels through grantmaking (Kiger, 2000; Parmar, 2012; Spero, 2010), their grantmaking approaches were globally transplanted and became seen as an essential foundation trait (Leat, 2016).

Secondly, due to longstanding concerns about foundations' social and political activities, legitimacy and influence (Arnove, 1980; Heydemann & Toepler, 2006; Krige & Rausch, 2012; Roelofs, 2003), grantmaking also provides foundations with an organizational shield and safety buffer. Giving resources to an intermediary rather than carrying out your own programmes represents a shift in responsibilities: the onus for achieving a specific purpose passes to the grantee. Thereby, as long as foundations operate within appropriate legal and accountability frameworks, they have limited direct answerability for the ways in which their grants are used by grantees and the outcomes they might – or might not – achieve (Leat, 2016).

Finally, academia, policy, and the media also appear to have played a role in raising awareness about and emphasizing the grantmaking foundation model. As operating foundations undertake their own activities and programmes, they are difficult to separate from the wider field of nonprofit organizations (Toepler, 1999). In comparison, grantmaking foundations provide a more bounded field for researchers. Being more easily identifiable does, however, also mean that foundations readily attract the attention of policymakers looking for new and alternative funding sources (Harrow & Jung, 2011), and that they offer an easy target for media in search of "stories," with the result that missteps by one foundation quickly lead to problematic generalizations across the wider body of foundations (Gaul & Borowski, 1993; Whitaker, 1974).

While the distinction between grantmaking and operating is a convenient shorthand, pure grantmaking foundations appear to be on the decline. With a wider move towards more engaged grantmaking approaches, outlined below, foundations increasingly combine grantmaking and operating approaches in their activities. What, then, constitutes grantmaking?

Grantmaking

At its most basic, grantmaking can be seen as "awarding gifts of cash (grants) . . . in support of projects" (Orosz, 2004, p. 204). It thus seems to be a reasonably straightforward activity: you pay somebody to do the work you are interested in. This, however, fails to acknowledge that grantmaking can be "a wearisome and complicated business" (Macdonald, 1956, p. 109). It masks that grantmaking is a highly diversified set of activities that incorporates numerous influences, traditions, styles, techniques, and expressions across a range of stages, such as: establishing a grantmaking strategy; developing appropriate decision-making procedures, protocols, and practices; creating and promoting priorities and application guidelines; assessing and selecting ideas worthy of support; communicating decisions and conditions; managing active grants, evaluating results, and making improvements; as well as addressing human temptations in the process (Association of Charitable Foundations, 2017; Cabinet Office, 2014b; DP Evaluation, 2012; Golden, 2004; Grant, 2016; Harrow & Fitzmaurice, 2011; Orosz, 2004; Sprecher, Egger, & von Schnurbein, 2016; Unwin, 2004). Thus, a large body of work providing guidance on grantmaking exists. Aspects that are emphasized include: focusing on those areas and approaches that are in line with the foundation's available resource base, having explicit funding criteria, offering accessible and user-friendly application forms and processes, using swift decision-making procedures and offering clear reasons for acceptances/rejections, and being honest and responsible in the grant terms, administration, and how conditions are managed (Grant, 2016, p. 415; Nielsen, 1985). These different facets of the grantmaking process present a range of issues to consider, and are outlined in Table 28.1.

Table 28.1 Key questions and issues that a grantmaking approach presents

What are the underlying drivers for grantmaking?	What type and degree of risk is the foundation willing to take? Is the focus on alleviating symptoms or supporting the delivery of services? Is the aim to build or broker knowledge and understanding? Is the aim to address root causes and work towards structural and/or policy change?
What does the foundation offer?	What kind of support is being offered (financial or also non-financial; direct or indirect)? What type of costs will be supported (capital, revenue, project, overheads, full, core)? How much is being offered and when (small or large grants, at which and for which part of the grantees' lifecycle)? What shape does the funding take (restricted, unrestricted; gift, grant, investment, prize, award; full, partial or matched)?
What is the funding timeframe and cycle?	Is the focus on short- or long-term grants? Is the emphasis on pro-cyclical (in line with the growth phase of an economic cycle) or countercyclical (in line with economic decline, challenges, and recessions) grantmaking?
What is the theory of change?	To whom are resources offered (established or emergent ideas/ organizations)? Is the focus on taking a top-down or a bottom-up approach?
What are the characteristics of the grant programme?	Is it responsive and open so that anybody who meets the foundation's criteria can apply? Is funding strategic and targeted to a specific outcome? Is it by invitation only?
Who benefits?	Explicitly? Implicitly?
What is the nature of the foundation's external relationships?	Is the relationship to grantees engaged or hands off? Direct or through intermediaries? Is it a gift, contractual, auditing, delegating, or collaborative relationship? Does the foundation encourage and seek collaborations with others or does it try to avoid them? Is the foundation pursuing a high or a low external profile?

Source: Based on Dietz, McKeever, Steele, & Steuerle, 2015; DP Evaluation, 2012; Frumkin, 2006; Leat, 2006; Ridley, 2017; Unwin, 2004.

The vocabulary that accompanies the resulting spectrum of grantmaking choices tends to be "coarse and imprecise" (Nielsen, 1985, p. 420). For example, the literature refers to scientific rather than indiscriminate grantmaking, to proactive rather than reactive approaches, to participatory rather than imposed grantmaking, to strategic or targeted grantmaking instead of "scatteration," to conservative grantmaking for traditional areas such as philanthropic mainstays of education, health, and culture, or to liberal grantmaking for reference to activities in more challenging areas such as social movements, controversial issues, and urgent social problems (Nielsen, 1985, p. 420; Fleishman, 2007; Gibson, 2017; Meachen, 2010; Orosz, 2004; Prewitt, 2006). The problem with such differentiations is that they tend to be value-laden and may often be portmanteaux (Nielsen, 1985), and that the empirical and theoretical underpinnings, as well as the practical applicability, of these labels is not always clear (Jung et al., 2018).

Within the context of grantmaking approaches, and responding to wider criticisms about the extent of philanthropy's actual achievements (e.g. Friedman, 2013; Goldberg, 2009; Singer,

2015), there has been a growing emphasis on maximizing foundations' grantmaking efficiency and effectiveness (Nielsen, 1985; Sprecher et al., 2016). Promoted ideas include becoming a "Total Impact" foundation, one that concentrates its resources on areas where it can achieve the largest impact (Cabinet Office, 2014a), using "catalytic philanthropy" as a way to apply "disruptive innovations and new tools" (Kramer, 2009), as well as conducting "venture philanthropy," the application of venture capital and business models to the foundation world (John, 2006). These ideas have been accompanied by an industry geared towards encouraging, developing, and measuring the impact and differences that foundations and other charities make (Inspiring Impact, 2017; National Committee for Responsive Philanthropy, 2009). The surrounding rhetoric and ideas seem, at least superficially, laudable and appealing. Whether or not more effective, efficient, and impactful philanthropy should indeed be the overarching focus of grantmaking foundations, however, needs unpacking.

As already Henry Ford pointed out, "charity and philanthropy are the repair shops and their efficiency, however high, does not remove the cause of human wrecks" (cited in Whitaker, 1974, p. 60). Thus, the extent to which foundations' approaches may need to be re-thought more broadly arises (e.g. Thümler, 2017). It also means that, rather than simply dismissing and discarding traditional grantmaking approaches and treating them with disdain, it is worth reflecting whether, with their focus on "gentle benevolence wrapped up in good intentions and support" and while a poor fit for the mushrooming emphasis on rationalism and audit cultures within the foundation field, traditional grantmaking approaches might actually be more appropriate and "relatively well adapted to the ambiguity, opportunism, and serendipity of foundation work" (Leat, 2017, p. 130). As such, other areas in need of further exploration include whether the drive for efficiency in grantmaking is predominantly beneficial to philanthropy or plays to other interests (such as consultancy profits, political control, or neoliberal agendas), and whether the surrounding shift in discourse is beneficial or harmful to the field (e.g. Leat, 2017; Scott, 2009; Thümler, 2016).

Foundations: Rich relations?

Foundations are generally perceived as the nonprofit sector's "rich relations" (Weissert & Knott, 1995), as "islands of money" (Smith, 2015). The robustness of these analogies is open to debate. Grantmaking foundations have a history of being reluctant to share data (Diaz, 2001). A substantial number of foundations prefers to keep information and data on their work private, being "cautiously transparent" (OECD, 2018, p. 93). Within this context, the relative imbalance of research on foundations does not help. Although 60 per cent of foundations identified in a recent global mapping are in Europe and only 35 per cent in North America (Johnson, 2018), most of the research on foundations comes from the US, with other countries, such as Canada, declaring the world of grantmaking foundations a "terra incognita," uncharted territory (Rigillo, Rabinowitz-Bussell, Stuach, & Lajevardi, 2018, p. 3). Thus, it is unsurprising that the mapping exercise concludes that surprisingly little is known about foundations' resources and the way these are used within, and across, national, regional, and global settings: "in much of the world, publicly available philanthropic data and knowledge are scarce" with insights being anecdotal, incomplete, and even inconsistent (Johnson, 2018, p. 9).

To map the foundation world, it is common practice to rank foundations by either their asset or grantmaking levels. The appropriateness of this approach has, however, been challenged. For example, foundations such as Stichting INGKA or Garfield Weston, whose main objective appears to be acting as corporate shells, might be resource-rich but could also be considered as philanthropic penny pinchers: their grantmaking levels appear relatively small when compared to their resources. The former CEO of Germany's Association of Charitable Foundation Felix Oldenburg put it bluntly: in the absence of standard reporting systems, a lot of the work on foundations is "ranking nonsense" with the only thing that we know for certain being that "the Bill & Melinda Gates Foundation is the world's largest foundation. That is pretty much it" (Oldenburg, 2018, n.p.; see also Grant, 2016).

At a global level, this lacuna of knowledge and patchwork quilt of information might be seen as a side-effect of the diverse socio-political and legal contexts within which foundations operate, or as arising from the divergent organizational expressions of the foundation form. However, even compiling data and information on grantmaking foundations at national levels remains problematic. This has repeatedly been highlighted by the authors of the one major ongoing survey of the UK's top-300 grantmaking foundations. Data come from a variety of sources, are derived using a diversity of methods, and cover different timeframes (Pharoah, Walker, & Goddard, 2017). The available data are also often quite dated. For example, at the point of writing, the latest available information on grantmaking foundations in the US offered by the Foundation Center (2018, n.p.), a self-described provider of "the most comprehensive, reliable information about the social sector" linked to the foundation field, is from 2014 – at least four years old.

Acknowledging that the data and knowledge base on grantmaking is thus not as good as one might hope for, what are the indicative insights that we do have? First of all, foundations appear to have global assets of around US$1.5 trillion, of which 60 per cent are held in the US and 37 per cent in Europe, leaving just 3 per cent of assets distributed across foundations in the rest of the world (Johnson, 2018). In light of these numbers and the geographic cluster in which these resources are distributed, critiques of foundations as instruments of cultural imperialism (Arnove, 1980) or as co-creators of world order (Krige & Rausch, 2012) seem unsurprising. However, two things need to be borne in mind. First of all, compared to spending by government and by major players on the international development scene, foundation monies actually tend to be relatively meagre (OECD, 2018; Pharoah et al., 2017). Secondly, it is important to consider the way in which these resources are distributed across the foundation landscape.

Notwithstanding the above criticism of foundation rankings, a look at the ten richest foundations in the world provides some useful insights on how foundation assets are distributed. Here, the endowments of the Bill & Melinda Gates Foundation, the Wellcome Trust, or the Lilly Endowment – approximately US$40 billion, US$27 billion, and US$10 billion respectively – do indeed dwarf the Gross Domestic Product (GDP) of a number of countries. What this sample also highlights, however, is the relatively quick decline in foundations' assets at the top end. This is not restricted to global foundation rankings. It tends to be replicated at national levels too: a very small number of very large foundations is followed by an increasingly large number of smaller and smaller foundations. Accordingly, there are indications that globally 90 per cent of foundations appear to have less than US$10 million, while 50 per cent of foundations have actually less than US$1 million in assets (Johnson, 2018), a long way from the "rich relative" analogy. Within the UK this "long tail of philanthropy" means that 20 of the 300 top grantmaking foundations account for more than half of all the grants made (Pharoah, Jenkins, Goddard, & Walker, 2016), while within the US the top 50 foundations are responsible for over a third (US$20 billion) of the total grantmaking of US$60 billion across the 87,000 foundations on the Foundation Center (2018) database. Independently of whether most foundations are thus actually "rich relations," are they at least "generous relations"?

Foundations: Generous relations?

Foundations have repeatedly been criticized for being "warehouses of wealth" (Gaul & Borowski, 1993) for hoarding their resources rather than using them to the best of their abilities. In its current form, this criticism goes back to the beginning of the 20th century (Clotfelter, 1985). Perceived as tax management vehicles and as representing "dangerous concentrations of unearned economic power" (Gaul & Borowski, 1993), widespread calls for corrective legal actions have led to various reforms over the years, most prominently to the Tax Reform Act of 1969 in the US (Troyer, 2000). Notwithstanding that commentators questioned the Act's "arbitrary rules," "esoteric concepts," and ambition to imagine and close "every possible loophole" for foundation abuse, independent of any compliance challenges and burdens (e.g. Worthy, 1975), the Act established a minimum payout requirement for foundations. Eventually fixed at 5 per cent, it raises interesting scenarios for reflecting on the philanthropic potential of the remaining resources. While qualifiers for foundations' minimum payout go beyond grant-making and include administrative expenditures, such as employee compensation and office maintenance (for current payout regulations see Internal Revenue Service, 2018), the payout requirement and the level at which it is set remain strongly contested (Billitteri, 2005; Levine & Sansing, 2014).

Since any level of payout influences the extent to which an organization that is reliant on its endowment can grow and thrive, central to the debate is whether foundations should exist in perpetuity or whether they should be expected to spend down (Steuerle, 1977). Those explicitly or implicitly in favour of foundations' perpetuity argue that increasing payout rates means to "cut off the dog's tail an inch at a time" (Worthy, 1975, p. 254), representing "a slow but certain death sentence to foundations" (Robert Smith, Pew Memorial Trust, cited in Steuerle, 1977; also Hamilton, 2011). Over the last 17 years, this view has been reiterated in a series of studies funded by US foundations and their umbrella bodies. The recurring argument is that a 5 per cent payout rate is "somewhat too high" and "challenging," with anything over and above 5 per cent portrayed as leading to a certain depletion of resources with an eventual liquidation of foundations (Bignami, 2013; Cambridge Associates, 2000).

Not everyone in the foundation field shares this perspective. The US National Network of Grantmakers, for example, has argued that "it makes no sense to limit total payout to only 5%" (Mehrling, 1999, p. 11); it has heavily criticized both foundations' obsession with investment banking at the expense of grantmaking, and the widespread tendency to equate and treat the required payout rate as a maximum level of giving (Mehrling, 1999). As the idea of spend-out or limited lifespan foundations has gained traction, the last few years have seen wider support for this sentiment (e.g. Waleson, 2007).

Recent findings, cutting across grantmaking and operating foundations, also indicate that there appear to be huge global variations in spending rates, ranging from 1.6 per cent in Nigeria to 37 per cent in Spain, with an average of 10.3 per cent (Johnson, 2018). Even in the US, a number of foundations regularly exceed the minimum payout requirement (Renz, 2012; Sansing & Yetman, 2002). In countries where a fixed legal payout requirement is absent, many already make grants around the 5 per cent mark anyway (Pharoah, Harrow, & Jung, 2017). Thus, there are questions whether a variable payout rate, or even its abandonment altogether, might be appropriate (Deep & Frumkin, 2001), or whether a minimum payout up to the point where foundations have made good on their received tax benefits should be required (Toepler, 2004). This then leads to broader questions about foundations. Where do their resources come from? What are the socio-political and economic roles that foundations play? What benefits do they provide, and to whom?

Are foundations' resources socially and morally acceptable?

From Andrew Carnegie to Bill Gates, from the pharmaceutical industry to tobacco, alcohol, oil and gas, the background of foundations' donors and resources, as well as the ways in which foundations invest and grow their assets can present various tensions. Are their resources socially and/or morally acceptable? As Francis Bacon (1886, p. 17) put it, "glorious gifts and foundations are like sacrifices without salt; and but the painted sepulchres of alms." Are foundations thus akin to an elaborate purification ritual for "bitter money," money that is obtained through theft or harm (Tasimi & Gelman, 2017)? Is it the case that "[t]o accept the reward of iniquity is to place upon our lips the seal of silence respecting its perpetrators" (Gladden, 1905, p. 23) when either the donor, his or her foundation, or the foundation's resources might be seen as "tainted"?

While from an economic perspective money is considered to be fungible (i.e. it represents a unit of exchange whose history and physicality are insignificant), psychological research shows that money is often also construed in terms of its physical substance and material background: it can be contaminated by, and carries traces of, its moral history (Tasimi & Gelman, 2017). As such, concerns about foundations' resources relate to a whole range of questions about (un) acceptable funds. These include: issues of illegality and whether resources are a by-product of any harmful activities; whether grants come with "strings attached" or violate moral codes; donors' own ethical stances and behaviours, and any "sins" they might have committed in the past; concerns about "guilt by association," the extent to which "all private sector money is morally tainted," and if certain sources are simply inherently unacceptable (Jones, 2014, pp. 195–199).

Even if the original resources of a foundation might not present any moral, ethical, or social challenges, the situation is further complicated by foundations' own investment strategies. Here, the view that higher investment returns translate into more resources for grantmaking – something to be desired – has tended to prevail across philanthropy. Questions about any negative social, political, or economic impact of foundations' investment activities are rarely explored or reflected upon (Dowie, 2002), resulting in situations where grantmakers' own investment of their resources can be diametrically opposed to their charitable activities (e.g. Mair, 2013). Where discussions about foundations' investment strategies do take place, the focus tends to be on short-term and narrow effects. While from an environmental and sustainability perspective the "keep it in the ground" initiative by the British newspaper *The Guardian* aimed at getting both the Bill & Melinda Gates Foundation and Wellcome Trust to divest from fossil fuels (Randerson, 2015) might be positive, from a social welfare perspective, it also might have severe negative impacts on the communities whose jobs and infrastructures such disinvestment affects (e.g. Humphrey, Johnson, Lang, Roswell, & Korn, 2014). This highlights the need for foundations and their critics to take a broader perspective and pursue strategies that go well beyond addressing immediate investment issues.

All these questions are of specific importance to grantees. Interestingly, and running counter to public discussions about acceptable funds, there is an argument that in relation to grants, nonprofits are in a different moral zone than individuals (Morris, 2008). While individuals are perceived as being in a position to refuse gifts if the individual disapproves of its origin, nonprofits may face more restricted moral, though not necessarily legally sanctioned, autonomy; their refusal of resources on moral grounds might be "comparable to mismanagement in squandering scarce resources or tolerating other operational inefficiencies. In its quest for moral purity, the charity may be doing less good than it might" (Morris, 2008, p. 752). Indeed, there are indications that some charity trustees "prioritise raising funds over upholding their personal values or ethics," that in their view "all donations should be accepted irrespective of its provenance or the values of the donor organisations" (Harrow & Pharoah, 2010, p. 6). Rather than reflecting on these issues in an abstract way, however, it is worth considering them within the context of foundations' roles more broadly.

Foundations' roles and purposes

What is the actual purpose of grantmaking as a practice (Leat, 2006)? As the wife of a Ford Foundation executive reportedly asked: "Why don't you boys just give everybody in the country two bucks apiece and quit?" (cited in Macdonald, 1956, p. 108). Indeed, while grantmaking offers "a lifeline for a startlingly high number of academic research teams and fledgling non-profit organisations" (McGoey, 2015, p. 19), understanding of grantmaking foundations' actual roles and purposes has always been sketchy.

One challenge in trying to understand foundations' roles and contributions is the unresolved issue of whether foundations and/or their resources are of a public or a private nature. Both "public" and "private" are contested terms. They can relate to: legal and regulatory contexts of how organizations are differentiated into these two categories; the political context of whether foundations serve public or private interests; the economic context, that is if something is of collective or individual concern; and, finally, the social context, things that are consequential or inconsequential for the public or an individual (Fernandez & Hager, 2014). While traditionally foundations can be seen as, and consider themselves to be, private – that is, distinct from public, governmental organizations – and behave accordingly, they are all public institutions as well, at least under the political context perspective: "their areas of engagement in society and justification for existence are outwardly focused" (Fernandez & Hager, 2014, p. 431). This then makes them hybrids in the sense that foundations have simultaneously public and private claims (Fernandez & Hager, 2014). This needs to be remembered when examining foundations' roles.

In their own words, grantmaking foundations do, and achieve, a lot of things. For example, the Mastercard Foundation (2018) "catalyzes prosperity in developing countries," the Rockefeller Foundation (2018) is "promoting the well-being of humanity throughout the world," and, as "impatient optimists," the Bill & Melinda Gates Foundation (2018) is "working to reduce inequity." Proactive and comforting, these slogans paint an encouraging picture. Notwithstanding grandiose rhetoric, being a grantmaking foundation in itself can, however, be seen as entirely and utterly unproductive: "funds do nothing productive until they are transferred to a person or organisation that puts them to use" (Grant, 2016, p. 408). Grantmakers' only "product" is "an empty cheque book" (Leat, 1995, p. 323). Thus, more critical voices compare foundations to "old-fashioned slot machines" in that "they have one arm and are known for their occasional payout" (Viederman, 2011, n.p.), to Don Quixotes in limousines – simultaneously comic and tragic characters fighting windmills – (Whitaker, 1974, p. 20), and to "the cadaver at a family wake – their presence is essential, but not very much is expected of them" (foundation president cited in Emerson, 2004, p. 2).

Synthesizing the diverse imagery on US foundations, McIlnay (1998) highlights six analogies for foundations' overarching roles that are perpetuated across foundation discourse. Accordingly, foundations can act as judges (of what and who gets funded, where, and why), editors (fulfilling an intermediary function), citizens (having legal and voluntary responsibilities and obligations to others), activists (associated with the idea of social change and social movements), entrepreneurs (innovators and risk takers), and partners (working with others across the private, public, and nonprofit sector). While most of these images appear to be mythical rather than actual representations (McIlnay, 1998), they do resonate with the growing body of work on foundations' socio-economic roles. Here, a number of overarching perspectives can be identified (Healy & Donnelly-Cox, 2016; Toepler, 2018a). Firstly, foundations are an expression of pluralism. They enable and allow the expression of a multitude of perspectives on what counts as public good and how this is provided and achieved. Secondly, they can fulfil a role in the voluntary redistribution of wealth. Thirdly, they can act as supplementary or substitutional funders in the provision of the public good or public services. Finally, due to their organizational independence and freedom – unrivalled by any other contemporary organizational form or institution (Anheier & Leat, 2013) – they are seen as potential change agents and risk takers, as catalysts for innovation. The way these relationships between foundations and society play out has been cast alternately as a partnership model, as a perfect match where both foundations and the state are reliant on each other to achieve the best outcomes (Macdonald & Szanto, 2007); as a mismatch, where foundations are part of a "shadow state" (Lipman, 2015); as an expression and enforcer of elite interests (McGoey, 2015); and as the institutional equivalent of a game of ping-pong, where foundations act as a prelude or post-script to public policy initiatives and state activities (Jung & Harrow, 2019).

Closely related to questions of foundations' roles and activities, is the position that foundations assume vis-à-vis each other and in relation to different actors across the public, private, and non-profit sectors (e.g., Förster, 2018; Mangold, 2018). In this regard, Anheier and Daly (2007, pp. 17–20) use countries' regime types and draw on comparative data on foundations from the US and 18 European countries to point to six clusters of foundation–state relationships:

- *Social democratic model* – in a well-developed welfare state, foundations complement or supplement state activities;
- *State-controlled model* – foundations are subservient to, and closely controlled by, the state;
- *Corporatist model* – foundations are subservient to the state and form part of the wider welfare system;
- *Liberal model* – foundations coexist in parallel and as a potential alternative to the state;
- *Peripheral model* – foundations are insignificant, albeit worthwhile if refraining from challenging the status quo;
- *Business model* – foundations are an expression of self-interest and aligned to corporate citizenship.

Inherently, these six clusters point to questions about foundations' legitimacy: how do foundations get the authority and credibility to perform these roles? Here, the literature refers to three types of legitimacy: normative, procedural, and empirical legitimacy (Beetham, 2013; Harman, 2016; Heydemann & Toepler, 2006). Normative legitimacy focuses on philosophical issues around the values and criteria that are, and should be, used to determine foundations' legitimacy in different settings. Procedural legitimacy looks at foundations' adherence to, and fulfilment of, legal frameworks, laws, and socio-political contracts, while empirical legitimacy addresses the social, political, and economic perceptions of, and perspectives on, whether foundations are legitimate. Although there have been longstanding debates about foundations' normative legitimacy (e.g. Reich, Cordelli, & Bernholz, 2016) and the extent to which foundations live up to their promises (e.g. Thümler, 2011), the third aspect seems rarely to be challenged: despite widespread debates about foundations' governance, transparency, and accountability, as well as prominent examples of scandals, corruptions, and mismanagement in the foundation world, overall confidence in, support of, and ambitions for the foundation form continue to appear strong (Anheier, 2018; Heydemann & Toepler, 2006).

Alongside their portrayed public roles and positioning, foundations can also fulfil more private, indirect, functions. Akin to the organizational equivalent of a "magic potion," their addressing of charitable issues can go hand-in-hand with solving business difficulties and family troubles (Lepaulle, 1927, p. 1126). Such functions are at their most noticeable in the history of those foundations with a family or industrial background. They include the use of foundations for managing tax issues to maintain family ownership and control of a corporate entity, as well as for enshrining a specific corporate vision or direction. Examples of such uses range from the establishment of the Ford Foundation in the US (Macdonald, 1956), to the Robertson Trust in Scotland (Maclean, 2001), Denmark's Carlsberg Foundation (2014), or the Stichting INGKA foundation in the Netherlands (Thomsen, 2017). Beyond this, foundations' structures and activities can also be used to keep the family happy: from grantee site visits offering entertainment opportunities for family members, to board meetings acting as family reunions (Oelberger, 2016).

While anathema to dominant contemporary perspectives on foundations – in which foundations are inferred to be linked to altruistic motives for wider good, and where the use of foundations for personal benefits can be an abuse of the foundation form (e.g. Charity Commission for England and Wales, 2017) – from a historical, anthropological, or sociological perspective such private aims should not come as a surprise. Here, the practice and casting of gifts, altruism, and egoism have not been considered as conceptual counterpoints but rather as symbiotic, offering a win–win situation for private and public interests in philanthropic acts (Davis, 2000; von Reden, 2015).

Concluding thoughts

Given the complexities of the foundation field, there are ongoing questions about the actual and potential contributions that foundations can make in addressing and solving social problems. In light of growing expectations of philanthropy more broadly, these appear particularly pertinent. Here, foundations' explicit track record appears chequered. Exercising social control and maintaining social stability, as well as giving legitimacy to themselves and their partners, sit alongside foundations' contributions to building social welfare, healthcare, and education (Berman, 1983; Thümler, 2011). While this chapter has pointed to some of the key issues surrounding grantmaking foundations, other areas, such as power and donor voice, as well as wider debates about risk, have been left open (e.g., Grant, 2016; Orosz, 2004; Reich et al. 2016; Winkelstein & Whelpton, 2017). As part of taking the foundation field forward, more nuanced perspectives are needed. Simplistic enchantments with grandiose visions, ambitions for and claims of foundations need to be recast in more modest, realistic, terms (Anheier & Leat, 2013; Harrow & Jung, 2011). As foundations generally appear to be far from the "rich relations" image, recent ideas encouraging foundations to be more pragmatic in their philanthropic endeavours by focusing on clearly bounded issues and niches (see Thümler, 2017) appear promising. So, too, is the growing interest in more communal approaches to grantmaking by foundations. These try to move away from top-down, prescriptive perspectives on what should be done towards more inclusive approaches to working with grantees. Examples from the UK include the Rank Foundation's engaged philanthropy approach, the Grants Plus programme advocated by the Esmée Fairbairn Foundation and others, as well as the John Ellerman Foundation's emphasis on being a "responsive funder"; internationally, this trend is illustrated by the Rockefeller Foundation's ENGAGE initiative aimed at supporting networks, and the Case Foundation's "Make it your own" awards programme. While still relatively emergent, they draw on traditional models of community philanthropy, social inclusion, and community development and thus may offer a way to address some of the challenges highlighted in this chapter.

References

Anheier, H. K. (2018). Philanthropic Foundations in Cross-National Perspective: A Comparative Approach. *American Behavioral Scientist, 62*(12), 1591–1602.

Anheier, H. K., & Daly, S. (2007). *The Politics of Foundations*. London: Routledge.

Anheier, H. K., & Leat, D. (2006). *Creative Philanthropy*. London: Routledge.

Anheier, H. K., & Leat, D. (2013). Philanthropic Foundations: What Rationales? *Social Research, 80*(2), 449–472.

Anheier, H. K., & Toepler, S. (Eds.). (1999). *Private Funds, Public Purpose: Philanthropic Foundations in International Perspective*. New York: Kluwer.

Arnove, R. F. (Ed.). (1980). *Philanthropy and Cultural Imperialism. The Foundations at Home and Abroad*. Boston: G.K. Hall.

Association of Charitable Foundations. (2017). *Introduction to Grant-Making Series*. London.

Association of Charitable Foundations. (2018). What is a foundation? www.acf.org.uk/about/what-is-a-foundation/

Bacon, F. (1886). Of Riches. In E. A. Abbott (Ed.), *Bacon's Essays* (Vol. II). London: Longmans, Green.

Beetham, D. (2013). *The Legitimation of Power* (2nd ed.). London: Palgrave Macmillan.

Berman, E. H. (1983). *The Influence of the Carnegie, Ford and Rockefeller Foundations on American Foreign Policy: The Ideology of Philanthropy*. Albany: State University of New York Press.

Bignami, P. G. (2013). *Sustainable Payout for Foundations. 2013 Update Study*. Cambridge Associates.

Bill & Melinda Gates Foundation. (2018). Homepage. https://www.gatesfoundation.org

Billitteri, T. J. (2005). *Money, Mission, and the Payout Rule: In Search of a Strategic Approach to Foundation Spending*. Washington, DC: Aspen Institute.

Brealey, P. (2013). The Charitable Corporation for the Relief of Industrious Poor: Philanthropy, Profit and Sleaze in London, 1707–1733. *History, 98*(333), 708–729.

Brown, E. R. (1979). *Rockefeller Medicine Men*. Berkeley: University of California Press.

Cabinet Office. (2014a). How foundations are using Total Impact approaches to achieve their charitable mission. London: https://www.gov.uk/government/uploads/system/uploads/attachment_data/file/386335/2903051_ImpactFoundations_acc.pdf

Cabinet Office. (2014b). Using a total impact approach to achieve social outcomes. https://www.gov.uk/government/publications/using-a-total-impact-approach-to-achieve-social-outcomes

Cambridge Associates. (2000). *Sustainable Payout for Foundations*. Grand Haven, MI.

Carlsberg Foundation. (2014). *Pursue Perfection*. Copenhagen: Kontrapunkt.

Carnegie, A. (1901). *The Gospel of Wealth and Other Timely Essays*. New York: Century.

Charity Commission for England and Wales. (2017). Update on Cup Trust Inquiry.

Clotfelter, C. T. (1985). Foundations. In C. T. Clotfelter (Ed.), *Federal Tax Policy and Charitable Giving* (pp. 253–272). Chicago: University of Chicago Press.

Council on Foundations. (2018). What is a foundation? www.cof.org/content/foundation-basics#what_is_a_foundation

Cunningham, H. (2016). The Multi-layered History of Western Philanthropy. In T. Jung, S. D. Phillips, & J. Harrow (Eds.), *The Routledge Companion to Philanthropy* (pp. 42–55). London: Routledge.

Davis, N. Z. (2000). *The Gift in Sixteenth-Century France*. Oxford: Oxford University Press.

Deep, A., & Frumkin, P. (2001). *The Foundation Payout Puzzle*. http://ksghauser.harvard.edu/index.php/content/download/68878/1248322/version/1/file/workingpaper_9.pdf

Diaz, W. A. (2001). The Lost Inner World of Grantmaking Foundations (or, as Willie Sutton once said, "That's Where the Money Is"). *Nonprofit Management & Leadership, 12*(2), 213–218.

Dietz, N., McKeever, R., Steele, E., & Steuerle, C. E. (2015). *Foundation Grantmaking over the Economic Cycle*. Washington, DC: Urban Institute.

Dowie, M. (2002). *American Foundations. An Investigative History*. Cambridge MA: MIT Press.

DP Evaluation. (2012). *A Funder Conundrum. Choices that funders face in bringing about positive social change*. London.

Emerson, J. (2004). Reflections on Philanthropic Effectiveness. www.issuelab.org/resource/reflections_on_philanthropic_effectiveness

European Foundation Centre. (2015). *Comparative Highlights of Foundation Laws*. Brussels.

Fernandez, K. M., & Hager, M. A. (2014). Public and Private Dimensionns of Grantmaking Foundations. *Public Administration Quarterly, 38*(3), 405–439.

Fleishman, J. L. (2007). *The Foundation*. New York: Public Affairs.

Förster, S. (2018). Foundations in Germany: Social Welfare. *American Behavioral Scientist, 62*(12), 1715–1734.

Foundation Center. (2018). Foundation Stats. http://data.foundationcenter.org

Friedman, E. (2013). *Reinventing Philanthropy*. Washington, DC: Potomac Books.

Frumkin, P. (2006). *Strategic Giving: The Art and Science Of Philanthropy*. Chicago: Chicago University Press.

Frumkin, P. (2014). New Forms of Grantmaking: Competitions, Prizes and Crowd Sourcing. In L. M. Salamon (Ed.), *New Frontiers of Philanthropy* (pp. 514–535). Oxford: Oxford University Press.

Gaul, G. M., & Borowski, N. A. (1993). *Free Ride. The Tax-exempt Economy*. Kansas City, MO: Andrews and McMeel.

Gibson, C. M. (2017). *Participatory Grantmaking: Has Its Time Come?*: Ford Foundation.

Gladden, W. (1905). *The New Idolatry and Other Discussions*. New York: McClure, Phillips.

Goldberg, S. H. (2009). *Billions of Drops in Millions of Buckets*. Hoboken, NJ: Wiley.

Golden, S. L. (2004). Grantseeking. In D. F. Burlingame (Ed.), *Philanthropy in America: A Comprehensive Historical Encyclopedia*. (Vol. 1, pp. 209–211). Denver, CO: ABC-Clio.

Goldsworth, J. G. (2016). *Lexicon of Trust & Foundation Practice*. Huntingdon, Cambs: Mulberry House Press.

Gordon, J., Harvey, C., Shaw, E., & Maclean, M. (2016). Entrepreneurial Philanthropy. In T. Jung, S. D. Phillips, & J. Harrow (Eds.), *The Routledge Companion to Philanthropy* (pp. 334–347). London: Routledge.

Grace, K. S., & Wendroff, A. L. (2000). *High Impact Philanthropy*. London: John Wiley.

Grant, P. (2016). Directing and Managing Grantmaking. In T. Jung, S. Phillips, & J. Harrow (Eds.), *The Routledge Companion to Philanthropy* (pp. 408–422). London: Routledge.

Hamilton, C. H. (2011). Payout Redux. *Conversations on Philanthropy, 8*, 28–38.

Harman, S. (2016). The Bill and Melinda Gates Foundation and Legitimacy in Global Health Governance. *Global Governance: A Review of Multilateralism and International Organizations, 22*(3), 349–368.

Harrow, J., & Fitzmaurice, J. (2011). *The Art of Refusal: Promising Practice for Grant Makers and Grant Seekers*. London: Centre for Charity Effectiveness, Cass Business School City University London.

Harrow, J., & Jung, T. (2011). Philanthropy Is Dead; Long Live Philanthropy? *Public Management Review, 13*(8), 1047–1056.

Harrow, J., & Pharoah, C. (2010). How do you ask difficult questions? Shared challenges and practice amongst fundraisers and researcher. CGAG Briefing Note 4. London: Centre for Charitable Giving and Effectiveness, Cass Business School City University London.

Healy, J., & Donnelly-Cox, G. (2016). The Evolving State Relationship: Implications of 'Big Societies' and Shrinking States. In T. Jung, S. D. Phillips, & J. Harrow (Eds.), *The Routledge Companion to Philanthropy*. London: Routledge.

Heydemann, S., & Toepler, S. (2006). Foundations and the Challenge of Legitimacy in Comparative Perspective. In K. Prewitt, M. Dogan, S. Heydemann, & S. Toepler (Eds.), *The Legitimacy of Philanthropic Foundations* (pp. 3–26). New York: Russell Sage Foundation.

Humphrey, J., Johnson, B., Lang, K., Roswell, D., & Korn, S. (2014). *Fossil-Free Investment for a Just Appalachian Transition. Obstacles and Opportunities*. Durham, NC: Croatan Institute.

Inspiring Impact. (2017). Our vision. http://inspiringimpact.org/about/our-vision/

Internal Revenue Service. (2018). Tax on Private Foundation Failure to Distribute Income: "Distributable amount." https://www.irs.gov/charities-non-profits/private-foundations/tax-on-private-foundation-failure-to-distribute-income-distributable-amount

John, R. (2006). *Venture Philanthropy: The evolution of high engagement philanthropy in Europe*. Oxford. www.sbs.ox.ac.uk/sites/default/files/Skoll_Centre/Docs/Venture%20philanthropy%20in%20Europe.pdf

Johnson, P. D. (2018). *Global Philanthropy Repor*. Hauser Institute for Civil Society and the Center for Public Leadership.

Jones, C. (2014). Dirty Money. *Journal of Academic Ethics, 12*, 191–207.

Jung, T., & Harrow, J. (2019). Providing Foundations: Philanthropy, Global Policy and Administration. In D. Stone & K. Moloney (Eds.), *Oxford Handbook on Global Public Policy and Transnational Administration* (pp. 619–637). Oxford: Oxford University Press.

Jung, T., Harrow, J., & Leat, D. (2018). Mapping Philanthropic Foundations' Characteristics: Towards an International Integrative Framework of Foundation Types. *Nonprofit and Voluntary Sector Quarterly, 47*(5), 893–917.

Katz, S. N. (2005). What Does It Mean to Say That Philanthropy Is "Effective"? The Philanthropists' New Clothes. *Proceedings of the American Philosophical Society, 149*(2), 123–131.

Kiger, J. C. (Ed.). (2000). *Philanthropic Foundations in the Twentieth Century*. Westport, CT: Greenwood Press.

Kramer, M. R. (2009). Catalytic Philanthropy. *Standford Social Innovation Review, Fall*, 30–35.

Krige, J., & Rausch, H. (Eds.). (2012). *American Foundations and the Coproduction of World Order in the Twentieth Century*. Göttingen: Vandenhoeck & Ruprecht.

Leat, D. (1995). British Foundations: The Organisation and Management of Grant-making. *VOLUNTAS: International Journal of Voluntary and Nonprofit Organizations, 6*(3), 317–329.

Leat, D. (2006). Grantmaking Foundations and Performance Measurement: Playing Pool? *Public Policy and Administration, 21*(3), 25–37.

Leat, D. (2016). Private and Family Foundations. In T. Jung, S. D. Phillips, & J. Harrow (Eds.), *The Routledge Companion to Philanthropy*. London: Routledge.

Leat, D. (2017). Grantmaking in a Disorderly World: The Limits of Rationalism. *Australian Journal of Public Administration, 77*(1), 128–135.

Lepaulle, P. (1927). Civil Law Substitutes for Trusts. *Yale Law Journal, 36*(8), 1126–1147.

Levine, C. B., & Sansing, R. C. (2014). The Private Foundation Minimum Distribution Requirement and Public Policy. *Journal of the American Taxation Association, 36*(1), 165–180.

Lipman, P. (2015). Capitalizing on Crisis: Venture Philanthropy's Colonial Project to Remake Urban Education. *Critical Studies in Education, 56*(2), 241–258.

Macdonald, D. (1956). *The Ford Foundation. The Men and the Millions – An Unauthorized Biography*. New York: Reynal.

Macdonald, G., & Szanto, A. (2007). Private Philanthropy and Government: Friends or Foes? In S. U. Raymond & M. B. Martin (Eds.), *Mapping the New World of American Philanthropy – Causes and Consequences of the Transfer of Wealth* (pp. 235–239). Hoboken, NJ: John Wiley.

Maclean, C. (2001). *The Robertson Trust*. Edinburgh: Maclean Dubois.

Mair, V. (2013, 10 December). Comic Relief Coverage Highlights Charities' Investment Dilemmas. *Civil Society*. https://www.civilsociety.co.uk/news/comic-relief-coverage-highlights-charities--investment-dilemmas.html

Mangold, J. (2018). Foundations in Germany: Higher Education. *American Behavioral Scientist, 62*(12), 1695–1714.

Mastercard Foundation. (2018). About us. www.mastercardfdn.org/about/

McGoey, L. (2015). *No Such Thing as a Free Gift. The Gates Foundation and the Price of Philanthropy*. London: Verso.

McIlnay, D. P. (1998). *How Foundations Work*. San Francisco: Jossey-Bass.

Meachen, V. (2010). *An Introductory Guide to Grantmaking*. Melbourne: Philanthropy Australia.

Mehrling, P. (1999). *Spending Policies for Foundations. The Case for Increased Grants Payout*. San Diego, CA: National Network of Grantmakers.

Morris, D. (2008). Tainted Money and Charity. Do 501(c)(3)s Have a Right to Refuse a Gift? *Nonprofit and Voluntary Sector Quarterly, 37*(4), 743–755.

Murphy, E. J. (1976). *Creative Philanthropy. Carnegie Corporation and Africa 1953–1973*. New York: Carnegie Corporation of New York.

National Committee for Responsive Philanthropy. (2009). *Criteria for Philanthropy at Its Best*. Washington, DC. www.ncrp.org/wp-content/uploads/2016/10/paib-fulldoc_lowres.pdf

Nielsen, W. A. (1985). *The Golden Donors. A New Anatomy of the Great Foundations*. New York: Truman Talley Books.

OECD. (2018). *Private Philanthropy for Development. The Development Dimension*. Paris: OECD Publishing.

Oelberger, C. R. (2016). Cui Bono? Private Goals in the Design of Public Organizations. *Administration & Society*, Online First.

Oldenburg, F. (2018). Oldenburgs Impuls – Ranking Nonsense. https://www.stiftungen.org/stiftungen/blogs/stiftungsblog/ranking-nonsense.html

Orosz, J. J. (2004). Grantmaking. In D. F. Burlingame (Ed.), *Philanthropy in America: A Comprehensive Historical Encyclopedia* (Vol. 1, pp. 204–209). Denver, CO: ABC-Clio.

Parmar, I. (2012). *Foundations of the American Century: The Ford, Carnegie, and Rockefeller Foundation in the Rise of American Power*. New York: Columbia University Press.

Pharoah, C., Harrow, J., & Jung, T. (2017). *Examining payout in UK philanthropic foundations*. Centre for Charitable Giving and Philanthropy.

Pharoah, C., Jenkins, R., Goddard, K., & Walker, C. (2016). *Giving Trends. Top 300 Foundation Grant-Makers.* London: Association of Charitable Foundations.

Pharoah, C., Walker, C., & Goddard, K. (2017). *Giving Trends 2017. Top 300 Foundation Grantmakers.* London: Association of Charitable Foundations.

Prewitt, K. (2006). Foundations. In W. W. Powell & R. Steinberg (Eds.), *The Nonprofit Sector. A Research Handbook* (2nd ed., pp. 355–377). New Haven, CT: Yale University Press.

Randerson, J. (2015). A Story of Hope: The Guardian Launches Phase II of its Climate Change Campaign. *The Guardian.* https://www.theguardian.com/environment/2015/oct/05/a-story-of-hope-the-guardian-launches-phase-two-of-its-climate-change-campaign

Reich, R., Cordelli, C., & Bernholz, L. (2016). *Philanthropy in Democratic Societies.* Chicago: University of Chicago Press.

Renz, L. (2012). *Understanding and Benchmarking Foundation Payout.* New York: Foundation Center.

Ridley, S. (2017) Firm Foundations. Setting your Grant-making Strategy. Vol. 1. London: Association of Charitable Foundations.

Rigillo, N., Rabinowitz-Bussell, M., Stuach, J., & Lajevardi, N. (2018). *Grantmaking in Canada and the United States: A Comparative Review and Analysis of the Literature.* Montréal: PhiLab.

Rockefeller Foundation. (2018). Homepage. https://www.rockefellerfoundation.org

Roelofs, J. (2003). *Foundations and Public Policy. The Mask of Pluralism.* New York: State University of New York Press.

Salamon, L. M. (Ed.). (2014). *New Frontiers of Philanthropy.* Oxford: Oxford University Press.

Sansing, R., & Yetman, R. (2002). *Distribution Policies of Private Foundations.* Hanover, NH: Tuck School of Business.

Schoon, N. (2015). Islamic Finance as Social Finance. In A. Nicholls, R. Paton, & J. Emerson (Eds.), *Social Finance* (pp. 572–588). Oxford: Oxford University Press.

Scott, J. (2009). The Politics of Venture Philanthropy in Charter School Policy and Advocacy. *Educational Policy, 23*(1), 106–136.

Shapiro, R. A., Mirchandani, M., & Jang, H. (Eds.). (2018). *Pragmatic Philanthropy. Asian Charity Explained.* Singapore: Palgrave Macmillan.

Singer, P. (2015). *The Most Good You Can Do.* New Haven, CT: Yale University Press.

Smith, B. (2015). Foundation Strategy . . . the Enemy of Collaboration? http://www.grantcraft.org/blog/foundation-strategy . . . the-enemy-of-collaboration

Spero, J. E. (2010). *The Global Role of U.S. Foundations.* New York: Foundation Center.

Sprecher, T., Egger, P., & von Schnurbein, G. (2016). *Swiss Foundation Code 2015.* Basel: Helbing Lichtenhahn.

Steuerle, E. (1977). Pay-out Requirements for Foundations. *Research Papers sponsored by The Commission on Private Philanthropy and Public Needs* (pp. 1663–1678). Washington, DC: US Department of Treasury.

Stone, L. M. (1975). The Charitable Foundation: Its Governance. *Law and Contemporary Problems, 39*(4), 57–74.

Tasimi, A., & Gelman, S. A. (2017). Dirty Money: The Role of Moral History in Economic Judgments. *Cognitive Science, 41*(S3), 523–544.

Thomsen, S. (2017). *The Danish Industrial Foundations.* Copenhagen: Djøf Publishing.

Thümler, E. (2011). Foundations, Schools and the State: School Improvement Partnerships in Germany and the US as Legitimacy-Generating Arrangements. *Public Management Review, 13*(8), 1095–1116.

Thümler, E. (2016). Financialization of Philanthropy: The Case of Social Investment. In T. Jung, S. D. Phillips, & J. Harrow (Eds.), *The Routledge Companion to Philanthropy* (pp. 362–374). London: Routledge.

Thümler, E. (2017). *Philanthropy in Practice: Pragmatism and the Impact of Philanthropic Action.* London: Routledge.

Toepler, S. (1999). Operating in a Grantmaking World: Reassessing the Role of Operating Foundations. In H. Anheier & S. Toepler (Eds.), *Private Funds, Public Purpose. Philanthropic Foundations in International Perspective* (pp. 163–181). New York: Kluwer Academic.

Toepler, S. (2004). Ending Payout as We Know It: A Conceptual and Comparative Perspective on the Payout Requirement for Foundations. *Nonprofit and Voluntary Sector Quarterly, 33*(4), 729–738.

Toepler, S. (2018a). Public Philanthropic Partnerships: The Changing Nature of Government/Foundation Relationships in the US. *International Journal of Public Administration,* 41(8), 657–669.

Toepler, S. (2018b). Toward a Comparative Understanding of Foundations. *American Behavioral Scientist,* 62(13), 1956–1971. 0002764218773504.

Troyer, T. A. (2000). The 1969 Private Foundation Law: Historical Perspective on Its Origins and Under-pinnings. *The Exempt Organization Tax Review, 27*(1), 52–65.

Unwin, J. (2004). *The Grantmaking Tango: Issues for Funders.* London: The Baring Foundation.

Viederman, S. (2011). Foundations don't practice what they preach. http://www.marcgunther.com/stephen-viederman-foundations-dont-practice-what-they-preach/

von Reden, S. (Ed.). (2015). *Stiftungen zwischen Politik und Wirtschaft.* Oldenburg: DeGruyter.

Waleson, H. (2007). *Beyond Five Percent: The New Foundation Payout Menu.* San Francisco, CA and New York, NY: Northern California Grantmakers and New York Regional Association of Grantmakers.

Weissert, C. S., & Knott, J. H. (1995). Foundations' Impact on Policymaking: Results from a Pilot Study. *Health Affairs, 14,* 275–286.

Whitaker, B. (1974). *The Foundations. An Anatomy of Philanthropy and Society.* London: Eyre Methuen.

Winkelstein, M., & Whelpton, S. (2017). Foundations Don't Know What They Are Risking. *The Foundation Review, 9*(2), 93–108.

Worthy, M. K. (1975). The Tax Reform Act of 1969: Consequences for Private Foundations. *Law and Contemporary Problems, 39*(4), 232–254.

29

CORPORATE PHILANTHROPY

Lonneke Roza

ASSISTANT PROFESSOR, BUSINESS-SOCIETY MANAGEMENT DEPARTMENT, ROTTERDAM SCHOOL
OF MANAGEMENT, ERASMUS UNIVERSITY, ROTTERDAM, THE NETHERLANDS

Lucas C.P.M. Meijs

PROFESSOR OF STRATEGIC PHILANTHROPY AND VOLUNTEERING, BUSINESS-SOCIETY
MANAGEMENT DEPARTMENT, ROTTERDAM SCHOOL OF MANAGEMENT, ERASMUS
UNIVERSITY, ROTTERDAM, THE NETHERLANDS

Introduction

Corporate Social Responsibility (CSR) has become indispensable in modern business. As early as the late 1920s, scholars started to suggest the necessity for businesspeople to assume some responsibility for the well-being of the community (Donham, 1927, 1929). It was, however, not until the 1950s that CSR found its more popular beginnings, especially in the wake of the publication of the book *Social Responsibilities of the Businessman* (Bowen, 1953). Since the 1970s, many different definitions have emerged for the concept of CSR. Some definitions (e.g., Carroll, 1979) focus on types of responsibility (i.e., financial, legal, ethical, and philanthropic); others (e.g., Freeman, 1984) focus on the relationship with and responsibility to stakeholders, and still others focus on the responsible actions taken (Aguinis and Glavas, 2012). Mostly, CSR is considered as a broad umbrella term that encompasses "a broad, integrated and strategic vision on the roles and responsibilities of a company in every society, national as well as international" (Wartick and Wood, 1998, p. 70).

Over the past half-century, the concept has received increasing attention in both research and practice. This is not surprising given the increasing urgency of CSR, due to the changing role of companies but also governments in social issues and a widely held belief among consumers, employees, and other stakeholders that CSR should be regarded as part of overall business performance. Though some might argue that CSR was considered illegitimate in the early days of the development of this concept, it seems in contemporary society it is rather illegitimate for corporations *not* to engage in CSR activities (Seghers, 2007).

Within the realm of CSR, Corporate Philanthropy (CP) is the most implemented CSR strategy in large multinational as well as in small- and medium-sized companies worldwide. CP is understood as "the voluntary business of giving of money, time or in-kind goods, without any *direct* commercial benefit, to one or more organizations whose core purpose is to benefit the community's welfare" (Madden et al., 2006, p. 49, italics in the original). According to Meijs and Van der Voort (2004), CP can be operationalized based on five Ms: (1) Money: donating financial resources directly or through supporting pay roll giving, (2) Means: donating products or tangible goods such as sharing office space and equipment, (3) Manpower: which refers to corporate volunteering, (4) Mass: sharing corporate networks and creating influence by introducing the nonprofit organization to the company's stakeholders, and (5) Media: Cause Related Marketing (CRM) and other joint media exposure that supports the nonprofit to campaign on, or promote a particular social issue.

Companies are increasingly allocating their resources to CP (Campbell et al., 2002). In both the United States and Europe, more than 20 billion dollars was given by companies (Giving USA, 2019; Giving in Europe, 2017). However, the relative importance of the contributions does differ between the two regions. Whereas giving by corporations is relatively low compared to other forms of giving in the United States (only 5 per cent of total giving), it is relatively high in Europe (25 per cent of total giving).[1] It is expected that the numbers will only rise, as the investments in corporate philanthropy have been rising since 2007 (Charities Aid Foundation, 2014). In addition, research among 261 international companies confirms that a majority of these companies (64 per cent) had increased their total community contributions between 2010 and 2013 (Stroik, 2014).

Moreover, there is a growing interest among companies to engage in corporate volunteering. Corporate volunteering (also known as employee volunteering, employer-supported volunteering, and workplace volunteering) refers to volunteer activities that are performed by employees and encouraged (or even facilitated) by their employing organizations (Roza, 2016). Corporate volunteering can be performed either in the employee's own time (e.g., with unpaid leave or other support from the employer) or during official working hours. For this reason, companies are likely to adopt formal and informal policies that involve volunteering. Corporate volunteering practices vary widely. For instance, some organizations adopt turnkey activities, such as employees volunteering to paint classrooms and plant flowers at a local elementary school. Others focus more on customized activities. For example, IBM sends individual employees on overseas sabbaticals where they use their business skills to advance technological capacity in other countries (Raffaelli and Glynn, 2014).

Motivations to engage in corporate philanthropy

Clearly, business and nonprofit organizations have their own motives to engage in CP. Even though the operationalization of the motives might differ, for each of the actors, the motives for engaging in CP can be segmented into four approaches: descriptive, instrumental, normative, and reactive (Liu et al., 2013). These four approaches are discussed for both companies and nonprofits.

Corporate motivations

First, the descriptive approach explains corporate managers' attempt to present their organizations to the outside world. In this approach to CP, managers focus on identifying who the community stakeholders are, what their claims are on the corporation, and how the potential nonprofit partner proposes to address these claims to act in accordance with their shared values; not at the least the value that is highly weighted by the community stakeholders (Liu et al., 2013). Here, managers can build a corporation's identity, and express their corporate values to a company's community stakeholders by protecting and promoting the welfare of the community (Bartel, 2001; Maignan and Ferrell, 2001). Alignment between the corporate values and the nonprofit partner's values can help a company to strengthen its relationship with its local community, because the nonprofits feel that companies are part of the same community (Roza, 2016).

Second, in the instrumental approach, which is the prevailing motive in business literature (Liket and Simaens, 2015), managers view CP as a means to an end (Liu et al., 2013). In other words, they use CP to reach certain organizational goals. In this quest, managers focus on how and whether engagement with nonprofit organizations can benefit the company and thereby strengthen organizational performance. This approach resonates with the growing attention in literature on strategic CP (Porter and Kramer, 2002). Strategic CP argues that CP should only be executed if companies can use their charitable efforts to simultaneously create social value as well as strengthening the competitive context of their company. For example, companies should allocate their CP into creating a favourable business climate in the direct surroundings of their company. Investing their resources into these specific projects in local communities creates value for the community while also benefiting the company. There is a clear business case for e.g., corporate volunteering in this, as a strong connection between employees and their working environments creates employer branding and leads to potential personal and professional development while volunteering. Although direct effects on the financial bottom line are less obvious, as CP excludes sponsoring and cause-related marketing, they do exist when local consumers favour locally embedded companies. CP from an instrumental perspective is thus linked to the company directly benefiting from it.

Third, the normative approach casts the motives of CP as based on it being the right thing to do (Liu et al., 2013). Managers take action based on the interests of the community stakeholders as a moral obligation, although it may not necessarily be in immediate business interest of the corporation. This could include supporting local nonprofit organizations to strengthen the community in which the company operates or benefit certain groups that are not able to be served commercially, such as supporting organizations that serve the homeless.

Lastly, there is a reactive approach to CP where companies engage in these interactions simply because they are pressured to do so (e.g., Van der Voort et al., 2009). Increasingly, governments, local communities, consumers, and even employees are putting pressure on companies to be active in the community to strengthen civil society and to resolve government and market failures. In some countries such as India (Gupta, 2014), CP is even required and enforced by law, raising conceptual questions of whether such legally coerced activity is truly CP, at least according to Western standards and academic definitions.

Nonprofit motivations

Nonprofit organizations can likewise have motivations based on the descriptive approach as to why they engage in partnerships with companies. As this approach is very much value-driven, nonprofit organizations engage in corporate philanthropic relations to express and further their own values. Here, nonprofit organizations feel that collaborating with companies is simply what they must do. These are nonprofit organizations that entirely build their business model on corporate giving and partnerships, simply because they believe that this is in their mutual interest. For example, organizations that support youngsters in deprived areas towards employment collaborate with corporate coaches because they represent the business community in which the nonprofit organizations would like to see their clients employed.

Similar to how companies could instrumentally approach their CP, nonprofit organizations also use CP instrumentally (Roza et al., 2017). For instance, they could use it as a signal to other donors, to enhance their legitimacy in society, obtain more resources for their mission, or even to serve their clients better. From a nonprofit perspective, strategic CP is defined as "utilizing the contributions of any 'responsible' activity of companies to allow a nonprofit organization to achieve its mission" (Roza, 2016, p. 330). In this perspective, nonprofit organizations should only engage in relationships based on CP that are directly – albeit perhaps only in the long term – beneficial for their organization. This challenges the general assumption that prevails in business literature and business practice that nonprofit organizations benefit from CP, regardless of which resources companies share and under which conditions. What might be strategic and instrumental for the company might not be strategic or instrumental for the nonprofit organization (Roza, 2016). Just like companies stay away from certain political and religious nonprofit organizations, nonprofit organizations stay away from companies in contested businesses such as tobacco and weapons.

Although perhaps less morally inclined, nonprofit organizations also engage in accepting CP because it is the right thing to do, for instance for their beneficiaries. This is the normative approach in which they feel the obligation towards their primary stakeholders to involve companies to provide their services. Organizations that focus on the employability of veterans or disadvantaged youth utilize their relationships based on CP with companies to directly serve the mission and the beneficiaries.

Lastly, nonprofit organizations sometimes feel they are being pressured to collaborate with companies (Shachar et al., 2018). This could resonate from corporate executives who are board members themselves, which is common in the United States. However, in countries where corporate giving is not yet a longstanding tradition (e.g., the Netherlands) and where CP is seen as an opportunity on the rise for nonprofit organizations, donors such as grant-making foundations and governmental institutions increasingly stimulate nonprofit organizations to work with companies and to seek their support (Roza, 2016). In addition, changing roles of governments in welfare states such as in the European Union increasingly pressures nonprofit organizations to seek their support elsewhere. Moreover, the general public (i.e., private donors) expects more entrepreneurial behaviour and cross-sectoral collaboration from nonprofit organizations.

Allocation of responsibility for corporate philanthropy

Companies organize their CP in various ways. First, firms choose to allocate the responsibility for CP to one (or multiple) company agent(s), such as the CEO or another member of upper management. This agent makes voluntary donations in the form of direct grants towards social, charitable, or nonprofit organizations (Gautier and Pache, 2015). This model is certainly still true for owners of small- and medium-sized (family) companies (Fitzgerald et al., 2010). The advantage of such an approach is that it is very clear to internal (e.g., employees, boards) and some external stakeholders (charitable organizations) who is making decisions on CP spending. Nevertheless, this might be problematic for the company, as it creates issues of transparency and accountability when agents' decision-making is entirely discretionary rather than based on firm guidelines. As CP is oftentimes still assigned to corporate elites with little involvement of employees (Breeze and Wiepking, 2017), there is little oversight of their spending. As such, there is a fair chance that they allocate the company's resources to their self-interested pet causes, disregarding any interest of corporate stakeholders internally and/or externally. Despite the potentially problematic nature of allocating CP to particular agents within the company, it offers opportunities for nonprofits that involve corporate representatives in their boards. These non-profits have the benefit to have close relationships with a potential (large) donor, and therefore solicitation for grants are easily made and potentially very successful (Walker, 2002).

Second, companies allocate CP to an in-house department, such as the Corporate Social Responsibility department or the Public Relations department (e.g., Altuntas and Turker, 2015; Husted, 2003). Here, the aim is to centralize all corporate giving and reduce issues around transparency and accountability. These departments have policies, strategies, and guidelines in place to be clear on the philanthropic rules of the game. Here, the difference between philanthropy, other corporate social responsibility activities, and corporate sponsoring will be clearly articulated and responsibilities will be allocated accordingly (Seitanidi and Ryan, 2007). For nonprofit organizations, it should be easier to select their partners, as they can select them based on the match with the company's philanthropic goals.

In addition, rather than allocating the responsibility for CP to a specific department, companies may set up a separate entity with a public benefit mission, e.g., a corporate foundation (Gautier and Pache, 2015; Petrovits, 2006; Webb, 1994). Here, the corporate foundation is responsible for the decision-making on allocating money, time, products, services, or other resources that have been allocated to them by the firm. These foundations are often linked to the founding company through their name, funding, trustees, administration, and potential employee involvement (Westhues and Einwiller, 2006). Corporate foundations are complex partners for nonprofits, as it is unclear how to approach them: as a company or as a foundation. Corporate foundations are not operating as regular grant-making foundations, nor as government institutions, business departments, or other traditional private foundations. Indeed, corporate foundations are hybrid entities in which they – in various degrees – adopt the logic (e.g., governance frames, language, value orientation) of both private foundations as well as businesses. Furthermore, although some corporate foundations may seem to be fully philanthropic (Swen et al., 2019), they are never truly independent from companies, again reinforcing the hybrid nature of corporate foundations.

Finally, firms can allocate the implementation of CP to an outside agent, such as an intermediary, broker, or matchmaker (Lee, 2011, 2015; Maas and Meijs, 2018). These third parties or intermediaries form the bridge between companies and nonprofit organizations, and also act as mediating agents between these organizations. Most of these intermediary organizations are familiar, experienced, and well known with the business and nonprofit rationales and able to bridge the interests and needs of both actors.

Business strategies for corporate philanthropy

Companies have various strategies to operationalize their CP. Generally, there are four strategies: a "cluster strategy," a "diffuse strategy," a "focused strategy," and a "coalition strategy" (see also Hills and Bockstette, 2015; Roza, 2017). Each approach comes with a different set of objectives and challenges.

Cluster strategy

A cluster strategy involves companies first determining which types or categories of social issues fit best with their core values and then selecting nonprofit partners that can help them to catalyse change on these social issues. In the cluster strategy, the company determines multiple social issues (usually two to four) which fit best with their core values and seek nonprofit partners that can help them to catalyse change on these social issues. For instance, Google allocates 1 billion dollars and 1 million employee volunteer hours in three clusters which are close to their corporate values: Education, Economic Opportunity, and Inclusion. Aligning on corporate values plays a key role in aligning CP with internal and external stakeholders (Roza, 2016). Here, alignment between the values of the organization and its employees has shown various benefits for both the company and the employee, including higher employee engagement and a better connection between the employees and the working environment, such as with their organization, their jobs, and their colleagues (Roza, 2016). Alignment between the company and nonprofit organizations based on shared values also leads to positive outcomes for both organizations involved, such as transformative learning (e.g., adapting individual worldviews). Furthermore, by jointly reaching goals based on shared beliefs, this strategy enhances satisfaction and pride, which strengthens the relationship between both organizations.

This type of strategy has the potential for developing long-term partnerships between companies and nonprofit organizations. For instance, the internationally renowned Dutch Rijksmuseum has had partnerships with Dutch multinational company Philips for more than 15 years (in 2018) because Philips values the convening power of the Dutch cultural history. Similarly, ABN AMRO, a financial services company, has multiyear alliances between the ABN AMRO Foundation and youth organizations that support children in developing their talents, which is one of the core values of the company. In addition, by living their core values through CP, this strategy has a great potential to engage employees in their efforts, at the very least by supporting those who share an affinity with the organization's core values (Haski-Leventhal et al., 2017).

Diffuse strategy

In a diffuse strategy, the focus of CP is not so much on a specific theme or cluster of issues, but rather on what certain stakeholders, e.g., employees or consumers, expect or require of nonprofit organizations or even governments. Many workplace volunteering programmes and matched giving programmes are an example of this. Here, the activities the companies support are very diverse, because the strategy is aimed at encouraging people to volunteer in areas that match their personal interests (Roza, 2016). Another type of diffuse strategy occurs when CP focuses on individuals or (potential) consumers and the social initiatives these individuals undertake to strengthen civil society. Here, the company could award grants to highly diverse projects based on the interest of their (potential) consumers – as determined, for example, by organizing voting schemes amongst consumers that award many small donations for projects proposed by other consumers. In fact, part of the diffuse strategy is to share with many stakeholders the decision on what to support and only set broad guidelines for what is not eligible for support. For instance, ING Nederland Fonds (corporate foundation of ING Group) includes a diffuse strategy in which they ask grassroots organizations in the Netherlands to apply for a grant, stimulating them to get support from their communities by letting them vote for the organization. Ultimately, these votes determine how much is granted to the grassroots organizations.

This strategy is effective if a company seeks to be actively facilitating a certain group of stakeholders. This results in a favourable image from these stakeholders. The challenge in such a strategy is to ensure that the company or corporate foundation receives sufficient high-quality applications, and/or gets its people (e.g., employees or consumers) to take action on their own accord and/or (partially) organize their volunteer or fundraising efforts themselves.

Focused strategy

In the focused strategy, the company focuses on one social issue and allocates all of its CP resources to this single issue. This strategy is the strategy most commonly used when a company's CP programme is linked to its core business. Such companies will often issue statements such as "we give according to what we do best" and either donate money and or/products related to what they produce themselves (e.g., donating medication, technological solutions) or let their employees apply their knowledge and expertise. For instance, many financial services organizations support financial literacy programmes. The advantages of this strategy are that there is great potential in the amount and diversity of resources the company can use and that it is an easy story to explain to external parties. After all, if you are a company in cell phones, it is logical to others that your CP also focuses on connecting people.

The challenge here is that people – including even a company's own employees – may be a little sceptical of the intentions and actual methods of such programmes. For instance, CP could be used to explore new markets, and might even serve commercial purposes which may harm the perceived authenticity of the philanthropic efforts. Take for instance Microsoft, which introduces their products to potential future customers through school programmes. Similarly, an insurance company may send trainees to a less developed country to introduce new systems of claiming damages that have not yet been tested in other markets.

Coalition strategy

In a coalition strategy, several parties enter into a partnership to be able to address a specific social issue. For instance, a Dutch corporate foundation called "From Debts to Chances" (formerly known as Delta Lloyd Foundation) aims to reduce poverty, in particular debts that poor people oftentimes have. They initiated "The Debt Coalition," in which governmental actors, companies and foundations, nonprofit organizations and educational institutions join forces to reduce debts and poverty. In practice, such a strategy may involve actual business rivals collaborating in order to solve a social problem. Although this strategy is also a single-issue strategy, the fact that there is a multiparty commitment on a jointly formulated social mission sets such a strategy apart from the "focused strategy," in which there is just one company committed to helping resolve a certain problem.

The advantage of such a strategy is the potential for social impact and innovation, which is greater if multiple stakeholders or problem owners are united. However, collaboration sometimes involves waiting for the various parties to arrive at a consensus, which means the process can be slow. Management of coalitions born out of such partnerships tends to be very time-intensive and complex due to the involvement of different parties which all have their own interests and priorities. Moreover, the various parties often all have their own jargon and corporate cultures, which can be hard to unite.

Once a strategy has been implemented, it is vital that companies (re)consider the pros and cons of said strategy every once in a while. For instance, it is quite possible that a particular strategy works well for a period of time and helps the company realize its CP aspirations and objectives, but has to be revised anyway due to changes in society, in the company, or regarding the company's relationship with major stakeholders, such as nonprofit organizations, shareholders, or government.

Nonprofit strategies to corporate philanthropic partner selection

Traditionally, when nonprofit organizations were seeking corporate partners, they oftentimes posed a moral appeal to the company to contribute to their social mission. This worked very well in situations in which one particular person within the company was responsible for CP, without any formal strategy and vision in place on the corporate level. However, as CP has become increasingly professionalized, this is no longer effective. Now, nonprofit organizations need to look at the (strategic) fit between the nonprofit organization and the company. This fit can be based on three logics: business fit, familiarity fit, and activity fit (Kim et al., 2010).

First, nonprofit organizations could select their partners based on similarities in their "business." This does not have to do with the core business of the company and the nonprofit, but rather with the purpose or mission of both organizations. Imagine a community restaurant that aspires to create social cohesion and aims to connect people in a certain geographical area. For a business fit, they should solicit for collaborations with companies with the same aspiration. For instance, a telecom company that defined their purpose as connecting people through their services would fit well. Here, nonprofit organizations appeal to companies with having similar goals in society, albeit for different audiences.

Another logical fit that nonprofit organizations might seek is based on joint brand recognition (i.e., familiarity fit). Here, well-known nonprofit organizations seek corporate partners that have the same familiarity as they do and appeal to them based on the notion of bettering their reputation. Many renowned museums around the world attract large companies because companies perceive famous cultural heritage as a brand that they want to be associated with. Very local nonprofit organizations seek local companies as they appeal to the joint familiarity in their community, which also opens up a broader audience for local companies.

Third, nonprofit organizations can seek an activity fit. Here, nonprofit organizations appeal to companies based on a specific need that can be fulfilled by the core business or major business unit within the company. Here the solicitation is based on "we need what you can do best." For instance, Philips Foundation aims to improve access to quality healthcare. In this light, the Dutch Heart Foundation collaborates with Philips Foundation to make the Netherlands a "six-minute cardiac arrest" zone by helping to expand the network of community first responders and automated external defibrillators (AEDs) across the entire country, especially in more remote areas.

Business and nonprofit case for corporate philanthropy

As mentioned earlier in this chapter, most studies on CP are based on instrumental theories, which treat CP as a tool with which to achieve direct or indirect economic results for the company. Many companies justify their CP based on the business case they can create. Indeed, much research has been dedicated and has built strong evidence for companies to claim a business case for CP (Liket and Simaens, 2015). For instance, CP has been found to strengthen marketing efforts by enhancing corporate reputation (Brammer and Pavelin, 2006), consumer evaluations (Kim et al., 2010), and consumer loyalty (Maignan et al., 1999).

Recently, there has also been more attention on the contribution of CP to human resource management (Roza, 2016) and issues such as attracting a talented workforce (Kim and Park, 2011; Roza, 2016), organizational socialization (Gully et al., 2013; Rupp et al., 2013), and cultivating employee engagement, organizational commitment, and organizational identification (Caligiuri et al., 2013; Grant et al., 2008; Kim et al., 2010; Turker, 2009). Additional ways in which companies can benefit from CP involve the reinforcement of community relations and legitimacy amongst stakeholders (Porter and Kramer, 2002). For example, corporate giving may strengthen the trust that local communities have in particular companies, thereby bestowing or enhancing legitimacy (Chen et al., 2008). Other studies have suggested that community involvement can improve community networks, trust, and the willingness to cooperate (Muthuri et al., 2009).

Far too little attention has been given to how CP impacts nonprofit organizations. Many academics and practitioners seem to assume that whatever companies give is useful and welcome for nonprofit organizations. Although financial support is in many cases most welcome, the particular restrictions, expectations, and project orientation of many companies may cause additional burdens to operational staff or even mission drift (Shachar et al., 2018). Indeed, CP incurs transaction and direct costs for nonprofits that may exceed the benefits. In many cases, nonprofit organizations must adapt their regular tasks to customize to the demands of corporate donors.

Specific attention in this nonprofit business case should be given particularly to corporate volunteering, as this complicates the relationship by a shift from a simple technical monetary transaction between two organizations to one which brings in the personal involvement of corporate employees, nonprofit employees and oftentimes their beneficiaries (Roza, 2016; Roza et al., 2017). Austin and Seitanidi (2012) claim that the relation becomes more complicated – though potentially also more rewarding for the nonprofit – when the corporate volunteering programme moves from a simple one-day event to more complex involvement schemes. Following Roza et al. (2017), the nonprofit case for CP and corporate volunteering should be viewed as multilevel: what are the consequences (positive and negative) for the nonprofit organization, employees, and beneficiaries? In other words, to really access the value of CP, we need a multi-stakeholder assessment of a CP case including both benefits and challenges (Roza et al., 2017).

On an organizational level, engaging employees in corporate volunteering at nonprofit organizations can also be seen as a stepping stone to being able to influence the company in different ways. Through transformative learning experiences (or experiential learning), employees can take their experiences back into their roles within a company. Second, it can be used to enhance recruitability of potential volunteers and financial donors (Haski-Leventhal et al., 2010; Roza et al., 2017), since engaging in CP also creates additional personal networks for the nonprofit organization. Third, corporate involvement broadens and deepens also the legitimacy of the nonprofit organization in society. Nevertheless, there are also organizational-level risks involved. Partnerships can lead to reputational damage for nonprofit organizations if the corporate donor receives bad publicity, gets involved in public scandals, or if the partnership is received by the general public as unauthentic. The latter happened to the Word Wide Fund for Nature (WWF) in Germany, although the short-term consequences seemed to be limited (Anheier et al., 2013).

On the individual level, corporate volunteering may lead to personal and professional development of the nonprofit employees, work relief, appreciation for their jobs, and, in many cases, they can provide additional services to their beneficiaries. Nevertheless, in many cases corporate volunteers are (albeit unintentionally) cherry picking, allowed to do all the fun activities with beneficiaries. Sometimes corporate volunteers replace paid jobs or regular volunteers as the nonprofit realizes that they can either cut their budget by these areas or increase budgets in corporate volunteers, which also brings along additional resources. Perhaps most damaging is when services provided by corporate volunteers do not meet the level of quality needed by the nonprofit organization. For instance, there is a health risk when incapable corporate volunteers are allowed to work with people with mental or physical challenges (Samuel et al., 2016).

Conclusions

CP seems increasingly important for both the corporate and the nonprofit world. On the sector level, both actors are essentially motivated through similar structures, but the operationalization and visibility of those motivations differ greatly between the two actors. Also, strategies for CP differ greatly: companies are more oriented toward business stakeholders in shaping their strategy, whereas nonprofit organizations orient their strategy primarily on finding the logical business partner. On the organizational level the picture becomes more diverse, as companies and nonprofit organizations make their own decisions on what motives and organizational practices fit them best. Both companies and nonprofit organizations are currently searching for new forms of collaboration, particularly in terms of allocating alternative ways of distributing resources beyond the traditional (financial) support, such as impact investing. Additionally, companies worldwide are experimenting with new or alternative forms to distribute their philanthropic giving such as the increasing interest of developing corporate foundations in Europe, Russia, and China (Roza et al., 2019, or creating corporate social impact funds. These organizations function as intermediary organizations, controlled by the company at arm's length. This makes CP more complex, but also with many more opportunities for both parties than ever before.

Note

1 Unfortunately, the numbers in Europe and the United States are not entirely comparable as the measurement of what is giving differs among the research. However, it does give a good indication of the size of the subsector in philanthropy.

References

Aguinis, H., & Glavas, A. (2012). What we know and don't know about corporate social responsibility: A review and research agenda. *Journal of Management, 38*(4), 932–968. DOI: 10.1177/0149206311436079

Altuntas, C., & Turker, D. (2015). Local or global: Analyzing the internationalization of social responsibility of corporate foundations. *International Marketing Review, 32*(5), 540–575. DOI: 10.1108/IMR-03-2014-0092

Anheier, H.K., Hass, R., & Beller, A. (2013). Accountability and transparency in the German nonprofit sector: A paradox?. *International Review of Public Administration, 18*(3), 69–84.

Austin, J.E., & Seitanidi, M.M. (2012). Collaborative value creation: A review of partnering between non-profits and businesses: Part 1. Value creation spectrum and collaboration stages. *Non-profit and Voluntary Sector Quarterly, 41*(5), 726–758. DOI: 10.1177/0899764012450777

Bartel, C.A. (2001). Social comparisons in boundary-spanning work: Effects of community outreach on members' organizational identity and identification. *Administrative Science Quarterly, 46*(3), 379–413. DOI: 10.2307/3094869

Bowen, H.R. (1953). *Social Responsibilities of the Businessman.* New York, NY: Harper.

Brammer, S.J., & Pavelin, S. (2006). Corporate reputation and social performance: The importance of fit. *Journal of Management Studies, 43*(3), 435–455. DOI: 10.1111/j.1467-6486.2006.00597.x

Breeze, B., & Wiepking, P. (2017). A Different Driver? Exploring Employee Engagement in Corporate Philanthropy. Paper presented at the European Research Network on Philanthropy (ERNOP) Conference in Copenhagen.

Caligiuri, P., Mencin, A., & Jiang, K. (2013). Win–win–win: The influence of company-sponsored volunteerism programs on employees, NGOs, and business units. *Personnel Psychology, 66*(4), 825–860. DOI: 10.1111/peps.12019

Campbell, D., Moore, G., & Metzger, M. (2002). Corporate philanthropy in the UK, 1985–2000: Some empirical findings. *Journal of Business Ethics, 39*(1–2), 29–41. DOI: 10.1023/A:1016371731732

Carroll, A.B. (1979). A three-dimensional conceptual model of corporate performance. *Academy of Management Review, 4*(4), 497–505. DOI: /10.5465/amr.1979.4498296

Charities Aid Foundation (2014). *Corporate giving by the FTSE 100.* Retrieved from CAF: https://www.cafonline.org/docs/default-source/about-us-publications/corporate_giving_ftse100_august2014.pdf

Chen, J.C., Patten, D.M., & Roberts, R.W. (2008). Corporate charitable contributions: A corporate social performance or legitimacy strategy? *Journal of Business Ethics, 82*(1), 131–144. DOI: 10.1007/s10551-007-9567-1

Donham, W.B. (1927). The social significance of business. *Harvard Business Review, 5*(4), 406–419.

Donham, W.B. (1929). Business ethics – A general survey. *Harvard Business Review, 7*(4), 385–394.

Fitzgerald, M.A., Haynes, G.W., Schrank, H.L., & Danes, S.M. (2010). Socially responsible processes of small family business owners: Exploratory evidence from the national family business survey. *Journal of Small Business Management, 48*(4), 524–551. DOI: 10.1111/j.1540-627X.2010.00307.x

Freeman, R.E. (1984). *Stakeholder Management: Framework and Philosophy.* Mansfield, MA: Pitman.

Gautier, A., & Pache, A.C. (2015). Research on corporate philanthropy: A review and assessment. *Journal of Business Ethics, 126*(3), 343–369. DOI: 10.1007/s10551-0131969-7

Giving in Europe (2017). *The State of Research on Giving in 20 European Countries.* Barry Hoolwerf & Theo Schuyt (Eds.). Amsterdam: Lenthe Publishers.

Giving USA (2019). *Giving USA 2019: The Annual Report on Philanthropy for the Year 2018*. Chicago: Giving USA Foundation.

Grant, A.M., Dutton, J.E., & Rosso, B.D. (2008). Giving commitment: Employee support programs and the prosocial sensemaking process. *Academy of Management Journal, 51*(5), 898–918. DOI: 10.5465/amj.2008.34789652

Gully, S.M., Phillips, J.M., Castellano, W.G., Han, K., & Kim, A. (2013). A mediated moderation model of recruiting socially and environmentally responsible job applicants. *Personnel Psychology, 66*(4), 935–973. DOI: 10.1111/peps.12033

Gupta, A. D. (2014). Implementing corporate social responsibility in India: Issues and the beyond. In *Implementing Corporate Social Responsibility* (pp. 19–29). New Delhi: Springer. DOI: 10.1007/978-81-322-1653-7_2

Haski-Leventhal, D., Meijs, L.C.P.M., & Hustinx, L. (2010). The third-party model: Enhancing volunteering through governments, corporations and educational institutes. *Journal of Social Policy, 39*(1), 139–158. DOI: 10.1017/S004727940990377

Haski-Leventhal, D., Roza, L., & Meijs, L.C. (2017). Congruence in corporate social responsibility: Connecting the identity and behavior of employers and employees. *Journal of Business Ethics, 143*(1), 35–51. DOI: 10.1007/s10551-015-2793-z

Hills, G., & Bockstette, V. (2015) *Simplifying Strategy. A practical toolkit for corporate societal engagement.* Retrieved from: https://www.fsg.org/tools-and-resources/simplifying_strategy

Husted, B. (2003). Governance choices for corporate social responsibility: To contribute, collaborate or internalize? *Long Range Planning, 36*(5), 481–498. DOI: 10.1016/S0024-6301(03)00115-8

Kim, H.R., Lee, M., Lee, H.T., & Kim, N.M. (2010). Corporate social responsibility and employee–company identification. *Journal of Business Ethics, 95*(4) 557–569. DOI: 10.1007/s10551-010-0440-2

Kim, S.Y., & Park, H. (2011). Corporate Social Responsibility as an organizational attractiveness for prospective public relations practitioners. *Journal of Business Ethics, 103*(4), 639–653. DOI: 10.1007/s10551-011-0886-x

Lee, L. (2011) Corporate volunteering: Understanding business implementation issues. *International Journal of Business Environment, 4*(2), 162–182. DOI: 10.1504/IJBE.2011.040173

Lee, L. (2015). Understanding the role of the broker in business non-profit collaboration. *Social Responsibility Journal, 11*(2), 201–220. DOI: 10.1108/SRJ-05-2013-0050

Liket, K., & Simaens, A. (2015). Battling the devolution in the research on Corporate Philanthropy. *Journal of Business Ethics, 126*(2), 285–308. DOI: 10.1007/s10551-013-1921-x

Liu, G., Eng, T. Y, & Ko, W.W. (2013). Strategic directions of corporate community involvement. *Journal of Business Ethics, 115*(3), 469–487. DOI: 10.1007/s10551-012-1418-z

Maas, S.A. & Meijs, L.C.P.M. (2018). Intermediary organizations as catalysts for corporate giving: Broker's involvement and impact on corporate charity undertakings. Paper presented at the Symposium on Philanthropy and Commerce (SPC) Conference in Beijing, China (October).

Madden, K., Scaife, W., & Crissman, K. (2006). How and why small to medium size enterprises (SMEs) engage with their communities: An Australian study. *International Journal of Nonprofit and Voluntary Sector Marketing, 11*(1), 49–60. DOI: 10.1002/nvsm.40

Maignan I., Ferrell, O.C., & Hult, H.T. (1999). Corporate citizenship: Cultural antecedents and business benefits. *Journal of the Academy of Marketing Science, 27*(4), 455–469. DOI: 10.1177/0092070399274005

Maignan, I., & Ferrell, O.C. (2001). Antecedents and benefits of corporate citizenship: An investigation of French businesses. *Journal of Business Research, 51*(1), 37–51. DOI: 10.1016/S0148-2963(99)00042-9

Meijs, L.C.P.M., & Van der Voort, J. (2004). Corporate volunteering: From charity to profit–non-profit partnerships. *Australian Journal on Volunteering, 9*(1), 21–31.

Muthuri, J.N., Matten, D., & Moon, J. (2009). Employee volunteering and social capital: Contributions to corporate social responsibility. *British Journal of Management, 20*(1), 75–89. DOI: 10.1111/j.1467-8551.2007.00551.x

Petrovits, C. (2006). Corporate-sponsored foundations and earnings management. *Journal of Accounting & Economics, 41*(3), 335–335. DOI: 10.1016/j.jacceco.2005.12.001

Porter, M.E., & Kramer, M.R. (2002). The competitive advantage of corporate philanthropy. *Harvard Business Review, 80*(12), 56–69.

Raffaelli, R., & Glynn, M.A. (2014). Turnkey or tailored? Relational pluralism, institutional complexity, and the organizational adoption of more or less customized practices. *Academy of Management Journal, 57*(2), 541–562. DOI: 10.5465/amj.2011.1000

Roza, L. (2016). *Employee engagement in corporate social responsibility*. Doctoral Thesis. Erasmus University, Rotterdam.

Roza, L. (2017). One size fits all? Four strategies for an effective corporate citizenship programme. RSM Discovery, Rotterdam. Retrieved September 17, 2018 from https://discovery.rsm.nl/articles/detail/284-one-size-fits-all-four-strategies-for-an-effective-corporate-citizenship-programme/

Roza, L., Meijs, L.C.P. M., Von Schnurbein, G., & Bethmann, S. (Eds.) (2019). *Research Handbook on Corporate Foundations: Civil Society & Corporate Philanthropy Perspectives. New Delhi: Springer.*

Roza, L., Shachar, I., Meijs, L., & Hustinx, L. (2017). The nonprofit case for corporate volunteering: A multi-level perspective. *Service Industries Journal, 37*(11–12), 746–765.

Rupp, D.E., Shao, R., Thornton, M.A., & Skarlicki, D.P. (2013). Applicants' and employees' reactions to corporate social responsibility: The moderating effects of first-party justice perceptions and moral identity. *Personnel Psychology, 66*(4), 895–933. DOI: 10.1111/peps.12030

Samuel, O., Roza, L., & Meijs, L.C.P.M. (2016). Exploring partnerships from the perspective of HSO beneficiaries: The case of corporate volunteering. *Human Service Organizations: Management, Leadership & Governance, 40*(3), 220–237. DOI: 10.1080/23303131.2015.1117552

Seghers, V. (2007). *Ce qui motive les entreprises mécènes philanthropie, investissement, responsabilité sociale?* (Acteurs de la société). Paris: Editions Autrement.

Seitanidi, M.M., & Ryan, A. (2007). A critical review of forms of corporate community involvement: From philanthropy to partnerships. *International Journal of Non-profit and Voluntary Sector Marketing, 12*(3), 247–266. DOI: 10.1002/nvsm.306

Shachar, I., Hustinx, L., Roza, L., & Meijs, L.C.P.M. (2018). A new spirit across sectors: Constructing a common justification for corporate volunteering. *European Journal of Cultural and Political Sociology, 5*(1–2), 90–115. DOI: 10.1080/23254823.2018.1435293

Stroik, M. (2014). *Giving in numbers. The 2014 edition. An in-depth analysis of corporate giving and employee engagement data from 261 of world's leading companies.* Retrieved September 17, 2018 from CECP: http://cecp.co/home/resources/giving-in-numbers/?tid=90

Swen, S., Roza, L., Meijs, L.C.P.M., & Maas, A.M.M. A (2019). Non-profit organizations' sensemaking of corporate foundations. In: Roza, L., Meijs, L.C.P.M., Von Schnurbein, G., & Bethmann, S. (Eds.) *Research Handbook on Corporate Foundations: Civil Society & Corporate Philanthropy Perspectives. New Delhi: Springer.*

Turker, D. (2009). How corporate social responsibility influences organizational commitment. *Journal of Business Ethics, 89*(2), 89–204. DOI: 10.1007/s10551-008-9993-8

Van der Voort, J.M., Glac, K., & Meijs, L.C.P.M. (2009). "Managing" corporate community involvement. *Journal of Business Ethics, 90*(3), 311–329. DOI: 10.1007/s10551-009-0051-y

Walker, C. (2002). Philanthropy, social capital or strategic alliance? The involvement of senior UK business executives with the voluntary sector and implications for corporate fundraising. *International Journal of Non-profit and Voluntary Sector Marketing, 7*(3), 219–228. DOI: 10.1002/nvsm.181

Wartick, S., & Wood, D. (1998). *International Business and Society.* Malden, MA: Blackwell.

Webb, N.J. (1994). Tax and government policy implications for corporate foundation giving. *Nonprofit and Voluntary Sector Quarterly, 23*(1), 41–67. DOI: 10.1177/0899764094231004

Westhues, M., & Einwiller, S. (2006). Corporate foundations: Their role for corporate social responsibility. *Corporate Reputation Review, 9*(2), 144–153. DOI: 10.1057/palgrave.crr.1550019

30

GOVERNMENT FUNDING

Michaela Neumayr

ASSISTANT PROFESSOR, INSTITUTE FOR NONPROFIT MANAGEMENT, WU VIENNA
UNIVERSITY OF ECONOMICS AND BUSINESS, VIENNA, AUSTRIA

Astrid Pennerstorfer

ASSISTANT PROFESSOR, INSTITUTE FOR SOCIAL POLICY, WU VIENNA
UNIVERSITY OF ECONOMICS AND BUSINESS, VIENNA, AUSTRIA

Introduction

Government funding of nonprofit organizations has perennially changed over the last decades. In the most recent past, these changes usually implied a decline in government support, motivated by either welfare state retrenchment or modernization of service provision, putting pressure on nonprofit revenues (e.g., Abramson & Salamon, 2016). In several countries the shrinking levels of nonprofits' public funding can also be traced back to the global financial crisis, as governments responded to the crisis by implementing austerity policies and decreasing public welfare spending (Cunningham et al., 2016; Pape et al., 2016). While the direct effects of altered government support on nonprofit organizations differed by field of activity and country, many saw themselves forced to search for alternative sources of income, such as philanthropic or commercial revenue (e.g., Eikenberry & Kluver, 2004; Guo, 2006; Pettijohn & Boris, 2013). Nevertheless, government funding still serves as one of the most important sources of nonprofits' revenue in many countries.

In Germany, Israel and the Netherlands, for instance, more than 60 per cent of nonprofit sectors' income stems from government funding (Salamon et al., 2017), while it is 45 per cent across countries in Western Continental Europe and 42 per cent across countries in Central and Eastern Europe (see Chapter 3 by von Schnurbein & Hengevoss, this volume). In the United States and Australia, the respective share is about 30 per cent (Pettijohn & Boris, 2013; Salamon et al., 2017) and in South America it is 19 per cent. This implies that on average one-third of nonprofit organizations' income around the world stems from the state (41-country average, Salamon et al., 2017, p. 276f.).

Receiving funding from government can be evaluated positively as it enables nonprofit organizations to fulfil their mission-related purpose, to increase legitimacy, enhance reputation or build capacity (e.g., Salamon, 1995). Government funding, however, may also come along with undesirable implications, such as mission drift, bureaucratization, reduction in political advocacy or increased commercialization (e.g., Chaves et al., 2004; Galaskiewicz & Bielefeld, 1998). Depending on the mechanism used for public funding, e.g., direct grants, contract payments, fees, reimbursements for services rendered to eligible private parties or indirect tax reductions, the (un-)desired side effects may differ.

This chapter provides a systematic overview of the implications of public funding on nonprofit organizations. It starts with a synopsis of key theories on the mode of nonprofit–government relations including the concepts of nonprofit regimes and of nonprofits' functions. We subsequently describe when and why different mechanisms of government funding have come into place and outline their current size and scope. The chapter continues with a discussion of both desired and undesired side effects of direct government funding in general, and government contracting in particular. After delineating the implications of impact-related funding mechanisms, the chapter closes with concluding remarks.

Theory of government–nonprofit relationships

Government *funding* is one of the facets of the relationship between the nonprofit sector and the government which cannot be isolated from the role of the nonprofit sector in public service provision or the function of the nonprofit sector in society in general, as will be discussed below.

Young (2006) proposed three theoretical modes of government–nonprofit interaction: a supplementary, a complementary and an adversarial mode. In a supplementary relationship, nonprofits fulfil (heterogeneous) demand for public goods that is left unsatisfied by the government. Nonprofit organizations and the public sector in this relation work separately, in parallel. In a complementary relation, the two institutional sectors closely work together. They act as partners in providing public services with the government being an important funder for these services and nonprofits having the capacity and knowhow to deliver them. Finally, in an adversarial relationship, nonprofits focus on advocacy rather than service provision, and the relation essentially consists of the nonprofit organization's attempts to influence the public sector in its doing.

The modes of government–nonprofit interaction are linked with nonprofits' functions. Out of a variety of functions ascribed to nonprofit organizations (e.g., James & Rose-Ackerman, 1986; Kramer, 1981), a recent concept defines three key functions: service delivery, advocacy and community building (Neumayr et al., 2009). Service delivery is the function for which the nonprofit sector is most well known, and it is often used to assess its economic relevance, e.g., by estimating the contribution of the provided services to GDP. The link between service delivery and government funding is most obvious when a complementary mode of interaction is prevailing.

Advocacy is the function attributed to the political sphere and it refers to nonprofits' activities aiming to "correct imbalanced political representation by ensuring that a broader set of interests are voiced" (Jenkins, 2006, p. 308). Advocacy is linked with government funding as it is widely supposed that nonprofits will reduce or even abandon their political activities when receiving public funds (see also Chapter 23 by Mosley, Weiner-Davis & Anasti, this volume).

The third function labelled community building (Kendall, 2003) refers to nonprofits' efforts in bringing people together and in fostering social cohesion. It is often seen as a by-product of the way nonprofits work, for example when mutual trust and reciprocity are built among members who meet on a regular basis, for example in nonprofits active in sports, culture or recreation. Government funding is again supposed to reduce nonprofits' community building in favour of other activities (e.g., Eikenberry & Kluver, 2004).

The fulfilment of these functions by the nonprofit sector, above all service delivery, is accompanied however by a set of elements that have been described as voluntary failures (Salamon, 1995). *Philanthropic insufficiency* deals with inadequate funding levels in relation to necessary public goods. *Philanthropic particularism* is concerned with the problem that nonprofit organizations often focus on servicing a narrow range of target groups of certain religions, ethnicities, ideologies or regions, while ignoring others. *Philanthropic paternalism* is mentioned as a third voluntary failure and describes the top-down approach, in which concerned clients might not have a say in programme design, and lacks democratic legitimation. Finally, *philanthropic amateurism* describes a lack of professionalism. Interaction with government can potentially remedy these failures, since comparative advantages of the government are the power to tax facing philanthropic insufficiency, concern for equity facing particularism, democratic legitimation and democratic decision-making procedures facing paternalism, and finally the ability to issue regulation and quality standards reducing amateurism (Toepler, 2018). This view directs attention to the advantage of a coexistence of both sectors, the nonprofit and the public, that cancels out the deficiencies of each other, at least partially and with collaborative governance.

Whether the mode of government–nonprofit interaction is complementary, supplementary or adversarial varies between countries, determined by past political and economic struggles between social classes in the respective countries (e.g., Esping-Andersen, 1990). Building on this, Salamon and Anheier (1998) describe four different nonprofit regimes. The first nonprofit regime is called *government-dominant* or *social-democratic*, and countries typically mentioned in this model are Sweden or Norway (Salamon & Sokolowski, 2017). This model is characterized by an extensive publicly funded and publicly provided welfare state, going along with a diminished social service role of nonprofits. Thus, the size of the nonprofit sector, measured by the share of employees working in nonprofits, is quite small (Salamon & Anheier, 1998, p. 228). Instead, its activities mostly lie outside the scope of the welfare state, such as culture, adult education, recreation, sports or advocacy; and public funding does not play the most important role (compare Table 3.2 in von Schnurbein & Hengevoss, this volume). In contrast, in countries of the *liberal* or *third-sector dominant* regime, low levels of government social welfare spending are accompanied with a rather large nonprofit sector. Social services are predominately provided by nonprofits, which themselves rely on private funding (e.g., philanthropic income, fees, commercial income) to a larger extent. Typical representatives of this type are the United States, Australia or the United Kingdom (Salamon & Sokolowski, 2017). Supplementation is seen as the dominant mode of government–nonprofit interaction in this regime (Salamon, 2006). Countries belonging to the third, the *corporatist* or *welfare-partnership* regime, usually have a large, mainly government-funded nonprofit sector, which is the main provider of social services. This is the case due to government reliance on the nonprofit sector for implementing its sizeable welfare-state policies (Salamon & Anheier, 1998, p. 228). Not surprisingly, the relationship can be described as complementary in this type. Germany, France or the Netherlands serve as example countries. In the fourth model, labelled *statist* regime (Salamon & Anheier, 1998, p. 228), both welfare spending and the nonprofit sector are small. Mexico, Brazil or Russia have been mentioned as examples in this category (Salamon & Sokolowski, 2017). Obviously, the importance of government funding varies between the four models, it is especially important in the corporatist regime, while it is of comparatively lower importance in the other three.

Modes of interaction between the government and the nonprofit sector may not only vary between countries, but also between different fields of activities within a country. For instance, while in Austria the delivery of mobile elderly care is provided in a complementary way (i.e., the government funds and nonprofits deliver care services), we find a prevailing supplementary mode in the fields of health and education, with the government being the main provider and nonprofits solely filling particular niches of demand, for example schools with alternative pedagogical concepts (Neumayr et al., 2017; Pennerstorfer, 2016). Empirically, we may also find different modes of interaction within one field of activity or even within one organization.

Change of government-funding mechanisms over time

Governments use various mechanisms for funding nonprofit organizations, which in turn influence the latter in different ways and to varying extents. Currently, the two primary funding mechanisms used are grants and contracts. Other forms of public funding include vouchers, reimbursements, fee income from government sources (e.g., Medicare and Medicaid for the US) and tax-credits. The relevance of the respective mechanisms may change according to country and over time.

For much of the second half of the 20th century, when the post-war influx of government money enabled the nonprofit sector to scale up and reach its current prominence in most Western countries (Toepler, 2018), the prevailing funding mechanism clearly was public grants. Usually, grants are supplied by governments to support a nonprofit organization and its mission-related work, with the government requesting a subsequent report on how the money was spent and the purposes achieved. This practice reflects the prevailing paradigm of public administration by that time, emphasizing inputs (see Figure 30.1) (Osborne, 2006).

From the early 1980s onwards, governments increasingly implemented contract payments to fund nonprofit organizations. Contrary to grants, the purpose of contract payments is to enable nonprofits to deliver a specific, government-defined service for a specified target group in a certain amount and quality in a given period of time for a fixed amount of funding. The growing use and reliance on contracts was motivated by several reasons. The prime motivation was the desire to improve the efficiency and effectiveness of service delivery. Therefore, emphasis was placed on input–output relations which required accurate documentation and reporting of all services delivered by nonprofits as well as on competitive processes in the selection of the service provider (e.g., tenders, competitive tenders). The latter implies not only competition among nonprofits, but also between nonprofit and for-profit providers. The underlying idea of this approach arises from New Public Management (NPM), which was the prevailing paradigm of public sector management at that time. Generally speaking, NPM builds on the assumption that the application of private-sector management models to public services, such as audits, benchmarks, monitoring, customer orientation, output control and also contracting, improves the efficiency of these services, influenced by the more profound trend of steady rationalization and marketization in all three sectors (Eikenberry & Kluver, 2004; Maier et al., 2016; Osborne, 2006; Smith & Lipsky, 1993).

At the same time, contract payments gained in importance because governments increasingly outsourced the delivery of services to nonprofit organizations, as it was the case in the UK and Australia, countries in which a rather supplementary mode of nonprofit–government interaction prevails. The massive wave of outsourcing services that had previously been provided

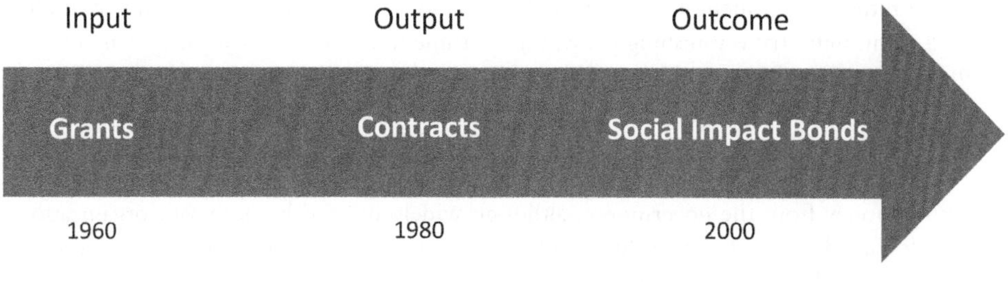

Input	Output	Outcome
Grants	Contracts	Social Impact Bonds
1960	1980	2000

Figure 30.1   Government-funding mechanisms subject to prevailing mode of governance

by the public sector was also inspired by the NPM trend (Bennett & Savani, 2011; Housego & O'Brien, 2012). Potential benefits of outsourcing are lower cost for the government and improved efficiency in the provision of services due to nonprofits' higher proximity to service users and better knowledge about their needs, the use of volunteers and the ability to receive donations (e.g., Gazley & Brudney, 2007; Knutsen, 2017). Further reasons for outsourcing public services also potentially include more professionalized service delivery, increased transparency and improved outcomes for service users due to a higher innovativeness (Housego & O'Brien, 2012).

The swift increase in the use of contract payments was also fostered by changes in legal regulations such as in countries belonging to the European Union (EU). Governments of countries in the EU have to comply with the European competition policy, public procurement law and state aid law, which to a large extent prohibit them supporting private organizations – which also applies to nonprofits – via grants, as this is regarded as a subsidy favouring a particular organization and as distorting the market for tradable services. Contract payments, in contrast, are more compatible with the EU's competition policy, especially as they can be drafted in ways that comply with the requirements, including tenders that also invite for-profit businesses to deliver social services.

Empirical data confirm that contracts indeed have outweighed grants by number and volume over the last decades, which have been the most important channel of public funding for a long time. In the UK, for instance, the relative importance of contract payment rose from 48 per cent in 2001 to 71 per cent in 2007, while the share of grants fell from 52 per cent to 29 per cent (Bennett & Savani, 2011, p. 218f.). In the US in 2013, the share of government funding deriving from fees as compared to grants was larger in almost all fields of nonprofit activities (e.g., health, social services) except the fields of arts and culture and international issues. The latter, however, only received about 3 per cent of total government revenues (Pettijohn & Boris, 2013; Toepler, 2018, p. 11).

In the early 2000s and about two decades after contract payments gained ground, much attention by both private and public actors was given to the concept of impact, manifested in attempts to measure the (social) impact of services and of social investments. Here, emphasis is put on the relation of input and impact and not any longer of input and output, also including longer time horizons (Osborne, 2006). The most often discussed impact-related mechanism of public funding is the Social Impact Bond (SIB). SIBs are financial products aiming to encourage private philanthropic investors to provide upfront capital for project-based service delivery by a nonprofit. The government has to pay for these services only if a defined impact is finally accomplished, typically evaluated about five to ten years after the implementation of the SIB. Otherwise, the philanthropic investor has to bear the costs (e.g., Joy & Shields, 2013; Maier et al., 2017). As the first SIB was introduced in the UK in 2010, the instrument is still in its infancy and we will see whether this or other impact-related funding mechanisms will gain ground in future government–nonprofit funding relations. So far, the total amount of funding channelled through SIBs is vanishingly low; the instrument, however, has already been deployed in 19 countries around the world (see Chapter 33 by Han, Chen & Toepler).

Aspects arising from increased government funding

Accepting money from the government, although widely utilized by nonprofit organizations, is a double-edged sword. For one thing, public support is evaluated very positively as government funding enabled a significant scaling up of nonprofit activity, increased their legitimacy and brought the sector to its current position. At the same time, however, public money is accompanied with a number of undesired effects which come along with regulation, implemented to ensure accountability and public interest, which, above all, reduce nonprofits' autonomy (Toepler, 2018).

Enlarged organizational scale, stability and legitimacy

Government funding enables nonprofit organizations to increase their activities, i.e., to reach more of their core clientele, to replicate successful programmes to new regions, or to implement additional programmes to serve new clientele (Toepler, 2018). As public funding has often been ascribed as more predictable than other sources, long-term funding arrangements with the government also contribute to nonprofits' financial security and thus financial and organizational stability. Another issue contributing to nonprofits' stability is the reputational effect of government funding. It signals that the government perceives a nonprofit as trustworthy, which in turn increases its recognition and reputation, validating its organizational legitimacy (Jung & Moon, 2007).

Empirical evidence for nonprofits' increased credibility by government funding is, however, rather scarce. A study on art nonprofits in South Korea shows how public funding is perceived as an affirmation of their status and programme. The legitimacy effect of funding from central government was found to be larger compared to local government, and larger compared to funding from foundations (Jung & Moon, 2007, p. 219). In contrast, Kim and van Ryzin (2014), also studying the arts sector, find no evidence of a signalling function of prestigious government grants.

Crowding-in and crowding-out of donations

The signalling value of government expenditure is also the underlying mechanism for the crowding-in pattern, describing a positive association of government funding and nonprofits' philanthropic income. As donors generally prefer to give to nonprofits that are well established, reliable and trustworthy, nonprofits' revenue from government here serves as a seal of approval which reduces donors' time and cost to monitor and judge the nonprofit themselves. In addition, government support leads to scaling advantages in nonprofits' operations which might increase the impact of a donor's contribution (Khanna & Sandler, 2000, p. 1544; Rose-Ackerman, 1981).

The adverse effect of the crowding-in pattern is crowding-out, bringing us to our first negative consequence of government funding. It posits that an increase in public funding would discourage donors' own initiative, which in turn reduces nonprofits' philanthropic income. The reasoning for crowding-out refers to the model of an altruistic donor who is interested in the provision of a certain amount of a public good. In the case where a nonprofit's government funding (stemming from donors' taxed money) increases in order to provide this amount of the public good, donors just reduce their own voluntary donations so that the amount of the public good is kept constant (Brooks, 2004; Payne, 1998).

The majority of prior studies examining the association between government funding and nonprofits' philanthropic income find some form of partial crowding-out, meaning that an increase in one dollar of government funding reduces private donations by less than one dollar (Brooks, 2004), while other studies find no significant effect or find crowding-in (Andreoni & Payne, 2011; Brooks, 1999; Hughes & Luksetich, 1999; Payne, 1998). The inconsistency of prior findings could partly be clarified by a recent meta-analysis that revealed that the results largely depend on contextual issues and methods used (De Wit & Bekkers, 2014). While experimental studies, for instance, identified crowding-out, results based on nonexperimental data reveal crowding-in effects due to the fact that donors usually do not know whether government has increased or decreased funding to a particular nonprofit in real-life situations. Nonprofits' field of activity is another important issue as crowding-out is more likely in social services and health where the government and donors fund similar public goods but less likely in arts and international relief (De Wit et al., 2018; Pennerstorfer & Neumayr, 2017).

Decrease of political activity due to loss of autonomy

Among the most frequently cited concerns about public funding is nonprofits' loss of autonomy due to financial dependency. The argument draws on resource dependence theory, implying that organizations are not autonomous in achieving their desired ends at their own discretion, but rely on resources from their environment to secure their survival (Pfeffer & Salancik, 1978). To maintain access to these resources, they are prepared to adapt to the perceived needs and expectations of important resource providers, in this case the government. The more important the funding resources are, the higher the perceived dependence and nonprofits' loss of autonomy in goal setting, resource allocation and programme selection (Jung & Moon, 2007).

Autonomy from the state is particularly crucial for nonprofits in carrying out the function of policy advocacy. Dependency threatens nonprofits' political activity as nonprofits might fear a cut of public funding or other negative sanctions (e.g., being excluded from meetings, loss of access to the legislative process or reduction in clients assigned) in the event of any undesired, oppositional advocacy (Chaves et al., 2004). Also, some nonprofits believe that they are prohibited from engaging in advocacy-related activities while receiving public funds (Bass et al., 2007).

Empirical evidence on the relationship of government funding and nonprofits' engagement in advocacy is mixed. While a few studies find that government support reduces nonprofits' advocacy (e.g., Bloodgood & Tremblay-Boire, 2017), others find no relationship (e.g., Neumayr et al., 2015). The majority of studies find a slightly positive association as a recent meta-study covering 38 investigations in Europe and the US revealed (Lu, 2015). Though the meta-study concludes that government funding does not seem to be a barrier for advocacy, it relies on quantitative measures of advocacy activities. Qualitative studies, however, argue that nonprofits do not necessarily reduce the amount of advocacy, but it is directed towards less critical or even welcome policy advocacy (e.g., Mosley, 2012).

Effects on the size, composition and performance of nonprofit boards

Another consequence of increased government funding is a possible change of nonprofit governance, most notably concerning the role, composition and performance of nonprofit boards (Considine et al., 2014; Hodge & Piccolo, 2005; O'Regan & Oster, 2002; Smith & Lipsky, 1993, p. 76; Stone et al., 2001). Traditional roles of effective nonprofit boards have been described both as being involved in operational activities and in monitoring the organization (e.g., Ostrower & Stone, 2006). Boards with high degrees of government funding have to focus less on typical roles, such as fundraising because it is less relevant in government-funded organizations (O'Regan & Oster, 2002). Since boards have to be more businesslike, and monitoring of government-funded organizations is a more complex task, boards must be professionalized and accordingly members have to be chosen according to skills. Consequently, the composition of boards is different when an organization receives a large share of government funding and it is harder for volunteer boards to exercise close supervision.

Empirically, boards have been found to be less able to represent community interests (Considine et al., 2014). Boards have also been found to be smaller (O'Regan & Oster, 2002; Stone et al., 2001). Research on the performance of nonprofit boards in organizations with a higher degree of government funding points towards less effective boards, although it is difficult to assess board performance objectively (O'Regan & Oster, 2002). Boards are found to be less involved and more passive (Hodge & Piccolo, 2005; O'Regan & Oster, 2002; Smith & Lipsky, 1993). Guo (2007) also found this negative association between government funding and the probability of an organization having a strong community board. Instead, boards "might be treated as a co-optive or legitimizing device rather than as an independent governing body that should be representative of community interests and responsible for the mission, direction, and policies of the organization" (Guo, 2007, p. 466).

It is noticeable that the discussion on the effects of government funding on nonprofit boards is mainly US-centred. One explanation for this could be that in other countries, especially in those with a strong complementary relation between the nonprofit sector and the government, nonprofits often are much more closely affiliated with political parties (e.g., Anheier et al., 1997; Neumayr et al., 2017). In their complementary role, they mainly provide services that are funded by the government, and board members of these organizations often are delegated by political parties.

Aspects arising from increased contracting

So far, potential consequences of government funding in general were highlighted. In doing this, the precise mode of government funding has been neglected. There are, however, multiple ways in which government funds are channelled to a nonprofit organization, as discussed previously. This section focuses on possible consequences that predominantly arise from contract payments. In a first step, underlying theories describing the contractual relationship between the government and the nonprofit organization are described. Subsequently, we discuss favourable and undesirable side effects of contracting, both from a theoretical and an empirical angle.

A fundamental theory concerned with the government–nonprofit contracting relationship is the principal–agent theory (Van Slyke, 2007). In this model, the government acts as the principal that chooses to contract with an agent (in our case the nonprofit organization), who carries out tasks on the principal's behalf. The agent, however, may have different goals than the principal and can exploit information asymmetries to maximize its own utility at the cost of collective or government interests. Consequently, for the principal it is important to correct for this "with a mix of incentives, sanctions, information systems (such as reporting procedures), and monitoring mechanisms" (Van Slyke, 2007, p. 162).

In this relationship, a central question is how to keep the agent accountable. While contracting is seen as the most feasible instrument to do so, the question of how to best design such contracts remains. Contracts for complex service provision on the one hand have to be specific enough to prevent the exploitation of information asymmetries, but on the other hand have to leave room for flexibility necessary to account for shifting needs of service users. In reality, it is practically impossible to specify every imaginable situation that could arise in the contract, so that contracts always remain incomplete (Isaksson et al., 2017). Monitoring the contracts is costly and time-consuming. Moreover, in contrast to goods, quality and organizational performance in service production are often hard to assess, making the problem of asymmetric information even more virulent. Often, it is not even fully established how to define quality for a particular service. If there are concrete performance measures, previous research has pointed to the risk that providers become too focused on the quality measures used at the cost of other, less-measurable quality aspects in service provision (Isaksson et al., 2017). In sum, the involved parties have to deal with "incomplete contracts in imperfect markets" (Van Slyke, 2007, p. 161).

One remedy to incomplete contracting is "relational contracting" which emphasizes long-term relationships, trust and reputation among the involved parties (Bertelli & Smith, 2010; Brown & Troutt, 2004; Christensen & Lægreid, 2010; Isaksson et al., 2017). A suitable theory to this approach is the stewardship theory (Van Slyke, 2007), which in contrast to the agency model assumes goal convergence between the two contracting parties because of shared collective interests. The steward makes decisions in the interest of its principal rather than maximizing its own utility, and greater value is placed on cooperation. Joint decision making and exchange of information point towards a more collaborative governance, which over time reduces transaction costs.

While there are reasonable grounds why the government might want to use contract payments, most existing research points towards negative consequences of such contractual arrangements for nonprofits.

Increase of accountability and bureaucratization

Contracting is often accompanied by increased administrative accountability requirements, performance measurement and competition in form of public tendering or grant applications. Theoretically, accountability requirements can be attributed to the principal–agent problem that entails supervision and reporting specifications. Empirically, various researchers have pointed to an increase of administrative work for nonprofit organizations, leading to a bureaucratization of the organization and diverting time from organizational core activities (e.g., Anheier et al., 1997; Knutsen, 2017). Obtaining and renewing contracts or participating in public tendering processes is often complex and time-consuming. Later, while fulfilling a contract, organizations often have to conform to documentation requirements that are similar to state accounting and reporting procedures, which might diverge from internal management control systems and documentation procedures. In addition, reporting requirements have been found to frequently change (Pettijohn & Boris, 2013). This becomes even more burdensome when an organization has a multitude of contracts with different governing bodies. For instance, nonprofit organizations in the US on average have six contracts or grants (Pettijohn & Boris, 2013). Marwell and Calabrese (2015, p. 1037) bring an example for child welfare providers in New York, which have to manage an average of 38 separate contracts with 20 different government bodies. Managing these contracts obviously causes transaction costs in a number of ways. Contracts are often relatively short, leading to uncertainty and unpredictability of the future and the problem of the "contract renewal dance" (Smith & Lipsky, 1993). Contract payments can be delayed, causing short-term cash flow problems. To manage the contracts administratively, nonprofits also require greater managerial professionalism and support staff, leading to a more complex organizational structure and an increase in organizational capacity. The additional administrative load can also crowd-out volunteers (Knutsen, 2017; Smith & Lipsky, 1993).

Growing commercialization

Another phenomenon closely connected to the contracting culture is commercialization, defined as nonprofits' increasing reliance on revenues from sales of goods and services (Salamon, 1993). The term *commercialization* is often associated with contracting in the context of state retrenchment and a reduction of income from public agencies (Smith, 2006). In this argument, the term commercialization is used to describe increases in income from commercial activities that are used to help offset losses in government income (Pettijohn & Boris, 2013). Such commercial income can comprise rental or retail income, or income from selling services directly to clients. Smith (2006) further illustrates such activities with diverse examples such as a jazz concert series organized by a museum to acquire new members, or the creation of a catering business by a low-income housing agency in order to create additional income.

Strictly speaking, further meanings of the term commercialization should be mentioned in this context. First, selling specified services for a specified price to the government is a commercial act by itself. In contrast to grants, income from fee-for-service payments are a sales revenue and thus commercial income. Also, income from selling services to service users directly is commercial income. Recent developments, such as the introduction of voucher systems, individual tax benefits or individualized budgets, have fostered the importance of such commercial income (e.g., Glasby & Littlechild, 2016). These new funding modes have been introduced as ways to strengthen consumer choice and personalization, turning clients to actual customers in a market. This often forces nonprofits to compete more directly with one another and also to compete with for-profit organizations.

Research on consequences of commercialization is quite abundant (see Maier et al., 2016, for an overview). A major concern that has been raised as a consequence of commercialization is mission drift, which will be discussed in more detail next.

Mission drift

Mission drift is defined as the goal displacement that occurs when organizations give priority to aims and activities that enable their survival and sustain their operations at cost of their original core purpose. Such goal distortion may result from the broader trend of commercialization, marketization and professionalization, but it is also discussed as a direct consequence of funding that comes with strings attached, as contracting does (Ebrahim et al., 2014; Jones, 2007). Although mission drift may take place in all kinds of organizations, for nonprofit organizations it "is particularly severe as it threatens their very raison d'être": if they move away from their core mission, they will lose their distinctive role that sets them apart from other sectors, namely in delivering social value to their beneficiaries (Ebrahim et al., 2014, p. 82). The link between government contracting and mission drift relates to nonprofits' dependence on income from contracts, which compromises their autonomy in goal setting and programme or service selection due to power asymmetries that make them match with the funders' requirements (Jung & Moon, 2007; Pfeffer & Salancik, 1978), again based on resource dependence theory.

Mission drift due to contracting may appear in many manifestations. Among the most crucial is nonprofits shift away from carrying out the functions of advocacy and community building (e.g., Eikenberry & Kluver, 2004; Housego & O'Brien, 2012). The mechanisms behind this are twofold: either because grant writing or other bureaucratic activities redirect organizational resources away from these functions or simply because contracts do not refund advocacy and community-building activities as they are almost exclusively dedicated to service provision. Mission drift may also refer to service delivery itself, resulting in changes of the core clientele or in "cherry picking" or "creaming" of clients, implying that nonprofits choose to serve only those clients that enable them to more easily fulfil stipulated output criteria (e.g., bringing a particular number of clients into employment) or that are just cheaper to serve (e.g., clients with less elderly care needs) (Eikenberry & Kluver, 2004).

Empirically, the results are somewhat mixed. Several studies confirm that nonprofits perceive mission drift (e.g., Bennett & Savani, 2011). Some report that nonprofits drift away from advocacy and community building towards service provision and undertake client creaming (e.g., Alexander et al., 1999; Bailis et al., 2009). There is also evidence that nonprofits start to operate in fields that are well outside their original mission, particularly when they contract with supranational agencies.

Worsening working conditions due to state underfunding

State underfunding implies that government contracts for the provision of public welfare services do not cover total costs, forcing nonprofit organizations to privately subsidize the government in order to provide these services and receive the contract. A main reason for this is that government contracts limit cost of living adjustments. Over the years, inflation thus leads to a real income decline for the nonprofits, when financial arrangements are not adjusted accordingly. In this context, a deficit model of collaborative governance has been proposed which comprises financial arrangements with the government that do not cover the full costs for providing welfare services (Marwell & Calabrese, 2015).

In order to cope with this insufficient public funding, organizations can try to obtain donations, borrow money, use their reserves or reduce costs. As a next step, the question of how nonprofits reduce costs arises. This could be through under-investment in infrastructure or reducing service quality. A number of authors from different countries address a similar topic that has become even more pertinent after the Great Recession in 2008 onwards, dealing with coping strategies of nonprofit organizations that operate in an environment of austerity and welfare state retrenchment (e.g., Cunningham et al., 2016; Jones et al., 2015; Milbourne & Cushman, 2015; Never & de Leon, 2014; Pape et al., 2016). Often, they draw attention to the workforce of nonprofit service providers, as human resources represent a major cost factor for service-providing nonprofit organizations and are consequently an obvious starting point for an organization to save costs.

The workforce is found to be increasingly confronted with a freeze or deterioration of pay, worsening working conditions and job insecurity. A low rate of unionization in many nonprofit sectors (e.g., Cunningham et al., 2016) further weakens the positions of employees in nonprofit organizations. Short-term and flexible contracts with the government are also reflected in contractual arrangements with workers. Cunningham (2016, p. 662) reports of "zero hours contracts" for Scottish nonprofit social care providers with the government, an agreement with a fixed number of a few hundred hours of service provision and additional time contracted on a casual basis in line with demand. Accordingly, workers in these organizations were also recruited with zero-hour contracts, thus passing insecurity to the employees. Concern is also voiced over the consequences of staff cuts and increasingly precarious work. Workers remaining in the organizations are faced with expectations of "doing more with less." This work intensification often goes along with fewer opportunities for promotion and training, and deskilling (Cunningham, 2016). In the future, this situation could further aggravate labour shortages and jeopardize the ability of the nonprofit sector to provide sufficient good-quality social services.

Reduced innovation due to state underfunding

Finally, a lack of innovation and the prevalence of standardization have been mentioned in the context of contracting (e.g., Knutsen, 2017). Contracts usually are made for specific, standardized services, and typically do not encourage innovative approaches in services delivery. Resources are a key to innovative actions, and an organizations' human resources and financial slack are found to be influential in determining innovative behaviour (e.g., Meyer & Leitner, 2018; Ruiz-Moreno et al., 2008). Constant state underfunding could thus jeopardize innovative behaviour of nonprofits.

There are, however, ways how public authorities can foster innovative behaviour through contracting. Davidson (2011) provides an example for Australian community aged care where both price and output are set in the tendering process by the public funder. Competition between providers is, instead, on other criteria such as quality or local appropriateness, and this has been found to stimulate innovativeness.

Aspects arising from impact-oriented public funding

More recently, impact-oriented measures have gained importance in the relation between the government and nonprofit organizations and also found their way into contractual arrangements such as performance-based contracts, meeting governments' increased accountability demands (cf. Smith, 2010). An entirely impact-related funding instrument is the Social Impact Bond (SIB). It is supposed to pay more attention to the actual impact of social policy, to innovative service provision, to devote resources to the prevention of social problems instead of curing them, and to encourage private philanthropy in order to fill gaps in public funding (Maier et al., 2017). Though SIBs have existed for a short time, these promises are already discussed controversially. Critical scholars assume that SIBs may fundamentally alter the provision of public welfare services as they rearrange responsibilities and rewards among governments, nonprofits and private investors and foster financialization (e.g., Dowling, 2017; Maier et al., 2017). For nonprofits, SIBs are said to provide stable (long-term) funding as well as freedom to innovate and personalize services according to client needs (Maier et al., 2017). So far, empirical evidence on the effects of SIBs are rare and general conclusions are hard to draw as the instrument itself is very vague and largely depends on the actual arrangements.

Concluding remarks

For many nonprofit organizations throughout the world, government funding (still) is a very important source of income and the government often the most important partner for collaboration (Toepler, 2018). Yet, the mode of government–nonprofit relations as well as the funding mechanisms have undergone remarkable changes over the last decades. In particular, grants have largely been outplaced by contract payments, and newer impact-related arrangements such as SIBs have emerged, notably driven by the prevailing paradigm of public sector management at the time.

Research that addresses these changes in government funding and its consequences for nonprofit organizations' behaviour, overall, draws a rather negative picture. Public funding and particularly contract payments, for instance, come along with a loss of autonomy, an increase of accountability and negative consequences of chronic state underfunding. However, we must be cautious not to jump to premature policy conclusions or managerial recommendations.

First of all, we should not overlook the fact that the observed pathologies may not only be a consequence of public funding in particular, but that income from other sources such as donations or commercial income can have (negative) effects on nonprofit organizations, too. Accordingly, practitioners need to consider whether the consequences associated with public funding are worse than those associated with private funding. Positive and negative effects of all different income categories should therefore be carefully balanced before concluding whether one income source outmatches the other. Second, there is also a risk of overgeneralizing. As mentioned, there are many different modes of government–nonprofit interaction, and it is important to look closely at the exact conditions of nonprofit–government collaboration and their implications on the organization in each case. Third, it is not always that consequences have to be passively accepted and taken, they often can proactively be directed and controlled in ways that possibly might turn them into positive consequences. Fourth, and finally, it is important to further distinguish between problems that are inherent in government funding or government contracting and those relating to problems in the implementation of such arrangements. By improving the implementation of contractual arrangements, much can be gained.

References

Abramson, A.J. and Salamon, L.M. (2016) Prospects for nonprofits and philanthropy in the Trump presidency, *Nonprofit Policy Forum, 7*(4): 565–571.

Alexander, J., Nank, R. and Stivers, C. (1999) Implications of Welfare Reform: Do Nonprofit Survival Strategies Threaten Civil Society?, *Nonprofit and Voluntary Sector Quarterly, 28*(4): 452–475.

Andreoni, J. and Payne, A.A. (2011) Is crowding out due entirely to fundraising? Evidence from a panel of charities, *Journal of Public Economics, 95*(5–6): 334–343.

Anheier, H.K., Toepler, S. and Sokolowski, S.W. (1997) The implications of government funding for non-profit organizations: Three propositions, *International Journal of Public Sector Management, 10*(3): 190–213.

Bailis, R., Cowan, A., Berrueta, V. and Masera, O. (2009) Arresting the killer in the kitchen: The promises and pitfalls of commercializing improved cookstoves, *World Development, 37*(10): 1694–1705.

Bass, G.D., Arons, D.F., Guinane, K., Carter, M.F. and Rees, S. (2007) *Seen but Not Heard: Strengthening Nonprofit Advocacy*. Washington, DC: The Aspen Institute.

Bennett, R. and Savani, S. (2011) Surviving mission drift how charities can turn dependence on government contract funding to their own advantage, *Nonprofit Management & Leadership, 22*(2): 217–231.

Bertelli, A. M. and Smith, C.R. (2010) Relational contracting and network management, *Journal of Public Administration Research & Theory, 20*(suppl_1): i21–i40.

Bloodgood, E. and Tremblay-Boire, J. (2017) Does government funding depoliticize non-governmental organizations? Examining evidence from Europe, *European Political Science Review, 9*(3): 401–424.

Brooks, A.C. (1999) Do Public subsidies leverage private philanthropy for the arts? Empirical evidence on symphony orchestras, *Nonprofit and Voluntary Sector Quarterly, 28*(1): 32–45.

Brooks, A.C. (2004) The effects of public policy on private charity, *Administration & Society, 36*(2): 166–185.

Brown, L.K. and Troutt, E. (2004) Funding relations between nonprofits and government: A positive example, *Nonprofit and Voluntary Sector Quarterly, 33*(1): 5–27.

Chaves, M., Stephens, L. and Galaskiewicz, J. (2004) Does government funding suppress nonprofits' political activity?, *American Sociological Review, 69*(2): 292–316.

Christensen, T. and Lægreid, P. (2010). Beyond NPM? Some Development Features. In T. Christensen and P. Lægreid (Eds.). *The Ashgate Research Companion to New Public Management*. London: Routledge, 391–403.

Considine, M., O'Sullivan, S. and Nguyen, P. (2014) Governance, boards of directors and the impact of contracting on not-for-profit organizations – An Australian study, *Social Policy & Administration, 48*(2): 169–187.

Cunningham, I. (2016) Non-profits and the 'hollowed out' state: The transformation of working conditions through personalizing social care services during an era of austerity, *Work, Employment & Society, 30*(4): 649–668.

Cunningham, I., Baines, D., Shields, J. and Lewchuk, W. (2016) Austerity policies, 'precarity' and the nonprofit workforce: A comparative study of UK and Canada, *Journal of Industrial Relations, 58*(4): 455–472.

Davidson, B. (2011) Contestability in human services markets, *Journal of Australian Political Economy, 68*: 213–239.

De Wit, A. and Bekkers, R. (2014) Government support and charitable donations: A meta-analysis of the crowding-out hypothesis, Working Paper of the Center for Philanthropic Studies, VU University Amsterdam.

De Wit, A., Neumayr, M., Handy, F. and Wiepking, P. (2018) Do government expenditures shift private philanthropic donations to particular fields of welfare? Evidence from cross-country data, *European Sociological Review, 34*(1): 6–21.

Dowling, E. (2017) In the wake of austerity: Social Impact Bonds and the financialisation of the welfare state in Britain, *New Political Economy, 22*(3): 294–310.

Ebrahim, A., Battilana, J. and Mair, J. (2014) The governance of social enterprises: Mission drift and accountability challenges in hybrid organizations, *Research in Organizational Behavior, 34*: 81–100.

Eikenberry, A. M. and Kluver, J.D. (2004) The marketization of the nonprofit sector: Civil society at risk?, *Public Administration Review, 64*(2): 132–140.

Esping-Andersen, G. (1990) *The Three Worlds of Welfare Capitalism.* Cambridge: Polity Press.

Galaskiewicz, J. and Bielefeld, W. (1998) *Nonprofit Organizations in an Age of Uncertainty: A Study of Organizational Change.* New York: Aldine de Gruyter.

Gazley, B. and Brudney, J.L. (2007) The Purpose (and perils) of government–nonprofit partnership, *Nonprofit and Voluntary Sector Quarterly, 36*(3): 389–415.

Glasby, J. and Littlechild, R. (2016) *Direct Payments and Personal Budgets* (Revised and substantially updated 3d ed.). Bristol: Policy Press.

Guo, B. (2006) Charity for profit? Exploring factors associated with the commercialization of human service nonprofits, *Nonprofit and Voluntary Sector Quarterly, 35*(1): 123–138.

Guo, C. (2007) When government becomes the principal philanthropist: The effects of public funding on patterns of nonprofit governance, *Public Administration Review, 67*(3): 458–473.

Hodge, M.M. and Piccolo, R.F. (2005) Funding source, board involvement techniques, and financial vulnerability in nonprofit organizations: A test of resource dependence, *Nonprofit Management and Leadership, 16*(2): 171–190.

Housego, A. and O'Brien, T. (2012) Delivery of public services by non-government organisations, *Australian Journal of Public Administration, 71*(2): 211–220.

Hughes, P.N. and Luksetich, W.A. (1999) The relationship among funding sources for art and history museums, *Nonprofit Management and Leadership, 10*(1): 21–37.

Isaksson, D., Blomqvist, P. and Winblad, U. (2017) Privatization of social care delivery – How can contracts be specified?, *Public Management Review, 20*(11): 1643–1662.

James, E. and Rose-Ackerman, S. (1986) *The Nonprofit Enterprise in Market Economics.* London: Harwood Academic.

Jenkins, J.C. (2006) Nonprofit Organizations and Political Advocacy. In W.W. Powell and R. Steinberg (Eds.). *The Nonprofit Sector: A Research Handbook* (Vol. 2). New Haven, CT: Yale University Press, 307–331.

Jones, G., Meegan, R., Kennett, P. and Croft, J. (2015) The uneven impact of austerity on the voluntary and community sector: A tale of two cities, *Urban Studies, 53*(10): 2064–2080.

Jones, M.B. (2007) The multiple sources of mission drift, *Nonprofit and Voluntary Sector Quarterly, 36*(2): 299–307.

Joy, M. and Shields, J. (2013) Social Impact Bonds: The Next phase of third sector marketization?, *Canadian Journal of Nonprofit and Social Economy Research, 4*(2): 39–55.

Jung, K. and Moon, M.J. (2007) The double-edged sword of public-resource dependence: The impact of public resources on autonomy and legitimacy in Korean cultural nonprofit organizations, *Policy Studies Journal, 35*(2): 205–226.

Kendall, J. (2003) *The Voluntary Sector: Comparative Perspectives in the UK.* London: Psychology Press.

Khanna, J. and Sandler, T. (2000) Partners in giving: The crowding-in effects of UK government grants, *European Economic Review, 44*(8): 1543–1556.

Kim, M. and Van Ryzin, G.G. (2014) Impact of government funding on donations to arts organizations: A survey experiment, *Nonprofit and Voluntary Sector Quarterly, 43*(5): 910–925.

Knutsen, W.L. (2017) Retaining the benefits of government–nonprofit contracting relationship: Opposites attract or clash?, *Voluntas: International Journal of Voluntary and Nonprofit Organizations, 28*(4): 1373–1398.

Kramer, R.M. (1981) *Voluntary Agencies in the Welfare State.* Berkeley: University of California Press.

Lu, J. (2015) Which nonprofit gets more government funding?, *Nonprofit Management and Leadership, 25*(3): 297–312.

Maier, F., Barbetta, G.P. and Godina, F. (2017) Paradoxes of Social Impact Bonds, *Social Policy & Administration.*

Maier, F., Meyer, M. and Steinbereithner, M. (2016) Nonprofit organizations becoming business-like: A systematic review, *Nonprofit and Voluntary Sector Quarterly, 45*(1): 64–86.

Marwell, N.P. and Calabrese, T. (2015) A deficit model of collaborative governance: Government–nonprofit fiscal relations in the provision of child welfare services, *Journal of Public Administration Research and Theory, 25*(4): 1031–1058.

Meyer, M. and Leitner, J. (2018) Slack and innovation: The role of human resources in nonprofits, *Nonprofit Management and Leadership 29*(2): 181–201.

Milbourne, L. and Cushman, M. (2015) Complying, transforming or resisting in the new austerity? Realigning social welfare and independent action among English voluntary organisations, *Journal of Social Policy, 44*(03): 463–485.

Mosley, J.E. (2012) Keeping the lights on: How government funding concerns drive the advocacy agendas of nonprofit homeless service providers, *Journal of Public Administration Research and Theory, 22*(4): 841–866.

Neumayr, M., Meyer, M., Pospíšil, M., Schneider, U. and Malý, I. (2009). The Role of Civil Society Organisations in Different Nonprofit Regimes: Evidence from Austria and the Czech Republic. In B. Enjolras and K.H. Sivesind (Eds.). *Civil Society in Comparative Perspective*: Bingley: Emerald, 167–196.

Neumayr, M., Schneider, U. and Meyer, M. (2015) Public funding and its impact on nonprofit advocacy, *Nonprofit and Voluntary Sector Quarterly, 44*(2): 297–318.

Neumayr, M., Schneider, U., Meyer, M., Pennerstorfer, A., Sokolowski, S.W. and Salamon, L.M. (2017). Austria. A Dualistic Pattern of Civil Society Development. In L.M. Salamon, S.W. Sokolowski and M.A. Haddock (Eds.). *Explaining Civil Society Development. A Social Origins Approach*. Baltimore, MD: Johns Hopkins University Press, 197–210.

Never, B. and de Leon, E. (2014) The effect of government contracting on nonprofit human service organizations: Impacts of an evolving relationship, *Human Service Organizations Management, Leadership & Governance, 38*(3): 258–270.

O'Regan, K. and Oster, S. (2002) Does government funding alter nonprofit governance? Evidence from New York City nonprofit contractors, *Journal of Policy Analysis and Management, 21*(3): 359–379.

Osborne, S.P. (2006) The New Public Governance?, *Public Management Review, 8*(3): 377–387.

Ostrower, F. and Stone, M.M. (2006). Governance: Research Trends, Gaps, and Future Prospects. In W.W. Powell and R. Steinberg (Eds.). *The Nonprofit Sector. A Research Handbook*. New Haven, CT: Yale University Press, 612–628.

Pape, U., Chaves-Ávila, R., Pahl, J.B., Petrella, F., Pieliński, B. and Savall-Morera, T. (2016) Working under pressure: Economic recession and third sector development in Europe, *International Journal of Sociology and Social Policy, 36*(7/8): 547–566.

Payne, A.A. (1998) Does the government crowd-out private donations? New evidence from a sample of non-profit firms, *Journal of Public Economics, 69*(3): 323–345.

Pennerstorfer, A. (2016) Die volkswirtschaftliche Bedeutung gemeinnütziger Organisationen in Österreich, *Der öffentliche Sektor, 42*(2): 7–13.

Pennerstorfer, A. and Neumayr, M. (2017) Examining the association of welfare state expenditure, nonprofit regimes and charitable giving, *Voluntas: International Journal of Voluntary and Nonprofit Organizations, 28*(2): 532–555.

Pettijohn, S.L. and Boris, E.T. (2013). *Nonprofit–Government Contracts and Grants. Findings from the 2013 National Survey*. Washington, DC: Urban Institute. Retrieved from: https://www.urban.org/sites/default/files/publication/24231/412962-Nonprofit-Government-Contracts-and-Grants-Findings-from-the-National-Survey.PDF?utm_source=Forum%20Bits%3A%2012–6-13&utm_campaign=Forum%20Bits%3A%2012/6/13&utm_medium=email

Pfeffer, J. and Salancik, G.R. (1978) *The External Control of Organizations: A Resource Dependence Perspective*. New York: Harper & Row.

Rose-Ackerman, S. (1981). Do government grants to charity reduce private donations? In M. White (Ed.). *Nonprofit Firms in a Three Sector Economy*. Washington, DC: Urban Institute, 95–114.

Ruiz-Moreno, A., García-Morales, V.J. and Llorens-Montes, F.J. (2008) The moderating effect of organizational slack on the relation between perceptions of support for innovation and organizational climate, *Personnel Review, 37*(5): 509–525.

Salamon, L.M. (1993) The marketization of welfare: Changing nonprofit and for-profit roles in the American welfare state, *Social Service Review, 67*(1): 16–39.

Salamon, L.M. (1995) *Partners in Public Service*. Baltimore, MD: Johns Hopkins University Press.

Salamon, L.M. (2006). Government–Nonprofit Relations from an International Perspective. In E.T. Boris and C.E. Steuerle (Eds.). *Nonprofits & Government: Collaboration & Conflict* (2nd ed.). Washington, DC: Urban Institute, 399–435.

Salamon, L.M. and Anheier, H. (1998) Social origins of civil society, *Voluntas: International Journal of Voluntary and Nonprofit Organizations, 9*(3): 213–248.

Salamon, L.M. and Sokolowski, S.W. (2017). Testing the Social Origins Theory of Civil Society Development. In L.M. Salamon, S.W. Sokolowski and M.A. Haddock (Eds.). *Explaining Civil Society Development. A Social Origins Approach*. Baltimore, MD: Johns Hopkins University Press, 91–124.

Salamon, L.M., Sokolowski, S.W. and Haddock, M.A. (2017) *Explaining Civil Society Development. A Social Origins Approach*. Baltimore, MD: Johns Hopkins University Press.

Smith, S.R. (2006). Government Financing of Nonprofit Activity. In E.T. Boris and C.E. Steuerle (Eds.). *Nonprofits & Government: Collaboration & Conflict* (2nd ed.). Washington, DC: Urban Institute, 219–256.

Smith, S.R. (2010) Nonprofits and public administration: Reconciling performance management and citizen engagement, *American Review of Public Administration, 40*(2): 129–152.

Smith, S.R. and Lipsky, M. (1993) *Nonprofits for Hire*. Cambridge, MA: Harvard University Press.

Stone, M.M., Hager, M.A. and Griffin, J.J. (2001) Organizational characteristics and funding environments: A study of a population of United Way–affiliated nonprofits, *Public Administration Review, 61*(3): 276–289.

Toepler, S. (2018). Government Funding Policies. In B.A. Seaman and D.R. Young (Eds.). *Handbook of Research on Nonprofit Economics and Management* (2nd ed.). Cheltenham: Edward Elgar.

Van Slyke, D.M. (2007) Agents or stewards: Using theory to understand the government–nonprofit social service contracting relationship, *Journal of Public Administration Research and Theory, 17*(2): 157–187.

Young, D.R. (2006). Complementary, Supplementary, or Adversarial? Nonprofit–Government Relations. In E.T. Boris and C.E. Steuerle (Eds.). *Nonprofits & Governments. Collaboration & Conflict* (2nd ed.). Washington, DC: Urban Institute, 37–79.

PART VI

The social enterprise space

31

SOCIAL ENTERPRISE[1]

Janelle A. Kerlin

ASSOCIATE PROFESSOR, DEPARTMENT OF PUBLIC MANAGEMENT AND POLICY,
GEORGIA STATE UNIVERSITY, ATLANTA, GEORGIA, UNITED STATES

Introduction

Use of the term *social enterprise* has been growing in popularity since the mid-1980s, though the activity itself has long been in existence. Generally defined as any market-based activity to address a social issue, social enterprise has by some accounts become a global movement to sustain socially beneficial activities largely by means other than traditional government and philanthropic resources. Though the value added from undertaking social enterprise can be emphasized differently depending on geographic context, social enterprise generally speaks to increasing the self-sufficiency, long-term sustainability, programmatic autonomy, and beneficiary empowerment of organizations involved in pursuing a social mission (Kerlin, 2009, 2017).

Looking globally, the social enterprise movement of the last three decades has been spurred on by the need for resources or programming or both to fill gaps in public and private systems attempting to serve the disadvantaged (Kerlin, 2010; Bull, 2008). Largely as an outlier, social enterprise in the United States (U.S.) also encompasses activities that support the improved well-being of populations beyond the disadvantaged. The term can include both whole organizations as well as program activities within an organization. Typical examples include organizations that provide work for the hard-to-employ, thrift stores that sell second-hand goods to support a social purpose, scouts that sell cookies or other items to fund their youth programming, microfinance organizations that lend money to the poor for their small business start-ups, and museum stores, among many others.

Definitions

The exact definition of social enterprise is often contested along its commercial and social boundaries. Indeed, Dart (2004, p. 415) speaks of social enterprise as "blurring the boundary between nonprofit and profit." Some in the burgeoning social enterprise field, however, appear to be coalescing around broad parameters for the term. Social enterprise is increasingly defined as distinct from corporate social responsibility (CSR), where profit-driven businesses donate only a fraction of their funds or employee time to social projects. Corporate philanthropy is also often seen as separate from social enterprise due to the primacy of the profit motive in the corporate generation of revenue relative to the comparably small social cause work of the organization.

Indeed, some definitions speak directly to business-engaged organizations seeking to "maximize improvements in society instead of owner or shareholder earnings" (Africa Social Enterprise, 2018). Other discussions exclude charitable/nonprofit organizations that generate only a small amount of commercial revenue. While the broadest definitions may include all of these forms of commercially backed social efforts (Young et al., 2016), definitions of social enterprise, either inherently or explicitly, often exclude undertakings that are relatively lacking in either the social or commercial aspect (European Commission, 2016; Kerlin, 2017; DTI, 2002).

More precise understandings of the concept of social enterprise and what it is associated with can vary across global regions as well as individual countries and even subnational spaces (Borzaga and Defourny, 2001; Kerlin 2006, 2009; Fisac and Moreno-Romero, 2015). Indeed, Europeans and Americans often define social enterprise differently. In the U.S., there are, broadly speaking, two principal schools of thought. The *earned-income school* focuses on social enterprise organizations and activities that generate commercial revenue in support of social goals. Indeed, a version of this definition is used by the U.S. professional association, the Social Enterprise Alliance, as well as among many social science scholars. In this perspective, social enterprise encompasses a variety of forms along a continuum from dual-purpose businesses that mediate profit goals with social objectives (hybrids) to nonprofit organizations engaged in mission-supporting commercial activity (social purpose organizations, for-profit subsidiaries of nonprofits, nonprofit-business partnerships, etc.). This is sometimes referred to as the spectrum school (Dees, 1996; Dees and Anderson, 2006; Alter, 2007).

The second school of thought, the *social innovation school*, is more focused on the individual (as opposed to the organization) and is embodied in the innovative social entrepreneur with the social enterprise as the vehicle through which a social innovation is delivered with or without a commercial base (Zeyen et al., 2013; see also Young, 2013; Chapter 32 by Mildenberger and Krlev, this volume). Business schools and foundations in the U.S. largely espouse the social innovation school. Some authors, however, promote a distinction in the use of these terms that aligns with the two schools of thought. Citing Dees (2003), Paul Light (2008) argues that on an academic level, there is increasing agreement that social enterprise is distinct from the foundation definition of social entrepreneurship due to its connection with revenue generation. Light (2008, p. 5) states, "Whereas social entrepreneurship seeks tipping points for innovation and change, social enterprise seeks profits for reinvestment and growth."

In Europe, the EMES International Research Network established a set of loose criteria to use in identifying social enterprises in that context. These include the economic/entrepreneurial criteria of "a continuous activity producing goods and/or selling services; a high degree of autonomy; a significant level of economic risk; a minimum amount of paid work." They also include the social criteria of "an explicit aim to benefit the community; an initiative launched by a group of citizens; a decision-making power not based on capital ownership; a participatory nature, which involves various parties affected by the activity; a limited profit distribution" (Defourny and Nyssens, 2010b, p. 43). This approach differs from the ways social enterprise is typically conceived of in U.S. circles. One key difference is the European focus on having a multi-stakeholder governing body, as well as a lack of emphasis of social enterprise involving "innovation." It should be added that in the European approach, not every criterion listed above needs to be met precisely in order to place an organization in the social enterprise sphere.

Given the above (and below) discussions, a precise definition of social enterprise has not been agreed upon by the social enterprise community, and approaches to understanding the concept continue to be debated in the social enterprise literature (Peattie and Morley, 2008; Teasdale, 2012; Young and Lecy, 2014; Young et al., 2016; Defourny and Nyssens, 2017a). Indeed, more recent attempts abandon the quest for a single unified definition and provide conceptual frameworks that allow for subjective selection against a range of possible scenarios. Young and Longhofer (2016, p. 24), speaking to a "social efficiency frontier," propose an inclusive range of individual types of organizations that adhere to a "mildly restrictive" definition based on the overall performance of an organization including its net social impact and financial sustainability. Defourny and Nyssens (2017a, 2017b), on the other hand, offer a more narrowly constructed grouping of four broad types of social enterprise organizations based on their international research. Drawing on her macro-institutional social enterprise framework, Kerlin (2013, 2017) identifies country models of social enterprise that can be refined at the national or subnational level. Some authors argue that such conceptual frameworks provide the most appropriate approach to the definitional question because particular environments shape the contours of the phenomenon for the best fit for social enterprise in that context (Young et al., 2016; Young and Lecy, 2014; Kerlin, 2006, 2016). Applicable to social enterprise, Mair, Robinson, and Hockerts (2006, p. 7) also state that, "Narrowing [social entrepreneurship] down to a uniformly agreed upon definition would probably make it applicable only to a limited set of problems and issues."

While the term 'social enterprise' has American and West European roots, the basic idea behind social enterprise, that of commercial revenue generation for social benefit, can been found indigenously in many other countries. With the international diffusion of the term 'social enterprise' and its Western conceptualization, many countries have not only applied the term to their own indigenous manifestations that fall under the broad definition, they have also taken Western examples of social enterprise policy and organizations and adjusted them for use in their own country contexts. This process can be seen in countries as diverse as Poland, Romania, South Korea, China, Chile, and Argentina (Kerlin, 2009, 2017), and can be facilitated by regional and international networks such as the Asian Venture Philanthropy Network (AVPN), the Global Impact Investing Network (GIIN), and the Global Social Entrepreneurship Network (GSEN), and international intermediaries including Socialab, the Social Enterprise Academy, and the British Council (Cui and Kerlin, 2017).

Activities, government involvement, and specific legal forms

Indeed, variation in social enterprise can be seen in the predominant activities, beneficiaries, outcome focus, funders, regulation, and legal forms for social enterprise in different contexts (Kerlin, 2010). In Europe, a number of countries provide strong national government support for social enterprise, including some welfare states that are viewed as having co-opted social enterprise for their own policy purposes, namely the work integration of the hard-to-employ (often through social cooperatives that enjoy substantial government subsidies, though there are variations on this model). Strong government support for this particular type of social enterprise activity has led to the term's association with the provision of employment and less so with other social purposes though this is more the case on the continent than in the United Kingdom (Defourny and Nyssens, 2010a; Nyssens, 2006). There is also a growing list of countries with specific legislation for social enterprise legal forms on the national level, many of which are adaptations of the cooperative form. In 1991, Italy was the first to adopt the social cooperative legal form with a number of other countries later following suit including France, Greece, Poland, Portugal, and Spain. Alternatively, in 2005, the U.K. implemented a new legal form, the Community Interest Company (CIC), to address the call to combine social mission and investment options in one organization (Brewer, 2016).

Social enterprise in the United States is, by comparison, largely left to the private and civil society sectors even though there is a comparatively strong national government presence, globally speaking. Here a national-level legal form has not been created for social enterprise, though there is significant state-level tinkering with different business forms that legally allow social and profit goals to coexist, such as the low-profit limited liability corporation (L3C), the social purpose corporation, and the benefit corporation (Brewer, 2016; Chapter 35 by Abramson and Billings, this volume). The cooperative form has historically not been associated with the term social enterprise in the U.S.; however, this is changing with the emergence of such entities as the Evergreen Cooperatives in Ohio and the Cooperative Home Care Associates in New York (Brewer, 2016). Also by contrast, in the U.S. there is generally more emphasis on revenue generation in support of a wide range of potential social purposes that may or may not involve beneficiaries in the earned income activity (Ebrahim et al., 2014) and that focus on the disadvantaged as well as improved well-being more generally. Historically, the development of social enterprise has involved more foundation than government support in the U.S. (Kerlin, 2006, 2009).

Organizational arrangements

Typical organizational arrangements for social enterprise in the U.S. context[2] span both nonprofit and for-profit legal forms (Alter, 2007). In terms of nonprofits, the social purpose organization involves the generation of earned income through the in-house sale of products or services. An example is the physical fitness and recreational services provided by the Young Men's Christian Association (YMCA). Also included in this category are sheltered workshops for those with disabilities, job training initiatives, and nonprofit-owned franchises.

The sale of products or services can also be arranged through a nonprofit or for-profit subsidiary. The creation of subsidiaries allows a nonprofit to engage in activities that may only be peripherally related to its mission or to reduce its risk as it experiments with new program or business ideas. Such subsidiaries are considered social enterprises when they include an earned income component. For example, a comprehensive social service provider might establish an employment agency for hard-to-place inner city residents as a separate nonprofit subsidiary. While the parent organization may provide start-up funding and administrative services, the subsidiary is able to adopt its own structure and create a business-like culture (Cordes et al., 2002).

The for-profit subsidiary is chosen most often when a nonprofit seeks to protect its tax-exempt status while engaging in substantial business activity that is not related to its charitable exempt purpose. Profits from the for-profit subsidiary are taxed at normal corporate income tax rates even though they support the charitable activities of the nonprofit. The Sustainable Community Initiatives' establishment of a for-profit subsidiary called Community Forklift (a recovered building materials store) is an example of this. At times, nonprofits go a step further and establish a network of nonprofit and for-profit subsidiaries creating a nonprofit conglomerate such as Housing Works, which serves the homeless with HIV/AIDS in New York City (Cordes et al., 2002).

Nonprofits in the U.S. also form partnerships with for-profits and act as trade intermediaries between small, local producers and markets for their products. These organizations either sell the locally acquired goods themselves or link local producers directly with buyers in distant markets. An example is Peoplink, Inc., an Internet-based service that connects artisan groups in developing countries directly with buyers in the United States. As a "trust broker," they handle promotion, payment, and returns for a 7 percent commission and direct expenses.

Social enterprises in the U.S. can also be housed within a for-profit business. Dual-purpose businesses (hybrids) mediate profit goals with internally realized social objectives to achieve either a double-bottom line (financial and social returns) or triple-bottom line (financial, social, and environmental returns) (see Chapter 35 by Abramson and Billings, this volume). An example is Puravida Coffee's mission, which calls for providing living wages for farmers and producers in Latin America through the sale of fair trade coffee, the education of consumers and business leaders to take action towards social good, and serving at-risk children and families in Latin American communities.

In the European context, there can be variations on these organizational arrangements with the for-profit and charity/association (similar to nonprofit) legal forms found there in addition to the cooperative. However, the use of a single organization appears to predominate over a conglomerate with this typically being the cooperative or social cooperative legal form (when such legislation is present). Associations may also house a revenue-generating component; however, this is only where laws allow business activity within the association legal form. The public sector social enterprise is also becoming an accepted form of social enterprise by some American and European observers. These typically involve local government entities that establish, control, and fund usually nonprofit organizations or associations involved in community development activities (Brewer, 2016; Defourny and Nyssens, 2017b).

Internal governance

Another point of differentiation across Europe and the U.S is the internal governance of the social enterprise. In the European context, the governance of the organization carries greater importance due to its expected role in the democratic advancement of the economy (Defourny and Nyssens, 2010b). Indeed, the European social enterprise focus on autonomous development, decision-making exclusive of capital ownership, and the participation of multi-stakeholders in the governance of the organization all speak to the cooperative roots of social enterprise in Europe. In terms of autonomy, a hallmark of European social enterprises is that they are established and managed by citizen groups rather than public or private entities though they can receive significant funding from these sources. As such, public–private partnerships are not included in their conceptualization of social enterprise (Defourny and Nyssens, 2010b), though they can be at times in the U.S. context (Young et al., 2016). Decision-making in European social enterprises is based on the premise of one-member-one-vote and is not determined by capital ownership, as it can be in the U.S. with for-profit social enterprises. The involvement of multiple stakeholders, including employees, beneficiaries, volunteers, sponsors and government and business actors from the local community, either on the board or as members, creates a situation of multi-stakeholder ownership and governance of the social enterprise. These last two characteristics are captured as requirements in the legislation for social enterprise legal forms in some European countries (Defourny and Nyssens, 2010b).

In the U.S. context, democratic governance of the social enterprise receives less attention and more focus is placed on ensuring business management expertise, especially in the case of the nonprofit social enterprise (Young and Lecy, 2014). Dees, Emerson, and Economy (2001) discuss many alternatives to the traditional nonprofit board structure that can help facilitate governance. Depending on how the social enterprise is structured in relation to the originating nonprofit, alternative board structures might include an advisory board or a business enterprise board. If the enterprise is located inside the nonprofit, an advisory board can be established to specifically provide support and counsel on the enterprise side. Such advisory boards typically have more representation from clients and the community and can be formal or informal. When the social enterprise is housed in a legally separate for-profit subsidiary, a business enterprise board can be established at its head with a focus on profit-making. Writing from the United Kingdom perspective, Spear et al. (2009) note that social enterprises can experience specific governance challenges depending on the type of organizational form for the social enterprise. These can include recruiting board members with the right skills and experience, the absence of a dominant external stakeholder, managing the membership, board power to control management, managing board and management interdependencies, and balancing social and financial goals.

Financial resources

Social enterprises draw on a variety of resources beyond commercial revenue to support their activities. The specific mix of resources for a social enterprise can depend on its legal form, life stage, the activities of the organization, and who it benefits (see benefits theory in Young 2015, 2017), as well as the availability of different types of resources. A nonprofit- or association-based social enterprise can draw on individual donations, membership fees, loans, foundation grants, government grants and contracts, and earned income from both individual and third-party payers, such as government insurance and voucher programs (Searing et al. 2016). Some legal forms, including the social cooperative type, specify preferential treatment when competing for government contracts in addition to tax benefits (Borzaga, 1996). For-profit and cooperative social enterprises can rely on financing by private investors in addition to many of the same financial resources for nonprofits and associations because they are not bound by a nondistribution constraint, as is often found with nonprofits and associations. While typical for-profit forms allow for a full return on investment for investors, some for-profit legal forms supporting social enterprise provide for a limited distribution of investment income (Brewer, 2016).

A number of new or restructured financial resources have become available for social enterprises (see Chapter 33 by Han, Chen, and Toepler, this volume). Crowdsourcing allows an organization to fundraise widely by soliciting many small donations through the use of an Internet platform such as GoFundMe or Kickstarter (Searing et al., 2016). Social impact bonds often involve a financial agreement between public and private stakeholders to provide funding for predetermined social outcomes by a social service delivery organization that can be a social enterprise. If the agreed-upon social outcome is achieved by the social service organization, the public entity then repays the cost of the program with agreed interest to the private investors (OECD, 2016). Other new types of financing for social enterprises include loan guarantees by foundations for access to low-interest loans and quasi-equity debt securities which combine features of equity and debt and allow nonprofit social enterprises to access important properties of equity investment (Bugg-Levine et al., 2012; Searing et al., 2016).

Critiques of social enterprise

Practitioners and researchers are increasingly aware that realizing the potential of social enterprise can be a challenge and is not without its pitfalls. Among the first critiques were those that spoke to the possible downsides of commercial revenue generation activity in nonprofit organizations. Eikenberry and Kluver (2004) and Weisbrod (2004) in the U.S. spoke to the risks to nonprofit organizations and civil society more broadly due to nonprofit marketization. European authors also added critical perspectives on social enterprise (Bull, 2008). Teasdale (2012) and Mason (2012) undertook critical discourse analyses of the fluid meaning of social enterprise in the United Kingdom. Dey and Steyaert (2012) published an overview of critical work on social enterprise that identified four types of critical research approaches and proposed a fifth more interventionist approach. More recently Sinclair et al. (2018), in a critical investigation of social enterprise in Scotland, found that structural conditions and institutional factors could constrain its impact.

Most recently, Pascal Dey and Chris Steyaert (2018) published an edited collection of papers written by scholars in North America and Europe that critique social entrepreneurship and enterprise. The five sections in the book bring awareness to and open a discourse around assumptions about social entrepreneurship, its political and ideological representations, how it is enacted through language, trust, and compassion with sometimes unintended consequences, its moral predicaments and limitations with respect to participation and democracy, and how newly understanding it from a relational view can shift thinking around what is possible including systems change. Their "affirmative critique," which positions the current phenomenon of social entrepreneurship and enterprise as "inadequate yet necessary" (Dey and Steyaert, 2018, p. 2), challenges stakeholders to not settle for the status quo, but rather push the field's frontiers to achieve the full potential of social enterprise and address any needed correctives along the way.

Theoretical and other research trends

Research in the area of social enterprise is an important part of moving the field and its practice forward. However, the use of theoretical approaches to explain and predict social enterprise processes and phenomenon has only slowly been developing (Haugh, 2012). Some of the prominent theories researchers have drawn on include institutional theory (Agrawal and Hockerts, 2013) and a number of its offshoots including institutional isomorphism (Nicholls, 2010), historical institutionalism (Kerlin, 2013, 2017), and institutional logics, which addresses social mission and market tensions (Pache and Santos, 2013; Cooney, 2006; Battilana and Lee, 2014; Vickers et al., 2017; Fitzgerald and Shepherd, 2018). Other theoretical approaches used include social network theory (Dufays and Huybrechts, 2014; Atsan, 2018), resiliency theory (Young and Kim, 2015), and ethnography (Mauksch et al., 2017), among others.

A number of authors have called for more research on social-enterprise related topics generally (Doherty et al., 2014; Smith et al., 2013; Mueller et al., 2011). Some recent topics researchers have examined include social enterprise as an organizational innovation and its institutionalization in a new context (Kerlin et al., 2017, 2018), its sustainability (Battilana and Dorado, 2010; Teasdale et al., 2013), scaling up (Lyon and Fernandez, 2012; Scheuerle and Schmitz, 2016; Bloom and Skloot, 2010; Agapitova and Linn, 2016; Seelos and Mair, 2017), the measurement of social outcomes, impact and value (Molecke and Pinkse, 2017; Grieco, 2015; Bagnoli and Megali, 2011; Nicholls et al., 2015), and social enterprise ecosystems (European Commission, 2016; Hazenberg et al., 2016; Searing et al., 2016), among many others including the topics addressed in this chapter.

Notes

1   Sections of this chapter were first published in the article, "Social Enterprise: What the U.S. and European Experience Can Teach Us—And Where to Now?" in the *Nonprofit Quarterly*, July 2018. The author would like to thank Dennis Young, Simon Teasdale, Cassady Brewer, and Meng Ye for their comments on drafts of this chapter.
2   This section largely excerpted from Kerlin and Gagnaire (2009).

References

Africa Social Enterprise (2018) Definition: Social Enterprise. Available at: https://www.africasocialenter prise.com/ (Accessed July 26, 2018).

Agapitova, N. and Linn, J.F. (2016) *Scaling up social enterprise innovations: approaches and lessons.* Global Economy & Development Working Paper 95. The Brookings Institution. Available at: https://www. brookings.edu/wp-content/uploads/2016/07/WorkingPaper95ScalingUpSocialEnterpriseInnova tionsRev.pdf

Agrawal, A. and Hockerts, K. (2013) 'Institutional theory as a framework for practitioners of social entre-preneurship', in Osburg, T. and Schmidpeter, R. (eds.) *Social Innovation: Solutions for a Sustainable Future*. New York: Springer, 119–129.

Alter, K. (2007) Social enterprise typology. *The Four Lenses Strategic Framework* [Online]. Available at: www.4lenses.org/setypology (Accessed June 5, 2018).

Atsan, N. (2018) 'Utilizing social networks in social entrepreneurship', in Iyigun, N.O. (ed.) *Creating Business Value and Competitive Advantage with Social Entrepreneurship*. Hershey, PA: IGI Global.

Bagnoli, L. and Megali, C. (2011) 'Measuring performance in social enterprises', *Nonprofit and Voluntary Sector Quarterly*, 40(1), 149–165.

Battilana, J., and Dorado, S. (2010) 'Building sustainable hybrid organizations: The case of commercial microfinance organizations', *Academy of Management Journal*, 53, 1419–1440.

Battilana, J. and Lee, M. (2014) 'Advancing research on hybrid organizing – insights from the study of social enterprises', *Academy of Management Annals*, 8(1), 397–441.

Bloom, P.N. and Skloot, E. (eds.) (2010) *Scaling Social Impact: New Thinking*. New York: Palgrave Macmillan.

Borzaga, C. (1996) 'Social cooperatives and work integration in Italy', *Annals of Public and Cooperative Economics*, 67, 209–234.

Borzaga, C. and Defourny, J. (eds.) (2001) *The Emergence of Social Enterprise*. New York: Routledge.

Brewer, C.V. (2016) 'The ongoing evolution in social enterprise legal forms', in Young, D.R., Searing, E.A.M, and Brewer, C.V. (eds.) *The Social Enterprise Zoo: A Guide for Perplexed Scholars, Entrepreneurs, Philanthropists, Leaders, Investors, and Policymakers*. Northampton, MA: Edward Elgar.

Bugg-Levine, A., Kogut, B. and Kulatilaka, N. (2012) 'A new approach to funding social enterprises', *Harvard Business Review*, January–February.

Bull, M. (2008) 'Challenging tensions: Critical, theoretical and empirical perspectives on social enterprise', *International Journal of Entrepreneurial Behavior & Research*, 14(5), 268–275.

Cooney, K. (2006) 'The institutional and technical structuring of nonprofit ventures: Case study of a U.S. hybrid organization caught between two fields', *Voluntas: International Journal of Voluntary and Nonprofit Organizations*, 17(2), 137–155.

Cordes J., Steuerle, E. and Poletz, Z. (2002) 'Examples of nonprofit/for-profit hybrid business models', Unpublished Paper. Washington, DC: Urban Institute.

Cui, T.S. and Kerlin, J.A. (2017) 'China: The diffusion of social enterprise innovation: exported and imported international influence', in Kerlin, J.A (ed.) *Shaping Social Enterprise: Understanding Institutional Context and Influence*. Bingley: Emerald.

Dart, R. (2004) 'The legitimacy of social enterprise', *Nonprofit Management & Leadership*, 14(4), 411–424.

Dees, J.G. (1996) 'The social enterprise spectrum: Philanthropy to commerce', Boston: Harvard Business School: Publishing Division, 9-393-343.

Dees J.G. (2003) 'Social entrepreneurship is about innovation and impact, not income', [online]. Available at: https://centers.fuqua.duke.edu/case/wp-content/uploads/sites/7/2015/02/Article_Dees_SEisAb outInnovationandImpactNotIncome_2003.pdf

Dees, J.G., Emerson, J. and Economy, P. (2001) *Enterprising Nonprofits: A Toolkit for Social Entrepreneurs*. New York: Wiley.

Dees, J.G. and Anderson, B.B. (2006) 'Framing a theory of social entrepreneurship: Building on two schools of practice and thought', in Mosher-Williams, R. (ed.) *Research on Social Entrepreneurship: Understanding and Contributing to an Emerging Field*, 1(6), Washington, DC: ARNOVA Occasional Paper Series.

Defourny, J. and Nyssens, M. (2010a) 'Social enterprise in Europe: At the crossroads of market, public policies and third sector', *Policy and Society*, 29(3), 231–242.

Defourny, J. and Nyssens, M. (2010b) 'Conceptions of social enterprise and social entrepreneurship in Europe and the United States: Convergences and divergences', *Journal of Social Entrepreneurship*, 1(1), 32–53.

Defourny, J. and Nyssens, M. (2017a) 'Fundamentals for an international typology of social enterprise models', *Voluntas: International Journal of Voluntary and Nonprofit Organizations*, 28(6), 2469–2497.

Defourny, J. and Nyssens, M. (2017b) 'Mapping social enterprise models: Some evidence from the "ICSEM" project', *Social Enterprise Journal*, 13(4), 318–328.

Dey, P. and Steyaert, C. (2012) 'Social entrepreneurship: Critique and the radical enactment of the social', *Social Enterprise Journal*, 28(2), 90–107.

Dey, P. and Steyaert, C. (eds.) (2018) *Social Entrepreneurship: An Affirmative Critique*. Cheltenham: Edward Elgar.

Doherty, B., Haugh, H. and Lyon, F. (2014) 'Social enterprises as hybrid organizations: A review and research agenda', *International Journal of Management Reviews*, 16(4), 417–436.

DTI (2002) *Social Enterprise. A Strategy for Success*. London: Department of Trade and Industry. Accessible at www.faf-gmbh.de/www/media/socialenterpriseastrategyforsucess.pdf

Dufays, F. and Huybrechts, B. (2014) 'Connecting the dots for social value: A review on social networks and social entrepreneurship', *Journal of Social Entrepreneurship*, 5(2), 214–237.

Ebrahim, A., Battilana, J. and Mair, J. (2014) 'The governance of social enterprises: Mission drift and accountability challenges in hybrid organizations', *Research in Organizational Behavior*, 34, 81–100.

Eikenberry, A. and Kluver, J. (2004) 'The marketization of the nonprofit sector: Civil society at risk?', *Public Administration Review*, 64(2), 132–140.

European Commission. (2016) *Social Enterprises and their Eco-systems: Developments in Europe 2016*, Directorate-General for Employment, Social Affairs and Inclusion.

Fisac, R. and Moreno-Romero, A. (2015) 'Understanding social enterprise country models: Spain', *Social Enterprise Journal*, 11(2), 156–177.

Fitzgerald, T. and Shepherd, D. (2018) 'Emerging structures for social enterprises within nonprofits: An institutional logics perspective', *Nonprofit and Voluntary Sector Quarterly*, 47(3), 474–492.

Grieco, C. (2015) *Assessing Social Impact of Social Enterprises: Does One Size Really Fit All?* New York: Springer.

Haugh, H. (2012) 'The importance of theory in social enterprise research', *Social Enterprise Journal*, 8(1), 7–15.

Hazenberg, R., Bajwa-Patel, M., Mazzei, M., Roy, M.J. and Baglioni, S. (2016) 'The role of institutional and stakeholder networks in shaping social enterprise ecosystems in Europe', *Social Enterprise Journal*, 12(3), 302–321.

Kerlin, J.A. (2006) 'Social enterprise in the United States and Europe: Understanding and learning from the differences', *Voluntas: International Journal of Voluntary and Nonprofit Organizations*, 17(3), 247–263.

Kerlin, J.A. (ed.) (2009) *Social Enterprise: A Global Comparison*. Lebanon, NH: Tufts University Press.

Kerlin, J.A. (2010) 'A comparative analysis of the global emergence of social enterprise', *Voluntas: International Journal of Voluntary and Nonprofit Organizations*, 21(2), 162–179.

Kerlin, J.A. (2013) 'Defining social enterprise across different contexts: A conceptual framework based on institutional factors', *Nonprofit and Voluntary Sector Quarterly*, 42(1), 84–108.

Kerlin, J.A. (2016) 'Habitats in the zoo', in Young, D.R., Searing, E.A.M. and Brewer, C. (eds.) *The Social Enterprise Zoo: A Guide to Perplexed Entrepreneurs, Philanthropists, Investors, and Policymakers*. Northampton, MA: Edward Elgar.

Kerlin, J.A. (ed.) (2017) *Shaping Social Enterprise: Understanding Institutional Context and Influence*. Bingley: Emerald.

Kerlin, J.A. and Gagnaire, K. (2009) 'Social Enterprise in the United States', in Kerlin, J.A. (ed.) *Social Enterprise: A Global Comparison*. Lebanon, NH: Tufts University Press.

Kerlin, J.A., Peng, S. and Cui, T.S. (2017) 'Social enterprise as an institutional innovation in China: Challenges to institutional isomorphism?', *Academy of Management Proceedings 2017 Conference*.

Kerlin, J.A., Lall, S., Peng, S. and Cui, T.S. (2018) 'Organizational responses to institutional pressures on social enterprises in China', *Academy of Management Proceedings 2018 Conference*.

Light, P.C. (2008) *The Search for Social Entrepreneurship*. Washington, DC: Brookings Institution Press.

Lyon, F. and Fernandez, H. (2012) 'Strategies for scaling up social enterprise: Lessons from early years providers', *Social Enterprise Journal*, 8(1), 63–77.

Mair, J., Robinson, J. and Hockerts, K. (2006) 'Introduction', in Mair, J., Robinson, J. and Hockerts, K. (eds.) *Social Entrepreneurship*, New York: Palgrave Macmillan.

Mason, C. (2012) 'Up for grabs: A critical discourse analysis of social entrepreneurship discourse in the United Kingdom', *Social Enterprise Journal*, 8(2), 123–140.

Mauksch, S., Dey, P., Rowe, M. and Teasdale, S. (2017) 'Ethnographies of social enterprise', *Social Enterprise Journal*, 13(2), 114–127.

Molecke, G. and Pinkse, J. (2017) 'Accountability for social impact: A bricolage perspective on impact measurement in social enterprises', *Journal of Business Venturing*, 32(5), 550–568.

Mueller, S., Nazarkina, L., Volkmann, C. and Blank, C. (2011) 'Social entrepreneurship research as a means of transformation: A vision for the year 2028', *Journal of Social Entrepreneurship*, 2(1), 112–120.

Nicholls, A. (2010) 'The legitimacy of social entrepreneurship: Reflexive isomorphism in a pre-paradigmatic field', *Entrepreneurship Theory and Practice*, 34(4), 611–633.

Nicholls, A., Nicholls, J. and Paton, R. (2015) 'Measuring social impact' in Nicholls, A., Nicholls, J. and Paton, R. (eds.) *Social Finance*. Oxford: Oxford University Press.

Nicholls, A., Paton, R. and Emerson, J. (eds.) (2015) *Social Finance*. Oxford: Oxford University Press.

Nyssens, M. (ed.) (2006) *Social Enterprise – At the Crossroads of Market, Public Policies and Civil Society*. London: Routledge.

OECD (2016) *Understanding Social Impact Bonds.* OECD LEED Working Paper. OECD Publishing. Accessible at: www.oecd.org/cfe/leed/UnderstandingSIBsLux-WorkingPaper.pdf (Accessed July 20, 2018).

Pache, A.C. and Santos, F. (2013) 'Inside the hybrid organization: Selective coupling as a response to competing institutional logics', *Academy of Management Journal,* 56, 972–1001.

Peattie, K. and Morley, A. (2008) 'Eight paradoxes of the social enterprise research agenda', *Social Enterprise Journal,* 4(2), 91–107.

Scheuerle, T. and Schmitz, B. (2016) 'Inhibiting factors of scaling up the impact of social entrepreneurial organizations – A comprehensive framework and empirical results for Germany', *Journal of Social Entrepreneurship,* 7(2), 127–161.

Searing, E.A.M., Lecy, J.D. and Andersson, F.O. (2016) 'Ecologies within the habitats of the zoo', in Young, D.R., Searing, E.A.M. and Brewer, C.V. (eds.) *The Social Enterprise Zoo: A Guide for Perplexed Scholars, Entrepreneurs, Philanthropists, Leaders, Investors, and Policymakers.* Northampton, MA: Edward Elgar.

Seelos, C. and Mair, J. (2017) *Innovation and Scaling for Impact. How Effective Social Enterprises Do It.* Stanford, CA: Stanford University Press.

Sinclair, S., Mazzei, M., Baglioni, S. and Roy, M.J. (2018) 'Social innovation, social enterprise, and local public services: Undertaking transformation?', *Social Policy and Administration,* [online] https://doi.org/10.1111/spol.12389

Smith, W.K., Gonin, M. and Besharov, M.L. (2013) 'Managing social-business tensions: A review and research agenda for social enterprise', *Business Ethics Quarterly,* 23, 407–442.

Spear, R., Cornforth, C. and Aiken, M. (2009) 'The governance challenges of social enterprises: Evidence from a UK empirical study', *Annals of Public and Cooperative Economics,* 80(2), 247–273.

Teasdale, S. (2012) 'What's in a name? Making sense of social enterprise discourses', *Public Policy and Administration,* 27(2), 99–119.

Teasdale, S., Kerlin, J.A., Young, D.R. and Soh, J.I. (2013) 'Oil and water rarely mix: Exploring the relative stability of nonprofit revenue mixes over time', *Journal of Social Entrepreneurship,* 4(1), 69–87.

Vickers, I., Lyon, F., Sepulveda, L. and McMullin, C. (2017) 'Public service innovation and multiple institutional logics: The case of hybrid social enterprise providers of health and wellbeing', *Research Policy,* 46(10), 1755–1768.

Weisbrod, B. (2004) 'The pitfalls of profits', *Stanford Social Innovation Review,* 2, 41–47.

Young, D.R. (2013) *If Not For Profit, For What? A Behavioral Theory of the Nonprofit Sector Based on Entrepreneurship.* Lexington, MA: Lexington Books. Atlanta: Georgia State University Library Digital Archive, http://scholarworks.gsu.edu/facbooks2013/1/ (digital reissue of Young, D.R. (1983)).

Young, D.R. (2015) 'Financing social innovation', in Nicholls, A., Paton, R. and Emerson, J. (eds.) *Social Finance.* Oxford: Oxford University Press.

Young, D.R. (2017) *Financing Nonprofits and Other Social Enterprises: A Benefits Approach.* Northampton, MA: Edward Elgar.

Young, D.R. and Lecy, J. (2014) 'Defining the universe of social enterprise: Competing metaphors', *Voluntas: International Journal of Voluntary and Nonprofit Organizations,* 25(5), 1307–1332.

Young, D.R. and Kim, C. (2015) 'Can social enterprise remain sustainable and mission-focused? Applying resiliency theory', *Social Enterprise Journal,* 11(3), 139–157.

Young, D.R., Searing, E.A.M. and Brewer, C.V. (eds.) (2016) *The Social Enterprise Zoo: A Guide to Perplexed Entrepreneurs, Philanthropists, Investors, and Policymakers.* Northampton, MA: Edward Elgar.

Young, D.R. and Longhofer, W. (2016) 'Designing the zoo', in Young, D.R., Searing, E.A.M. and Brewer, C.V. (eds.) *The Social Enterprise Zoo: A Guide for Perplexed Scholars, Entrepreneurs, Philanthropists, Leaders, Investors, and Policymakers.* Northampton, MA: Edward Elgar.

Zeyen, A., Beckmann, M., Mueller, S., Dees, J.G., Khanin, D. and Krueger, N. (2013) 'Social entrepreneurship and broader theories: Shedding light on the bigger picture', *Journal of Social Entrepreneurship,* 4(1), 88–107.

32

SOCIAL INNOVATION

What it is, why it matters and
how it can be studied

Gorgi Krlev

POSTDOCTORAL RESEARCHER, CENTRE FOR SOCIAL INVESTMENT (CSI),
UNIVERSITY OF HEIDELBERG, HEIDELBERG, GERMANY

Georg Mildenberger

HEAD OF RESEARCH, CENTRE FOR SOCIAL INVESTMENT (CSI),
UNIVERSITY OF HEIDELBERG, HEIDELBERG, GERMANY

Social innovations have long been recognized (see Zapf, 1989). However, systematic research on social innovation has only recently gained momentum (Cajaiba-Santana, 2014; Moulaert, MacCallum, Mehmood, & Hamdouch, 2013; Pol & Ville, 2009; Rao-Nicholson, Vorley, & Khan, 2017; van der Have & Rubalcaba, 2016; van Wijk, Zietsma, Dorado, Bakker, & Martí, 2018). A substantial share of the existing research stems from cross-national research projects funded by the European Commission which covers mapping the phenomenon (Pelka & Terstriep, 2016), its measurement (Krlev, Bund, & Mildenberger, 2014), financing (Glänzel, Krlev, Schmitz, & Mildenberger, 2013), the actors involved, their roles and capacities (Anheier, Krlev, & Mildenberger, 2018) as well as first attempts at theorizing it (Howaldt & Schwarz, 2016). Social innovation has for instance been examined by means of Amartya Sen's Capability Approach and thus in relation to how it helps decrease marginalization of certain groups in society (Jacobi, Nicholls, & Chiappero-Martinetti, 2017; Jacobi, Chiappero-Martinetti, Ziegler, van der Linden, van Beers 2019; Nicholls & Ziegler, 2019). There have also been new insights as to the historical dimensions of social innovation (McGowan & Westley, 2015; McGowan, Westley, & Tjörnbo, 2017; Schimpf, Mildenberger, Giesecke & Havas 2019 more specifically on social housing and Schimpf & Ziegler on freshwater supply), and the impact of social innovation on broader transformations in societies (Haxeltine et al., 2016, on sustainability transitions).

Despite these advances, the field is characterized by some definitional looseness and a lack of systematic evidence. First, some promote the normative dimension of social innovation and define social innovation as improved ways of dealing with pressing social needs or addressing "wicked" social problems (Churchman, C. West, 1967, as outlined in Krlev, Anheier, & Mildenberger, 2018a). Others use social innovation as a synonym to any social change or transformed social practice (Franz, Hochgerner, & Howaldt, 2015; Howaldt & Schwarz, 2010). In the latter interpretation, industrial assembly-line production and fast food are considered social innovation. Whereas in the former approach the assembly line is a technological innovation with significant social consequences and fast food fashion a lifestyle (see Bliss, 1993, on the idea of 'lifestyles').

Second, most research is focused on single organizations and marked by a relative neglect for broader social innovation developments. This goes for research relating to 'business' or 'social innovation biographies' (Howaldt, Schröder, Kaletka, Rehfeld, & Terstriep, 2016; Terstriep, Kleverbeck, Deserti, & Rizzo, 2015) just as for case studies originating from the research on social entrepreneurship that retrospectively receives the label of social innovation (for example Mair, Marti, & Ventresca, 2012; Reay & Hinings, 2005 or Battilana & Dorado, 2010). While important to unpack micro processes and antecedents of the social innovation debate (see Ayob, Teasdale, & Fagan, 2016, for more), finding responses to the grand challenges of our times (Ferraro, Etzion, & Gehman, 2015) as manifested in the sustainable development goals (George, Howard-Grenville, Joshi, & Tihanyi, 2016) may benefit from larger and comparative research designs. To assess social innovation comprehensively these could benefit from taking on a systems approach, more common for instance in ecological economics (see Sedlacko, Martinuzzi, Røpke, Videira, & Antunes, 2014), or a 'strategic action fields' perspective (Fligstein & McAdam, 2011; Fligstein & McAdam, 2012). Due to the infancy of the field, but also because positive social change triggered through social innovation necessitates multiple levels of analysis, building bridges between the studies of organizations, those of organizational fields and wider regional contexts is a key challenge.

In this chapter, we first outline why there is increasing interest in social innovation and which socio-economic and socio-political developments have led to it. Second, we trace the origins of the social innovation discourse by relating it to that of social entrepreneurship, where the 'social innovation school of thought' has been identified as one of two main approaches to the phenomenon (the 'enterprising school of thought' being the complementary one; Dees, 2001; Dees & Anderson, 2006a, 2006b; see also Chapter 31 by Kerlin in this volume). We also address why and how social innovation can be performed not only in new ventures but also within existing organizations as well as at the interfaces between organizations (Tracey & Stott, 2016). Third, we outline in more detail which benefits a "systems perspective" to social innovation brings. Fourth, and in relation to all the latter, we derive a rationale for the normative grounding of social innovation against competing value-neutral definitions and lines of inquiry. We do so in view of very recent evidence on social needs orientation and proximity to target groups being pivotal elements for producing social innovation (Krlev, Anheier, Behrendt, & Mildenberger, 2017; Krlev, Anheier, & Mildenberger, 2018c), in particular when it is in an early state of emergence. We close with reflections of promising future pathways for social innovation research.

Origins of social innovation

Today, the need to manage social change is expressed across policy and sector borders and social innovation is seen as a vehicle to do it (Krlev, Einarsson, Wijkström, Heyer, & Mildenberger, forthcoming). The European Commission has been one of the primary drivers promoting the term and its conceptualization (European Commission, 2013b). In particular, in the European context we clearly witnessed a policy-led agenda of research and practice in social innovation over the last decade.

The concept's origins, however, are placed earlier and elsewhere. The fascination for social innovation is primarily fed from economics and business studies, in which individual creativity and problem solving are extended from being a source of competitive advantage (see Saxenian, 1994, on Silicon Valley) to a source of social renewal and sustainable change (Martin & Osberg, 2007; Schaper, 2016). Global network and advocacy organizations such as Ashoka have done a lot to popularize the term, for example by proclaiming "everyone a change maker" (Bornstein, 2007; Nicholls, 2010). The link between societal renewal and entrepreneurship goes back to Schumpeter's theory, which, if carefully read, incorporates aspects of 'non-economic entrepreneurship' and "recombinant innovation [that] is pushed forward in e.g. politics, science or social life" (Krlev, 2012, p. 65, in relation to Schumpeter, 1911, 105ff.; and Swedberg, 2009). Further parallels can be drawn to later studies on the interplay between technology and society when former niche solutions intrude into existing 'regimes' and become the 'new normal.' Such studies were promoted in 'evolutionary economics' some time ago (Nelson & Winter, 1982), and recently renewed in studies of socio-technological change (Geels, 2012).

The social innovation discourse is also tied to major themes in other social sciences. It is for instance related to the incremental, small-scale changes that make Karl Popper's 'piecemeal engineering' (Popper, 1966) – a concept that embraces the idea of directed change but abstracts from the great master plans and advocates for a more limited and clear-cut agent-led process of societal renewal. Parallels can also be found between social innovation and Max Weber's sociology (Weber, 1921, 1978, p. 321; see also Radkau, 2013). In line with Schumpeter's thinking, Weber argued that change and renewal of regulated institutional fields is driven primarily by actors that have made 'abnormal experiences.' A shared theme of the discourse is thus that innovation often occurs in decentralized settings and outside centers of power (Anheier, 2013).

Clarifying the social innovation concept[1]

"Social innovations [are] new ideas (products, services and models) that simultaneously meet social needs (more effectively than alternatives) and create new social relationships or collaborations. They are innovations that are not only good for society but also enhance society's capacity to act" (Bureau of European Policy Advisers (BEPA), 2011; compare also to European Commission, 2013a; The Young Foundation, 2012). This definition of social innovation is among the most widely applied and promoted. The concept of social innovation underscores novelty, but it typically embeds the dimension of novelty with respect to time and geographic contexts. A replication and clever adaption of a new approach that emerged elsewhere can still qualify as social innovation. The criterion that it needs to address a problem or challenge previously unaddressed in the specific context is more essential. Looking back, the establishment of freshwater supply in households used to be a social innovation in the 19th century in Western Europe (Schimpf & Ziegler, 2019), with limited room for further improvement today. In contrast, innovations relating to new ways of establishing freshwater supply and providing clean potable water could still be a social innovation if observed in one of the least developed countries. Inherent in the concept of social innovation is that it increases efficiency, but more importantly effectiveness (functionalist perspective) and that it leads to positive social change (transformationalist perspective) (Krlev et al., 2018a). This does not mean that it may not have unintended negative consequences.

Social innovation as a concept is closely linked to the literature on social entrepreneurship, which has a longer tradition as a fairly cohesive strand of research. Dees and Anderson (2006a) have distinguished two schools of thought with regard to social entrepreneurship: The 'Social Enterprise School' on the one side and the 'Social Innovation School' on the other. The functionalist aspects of social innovation are more connected to the element of "enterprising" in that discourse, and the transformationalist aspects to the notion of "entrepreneurial innovation." This is explained in more detail below.

Social innovation and enterprise

Right from its emergence, the concept of social entrepreneurship took a middle ground located between nonprofit and for-profit activity (Nyssens, 2006, p. 325). This was seen to be a result of converging forces situated between the two sectors.

First, nonprofits still depend on a mix of revenue sources, and private giving (accounting for 10 percent) as well as public sector funding (accounting for 35 percent) constitute a substantial share of their income (Weisbrod, 1998, pp. 48–49). However, as Weisbrod also showed, nonprofits have been becoming more 'enterprising' for a long time, seeking to generate more earned income, with private charges and fees amounting to more than 50 percent. Now does that mean most nonprofits have become, or have always been, social enterprises? No, since the social enterprise concept has a strong stress on the creation of mission-related revenue streams. Social enterprises for example enable beneficiaries to pay for services by splitting payments over a period of time, or operating on cross-subsidization models, where services sold to wealthier customers enable service at lower or no costs to more disadvantaged customers. A prime example is the Aravind Eyecare Hospital that provides eye-surgery to poor customers for free (Seelos & Mair, 2017).

Second and towards the other end of the continuum of the 'enterprising dimension,' social entrepreneurship is delimited by the profit motive. A sub-concept of Social Entrepreneurship for instance is 'Social Business' (Yunus, Moingeon, & Lehmann-Ortega, 2010), which incorporates economic self-sufficiency as a definitional criterion, which means full independence from donations or state subsidies. It is therefore more strongly linked to the for-profit area, with the main difference from responsible businesses lying in its strict retention and reinvestment of all firm profits. Another neighboring concept is that of corporate social responsibility (CSR) (Dacanay, 2009), in particular when the latter is applied by firms in an 'instrumental' way, that is in order to increase economic success along the way, or in a 'political' way to add to their societal influence and bargaining power (Garriga & Melé, 2004). Two among several different options of how firms apply CSR are first to conduct their business in a way that is socially beneficial beyond legal compliance, and second to perform business-unrelated philanthropic activity (Crane, Matten, & Spence, 2014; also Carroll, 2008).

Another version of responsible corporate action that is in contrast to these 'responsive' types of CSR, is Porter and Kramer's (2011) concept of 'shared value' which they also sometimes label 'strategic CSR' (Porter & Kramer, 2006). It points to an integration of social activities and business activities in a way that enables the production of sustainable competitive advantage. One of the examples that Porter and Kramer discussed in their 2006 work were Nestlé's 'Milk Districts,' in which the company performed capacity building for and with local dairy farmers in developing countries. Such examples in turn provide some overlap with base-of-the-pyramid (BoP) business activities that are meant to address and provide services to the world's poorest population groups (Milstein, Simanis, Duke, & Hart, 2008, p. 41), with the hope of increasing their livelihoods while tapping a neglected economic potential (Prahalad & Hammond, 2002; Prahalad & Hart, 2002). Entrepreneurship and innovation are often closely tied to the concept (Hall, Matos, Sheehan, & Silvestre, 2012). This discussion about socially minded business practices has recently been complemented by a focus on responsible innovation, which denotes "forms of participative and reflexive governance [that] can help address the social and environmental challenges that society faces," that is corporate activities that move from avoiding harm to doing good (Scherer & Voegtlin, 2018).

Social innovation and entrepreneurship

The Social Innovation School of thought brings in an increasing orientation towards models that address, serve and involve beneficiaries or customers in an often unprecedented way, for instance by turning "antagonistic assets into complementarities" (Hockerts, 2015). One example that Hockerts refers to is the employment of people with autism as software testers instead of workers in sheltered workshops. This second school of thought within social entrepreneurship is mainly associated with Bill Drayton's organization Ashoka and is therefore rooted in developing countries. In the early 1980s Drayton started to spot and support individuals in developing countries whom he suspected could foster major social change through small-scale yet highly innovative ventures. Drayton first referred to these individuals as 'public entrepreneurs.' Ashoka and others adopted the term 'social entrepreneur' in the mid-1990s (Dees & Anderson, 2006a, pp. 44–46), although historic examples of such individuals could be found much earlier (see Alvord, Brown, & Letts, 2004; Bornstein, 2007, pp. 40–47).

It is important to note that, while a distinct emphasis is set in the two schools, it does not mean that innovation plays no role in social enterprises, nor that earned income is meaningless to the social innovator. Dees and Anderson (2006a, p. 50) have advocated for discussing social entrepreneurship as "enterprising social innovation" and considering "social entrepreneurs who carry out innovations that blend methods from the worlds of business and philanthropy to create social value that is sustainable and has the potential for large-scale impact."

Organizational localization of social innovation

All of the discussed phenomena can in principle embrace the element of innovation, but they differ in terms of (1) the organizational population they refer to and (2) the motivational character of the action performed. CSR, BoP business and 'shared value' focus mostly on large for-profit organizations that perform activities at least in part to benefit themselves. The social enterprise discourse instead focuses mostly on small-scale organizations with the motivation of responding to social challenges and the aim of creating social impact (Dees, 2001; Schröer, Eurich, & Mildenberger, 2015, pp. 16–18). There is therefore also different weight on the profit motive versus that of creating positive social change through innovation, which we know from other areas such as impact investing or venture philanthropy (Mair & Hehenberger, 2014).

Figure 32.1 maps the different concepts against each other. Since innovation is only one pathway to generating social impact the latter instead of the former is used in the classification scheme. Social impact may comprise different notions and is therefore split into categories ranging from 'socially responsible acting,' for example in ordinary business activity, to 'unprecedented solutions to social problems.' The innovation aspect discussed is incorporated into the upper end of the social impact dimension by addressing 'unprecedented solutions' or the 'improvement of existing solutions.' This resonates with the common definitional elements of social innovation, such as the superiority of actions provided versus the status quo or an increase in societal capabilities (Anheier et al., 2018; Nicholls & Murdock, 2012; The Young Foundation, 2012). The last two stages are contrasted with 'mitigating social problems' by for instance providing shelter for homeless people or 'cultural societal advancement' such as the sponsoring of public concerts or sports competitions.

The horizontal dimension is 'economic self-sufficiency,' contrasting 'earned income' with 'external contributions' in the forms of donations or government subsidies. Volunteering time as a philanthropic contribution plays a role in sketching the 'traditional' nonprofit sector. According to long-standing data (Salamon, Sokolowski, & List, 2003), earned income typically makes up about 40 percent of nonprofit income when volunteering is included as a philanthropic input (see the black dotted line) and 50 percent when volunteering is excluded. Government funding

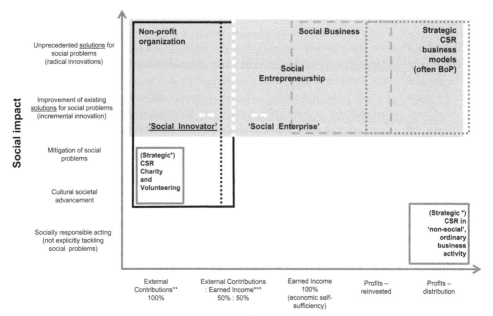

Figure 32.1 Organizational localization of social innovation

Notes

★ May also be responsive; ★★ Donations from individuals, foundations and corporations; Government subsidies; Volunteering time as philanthropic contribution included (long dotted line); ★★★ Mission-related fees (directly or indirectly), Ancillary/Unrelated business income.

Source: Krlev, 2011.

tendered for in competitive quasi-markets, in contrast to non-performance-based and service unrelated subsidies, is considered earned income in Figure 32.1.

The area of social entrepreneurship is divided into a 'social enterprise' section which stresses the earned income generation on the one side, and the 'social innovator' dimension on the other. The border is at 50 percent earned income, that is above the share of income earned by 'traditional' nonprofits at a maximum. The borderline is dotted and permeable and the two spheres are interconnected as marked by two-headed arrows. One reason for this fuzziness is that income patterns vary significantly, for instance depending on fields of activity (Salamon et al., 2003). What is more, there is no strict separation between the two types of entrepreneurial organizations: a 'social innovator' can be enterprising, just as a 'social enterprise' can be innovative.

To complete the picture, it remains for us to relate the other concepts to the latter two. A 'social business' needs to be financially self-sufficient and potentially profit-generating, but it also includes a non-distribution constraint. CSR can focus on shaping 'non-social' business activity as well as on charitable activities including volunteering. These activities are likely to be responsive, but may also be strategic. Strategic CSR or 'shared value' activities instead are always linked to the company's core competencies and may include the earning and distribution of profits. When the profit-generating and distributing aspect becomes dominant and social or environmental goals of the business fall behind or are only byproducts, the respective activity is clearly different from the social entrepreneurship concept. Otherwise, there might be overlaps.

BoP business can be considered a part of the 'strategic CSR' concept, when such activities are performed in developing countries.

Social innovation is still tied to these organizational phenomena, and most closely to social entrepreneurship, but in recent years the social innovation discourse has started to decouple from organizational archetypes and spheres of influences to being more of a 'supra-concept' of targeted social change. We will sketch out the most prominent lines of recent inquiry in the next section.

Social innovation as a source of societal renewal

Social innovation through its link to social entrepreneurship has often been tied to new and small organizations that are supposedly more agile, flexible and creative than established welfare providers for instance (see Cameron & Quinn, 1983, for a classic, and Blättel-Mink, 2006, for more recent work on life-cycle perspectives that uncover the advantages of start-ups in technological innovation). There is also evidence to the contrary though and a recognition that major organizations can play a role in social innovation, in particular when it comes to diffusion and scaling (see Heinze, Schönauer, Schneiders, Grohs, & Ruddat, 2013; Nock, Krlev, & Mildenberger, 2013, on the German Free Welfare Associations). The focus in social innovation has shifted from being driven by individual entrepreneurs to also being promoted by actors within larger and established organizations. The latter is often referred to as 'social intrapreneurship' (Grohs, Schneiders, & Heinze, 2015; Schmitz & Scheuerle, 2012). In addition to growing appreciation of the capacities of established welfare providers, new individual actors (potentially) engaged in the social innovation process have gained more attention, for instance volunteers (Wit, Mensink, Einarsson, & Bekkers, 2017).

The extension of social innovation research to new types of organizations and actors, has been taken further by studying inter-organizational and platform-based action addressing social challenges (Phillips, Alexander, & Lee, 2017; Tracey & Stott, 2016). Tracey and Stott refer to the latter as 'social extrapreneurship,' which they align with concepts of 'institutional work' or 'institutional entrepreneurship' that is concerned with the interplay of actors rather than single organizational analysis (for example Zietsma & Lawrence, 2010). The focus in social innovation research has swayed towards 'embedded' approaches that take norms and values into account and investigate how these are shaped through the innovation process (Purtik & Arenas, 2017). Previous examples of such thinking place social innovation into an ecosystem that is marked by entrepreneurial action (Phillips, Lee, Ghobadian, O'Regan, & James, 2015; Roundy, 2017; Slimane & Lamine, 2017) – be it within or outside organizations. The entrepreneurial action is thus embedded into framework structures that spread from societal perceptions, to policy, to resources, to formalized institutions (Krlev et al., 2014). The interplay of the relevant spheres and levels determines the social innovation capacity of regional settings.

Examples of recent studies applying an ecosystems logic include the investigation of the interplay between social movements and corporations in driving the firms' involvement in social innovation (Carberry, Bharati, Levy, & Chaudhury, 2017). Particular geographic contexts populated by diverse actors and across a range for fields of activity have also become primary places in which social innovation is studied. They may be rural (Neumeier, 2017; Richter, Fink, Lang, & Maresch, 2020), but are more often urban (Brandsen, Cattacin, Evers, & Zimmer, 2016; Moulaert, Martinelli, Gonzalez, & Swyngedouw, 2007).

The ecosystems or innovation systems perspective culminates in research that abstracts from organizational practices, or sees them as subordinate to broader innovation process located above and beyond organizations. This research is cross-national and ranges across multiple fields of activity. It starts by identifying recognized social innovation streams (SI streams), which are defined by several criteria (Krlev, Anheier, & Mildenberger, 2018b, p. 60). They are (1) new approaches, principles of action, governance forms or modes of organization; they have (2) fundamentally affected a field of activity, that is coined practice in the field in a significant and recognizable way; (3) they have been around for a considerable period of time, that is they are not so new that they are more of a particular than a universal character; (4) they are not geographically restricted, that is they occur in different regions within a country and across countries.

Examples for such SI streams are manifold. Arts-based interventions applied to rejuvenate abandoned urban areas are one of them (Cancellieri et al., 2018). The 'recovery approach' in mental health treatment that uses the self-healing capacities of the individual and draws on the competencies of individuals with 'lived-experience' is another (Bauer, Hyanek, Figueroa, & Sandford, 2018). A third is the formation of cross-sector partnerships to realize a successful qualification and work integration of socially excluded groups, for instance refugees (Leca et al., 2018).

Taking such an approach involves a rather high degree of abstraction and introduces "noise" into the analysis, because conditions and maturity of social innovations vary across contexts (Krlev et al., 2018c). The benefit of locating the investigation of social innovation at the aggregate level, however, is that it enables the identification of relevant actors independent of organizational sectors, types or traditions. It is ideal for exploratory investigation, which is much needed against the current state of research on social innovation. 'Process tracing' (Beach & Pedersen, 2016; Bengtsson & Ruonavaara, 2017; Bennett & Checkel, 2017; Collier, 2011) or other time-based methods of inquiry (Langley, 1999; Langley, Smallman, Tsoukas, & van de Ven, 2013) help identify milestones in the development of the SI stream, critical junctions as well as the promoters and opponents of the development. They serve to derive a rich and thick description, not only of the studied social innovation ecosystem as of the time of the study, but also of its evolution over time. Once this description has been compiled, scholars can move on to identify the individual organizations and institutions involved in the process and test for traits that have enabled them to play a significant role in it. We have ourselves performed and directed such research with some surprising results that can enhance the theorizing of social innovation and inform future research (Anheier et al., 2018).

One of the core findings of our research was that organizational behavior and resources were much more central to making a considerable contribution to the SI stream than organizational structure. This calls into question the prevalent focus in previous research on new and small organizations as drivers of social innovation. As regards behavior and resources, three characteristics stood out. First, the actors that had promoted the SI stream most strongly were social needs oriented. This sounds trivial at first, since the very definition of social innovation entails social needs orientation (Nicholls & Murdock, 2012). However, it clearly opposes simple extrapolations from entrepreneurial creativity and innovation in the commercial area, whose orientation is at potential customer demands not the satisfaction of social needs, from that in the realm of social challenges. It may also provide ground to challenge the assumption underlying strategic CSR, shared value or BoP in particular, which is that what benefits corporations can and should also benefit society and that it only takes a shift in corporate strategy to reconcile the two (compare to previous criticism of the concept Crane, Palazzo, Spence, & Matten, 2014). It furthermore casts doubts on whether a mere 'moralization of markets' (Stehr, Henning, & Weiler, 2010) or a 'caring' version of capitalism (Barman, 2016) will be strong enough drivers of social innovation. Against our findings, it does not seem sufficient to 'care' while striving for profits. Instead, an emphasis on meeting neglected social needs is vital and we could find the latter more often among the nonprofit and public organizations we studied than among firms.

Second, social innovators mostly needed to be locally embedded. This came in the form of knowing the operating context and the stakeholders placed in it well, but also as a close connection to the target group of the social innovation. Nonprofit organizations were particularly strong on this account, in particular because of previous experience of working with the target group. In the work integration SI stream of cross-sector partnerships for example (Leca et al., 2018), nonprofits typically had long since been providing training, language courses or coaching to refugees, while firms and public sector actors were less familiar with the target group before the joint initiative.

Third, the promoters of social innovation exhibited a high degree of organizational openness, including regular exchange with other organizations, membership in umbrella organizations, embracement of user feedback, etc. This confirms previous suppositions that social innovation is in fact a cross-sector phenomenon, which is strongest when diverse actors come together (Murray, Caulier-Grice, & Mulgan, 2010). It thereby underlines the need for studying social innovation from a 'systems perspective.' This need is further underlined by the importance of local embeddedness and the orientation at social needs, the definition and identification of which always entails a societal negotiation process (Krlev et al., 2014).

The normative grounding of social innovation and future pathways

Social change is currently discussed with a special taste for evidence-based action and a shift in the perception of societies, marked by a focus on for instance self-regulation and inclusive growth and progress (European Commission, 2012). The terms 'revolution' or 'reform' are being replaced by the term 'social innovation,' referring to an improvement of social practices and societal outcomes (European Commission, 2013a). This is not least because innovation seems to represent a more flexible, experiment-based and simultaneously more potent course of action, both at the level of society and that of organizations.

A systems approach to studying social innovation comes with the challenge of embracing breadth instead of depth in the initial setup of the research. Taking this stance is supported by the recognition that social innovations in themselves are almost never entirely new and that they can be studied in relation to past events, such as the establishment of social housing in Western Europe (Schimpf et al., 2019), or the foundation of the modern university (Drucker, 1985). However, when the geographic range, timeframe and considered actors are broad, we need to make every effort to clearly outline the social innovation studied and its conceptual grounding. We believe the concept of 'social innovation streams' and their definitional characteristics can provide guidance in this regard. One of the central threads of the concept is its normative grounding in being intentional and directed social change that *aims at* reaching a state that is superior to the status quo.

This angle also helps identifying social innovations by means of expert consultations. Bartels (2017) is of course right in pointing out that (unintended) consequences of social innovation might produce tensions and that in consequence social innovations are not purely 'good.' However, this does not provide sufficient ground for arguing for a value-neutral concept of social innovation (Howaldt & Schwarz, 2010), since the latter entails the risk of mixing up social innovation with other changes such as new lifestyles, institutional transformations or new social practices. A value-neutral interpretation of social innovation would also fall out of sync with the theory of technological innovation, in which innovation is defined as shifts in productivity occurring through *improved* capital equipment (Salter, 1969). Following this definition innovation always entails the element of being *better* than what was previously available and negating this distinctive criterion would rob the concept of its theoretical and empirical value.

In this chapter we have tried to show that although the social innovation discourse should remain connected to current strands of research on institutional change or innovation management, for example, it has done well to make a step beyond it. Social innovation as an overarching concept holds great promise and will hopefully not turn out to be a fad. To avoid this, researchers will need to promote two things: First, they should more closely tie social innovation to the grand theories of societal renewal to strengthen its conceptual grounding. Second, they should critically assess the present and historic significance of social innovation processes, and in particular probe deeper into the capacities and roles of actors driving the social innovation process over time. We have generated insights on actor roles and functions. In order to expand our understanding of social innovation, and also in order to provide practical and policy relevant advice on how to govern it, we will need to promote further system-based, process-oriented and cross-sector research of the phenomenon. Nonprofit scholars should be particularly interested in investigating this further for the central functions in the social innovation process that (only) nonprofit organizations seem to be able to perform.

Note

1   The next two sections in part reproduce the content of Krlev's (2011) working paper.

References

Alvord, S.H., Brown, L.D., & Letts, C.W. (2004). Social entrepreneurship and societal transformation: An exploratory study. *Journal of Applied Behavioral Science*, 40(3), 260–282.

Anheier, H.K. (Ed.). (2013). *Governance challenges & innovations: Financial and fiscal governance.* Oxford: Oxford University Press.

Anheier, H.K., Krlev, G., & Mildenberger, G. (Eds.). (2018). *Social innovation: Comparative perspectives.* New York: Routledge. Retrieved from https://www.routledge.com/Social-Innovation-Open-Access-Comparative-Perspectives/Anheier-Krlev-Mildenberger/p/book/9781138068360

Ayob, N., Teasdale, S., & Fagan, K. (2016). How social innovation 'came to be': Tracing the evolution of a contested concept. *Journal of Social Policy*, 45(04), 635–653. doi:10.1017/S004727941600009X

Barman, E. (2016). *Caring capitalism: The meaning and measure of social value.* New York: Cambridge University Press.

Bartels, K. (2017). The double bind of social innovation: Relational dynamics of change and resistance in neighbourhood governance. *Urban Studies*, 54(16), 3789–3805.

Battilana, J., & Dorado, S. (2010). Building sustainable hybrid organizations: The case of commercial microfinance organizations. *Academy of Management Journal*, 53(6), 1419–1440. doi:10.5465/AMJ.2010.57318391

Bauer, A., Hyanek, V., Figueroa, M., & Sandford, S. (2018). Health care: The recovery approach to mental health. In H.K. Anheier, G. Krlev, & G. Mildenberger (Eds.), *Social innovation. Comparative perspectives* (pp. 130–148). New York: Routledge.

Beach, D., & Pedersen, R.B. (2016). *Process-tracing methods: Foundations and guidelines.* Ann Arbor: University of Michigan Press.

Bengtsson, B., & Ruonavaara, H. (2017). Comparative process tracing: Making historical comparison structured and focused. *Philosophy of the Social Sciences*, 47(1), 44–66. doi:10.1177/0048393116658549

Bennett, A., & Checkel, J.T. (2017). *Process tracing: From metaphor to analytic tool* (6th printing). *Strategies for social inquiry.* Cambridge: Cambridge University Press.

Blättel-Mink, B. (2006). *Kompendium der Innovationsforschung.* Wiesbaden: Verlag für Sozialwissenschaften.

Bliss, C.J. (1993). Life-style and the standard of living. In M. Nussbaum & A. Sen (Eds.), *The quality of life* (pp. 417–436). Oxford: Oxford University Press.

Bornstein, D. (2007). *How to change the world* (updated ed.). New York: Oxford University Press.

Brandsen, T., Cattacin, S., Evers, A., & Zimmer, A. (Eds.). (2016). *Social innovations in the urban context.* Cham: Springer.

Bureau of European Policy Advisers (BEPA). (2011). *Empowering people, driving change: Social innovation in the European Union.* Luxembourg: Publications Office of the European Union.

Cajaiba-Santana, G. (2014). Social innovation: Moving the field forward. A conceptual framework. *Technological Forecasting & Social Change, 82*, 42–51.

Cameron, K. S., & Quinn, R. E. (1983). Organizational life cycles and shifting criteria for effectiveness: Some preliminary evidence. *Management Science, 29*(1), 33–51.

Cancellieri, G., Turrini, A., Sanzo Perez, M.J., Salido Andrés, N., Kullberg, J., & Cognat, A. (2018). Social innovation in arts & culture: Place-regeneration initiatives driven by arts & culture to achieve social cohesion. In H.K. Anheier, G. Krlev, & G. Mildenberger (Eds.), *Social innovation. Comparative perspectives* (pp. 79–103). New York: Routledge.

Carberry, E.J., Bharati, P., Levy, D.L., & Chaudhury, A. (2017). Social movements as catalysts for corporate social innovation: Environmental activism and the adoption of green information systems. *Business & Society*, 1–45.

Carroll, A. (2008). Corporate social responsibility. In W. Visser, D. Matten, M. Pohl, & N. Tolhurst (Eds.), *The A to Z of corporate social responsibility. A complete reference guide to concepts, codes and organizations* (pp. 122–131). Chichester: Wiley.

Churchman, C. West. (1967). Guest Editorial: Wicked problems. *Management Science, 14*(4), B141–B142. Retrieved from http://www.jstor.org/stable/2628678

Collier, D. (2011). Understanding process tracing. *PS: Political Science & Politics, 44*(04), 823–830. doi:10.1017/S1049096511001429

Crane, A., Matten, D., & Spence, L.J. (2014). Corporate social responsibility in a global context. In A. Crane, D. Matten, & L.J. Spence (Eds.), *Corporate social responsibility. Readings and cases in a global context* (2nd ed., pp. 3–26). New York: Routledge.

Crane, A., Palazzo, G., Spence, L.J., & Matten, D. (2014). Contesting the value of "creating shared value". *California Management Review, 56*(2), 130–153. doi:10.1525/cmr.2014.56.2.130

Dacanay, M.L.M. (2009). Social entrepreneurship: An Asian perspective. In J.A. Robinson, J. Mair, & K. Hockerts (Eds.), *International perspectives on social entrepreneurship* (pp. 163–182). Basingstoke: Palgrave Macmillan.

Dees, J.G. (2001). *The meaning of social entrepreneurship*. Occasional Paper. Durham, NC.

Dees, J.G., & Anderson, B.B. (2006a). Framing a theory of social entrepreneurship: Building on two schools of practice and thought. In R. Mosher-Williams (Ed.), *ARNOVA Occasional Paper Series*: Vol. 1, No. 2. *Research on Social Entrepreneurship. Understanding and Contributing to an Emerging Field* (pp. 39–65). Indianapolis.

Dees, J.G., & Anderson, B.B. (2006b). Rhetoric, reality, and research: Building a solid foundation for the practice of social entrepreneurship. In A. Nicholls (Ed.), *Social entrepreneurship. New models of sustainable social change* (pp. 144–168). Oxford: Oxford University Press.

Drucker, P.F. (1985). *Innovation and entrepreneurship: Practice and principles. Classic Drucker Collection*. New York: Harper & Row.

European Commission. (2012). *Europe 2020*. Retrieved from http://ec.europa.eu/europe2020/europe-2020-in-a-nutshell/flagship-initiatives/index_en.htm

European Commission. (2013a). *Guide to social innovation*. Brussels. Retrieved from http://ec.europa.eu/regional_policy/sources/docgener/presenta/social_innovation/social_innovation_2013.pdf

European Commission. (2013b). *Social innovation research in the European Union: Approaches, findings and future directions*. Brussels.

Ferraro, F., Etzion, D., & Gehman, J. (2015). Tackling grand challenges pragmatically: Robust action revisited. *Organization Studies, 36*(3), 363–390. doi:10.1177/0170840614563742

Fligstein, N., & McAdam, D. (2011). Toward a general theory of strategic action fields. *Sociological Theory, 29*(1), 1–26.

Fligstein, N., & McAdam, D. (2012). *A theory of fields*. New York: Oxford University Press.

Franz, H.-W., Hochgerner, J., & Howaldt, J. (Eds.). (2015). *Challenge social innovation: Potentials for business, social entrepreneurship, welfare and civil society* (Aufl. 2012). Berlin: Springer Berlin.

Garriga, E., & Melé, D. (2004). Corporate social responsibility theories: Mapping the territory. *Journal of Business Ethics, 53*, 51–71.

Geels, F.W. (2012). A socio-technical analysis of low-carbon transitions: Introducing the multi-level perspective into transport studies. *Journal of Transport Geography, 24*, 471–482.

George, G., Howard-Grenville, J., Joshi, A., & Tihanyi, L. (2016). Understanding and tackling societal grand challenges through management research. *Academy of Management Journal, 59*(6), 1880–1895.

Glänzel, G., Krlev, G., Schmitz, B., & Mildenberger, G. (2013). *Report on the feasibility and opportunities of using various instruments for capitalising social innovators*. A deliverable of the project: "The theoretical, empirical and policy foundations for building social innovation in Europe" (TEPSIE), European Commission – 7th Framework Programme. Brussels.

Grohs, S., Schneiders, K., & Heinze, R.G. (2015). Social entrepreneurship versus intrapreneurship in the German social welfare state: A study of old-age care and youth welfare services. *Nonprofit and Voluntary Sector Quarterly, 44*(1), 163–180.

Hall, J., Matos, S., Sheehan, L., & Silvestre, B. (2012). Entrepreneurship and innovation at the base of the pyramid: A recipe for inclusive growth or social exclusion? *Journal of Management Studies, 49*(4), 785–812.

Haxeltine, A., Avelino, F., Pel, B., Dumitru, A., Kemp, R., Longhurst, N., et al. (2016). *A framework for transformative social innovation.* TRANSIT Working Paper # 5, TRANSIT: EU SSH.2013.3.2-1 Grant agreement no: 613169.

Heinze, R.G., Schönauer, A., Schneiders, K., Grohs, S., & Ruddat, C. (2013). Social Entrepreneurship im etablierten Wohlfahrtsstaat. Aktuelle empirische Befunde zu neuen und alten Akteuren auf dem Wohlfahrtsmarkt. In S.A. Jansen, R. Heinze, & M. Beckmann (Eds.), *Sozialunternehmen in Deutschland. Analysen, Trends und Handlungsempfehlungen* (pp. 315–346). [S.l.]: Vs Verlag fuer Sozialwissenschaften.

Hockerts, K. (2015). How hybrid organizations turn antagonistic assets into complementarities. *California Management Review, 57*(3), 83–106. doi:10.1525/cmr.2015.57.3.83

Howaldt, J., Schröder, A., Kaletka, C., Rehfeld, D., & Terstriep, J. (2016). *Mapping the world of social innovation: A global comparative analysis across sectors and world regions.* D 1.4 SI-DRIVE Social Innovation: Driving Force of Social Change.

Howaldt, J., & Schwarz, M. (2010). *'Soziale Innovation' im Fokus: Skizze eines gesellschaftstheoretisch inspirierten Forschungskonzepts* (1st ed.). Bielefeld: Script.

Howaldt, J. & Schwarz, M. (2016). *Social innovation and its relationship to social change: Verifying existing social theories in reference to social innovation and its relationship to social change.* Working Paper TU Dortmund.

Jacobi, N. von, Nicholls, A., & Chiappero-Martinetti, E. (2017). Theorizing social innovation to address marginalization. *Journal of Social Entrepreneurship, 8*(3), 265–270. doi:10.1080/19420676.2017.1380340

Jacobi, Nadia von; Chiappero-Martinetti, Enrica; Ziegler, Rafael; van der Linden, Martijn Jeroen; van Beers, Cees (2019): Social Innovation and Agency. In: Alex Nicholls und Rafael Ziegler (Hg.): Creating economic space for social innovation: Oxford University Press.

Krlev, G. (2011). *Mapping the area of social entrepreneurship: The social entrepreneurship scheme.* Working Paper. Retrieved from http://ssrn.com/abstract=1871907

Krlev, G. (2012). Strategies in social entrepreneurship: Depicting entrepreneurial elements and business principles in SEOs from Germany and Bangladesh. *Journal of Entrepreneurship Perspectives, 1*(1), 61–96.

Krlev, G., Anheier, H.K., Behrendt, C., & Mildenberger, G. (2017). The who, what and how of social innovation. A qualitative comparative analysis. *Academy of Management Proceedings, 2017*(1), 14266. doi:10.5465/AMBPP.2017.14266abstract

Krlev, G., Anheier, H.K., & Mildenberger, G. (2018a). Introduction: Social innovation – What is it and who makes it? In H.K. Anheier, G. Krlev, & G. Mildenberger (Eds.), *Social innovation. Comparative perspectives* (pp. 3–35). New York: Routledge.

Krlev, G., Anheier, H.K., & Mildenberger, G. (2018b). Methods: Indentifying and analysing the social innovation streams. In H.K. Anheier, G. Krlev, & G. Mildenberger (Eds.), *Social innovation. Comparative perspectives* (pp. 49–76). New York: Routledge.

Krlev, G., Anheier, H.K., & Mildenberger, G. (2018c). Results: The comparative analysis. In H.K. Anheier, G. Krlev, & G. Mildenberger (Eds.), *Social innovation. Comparative perspectives* (pp. 257–279). New York: Routledge.

Krlev, G., Bund, E., & Mildenberger, G. (2014). Measuring what matters – Indicators of social innovativeness on the national level. *Information Systems Management, 31*(3), 200–224. doi:10.1080/10580530. 2014.923265

Krlev, G., Einarsson, T., Wijkström, F., Heyer, L., & Mildenberger, G. (forthcoming). The policies of social innovation – a cross-national analysis. *Nonprofit and Voluntary Sector Quarterly.*

Langley, A. (1999). Strategies for theorizing from process data. *Academy of Management Review, 24*(4), 691. doi:10.2307/259349

Langley, A., Smallman, C., Tsoukas, H., & van de Ven, A.H. (2013). Process studies of change in organization and management: Unveiling temporality, activity, and flow. *Academy of Management Journal, 56*(1), 1–13. doi:10.5465/amj.2013.4001

Leca, B., Sandford, S., Cognat, A., Pache, A.-C., Mato Santiso, V., Hyanek, V., & Krlev, G. (2018). Cross-sector partnerships: A social innovation in the European work integration sector. In H.K. Anheier, G. Krlev, & G. Mildenberger (Eds.), *Social innovation. Comparative perspectives* (pp. 201–223). New York: Routledge.

Mair, J., & Hehenberger, L. (2014). Front-stage and backstage convening: The transition from opposition to mutualistic coexistence in organizational philanthropy. *Academy of Management Journal, 57*(4), 1174–1200. doi:10.5465/amj.2012.0305

Mair, J., Marti, I., & Ventresca, M.J. (2012). Building inclusive markets in rural Bangladesh: How intermediaries work institutional voids. *Academy of Management Journal, 55*(4), 819–850. doi:10.5465/amj.2010.0627

Martin, R.L., & Osberg, S. (2007). Social entrepreneurship: The case for definition. *Stanford Social Innovation Review*, (Spring), 28–39.

McGowan, K., & Westley, F.R. (2015). At the root of change: The history of social innovation. In A. Nicholls, J. Gundelfinger, & M. Gabriel (Eds.), *New frontiers in social innovation research* (pp. 52–68). Basingstoke: Palgrave Macmillan.

McGowan, K., Westley, F., & Tjörnbo, O. (2017). The history of social innovation. In Westley, F., McGowan, K., & Tjörnbo, O. (Eds.), *The evolution of social innovation: Building resilience through transitions* (pp. 1–17). Cheltenham: Edward Elgar.

Milstein, M.B., Simanis, E., Duke, D., & Hart, S. (2008). Base of the Pyramid (BoP) model. In W. Visser, D. Matten, M. Pohl, & N. Tolhurst (Eds.), *The A to Z of corporate social responsibility. A complete reference guide to concepts, codes and organizations* (pp. 40–43). Chichester: Wiley.

Moulaert, F., MacCallum, M., Mehmood, A., & Hamdouch, A. (2013). *The international handbook on social innovation: Collective action, social learning and transdisciplinary research.* Cheltenham: Edward Elgar.

Moulaert, F., Martinelli, F., Gonzalez, S., & Swyngedouw, E. (2007). Introduction: Social innovation and governance in European cities: Urban development between path dependency and radical innovation. *European Urban and Regional Studies, 14*(3), 195–209.

Murray, R., Caulier-Grice, J., & Mulgan, G. (2010). *The open book of social innovation.* London: The Young Foundation and Nesta.

Nelson, R.R., & Winter, S.G. (1982). *An evolutionary theory of economic change.* Cambridge, MA: Belknap Press.

Neumeier, S. (2017). Social innovation in rural development: Identifying the key factors of success. *Geographical Journal, 183*(1), 34–46.

Nicholls, A. (2010). The legitimacy of social entrepreneurship: Reflexive isomorphism in a pre-paradigmatic field. *Entrepreneurship Theory and Practice, 34*(4), 611–633.

Nicholls, A., & Murdock, A. (2012). The nature of social innovation. In A. Nicholls & A. Murdock (Eds.), *Social innovation. Blurring boundaries to reconfigure markets* (pp. 1–32). New York: Palgrave Macmillan.

Nicholls, A., & Ziegler, R. (Eds.). (2019). *Creating economic space for social innovation.* Oxford: Oxford University Press.

Nock, L., Krlev, G., & Mildenberger, G. (2013). *Soziale Innovationen in den Spitzenverbänden der Freien Wohlfahrtspflege: Strukturen, Prozesse und Zukunftsperspektiven.* Retrieved from http://www.bagfw.de/uploads/media/2013_12_17_Soziale_Innovationen_Spitzenverbaenden_FWp.pdf

Nyssens, M. (2006). Social enterprise at the crossroads of market, public policies and civil society. In M. Nyssens (Ed.), *Social enterprise. At the crossroads of market, public policies and civil society* (pp. 313–328). London: Routledge.

Pelka, B., & Terstriep, J. (2016). Mapping social innovation maps: State of research practice across Europe. *European Public and Social Innovation Review, 1*(1), 3–16.

Phillips, W., Alexander, E.A., & Lee, H. (2017). Going it alone won't work!: The relational imperative for social innovation in social enterprises. *Journal of Business Ethics, 14*(2), 32. doi:10.1007/s10551-017-3608-1

Phillips, W., Lee, H., Ghobadian, A., O'Regan, N., & James, P. (2015). Social innovation and social entrepreneurship: A systematic review. *Group & Organization Management, 40*(3), 428–461.

Pol, E., & Ville, S. (2009). Social innovation: Buzz word or enduring term? *Journal of Socio-Economics, 38*, 878–885.

Popper, K.R. (1966). *The open society and its enemies.* Princeton, NJ: Princeton University Press.

Porter, M.E., & Kramer, M.R. (2006). Strategy & society: The link between competitive advantage and corporate social responsibility. *Harvard Business Review*, (December), 2–17.

Porter, M.E., & Kramer, M.R. (2011). Creating shared value: How to reinvent capitalism – and unleash a wave of innovation and growth. *Harvard Business Review*, (January–February), 2–17.

Prahalad, C.K., & Hammond, A. (2002). Serving the world's poor profitably. *Harvard Business Review, 80*(9), 48–57.

Prahalad, C.K., & Hart, S.L. (2002). The fortune at the bottom of the pyramid. *Strategy + Business, 26*(First Quarter), 2–14.

Purtik, H., & Arenas, D. (2017). Embedding social innovation: Shaping societal norms and behaviors throughout the innovation process. *Business & Society*, 1–40.

Radkau, J. (2013). *Max Weber: A biography*. Hoboken, NJ: Wiley.

Rao-Nicholson, R., Vorley, T., & Khan, Z. (2017). Social innovation in emerging economies: A national systems of innovation based approach. *Technological Forecasting and Social Change, 121*, 228–237. doi:10.1016/j.techfore.2017.03.013

Reay, T., & Hinings, C.R. (2005). The recomposition of an organizational field: Health care in Alberta. *Organization Studies, 26*(3), 351–384. doi:10.1177/0170840605050872

Richter, R., Fink, M., Lang, R., & Maresch, D. (2020). *Social entrepreneurship and innovation in rural Europe*. New York: Routledge.

Roundy, P.T. (2017). Social entrepreneurship and entrepreneurial ecosystems: Complementary or disjoint phenomena? *International Journal of Social Economics, 44*(9), 1252–1267.

Salamon, L.M., Sokolowski, W., & List, R. (2003). *Global civil society: An overview*. Johns Hopkins Comparative Nonprofit Sector Project. Baltimore, MD.

Salter, W.E.G. (1969). *Productivity and technical change*. Department of Applied Economics Monographs. Cambridge: Cambridge University Press. Retrieved from http://books.google.de/books?id=1Lu4 AAAAIAAJ

Saxenian, A.L. (1994). *Regional advantage: Culture and competition in Silicon Valley and Route 128*. Cambridge, MA: Harvard University Press.

Schaper, M. (2016). *Making ecopreneurs: Developing sustainable entrepreneurship* (2nd ed.). London: Routledge.

Scherer, A.G., & Voegtlin, C. (2018). Corporate governance for responsible innovation: Approaches to corporate governance and their implications for sustainable development. *Academy of Management Perspectives*. doi:10.5465/amp.2017.0175

Schimpf, Gudrun-Christine; Mildenberger, Georg; Giesecke, Susanne; Havas, Attila (2019): *Trajectories of social innovation: housing for all?* In: Alex Nicholls und Rafael Ziegler (Hg.): Creating economic space for social innovation: Oxford University Press.

Schimpf, Gudrun-Christine; Ziegler, Rafael (2019): *Trajectories of Social Innovation: water for all?* In: Alex Nicholls und Rafael Ziegler (Hg.): Creating economic space for social innovation: Oxford University Press. Schmitz, B., & Scheuerle, T. (2012). Founding or transforming? – A comparative case study of social intrapreneurship in three German Christian based NPOs. *Journal of Entrepreneurship Perspectives, 1*(1), 13–35.

Schröer, A., Eurich, J., & Mildenberger, G. (2015). Soziale Innovationen. gesellschaftliche Relevanz, Definition und Förderung. In M. Vilain & S. Wegner (Eds.), *Am Wendepunkt? InnenPerspektiven der Sozialwirtschaft* (epd-Dokumentation 29/2016, pp. 57–64). Darmstadt.

Schumpeter, J.A. (1911). *Theorie der wirtschaftlichen Entwicklung*. Leipzig: Duncker & Humblot.

Sedlacko, M., Martinuzzi, A., Røpke, I., Videira, N., & Antunes, P. (2014). Participatory systems mapping for sustainable consumption: Discussion of a method promoting systemic insights. *Ecological Economics, 106*, 33–43. doi:10.1016/j.ecolecon.2014.07.002

Seelos, C., & Mair, J. (2017). *Innovation and scaling for impact: How effective social enterprises do it*: Stanford, CA: Stanford University Press.

Slimane, K.B., & Lamine, W. (2017). A transaction-based approach to social innovation. *International Journal of Entrepreneurship and Innovation, 18*(4).

Stehr, N., Henning, C., & Weiler, B. (2010). *The moralization of the markets* (First paperback printing). London: Transaction Publishers.

Swedberg, R. (2009). Schumpeter's full model of entrepreneurship: Economic, non-economic and social entrepreneurship. In R. Ziegler (Ed.), *An introduction to social entrepreneurship. Voices, preconditions, contexts* (pp. 77–106). Cheltenham: Edward Elgar.

Terstriep, J., Kleverbeck, M., Deserti, A., & Rizzo, F. (2015). *Comparative report on social innovation across Europe*. SIMPACT Project Report D 3.2.

The Young Foundation. (2012). *Social innovation overview: Part I – Defining social innovation*. A Deliverable to the Project "The Theoretical, Empirical and Policy Foundations for Building Social Innovation in Europe" (DG Research). Brussels.

Tracey, P., & Stott, N. (2016). Social innovation: A window on alternative ways of organizing and innovating. *Innovation, 19*(1), 51–60. doi:10.1080/14479338.2016.1268924

van der Have, R.P., & Rubalcaba, L. (2016). Social innovation research: An emerging area of innovation studies? *Research Policy, 45*(9), 1923–1935. doi:10.1016/j.respol.2016.06.010

van Wijk, J., Zietsma, C., Dorado, S., Bakker, F.G.A. de, & Martí, I. (2018). Social innovation: Integrating micro, meso, and macro level insights from institutional theory. *Business & Society, 57*(2), 000765031878910. doi:10.1177/0007650318789104

Weber, M. (1921). *Wirtschaft und Gesellschaft: Grundriss der verstehenden Soziologie.* Tübingen: Mohr-Siebeck.

Weber, M. (1978). *Economy and society: An outline of interpretive sociology.* Berkeley: University of California Press.

Weisbrod, B.A. (1998). *To profit or not to profit: The commercial transformation of the nonprofit sector.* Cambridge: Cambridge University Press.

Wit, A. de, Mensink, W., Einarsson, T., & Bekkers, R. (2017). Beyond service production: Volunteering for social innovation. *Nonprofit and Voluntary Sector Quarterly, 43*, 089976401773465. doi:10.1177/08997 64017734651

Yunus, M., Moingeon, B., & Lehmann-Ortega, L. (2010). Building social business models: Lessons from the Grameen experience. *Long Range Planning, 43*(2–3), 308–325. doi:10.1016/j.lrp.2009.12.005

Zapf, W. (1989). Über Soziale Innovationen. *Soziale Welt, 40*(1–2), 170–183.

Zietsma, C., & Lawrence, T.B. (2010). Institutional work in the transformation of an organisational field: The interplay of boundary work and practice work. *Administrative Science Quarterly, 55*, 189–221.

33

SOCIAL FINANCE FOR NONPROFITS

Impact investing, social impact bonds, and crowdfunding

Jun Han

ADJUNCT PROFESSOR, MCCOURT SCHOOL OF PUBLIC POLICY,
GEORGETOWN UNIVERSITY, WASHINGTON, DC, USA

Wendy Chen

PHD CANDIDATE, SCHAR SCHOOL, GEORGE MASON UNIVERSITY, ARLINGTON, VA, USA

Stefan Toepler

PROFESSOR OF NONPROFIT STUDIES AND MPA DIRECTOR, SCHAR SCHOOL OF
POLICY AND GOVERNMENT, GEORGE MASON UNIVERSITY, ARLINGTON, VA, USA

Introduction

In its simplest terms, social finance refers to "the allocation of capital primarily for social and environmental returns, as well as in some cases, a financial return" (Nicholls et al., 2015: 3). Within the broad definition, a spectrum of diverse social finance approaches exists, that spans from the sole focus on social return on the one end to the sole focus on financial return on the other (Nicholls et al., 2015: 4–5). In general, social finance includes social investments (a term often used in the United Kingdom), impact investing (a term mainly used in the United States), social impact bonds (or pay for success), crowdfunding, microfinance, green finance, and so on.

Many debates around social finance and its forms are often focused on the "financial return" part of the spectrum, or on pursuing broad goals through investments in commercial applications (e.g., green finance, which seeks ecological transformations of the economy), in which nonprofits are typically not centrally involved if at all. In this chapter, we focus on the forms of social finance that benefit or engage nonprofit organizations more closely, rather than the ones that pursue broader social and public goals by commercial means, in particular the three forms of Impact Investing, Social Impact Bonds, and Crowdfunding.

The historical context of social finance

Although interest has increased exponentially since the turn of the millennium, some analysts suggest that the roots of social finance date back to the religious campaigns against slavery and the slave trade in the 18th and 19th centuries. In 1758, the Religious Society of Friends, known as Quakers, declared that involvement in the slave trade would lead to exclusion from society (David, 2007). In 1760, John Wesley, the founder of Methodism, delivered the well-known sermon "The Use of Money," which claimed that "evil could not be found in money itself, but rather in how it was used" (Finkelman and Huntington, 2017: 2). In 1928, a group of Quakers launched the Pioneer Fund, the first mutual fund to avoid investments in some "sin" industries (Lumberg, 2017).

The emergence of broad social movements in the second half of the 20th century ushered in an era of greater public scrutiny of business practices. In the 1950s and 1960s, during the civil rights struggle, university students and labor unions urged universities to stop unethical investments. During the Vietnam War, the students and anti-war movements led to the protests against the arms industry (Donovan, 2017). The Civil Rights Act of 1964 and the Voting Rights Act of 1965 in the US opened the door to the establishment of community development banks in low-income and minority communities (Donovan, 2017). In 1968 and 1969, the Ford Foundation organized a series of conferences at Yale University for "universities and other non-profit institutions to consider the social consequences of corporate activities from which these institutions derive an endowment return" (Trelstad, 2016: 6; Simon et al., 1972). The Ford Foundation simultaneously developed "program related investments" to "shift from using grants to low-interest loans to finance programs like urban redevelopment or affordable housing" (Trelstad, 2016: 6).

In the 1970s, socially responsible investing appeared. Socially responsible investment funds were established, which avoided investments in arms, alcohol, tobacco, and gambling; and on occasion in countries with oppressive political regimes, such as South Africa under apartheid (Donovan, 2017). A milestone was the founding of the first asset management company dedicated to socially responsible investing, Franklin Research & Development, by Joan Bavaria in 1982, later rebranded as Trillium Investments (Trelstad, 2016: 6). As socially responsible investments and mutual funds proliferated, the Domini Social Index was launched, consisting of 400 large corporations in the US. Compared to the S&P 500, these companies were selected based on a wide range of social and environmental criteria (Donovan, 2017).

Since 2000, the scope of social finance has been extended, from passively avoiding investing in industries with negative social externalities to actively seeking to generate social and financial returns at the same time. Moreover, social investment has also expanded to a global scale. The 2005 report "Who Cares Wins" by the United Nations Environment Programme (UNEP) Finance Initiative coined the term "Environment, Social and Governance (ESG)", which called for the integration of ESG factors into investment and decision-making (Kell, 2018). In the following year, the United Nations released the Principles for Responsible Investment (PRI) that "offer a menu of possible actions for incorporating ESG issues into investment practice" (UNEP Finance Initiative, 2019). Since 2006, the number of signatories of the PRI has grown from 100 to over 2,300, managing more than 80 trillion US dollars (UNEP Finance Initiative, 2019). In 2015, the United Nations estimated that it will cost between $50 trillion and $70 trillion to achieve the Sustainable Development Goals (SDGs), which led the Rockefeller Foundation to call for leveraging innovative finance to tap into the over $200 trillion in private capital to help implement the SDGs (Keohane and Madsbjerg, 2016).

Crowdfunding antecedents have likewise been traced over a long period of time. The broader concept of crowdsourcing (Bretschneider et al., 2014; Kuppuswamy & Bayus, 2015; Thurridl & Kamleitner, 2016) has also been dated back to the 1700s and was established to help a firm gain access to resources and knowledge that traditionally it may not have been able to obtain through other means (Jeppesen & Lakhani, 2010; Mollick, 2014). This has led to the evolutionary process that crowdfunding is still undergoing today. Notable examples include the construction of the Statue of Liberty's pedestal which was paid for by the people of New York in 1886. With the campaign started by the publisher Joseph John Pulitzer in his newspaper *New York World* urging citizens to donate to the completion of the pedestal, over $100,000 was raised with most donations being $1 or less.[1] Then, when Dr. Muhammad Yunus launched Grameen Bank in Bangladesh in 1976, the microfinance model began to take root (Khandker et al., 1995) and spread to other countries like China (Zhao & Han, 2019). It laid the groundwork for the evolution of digital crowdfunding later.

Key concepts and forms of social finance

Social investment or impact investing

Social investment, or impact investing, is one of the main forms of social finance. In many cases, the three terms, social finance, social investment, and impact investing, are used interchangeably. In general, social investment as a term is more commonly used in the United Kingdom, while impact investing is more prevalent in the United States.

Big Society Capital (BSC), the first social investment wholesale bank in the world, was founded in London in April 2012.[2] BSC defines social investment as "repayable finance for charities and social enterprises that targets both financial and social returns for investors." BSC believes that

> charities and social enterprises can use repayable finance to help them increase their impact on society, for example by maintaining cash flow, buying an asset, growing or kick starting their organization. They can choose to access this finance from social investors, who will be motivated by their social missions. For investors, social investment is part of the spectrum of impact investment. It actively targets high impact in investments by focusing on charities and social businesses. Sometimes investors will accept lower returns or take greater risks to achieve this.

According to BSC data, by 2019, BSC had spent about £1 billion on social investment including £291 million of its own funds and £752 million from its co-investors. Of the BSC social investment, 65 percent is capital for charities and social enterprises, and 4 percent is helping charities deliver services through social impact bonds with other investments as remainder.[3]

The Global Impact Investing Network (GIIN) defines impact investments as "investments made with the intention to generate positive, measurable social and environmental impact alongside a financial return."[4] The creation of the term dates back to 2007, when it was coined at a conference organized by the Rockefeller Foundation in its Bellagio Centre in Italy (The Rockefeller Foundation 2019; Han & Shah, 2019). This event is usually regarded as a milestone that initiated the impact investing movement in the modern era. A second major milestone galvanizing the field's development, was the release of a report by the G8 Taskforce on Social Impact Investment, set up by the then UK prime minister David Cameron and chaired by venture capitalist Sir Ronald Cohen, in September 2014. Titled "Impact Investment: The Invisible Heart of Markets: Harnessing the power of entrepreneurship, innovation and capital for public good" (Cohen, 2014), this report called on governments and the financial sector to grow the social investment market by unleashing the billions of dollars locked up in charitable endowments, pension funds, and private wealth (Grave, 2014). According to the GIIN, over 1,340 organizations currently manage $502 billion in impact investing assets worldwide.[5] Participants in the impact investment markets range from major banks and financial institutions, such as Bank of America, Deutsche Bank, and Goldman Sachs, to large philanthropic foundations, including the Rockefeller Foundation, Ford Foundation, and Bill & Melinda Gates Foundation. Other impact investors include development finance institutions, pension funds and insurance companies, and even NGOs and religious institutions.[6]

Social impact bond or pay for success

A Social Impact Bond (SIB) is a model of social finance that has drawn the most public and policy interest so far, although the initial uptake (i.e., actual diffusion and adoption) of these schemes has been modest (Arena et al., 2016). The term "social impact bond" was originally coined by Geoff Mulgan, former chief executive of the Young Foundation in the UK, in a paper as one of several new social investment models in 2008 (Nicholls & Tomkinson, 2015). It was first launched by Social Finance UK, led by Sir Ronald Cohen in 2010. According to the Government Outcomes Lab project database at the University of Oxford, as of May 2019, 68 social impact bonds are operating or have been completed in the UK.[7]

Social impact bonds are "a form of payment by results but extend this by harnessing social investment from capital markets to cover the up-front costs of service intervention" (Edmiston & Nicholls, 2018). They consist of "a set of contracts, the basis of which is an agreement by the government to pay investors for an improvement in a specific social outcome once it has been achieved" (Nicholls & Tomkinson, 2015, p. 336). The analogy to financial bonds is that investors will receive a pre-specified annual return over the lifetime of the SIB akin to a bond's interest rate. However, as existing research points out, the bond analogy is somewhat misleading as interest in financial bonds is guaranteed but returns for SIB investors are contingent on performance and meeting a set of outcome goals (Fraser et al., 2018). Moreover, SIBs involve multilateral contractual collaborations that financial bonds do not (Dey & Gibbon, 2018).

The difference between traditional commissioning (or tendering) and social impact bonds is demonstrated in Figure 33.1. On the left side is the traditional commission process, where governments provide grants to, or contract with (purchase of service – PoS), nonprofits, and nonprofits deliver services to the target population in turn. On the right side of the figure is the simplified model of a social impact bond. Upon negotiation of the SIB contract, investors first provide the impact investments to nonprofits to finance the delivery of services to the target population. Then social outcomes are generated, measured, evaluated, and reported to government agencies. Governments then will pay impact investors based on the measured social outcomes if goals are met. The innovation of the SIB model is that impact investors will first take the risk, and when the improved outcomes are achieved, governments then will pay for the success. Since the payment relies on the success of achieving social outcomes, SIBs are usually called Pay for Success schemes in the US, a term coined by Social Finance US. In principle, the SIB concept is a win–win scenario for all parties involved: investors stand to make profits from their investments; nonprofits gain access to new financing; and governments benefit by having the risk for failed interventions shifted to the investors and by realizing cost savings from reduced need for future interventions if the SIB succeeds (Dey & Gibbon, 2018).

In 2010, Social Finance, Ltd., signed the first social impact bond contract with the UK Ministry of Justice, designed to end the cycle of reoffending, or recidivism, among prisoners from the Peterborough prison (Mirchandani, 2018). The 17 impact investors, including the Rockefeller Foundation, invested £5 million to provide financial support for nonprofits and social enterprises to lower reoffending rates of some 3,000 male prisoners serving prison sentences of 12 months or less (Mirchandani, 2018). Frontline service delivery was managed by One Service, created by Social Finance, with contractual collaborations with service partners,

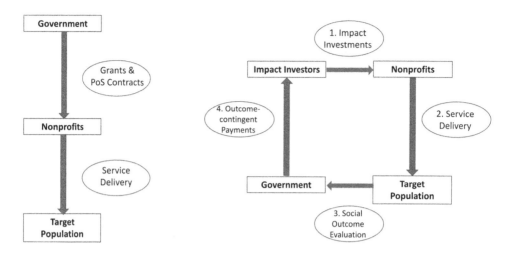

Figure 33.1   The difference between traditional commissioning and social impact bonds

including the St Giles Trust, Ormiston, SOVA, YMCA, and Mind (Nicholls & Tomkinson, 2015, pp. 345–356). The condition for the SIB is that the project would be conducted over a 7-year period with three cohorts of 1,000 prisoners each, and if the recidivism rate decreased by a specific rate (at least 7.5 percent), then a fixed payment per unit decrease in the recidivism rate (a minimum repayment of 2.5 percent) would be paid from the UK Ministry of Justice to the investor group (Nicholls & Tomkinson, 2015, p. 342; Schinckus, 2018, p. 2). Five years later, convictions fell by 9 percent, and the investors received the returns in full, plus 3.1 percent a year (Ebrahimi, 2017).

The first US social impact bond was piloted in New York in 2012 with the goal of reducing the recidivism rate of young people in the Rikers Island prison. This impact bond was funded by Goldman Sachs and guaranteed by Bloomberg Philanthropies. As mentioned earlier, in the US, social impact bonds are usually called Pay for Success (PFS). By October 2018, 25 PFS projects had been launched in the US, with the scale between $5 and $10 million as the minimum threshold (Nonprofit Finance Fund, 2019, p. 4).

Beyond these early efforts, the impact bonds have spread globally. According to the Impact Bond Global Database developed by Social Finance UK, there are 132 impact bonds operating in 25 countries, which raised $431 million in capital, and impacted 1,064,030 people, as of May 10, 2019.[8] The United Kingdom (47), the United States (26), the Netherlands (11), and Australia (9) are the top four countries with the largest number of SIBs. The issue areas of SIBs are extended from reducing recidivism to workforce development, housing, health, child and family welfare, criminal justice, education and early years, and poverty and environment.[9]

Crowdfunding

Another major, albeit quite different type, of social finance emerged in force almost simultaneously with the SIB concept. Similar to the practice of crowdsourcing which solicits information and knowledge from the crowd, "crowdfunding" (i.e., fundraising from a crowd) as a new digital form of raising funds or capital for projects essentially appeared in the late 2000s, due to the digital revolution and changing public policies (Renko et al., 2019). In general, crowdfunding can be defined as "the efforts by entrepreneurial individuals and groups – cultural, social, and for-profit – to fund their ventures by drawing on relatively small contributions from a relatively large number of individuals using the Internet, without standard financial intermediaries" (Mollick, 2014). So far, there are three major types of crowdfunding through which both individuals and organizations can seek funding from the crowd and offer either rewards, interest, or equity in return (Renko et al., 2019).

The crowdfunding market has been growing drastically over the last decade. Since President Obama signed the Jumpstart Our Business Startups (JOBS) Act enabling individuals to conduct equity-based crowdfunding on April 5, 2012, the crowdfunding market has become even bigger (Zhao et al., 2019). For 2017, funds raised were estimated at $17.2 billion in North America, $10.5 billion in Asia, and $6.5 billion in Europe[10] and the World Bank predicted that it could potentially reach over $96 billion by 2025.[11] Crowdfunding has become more prevalent over recent years as it provides an alternative to other funding methods such as venture capitalists or bank loans by utilizing online platforms designed to draw on the funding power of relatively large numbers of people who wish to back or support projects that they have an interest in (Mollick, 2014). These projects could come from nonprofits that wish to raise money for social causes, such as building schools in Africa, or as an online platform, or for-profit ventures that wish to develop and sell new products in commercial markets. The amounts that these projects individually raise depends on a variety of elements, and those amounts especially vary when comparing commercially oriented projects to socially oriented ones.

For chronically underfunded nonprofits hampered by the free-rider problem in fundraising (Anheier, 2014), crowdfunding presents an especially attractive proposition as an alternative funding method (Lehner, 2013), providing access to new streams of support as well as new supporters. Despite this appeal, most of the crowdfunding research to date has focused on commercial projects. Moreover, early evidence suggests that, just as nonprofits have a harder time procuring funds through traditional means as compared to commercially oriented firms, they also lag behind their commercial counterparts on crowdfunding sites (Chen, 2018).

The first iteration of digital crowdfunding as we know it today began when ArtistShare, a platform designed for musicians who wish to grow their careers, was created in 2001. On this platform, artists are connected with fans who can follow along with the artists' creative process and contribute to support an artist's musical projects via donation (ArtistShare, 2019). That same year, JustGiving was launched which was more focused on social causes and since then has helped raise over $4.5 billion in over 164 countries.[12]

Another notable entry to the crowdfunding space appeared in 2005 with the addition of Kiva, a nonprofit microloan platform designed to lift up individuals in the Global South. Kiva presents its mission as "expanding financial access to help underserved communities thrive."[13] The year 2005 also saw the launch of the first British peer-to-peer lending platform Zopa which aimed "to give people access to simpler, better-value loans and investments."[14] Shortly thereafter, the founder of FundaVlog[15] Michael Sullivan coined the term "crowdfunding" in 2006, which was rapidly adapted (Zhao et al., 2019).

The financial crisis of 2007–2008 had two major impacts on the emerging field of crowdfunding, which both accelerated the development of crowdfunding. First, big banks took this crash as a signal to reduce the amount of lending they would provide to small businesses. From this, for-profits and nonprofits alike would now need to find alternative funding methods as one of the fundamental funding sources was now scaling back access to loans (Zhao et al., 2019). Second, in the years following the crisis, financially distressed individuals turned to crowdfunding as well seeking funding for personal expenses, such as medical bills, due to their lack of personal wealth (Berliner & Kenworthy, 2017). This increased usage brought a greater public awareness to these platforms and thus drove up the userbase. Against this backdrop, some of the larger crowdfunding platforms, including Indiegogo, Kickstarter, GoFundMe, Crowdfunder, and CircleUp, began to emerge.

The top two reward-based crowdfunding platforms, Indiegogo and Kickstarter, were formed in 2008 and 2009. Both of these platforms focused on providing individuals with specific projects, mainly art projects at the beginning, to seek funding from the crowd in exchange for small rewards. Then, 2009 saw the beginning of GoFundMe, a charity-based crowdfunding platform, while Obama launched the Startup America Initiative in 2011 which was designed to reboot small business. In the same year, Crowdfunder and CircleUp were both launched which allowed users to gain equity in the companies which they crowdfunded. Then following the precedent set in 2011, Obama launched the Jumpstart Our Business Startups (JOBS) Act in 2012 which laid the groundwork for allowing non-accredited investors to gain equity in companies (Zhao et al., 2019). However, the JOBS Act was primarily designed to help equity-based firms, or commercially oriented firms, and did less to aid nonprofits.

There are at least three methods in which individuals and organizations including nonprofits can raise funds via crowdfunding. The first method is when nonprofits participate directly as the campaigner to solicit funds for their particular causes (Renko et al., 2019). This crowdfunding typically takes place on rewards or donation-based platforms such as GoFundMe or Indiegogo. In these cases, individuals post projects that can be either commercial or social in nature which seek a specific goal set for their project. Indiegogo began with an aim to help many different types of products from consumer goods to socially oriented projects,[16] while Kickstarter, founded a year later, aims to "helps artists, musicians, filmmakers, designers, and other creators find the resources and support they need to make their ideas a reality."[17] Depending on the individual platform's rules, campaigners may or may not be able to keep the amount raised if the goal amount is not met.[18] Similarly, donation-based platforms exist such as GoFundMe which allow for mission-based crowdfunding projects to raise funds for their causes. These can be for issues ranging from supporting Little League youth sports teams to disaster relief and can be posted by organizations or individuals (Freedman & Nutting, 2015).

The second method is through microloan enterprises or debt-based crowdfunding, such as Kiva, which allows individuals to make small loans to impoverished individuals from around the world (Renko et al., 2019). With this method, nonprofits or social entrepreneurs can seek funding from individuals willing to provide small repayable loans according to the agreed upon terms.

However, in many cases, the projects that are posted on these sites are not primarily socially oriented. For instance, Kiva's mission is to "expand financial access to help underserved communities thrive,"[19] but the focus is on the business, educational, or other needs of small-scale entrepreneurs, farmers, and others. Individuals are able to request loans for virtually anything ranging from cattle to business supplies to television sets. In this debt-based model, the platforms screen the fund seekers who are expected to pay back the loan amount plus interest (Freedman & Nutting, 2015). Kiva, for example, works with local partner NGOs that vet, select, and propose clients to be featured on the Kiva website. While this avenue may be feasible for nonprofits to pursue funding for social and development projects, it is still primarily being used for personal and commercial purposes.

The third method in which nonprofits seek funds through crowdfunding is when the crowdfunding platform is to operate as a social enterprise or nonprofit itself (Renko et al., 2019). These organizations specifically target other nonprofits and help to expose them to large groups of people to invest in their projects through their platforms. One example of these platforms is Crowdrise. Despite being founded as a for-profit enterprise in 2010, Crowdrise focuses on helping nonprofits raise funds. Crowdrise was acquired in 2017 by the mission-based crowd-funding platform GoFundMe (Lunden, 2017).

Key social finance policies in the UK and US

A series of pioneering practices in modern social finance first emerged in the UK, fostered by a range of supportive policies by the British government in recent years. In 2002, the largest social enterprise supporting network in the UK, UnLtd, funded by an endowment from the Millennium Commission, was created to conduct social investment (UnLtd, 2019). In 2009, the Department of Health in the UK launched the Social Enterprise Investment Fund (SEIF) to support social enterprises in delivering health and social care services; followed in 2011 by the first launch of a social impact bond in London; and the establishment of Big Society Capital also in London in 2012 (Han, 2017, p. 1212). In 2013, the Public Services Act or Social Value Act came into force, the Social Stock Exchange was launched, and the G8 Social Investment Task Force was launched when the UK hosted the G8 (Han, 2017, p. 1212). The Social Value Act requires the public sector agencies that commission public services to think about how they can secure wider social, economic, and environmental benefits, rather than only considering the lowest price.[20] Social Stock Exchange provides a directory of companies that passed a "social impact test," and the businesses on the list can get much visibility from impact investors (Chhichhia, 2015).

As a fiscal support for social finance or social investment, the UK implemented the Community Investment Tax Relief (CITR) in 2012 and Social Investment Tax Relief (SITR) in 2014. The CITR encourages investment in disadvantaged communities by giving tax relief to investors who back businesses and other enterprises.[21] Social Investment Tax Relief (SITR) encourages individuals to invest into social enterprises, charities, and community businesses by receiving a 30 percent tax break on SITR investments.[22]

Similar to the United Kingdom, the United States has also introduced a series of legal and policy measures to support social finance. The Community Reinvestment Act of 1977, which prohibited discriminatory lending practices in low-income communities, the launch of the US Sustainable Investment Forum (US SIF) in 1984 (Lumberg, 2017), the Community Development Financial Institutions (CDFI) Act of 1994, and the US Treasury's Community Development Financial Institutions Fund are widely seen as antecedents (Nicholls et al., 2015, p. 473). In 2009, the Obama Administration launched the Office of Social Innovation and Civic Participation and created the Social Innovation Fund and other initiatives seeking to involve philanthropic partners (Toepler, 2018a). The Global Impact Investing Network (GIIN) was launched at the same time as the institutional infrastructure for impact investing. In 2011, the GIIN launched an online directory, namely ImpactBase, which is a searchable online database of 443 impact investment funds.[23] Similarly, the Case Foundation developed an online tool, namely "Impact Investing Network Map," which demonstrates the publicly available transactions between impact investors and investees.[24] In 2013, the National Advisory Board of the US was launched, led by the Omidyar Network and the Social Finance US, to promote a policy agenda for US impact investment.[25]

Additional energy went into creating new hybrid legal forms as investees of social finance to create options beyond the nonprofit/for-profit dichotomy (see Chapter 34 by Krlev & Anheier, this volume). Social enterprises can register as low-profit limited liability companies (L3C) and Benefit Corporations in the US (Chapter 35 by Abramson & Billings, this volume). In 2008, Vermont was the first state to create the low-profit limited liability company (L3C) as an official legal status for social enterprises. L3C was primarily designed to facilitate program-related investments from philanthropic foundations to social enterprises without charitable nonprofit status (Schmidt, 2010; Chan, 2011). In 2010, the first benefit corporation legislation was passed in Maryland; this legal construct attempts to anchor the pursuit of social benefit in the corporate charter (Toepler, 2018b). According to the database of Social Enterprise Law Tracker, developed by New York University, as of April 2019, 34 states in the US had enacted the Benefit Corporation legislation, and 8 states are now considering passing the legislation. By 2018, 8 states in the US recognized low-profit limited liability company (L3C) as an official legal status, and 3 states were considering doing so.[26]

Discussion and conclusion

In a little over a decade, social finance has gathered significant, and increasingly global, scholarly and policy interest. It has been driven by the prospect of potentially drawing trillions of private capital into solving social, environmental, and economic problems, even at a global scale. Yet while the dollar numbers engaged in various forms of social finance seem impressive, they are still far from the panacea that supporters predict them to become. The $17 billion raised in 2017 through crowdfunding in North America, for example, compares to $410 billion in US private giving in the same year (Giving USA, 2018). What is more, much, if not most, of the crowd-raised funds benefit commercial projects or individuals, calling the current revenue potential of this type of social finance for social enterprises, nonprofits, and public institutions into question, just as some of them are beginning to consider crowdfunding as a method to compensate for dwindling subsidies (e.g., Cappelle, 2019). When comparing social and commercial crowd-funded projects, commercial projects are much more likely to generate surplus funding, or amounts exceeding the original goal amount set by the owner of the project. Furthermore, the total amount of funding raised by commercial projects dwarfs the amounts raised by social ones (Chen, 2018). Similar issues arise with other social finance mechanisms.

Social impact bonds have great potential applications for nonprofits, which occupy a clearly prescribed role within the overall contractual arrangements. Yet despite the broad appeal and the intense policy interest in this instrument, the actual number of SIBs that developed to the implementation stage has remained minuscule on a global scale (Arena et al., 2016), which may be due to the barriers to pushing the model of social impact bond or pay for success forward. One of the main barriers now that the first SIBs have reached the end of their initial lifetime, is that there still is a lack of conclusive evidence of their effectiveness (Eames et al., 2014). With few SIBs having run their course so far, results remain mixed. After starting off well, the Peterborough SIB's effectiveness declined over time and was closed recently; the Riker's Island SIB was considered a failure (Dey & Gibbon, 2018). Contributing to the difficulties is the fundamental problem of devising appropriate success and outcome measurements (Arena et al., 2016). This may be addressed through carefully calibrated cost–benefit analyses, but the complex principal–agent relationships introduce openings for opportunistic behaviors that may undermine successful implementation (Pandey et al., 2018). More broadly, impact bonds push service providers towards financial accountability and more easily measurable projects, while undermining accountability relations between government and service providers and between the latter and the target populations (Balboa, 2016). Social finance holds considerable promise for social enterprise and nonprofits, but also considerable roadblocks remain before its promise can be fully realized.

Notes

1   Source: https://www.nps.gov/stli/learn/historyculture/joseph–pulitzer.htm
2   See more information at the website: https://www.bigsocietycapital.com

3 Source: https://bigsocietycapital.fra1.cdn.digitaloceanspaces.com/media/documents/Big_Society_Capital_2018_Annual_Review.pdf

4 Source: https://thegiin.org/impact-investing/need-to-know/#what-is-impact-investing

5 Source: https://thegiin.org/impact-investing/need-to-know/#what-is-the-current-state-of-the-impact-investing-market

6 Source: https://thegiin.org/impact-investing/need-to-know/#what-is-the-current-state-of-the-impact-investing-market

7 Source: https://golab.bsg.ox.ac.uk/our-projects/go-labs-project-database

8 See the website of the database: https://sibdatabase.socialfinance.org.uk

9 Source: https://sibdatabase.socialfinance.org.uk

10 Source: https://www.statista.com/statistics/946659/global-crowdfunding-volume-worldwide-by-region/

11 Source: http://documents.worldbank.org/curated/en/409841468327411701/pdf/840000WP0Box380crowdfunding0study00.pdf

12 Source: https://www.justgiving.com/about-us

13 Source: https://www.kiva.org/about

14 Source: https://zopa.com

15 FundaVlog was a crowdfunding site that sought to help raise funds for videoblog-related projects and events. It does not exist anymore (Hanson, 2016).

16 Source: www.indiegogo.com

17 Source: https://www.kickstarter.com/about?ref=global-footer

18 Sources: https://support.indiegogo.com/hc/en-us/articles/204456408-Fees-Pricing-for-Campaigners-How-much-does-Indiegogo-cost-; https://www.kickstarter.com/help/fees

19 Source: https://www.kiva.org/about

20 See more information on the Social Value Act at the website: https://www.gov.uk/government/publications/social-value-act-information-and-resources/social-value-act-information-and-resources

21 See more information on the Community Investment Tax Relief (CITR) at the website: https://www.gov.uk/government/publications/community-investment-tax-relief-citr

22 See more information on the Social Investment Tax Relief (SITR) at the website: https://www.bigsocietycapital.com/what-we-do/current-projects/social-investment-tax-relief/get-sitr

23 See the website: https://www.impactbase.org

24 See the website: https://casefoundation.org/networkmap

25 See the website: http://impinvalliance.org

26 See the website: https://socentlawtracker.org

References

Anheier, H. K. (2014). *Nonprofit Organizations: Theory, Management Policy*. New York: Routledge.

Arena, M., Bengo, I., Calderini, M., and Chiodo, V. (2016). Social impact bonds: Blockbuster or flash in a pan? *International Journal of Public Administration*, 39(12), 927–939.

ArtistShare. Retrieved from ArtistShare.com. (Accessed May 20, 2019).

Austin, J., Stevenson, H., and Ii-Skillern, J. (2006). Social and commercial entrepreneurship: Same, different, or both? *Entrepreneurship Theory and Practice,* 30(1), 1–22.

Balboa, C. M. (2016). Accountability of environmental impact bonds: The future of global environmental governance? *Global Environmental Politics*, 16(2), 33–41.

Berliner, L. S., and Kenworthy, N. J. (2017). Producing a worthy illness: Personal crowdfunding amidst financial crisis, *Social Science and Medicine*, 187, 233–242.

Bretschneider, U., Knaub, K., and Wieck, E. (2014). Motivations for crowdfunding: What drives the crowd to invest in start-ups? *Twenty Second European Conference on Information Systems*, 1–11.

Cappelle, L. (2019). Is crowdfunding the future of opera and ballet? *Financial Times*, May 27. Available at: https://www.ft.com/content/1beb4c1e-763c-11e9-b0ec-7dff87b9a4a2

Chan, E. (2011). The L3C – 3 Years Later, Nonprofit Law Blog. Available at: www.nonprofitlawblog.com/the-l3c-3-years-later/

Chen, W. (2018). Does Crowdfunding Benefit Social Entrepreneurship? Paper presented at the 47th Annual Conference of ARNOVA, Austin, TX, November 15–17.

Chhichhia, B. (2015). The rise of social stock exchanges: A new, innovative platform is helping more investors support social enterprises, *Stanford Social Innovation Review*, https://ssir.org/articles/entry/the_rise_of_social_stock_exchanges

Cohen, R. (2014). Impact Investment: The Invisible Heart of Markets: Harnessing the power of entrepreneurship, innovation and capital for public good. G8 Social Impact Investment Taskforce. Available at www.ietp.com/sites/default/files/Impact%20Investment%20Report%20FINAL.pdf

David, H. T. (2007). Transnational advocacy in the eighteenth century: Transatlantic activism and the anti-slavery movement, *Global Networks,* 7(3), 367–382.

Dey, C., and Gibbon, J. (2018). New development: Private finance over public good? Questioning the value of impact bonds, *Public Money & Management,* 38(5), 375–378.

Donovan, W. (2017). A short history of socially responsible investing: Investing from the Methodists to South Africa to Domini, *The Balance.* Available at: https://www.thebalance.com/a-short-history-of-socially-responsible-investing-3025578.

Eames, S., Terranova, V., Battaglia, L., Nelson, I., Riesenberg, C., and Rosales, L. (2014). A review of Social Impact Bonds: Financing social service programs through public–private partnerships. Working Paper. University of Texas at Austin, School of Social Work.

Ebrahimi, H. (2017). 'Forget capitalism – profit will soon be a dirty word', Sir Ronald Cohen has swapped private equity for social investment, *The Times*, October 25. Available at: https://www.thetimes.co.uk/article/forget-capitalism-profit-will-soon-be-a-dirty-word-gfmhv9tk0.

Edmiston, D., and Nicholls, A. (2018). Social Impact Bonds: The role of private capital in outcome-based commissioning, *Journal of Social Policy,* 47(1), 57–76.

Finkelman, J., and Huntington, K. (2017). *Impact Investing: History & Opportunity.* Athena Capital Advisors LLC.

Fraser, A., Tan, S., Lagarde, M., and Mays, N. (2018). Narratives of promise, narratives of caution: A review of the literature on Social Impact Bonds. *Social Policy & Administration*, 52(1), 4–28.

Freedman, D. M., and Nutting, M. R. (2015). Brief History of Crowdfunding Including Rewards, Donation, Debt, and Equity Platforms in the USA. http://freedman-chicago.com/ec4i/History-of-Crowdfunding.pdf

Giving USA. (2018). Giving USA 2018: The Annual Report on Philanthropy for the Year 2017. Chicago: Giving USA Foundation. Researched and written by the Indiana University Lilly Family School of Philanthropy.

Grave, I. D. (2014). Sir Ronald's G8 Taskforce plan to unleash $1 trillion in social impact investment, *Pioneers Post.* Available at: https://www.pioneerspost.com/news-views/20140915/sir-ronalds-g8-taskforce-plan-unleash-1-trillion-social-impact-investment.

Han, J. (2017). Social marketisation and policy influence of third sector organisations: Evidence from the UK, *Voluntas: International Journal of Voluntary and Nonprofit Organizations,* 28(3), 1209–1225. https://link.springer.com/article/10.1007/s11266-017-9853-1

Han, J., and Shah S. (2019). The ecosystem of scaling social impact: A new theoretical framework and two case studies, *Journal of Social Entrepreneurship,* 1–25, http://dx.doi.org/10.1080/19420676.2019.1624273

Hanson, J. (2016). *The Social Media Revolution: An Economic and Encyclopedia of Friending, Following, Texting, and Connecting.* Santa Barbara, CA: ABC-CLIO, pp. 98–103.

Jeppesen, L. B., and Lakhani, K. R. (2010). Marginality and problem-solving effectiveness in broadcast search, *Organization Science*, 21, 1016–1033.

Kell, G. (2018). The Remarkable Rise of ESG, Forbes. Available at: https://www.forbes.com/sites/georgkell/2018/07/11/the-remarkable-rise-of-esg/#54982eb71695.

Keohane, G. L., and Madsbjerg, S. (2016). The innovative finance revolution: Private capital for the public good, *Foreign Affairs*, 95 (special edition). Available at: https://www.rockefellerfoundation.org/our-work/initiatives/innovative-finance/

Khandker, S. R., Khalily, B., and Khan, Z. (1995). *Grameen Bank: Performance and Sustainability.* Washington, DC: International Bank for Reconstruction and Development/The World Bank.

Kuppuswamy, V., and Bayus, B. L. (2015). A Review of Crowdfunding Research and Findings. Available at SSRN: https://ssrn.com/ abstract=2685739. (Accessed on May 20, 2019).

Lehner, O. M. (2013). Crowdfunding social ventures: A model and research agenda. *Venture Capital*, 15(4), 289–311.

Lunden, I. (2017). GoFundMe Acquires CrowdRise to Expand to Fundraising for Charities. Retrieved from: https://techcrunch.com/2017/01/10/gofundme-buys-crowdrise-to-expand-to-fundraising-for-charities/ (Accessed on May 20, 2019).

Lumberg, J. (2017). A History of Impact Investing, *Investopedia.* Available at: https://www.investopedia.com/news/history-impact-investing/#ixzz4xTHt2p00.

Mirchandani, B. (2018). Voices from the field: Social Impact Bonds and the search for ways to finance public sector R&D, *Nonprofit Quarterly*. Available at: https://nonprofitquarterly.org/2018/03/30/voices-field-social-impact-bonds-search-ways-finance-public-sector-rd/

Mollick, E. (2014). The dynamics of crowdfunding: An exploratory study, *Journal of Business Venturing*, 29(1), 1–16.

Nicholls, A., Paton, R., and Emerson, J. (eds.). (2015). *Social Finance*. Oxford: Oxford University Press.

Nicholls, A., and Tomkinson, E. (2015). The Peterborough Pilot Social Impact Bond, in Nicholls, A., Paton, R. and Emerson, J. (eds.) *Social Finance*. Oxford: Oxford University Press, pp. 335–380.

Nonprofit Finance Fund. (2019). *Pay for Success: The First 25*. Available at: https://nff.org/sites/default/files/paragraphs/file/download/pay-for-success-first-25.pdf?mc_cid=be6d2d4ba4&mc_eid=36bc6a7aea.

Pandey, S., Cordes, J. J., Pandey, S. K., and Winfrey, W. F. (2018). Use of social impact bonds to address social problems: Understanding contractual risks and transaction costs, *Nonprofit Management and Leadership*, 28(4), 511–528.

Renko, M., Moss, T., and Llloyd, A. (2019). Crowdfunding by Non-profit and Social Ventures, in Landström, H., Parhankangas, A., and Mason, C. (eds.) *Handbook of Research on Crowdfunding*. Cheltenham: Edward Elgar.

Schinckus, C. (2018). The valuation of social impact bonds: An introductory perspective with the Peterborough SIB, *Research in International Business and Finance*, 45, 1–6.

Schmidt, Elizabeth. (2010). Vermont's social hybrid pioneers: Early observation and questions to ponder, *Vermont Law Review*, 35(1), 163–209.

Simon, J. G., Powers, C. W., and Gunnemann, J. P. (1972). *The Ethical Investor*. New Haven, CT: Yale University Press.

The Rockefeller Foundation. (2019). The Bellagio Center. https://www.rockefellerfoundation.org/our-work/bellagio-center

Thurridl, C., and Kamleitner, B. (2016). What goes around comes around? Rewards as Strategic assets in crowdfunding, *California Management Review*, 58(2), 88–110.

Toepler, S. (2018a). Public philanthropic partnerships: The changing nature of government/foundation relationships in the US, *International Journal of Public Administration*, 41(8), 657–669.

Toepler, S. (2018b). Do benefit corporations represent a policy threat to nonprofits? *Nonprofit Policy Forum*, 9(4), 1–9.

Trelstad, B. (2016). Impact investing: A brief history, *Capitalism & Society*, 11(2).

UNEP Finance Initiative. (2019). About the PRI. Available at: https://www.unpri.org/about-the-pri/about-the-pri/322.article.

UnLtd. (2019). Our Story so Far. Available at: https://www.unltd.org.uk/about-us/what-we-do/

Zhao, M., and Han, J. (2019). Tensions and risks of social enterprises' scaling strategies: The case of microfinance institutions in China, *Journal of Social Entrepreneurship*, doi:10.1080/19420676.2019.1604404

Zhao, Y., Harris, P., and Lam, W. (2019). Crowdfunding industry – History, development, policies, and potential issues, *Journal of Public Affairs*, 19(1921), 1–9.

34

HYBRIDITY

Origins and effects

Gorgi Krlev

POSTDOCTORAL RESEARCHER, CENTRE FOR SOCIAL INVESTMENT (CSI),
UNIVERSITY OF HEIDELBERG, HEIDELBERG, GERMANY

Helmut K. Anheier

PROFESSOR, HERTIE SCHOOL, BERLIN, GERMANY, AND LUSKIN
SCHOOL OF PUBLIC AFFAIRS, UCLA, CA, USA

Introduction

Hybridity has become a growing focus in management and governance research generally, and it has achieved increasing attention across theories and research fields (see Battilana, Besharov, & Mitzinneck, 2017, for a comprehensive overview). Fields of study include business ethics (e.g., Haigh & Hoffman, 2012), nonprofit sector research (e.g., Brandsen, Donk, & Putters, 2005; Cooney, 2006; Smith, 2010), public management (e.g., Caldwell, Roehrich, & George, 2017; Thomasson, 2009), political economy (e.g., Koppell, 2010), and organization studies (e.g., Battilana & Lee, 2014; Clegg & Courpasson, 2004; Fosfuri, Giarratana, & Roca, 2016; Hasenfeld & Gidron, 2005; Pache & Santos, 2013). Among the dominant theoretical approaches are neo-institutionalism (e.g., Mair & Marti, 2009), welfare regimes (e.g., Anheier & Krlev, 2014; Evers, 2005), and entrepreneurship (e.g., Austin, Stevenson, & Wei-Skillern, 2006; Battilana & Dorado, 2010; Steyaert & Hjorth, 2006).

Despite variations in focuses and approaches the research shares a central thread: Hybridity is seen against the notion of a traditional steady state of form purity – be it the Weberian public agency (1978), the Coaseian business firm (1937), or the Titmuss voluntary agency (1970). The argument being that organizational forms once distinct are becoming less distinguishable, with sector borders fuzzier (Billis, 2010; Evers, 2005) – be it public agencies seeking greater fee income, nonprofits assuming nearly statutory functions, social entrepreneurs creating start-ups, or public–private partnerships of many kinds. What is more, hybridity by diversifying the directive orders governing organizations (Alford & Friedland, 1985) is seen as something less stable, yet more complex and tension-ridden, and ultimately more of a transitory nature. And while hybridization is mostly viewed in a positive light (Anheier & Krlev, 2015), it also produces greater management and governance issues, for instance accountability disorders (Koppell, 2005) or more demanding prerequisites for leadership (Schröer & Jäger, 2011).

The civil society context is among the most frequent settings of hybridity research, which in this strand looks at how nonprofits start to deviate from their prototypical outfit and practices by combining seemingly incompatible elements (see Battilana & Lee, 2014; Billis, 2010; Cornforth & Spear, 2010; Hasenfeld & Gidron, 2005). To date scholars mostly focused on how hybrids are managed and governed (see for instance the special issue by Anheier & Krlev, 2015). Although the literature has probed into the origins, task environments, and behaviors of hybrids (Battilana et al., 2017), it has often been only loosely coupled to the theoretical repertoire of organization studies, with some exceptions (Haveman & Rao, 2006). Therefore, guided by the literature on organizational evolution and ecologies (Aldrich & Ruef, 2006; Hannan, Pólos, & Carroll, 2007; Romanelli, 1991), we explore the question: *What does extant research tell us about the context conditions in which hybrids occur, and how do these relate to existing knowledge about organizations' forms and practices in response to their environments?* Second, and in the tradition of new institutionalism, which suggests that organizations assimilate to others due to isomorphic pressures (DiMaggio & Powell, 1983) and thereby gain legitimacy (Heugens & Lander, 2009), we probe the question: *Do hybrids, as a perceptibly new organizational phenomenon, conform with or deviate from what we know about the typical interplay between field structure and organizational agency?*

Our analysis suggests that hybridization can be seen as a procedural evolution that increases organizations' acting capacity within dynamic context conditions and complex task environments. This comes at the expense of higher transaction costs of management, which are however accepted, even embraced, as a necessary trade-off. What is more, hybrids willingly enter continuous struggles for legitimacy and seem to favor contingency fit over institutional fit with their field. This means they seek to align more with the tasks to be achieved than with what is demanded by them from their field. Often they temporarily defy both reference frames with the goal of changing their field environment according to their own example and avoid the need to adapt themselves. This may bring hybrids to the brink of organizational collapse. Hybridization and the practices associated with it are thus a potent process for organizations, in particular as regards the capacity to cope with challenging field conditions, or even changing the rules of the game. But hybridization may also increase organizations' fragility.

Hybridity: Where does it come from and what does it lead to?

A persistent challenge in the study of hybrids is the ambiguity in the very definition of what constitutes hybridity. Most studies of both the nature and consequences of hybridity take on an institutional logics perspective (Friedland & Alford, 1991; Thornton, Ocasio, & Lounsbury, 2012), be it conceptual articles (see Besharov & Smith, 2014; Seibel, 2015; Skelcher & Smith, 2015, the last one with some deviation) or empirical work (Kim, Shin, & Jeong, 2016; Pache & Santos, 2013). The potential clash of logics is undoubtedly an important definitional criterion of hybridity (Battilana & Lee, 2014). It has been quite prominently studied in relation to work integration organizations that seek to be "enterprising" and "caring" at the same time (Battilana, Sengul, Pache, & Model, 2015; Bode, Evers, & Schulz, 2006; Pache & Santos, 2013; Vidal, 2005). There is increasing evidence that hybrids find ways of maintaining organizational stability even under competing logics, for instance by "selective coupling" of elements that to a varying intensity speak to the multiple stakeholders engaged (Pache & Santos, 2013). Other strategies are "strategic defiance" and "innovation" to harness or revert tensions where logics or stakeholder preferences clash (Mair, Mayer, & Lutz, 2015, also Jay, 2013). In yet other cases, logics might remain incompatible or at least "uncombined" and continue to exist in parallel but on their own. Skelcher and Smith (2015) speak of "segregated" or "blocked" types of hybrids. Besharov and Smith (2014) suggest there are situations where logics are "contested" and lead to a high level of conflicts. All these cases, one might argue, point at cases of weak, temporary, or unstable hybridity that are likely to fall back into states of non-hybridity in the longer term. Overall, the literature provides advanced knowledge on strategies employed by hybrids to maintain organizational stability as well as it outlines cases where hybridity might not be lasting. Less attention has been given to the questions of why hybridity emerges at all as well as how hybridization may affect organization-field interactions, in other words the connection between social structure and organizational agency.

Conditions of emergence

While hybridity is the property of a given organization, its causes and wider consequences may be less so, and more likely found in the immediate task environment and the wider organizational field. Literature on organizational ecologies has provided us with a conceptual and theoretical repertoire potentially relevant to the study of hybridity (Minkoff, 2002). It has discussed refunctionality and recombinations of organizational and institutional traits, punctuated equilibria and major change in organizational fields as well as inertia of actors in these fields, or organizational niching strategies (Gersick, 1991; Hannan et al., 2007; Hannan & Freeman, 1977; Romanelli, 1991; Romanelli & Tushman, 1994; Tushman & O'Reilly, 2002).

Much of that applies to hybridity: Hybrids seem an example of recombinant innovation of organizational types and practices, and they apply processes in their management and governance that are non-standard. The emergence of hybridizing also coincides with changes in surrounding environments. There clearly is a stronger awareness of and urge to address what has been described as wicked problems some time ago (Churchman, C. West, 1967) and has recently been re-labeled "grand challenges" of our time (Ferraro, Etzion, & Gehman, 2015). The economic crisis of 2008 and other events have done their part in driving the perceived urgency of finding new responses, one result of that being the blend of separated worlds visible in the merging of "care" and "capitalism" (Barman, 2016), "social" and "investment" (Nicholls, 2010a), or "government control" and "enterprise" (Koppell, 2001). Although these are broad trends affecting organizations, hybridity to date seems to remain the exception rather than the rule in view of organizational populations more broadly. Genuine hybridity is hard to find with the label being used by some only as a signaling device (Mair et al., 2015). It is thus (still) a niching strategy.

While the above reflections provide some idea of what hybridity is accompanied by, it is less certain what conditions in particular hybridity has evolved as a response to. Literature on the evolution of organizational forms can help explore reasons for the emergence of hybridity (see Anheier, 2014, on form evolution in the context of nonprofit studies). That literature makes one point in particular: Some task environments lead to specific and dominant organizational forms rather than others (Aldrich & Ruef, 2006). The prototypical organizational form in settled context conditions and established institutional fields would be the U-form according to organizational theorists. Under such conditions, organizations are handled by what Mintzberg (1983) identified as the professional bureaucracy, whereby dominant professions assume control and succeed in organizational capture, e.g., the professoriate in universities, or the medical profession in hospitals. Based on what theory tells us, hybridity may occur but is unlikely to be strong and prevail in such contexts, although there certainly have been shifts in how universities, in particular in the medical sciences, engineering and business departments, need to behave nowadays with evidence of hybridity occurring (Jongbloed, 2015; also Murray, 2010; Schildt & Perkmann, 2016). Hybridity may also occur after punctuated equilibria, but remain transitory as dominant stakeholders are likely to emerge, e.g., curators reassuming control of a museum after a financial crisis when the chief finance officer took charge, or a school district in temporary receivership.

For Chandler (1990) and Powell (1990), the emergence of the M-form and later the N-form were responses to shifts in task environments and fields – in other words the supply and demand conditions and the constraints and opportunities presented. Powell posits, and this has been confirmed later, that there is no single explanation for the emergence of the network form (see Jones, Hesterly, & Borgatti, 1997, as an example of theory building or Reficco & Marquez, 2012, for recent empirical research). Rather it is dependent on a number of factors, among which the reduction of transaction costs is not a primary aim. The reverse seems true. Networks "actually increase transaction costs, but in return they provide concrete benefits or intangible assets that are far more valuable," among them "[t]he reduction of uncertainty, fast access to information, reliability, and responsiveness" (Powell, 1990, p. 323).

The question for hybridity then becomes: what supply and demand conditions (and the legal, regulatory, social, and political factors implied) have made the emergence of multiple stakeholder configurations and shifts in agency within organizations more likely?

Interplay between field structure and agency

There is an age long debate on whether the course organizations take is determined by themselves or actually the result of forces located at the field level (DiMaggio & Powell, 1983). Heugens and Lander's (2009) meta-analysis on the question provides some key insights, which confirm, relativize, and extend our knowledge in this regard. First, they relativize the implications of institutional theory by concluding that "organizations enjoy at least some discretion in crafting responses to institutional processes" (Heugens & Lander, 2009, p. 76). At the same time, they confirm the central claim of institutional theory, namely that conformity with templates for organizing available in organizational fields, increases organizations' symbolic performance, that is legitimacy. More surprisingly, they extend institutional theory in finding that isomorphism not only levers organizations' symbolic performance, but has direct effects on their substantive performance. This latter effect was reproduced in later empirical studies, for instance in Miller et al.'s (2012) work on strategic conformity among Fortune 1000 firms, which increased returns on assets. It has also been confirmed in Volberda et al.'s (2011) examination of the link between the institutional fit and performance of 1,904 Dutch companies.

What Volberda and colleagues bring to the table as an important add-on is the discussion of contingency fit – defined as the match between the organization's technology, structure and culture and its task environment – on firm performance. From their combined investigation of institutional fit and contingency fit, the authors deduct synergies when both contingency fit and institutional fit are increased, and a potential for hedging one against the other in periods of misfit. Under conditions of "suddenly unfamiliar task and institutional environments, such as in cases of radical innovation [. . .], and radical regulatory reform" (Volberda et al., 2011, p. 1051), their data suggests organizations will be better off fixing institutional misfit before contingency misfit. So essentially, they suggest mimicking the industry leaders in phases of turmoil pays off more for organizations, at least in the short run, than finding adequate responses to changes in the environment. This enlightens an open question, which Heugens and Lander (2009) have pointed out, namely that of whether substantive performance is spurred by both competitive isomorphism – as a result of a survival of the fittest within organizational fields – and mimicry, that is deliberate assimilation to acquire legitimacy. Volberda et al.'s evidence suggests that mimicking can have significant effects on substantive performance.

A debate of these issues has started to unfold within the study of hybridized organizational phenomena. Nicholls (2010b) sensitized scholars of social entrepreneurship, inarguably the research area with the most frequent references to hybridity (Doherty, Haugh, & Lyon, 2014), to the "reflexive isomorphism" observable in the field and promoted by resource-rich actors within the discourses of "philathrocapitalism" and "marketization." Steyaert and Dey (2010) and later Ruebottom (2013) echo the prevalence of "hero narratives" in the field. However, it is not only the observers and advocates shaping the institutional structures of the field who deliberately push such narratives. Ruebottom gives insights on how organizations operating on the ground employed strategic rhetoric dichotomizing practices of protagonists and antagonists in a struggle for improved solutions to social challenges. Dart has put forth much earlier that "social enterprise" as a label has gained moral legitimacy, in particular in the Anglo-Saxon context, by assimilating to "business structures and market models [that] have become a sine qua non" (Dart, 2004, p. 419, in relation to Kuttner, 1999).

Mair et al.'s (2015) findings sensitize us for the fact that there might be more to this. Among those signaling to be part of the protagonists of a supposedly hybrid field, there are differences in whether and how far hybridity is effectively embodied within the organization. While Mair and colleagues find that some organizations behave and look more like "ideal types" of organizations, others deviate significantly from them, for instance in terms of board composition and stakeholders' strategic engagement. It therefore stands to reason that there will be variation in how hybrids deal with the challenge of gaining legitimacy. While seeming hybrids in particular are likely to behave as organizations at large because they resemble more than they differ from them, that is favor institutional fit over contingency fit in relation to their field, this seems less clear with regard to genuine hybrids.

The question as regards hybrids' agency relative to field structure then results in: does hybridization in organizations trigger behavior in relation to their institutional environment that is different to what institutional theory would generally suggest?

Method

To answer the questions on hybrids' origins and behavior, we review recent and prominent empirical studies of hybridity. To compile this collection of studies, we carried out a literature review, which was completed in November 2017 and is documented in the Appendix to this chapter. After the initial steps of the search, a subsequent screening of the remaining papers revealed that the label "hybridity" referred to a range of aspects – spanning from human resource issues within organizations, to inter-organizational collaboration, to the hybrid nature of market arrangements. There was a wide range of thematic focuses too, with the effects of multiple institutional logics being most prominent.

We therefore structured the remaining papers with regards to two dimensions (see also Table 34.2 in the Appendix): (1) the subject of research, comprising (a) institutional logics, (b) governance of hybrids, (c) organizational learning, and (d) organizational change; and (2) the level of analysis ranging from (a) cross-level investigations with sporadic insights on hybridity within organizations, to (b) the field level (for instance markets) abstracting largely from individual organizations, to (c) issues of structures and management in organizations relative to their surrounding field, to (d) studies within organizations relating to groups or individual practices. While the first dimension was mainly meant to highlight key research themes, the second dimension served as a selection criterion with an obvious focus on studies in the (c) and (d) categories.

Further in line with our research focus, we made sure that articles in the final selection gave sufficient detail on the individual organization so as to allow judgment on their state of hybridity and the effects of hybridization. We therefore excluded quantitative studies that dealt with hybridity in an aggregated way or qualitative ones that performed superficial analyses for the sake of illustration only.

The eventual sample comprised 13 articles which are summarized in Table 34.1, including a short reference to the type of organization the articles deal with. We then performed an analysis

Table 34.1 Final sample of empirical articles

Author & Year	Title	Journal	Organizational focus
Ashforth & Reingen, 2014	Functions of Dysfunction	ASQ	Natural food cooperative
Battilana & Dorado, 2010	Building Sustainable Hybrid Organizations	AMJ	Microfinance organizations
Battilana et al., 2015	Harnessing Productive Tensions in Hybrid Organizations	AMJ	Work integration social enterprises
Cooney, 2006	The Institutional and Technical Structuring of Nonprofit Ventures	Voluntas	Social enterprise in the field of welfare-to-work projects
Foreman & Whetten, 2002	Members' Identification with Multiple-Identity Organizations	Org. Science	Rural cooperatives
Hockerts, 2015	How Hybrid Organizations Turn Antagonistic Assets into Complementarities	CMR	Work integration social enterprise, base-of the pyramid, fair trade
Hustinx & Waele, 2015	Managing Hybridity in a Changing Welfare Mix	Voluntas	"Social grocery" project in entrepreneurial non-profit
Jay, 2013	Navigating Paradox as a Mechanism of Change and Innovation in Hybrid Organizations	AMJ	Public–private Cambridge Energy Alliance
Liu & Ko, 2012	Organizational Learning and Marketing Capability Development	NVSQ	Charity-retailers as social enterprises
Pache & Santos, 2013	Inside the Hybrid Organization	AMJ	Work integration social enterprises
Schemeil, 2013	Bringing International Organization In	Org. Studies	International organizations
Tracey & Phillips, 2016	Managing the Consequences of Organizational Stigmatization	AMJ	Social enterprise working with migrants
York et al., 2016	Exploring Environmental Entrepreneurship	JMS	Environmental entrepreneurs in renewable energy

of the selected papers as to conditions of emergence and structure-agency interactions relative to the organizations' field.

Why and where hybridization occurs

Schemeil (2013) in his study of a variety of international organizations (including for example nonprofit human rights organizations) examines their ways to persist in highly unstable environments. He describes these organizations as complex, multifaceted, and multileveled entities and finds that those able to overcome states of vulnerability and episodes due to changing circumstances exhibit strong traits of hybridity. Schemeil refers to the redefinition of organizational mission, mandate enlargement, and engagement in large and durable but changing networks in particular. Jay's (2013) study of a public–private partnership to promote energy efficiency goes further. It posits the evolution of varying stakeholder influence, at different points in time, which enables hybrids not only to navigate challenging environments; instead it enables organizations to innovate on paradoxes evolving during the process, such as the ambiguity whether certain outcomes are to be judged as a success or a failure, for instance the indirect effects of reducing energy use outside the own coalition of partners. The realization that provisioned organizational identities such as that of a business provider were not compatible with the emergent paradoxes did not hamper but spur further transformations and positive externalities as well as other innovations within the alliance.

Similarly, Hockerts (2015) study of three distinct types of hybrids looks at the ways in which they can reverse disadvantageous situations into more favorable ones, by challenging and adapting the predominant perspective on existing challenges. More specifically, by employing new and different cognitive models, hybrids create demands for antagonistic assets, such as disability, autism. Hockerts shows that harnessing rather than opposing seeming deficiencies enables hybrids' readiness to thrive in highly competitive markets such as software testing. Tracey and Phillips (2016) examine how hybrids manage to resist even more unfavorable context conditions. They study how a social enterprise redeemed its organizational identity after stigmatization by its local community. After the social enterprise they study had initiated a support program for migrants, the organization was blamed for "supporting an unwelcome group" by the original community it served. Key to overcoming this stigmatization were the internal organizational dynamics initiated by the social enterprise's management. Advocacy and valorization contributed to a new shared identity of social justice among staff and beneficiaries, which built on the revised perception of migrants being providers rather than users of public services through prospects of future jobs and *contributions to* rather than *use of* social welfare systems. Through this process, the organization did not only create profits for itself and its target group, but succeed in convincing market players to recognize the value of underutilized resources. It thus extended its market share and social impact at the same time.

Hybridity as an organizational property furthermore enables actors to fulfill the demands of, and actively involve, a diverse range of internal and external stakeholders. This can be observed in fields as disparate as work integration (Pache & Santos, 2013) and renewable energy production (Patriotta, Gond, & Schultz, 2011, without an explicit focus on hybridity and thus not in the review). Pache and Santos show how a "selective coupling" of logics can be used to deal with competing claims and expectations, while York et al. (2016) describe hybrid ventures that enable "self-selection" by all potential stakeholders. With the latter, York et al. refer to the practice of deliberately formulating a wide set of goals and allowing for a wide range of interpretations, so that as many stakeholders as possible can identify with the organizations. These examples support the reasoning that hybrids have an enhanced ability to master and utilize challenging environments for their organizational purposes.

The enabling functions of hybridity come at the cost of trade-offs in organizational management. Ashforth and Reingen (2014) provide valuable insights into processes on the group and individual level in a hybrid organization. In their analysis of a natural food cooperative, the authors identify patterned social–psychological dynamics in which the duality between pragmatism and idealism plays out. The cooperative achieved sustainable functionality at the organizational level only at the expense of partial dysfunctionality at the group level. Members' unease with a hybrid identity led to "mission splits," in which members claimed either cooperative ideals or business practices for themselves and projected the logic they embraced less onto others. This led to serious inter- and intragroup conflicts. Battilana and Dorado's (2010) study of two pioneering commercial microfinance organizations, too, points at the increased effort that needs to be put into managing hybrid organizations placed in emergent industries. The authors describe targeted hiring and socialization policies as important "early levers" to achieve a durable balance between the conflicting logics of development and banking, to rule out fundamental incompatibilities in stakeholder preferences and to avoid mission drift.

Battilana et al. (2015) analyze internal identity challenges that hybrids face in the context of work integration social enterprises. The authors emphasize the favorable function of "spaces of negotiation" as arenas of interaction that allowed sub-groups in an organization to discuss the trade-offs they faced by the hybrid nature of the enterprise. By structurally differentiating between groups of different responsibilities in the organization and by carefully coordinating their frequent meetings and exchange, intra-organizational conflict was mitigated and transformed into productive tension. In addition to mandatory meetings and formal processes, social events such as annual collective company retreats were needed to support "socialization" and "nurture conviviality." Cooney (2006) sheds light on another complication that may arise in hybrids in the field of work integration. Organizations in the field may struggle to combine the demands from the social service field, such as meeting grant requirements, with demands from the business field, such as operating according to efficient production schedules that are prerequisite in the industrial niches in which the enterprises compete. The challenge here is not only competing demands, but also that the two action fields "move at a different pace" (Cooney, 2006, p. 157).

How hybrids behave in relation to their field

Hustinx and de Waele's (2015) study on managing practices in an entrepreneurial nonprofit social grocery illustrates how adverse organizational identities can pose severe threats to a venture's legitimacy. The particularity of the case lies in that people who had deep experience with poverty were enabled through a participatory process that built strongly on volunteer engagement to deliver services to people currently living in poverty. As a result of an institutional environment focused on principles of (social) innovation and entrepreneurship, the organization developed a model of "blended hybridity," combining a managerial logic with its original emancipatory one. This hybridity was held up high and presented to stakeholders for its symbolic function, with the eventual goal to change the institutional environment. To live up to the expectations of stakeholders that were meant to be served by this model, strong elements of the managerial logic were implemented and maintained in everyday practices. To meet managerial requirements, staff applied latent categorization and differential involvement of participants/volunteers. Staff members often took over tasks themselves instead of providing supportive assistance to participants, and even pragmatically ex- and included participants, if that was to the economic benefit of the organization. It did so risking temporary organizational dysfunction through conflicting demands, sometimes referred to as "blocked hybridity" (Hustinx & Waele, 2015, in relation to Skelcher & Smith, 2015).

Elucidating the structural tensions that can emerge inside hybrid organizations and between them and their environment, Cooney (2006) too refers to threats to legitimacy stemming from the managerial logic and commercial pressures to the venture that might at first be accepted for gaining more access to resources and a wider standing. Her case study of a US nonprofit organization in work integration points out how a strategic response to one of the main tensions produced by hybridity threatened the organization's viability. The nonprofit tried to balance conflicts between providing effective service to its work integration clients and the commercial pressures in the worksites by scaling the business in the hope that this would be to the benefit of both goals. However, this led to an erosion of integrity towards those stakeholders that were more interested in social service provision and thereby undermined its legitimacy substantively. Despite the resulting threat, the organization maintained its practice without giving in to either extreme. It managed to do so by operating on a multidivisional structure exerted simultaneously to competitive isomorphism, or contingency fit for that matter, and institutional isomorphism, yet with varying intensity and priorities over time.

Foreman and Whetten's (2002) study underscores this very point with a more narrow focus on different types of members within rural cooperatives and how shifts in their perceptions about the hybrid character of such organizations may affect legitimacy. The authors develop a model in which a members' organizational identification is conceptualized by an identity comparison process, that is a match between members' perception of what an organization is and what it should be, relative to and influenced by its context. They apply this model empirically and find that rural cooperatives, embodying both business and family identities, are challenged by the need to secure organizational identity congruence. If members of the coop conceived experienced and ideal identities as incongruent, this had significant effects on member commitment as well as cognitive and pragmatic legitimacy granted by the members. A similar process of legitimacy formation is what Jay (2013) refers to when highlighting the role of "sensemaking" between involved stakeholders and subsequent form transitions in his study of the public–private Cambridge Energy Alliance. In his case, stakeholders were able to harness tensions in productive ways and turn them into sources of innovation, which helped secure or open new channels of legitimacy.

Finally, Liu and Ko's (2012) work which examines charity retailers' ability to employ marketing capabilities in creating rather than acquiring legitimacy for the hybrid venture. The authors identify learning and knowledge accumulation as the most central elements in the process of implementing marketing instruments into charities to make them more apt for performing to the expectations of a wider range of stakeholders. At the same time radical or controversial innovations such as "providing bonus incentives for salespeople" are unlikely to be implemented into hybridized nonprofits "until most of their stakeholders (i.e., donors, volunteers, customers, and so on) in the sector collectively shift their perspectives about how charity retail stores should be operated" (Liu & Ko, 2012, p. 603).

Discussion

Conceptualizing conditions of emergence

The synthesis of research provided on *conditions of emergence* suggests that hybridity increases organizations' ability to navigate dynamic context conditions and to manage complex task environments. Dynamism (Burns & Stalker, 1994), referring to the rate of change in fields, means that stakeholders may come up with different assessments and hence goals and strategies given the volatility of the field, and the constraints and opportunities involved. Field conditions of dynamism are to be found when there is a perceptional shift on what represents a viable solution, for instance the idea of exploiting assets that might otherwise be thought of as a liability (such as disabled employees). Dynamism is also found in fields that demand high degrees of innovation, such as renewable energy production. Other conditions can give rise to or involve dynamism too: Purdy and Gray (2009) for instance showed how multilevel dynamics, including interactions between entrepreneurial incidents as well as strategic positioning of new entrants versus incumbents, allowed multiple practices to evolve in the emergence of state offices for dispute resolution. Dunn and Jones (2010) analyzed how distinct groups of interest created dynamic tensions in how training of the medical profession should be shaped by pushing their favored logic of science or care respectively, including fluctuations over time.

Complexity, following Perrow (1979), addresses the number of elements and their interactions in task environments that stakeholders, and especially management, need take into account. In complex environments, stakeholders may be more likely to focus on some elements closer to their objectives than others, whereas in simpler environments such differences are less pronounced. What I refer to as complexity in task environments shares some commonalities with what is referred to as "institutional complexity" (Greenwood, Raynard, Kodeih, Micelotta, & Lounsbury, 2011) or "institutional plurality" (Schildt & Perkmann, 2016), but it is also distinct from those terms. Complexity in relation to hybrids seems to refer to the number of different tasks that must be dealt with simultaneously (Scott, 1992, p. 230), and not only clashes between incompatible logics, or the need to span and integrate a number of hierarchical levels (Anderson, 1999).

The above two elements, in combination with others, have been used to establish a matrix of different kinds of environments long since (Jurkovich, 1974). In short: Hybridization occurs when organizations invite and propel shifts in their active engagement with a range of stakeholders, which pursue different interests. They do so in order to cope with context conditions that are marked by (1) high rates and/or profundity of change occurring (dynamism) and (2) which demand simultaneous engagement at different levels of activity (complexity).

Schemeil's (2013) research has shown that hybridization was key to the organizations' adaptability to external change and empowered them to resist a potential lock-down through dominant stakeholder interests. Their ability to mobilize extensive internal and external resources at scale levered their ability to act within adverse context conditions. While hybrids may encounter as well as produce paradoxes, their multi-stakeholder nature and shifts in agency supports reflection on such paradoxes and makes them able to transform tensions into mechanisms of change. While Jay concludes that "innovation is by no means a guaranteed outcome of hybridity and navigating paradox" (Jay, 2013, p. 153), his study implies that hybrids are better positioned to adapt to dynamism and utilize complexity than non-hybrids. Hockerts' (2015) conclusion is that processes of hybridization can help organizations take on new viewpoints that do not only lever their own competitiveness but are to the benefit of those possessing antagonistic assets. A process of valorization could be initiated by the organization Tracey and Phillips (2016) dealt with due to its hybrid nature. The initiative of management and joint identity work among a group of internal and external stakeholders led to a reversal of stigma out of a major organizational crisis, more specifically to identity affirmation and resource augmentation speaking to the social welfare and business worlds alike.

In relation to organizational ecologies, hybridity might be seen as a procedural – since it lacks a characteristic organizational form and is marked by particular processes taking place – rather than a form evolution in response to field conditions. In consequence, the occurrence of hybridization is a function of greater dynamism in organizational fields and greater complexity in task environments. Conversely, rates would drop and conversions to non-hybridity increase as environments become less dynamic and complex. The procedural evolution of hybridization results in an increase in acting capacity in view of outcomes required in such environments. It enables the mobilization of different expertise and resources and invites renewed "search processes" of multiple stakeholders to find proposals to further their respective goals.

In contrast to what Schildt and Perkmann (2016) suggest, hybridization does not seem to be a merely temporary change process in the transition from one organizational settlement to another, but an adaptable procedure permanently upheld by some organizations or actor coalitions (see Chemin & Vercher, 2011, for the latter). While the formation of network structures represents a constellation *between* loosely coupled actors to respond to such circumstances (Powell, 1990), hybridization looks like a similar phenomenon occurring *within* organizations relative to their field environment. Curiously, it includes a tighter relational coupling of involved stakeholders on the one hand, but a less clearly embodied form and greater variability in its outfit, on the other, depending on fields of activity and even changing over time.

At the same time, hybridization complicates the management of the organization in that the shifts in stakeholder agency also produce higher costs in coordination and decision making. In Ashforth and Reingen's case (2014) some individuals had to act as "lightning rods" to absorb conflict so as to secure organizational survival. To maintain the organizational duality, the organization furthermore had to oscillate decisions and allow for frequent power shifts that resulted in tensions which had to be moderated by conflict management and persistent promotion of tolerance, respect, and forgiveness to maintain and repair damaged relationships. Bridging professional fields can play a role too. In Battilana and Dorado's (2010) case investments of considerable time and resources into training, promotion, and incentive systems were needed to "socialize" bank managers. In the less successful of their two cases, the failure to create a shared identity led to identity schisms, which needed to be mitigated by a significant number of control procedures. These in turn had negative effects on employees' work performance and commitment. What is more, when vulnerable staff is employed, hybrids are forced to hedge market risks and threats that might arise from broader economic cycles to protect their personnel (Cooney, 2006); a circumstance rendering them more inflexible and complicating effective strategizing.

In return for greater acting capacity with supposedly positive effects on the outcome level, hybrids typically have to cope with higher transaction costs in three areas: (1) procedural management and coordination; (2) strategizing and decision making; (3) stakeholder communication and conflict management. The performance uncertainty for management in multiple stakeholder configurations suggests a high potential for organizational failures, inviting contract defects (e.g., moral hazards, gaming, shirking, creaming), select satisficing, rent-seeking, and other strategies.

Conceptualizing behavior

The within organization struggles triggered by hybridization find some counterparts in relation to the field level. As to what we've learned here about the *relation between organizational agency and field structure*, hybrids seem to exhibit a range of behaviors, which are not in line with what existing research suggests. Applying different institutional logics and inviting different stakeholders to take precedence over the organizations' actions, entails a high degree of risk. The legitimization processes triggered by hybridization may bring the organization to the brink of collapse. This applies in particular when, although maintaining a state of hybridity, shifts in logics and agency make the organization sway away from the expectations of those stakeholders originally vital to the organization's survival, such as beneficiaries, regulators, or civil society at large. But the practice of doing just that – namely operating at this brink with constant renewals of legitimation processes – seems to be the rule rather than the exception for hybrids.

Foreman and Whetten (2002) argue that the dynamics of legitimacy with regard to hybrids is best understood by applying "organizational form-level identification," referring to an analysis that spans not only individual, group, and organization levels but extends to organizational form. What I've done here is take it a step further to include not only the latter, but also field level interactions. While benefiting the efficiency of operations in the short term, "more fundamental and less tangible 'social' goals were overruled" by the shift to hybridity that Hustinx and Waele

(2015, p. 1687) describe. This happened at the expense of legitimacy granted by the original core stakeholders, outside as well as within the organization. In this case, the organization acted in the interest of what seemed to be needed to provide an improved solution to the challenge of poverty, and disregarded what had typically been regarded as legitimate. In other words, the organization favored contingency fit over institutional fit and thus behaved contrary to Volberda et al.'s (2011) findings within established institutional fields.

Jay's (2013) research highlights that continuous innovation was needed to secure legitimacy of the energy alliance. The very fact that innovation was needed points at the risky nature of hybrids' struggle for organizational stability and evolution. In his case, the alliance underwent so fundamental changes over time that it temporarily defied both contingency and institutional fits, in order to affect the field in more fundamental ways by changing the rules of the game. Liu and Ko (2012) point into a similar direction. They show that if hybrids move too fast, they risk losing legitimacy altogether and they need to invest in producing mind shifts among stakeholders before they take action. This might make them risk-averse and sluggish at times, but enables them to actively create new patterns of legitimacy rather than having to adapt to available templates. What hybrids thus engage in are acts of (trans-)forming institutions. These acts typically range from micro practices referred to as institutional work (Lawrence & Suddaby, 2006; Lawrence, Suddaby, & Leca, 2010), to the grander designs of organizations' institutional strategies referring to a "comprehensive set of plans and actions" (Marquis & Raynard, 2015) or field level processes of institutional entrepreneurship (e.g., DiMaggio, 1988; Garud, Hardy, & Maguire, 2016).

Suddaby, Saxton, and Gunz (2015) for instance study how social media activities of professional firms can be seen as institutional work that has led to domain changes, here an extension and redefinition of expertise in the field of accounting. Lawrence and Dover show how institutional work, the purposeful influence of actors on "higher-order social arrangements that involve both patterns of activity and symbolic systems that infuse that activity with meaning" (2015, p. 372, in relation to Friedland & Alford, 1991), has contributed to forming local alliances in the provision of housing for the hard-to-house. Zietsma and Lawrence (2010) studied the institutional work involved in transforming the practices in the British Columbia coastal forestry industry. These underwent fundamental changes from institutional stability surrounding clearcutting until the 1990s to an institutional re-stabilization based on eco-system-based management in 2006. The evidence gathered on the agency of hybrids in relation to field structure shares some commonalities with these studies, in particular in view of the importance of individuals as agents of institutional change and the micro processes involved (Suddaby, 2010). There are also differences however: While all the cited research mainly looks at the reshaping of practice norms through "embedded agency" within established fields, hybrids are often placed between fields, or as Cooney (2006, p. 159) has suggested create new fields: while "functionally straddl[ing] both social service and business organizational fields [...] hybrid organizations are increasingly occupying their own separate organizational field."

In thus far hybridization is closer to acts of creating an institutional environment in emerging markets as discussed by Marquis and Raynard (2015). It also shares commonalities with Albertini and Muzzi's (2016) analysis of institutional entrepreneurship by low-status organizations promoting innovation in highly institutionalized fields. Hybrids' behavior appears to be a mix of more modest institutional work and more daring institutional entrepreneurship. While the latter has been criticized for presenting organizations as "hypermuscular supermen" (Suddaby, 2010, p. 15), hybrids seem to be marked by such an ambition at least to some degree. Although not explicitly about hybridity, previous work on social enterprises has shown how they engage in "institution building" (Mair & Marti, 2009) or close "institutional voids" (Mair, Marti, & Ventresca, 2012).

Conclusion

The lenses applied here have helped identify hybridity as a procedural evolution, affecting practices within organizations rather than necessarily their structure or form, in response to specific context conditions. In congruence with findings on the form evolution of networks (Powell, 1990), hybridity causes greater not lower transaction costs of management in return for greater acting capacity in view of complexity and dynamism. In contrast to Powell and others' work on networks, however, hybridization within organizations does not ease the acquisition of legitimacy and thus defy the suggestions of institutional theory that hold in many other settings. In further contrast to earlier suppositions on hybridity (Anheier & Krlev, 2015), the reviewed research suggests that hybrids' legitimacy does not stand on a broader basis than that of non-hybrids but that it is in fact much more fragile, at least until the institutional transformation hybrids seek has occurred. Such configurations and their implications represent inherently political organizations that operate under greater performance uncertainty than would be the case for those in states of non-hybridity.

The causes for such behavior at the expense of economic performance or the typical gains resulting from isomorphism (see Heugens & Lander, 2009; Miller, Le Breton-Miller, & Lester, 2012) are still unclear. In a civil society context compassion, not only to help neglected target groups (Miller, T.L. et al., 2012) but to lever effectiveness by changing the rules of the game, could play a role. However, this would require more targeted testing. This might also help enlighten the question: When is hybridity a reaction demanded by context conditions and when is it a deliberate strategy? In line with calls for studying "hybridity as a matter of degree rather than type" (Battilana et al., 2017), both the above suggest that we need better conceptualizations of different hybridization processes. These are likely to emerge only if there is more primary and in particular comparative in-depth research. The open questions also call for more sequential research that looks closely at the establishment of new or the revision of established organizational fields in relation to hybrid activity occurring in the field. Hybridization seems particularly apt a phenomenon for the conjoint application of organization ecology and institutionalism as recently advocated for by Lander and Heugens (2017). It is also a research theme where "organizational institutionalism" and "institutionalized organizationalism" (Kraatz & Block, 2008) are not only potentially but essentially symbiotic.

References

Albertini, S., & Muzzi, C. (2016). Institutional entrepreneurship and organizational innovation. *International Journal of Entrepreneurship and Innovation, 17*(2), 110–119. https://doi.org/10.1177/1465750316648578

Aldrich, H., & Ruef, M. (2006). *Organizations evolving.* London: Sage. Retrieved from http://books.google.de/books?id=DMbyE1S16kUC

Alford, R.R., & Friedland, R. (1985). *Powers of theory: Capitalism, the state, and democracy.* Cambridge: Cambridge University Press.

Anderson, P. (1999). Perspective: Complexity theory and organization science. *Organization Science, 10*(3), 216–232. https://doi.org/10.1287/orsc.10.3.216

Anheier, H.K. (2014). *Nonprofit organizations: Theory, management, policy* (2nd). London: Routledge.

Anheier, H.K., & Krlev, G. (2014). Welfare regimes, policy reforms, and hybridity: Introduction to the Special Issue. *American Behavioral Scientist, 58*(11), 1395–1411.

Anheier, H.K., & Krlev, G. (2015). Guest Editors' Introduction: Governance and management of hybrid organizations. *International Studies of Management and Organization, 45*(3), 193–206. Retrieved from 10.1080/00208825.2015.1006026

Ashforth, B.E., & Reingen, P.H. (2014). Functions of dysfunction. *Administrative Science Quarterly, 59*(3), 474–516. https://doi.org/10.1177/0001839214537811

Austin, J., Stevenson, H., & Wei-Skillern, J. (2006). Social and commercial entrepreneurship: Same, different, or both? *Entrepreneurship Theory & Practice*, *30*(1), 1–22.

Barman, E. (2016). *Caring capitalism: The meaning and measure of social value*. New York: Cambridge University Press.

Battilana, J., Besharov, M. L., & Mitzinneck. (2017). On hybrids and hybrid organizing: A review and roadmap for future research. In R. Greenwood, C. Oliver, T. B. Lawrence, & R. E. Meyer (Eds.), *The SAGE handbook of organizational institutionalism*. Los Angeles: Sage.

Battilana, J., & Dorado, S. (2010). Building sustainable hybrid organizations: The case of commercial microfinance organizations. *Academy of Management Journal*, *53*(6), 1419–1440. https://doi.org/10.5465/AMJ.2010.57318391

Battilana, J., & Lee, M. (2014). Advancing research on hybrid organizing – Insights from the study of social enterprises. *Academy of Management Annals*, *8*(1), 397–441. https://doi.org/10.1080/19416520.2014.893615

Battilana, J., Sengul, M., Pache, A.-C., & Model, J. (2015). Harnessing productive tensions in hybrid organizations: The case of work integration social enterprises. *Academy of Management Journal*, *58*(6), 1658–1685. https://doi.org/10.5465/amj.2013.0903

Besharov, M. L., & Smith, W. K. (2014). Multiple institutional logics in organizations: Explaining their varied nature and implications. *Academy of Management Review*, *39*(3), 364–381. https://doi.org/10.5465/amr.2011.0431

Billis, D. (Ed.). (2010). *Hybrid organizations and the third sector: Challenges for practice, theory and policy*. Basingstoke: Palgrave Macmillan.

Bode, I., Evers, A., & Schulz, A. (2006). Work integration social enterprises in Europe: Can hybridization be sustainable? In M. Nyssens (Ed.), *Social enterprise: At the crossroads of market, public policies and civil society* (pp. 237–258). London: Routledge.

Brandsen, T., Donk, W. van de, & Putters, K. (2005). Griffins or chameleons? Hybridity as a permanent and inevitable characteristic of the third sector. *International Journal of Public Administration*, *28*, 749–765.

Burns, T., & Stalker, G. M. (1994). *The management of innovation* (Rev. ed). Oxford: Oxford University Press.

Caldwell, N. D., Roehrich, J. K., & George, G. (2017). Social value creation and relational coordination in public–private collaborations. *Journal of Management Studies*, *50*, 930. https://doi.org/10.1111/joms.12268

Chandler, A. D. (1990). *Scale and scope: The dynamics of industrial capitalism* (1st ed.). Cambridge, MA: Harvard University Press.

Chemin, C., & Vercher, C. (2011). The challenge of activist coalition governance: Accommodating diversity to create institutions – an approach via the inter-relationships between action, project and instrument. *Voluntas: International Journal of Voluntary and Nonprofit Organizations*, *22*(4), 682. https://doi.org/10.1007/s11266-011-9201-9

Churchman, C. West. (1967). Guest Editorial: Wicked problems. *Management Science*, *14*(4), B141–B142. Retrieved from www.jstor.org/stable/2628678

Clegg, S., & Courpasson, D. (2004). Political hybrids: Tocquevillean views on project organizations. *Journal of Management Studies*, *41*(4), 525–547. https://doi.org/10.1111/j.1467-6486.2004.00443.x

Coase, R. (1937). The nature of the firm. *Economica*, *4*(16), 386–405. https://doi.org/10.1111/j.1468-0335.1937.tb00002.x

Cooney, K. (2006). The institutional and technical structuring of nonprofit ventures: Case study of a U.S. hybrid organization caught between two fields. *Voluntas: International Journal of Voluntary and Nonprofit Organizations*, *17*(2), 137–155.

Cornforth, C., & Spear, R. (2010). The governance of hybrid organizations. In D. Billis (Ed.), *Hybrid organizations and the third sector: Challenges for practice, theory and policy* (pp. 70–90). Basingstoke: Palgrave Macmillan.

Dart, R. (2004). The legitimacy of social enterprise. *Nonprofit Management and Leadership*, *14*(4), 411–424.

DiMaggio, P. (1988). Interest and agency in institutional theory. In L. G. Zucker (Ed.), *Institutional patterns and organizations: Culture and environment* (pp. 3–22). Cambridge, MA: Ballinger.

DiMaggio, P. J., & Powell, W. W. (1983). The iron cage revisited: Institutional isomorphism and collective rationality in organizational fields. *American Sociological Review*, *48*(2), 147–160.

Doherty, B., Haugh, H., & Lyon, F. (2014). Social enterprises as hybrid organizations: A review and research agenda. *International Journal of Management Reviews*, *16*(4), 417–436. https://doi.org/10.1111/ijmr.12028

Dunn, M. B., & Jones, C. (2010). Institutional logics and institutional pluralism: The contestation of care and science logics in medical education, 1967–2005. *Administrative Science Quarterly, 55*(1), 114–149. https://doi.org/10.2189/asqu.2010.55.1.114

Evers, A. (2005). Mixed welfare systems and hybrid organizations: Changes in the governance and provision of social services. *International Journal of Public Administration, 28*(9–10), 737–748. https://doi.org/10.1081/PAD-200067318

Ferraro, F., Etzion, D., & Gehman, J. (2015). Tackling grand challenges pragmatically: Robust action revisited. *Organization Studies, 36*(3), 363–390. https://doi.org/10.1177/0170840614563742

Foreman, P., & Whetten, D. A. (2002). Members' identification with multiple-identity organizations. *Organization Science, 13*(6), 618–635. https://doi.org/10.1287/orsc.13.6.618.493

Fosfuri, A., Giarratana, M. S., & Roca, E. (2016). Social business hybrids: Demand externalities, competitive advantage, and growth through diversification. *Organization Science, 27*(5), 1275–1289. https://doi.org/10.1287/orsc.2016.1080

Friedland, R., & Alford, R. R. (1991). Bringing society back in: Symbols, practices and institutional contradictions. In P. DiMaggio & W. W. Powell (Eds.), *The New Institutionalism in Organizational Analysis* (pp. 232–263). Chicago: University of Chicago Press.

Garud, R., Hardy, C., & Maguire, S. (2016). Institutional entrepreneurship as embedded agency: An introduction to the special issue. *Organization Studies, 28*(7), 957–969. https://doi.org/10.1177/0170840607078958

Gersick, C. J. G. (1991). Revolutionary change theories: A multilevel exploration of the punctuated equilibrium paradigm. *Academy of Management Review, 16*(1), 10–36. https://doi.org/10.2307/258605

Greenwood, R., Raynard, M., Kodeih, F., Micelotta, E. R., & Lounsbury, M. (2011). Institutional complexity and organizational responses. *Academy of Management Annals, 5*(1), 317–371. https://doi.org/10.1080/19416520.2011.590299

Haigh, N., & Hoffman, A. J. (2012). Hybrid organizations: The next chapter of sustainable business. *Organizational Dynamics, 41*(2), 126–134. https://doi.org/10.1016/j.orgdyn.2012.01.006

Hannan, M. T., & Freeman, J. (1977). The population ecology of organizations. *American Journal of Sociology, 82*(5), 929–964. https://doi.org/10.2307/2777807

Hannan, M. T., Pólos, L., & Carroll, G. (2007). *Logics of organization theory: Audiences, codes, and ecologies.* Princeton, NJ Princeton University Press.

Hasenfeld, Y., & Gidron, B. (2005). Understanding multi-purpose hybrid voluntary organizations: The contributions of theories on civil society, social movements and non-profit organizations. *Journal of Civil Society, 1*(2), 97–112.

Haveman, H. A., & Rao, H. (2006). Hybrid forms and the evolution of thrifts. *American Behavioral Scientist, 49*(7), 974–986. https://doi.org/10.1177/0002764205285179

Heugens, P. P. M. A. R., & Lander, M. W. (2009). Structure! Agency! (And other quarrels): A meta-analysis of institutional theories of organization. *Academy of Management Journal, 52*(1), 61–85. https://doi.org/10.5465/AMJ.2009.36461835

Hockerts, K. (2015). How hybrid organizations turn antagonistic assets into complementarities. *California Management Review, 57*(3), 83–106. https://doi.org/10.1525/cmr.2015.57.3.83

Hustinx, L., & Waele, E. de. (2015). Managing hybridity in a changing welfare mix: Everyday practices in an entrepreneurial nonprofit in Belgium. *Voluntas: International Journal of Voluntary and Nonprofit Organizations, 26*(5), 1666–1689. https://doi.org/10.1007/s11266-015-9625-8

Jay, J. (2013). Navigating paradox as a mechanism of change and innovation in hybrid organizations. *Academy of Management Journal, 56*(1), 137–159. https://doi.org/10.5465/amj.2010.0772

Jones, C., Hesterly, W. S., & Borgatti, S. P. (1997). A general theory of network governance: Exchange conditions and social mechanisms. *Academy of Management Review, 22*(4), 911–945.

Jongbloed, B. (2015). Universities as hybrid organizations. *International Studies of Management & Organization, 45*(3), 207–225. https://doi.org/10.1080/00208825.2015.1006027

Jurkovich, R. (1974). A core typology of organizational environments. *Administrative Science Quarterly, 19*(3), 380. https://doi.org/10.2307/2391979

Kim, T.-Y., Shin, D., & Jeong, Y.-C. (2016). Inside the "hybrid" iron cage: Political origins of hybridization. *Organization Science, 27*(2), 428–445. https://doi.org/10.1287/orsc.2016.1057

Koppell, J. G. S. (2001). Hybrid organizations and the alignment of interests: The case of Fannie Mae and Freddie Mac. *Public Administration Review, 61*(4), 468–482.

Koppell, J. G. S. (2005). Pathologies of accountability: ICANN and the challenge of "Multiple Accountabilities Disorder". *Public Administration Review, 65*(1), 94–108.

Koppell, J. G. S. (2010). *World rule: Accountability, legitimacy, and the design of global governance*. Chicago: University of Chicago Press.

Kraatz, M. S., & Block, E. S. (2008). Organizational implications of institutional pluralism. In R. Greenwood, C. Oliver, K. Sahlin, & R. Suddaby (Eds.), *The Sage handbook of organizational institutionalism* (pp. 243–275). Los Angeles: Sage. https://doi.org/10.4135/9781849200387.n10

Kuttner, R. (1999). *Everything for sale: The virtues and limits of markets*. New York: Random House.

Lander, M. W., & Heugens, P. P. M. A. R. (2017). Better together: Using meta-analysis to explore complementarities between ecological and institutional theories of organization. *Organization Studies, 38*(11), 1573–1601. https://doi.org/10.1177/0170840616677629

Lawrence, T., & Suddaby, R. (2006). Institutions and institutional work. In S. Clegg, C. Hardy, T. Lawrence, & W. R. Nord (Eds.), *Handbook of organization studies* (pp. 215–254). London: Sage.

Lawrence, T. B., & Dover, G. (2015). Place and institutional work: Creating housing for the hard-to-house. *Administrative Science Quarterly, 60*(3), 371–410. https://doi.org/10.1177/0001839215589813

Lawrence, T. B., Suddaby, R., & Leca, B. (Eds.). (2010). *Institutional work: Actors and agency in institutional studies of organization*. Cambridge: Cambridge University Press.

Liu, G., & Ko, W.-W. (2012). Organizational learning and marketing capability development. *Nonprofit and Voluntary Sector Quarterly, 41*(4), 580–608. https://doi.org/10.1177/0899764011411722

Mair, J., & Marti, I. (2009). Social entrepreneurship as institution building. In J. A. Robinson, J. Mair, & K. Hockerts (Eds.), *International Perspectives on Social Entrepreneurship* (pp. 144–160). Basingstoke, Hampshire: Palgrave Macmillan.

Mair, J., Mayer, J., & Lutz, E. (2015). Navigating institutional plurality: Organizational governance in hybrid organizations. *Organization Studies, 36*(6), 713–739. https://doi.org/10.1177/0170840615580007

Mair, J., Marti, I., & Ventresca, M. J. (2012). Building inclusive markets in rural Bangladesh: How intermediaries work institutional voids. *Academy of Management Journal, 55*(4), 819–850. https://doi.org/10.5465/amj.2010.0627

Marquis, C., & Raynard, M. (2015). Institutional strategies in emerging markets. *Academy of Management Annals, 9*(1), 291–335. https://doi.org/10.1080/19416520.2015.1014661

Miller, D., Le Breton-Miller, I., & Lester, R. H. (2012). Family firm governance, strategic conformity, and performance: Institutional vs. strategic perspectives. *Organization Science, 24*(1), 189–209. https://doi.org/10.1287/orsc.1110.0728

Miller, T. L., Grimes, M. G., McMullen, J. S., & Vogus, T. J. (2012). Venturing for others with heart and head: How compassion encourages social entrepreneurship. *Academy of Management Review, 37*(4), 616–640. https://doi.org/10.5465/amr.2010.0456

Minkoff, D. C. (2002). The emergence of hybrid organizational forms: Combining identity-based service provision and political action. *Nonprofit and Voluntary Sector Quarterly, 31*(3), 377–401.

Mintzberg, H. (1983). *Structure in fives: Designing effective organizations*. Englewood Cliffs, NJ: Prentice-Hall.

Murray, F. (2010). The oncomouse that roared: Hybrid exchange strategies as a source of distinction at the boundary of overlapping institutions. *American Journal of Sociology, 116*(2), 341–388. https://doi.org/10.1086/653599

Nicholls, A. (2010a). The institutionalization of social investment: The interplay of investment logics and investor rationalities. *Journal of Social Entrepreneurship, 1*(1), 70–100.

Nicholls, A. (2010b). The legitimacy of social entrepreneurship: Reflexive isomorphism in a pre-paradigmatic field. *Entrepreneurship Theory and Practice, 34*(4), 611–633.

Pache, A.-C., & Santos, F. (2013). Inside the hybrid organization: Selective coupling as a response to competing institutional logics. *Academy of Management Journal, 56*(4), 972–1001. https://doi.org/10.5465/amj.2011.0405

Patriotta, G., Gond, J.-P., & Schultz, F. (2011). Maintaining legitimacy: Controversies, orders of worth, and public justifications. *Journal of Management Studies, 48*(8), 1804–1836. https://doi.org/10.1111/j.1467-6486.2010.00990.x

Perrow, C. (1979). *Complex organizations: A critical essay* (2nd ed.). Glenview, IL: Scott, Foresman.

Powell, W. W. (1990). Neither market nor hierarchy: Network forms of organization. *Research on Organizational Behavior, 12*, 295–336.

Purdy, J. M., & Gray, B. (2009). Conflicting logics, mechanisms of diffusion, and multilevel dynamics in emerging institutional fields. *Academy of Management Journal, 52*(2), 355–380. https://doi.org/10.5465/AMJ.2009.37308255

Reficco, E., & Marquez, P. (2012). Inclusive networks for building BOP markets. *Business & Society, 51*(3), 512–556. https://doi.org/10.1177/0007650309332353

Romanelli, E. (1991). The evolution of new organizational forms. *Annual Review of Sociology, 17*, 79–103. https://doi.org/10.2307/2083336

Romanelli, E., & Tushman, M. L. (1994). Organizational transformation as punctuated equilibrium: An empirical test. *Academy of Management Journal, 37*(5), 1141–1166. https://doi.org/10.2307/256669

Ruebottom, T. (2013). The microstructures of rhetorical strategy in social entrepreneurship: Building legitimacy through heroes and villains. *Journal of Business Venturing, 28*(1), 98–116. https://doi.org/10.1016/j.jbusvent.2011.05.001

Schemeil, Y. (2013). Bringing international organization in: Global institutions as adaptive hybrids. *Organization Studies, 34*(2), 219–252. https://doi.org/10.1177/0170840612473551

Schildt, H., & Perkmann, M. (2016). Organizational settlements: Theorizing how organizations respond to institutional complexity. *Journal of Management Inquiry*. Advance online publication. https://doi.org/10.1177/1056492616670756

Schröer, A., & Jäger, U. (2011). *Leadership in Hybrid Organizations*. Paper presented at 2011 CSI Symposium "Leadership and Governance in Hybrid Organizations", Heidelberg, Germany, December.

Scott, W. R. (1992). *Organizations: Rational, natural, and open systems* (3rd ed.). Englewood Cliffs, NJ: Prentice Hall.

Seibel, W. (2015). Studying hybrids: Sectors and mechanisms. *Organization Studies, 36*(6), 697–712. https://doi.org/10.1177/0170840615580005

Skelcher, C., & Smith, S. R. (2015). Theorizing hybridity: Institutional logics, complex organizations, and actor identities: The case of nonprofits. *Public Administration, 93*(2), 433–448. https://doi.org/10.1111/padm.12105

Smith, S. R. (2010). Hybridization and nonprofit organizations: The governance challenge. *Policy and Society, 29*(3), 219–229. https://doi.org/10.1016/j.polsoc.2010.06.003

Steyaert, C., & Dey, P. (2010). Nine verbs to keep the social entrepreneurship research agenda 'dangerous'. *Journal of Social Entrepreneurship, 1*(2), 231–254. https://doi.org/10.1080/19420676.2010.511817

Steyaert, C., & Hjorth, D. (Eds.). (2006). *Entrepreneurship as social change: A third movements in entrepreneurship book*. Cheltenham: Edward Elgar.

Suddaby, R. (2010). Challenges for institutional theory. *Journal of Management Inquiry, 19*(1), 14–20. https://doi.org/10.1177/1056492609347564

Suddaby, R., Saxton, G. D., & Gunz, S. (2015). Twittering change: The institutional work of domain change in accounting expertise. *Accounting, Organizations and Society, 45*, 52–68. https://doi.org/10.1016/j.aos.2015.07.002

Thomasson, A. (2009). Exploring the ambiguity of hybrid organizations: A stakeholder approach. *Financial Accountability & Management, 25*(3), 353–366. https://doi.org/10.1111/j.1468-0408.2009.00481.x

Thornton, P. H., Ocasio, W., & Lounsbury, M. (2012). *The institutional logics perspective: A new approach to culture, structure, and process*. Oxford: Oxford University Press.

Titmuss, R. M., Oakley, A., & Ashton, J. (1970). *The gift relationship: From human blood to social policy*. New York: New Press.

Tracey, P., & Phillips, N. (2016). Managing the consequences of organizational stigmatization: Identity work in a social enterprise. *Academy of Management Journal, 59*(3), 740–765. https://doi.org/10.5465/amj.2013.0483

Tushman, M., & O'Reilly, C. A. (2002). *Winning through innovation: A practical guide to leading organizational change and renewal* (Rev. ed.). Boston, MA: Harvard Business School Press.

Vidal, I. (2005). Social enterprise and social inclusion: Social enterprises in the sphere of work integration. *International Journal of Public Administration, 28*(9–10), 807–825. https://doi.org/10.1081/PAD-200067347

Volberda, H. W., van der Weerdt, N., Verwaal, E., Stienstra, M., & Verdu, A. J. (2011). Contingency fit, institutional fit, and firm performance: A metafit approach to organization–environment relationships. *Organization Science, 23*(4), 1040–1054. https://doi.org/10.1287/orsc.1110.0687

Weber, M. (1978). *Economy and society: An outline of interpretive sociology*. Berkeley: University of California Press.

York, J. G., O'Neil, I., & Sarasvathy, S. D. (2016). Exploring environmental entrepreneurship: Identity coupling, venture goals, and stakeholder incentives. *Journal of Management Studies, 53*(5), 695–737. https://doi.org/10.1111/joms.12198

Zietsma, C., & Lawrence, T. B. (2010). Institutional work in the transformation of an organizational field: The interplay of boundary work and practice work. *Administrative Science Quarterly, 55*(2), 189–221. https://doi.org/10.2189/asqu.2010.55.2.189

Appendix

Our literature review proceeded as follows. We focused on the journals that were most likely to have been outlets for hybridity research in a civil society context with a focus on the intra-organizational as well as organization-field level perspectives needed to make a judgment on my research questions. We thus focused on journals with an emphasis on management theory and track-record of embracing research in relation to civil society, organization theory outlets, and specialized nonprofit journals.

The online archives of the most highly ranked journals in these areas were screened via EBSCOhost databases. The term "hybrid*" was applied for a search covering titles and abstracts of papers published between 2000 and 2017. This yielded the following results: *Academy of Management Journal* (AMJ): 16 articles; *Administrative Science Quarterly* (ASQ): 5 articles; *Journal of Management Studies* (JMS): 24 articles; *Organization Studies*: 17 articles; *Organization Science*: 26 articles; *Organization*: 12 articles; *Nonprofit & Voluntary Sector Quarterly* (NVSQ): 9 articles; *Voluntas*: 2 articles; *Journal of Management*: 0 articles. The search resulted in a total number of 109 articles referring to hybridity and hybrid organizing.

To make sure we had not overlooked other relevant research, we ran an extra search via Google Scholar and ISI Web of Knowledge. Again, the timeframe for documents was set between 2000 and 2017. This time the search was restricted to papers mentioning the search terms in the title. "Hybrid organization/organization" provided 88 results. Applying the search term "hybrid AND civil society" yielded 16 documents, while "hybrid AND third sector" resulted in 13 articles. The total number of 225 articles is close to what others have found, if with slightly different search strategies and analytic aims (Battilana et al., 2017). We only retained for further screening articles that in fact had an explicit focus on hybridity, that is employed the term rather than referring only to "conflicting logics" for instance. We also included only those articles published in journals of comparable scholarly impact to those initially listed judged by their current impact factor.

Starting from there, we performed a content-related screening of the articles and selected only those articles, which were of an empirical rather than a theoretical nature. This resulted in a body of 46 papers for further analysis that we structured along two dimensions: (1) thematic focus, (2) level of analysis (see Table 34.2).

Table 34.2 Thematic focus and level of analysis in initial sample

Level/Thematic focus	Multi-/Cross-level	Field/industry/market	Organization (management and relation to field)	Organization (group/team/individual)
Effects and moderation of competing logics	Hasenfeld, Gidron (2005) McKague, Zietsma, Oliver (2015) Quélin, Kivleniece, Lazzarini (2017) Skelcher, Smith (2015) Venkataraman, Vermeulen et al. (2016) York, Hargrave, Pacheco (2016)	Bushouse, Never et al. (2016) Calvo, Morales (2016) Chan, Ryan (2016) Cobb, Wry, Zhao (2016) Lee, Jay (2015) Mair, Hehenberger (2014) Seibel (2015) Traettberg (2015)	Battilana, Dorado (2010) Cooney (2006) Doherty, Haugh, Lyon (2014) Gibbons, Hazy (2017) Hockerts (2015) Knutsen (2013) Pache, Santos (2013) Santos, Pache, Birkholz (2015) Schemeil (2013) Weber, Weidner, Kroeger, Wallace (2017)	Battilana, Sengul et al. (2015) Hahn, Preuss, Pinkse, Figge (2014) Hustinx, de Waele (2015) Sharma, Bansal (2016) Sharp, Zaidman (2015) York, O'Neil, Sarasvathy (2016)
Governance of hybrids, including impact		Ashraf, Ahmadsimab, Pinkse (2017) Nicholls (2010) Holt, Littlewood (2015)	Cabral (2017) Cabral, Lazzarini et al. (2013) Caldwell, Roehrich et al. (2017) Haigh, Kennedy, Walker (2015) Mair, Mayer, Lutz (2015) Pestoff (2014)	
Organizational identity			Tracey, Phillips (2016)	Ashforth, Reingen (2014) Foreman, Whetten (2002)
Organizational change, learning, and actor collaboration	Rivera-Santos, Ruffin, Wassmer (2017) Tello-Rozas, Pozzebon, Mailhot (2015)		Jay (2013) Liu, Ko (2012)	

35

NEW LEGAL FORMS FOR HYBRID ORGANIZATIONS

Alan J. Abramson

PROFESSOR OF GOVERNMENT AND POLITICS, SCHAR SCHOOL OF POLICY AND
GOVERNMENT, GEORGE MASON UNIVERSITY, ARLINGTON, VA, USA

Kara C. Billings

GRADUATE RESEARCH ASSISTANT, SCHAR SCHOOL OF POLICY AND GOVERNMENT,
GEORGE MASON UNIVERSITY, ARLINGTON, VA, USA

Introduction

Recent decades have seen significant growth in hybrid, double-bottom-line organizations that aim both to "do good," like nonprofits and government, and "make money," like businesses (Young et al. 2016). Many businesses now seek to achieve some social and environmental good. TOMS is a well-known example, giving away a pair of shoes with every pair sold (TOMS n.d.). Meanwhile, many nonprofits are relying less on charitable donations and more on commercial strategies that emphasize earning income from fees for goods or services (Young et al. 2012; Kerlin and Pollak 2011). Goodwill, for example, earns more than half of its revenue from store sales (Goodwill n.d.). Unfortunately, however, existing for-profit and nonprofit laws do not always accommodate these new hybrid orientations very well. For-profit law generally prioritizes profit maximization over advancing social good, while nonprofit law may constrain organizations' commercial activity (Gottesman 2007; Krupkin and Looney 2017; Young et al. 2016; Kickul and Lyons 2012; Foster and Fine 2007).

New legal forms for hybrid organizations offer a potential solution to this dilemma. Over the past two decades, more and more countries have passed laws that recognize hybrid organizations which pursue social good and profit (Triponel and Agapitova 2017; Brakman Reiser and Dean 2017; Young et al. 2016). These new hybrid legal forms include businesses that advance social and environmental good as well as cooperatives focused on social impact rather than member benefit (Young et al. 2016). More than 30,000 organizations worldwide are utilizing these new forms, and their numbers are increasing (CIC Regulator 2017; Venturi and Zandonai 2012; B Lab 2017c; Cooney et al. 2014; Triponel and Agapitova 2017). However, hybrid laws are still being tested and questions remain about their ability to allow organizations to commit to both profit and social purpose while staying financially sustainable and accountable (Brakman Reiser and Dean 2017; Callison and Vestal 2010; Callison 2012; Tyler et al. 2015; Mickels 2009). This chapter discusses the growth of new legal forms for hybrid organizations, the strengths and weaknesses of the forms currently available, and what future, new legal forms for hybrids might look like.

Defining hybrid organizations

What constitutes a hybrid organization? This question has sparked considerable debate in recent decades. Oliver Williamson, a Nobel-Prize-winning economist, was one of the first to define hybrid organizations (Ménard 2009: 89). In his 1985 book *The Economic Institutions of Capitalism*, Williamson describes transactions such as franchising, joint ventures, and other forms of nonstandard contracting that do not fit neatly into the purview of business or government (Williamson 1985: 83). Williamson goes on to conceptualize hybrids as an organizational form that is "located between" the two sectors and better equipped to handle such "nonstandard" transactions (Williamson 1991: 281; Ménard 2009: 92).

Other scholars have since expanded on Williamson's definition of hybrid organizations. Some add a third sector to the mix – the nonprofit or voluntary sector – and argue that hybrids borrow elements from the business, government, and/or nonprofit sector (Borys and Jemison 1989; Powell 1990; Brandsen et al. 2005). Others broaden the discussion further, arguing that hybrids draw not only from different economic forms but also from different societal institutions, combining elements from different cultures, religions, and familial structures (Skelcher and Rathgeb Smith 2015: 437–439). Seibel (2015) emphasizes the importance of taking into account both formal and informal aspects of hybrids in understanding their operation. The diverse nature of hybrid organizations may materialize in the form of a dual mission (e.g., the pursuit of social good and profit), mixed ownership (e.g., public and private), and/or diverse funding streams (e.g., charitable donations and sales of goods and services) (Johanson and Vakkuri 2018: 3–4).

Today, the term "hybrid" generally signifies organizations that mix the do-good orientation of the nonprofit sector with the commercial logic of the for-profit sector. There are other types of hybrid organizations – for example, state-owned enterprises that combine logics from government and business – but the experience of nonprofit and for-profit hybrids seems to be the driving force behind recent changes in law. In fact, some have argued that hybrids will ultimately form a "fourth sector" of the economy that complements the government, business, and nonprofit sectors (Sabeti 2011).

Hybrids are sometimes conflated with "social enterprises," although this term does not yet have a universally agreed upon meaning (see Chapter 31 by Kerlin, this volume). Some use "social enterprises" to refer specifically to nonprofits with commercial income, while others would broaden the meaning to include businesses with a social orientation. In any case, "social enterprise" is a label that originated with the emergence of microfinance in the 1970s, but is used today to refer to organizations that are both financially sustainable and socially impactful (Young and Longhofer 2016: 24).

The contributors to *The Social Enterprise Zoo* (Young et al. 2016) detail a spectrum of social enterprises, ranging from public sector social enterprises (e.g., government-controlled nonprofits), to commercial nonprofits (nonprofits that rely on earned income), to social cooperatives (a cooperative with a social purpose), to social businesses (a business that reinvests all profits into the cause), to sustainable businesses (businesses with a net positive social impact). The existing, new, hybrid legal forms generally fall in the "sustainable business" and "social cooperative" categories on the social enterprise spectrum (Young and Longhofer 2016: 24).

Why the interest in new hybrid legal forms?

An increase in the number of entrepreneurs who combine an instinct for doing good and a business mindset has been accompanied by growing frustration with the current menu of options available for incorporation. These entrepreneurs don't want to sacrifice mission or profitability;

the trade-off they feel they have to make in choosing the current for-profit or nonprofit forms. They also want a way to signal their commitment to doing good to consumers and investors and to differentiate themselves from the multitude of companies claiming they are socially and environmentally responsible. Meanwhile, many policymakers support the creation of new legal forms for hybrids, viewing them as a promising new vehicle for attracting new resources and perhaps new efficiencies to social service provision. In summary, support for distinct legal forms for hybrids is driven by three main factors: (1) entrepreneurs' frustrations with the constraints of conventional legal forms; (2) entrepreneurs' beliefs that a new legal form will improve branding and credibility; and (3) policymakers' attempts to use market forces to increase funding for social services.

Constraints of current legal forms

While the nonprofit form confers several advantages, including tax benefits and a philan-thropic brand, it severely limits access to resources (Young and Brewer 2016: 6). Nonprofits rarely grow as large as for-profits; in the U.S., for example, only 144 nonprofits exceeded $50 million in revenue from the 1970s to the 2000s, compared to 50,000 new businesses (Foster and Fine 2007: 46; Social Impact Investment Taskforce 2014). Nonprofit law limits access to capital in two primary ways. First, nonprofits cannot distribute profits to owners, which means they cannot access equity capital, which is an appealing source of funding because it doesn't require repayment (Gottesman 2007: 348; Kickul and Lyons 2012: 122). Second, earned income generated by a nonprofit must be "related" to its charitable purpose or the income will be taxed as "unrelated" income and possibly put the nonprofit's tax-exempt status at risk. In addition to financial constraints, nonprofit law generally limits organizations to engaging in charitable activities including "education, social services, healthcare, environment, or the arts" – potentially precluding other forms of social good (Young and Brewer 2016: 7).

For-profit legal forms, in comparison, offer easier access to market-generated capital. At the same time, for-profits may be limited in the amount of good they can do, despite a trend towards corporate social responsibility over the past few decades (Galaskiewicz and Colman 2006: 185–186). To be sure, there is an ongoing legal debate over whether corporate law actu-ally requires directors to maximize shareholder wealth above all else (Bainbridge 1991; Stout 2012); however, in practice, for-profit directors tend to prioritize profit-seeking (Brewer 2016: 45). That is because they are beholden to shareholders, who have the ability to remove and/or bring lawsuits against directors who do not operate in their interests. While some countries have passed laws that protect directors from such lawsuits, they have largely failed to translate to a change in practice (Gottesman 2007: 350). In addition, for-profit legal forms come with heavier tax burdens that can limit the funds available to do good. Corporate forms generally require double taxation: one on the company and one on individual earnings. Pass-through forms, which include partnerships, sole proprietorships, and S-corporations, and comprise about 95 percent of businesses in the U.S., only require one tax on individual earnings, but have weaker protections against personal liability and/or a heavier administrative burden which can make them less appealing to entrepreneurs (Krupkin and Looney 2017; Brewer 2016: 63).

Cooperatives are a common legal form of organization outside of the U.S. However, the form is not entirely ready-made for hybrids, either. Because cooperatives exist to serve their members, they are limiting for those entrepreneurs who want to serve a broader population, and/or a population that does not have the ability to pay a membership fee. Cooperatives also have a democratic governing structure, giving the founders less control over the direction of the organization. While cooperatives can harness private market capital to some extent, they cannot trade ownership for equity from investors, and are therefore limited in how much capital they can raise (Brewer 2016: 64).

Improved branding

Aside from solving some of the shortcomings of conventional legal forms, there are other reasons why a new legal form for hybrids is attractive. Most notably, perhaps, is the branding that can come with a new legal form. Currently, entrepreneurs have a hard time sending a signal to customers, investors, partners, and others about their dual commitment to social purpose and profit (Brakman Reiser 2013: 684). In addition, they have trouble distinguishing their enterprises from the many companies claiming to do good without an actual commitment. There is a growing demand by consumers, investors, and entrepreneurs for socially conscious companies but a lack of "comprehensive and transparent standards . . . for a consumer to tell the difference between a 'good company' and just good marketing" (Clark and Vranka 2013: 3). A new legal form with adequate accountability mechanisms would serve to differentiate the organizations most strongly committed to social and environmental good.

Political appeal

New hybrid legal forms are also adopted for political reasons and are themselves shaped by the political and social system of which they are a part (Mair 2010). In many countries, policymakers see hybrid legal forms as a way to draw more non-governmental resources into social service provision and to provide these services more efficiently and effectively than government does on its own. In the U.K., for example, policymakers in the New Labour government of the 2000s viewed the creation of the community interest company as a way "to achieve the political objective of regenerating deprived communities" using market forces (Calo and Teasdale 2016: 198). In Italy, lawmakers legitimized social cooperatives in 1991 as a vehicle through which the government could provide increased funding for social services (Calo and Teasdale 2016: 194–195). Similarly, in South Korea, the creation of the social enterprise certification was a response to increasing public outcry over rising unemployment and a dearth of social services (Bidet and Eum 2011: 77). In the U.S., policymakers see new hybrid legal forms as "an opportunity to please the entire political spectrum without spending a dime" (Brakman Reiser and Dean 2017: 66).

What new legal forms are being developed?

Over the past two decades, a number of countries have passed laws creating new legal forms for hybrids. The most well-known forms include the social cooperative in Italy, the community interest company in the U.K., and the benefit corporation in the U.S. These and many other legal forms are available globally, particularly in North America, Europe, and parts of Asia (Triponel and Agapitova 2017; Orrick, Herrington & Sutcliffe LLP 2014; Young et al. 2016). New hybrid legal forms generally fall under the "sustainable business" and "social cooperative" categories on the social enterprise spectrum (Young et al. 2016).

The ones that qualify as sustainable businesses, such as the U.S. benefit corporation, share core elements of for-profit law. They have shareholders, allow profit distribution, and generally prioritize profit over social good (Tyler et al. 2015: 253). However, they deviate from for-profit law by requiring the pursuit of one or more social or environmental purposes and allowing directors some flexibility in considering non-shareholder interests in making business decisions.

In contrast, hybrid forms that draw from cooperative and nonprofit law, such as Italy's social cooperative and South Korea's social enterprise, place limits on profit distribution and put more emphasis on mission. They require an organization to select a specific social purpose that is paramount to profit. In addition, they often have an "asset lock" on the conversion or dissolution of the organization, meaning that any profits or assets are transferred to another organization or the government in such a case. As a result of these stronger accountability mechanisms, these forms usually offer some sort of tax benefits.

While there are some dominant new legal forms for hybrids, "diversity is an intrinsic characteristic of the social enterprise space," and many new hybrid legal forms are unique (Young and Longhofer 2016: 15). The specific features of new legal forms are important, determining the "instinct" of an organization (Brewer 2016: 35). Legal form influences organizational characteristics, including an organization's brand, ownership, governance, ability to raise capital, and accountability. Importantly for hybrids, a legal form can enable the coexistence of "logics and value systems" from two or more sectors (Doherty et al. 2014: 418). This chapter will discuss five hybrid legal forms that are widely known and demonstrate a breadth of legal characteristics (see Table 35.1).

Social cooperative (Italy)

Italy created a new type of cooperative in 1991 to fill a gap in government services related to welfare and employment (Triponel and Agapitova 2017: 24). Social cooperatives were arguably the first "specific legal form for social enterprise" (Young 2017: 32). While similar to traditional cooperatives in terms of member ownership and democratic governance, social cooperatives in Italy are required to provide social, educational, or health-related services or job opportunities for the hard-to-employ rather than serving the interests of their members (Brewer 2016: 47). In addition, they receive a number of tax benefits, including exclusion from the income tax, but are subject to stricter rules regarding their financing. They have a limit on distributable profits and an "asset lock," which means that profits are transferred to the government rather than members if the social cooperative is converted to a for-profit or dissolved (Brewer 2016: 47; Triponel and Agapitova 2017: 24–25).

Table 35.1 Features of hybrid legal forms

	Amends existing law or separate legal entity	Social purpose	Limits on profit distribution	Asset lock	Reporting requirements	Tax benefits
Social cooperative (Italy)	Amends nonprofit law	Specific	Yes	Yes	Yes	Yes
Low-profit limited liability company (U.S.)	Amends LLC law	Flexible	No	No	No	No
Benefit corporation (U.S.)	Separate	Broad	No	No	Yes	No
Social enterprise (South Korea)	Separate	Specific	Partial	Yes	Yes	Yes
Community interest company (U.K.)	Amends business law	Flexible	Partial	Yes	Yes	No

Low-profit limited liability company (U.S.)

The low-profit limited liability company (L3C) was the first hybrid legal form in the United States (Brakman Reiser 2011: 593). Vermont was the first state to enact the L3C form in 2008 and since then, seven additional states have authorized L3Cs (Social Enterprise Law Tracker 2017). As its name implies, the L3C is a variation on the limited liability company (LLC), and states amend LLC law to create the L3C (Esposito 2012: 682). The L3C shares the two dominant qualities of an LLC: limited liability of owners and pass-through tax treatment (Morrison & Foerster 2016: 47–76). The main differences between the two forms are that an L3C's articles of incorporation must specify a charitable or educational purpose as defined by the Internal Revenue Code, and income generation and appreciation of property cannot be significant purposes, thus establishing the precedence of a cause over profit (Brakman Reiser 2013: 690). One of the driving forces behind the creation of the L3C form was to create a safer way for foundations to make tax-exempt "program-related investments" (e.g., loans and equity investments) in LLCs (Esposito 2012: 682).

Benefit corporation (U.S.)

Benefit corporation legislation was first passed in the U.S. in Maryland in 2010 and, since then, almost three dozen U.S. jurisdictions have authorized the hybrid form (Social Enterprise Law Tracker 2017; Toepler 2018). Benefit corporations are similar to traditional corporations except that they must pursue a general public benefit – defined as "a material positive impact on society and the environment" – and can optionally pursue specific public benefits (Callison 2012: 92–94; B Lab 2017b: 3). This creates a "triple bottom line" of profits, social good, and environmental good (Mickels 2009). Benefit corporations are generally established through a separate state law rather than an amendment to corporate law (Brakman Reiser 2011: 595).

Though similar in name, benefit corporations are distinct from B Corps, which are corporations that have been independently certified by B Lab, a Pennsylvania-based nonprofit, as meeting "rigorous standards of social and environmental performance, accountability, and transparency" (B Lab 2017a). The B Corp designation is often utilized by corporations in states that do not yet have a legal benefit corporation form. In fact, B Lab authored the model legislation that most state benefit corporation laws are based on and requires its B Corps to become benefit corporations if they operate in a state where the form has been legalized (Brakman Reiser and Dean 2017: 60).

Nearly all states require benefit corporations to pursue the general public benefit with the exception of Delaware, which requires a specific benefit. Of note, four states in the U.S. have "social purpose corporations," which are very similar to benefit corporations except that they require a specific instead of a general social purpose. Directors of benefit corporations are required to "consider the effects of any action or inaction" on a long list of stakeholders, including shareholders, employees, customers, the community, the environment, and the corporation itself (Tyler et al. 2015). This requirement offers some protection for directors against shareholder lawsuits (Brakman Reiser and Dean 2017: 55). Benefit corporations are also required to publish an annual report that is available to the public and uses a third-party standard to evaluate its societal and environmental impact (Callison 2012: 95–97). In some states, these reports must be submitted to the secretary of state, but there are no penalties for noncompliance (Brakman Reiser and Dean 2017: 59). Benefit corporations are similar to regular corporations in most other ways. They are subject to the corporate tax rate, have no limits on profit distribution, and can be created, converted, or dissolved with a two-thirds majority vote of shareholders (Callison 2012: 93).

Social enterprise (South Korea)

In 2007, South Korea passed the Social Enterprise Promotion Act, creating the social enterprise. The social enterprise is a legal certification that for-profits, nonprofits, and cooperatives can apply for (Bidet and Eum 2011: 77). Organizations must be operational for at least six months before they can become a social enterprise in South Korea. In addition, they must have at least one employee, have a democratic governing structure, engage in activities related to a social purpose, generate profits that cover more than 30 percent of labor costs, and dedicate a large proportion of their profits to their social purpose (Triponel and Agapitova 2017: 26). When organizations satisfy these requirements, they can become certified as a social enterprise through the central government's Ministry of Labor and Employment. They must adopt one of four forms: (1) the work integration form, in which 50 percent or more of all *employees* are considered disadvantaged; (2) the social services provision form, in which 50 percent or more of *beneficiaries* are considered disadvantaged; (3) a form combining these elements, and (4) other types of social enterprise such as those with environmental missions (Triponel and Agapitova 2017: 26). Certification as a social enterprise comes with tax exemption, with a review and renewal process every four years (Jung et al. 2016). However, there is a partial limit on profit distribution – one-third of profits may be distributed – and an asset lock upon dissolution or conversion (Triponel and Agapitova 2017: 26).

Community interest company (U.K.)

The U.K. Parliament created the community interest company (CIC) in 2005. CICs must pursue community benefit, defined by whether a reasonable person would consider the company's activities "for the benefit of the community" (Triponel and Agapitova 2017: 21). CICs are subject to an asset lock and restrictions on distributable profits. CIC directors are also required to involve stakeholders in governance (Brewer 2016: 53). This was not a dramatic change for directors in the U.K., because U.K. law already allowed directors to consider "a wide group of stakeholder interests, such as employees, suppliers, local communities and the environment" in decision-making (Triponel and Agapitova 2017: 21). CICs are regulated by the Office of the Regulator of Community Interest Companies, which can "investigate complaints . . . change the makeup of the board, or even terminate the CIC when necessary" (Liao 2013: 80). While there are no direct tax benefits given to CICs, the U.K. recently instituted tax relief for impact investors who advance social purposes, which should benefit CICs (Brakman Reiser and Dean 2017).

How are new legal forms working?

The establishment of new hybrid legal forms is gaining momentum, but are these new forms working? There is no consensus among scholars and practitioners, but they all tend to agree that there is room for improvement. Some maintain that the forms will improve over time, as the kinks are worked out and a strong ecosystem is formed for hybrids that provides them with the financial and human resources and other supports they need (Battilana et al. 2012: 51). Others contend that new legal forms are not necessary to support the growth of hybrids, and that adjustments to nonprofit and for-profit law will suffice. Of course, new hybrid legal forms vary widely, and a criticism of one form may not apply to another. As with any new field of study, empirical research on hybrid legal forms is scarce. However, the current scholarship indicates that new legal forms offer improved branding for hybrids, but they beget challenges related to mission, accountability, financing, and organizational operations.

Utilization

One obvious marker of success is whether the new hybrid legal forms are being used. Utilization of forms differs by country. The community interest company (CIC) in the U.K. is the most utilized hybrid form thus far, with more than 13,000 registered CICs as of 2017 (CIC Regulator 2017: 6). CICs continue to grow rapidly in the U.K., with a 10 percent increase in the number of companies from 2016 to 2017 (CIC Regulator 2017: 12). Italy's social cooperatives have been around longer, since 1991, and they are similar in number, totaling more than 11,000 organizations in 2012 (Venturi and Zandonai 2012: 3). Forms in the U.S. are also relatively new, coming into existence after 2008. They have seen modest growth since that time, amounting to roughly 3,000 benefit corporations and 1,000 low-profit limited liability companies (L3Cs) (B Lab 2017c; Cooney et al. 2014). Social enterprises exist on a similar scale in South Korea, which has seen 2,000 social enterprises certified since 2007 (Triponel and Agapitova 2017: 27).

Branding

New legal forms are also offering an improved brand for hybrids. Branding is one of the key benefits entrepreneurs see in a designated legal form, as a way "to declare that their entities are committed to a new and different goal – pursuing both profit and social good" (Brakman Reiser 2013: 685). A clear brand fosters greater trust between organizations and investors, customers, and others (Triponel and Agapitova 2017: 17). For example, some for-profit colleges in the U.S. have transitioned to benefit corporations (Fain 2014), giving an oft-criticized sector an opportunity to adopt a potentially better-aligned brand and rebuild trust with its stakeholders.

Goals

At the same time, new hybrid legal forms are running into various roadblocks, the first of which has been aptly called "the problem of serving two masters" (Brakman Reiser and Dean 2017: 19). Organizations that adopt a hybrid legal form generally pursue dual goals of social good and profit. Some legal forms, including the social cooperative in Italy and the CIC in the U.K., more explicitly prioritize social good over profit. Others, namely the U.S. benefit corporation, do not specify one over the other. While affording more agency, this effectively negates accountability for achieving social goals. Two scholars summarize the dilemma: "over the long term, pursuit of profit and social good can be mutually reinforcing. But, at many individual moments, one goal will need to be sacrificed for the other" (Brakman Reiser and Dean 2017: 28). Moreover, the U.S. benefit corporations have the added task of achieving environmental good in addition to public benefit and profits. It is unlikely that one corporation can effectively advance these three lofty goals.

Accountability

Accountability is also lacking on other fronts. Regulatory accountability can take the form of a designated government agency with oversight and enforcement powers and annual reporting requirements (Brakman Reiser and Dean 2017: 37–39). In the U.S., such a government agency is lacking for both the benefit corporation and L3C. While benefit corporations are required to publish an annual report evaluating the organization's social and environmental performance against an independent third-party standard, "it is conceivable that some third-party standard-setters will establish very low, but transparent, standards" (Callison 2012: 94). In addition, no third-party organization or governmental agency has the power to take action against a benefit corporation that does not meet its objectives.

The U.K.'s CICs have stronger regulatory accountability. They are required to file annual reports publicly with a designated government agency, the CIC Regulator, which has oversight and enforcement powers (Brakman Reiser and Dean 2017: 74). The task has not been too hard. In 2017, the CIC Regulator received 53 complaints about CICs, "a very small figure in comparison to the 13,055 CICs on the register" (CIC Regulator 2017: 12). U.K. law also holds CIC directors accountable by giving the regulatory agency "the authority to bring claims challenging director's fiduciary compliance" and "to appoint and remove CIC directors" (Brakman Reiser and Dean 2017: 74). Hybrid forms in the U.S. fall short in this respect, with directors shielded from government, shareholder, and stakeholder lawsuits.

One reason for these differences between the two countries relates back to the way that directors are held accountable under hybrid law. According to legal scholars, "fiduciary duties can arise only if the language 'clearly and explicitly instruct[s] these leaders to prioritize social good'" (Tyler et al. 2015: 267). CICs must prioritize social good over profit to the extent that a "reasonable person" would consider the CIC's activities to be "carried on for the benefit of the community" (Brakman Reiser and Dean 2017: 74). Therefore, directors that do not prioritize community benefit can be held accountable. In contrast, U.S. benefit corporation directors must have merely "considered" the effects of decisions on stakeholders (Tyler et al. 2015: 264). Such ambiguity provides little basis for legal recourse for shareholders or other stakeholders who are displeased with directors' actions (Brakman Reiser and Dean 2017: 57). Of course, shareholders still have the power to remove directors, giving them substantial recourse (Tyler et al. 2015: 260). However, there is no guarantee shareholders will prioritize social good over profit, either. The L3C form provides a slightly stronger basis for a lawsuit against directors because its charitable or educational purpose must take priority over the pursuit of income. However, "actual legal accountability in the L3C is threatened by statutory provisions" that automatically convert a L3C to a traditional LLC if it does not prioritize its specified social purpose (Tyler et al. 2015: 267–268).

While current hybrid laws in the U.S. advance only relatively weak regulatory and fiduciary accountability, they enable some accountability through public pressure. Benefit corporations' mandatory, annual reports make information available to customers, investors, policymakers, and other stakeholders. However, the utility of these reports is limited by "the depth, quality, and accuracy of the information" and whether they are "available for the right reasons at the right time" (Tyler et al. 2015: 263). Ironically, benefit corporations in states without hybrid laws may experience stronger social accountability as they are "subject to audit by B Lab on an ongoing basis" rather than once a year (Brakman Reiser 2011: 594). Benefit corporation law also enables directors, shareholders, and stakeholders specified in the articles of incorporation to bring a "benefit enforcement proceeding" against the corporation. However, such proceedings constitute more of a slap on the wrist rather than any real penalties (Brakman Reiser and Dean 2017: 57). Inadequate accountability mechanisms threaten to weaken the brand of new hybrid legal forms and erode trust between organizations and their customers, partners, and investors.

Financing

Financing has also been a challenge for some hybrid legal forms, but not for others. Different hybrid legal forms "entail different constraints and incentives that are likely to influence the degree to which particular sources of income can be engaged" (Searing and Young 2016: 170). For example, government funding has sustained Italy's social cooperatives, as they were conceived as a vehicle for increased public support for social services. Meanwhile, the number of CICs has increased rapidly, thanks to a growing market for impact investors who seek both societal benefit and financial return (CIC Regulator 2017: 7). U.K. policymakers have incentivized impact investment by loosening restrictions on profit distribution and the asset lock, which had previously "made CIC status insufficiently attractive to investors" (Brakman Reiser and Dean 2017: 75). In the U.S., benefit corporations have the advantage of unlimited profit distribution, increasing their appeal to investors. Several benefit corporations in the U.S. have been able to access venture capital funds from top firms and are examples of successful organizations, including Patagonia, Kickstarter, and This American Life, which are incorporated as benefit corporations (Kannel and Samali 2017). However, benefit corporations have not been able to harness impact investment to the same extent as CICs because they are unable "to send a reliable signal of their commitment [to social good]" to such investors (Brakman Reiser and Dean 2017: 27).

Meanwhile, the U.S. L3C is struggling to deliver on its promise to facilitate greater program-related investments (PRIs) (e.g., loans or equity investments) by private foundations (Searing and Young 2016: 185). The L3C statute mimics the Internal Revenue Service's guidance on PRIs, reducing, but not entirely eliminating, the risk to a foundation of investing in a for-profit activity (Esposito 2012: 685). Early evidence from Vermont suggests that L3C leaders are interested in the prospect of PRIs but have not yet tapped them as a funding source (Schmidt 2010: 16). Scholars are skeptical that this concept will work, raising the point that a regular LLC already has the capacity to include the IRS guidance in its articles of incorporation, begging the question of whether there is a need for L3Cs (Callison and Vestal 2010: 291). Others worry that PRIs enable the transfer of "tax-exempt, foundation dollars that are subsidized by the government . . . to increase returns for private investors, an impermissible, non-charitable purpose" (Culley and Horwitz 2014: 17–18).

Hybrid legal forms have the potential to tap into novel financing mechanisms. For example, they may help organizations make use of social impact bonds, which involve a partnership between government and private investors "who agree to take on risk in the financing of an innovative social program in return for financial reward . . . contingent on program success" (Young 2017: 194). In social impact bond arrangements, hybrids may serve as service organizations responsible for achieving social good, a role currently assumed by nonprofits. They could also act as professional service organizations facilitating financial agreements between parties. While the social impact bond market is relatively small, it is expected to grow as governments continue to outsource social services and demand results (Social Impact Investment Taskforce 2014: 18).

Legitimized hybrid organizations may also fare better in the crowdsourcing market. Crowdsourcing entails "gathering resources through large numbers of small pledges from people outside [an organization's] traditional circle," usually through a website like GoFundMe, Indiegogo, or Kickstarter (Searing and Young 2016: 183). Crowdsourcing offers organizations diverse funding tools, sometimes taking the form of a grant, loan, or transaction (e.g., individuals may receive gifts for their donations) (Searing and Young 2016: 183–184). Social enterprises are already taking advantage of crowdsourcing, and it is likely that a legalized hybrid form would enhance organizations' ability to raise funds in this space. Individuals may be more willing to put their money towards an organization that is certified through an established process and has some accountability mechanisms.

New hybrid legal forms may also help to spur novel financing mechanisms. Within the impact investing market, for example, scholars have theorized an ideal form of financing for hybrids called FLY Paper: "a debt product with a modest financial yield" (Brakman Reiser and Dean 2017: 84). As with any impact investments, investors would trade larger financial gains for the promise of social good. However, FLY Paper purchasers can still reap some profits; they have priority over shareholders in trading their holdings for stock in the company in the case of substantial profits (Brakman Reiser and Dean 2017: 85). This tool would only work for legal forms that are able to distribute profits, such as the corporate hybrid forms.

Organizational governance and culture

Finally, hybrid legal forms create challenges in terms of organizational operations. A double or triple bottom line makes governance more complex and time-consuming. At a minimum, "benefit corporation board meetings will need to be much longer than traditional ones" to consider the interests of many different stakeholders and competing interests (Brakman Reiser and Dean 2017: 54). A double bottom line also affects organizational culture, creating conflicts between employees from the for-profit and nonprofit sectors who are accustomed to different norms (Battilana et al. 2012: 54). Corporate hybrid forms also complicate relationships between directors, shareholders, and stakeholders, providing little guidance to directors about whose interests to prioritize and when. Similarly, social cooperatives create new challenges for organizations that have to transition from a dues/fees model to government funding, the latter requiring a greater burden in terms of measurement and reporting. Finally, new legal forms invariably create areas of expertise that no one yet specializes in, meaning there are few lawyers, accountants, and other professionals to service such organizations. In the U.S., this issue is compounded because hybrid laws differ from state to state (Tyler et al. 2015: 273). However, this is likely a temporary problem that will be solved as particular forms gain traction.

The future of hybrid forms

The hybrid legal landscape is diverse, and some legal forms may thrive while others perish. There is a healthy scholarly debate about whether such forms are necessary, with some arguing that hybrid forms represent a critical part of the future global economy and others saying that tweaks to current nonprofit and for-profit laws would suffice to accommodate hybrids. One author who stands on the pro-new legal forms side likens them to "a massive software update and addition to the capitalism platform" that will "better accommodate social ventures as a new application of the system" (Tyler et al. 2015: 283). We will not take a position on this debate, but rather examine what improvements to current hybrid legal forms might look like and, lacking new legal forms, what changes would be necessary to nonprofit and for-profit law to accommodate hybrids.

Improving hybrid forms

A number of scholars have argued that social good must be explicitly prioritized in hybrid laws to ensure real accountability, create a meaningful brand, and build trust between an organization and its stakeholders (Brakman Reiser and Dean 2017: 26; Tyler et al. 2015: 284).

Prioritize social benefit

In their 2017 book, *Social Enterprise Law*, Dana Brakman Reiser and Steven A. Dean call the ideal legal form "a mission-protected hybrid" that "function[s] as a brand upon which investors and entrepreneurs will rely" (2017: 26). The form would include enforcement mechanisms that ensure the prioritization of social good. The authors argue that this is the only way to ensure accountability and the only legitimate case for an independent hybrid legal form, since for-profits already have the capability to pursue social good if it is in line with profits.

Brakman Reiser and Dean are skeptical of the current hybrid forms in the U.S., but they think that Delaware's public benefit corporation model holds promise (Brakman Reiser and Dean 2017: 65). Referring to Delaware as "corporate law's 800-pound gorilla," the authors argue that the form gets closer to prioritizing social good by requiring companies to "indicate one or more specific public benefits" and providing clear guidance to directors to "'balance' the financial interests of shareholders . . . other stakeholders impacted by the firm's conduct, and the public benefit the firm identifies in its charter" (Brakman Reiser and Dean 2017: 61–66). However, the form falls short in its accountability mechanisms, requiring annual reports to be distributed only to shareholders every two years and making the use of a third-party standard optional. Other authors agree with requiring a specific, "clearly defined" social purpose, adding that the law should "expressly provide for a fiduciary duty to maintain the primacy of the entity's social purpose(s)" (Tyler et al. 2015: 284).

Improve accountability and oversight

The balance between accountability and administrative burden in terms of documenting impact is tricky. However, there are ways to increase accountability without putting new hybrids out of business. Nonprofits are accountable to social mission because they lose their tax-exempt status if they deviate from the rules. Since most hybrid forms do not provide for tax benefits, there need to be other enforcement mechanisms. The U.K.'s CICs provide a good model. The CIC Regulator calls its role "light touch" oversight, stepping in in rare cases when a CIC is not fulfilling its stated purpose (CIC Regulator 2017: 18). Relatively simple reporting and disclosure requirements such as "(a) mandatory periodic reporting of activities to a regulatory oversight office that will be publicly available; and (b) public notice of entity conversion to another form" ensure a great deal of accountability (Tyler et al. 2015: 284).

Brakman Reiser and Dean theorize the ideal level of regulatory oversight and accountability mechanisms. They argue that accountability should occur at all phases of an organization's evolution: upon incorporation, on an ongoing basis once it adopts the form, and upon dissolution or conversion to another entity. Accountability on entry would simply mean filing paperwork with a regulatory agency for incorporation; investors will be doing much of the vetting themselves as they review the organization's business plan and other documents (Brakman Reiser and Dean 2017: 35–36). Ongoing compliance would have multiple elements, such as annual financial disclosures to a regulatory agency, with a balance sheet split between expenditures on profit and social good, "with dual-purpose expenditures allocated between the two categories" (Brakman Reiser and Dean 2017: 37). There would be penalties for organizations without a majority of expenditures in the "social good" category.

In addition, ongoing compliance would include internal accountability mechanisms by "empowering shareholders with informational, voting, and litigation rights" and giving them the ability to hold directors accountable (Brakman Reiser and Dean 2017: 36). However, the authors would not give other stakeholders litigation rights, given the risk of frequent lawsuits from individuals who are not actively engaged in the organization. Accountability upon dissolution or conversion would take the form of an alert to the regulatory agency and a two-thirds majority vote by shareholders; most corporate forms already have this (Brakman Reiser and Dean 2017: 47). A difference would be that there would be a limit on the percentage of profits owners could take upon converting or dissolving the organization, initially 60 percent, drawing down to 10 percent after 10 years, which the authors hope will weed out investors who are only interested in making a profit. Also, at formation, the organization would designate the charity to receive these extra profits, and the charity will have the right to sue if the organization dissolves without paying them (Brakman Reiser and Dean 2017: 48–49).

Provide tax benefits

Another question is tax benefits. Some have argued that without them, there are not enough benefits for adopting a hybrid form. The answer to this seems to be that hybrid forms with firmer restrictions – those that clearly prioritize a specific purpose, limit profit distribution, and have an asset lock – should offer some tax benefits. South Korea's social enterprise is an example. However, for the corporate hybrid forms in the U.S., it seems unreasonable to provide tax benefits. Two scholars argue that such a move would "undermine the much-touted flexibility offered by the hybrid forms" by stipulating a narrower definition of public benefit, and create too much work for any agency trying to ensure that profits are not excessive (Mayer and Ganahl 2014: 387). However, the authors suggest the adoption of indirect tax subsidies that would benefit hybrids doing good, including (1) "increasing the limit on deducting charitable contributions for hybrids classified as corporations for federal tax purposes, or permitting such entities to deduct more of their charitable spending as business expenses" and (2) "eliminating the automatic classification of S corporation income as unrelated business taxable income for tax-exempt shareholders when the income arises from ownership in a hybrid classified as an S corporation" (Mayer and Ganahl 2014: 422). The U.S. could follow the U.K.'s lead on this, with incentives provided to the impact investing market rather than tax breaks for CICs.

Scrapping hybrid legal forms

If new, legal forms for hybrids fail to develop a well-functioning fourth sector over time, or lack the accountability mechanisms to ensure that organizations are achieving real societal good, there may not be a need for them at all. Instead, policymakers may want to consider changes to nonprofit and for-profit law that better accommodate hybrids. For-profit law would need to allow for organizations that want to pursue social good alongside profits, although some point out that profit maximization is not necessarily the specified purpose of business to begin with (Stout 2012). There is, however, enough legal precedent standing against directors who do not maximize profit for shareholders that changes would be necessary for hybrids that want to adopt a corporate form (Tyler et al. 2015: 274–278). The for-profit sector in the U.S. has already started making such accommodations; since the 1980s, more than 30 states have passed laws permitting corporate leaders to consider the interests of parties other than shareholders in decision-making. Such laws, called "nonshareholder constituency statutes," allow leaders to consider stakeholders such as employees, customers, suppliers, and communities in decision-making (Bainbridge, 1991: 973; Brewer 2016: 45).

There are no clear adjustments to nonprofit law to accommodate hybrids, but rather greater awareness and guidance on how to use the nonprofit form could help. For example, contrary to popular belief, the legal definition of charity in the U.S. "is open-ended and designed to permit change as the needs of society change over time" (Fremont-Smith 2013). In addition, different nonprofit forms exist that can help organizations that want to rely more heavily on market-oriented capital. For example, the Green Bay Packers football team is a well-known example of a nonprofit stock corporation, a lesser-known model for nonprofits that does not require a charitable purpose and allows organizations to have shareholders with limits on profit distribution (Toepler 2014). In addition, nonprofits can earn substantial income through commercial activities, such as museum gift shops, if they get creative. There is also the option for nonprofits to establish a for-profit subsidiary or enter into a partnership with a business that can generate profits that are in part donated back to the nonprofit. However, such arrangements "come with additional compliance and overhead costs" (Toepler 2014: 8).

In the U.S., greater awareness and use of the cooperative form may also support hybrids. The cooperative sector in the U.S. is relatively small, comprising roughly 30,000 organizations (Young 2017: 31). Cooperatives can incorporate under for-profit or nonprofit law depending on the state, and there is no specific legal form for them (Young 2017: 32). The U.S. could follow Italy's lead and use cooperatives for social good rather than strictly member benefit (Young 2017: 32). This would require some adjustments to current cooperative law. There are some U.S. cooperatives that demonstrate the potential of the form. For example, REI, the outdoor gear and clothing retailer and largest cooperative in the U.S., has made a substantial commitment to environmental good (Acosta et al. 2013). There are also more than 1,000 child care cooperatives in the U.S. pursuing the social impact of providing affordable and high-quality care (Cooperatives for a Better World n.d.).

Conclusion

As hybrids become an increasing part of the global economy, new laws have sprung up to house these organizations. The new legal forms range from social cooperatives to sustainable businesses and they vary widely – some providing a stricter focus on social good and accompanying tax benefits, and others providing more flexibility to pursue profits in lieu of such perks. As the number of organizations using these new forms increases, the forms' advantages and disadvantages begin to show. Only time will tell whether the kinks will be worked out or some forms may need to be abandoned altogether. In either case, laws are only one part of the ecosystem that surrounds hybrid organizations, and the success of new hybrid legal forms will depend in large part on the functioning of other factors, including the funding streams and market demand for socially conscious organizations.

Acknowledgement

The authors are grateful to the Schar Initiative at George Mason University's Schar School of Policy and Government for funding support for the writing of this chapter.

References

Acosta, A., Trujillo, M., & Sawayda, J. (2013). Recreational Equipment Incorporated (REI): A Responsible Retail Cooperative. Daniels Fund Ethics Initiative, University of New Mexico, pp. 1–12.

B Lab (2017a). *About B Lab* [Online]. B Corporation. Available at: https://www.bcorporation.net/what-are-b-corps/about-b-lab (Accessed 22 September 2017).

B Lab (2017b). *Model Benefit Corporation Legislation* [Online]. B Corporation. Available at: http://benefitcorp.net/attorneys/model-legislation (Accessed 22 September 2017).

B Lab (2017c). *FAQ: General Questions* [Online]. B Corporation. Available at: http://benefitcorp.net/faq (Accessed 16 December 2017).

Bainbridge, S.M. (1991). Interpreting Nonshareholder Constituency Statutes. *Pepperdine Law Review, 19*, pp. 971–1025.

Battilana, J., Lee, M., Walker, J., & Dorsey, C. (2012). In Search of the Hybrid Ideal [Online]. *Stanford Social Innovation Review*. Available at: https://ssir.org/articles/entry/in_search_of_the_hybrid_ideal (Accessed 1 October 2017).

Bidet, E., & Eum, H.S. (2011). Social Enterprise in South Korea: History and Diversity. *Social Enterprise Journal*, 7(1), pp. 69–85.

Borys, B., & Jemison, D.B. (1989). Hybrid Arrangements as Strategic Alliances: Theoretical Issues in Organizational Combinations. *Academy of Management Review*, 14(2), pp. 234–249.

Brakman Reiser, D. (2011). Benefit Corporations: A Sustainable Form of Organization. *Wake Forest Law Review*, 46, pp. 591–624.

Brakman Reiser, D. (2013). Theorizing Forms for Social Enterprise. *Emory Law Journal*, 62, pp. 681–696.

Brakman Reiser, D., & Dean, S.A. (2017). *Social Enterprise Law: Trust, Public Benefit and Capital Markets.* Oxford: Oxford University Press.

Brandsen, T., Van de Donk, W., & Putters, K. (2005). Griffins or Chameleons? Hybridity as a Permanent and Inevitable Characteristic of the Third Sector. *International Journal of Public Administration*, 28(9–10), pp. 749–765.

Brewer, C.V. (2016). The Ongoing Evolution in Social Enterprise Legal Forms. In D.R. Young, E.A. Searing, & C.V. Brewer, eds., *The Social Enterprise Zoo: A Guide for Perplexed Scholars, Entrepreneurs, Philanthropists, Leaders, Investors, and Policymakers.* Northampton, MA: Edward Elgar, pp. 33–64.

Callison, J.W. (2012). Putting New Sheets on a Procrustean Bed: How Benefit Corporations Address Fiduciary Duties, the Dangers Created, and Suggestions for Change. *American University Business Law Review*, 2, pp. 85–114.

Callison, J.W., & Vestal, A.W. (2010). The L3C Illusion: Why Low-Profit Limited Liability Companies Will Not Stimulate Socially Optimal Private Foundation Investment in Entrepreneurial Ventures. *Vermont Law Review*, 35, pp. 273–294.

Calo, F., & Teasdale, S. (2016). Governing the Zoo. In D.R. Young, E.A. Searing, & C.V. Brewer, eds., *The Social Enterprise Zoo: A Guide for Perplexed Scholars, Entrepreneurs, Philanthropists, Leaders, Investors, and Policymakers.* Northampton, MA: Edward Elgar, pp. 193–209.

CIC Regulator (2017, July 19). *Annual Report 2016 to 2017* [Online]. The Office of the Regulator of Community Interest Companies. Available at: https://www.gov.uk/government/uploads/system/uploads/attachment_data/file/630211/cic-17-2community-interest-companies-annual-report-2016-2017.pdf (Accessed 2 October 2017).

Clark Jr., W.H., & Vranka, L. (2013). *The Need and Rationale for the Benefit Corporation* [Online]. Benefit Corporation. Available at: http://benefitcorp.net/sites/default/files/Benefit_Corporation_White_Paper.pdf (Accessed 1 January 2018).

Cooney, K., Koushyar, J., Lee, M., & Murray, H. (2014, December 5). Benefit Corporation and L3C Adoption: A Survey [Online]. *Stanford Social Innovation Review.* Available at: https://ssir.org/articles/entry/benefit_corporation_and_l3c_adoption_a_survey (Accessed 1 October 2017).

Cooperatives for a Better World (n.d.) *Social Co-ops Overview* [Online]. Cooperatives for a Better World. Available at: https://cooperativesforabetterworld.coop/learn-about-co-ops/types-of-cooperative-businesses/social-co-ops/ (Accessed 2 April 2018).

Culley, R., & Horwitz, J.R. (2014). Profits v. Purpose: Hybrid Companies and the Charitable Dollar. *University of Michigan Public Law* Research Paper No. 272, pp. 1–34.

Doherty, B., Haugh, H., & Lyon, F. (2014). Social Enterprises as Hybrid Organizations: A Review and Research Agenda. *International Journal of Management Reviews*, 16(4), pp. 417–436.

Esposito, R.T. (2012). The Social Enterprise Revolution in Corporate Law: A Primer on Emerging Corporate Entities in Europe and the United States and the Case for the Benefit Corporation. *William & Mary Business Law Review*, 4, pp. 639–714.

Fain, P. (2014). *Dropping Profit* [Online]. Inside Higher Ed. Available at: https://www.insidehighered.com/news/2014/07/17/few-profits-have-become-nonprofits-despite-regulatory-environment (Accessed 17 December 2017).

Foster, W., & Fine, G. (2007). How Nonprofits Get Really Big. *Stanford Social Innovation Review,* 5(2), pp. 46–55.

Fremont-Smith, M. (2013). Do We Need a Legal Definition of Charity? Institute for Civil Society, Harvard University and Urban Institute, pp. 1–20.

Galaskiewicz, J., & Colman, M.S. (2006). Collaboration between Corporations and Nonprofit Organizations. In W.W. Powell, & R. Steinberg, eds., *The Nonprofit Sector: A Research Handbook.* 2nd ed. New Haven, CT: Yale University Press, pp. 180–206.

Goodwill (n.d.). *Annual Report: Our Financials.* Goodwill Industries International, Inc. Available at: www.goodwill.org/annual-report/

Gottesman, M.D. (2007). From Cobblestones to Pavement: The Legal Road Forward for the Creation of Hybrid Social Organizations. *Yale Law & Policy Review*, 26(1), pp. 345–358.

Johanson, J.E., & Vakkuri, J. (2018). *Governing Hybrid Organizations: Exploring Diversity of Institutional Life.* Abingdon: Routledge, pp. 3–4.

Jung, K., Jang, H.S., & Seo, I. (2016). Government-driven Social Enterprises in South Korea: Lessons from the Social Enterprise Promotion Program in the Seoul Metropolitan Government. *International Review of Administrative Sciences*, 82(3), pp. 598–616.

Kannel, C., & Samali, M. (2017). *Startups: Should You Incorporate as a Public Benefit Corporation?* [Online]. VentureBeat.com. Available at: https://venturebeat.com/2017/04/30/startups-should-you-incorporate-as-a-public-benefit-corporation/ (Accessed 15 December 2017).

Kerlin, J.A., & Pollak, T.H. (2011). Nonprofit Commercial Revenue: A Replacement for Declining Government Grants and Private Contributions? *American Review of Public Administration*, 41(6), pp. 686–704.

Kickul, J., & Lyons, T.S. (2012). *Understanding Social Entrepreneurship: The Relentless Pursuit of Mission in an Ever Changing World.* New York: Routledge.

Krupkin, A., & Looney, A. (2017). *9 Facts about Pass-through Businesses* [Online]. Brookings Institution. Available at: https://www.brookings.edu/research/9-facts-about-pass-through-businesses/ (Accessed 20 December 2017).

Liao, C. (2013). The Next Stage of CSR for Canada: Transformational Corporate Governance, Hybrid Legal Structures, and the Growth of Social Enterprise. *McGill International Journal of Sustainable Development Law and Policy*, 9(1), pp. 53–85.

Mair, J. (2010). Social Entrepreneurship: Taking Stock and Looking Ahead. In A. Fayolle, & H. Matlay, eds., *Handbook of Research on Social Entrepreneurship.* Northampton, MA: Edward Elgar, pp. 15–28.

Mayer, L.H., & Ganahl, J.R. (2014) Taxing Social Enterprise. *Stanford Law Review*, 66, pp. 387–442.

Ménard, C. (2009). Oliver Williamson and the Logic of Hybrid Organization. In M. Morroni, ed., *Corporate Governance, Organization, and the Firm: Co-operation and Outsourcing in the Global Economy.* Northampton, MA: Edward Elgar, pp. 89–92.

Mickels, A. (2009). Beyond Corporate Social Responsibility: Reconciling the Ideals of a For-Benefit Corporation with Director Fiduciary Duties in the U.S. and Europe. *Hastings International and Comparative Law Review*, 32(1), pp. 271–304.

Morrison & Foerster LLP (2016). Which Legal Structure is Right for My Social Enterprise? A Guide to Establishing Social Enterprise in the United States [Online]. Thomson Reuters Foundation. Available at: https://www.trust.org/contentAsset/raw-data/1b34bbc3-de52-477a-adae-850a56c2aabe/file (Accessed 14 November 2017).

Orrick, Herrington & Sutcliffe LLP (2014). Balancing Purpose and Profit: Legal Mechanisms to Lock in Social Mission for "Profit with Purpose" Businesses across the G8 [Online]. Thomson Reuters Foundation. Available at: https://www.trust.org/contentAsset/raw-data/1d3b4f99-2a65-49f9-9bc0-39 585bc52cac/file (Accessed 20 May 2019).

Powell, W.W. (1990). Neither Market nor Hierarchy: Network Forms of Organization. In M.J. Handel, ed., *The Sociology of Organizations.* Thousand Oaks, CA: Sage, pp. 104–117.

Sabeti, H. (2011). The For-Benefit Enterprise [Online]. *Harvard Business Review*. Available at: https://hbr.org/2011/11/the-for-benefit-enterprise (Accessed 3 January 2018).

Schmidt, E. (2010). Vermont's Social Hybrid Pioneers: Early Observations and Questions to Ponder. *Vermont Law Review*, 35, pp. 163–210.

Searing. E.A.M., & Young, D.R. (2016). Feeding the Animals. In D.R. Young, E.A. Searing, & C.V. Brewer, eds., *The Social Enterprise Zoo: A Guide for Perplexed Scholars, Entrepreneurs, Philanthropists, Leaders, Investors, and Policymakers.* Northampton, MA: Edward Elgar, pp. 167–192.

Seibel, W. (2015). Studying Hybrids: Sectors and Mechanisms. *Organization Studies*, 36(6), pp. 697–712.

Skelcher, C., & Rathgeb Smith, S. (2015). Theorizing Hybridity: Institutional Logics, Complex Organizations, and Actor Identities: The Case of Nonprofits. *Public Administration*, 93(2), pp. 433–448.

Social Enterprise Law Tracker (2017). *Status Tool* [Online]. NYU School of Law and NYU Stern. Available at: http://socentlawtracker.org/#/spcs (Accessed 14 December 2017).

Social Impact Investment Taskforce (2014, September). *Impact Investment: The Invisible Heart of Markets* [Online]. Available at: www.ietp.com/sites/default/files/Impact%20Investment%20Report%20FINAL.pdf (Accessed 17 December 2017).

Stout, L.A. (2012). *The Shareholder Value Myth: How Putting Shareholders First Harms Investors, Corporations, and the Public.* San Francisco, CA: Berrett-Koehler.

Toepler, S. (2014). Between Markets and Charity: Understanding the Hybridization of Social Good Provision [Online]. Paper presented at the 11th bi-annual conference of the International Society for Third-Sector Research (ISTR), Munster, Germany, 22–25 July. Available at: www.doi.org/10.13140/RG.2.2.15735.11689/1 (Accessed 20 May 2019).

Toepler, S. (2018). Do Benefit Corporations Represent a Policy Threat to Nonprofits? *Nonprofit Policy Forum*, 9(4), https://doi.org/10.1515/npf-2018-0021

TOMS (n.d.). *One for One* [Online]. TOMS.com, LLC. Available at: https://www.toms.com/one-for-one-en/

Triponel, A., & Agapitova, N. (2017). Legal Framework for Social Enterprise: Lessons from a Comparative Study of Italy, Malaysia, South Korea, United Kingdom, and United States. World Bank Group Working Paper, pp. 1–41.

Tyler, J.E., Absher, E., Garman, K., & Luppino, A.J. (2015). Producing Better Mileage: Advancing the Design and Usefulness of Hybrid Vehicles for Social Business Ventures. *Quinnipiac University Law Review*, 33(2), pp. 237–323.

Venturi, P., & Zandonai, F. (2012). *Social Enterprise in Italy: Plurality of Models and Contribution to Growth* [Online]. Iris Network Report. Available at: www.irisnetwork.it/wp-content/uploads/2010/04/exsum_reportiris_socent_1-ENG.pdf (Accessed 17 December 2017).

Williamson, O. (1985). *The Economic Institutions of Capitalism*. New York: Free Press.

Williamson, O. (1991). Comparative Economic Organization: The Analysis of Discrete Structural Alternatives. *Administrative Science Quarterly*, 36, pp. 269–296.

Young, D.R. (2017). *Financing Nonprofits and Other Social Enterprises: A Benefits Approach*. Northampton, MA: Edward Elgar.

Young, D.R., & Brewer, C.V. (2016). Introduction. In D.R. Young, E.A. Searing, & C.V. Brewer, eds., *The Social Enterprise Zoo: A Guide for Perplexed Scholars, Entrepreneurs, Philanthropists, Leaders, Investors, and Policymakers*. Northampton, MA: Edward Elgar, pp. 3–14.

Young, D.R., & Longhofer, W. (2016). Designing the Zoo. In D.R. Young, E.A. Searing, & C.V. Brewer, eds., *The Social Enterprise Zoo: A Guide for Perplexed Scholars, Entrepreneurs, Philanthropists, Leaders, Investors, and Policymakers*. Northampton, MA: Edward Elgar, pp. 15–32.

Young, D.R., Salamon, L.M., & Grinsfelder, M.C. (2012). Commercialization, Social Ventures, and For-Profit Competition. In L.M. Salamon, ed., *The State of Nonprofit America*. 2nd ed. Washington, DC: Brookings Institution Press, in collaboration with the Aspen Institute, pp. 521–548.

Young, D.R., Searing, E.A., & Brewer, C.V., eds. (2016). *The Social Enterprise Zoo: A Guide for Perplexed Scholars, Entrepreneurs, Philanthropists, Leaders, Investors, and Policymakers*. Northampton, MA: Edward Elgar.

INDEX

For Product Safety Concerns and Information please contact our EU
representative GPSR@taylorandfrancis.com Taylor & Francis Verlag GmbH,
Kaufingerstraße 24, 80331 München, Germany

Printed and bound by CPI Group (UK) Ltd, Croydon, CR0 4YY
08/05/2025
01864329-0007